AF556967

SUSTAINING AIR POWER

SUSTAINING AIR POWER

ROYAL AIR FORCE LOGISTICS SINCE 1918

TREVOR STONE

FONTHILL

It's not my place to run the war.
A plane I cannot fly.
It's not my place to say how far
our radars probe the sky.
It's not my place to shoot off guns
nor even load a shell.
But let the blasted things run short
and see who catches hell!

Anon

Fonthill Media Language Policy

Fonthill Media publishes in the international English language market. One language edition is published worldwide. As there are minor differences in spelling and presentation, especially with regard to American English and British English, a policy is necessary to define which form of English to use. The Fonthill Policy is to use the form of English native to the author. Trevor Stone was born and educated in the United Kingdom and therefore British English has been adopted in this publication.

Fonthill Media Limited
Fonthill Media LLC
www.fonthillmedia.com
office@fonthillmedia.com

First published in the United Kingdom and the United States of America 2017

British Library Cataloguing in Publication Data:
A catalogue record for this book is available from the British Library

ISBN 978-1-78155-635-1

Typeset in 10.5pt on 13pt MinionPro
Printed and bound in England

Foreword

All armed forces, from the battles of the ancient world to the asymmetric conflicts of the twenty-first century, have faced the problem of supplying the weapons, equipment, and sustenance to sustain combat. Now covered by the term 'logistics', supply and resupply has often meant the difference between victory and defeat. The Mongol armies that marauded across Asia in the late Middle Ages were accompanied by camels and horses carrying huge quantities of new arrows and bows. The baggage train of European armies in the field stretched for miles behind the marching men. In the modern age, the capacity to supply by rail, road, or ship (and for the past century, by air) has been a critical factor. On the approaches to Stalingrad, German engineers and Russian labourers worked day and night to construct new rail links or to keep existing ones open, but when Stalingrad was finally cut off and surrounded, aircraft were used to bring in supplies. There were far too few, and the fate of the German 6th Army was sealed.

Logistics have nevertheless remained an unloved subject among historians, perhaps because the story of actual combat has all the drama. Slogging along behind the front with wagons and lorries full of equipment or running large depots and maintenance stores is the stuff of civilian life as much as the military. However, without those efforts and that organisation, waging war—particularly modern, large-scale, and technically sophisticated war—is out of the question. The logistical problems facing modern air forces have something in common with all issues of supply, but with a difference. Air combat is capital-intensive; complex aircraft engineering requires a regular flow of thousands of different components and small parts. The wrong parts, or interruptions in supply, keep aircraft grounded and useless. Air forces are only as good as the logistic and maintenance system allows. That is the lesson Trevor Stone presents in this first comprehensive study of the RAF's logistic organisation over the past century of its existence. This is a history of the enablers, those whose efforts made it possible to fight air war at all.

The logistics challenge for the RAF throughout that whole period has been shaped by deployment overseas. From the First World War to intervention in the current Middle East conflicts, supply has not been a simple process of moving goods from one part of the country to another, although this too was a critical factor in the Battle of Britain in 1940, all too often overlooked in accounts of the most important air-to-air battle the RAF has fought. Overseas logistic reach is a different managerial challenge. For the first half of the century covered here, Britain was a major imperial power, with a long tradition of moving goods around a truly global empire. That experience helped to shape RAF Logistics, from bases in Egypt and India to supporting conflict in multiple wartime theatres in the two world wars. Tens of thousands of RAF men and women have played their part in sustaining those overseas commitments, though they have tended to be voices off when it comes to explaining what the RAF was capable of doing. Trevor Stone was a logistics officer with the RAF for thirty-five years, and it is thanks to him that the unsung heroes of supply and distribution and maintenance will at last move out of the wings to have a place on stage.

Richard Overy
University of Exeter, February 2017

Preface

This book has been a long time in the making and is the culmination of some twenty-five years of research. I first became interested in the history of Royal Air Force (RAF) logistics just a few years after I had completed my supply officer training at the RAF College Cranwell in 1981. It was evident that there was a rich history behind the specialisation, but, surprisingly, no official history had ever been written. I vowed then that one day, I would put that right. This book is the result and is the first definitive history to be produced that tells the story of RAF Logistics since 1918. It is a story that opens the hangar doors on a discipline that has been critical to the sustainment of British air power for nearly 100 years.

Firstly, the subject itself needs to be defined. The art of logistics has been practised for thousands of years, although the origin of the term is subject to different interpretations. Many writers believe that it has its roots in the world of the military, although its etymology can be traced to the ancient Greek adjective, '*logistikus*', meaning skilled in calculating.[1] The military use of the term emerges much later in the French '*logistique*', a term believed to have been coined by Baron Jomini, defining an officer responsible for quartering troops and finding animal forage.[2] In British military history, the term has gained more popular use since the Second World War, a trend that seems to mirror its popularity in the commercial sector, particularly noticeable since the 1970s. The definition of the term though is more difficult to pin down, often depending on the inclusion (or not) of engineering activity, a debate that seems to be a preoccupation of the military; it is currently dormant, and it is not the intention of this book to reopen it.

For many years, there existed in the RAF a clear demarcation between Engineering and Supply, with both disciplines represented by a specialist ground branch and associated trades. This remained a clearly understood division of responsibilities for many years but, by the early 1990s, the service found the need to expand its scope of logistics with the introduction of what was known as Support Chain Management, a concept that included engineering as a 'link' in the chain. This perspective is similar to that of the North Atlantic Treaty Organisation (NATO), which includes maintenance activities in its definition, along with medical and health service support.[3] The fashion for an all-embracing term within the RAF faded, and the more traditional lines of demarcation were restored when the RAF's Supply Branch was renamed Logistics in 2009; technical activity remains the responsibility of the RAF Engineering Branch and Trades.

The question remains: what then is the scope of RAF Logistics? The deliberations of academics and military doctrine authors complicate the pursuit of a straightforward definition. The answer can be found in the work of one of the earliest writers on the topic in the modern era, the Frenchman Baron Jomini. In his work *The Art of War*, Baron Jomini includes in his definition 'the practical art of moving armies' and providing for the successive arrival of convoys of supplies and establishing and organizing lines of supplies'.[4] The historian Martin van Creveld, in *Supplying War* (his seminal work on military logistics), suggests that the elements of Baron Jomini's definition can be joined up to form 'the practical art of moving armies and keeping them supplied'.[5] This take on Jomini's views seems to get straight to the point—the broad definition of logistics need be no more complex. For the purpose of this book, therefore, the scope of the term is limited to Supply and Movements and excludes engineering activity, albeit the synergy with this is acknowledged where appropriate.[6]

In researching the book, the one real challenge I faced was how to present the story, especially as logistics is a multi-faceted discipline and consists of a diverse range of specialisations. Part One, as far as possible, tells the main story chronologically. To avoid over-complicating this, the finer detail of some of the more complex perspectives—such as tactical and expeditionary logistics, movements, fuels, supply chain management, information technology, and training—have been covered as dedicated chapters in Part Two. Finally, Part Three draws a number of conclusions on the complete work.

In the early days of research, I received much advice on what this history should look like. They were all valuable, but there was one comment in particular, expressed by a number of people, that stood out from the rest; this was to make sure that there was a human face to the complexities of logistics. Its work could not have been achieved without the commitment and professionalism of its men and women, both service and civilian. This has been an important factor in writing this book, and I have included a number of personal reminiscences and anecdotes that, I hope, 'humanises' the historical narrative. In taking this approach, a balance had to be struck; therefore, there have been a number of trade-offs between the historian's academic 'rigour' and keeping the subject alive. While my publisher has been extremely flexible with the overall size of the book, there was, of course, an upper limit and some areas have therefore only been covered superficially. This by no means indicates any degree of lesser importance. While every effort has been taken to verify facts, there are some areas where a lack of accessible archival material has made research difficult and the memory and personal papers of former and current logisticians has been the only way to piece the story together. Where there are omissions or inaccuracies, I should welcome the observers getting in touch with me via the publisher. Notwithstanding, I hope the result has achieved a readable balance.

Finally, and with research that has taken a long time to accumulate, there has been an ever-present question of when to stop. By its very nature, the RAF has been involved in new operations and its structure and organisation is subject to almost continual change. A key turning point, however, arose when the British Prime Minister David Cameron announced in November 2010 that British combat troops would be withdrawn from Afghanistan by 2014. This seemed to be a suitable point at which to bring the story to a close. The story of RAF Logistics will continue and I hope that a sequel is produced in years to come to ensure that its achievements are given due recognition and its continuing contribution to sustaining British air power is suitably acknowledged.

Trevor Stone
Cambridgeshire, February 2017

Acknowledgements

I would first like to thank the unfailing support of Air Commodores Nick Morris and Mike Allisstone, both highly experienced and much respected former senior RAF Supply Branch officers. Between them, they acted as an editorial team, reviewing the book as it developed and providing valuable, critical advice. This book could not have been completed without their help and I owe them a great deal; the result is as much theirs as mine.

I have been fortunate in having received assistance from many people, serving and retired, service and civilian, as well as from their families. Many of them have been acknowledged, but it was not possible to include them all, although their contribution has helped shape my understanding of the wider complexities of RAF Logistics. They will know who they are, and my heartfelt thanks go to them all. There have been a number of people who have provided a significant input, including suggested text, and I would like to express particular thanks to the following: Air Vice-Marshals Donald Hills and Matt Wiles; Air Commodores John Bessell, Ron Gladding, Paul Hedges, Les O'Dea, Gerry Pengelly, Andy Spinks, and Peter Whalley; Group Captains John Craven-Griffiths, Neil Cromarty, David Forsyth, Bill Girdwood, Duncan Grant, Steve Harpum, Richard Hills, Andrew Humphries, David Lester-Powell, Dai John, Chris Markey, Alan Matthews, David Packman, Ron Robertson, and Robin Springett; Wing Commanders Mike Barham, Paul Buxton, Jamie Cameron, Jo Lincoln, and Rob Sutton; and Squadron Leaders Tom Cousins, Roger Cresswell, Nigel Dabin, Richard Evans, Ken Felton, Bob Little, Andy Marshall, Jim Nadin, and David Sefton.

In addition to these contributors, I would like to acknowledge the support provided by the MOD Air Historical Branch (RAF) (Seb Cox and Graham Day) and the Trenchard Museum, RAF Halton (Francis Hanford). I am also indebted to Tim Pierce of the RAF College Cranwell Library and the UK National Archives at Kew. Thanks are also extended to a number of commercial companies for their assistance including: Boeing Defence UK (Debbie Docherty and Jeanine Swaine) and Systecon UK Ltd (Phil Bean, Phil Sturgess, and Olof Waak). My thanks are also extended to Professor Richard Overy who, in addition to writing the foreword, also patiently coached me in the historian's craft as he supervised me throughout my history doctorate with the University of Exeter. I am grateful to the Ministry of Defence for permission to use Crown Copyright material.

Throughout my research, I found military and veterans' magazines, newsletters, and commemorative booklets to be a rich source of detail and reminiscences. In many cases, the organisations concerned have long since been disbanded and it was not possible to trace any publisher, body, or individual from whom permission to quote or copy photographs could be obtained. Where I have used such material, due acknowledgement of the source has been made. I trust that if any author of these sources recognises his or her handiwork, they will forgive me for not paying due credit by name and I would welcome them getting in touch with me through the publisher. Last, and by no means least, I am particularly grateful to my wife, Lynne Joy, for her patience over many years of research and for her invaluable help with proofreading the manuscript and an independent view on what I had to say. The responsibility for any remaining mistakes is entirely mine.

CONTENTS

Foreword by Richard Overy 5
Preface 7
Acknowledgements 11
List of Abbreviations 15
Glossary 19

Part I: The Logistics Story

1 Building on the Foundations: 1918–1933 25
2 Biplanes to Monoplanes: 1934–1939 57
3 The Second World War: 1939–1945 89
4 The Cold War Years: 1946–1989 163
5 Towards the Future: 1990–2014 208

Part II: Perspectives

6 Tactical and Expeditionary Logistics 247
7 Movements 289
8 Post-war Management of POL and Compressed Gasses 346
9 Managing the Supply Chain 369
10 Information Technology 410
11 Training and Education 438

Part III: Conclusions

12 The Logistics Journey 457

Appendix I: Heads of the RAF Logistics Organisation, 1918–2014 460
Appendix II: Operational Honours and Awards 462

Endnotes 467
Bibliography 497
Index 506

List of Abbreviations

AAP	Army aircraft park (First World War)
AAP	Air ammunition park (Second World War)
ACE	Allied Command Europe
ACSSU	Air Combat Service Support Unit
AD	Ammunition depot
AD	Automatic data processing
AE	Aircraft establishment
AED	Aircraft equipment depot
AGS	Aircraft general spares (or stores)
AMF (A)	ACE Mobile Force (Air)
AMF (L)	ACE Mobile Force (Land)
AMSO	Air Member for Supply and Organisation
AMW	Air Mobility Wing
AMWO	Air Ministry weekly order
AOC	Air officer commanding
AOG	Aircraft on ground
AP	Air Publication
APFC	Air portable fuel container
ASP	Air Stores Park
AT	Air transport
BEM	Medal of the Order of the British Empire (British Empire Medal)
BFI	Bulk fuel installation
CAS	Chief of the Air Staff
CB	Companion of the Order of the Bath
CBE	Commander of the Order of the British Empire
CDL	Chief of Defence Logistics
CE	Chief executive
CGE	Controller-General of Equipment
CMG	Companion of St Michael and St George
CO	Commanding officer
CPX	Command post exercise

CSDE	Central Servicing Development Establishment
DD	Deputy directorate
DGE	Directorate or Director General of Equipment
DGS (RAF)	Director General of Supply (RAF)
DLO	Defence Logistics Organisation
DofE	Directorate or Director of Equipment
DSDA	Defence Storage and Distribution Agency
DTMA	Defence Transport and Movements Agency
EAW	Expeditionary Air Wing
EBFI	Emergency bulk fuel installation
ED	Equipment depot
EDP	Electronic data processing
EO	Equipment officer
EP	Equipment park
EPAS	Equipment Provisioning and Accounting Section
ESA	Explosives storage area
ESD	Equipment supply depot
ETA	Estimated time of arrival
EU	Embarkation unit
FAP	Fly away pack
FEAF	Far East Air Force
GD	General duties
GS	General service
HE	High explosive
HQ	Headquarters
HQ ASC	Headquarters Air Support Command
HQ RAFG	Headquarters RAF Germany
HQ RAFSC	Headquarters RAF Support Command
HQ STC	Headquarters Strike Command
IFOR	Implementation Force
IOT	Initial officer training
IPT	Integrated project team
IT	Information technology
JFLogC	Joint Force Logistics Component
JHC	Joint Helicopter Command
JNCO	Junior non-commissioned officer
JSC	Joint Supply Chain
LCC	Logistics Computer Centre
LPO	Local purchase order
MACE	Maintenance Analysis Computing Establishment
MAMS	Mobile Air Movements Squadron
MAXEVAL	Origin uncertain but likely to be maximum evaluation

MDC	Maintenance data centre
MBE	Member of the Order of the British Empire
MINEVAL	Origin uncertain but likely to be minimum/minimal evaluation
MOB	Main operating base
MOD	Ministry of Defence
MP	Military police/policeman
MPO	Master provisioning office
MSF	Mobility Supply Flight
MT	Motor transport
MU	Maintenance unit
NATO	North Atlantic Treaty Organisation
NCO	Non-commissioned officer
NEAF	Near East Air Force
OBE	Officer of the Order of the British Empire
OC	Officer commanding
ORB	Operations Record Book (RAF Form 540)
ORBAT	Order of battle
PFDS	Priority freight distribution system
PJHQ	Permanent Joint Headquarters
POL	Petroleum, oils, and lubricants
QRA	Quick reaction alert
RAF	Royal Air Force
RAFG	RAF Germany
RAuxAF	Royal Auxiliary Air Force
RAFLO	RAF liaison officer
RAFSADPS	RAF Supply ADP system
RAFVR	Royal Air Force Volunteer Reserve
RCT	Royal Corps of Transport
R&D	Receipt and despatch
RE	Royal Engineers
REME	Royal Electrical and Mechanical Engineers
RFC	Royal Flying Corps
RLC	Royal Logistic Corps
RMA	Rear maintenance area
RN	Royal Navy
RNAS	Royal Naval Air Service
SA	Stores accounting
SAA	Small arms ammunition
SAC	Senior aircraftsman
SACEUR	Supreme Allied Commander Europe
SADAC	Supply and Distribution Activity Complex
SAMO	Senior air movements officer

SCC	Supply Control Centre
SCCS	Supply Central Computer System
SD	Stores depot
SDR	Strategic Defence Review
SEO	Senior equipment officer
SEPECAT	*Société Européenne de Production de l'avion Ecole de Combat et d'Appui Tactique*
SESO	Senior Equipment staff officer
SH	Support helicopter
SMB	Supply/support management branch
SNCO	Senior non-commissioned officer
SSR (A)	SACEUR's Strategic Reserve (Air)
SWO	Station warrant officer
TACEVAL	Tactical evaluation
TAF	Tactical Air Force
TG	Trade group
TOR	Terms of reference
TSW	Tactical Supply Wing
TTF	Truck tanker fuel
TTW	Transition to war
UED	Universal equipment depot
UKMF	UK Mobile Force
UNPROFOR	United Nations Protection Force
UNSCR	United Nations security council resolution
UOR	Urgent operational requirement
USA	United States of America
USAS	Unit Supply ADP System
V&A	Valuable and attractive
VOG	Valiant/Victor/Vulcan on ground
WAAC	Women's Army Auxiliary Corps
WAAF	Women's Auxiliary Air Force
WRAF	Women's Royal Air Force
WO	Warrant officer
WT	Wireless telegraphy

Glossary

Computing Technology

The highly specialist discipline of computing technology has undergone a whole series of name changes since the RAF first became involved with this in the early 1960s. Various terms have been used including: electronic data processing (EDP), automatic data processing (ADP), information technology (IT), information and communications technology (ICT), and the more recent trend, which seems to be information systems (IS).

D-Day

Although the term 'D-Day' is commonly associated with the Allied invasion of Europe in June 1944, the term is a much wider-used military convention used to denote the actual day that an operation commences. Days prior to that are referred to as D minus (or -) 1, 2, 3 etc. and days after as D plus (or +) 1, 2, 3 etc. The actual time that an operation commences is referred to as H-hour.

Flag, General, and Air Rank 'Star' Convention

To provide a universal convention across Defence for officers above (and including) commodore in the Royal Navy (flag rank), brigadier in the Army (general rank), and air commodore in the RAF (air rank), a star system, similar to that used by US forces, has become commonplace. This is believed to derive from the star plates that are affixed to the front of such officer's staff cars. Thus, in the RAF, an air commodore would be referred to as a one-star officer, an air vice-marshal two-star, an air marshal three-star, and an air chief marshal four-star. The same principle applies to the equivalent ranks in the RN and the Army.

General Staff System

Although this convention has been around for many years, the RAF's increased involvement in joint operations has seen it adopt what is known as the general or continental staff system, where specific disciplines are referred to collectively by a number. This is generally prefixed with a 'C' for combined operations, 'J' for joint, 'N' for the naval, 'G' for land, and 'A' for air environments. Broadly speaking, 1 is personnel, 2 is intelligence and security, 3 is operations, 4 is logistics, 5 is plans, 6 is communications, 7 is education and training, 8 is finance, and 9 is civil or military affairs.

Materiel

Materiel (as distinct from material) relates to military equipment and supplies required by a military force. Derived from the French *matériel*, the term seems to have gained more widespread usage after the Second World War. See also stores and supplies.

Movements

Where referred to throughout this book, the term movements is a generic term that means everything connected with moving personnel and freight from one place to another. It also includes the control of movement and the means of transportation. It is acknowledged that this differs from the definition used by the British Army.

Operation Codenames

It has been a long-standing military practice to allocate a codename to operations. The aims of this are twofold. Firstly, from a security perspective, the codename does not give away the nature of the operation. For example, the Second World War codename Operation Torch does not provide any indication that it means the invasion of North Africa. Secondly, the codename is a specific and definitive term for what could be quite a complex and lengthy operational objective. It therefore minimises the opportunity for confusion and ambiguity.

Stores and Supplies

Throughout the period up until the end of the Second World War, this book refers to both stores and supplies. Stores were defined by the RAF as air force materiel other than supplies, while supplies were defined as food, forage, fuel, petrol, oil, light, disinfectants, and medical comforts. This practice seems to have been discontinued after the war.

Turnover

Where mentioned in the text, the term turnover is a figure that equates to the number of receipts plus the number of issues.

Weights and Measures

Although it now seems customary to convert weights and measures into metric equivalencies, this has been avoided as, for example, the term kilogram in a First World War context would clearly be out of place.

PART I

The Logistics Story

1

Building on the Foundations: 1918–1933

The RAF was formed in the closing months of the First World War following the merger of the Royal Flying Corps (RFC) and the Royal Naval Air Service (RNAS). The RAF's logistics organisation, structure, and procedures were shaped, initially by lessons learned from the First World War, then progressively developed to support operations in the 1920s and 1930s. Trenchard, often described as the 'father of the RAF', commented that in his formative structure of the service, he had 'laid the foundations for a castle'.[1] The post-war period saw the RAF building on those foundations, a process that saw logistics evolving to meet the needs of the new service. By the outbreak of the Second World War, however, RAF Logistics were very different, largely as a result of the transformation that took place during the expansion programme that began in 1934. This chapter examines the formative period up to the end of 1933.

Formation of the Royal Flying Corps

The RFC emerged from the work of a standing sub-committee of the Committee of Imperial Defence in November 1911, which recommended that a Flying Corps be established, consisting of a Military and Naval Wing, a Central Flying School, and an aircraft factory. Following ministerial approval, the RFC was established by Royal Warrant on 13 April 1912. Given the difference in Army and Navy operating requirements, however, the Naval Wing moved away from the RFC and soon evolved into what unofficially became known as the RNAS.

By July 1915, the Admiralty declared that officers of the Naval Wing would become part of the Military Branch of the Royal Navy, and in July 1915, the Admiralty officially constituted the RNAS. The Admiralty worked independently from the outset and had established its own Air Department.[2] While a degree of coordination was achieved between the two services through a Joint Air Committee from 1912, its meetings ceased in August 1914 with the outbreak of hostilities.[3] Consequently, by August 1914, logistic support for the RNAS had become quite separate from the RFC with the Admiralty's Air Department's civil assistant becoming responsible for the supply of stores, spares, freight, and transport for naval aircraft.[4]

Although the design, development, and manufacturing capability of the Royal Aircraft Factory at Farnborough was available to both services, the RNAS developed its own technical department. Such an arrangement enabled the Admiralty to source its aircraft, engines, and spares from the open market, while the RFC was largely dependent on the Royal Aircraft Factory. This inevitably led to friction between both air arms, who literally competed for resources, rather than working together.[5] The first attempt at addressing problems caused by the disparate approaches to logistics by the RFC and the RNAS came in May 1916 with the creation of the first Air Board. Much wider problems with the use and administration of both the flying services led to the formation of a new Air Board in January 1917. Notwithstanding these attempts at higher level coordination, both the RFC and the RNAS pursued their own logistic support procedures throughout the war.

Many members of the RFC's predecessor, the Air Battalion of the Royal Engineers (RE), transferred to the new Flying Corps, taking with them their logistic expertise gained from supporting the very beginnings of military aviation. One such individual who contributed a great deal to the formative years of logistics in the RFC and the RAF was Frank Howard Kirby. Born in 1871 at Thame in Oxfordshire, Kirby enlisted in the RE in 1892 and was sent to South Africa in 1899. He served in the South African War until 1902, gaining the Distinguished Conduct Medal (DCM) in

RNAS personnel pictured in Paris with a partially crated aircraft on a transport lorry, *c.* 1915. (*Author's collection*)

March 1900 for blowing up part of the Bloemfontein railway. He won the Victoria Cross (VC) for his part during a raid north of Kronstadt when, under enemy fire, he rode to the aid of a man whose horse had been shot and recovered him to safety. Kirby was also mentioned in despatches several times for the South African War. He was subsequently commissioned into the Air Battalion of the RE in 1911, becoming quartermaster of the Central Flying School on his transfer to the RFC in 1912. He served in France during 1916 and, by 1917, had become the commanding officer (CO) of No. 1 Stores Depot at Kidbrooke in the rank of lieutenant-colonel. Of the many contributions, which Kirby made to the development of early air logistics, the most notable and influential was his work in helping to shape store keeping and stores accounting procedures. He remained with the newly formed RAF in 1918, subsequently joining its Stores Branch in 1920, and retired from the service as a group captain in 1926, having been appointed a Commander of the Order of the British Empire (CBE) the same year. Kirby died on the 8 July 1956 at Sidcup, Kent, and his grave is located at the Streatham Vale crematorium. There is a memorial to him in the Chatham Garrison Church, Kent.

Initially, military aviation in the Army was administered by a small committee until June 1913 when a Directorate of Military Aeronautics (DMA) was established in the War Office. This new directorate was divided into three sections: Military Aeronautics (MA) 1 was responsible for policy, administration and personnel; MA2 was responsible for equipment; and MA3 looked after contracts, including the purchase of aeronautical materiel.[6] As a result of the rapid growth of the RFC, the Director-General of Military Aeronautics became a member of the Army Council in February 1917.

Logistics in the RFC

By the time the German Army entered Belgium on 4 August 1914 and the subsequent declaration of war by Britain, the RFC had just sixty-three aircraft and ninety-five motor transport (MT) vehicles.[7] The Corps deployed to France for the first time with the British Expeditionary Force in August 1914 with just four squadrons of aircraft and an Aircraft Park, which provided logistical support.[8]

One of the earliest difficulties that the RFC experienced was due to the relative infancy of aircraft production. At the outbreak of war, there were just twelve aircraft-manufacturing firms in Britain, three of which were producers of seaplanes. In terms of output, total production amounted to just 100 aircraft per year.[9] This limited manufacturing capacity meant that the British were largely dependent on France to meet their needs. Indeed, the demand for aircraft in the first six months of the war was so great that some 100 aircraft were bought from French companies; by the end of the war, 1,500 airframes had been acquired from this source.[10] Notwithstanding the problems with supply of whole aircraft, there was also a lack of suitable aero engines; in the spring of 1914, the Government had even resorted to offering a £5,000 prize for a British-designed engine. Here too, the British were reliant on engines of French design, especially for the first six months of the war. The engine supply situation was further compounded by, quite ironically, a pre-war dependence on Germany for the production and supply of magnetos. British production was woefully inadequate and the source of supply was based on just one company. As a result, both the War Office and the Admiralty relied heavily on the import of mainly German-built magnetos. The shortage came to a head in the summer of 1916 when pre-war delivered supplies of magnetos were exhausted; it was not until the autumn that reliable British-produced magnetos became available and then only at a rate of between twenty and thirty a week. Raw material supply was one of the main causes of the lack of progress, with some components being sourced from as far away as Japan and America. Spares for repair were in very short supply and spare magnetos were often obtained by diverting those destined for new engine production.[11]

Despite the popularly held view that aircraft of this time were primitive structures made from just wood, wire, and canvas, the reality was more complex. This was a factor that quickly began to complicate their logistical support. The fuselage of the R.E.8 aircraft, for example (excluding the wood itself), consisted of 273 individually referenced items, within which there was a total of some 800 parts including nuts, bolts, washers, rivets, split pins, bracing wires, and various metal jointing plates.[12] As aircraft designs matured, they became more complex machines and were more demanding to maintain. Aside from the main aircraft structure, the range of on-aircraft equipment, all of which required spares, expanded significantly to include: wireless sets; Lewis and Vickers machine guns (including magazines and mountings); bombs, bomb carriers, sights and release gears; cameras and photographic equipment. There was also a wide range of miscellaneous stores such as brass, copper, gun-metal, solder, mild-steel, tool-steel, tin, copper-tubing, acetone, beeswax, paint, soda, soap, tallow, varnish, carbide, oil, and timber.[13] By October 1918, excluding obsolete aircraft and engine types, the newly-formed RAF was still operating around forty-two aircraft makes and types and some fifty-two engine variants.[14] The significance for logistics is that the extent and diversity of aircraft and aero engines multiplied the required spare parts, many of which were unique to specific manufacturers and were not interchangeable. The quantity of required spares needed to be forecast and then orders placed through a multitude of contracts. The spares then had to be physically stocked, located, and accounted for.

As the war progressed, the maximum number of aircraft that a squadron was permitted to hold at any one time (known as the aircraft establishment or AE) increased; this led to a corresponding increase in the equipment and spares requirement. In March 1916, the squadron AE increased to eighteen aircraft, further expanding to twenty-four in March 1917.[15] Deliveries of new aircraft to meet the changing AE between 1914 and 1918 were quite dramatic, progressively increasing from eighty-four in 1914 to 7,230 in 1918.[16] The growth in aircraft numbers was not just to meet an expanding Flying Corps, but also to meet substantial shortfalls

Replica R.E.8 aircraft pictured at the Shuttleworth Trust, Old Warden. (*Author's collection*)

from attrition; in the period from 12 June 1915 to 1 March 1917, of the 7,137 aircraft taken into service, 4,047 were struck off service charge—some 57 per cent of the deliveries.[17] By the end of October 1918, the newly formed RAF had a total of 22,171 aircraft on charge but with a total of 37,702 aero engines; of these, 5,090 were in the process of repair and 4,880 in store (of which 2,741 were obsolete).[18] Although a significant number were purchased from overseas, 55,093 aircraft and 41,034 engines had been manufactured in Britain.[19]

The operation of aircraft also called for large quantities of petroleum, oils, and lubricants (POL) and the supply of these presented a significant challenge, not just in terms of the quality requirements, but also the sheer volume required to support the RFC's rapidly growing aircraft fleet; by 1916, the RFC was consuming some 200,000 gallons per month.[20] The supply of petrol in particular was challenging. Although distribution by lorries carrying fuel in fifty-gallon drums had been used in the early months of the war, this soon proved to be impractical as their weight made handling difficult. It was thus that for the rest of the war, fuel was generally transported in two or four-gallon tins packed in wooden cases.[21] Refuelling aircraft was carried out by hand and was a time-consuming and laborious process. The Sopwith Camel F.1 aircraft, for example, required the best part of ten tins of aviation spirit (four-gallon capacity) to fill its fuel tanks.[22] Due to the high quality control and safety requirements, the fuel tin filling operation for aviation spirit needed special supervision; this was carried out at Portishead (near Bristol) until the spring of 1918 when, due to the consumption (which had then increased to around 600,000 gallons per month), fuel tin filling was carried out in France at Rouen and Calais

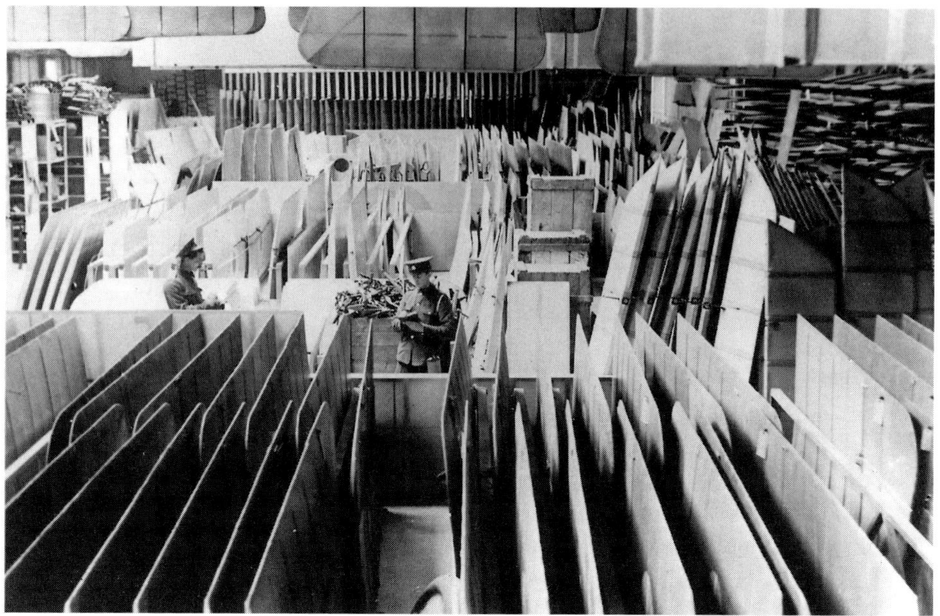

RFC wing store. (*IWM*)

from bulk storage tanks; these installations were supplied by tank steamers from the USA. From that point on, all fuel (aviation and MT) used overseas was filled and distributed from these installations. For units consuming large quantities of fuel, 3,000-gallon railway tank wagons and 600-gallon tank lorries were introduced in early 1917, although the use of two-gallon fuel tins still remained the most practical means of off-loading from these bulk carriers and transporting to the user units.[23]

Given these demands, it was essential that the RFC had an efficient and reliable logistics system; the Corps developed this, and it proved to be particularly effective throughout the war.[24] In essence, it consisted of four distinct elements, the first of which was procurement. From the formation of the RFC, complete aircraft were sourced by the Equipment Section of the DMA at the War Office, with quality standards monitored by an Aeronautical Inspection Department that had been formed in December 1913.[25] The uncoordinated approach to logistics by the RFC and the RNAS persisted throughout the early years of the war and, in March 1917, the responsibility for aeronautical supply was transferred to the Ministry of Munitions, albeit that responsibility for design, numbers to be ordered and allocation to the RFC and RNAS remained with the Air Board.[26] Stores and supplies for the RFC were ordered by the DMA through the Ordnance Aeronautical Stores Department (OASD) (part of the Army Ordnance Department) at Farnborough and were sourced from either the Royal Aircraft Factory or directly purchased from private manufacturers. This remained the arrangement until January 1917, when the OASD was absorbed into the Equipment Branch of Headquarters (HQ) RFC.[27] By the end of the war, this branch had developed into a well-organised structure, consisting of some twenty-five RFC officers in seven sub-sections responsible for both stores and technical activities.[28]

The second element of the logistic structure was the depot. The requirement for these had been evident from the very early days of the RFC as a location to hold the large volumes of spares being delivered from manufacturers, for the storage of complete aircraft awaiting allocation to units, and for a repair and maintenance capability that demanded a range of specialist workshops and specialist engineering equipment. The first of these establishments was formed at Farnborough in May 1912. Known as the Line of Communications Workshop, it was renamed the Flying Depot in 1913, before becoming the Aircraft Park in April 1914.[29] Up until the beginning of the First World War, the RFC's inventory was centrally administered by the Flying Depot, which replenished stores expended by squadrons and units on a monthly basis.[30] The sheer range and volume of equipment flowing into the depot, coupled with an ever-expanding workshop requirement, soon demanded additional space. Concurrent with this, it was found necessary to separate training aircraft and the storage of vehicle spares, paint, photographic and electrical equipment: the logistic task was beginning to grow. Consequently, additional facilities were established at Greenwich, Chelsea, and Ascot.[31] In early 1916, this home organisation was reorganised into what was known as the Southern and Northern Aircraft Depots. The Southern Depot was based on the original RFC location at Farnborough (where its HQ element was located) with a park on that site and at Chelsea and Ascot. Additionally, a Northern Aircraft Depot formed at Bradford was responsible for units north of an imaginary line drawn east and west through Nottingham.[32] Three further types of specialist unit were established in the United Kingdom (UK) during 1917: the first of these were Aircraft Acceptance Parks, which were responsible for receiving aircraft from manufacturers, examining and equipping them for operational service, before despatching them to units at home and overseas; the second type were Stores Distributing Parks (SDP) to supply the recently formed RFC Training Brigade and its flying training schools; and the third type were Stores depots (SD). These units were the genesis of the RAF's depot system, which developed after the First World War.[33]

The development of overseas depots followed similar principles but was more directly influenced by operational needs. The original aircraft park at Farnborough deployed with the RFC to France in August 1914 and by the end of October 1914 had become established at St Omer, with a port depot at Rouen. By the middle of 1915, the demands on the park had grown considerably and a second park was established at Candas, with a port depot at Boulogne. Both parks received their equipment by train from their respective port depots.[34] It quickly became apparent that the parks would become increasingly immobile unless they could be relieved of the heavy repair work commitment. With the decision to form brigades for each army, three new Army aircraft parks (AAP) were formed in December 1915, each allocated to one of the new brigades. The new parks were intended to remain as mobile as possible, situated to the

Engine change, RFC style. (*Crown Copyright—Air Historical Branch MoD*)

rear of each army and close to a railhead to enable rapid redeployment. Each park held between two weeks' and one month's stock of stores and looked after the daily needs of the flying squadrons in their respective army.[35] This was a particularly significant development as the mobility of these new parks would enable them to extend the supply chain if and when the supported flying squadrons moved forward any significant distance. This characteristic, which enables a supply chain to be extended from the home base to forward operating locations, is often referred to as logistical reach. Indeed, stores and supplies were packed into purpose-built cases, which could be easily loaded onto lorries and stock issued on the move if required.[36] This concept remained an important component of the RAF's logistic order of battle (ORBAT) and became a key part of the RAF's *War Manual* much later in 1928. With mobility largely preserved through the new AAPs, the former aircraft parks at St Omer and Candas became fixed repair and supply parks and were renamed aircraft depots on 15 December 1915. Each of the main depots held up to three months' stock of aircraft and vehicle stores, and received all new aircraft destined for front line squadrons. In terms of geographical distance, most of the flying squadrons were located six to eight miles from the front line with their new AAPs some five to ten miles further back.[37]

The third element of the logistic organisation was distribution. The movement of stores within the UK and to overseas theatres was heavily dependent on rail, sea, and inland waterways. As far as the campaign in France was concerned, most military stores were moved across the Channel by barge and then onwards by rail or inland waterways; in the case of the RFC, the majority of equipment was moved to the Continent via the port depots at Boulogne and Rouen. This total military task alone (of which the RFC's requirement was a relatively small component) was a sizeable undertaking. The quantity of stores and supplies conveyed by inland waterways in France rose from a weekly average of just over 19,000 tons in November 1916 to a peak of over 66,000 tons in October 1918.[38] The cross-Channel barge tonnage was also extensive, rising from a weekly average of 445 tons in December 1916 to a peak of just over 25,000 tons in October 1918.[39] The total figure for cross-Channel shipment between 9 August 1914 and 26 March 1920 was 27,566,245 tons. Of this figure, aircraft stores (excluding fuels, oils and ammunition) amounted to just 131,339 tons or 0.48 per cent.[40] By way of comparison, the figure for hay and oats for livestock (mainly horses and mules) was 5,919,427 tons or just over 21 per cent.[41]

The fourth element of the RFC's logistic organisation was squadron level support. At its heart was the maintenance of sufficient stocks to support flying and the wider needs of ground equipment and personnel. The growth in the diversity of equipment types led to an exponential increase in the size of the RFC's inventory, which required a sophisticated stock control and accounting system. The procedures used by the RFC were developed as early as March 1913 and were based on a modified version of the Regulations for Royal Engineers Services.[42] These were later promulgated as the official system of accounting for the RFC.[43] A number of the principles in this document continue to underpin the general supply accounting process in use by Defence logistics in the twenty-first century. A key feature of this system was that items in the RFC's inventory were clearly identified. This was especially important in the support of aircraft where much of their structure, especially aero engines, consisted of closely fitting components and the selection of exactly the right replacement part was essential. This required the allocation of a part or stock number, which was usually one that had already been given to the item by the original manufacturer. Up until 1918, there was no standard RFC system of identification and manufacturers often used quite complex systems. The Royal Aircraft Factory, for example, used a four-level identification system consisting of a unit, component, group, part number system to identify components in the R.E.8 reconnaissance aircraft.[44] Thus, for example, a straightforward washer for part of the aircraft's tail plane adjusting gear was identified as Unit No. 300, Component No. C.524, Group S.677, Part No. AGS.160D.

It was also necessary to know what stock was held, not just for visibility of holdings, but also for reasons of propriety as stores and supplies were, in theory, public property; even in war, the need to protect the 'public purse' was ever present. At the higher level, stores and supplies used by the RFC were classified using a categorization system: Class 'A' included complete items such as instruments, tools, plant and special stores, and Class 'B' items were components of complete items or consumable stores such as oils and paints; a further category, Class 'C', was later added to cover the consumable items.[45] This made the task of inventory management

RFC tyre store. (*IWM*)

more straightforward as initially, only Class 'A' items were accounted for throughout their in-service life. The overall system required manuscript ledgers to be kept; these formed the main stock record of equipment.[46] Of particular note is that the record of stock holdings was purely a local matter, and there was no overall master stock record balance maintained by the RFC at HQ level. Consequently, without a master record of stock, it was not possible to view the RFC's complete holdings and therefore extremely difficult to redistribute stores and supplies should they be required elsewhere. For example, a squadron might be short of a specific item, but the same item might be in plentiful supply at a neighbouring squadron. The challenge of this is best appreciated when set against the overall size of the RFC's inventory, which, by the end of the war, had grown to approximately 50,000 different types of item.[47] The requirement for overall visibility of stockholdings by managers remained a significant challenge for RAF Logistics throughout the inter-war and Second World War periods. Serious progress towards what was known as 'global' visibility of assets was not achieved until the RAF introduced computerised stock control in 1965.

Introduction of Equipment Officers

All this work required specialists who understood the finer points of managing stores and supplies. Prior to the First World War, this responsibility rested with just two quartermasters for the RFC: Lieutenant W. J. D. Pryce for the Military Wing (based at the Flying Depot and known as the Officer in Charge Stores) and Lieutenant F. H. Kirby VC for the Central Flying School.[48] For the flying squadrons though, there were no commissioned officers appointed as quartermasters and stores were the overall responsibility of the respective squadron CO. To assist them in this task, storekeepers were appointed for each of the flights within a squadron, with an assistant known as a storeman and a ledger keeper to maintain the records of account and the associated paperwork.[49]

This arrangement endured until the end of 1914, by which time operating experience had shown that there was a growing need for a specialist ground branch officer. This shortfall was addressed in January 1915 with the introduction of a new officer specialisation known as an Equipment officer, whose purpose was to 'to relieve the over-burdened pilots and observers'.[50] There were two grades: an Equipment officer (EO), in the rank of captain, for wings, and an assistant Equipment officer (AEO), in the rank of lieutenant or second lieutenant, for squadrons.[51] The title itself is misleading in that the specialisation was responsible for both supplies and engineering. Most of the new posts were filled by commissioning regular quartermaster sergeants of the RE and by calling for volunteers whose previous experience varied between general engineering and a basic knowledge of the internal combustion engine.

The rate of expansion was quite marked as, by July 1916, there were some 412 officers serving as EOs, AEOs, or quartermasters in the RFC.[52] As far as training was concerned, this was somewhat *ad hoc* until a dedicated school was set up near Reading in August 1917 and designated No. 1 Equipment Officers School of Instruction. By October 1917, the school had moved to Henley-on-Thames and was accommodated in a number of temporarily requisitioned premises in and around the town including the Imperial Hotel, Royal Hotel, Phyllis Court Club, and the Grosvenor Club in Remenham. At this time, the course was eight weeks in duration, the first two of which were spent studying various aspects of stores administration and then six weeks to become 'acquainted with technical terms to give them an elementary knowledge of engines, aeroplanes and MT'.[53] The ideal individuals for appointment as an EO or AEO were seen as 'incapacitated flying officers and observers (over twenty-five years old), trained RAF WOs and SNCOs (stores) and civilians of good education and business experience'.[54]

The RFC equipment organisation was by no means an all-male preserve. It relied quite heavily on women; by the middle of 1917, the newly formed Women's Army Auxiliary Corps (WAAC) was accepting applicants specifically for RFC service. In March 1918, there were some 1,322 female stores workers in the RFC.[55] The logistic organisation also had a significant number of civilians (men and women) in its workforce, especially at the UK Stores depots. At No. 1 SD Kidbrooke, of the 2,200 military and civilian staff working at the depot in 1917, about 20 per cent of the civilian staff were women.[56]

Left: A typical RFC airman. This style of tunic was popularly known as the 'maternity' jacket. (*Author's collection*)

Below: Group of RAF Equipment Officers pictured in 1918. Note the mixed style of very early RAF uniform. (*Author's collection*)

A Standardised Approach to Store Keeping and Accounting

Amid the broader description of how the RFC's logistics system developed, recognition needs to be given to a handful of RFC officers within the DMA at the War Office who, through dogged determination, managed to develop and implement a standardised method of store-keeping and accounting for the RFC. Towards the end of October 1917, a special branch was formed in the DMA initially consisting of Lieutenant-Colonel A. Fletcher (soon succeeded by Lieutenant-Colonel F. H. Kirby VC), Captain J. Rylands, Lieutenant A. Holmes, and Lieutenant Price. Their task was to introduce a standard system and uniformity into the RFC's stores accounting organisation. The team wasted no time in getting to grips with this significant challenge, with Lieutenant Kirby and Captain Rylands tackling the Stores depots, AAPs, and SDPs while Lieutenants Holmes and Price visited all home units. By consulting the reports of army local auditors who were carrying out their own personal audits and test stocktaking, a number of weaknesses were soon observed. It is not clear exactly when this work was completed but the findings and recommendations were submitted to and endorsed by the Air Board by the end of 1917. The results of this work formed the first standardised procedures for RFC store keeping and accounting and were promulgated by Air Board letter to all RFC HQs.

Mobile Logistics

One RFC initiative in particular had far-reaching implications for RAF Logistics and was a concept that underpinned the development of what were later to be known as Air Stores Parks in the 1930s. The German offensive during the spring of 1918 and the advance towards the rail junction at Amiens caused significant supply problems for the RFC and the far-sighted concept of mobility (despite the largely static nature of trench warfare that had prevailed for most of the war) came into its own. On the first day of the offensive, many of the RFC's aerodromes came under artillery fire. Consequently, new aerodromes had to be identified and occupied almost on a daily basis. Indeed, by 5 April 1918, forty-five new aerodromes had been secured.[57] This upheaval brought with it the need to maintain stores and supplies to the squadrons of the newly formed RAF, which became all the more difficult when their supplying units, the aircraft parks, had to move as a result of the threat from the enemy offensive.[58] To meet the need for these urgently required supplies, the Deputy Assistant Adjutant and Quartermaster-General at RFC HQ, Brigadier-General H. R. M. Brooke-Popham, introduced what were known as resupply convoys. His priority was to ensure that each new aerodrome location had adequate stocks of fuel and munitions and as soon as a new site had been identified, stocks were pre-positioned in order that the incoming squadrons could be re-armed and fuelled without delay. To support this concept, two convoys were set up, each of eight light tenders. One

Group of RFC airmen on a Leyland lorry in 1913. (*Crown Copyright—Air Historical Branch MoD*)

of the convoys was loaded with machine-gun ammunition and 25-lb bombs and could deploy at five minutes' notice, day or night; the second convoy provided a delivery service for urgently required spare parts.[59] This initiative enabled the flying squadrons to focus on their operational task and to remain mobile without the additional burden of maintaining their own resupply of critical stores and supplies.

Operations in the Middle East

Although much written about the RFC during the First World War focuses on the Western Front, it was also particularly active in the Middle East. The organisation chart of the RAF Middle East on 30 September 1918 shows deployments in Palestine, Salonika, Mesopotamia and India, each with its own Aircraft Park. Conditions at many locations were rudimentary to say the least, a fact that is well-illustrated by a description of the park, which had been established at Tanooma on the other side of Basra harbour to support operations in Mesopotamia in 1915. Conditions here were very basic and the park was located in a number of palm-leaf huts with a few iron-roofed brick sheds, surrounded by desert. Of particular difficulty was the provision of labour to unload supplies coming in by sea. Indeed, many ships were reported as lying in harbour for months with others returning to India having unloaded only a small part of their cargo.[60]

Formation of the RAF and the Air Ministry

As early as 1916, the overlapping responsibilities of the RFC and the RNAS, the competition for aircraft and engines, coupled with growing public concern over German bombing raids, led to consideration of the possible unification of the air services. Eventually, the Prime Minister, Lloyd George, appointed General Jan Christian Smuts to head a government committee to examine air defence and air organisation.[61] As part of his report, Smuts recommended the formation of a new service that would be independent from the Army and Navy; with the passing of the Air Force Bill in November 1917, the RAF officially came into being on 1 April 1918.

Smuts also recommended the formation of an Air Ministry and an Air Council (to replace the Air Board), and these were established on 3 January 1918 with Lord Rothermere as the first Secretary of State and President of the Council. Initially, responsibility for logistics (now in a Directorate of Equipment (DofE)), excluding aircraft production, was the responsibility of a Controller-General of Equipment (CGE), Major-General (later Air Vice-Marshal Sir) W. S. Brancker.

The RAF Establishes its Approach to Logistics

The logistic organisation and processes of the new RAF were largely based on the RFC's system. There is little in archival sources to account for this, but the fact that the Air Council was dominated by RFC officers, largely because their former corps was by far the larger of the two air arms, might go some way in providing an explanation. Indeed, of the nine key members (excluding the Secretary and Assistant Secretary), just two Naval officers were included—Rear-Admiral Kerr filling the post of Deputy Chief of the Air Staff and Commodore Paine as Master-General of Personnel. Thus, by the time the RAF was formed, the RNAS had limited influence as far as the development of logistics for the new service was concerned.[62]

Although aviation was a relatively new technology, it had quickly become apparent that the logistical needs of air power were considerable and statistics quoted earlier in this chapter only scratch the surface. This was further complicated by the diversity of aircraft and engine types in service; by November 1918, the RAF was operating over twenty aircraft types and twenty-three different engines. The overall cost had been high, both in terms of money and manpower. Indeed, by the Armistice, air expenditure was in the region of £1 million per day. Of all the lessons learned, perhaps the need for mobility would prove to be vital to future operations. It was a factor that was critical during the Second World War and has gained significance again, after not quite so much emphasis during the Cold War, in the evolving British Defence strategy of the twenty-first century.

One of the first priorities for RAF Logistics in the post-First World War period was to introduce a standardised peacetime approach to stores accounting and storekeeping, which would maintain a degree of propriety and public accountability. By and large, the system of accounting for RFC units had been adopted by the RAF from its formation; however, this reflected Army working practices and had evolved piecemeal to meet wartime needs.[63] It was thus that the Air Ministry's Establishment Committee, chaired by Bertram Jones (who had been transferred to the Air Ministry from the Ministry of Munitions to advise on finance), was tasked with conducting a review. The findings of the committee became known as the Jones Report and were presented to the Secretary of State in November 1918.[64]

The report was particularly insightful about logistics and recognised that careful reorganisation could enable things to be done more efficiently and economically. Moreover, with the imminent demobilisation following the cessation of hostilities, there was a pressing need to put in place an efficient logistics organisation that could handle the huge stocks of war surplus materiel. The report recommended that the DofE should be divided into five separate directorates: Aircraft Equipment, Provision, Stores, Parks and Depots, and a Record Branch. There was also a recommendation that an Accounting Committee be formed to review the methods of store keeping in the RAF to improve them where necessary and establish a standard system that was not to be deviated from without Air Ministry authority.[65]

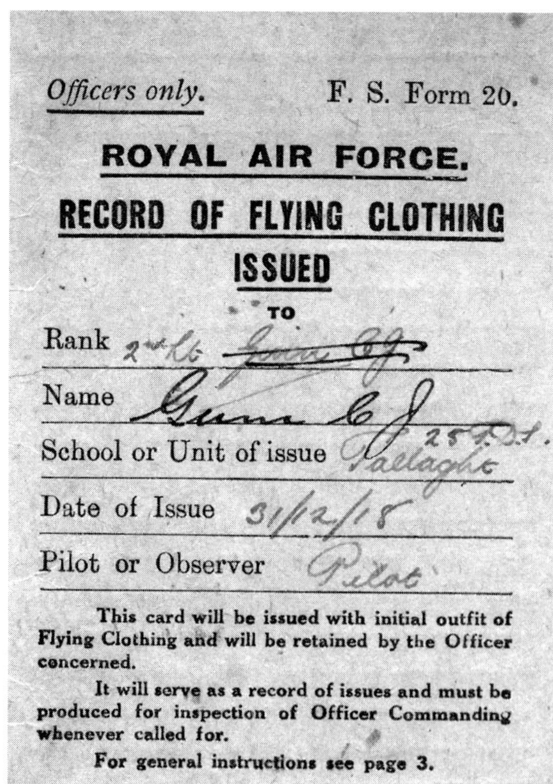

Officers only. F. S. Form 20.

ROYAL AIR FORCE.

RECORD OF FLYING CLOTHING ISSUED

TO

Rank 2nd Lt

Name Gunn C J

School or Unit of issue

Date of Issue 31/12/18

Pilot or Observer Pilot

This card will be issued with initial outfit of Flying Clothing and will be retained by the Officer concerned.

It will serve as a record of issues and must be produced for inspection of Officer Commanding whenever called for.

For general instructions see page 3.

One of the many standardised documents produced in 1918. (*Author's collection*)

The Jones Report was considered at the sixty-second meeting of the Air Council on 19 November 1918. However, it was decided that the recommendations could not be adopted during demobilisation; rather, the report should be passed to the CGE who 'should be guided by the principles laid down on reorganizing his department on a smaller scale'. The file was passed to the CGE for further action on 11 December 1918.[66] It is not clear if the five directorates were ever introduced, but the suggestion regarding the Accounting Committee most certainly was. Shortly after the referral to CGE, a part-time committee was formed to 'create a proper system for peace time working'; this committee was officially named as the Committee on Store Accounting and Storekeeping Procedure and put on a full-time basis in August 1919.[67]

The terms of reference bore a very close resemblance to the Jones Report recommendations, with the declared intentions of examining the store keeping methods in use at all types of RAF unit and to draw up a definitive storekeeping and accounting manual. Two more requirements in the terms of reference were, for the time, both innovative and consultative: firstly, the committee wished to obtain the opinions of RAF Equipment officers, and secondly, they would investigate storekeeping methods employed by civilian firms engaged in what it termed 'analogous trades'. The committee made a number of visits to Army ordnance and supply depots, Naval dockyards, railway clearing houses, and commercial firms handling similar stores to the RAF. Their work was not just theoretical and, in many cases, methods that looked suitable for use in the RAF were first tested in a stores facility at Andover, which had been made available to the committee for experimental purposes. Many of the new procedures had an immediate and, in some cases, quite a significant effect on the service. One major change was that responsibility for stores held by flights or sections was to be transferred from the stores officer to the inventory held by the respective flight officer. It is not clear from which date this change became effective, but the six-monthly return revealed that 75 per cent of equipment held by flights had been returned to stores.[68]

By November 1920, most of the new procedures and regulations had been introduced. Shortly afterwards, these regulations were published as Air Publication (AP) 830: *Instructions for Store Accounting and Store Keeping*, issued in August 1921. At the heart of these regulations was the principle that each self-accounting unit would be permitted to hold items on the basis of establishments; this was a set figure for each line item, which specified the maximum number that could be held at any one time. Once stock holdings dropped to a certain level, the unit concerned submitted a demand for stock replenishment that, in turn, was provided (or 'satisfied' as this later became known) by the appropriate Stores depot.[69] The AP830 became the day-to-day handbook of RAF Logistics, providing detailed policies and procedures for much of its activity. Additionally, this governance was supported by a whole range of other documents outlining agreed flying rates, weapons consumption, equipment scales, fuels, and explosives.

Another change at this time concerned identification of equipment. As highlighted earlier, there was no standard method of naming items (vocabulary) and the inventory contained items from both the army vocabulary and what was known as the Naval *Rate Book*. An example of the confusion that existed as a result of this lack of standardisation was that India rubber tubing appeared in no fewer than eleven different sections in stores ledgers. The opportunity was taken to standardise parts identification and the RAF introduced what was known as 'nomenclature', which divided the items within the RAF inventory into sections. This enabled each individual item (or line item as they became known) to be given a standard name and a unique identity. For example, a single spring washer (one quarter of an inch) was categorised in Section 54 and allocated the specific reference number of 162D; thus, this item's official stores identity became '54/162D, Spring, Single, ¼'.[70] This section and reference identification (known as domestic reference numbering) provided a logical, standardised, and flexible system that served the RAF well throughout the Second World War and beyond, until the North Atlantic Treaty Organisation (NATO) codification system was gradually adopted in the mid-1950s (see Chapter Nine).[71]

Challenges for RAF Logistics in the Early Post-war Period

The immediate post-war years saw the RAF move from a service on a war footing, consuming vast quantities of equipment and supplies, to a largely peacetime service with a significantly reduced support requirement. The RAF had demobilised some 275,565 people (officers, cadets and other ranks) during the period 11 November 1918 to 1 May 1920.[72] By October 1920, the strength was a mere 3,000 officers and 24,000 other ranks, a reduction to less than one-tenth of its wartime levels within two years.[73] The number of flying squadrons was also reduced substantially; by the beginning of 1921 there were just nineteen: five each in Britain and Egypt, four each in India and Iraq, and one in the Far East.[74]

In addition to existing Empire interests in India and Egypt, Britain also gained a responsibility for territories formerly occupied by the Imperial German and Ottoman dynasties under an initiative by the League of Nations, which included Palestine, Jordan, and Mesopotamia (Iraq). It was little surprise that this brought with it many tribal clashes and anti-British uprisings.[75] It was against this turbulent backdrop, and at a time of continuing debate regarding the need for an independent air force, that the RAF began to secure a key role in what became known as imperial policing.[76] As part of this, the RAF was employed as widely as possible to demonstrate just how effective (both in terms of cost and resources) air power could be.[77]

A significant step forward came in 1921 when, following the success of the RAF in the then British Somaliland policing operations, the Service took the lead role in action against dissident groups in Iraq and Transjordan.[78] A key point here is that the employment of air power represented significant value for money. For example, the total cost of using the RAF in the month-long operations against the so called 'mad' Mullah in Somaliland in 1920 came to just £70,000. This cost was placed in context by the Secretary of State for War at the time who declared to Parliament that 'the Royal Air Force on this expedition achieved more than we were able to do in one expedition before the war at an expenditure of over £2,500,000, and that would be £6,000,000 or £7,000,000 of the present currency'.[79] This 'imperial policing' provided 'a cheap and ubiquitous form of colonial control in the more inaccessible corners of the globe'.[80]

There was, however, a dichotomy here for logistics. On the one hand, the post-First World War run-down of the RAF had led to a substantial reduction in the levels of equipment stocks. Indeed, some 10,000 aircraft and 30,000 aero engines (along with accompanying spares) became surplus to requirements and were sold-off for £1 million and 50 per cent of future profits to the Aircraft Disposal Company.[81] On the other hand, the requirement to provide support for emerging but quite uncertain future commitments, required sufficient equipment to be retained and this became problematical. The Operations Record Book (ORB) for No. 3 SD at Milton, for example, makes the comment in 1920 that 'difficulties were experienced in framing an idea as to what quantity of stocks should be held to meet the requirements of the Royal Air Force units in peace time'.[82] It is likely that equipment disposal was achieved with relative ease, though it would have been a sizeable task in terms of the physical work involved to move this materiel from where it was located, to the Air Disposal Company. The question of maintaining sufficient equipment for the future, however, proved to be more difficult.

This was particularly evident in India. The availability of spares became critical here and the RAF was dependent on the financial vote of the Army in India. By the beginning of the 1920s, the position had become desperate and using parts from grounded aircraft to keep others serviceable, otherwise known as 'robbing' (Peter to pay Paul), had become increasingly commonplace. The memoirs of Marshal of the RAF Sir Arthur Harris provide an enlightening view of the situation at the time. Posted to the North West Frontier in 1919–20 as officer commanding (OC) No. 45 Squadron, Harris was especially critical of the logistics situation and described how his squadron 'lacked everything in the way of necessary accommodation and spares and materials for keeping our aircraft serviceable'.[83] What particularly infuriated him was that there were large numbers of dual-ignition engines available at home that were being sold as scrap by the Disposal Board for a few pounds.[84] The situation deteriorated to the point where Air Vice-Marshal Sir John Salmond (formerly air officer commanding (AOC) of the RAF Inland Area in Britain) was sent to India in early 1922 to conduct an urgent enquiry.[85] Salmond's report, which was delivered in August 1922, left no doubt as to the state of affairs, commenting in the opening paragraph that 'it is with regret that I have to report that the Royal Air Force in India is to all intents and purposes non-existent as a fighting force at this date'.[86] Indeed, of the seventy aircraft on the authorised establishment in August 1922, just seven were serviceable, a situation largely attributable to the lack of spares.[87] There were a number of other contributory factors, all of which were subject to wide ranging recommendations in Salmond's report. The position took time to recover and showed that operational effectiveness could deteriorate rapidly if logistics was neglected.[88]

There is little in archival sources to illustrate how these early overseas commitments were supported but the limited size of each would suggest that the self-sustaining design of squadrons and proximity to already established RAF bases in these theatres, such as Habbaniya in Iraq, were significant factors.[89] Nonetheless, their support remained a challenge for the early RAF stores organisation, which had only just managed to set in place its own procedures and was establishing resupply routes to places that, at the time, were difficult to access. The world today is a much smaller place, thanks largely to vastly improved telecommunications and long-range, high-speed transport aircraft; in the early 1920s, prior to the use of the air mail route in the Middle East, it took some six to seven weeks by sea just to get correspondence from the UK to Baghdad, let alone bulky stores and equipment.[90]

The Post-War Stores Depots

Responsibility for procurement of aircraft and equipment for the RAF was the overall responsibility of the Director General of Supply and Research. Once in service, responsibility for the ongoing supply support of aircraft, equipment and people rested with the DofE. Depots were the next key link in the supply chain but the number of these was drastically reduced in the immediate post-war period. By the end of 1918, the RAF in the UK had inherited eight Stores Distributing Parks (SDP) and seven SDs from the RFC's logistic organisation. There was little need for such an extensive depot structure post-war and these were rationalised by the Air Ministry, which decided that all stores distribution would be carried out from the main SDs. Consequently, the eight SDPs were closed, leaving in place Nos 1, 3, 4, and 5 SDs, plus the Packing Depot at Ascot (formerly No. 6 SD).[91]

Further rationalisation took place in September 1921 when No. 5 SD (Balloon Stores Depot) was closed and amalgamated with No. 4 SD at Ruislip; in 1924, the Army depot at Altrincham was taken over as No. 2 SD to accommodate the increasing RAF range of arms, ammunition, pyrotechnics, and bombs.[92] Thus, by 1933, the RAF was served by four SDs: No. 1 SD Kidbrooke, No. 2 SD Altrincham, No. 3 SD Milton, and No. 4 SD Ruislip. These depots received equipment and supplies from manufacturers, maintained a bulk stockholding for the replenishment of unit stocks, and acted as distribution centres for RAF stations at home and overseas. As far as overseas depots were concerned in 1920, a Stores depot was situated at Alexandria in Egypt with similar functions located within the aircraft parks at Baghdad in Iraq and Lahore in India. In 1924, a supply depot was constructed at

Sarafand in Palestine, followed by the establishment of a stores and supply depot at Steamer Point, Aden during 1929. To facilitate the conveyance of men and materiel abroad, a RAF embarkation office was established at the port of Southampton in 1921, with a port detachment at London's West India Dock in 1930. Port detachments were also established on the receiving end to serve their respective depots overseas in India, Egypt, Iraq, Palestine, and Aden.[93]

Most of the depots had an interesting story to tell in terms of their development, but none perhaps more so than No. 1 SD at Kidbrooke. The depot itself was originally established in October 1915 as an RFC storage centre for aircraft produced in excess of immediate requirements. Like many of the wartime depots, it had been set up as a temporary facility—in this case, in the former Thames Iron Works. Additional space was soon required and, by December 1915, extra storage was acquired at the Charlton Rope Works, which was quickly pressed into service storing MT spares, tools, electrical, wireless, and photographic equipment. During January 1916, the damp conditions at the iron works site were found to be unsuitable for the storage of aircraft so these were moved elsewhere, their place being taken by machine-guns, bomb dropping apparatus, and sights. Soon after, in March 1916, an explosives section was added at Charlton with the responsibility for small arms ammunition and various types of flares. With the rapid expansion of the RFC during the middle of 1916, further storage was needed; the Greenwich Linoleum Works at Blackwall Lane was hired and devoted to the storage of machine tools. Housed in temporary facilities, the depot did not really exist as a purpose-built entity.

By the beginning of January 1917, Lieutenant-Colonel Frank Kirby VC had assumed command of the Kidbrooke depot and its satellites. He had clearly inherited a very 'mixed bag' and it was increasingly difficult to operate quickly or efficiently from such a mixture of scattered hirings. Consequently, consideration was given to building a depot in an area adjacent to the Kidbrooke railway sidings, which had already been used for movement in and out of the existing hirings. The project was approved by the Air Board at a cost of £250,000, with work starting in June 1917. By August that year, the personnel strength of the depot was approximately twenty-four officers and 2,200 civilian staff. In the late summer of 1918 the building work was nearly complete and by the Armistice in November 1918, equipment had been moved into the new site from Greenwich and Charlton, along with the wireless repair section from No. 10 MT Depot at Wormwood Scrubs. With the formation of the then WRAF, a large number of the women already working at No. 1 SD Kidbrooke were enrolled into the WRAF along with a number of others by direct recruitment in the local area. This was not as good for the men as it might first appear as all those who were physically fit were subsequently transferred for duties on the Western Front. There must have been a sizeable intake of staff (presumably mostly women) as the strength of the depot on 11 November 1918 was approximately 100 officers and a mixture of 4,000 airmen, WRAF, and civilians.[94]

By 1 January 1920, Kidbrooke's strength had dropped to thirty-six officers, 687 airmen (there is no specific reference to the number of airwomen), 1,083 civilian men, and 124 civilian women. As part of the rapid demobilisation of airmen, the number of civilian employees had been increased, pending airmen on post-war engagements becoming available. During the winter of 1919–1920, the number of civilians was steadily reduced by discharge and replaced by airmen being posted in. This did not go down at all well with the civilian workforce and their representative obtained a hearing from the Prime Minister no less, as a result of which the Air Council agreed to staff the SDs with civilians under RAF officers. By 1 April 1920, the last of the airmen were posted away leaving a civilian strength of 1,894. The depot continued to take on more equipment ranges; by 1 January 1923, the number of civilian personnel had dropped to about 996. A further interesting change took place in April 1924 concerning security at Kidbrooke. The Metropolitan Police had been responsible for this since 1919, but were replaced by civilian warders as the cost of the police presence was perceived to be too high.

The RAF Stores Branch

On the formation of the RAF in 1918, the management of logistics below Air Ministry level still remained the responsibility of Equipment officers, a role which had been established as part of the RFC in 1915, although they still had a dual responsibility for both engineering and stores matters. This had never been an entirely satisfactory arrangement as each of these disciplines required quite different professional backgrounds and specialist knowledge. The requirement for an officer branch solely responsible for logistics (then referred to generically as stores) was championed by the RAF's second post-war DGE, Air Commodore (later Air Vice-Marshal Sir) Charles Lambe, who had taken up the post in June 1919.[95] In due course, Lambe proposed the formation of a Stores Branch with the intention that its officers be recruited largely from the ranks. The proposal was approved by the Secretary of State for War and Air (Winston Churchill) in mid-October 1919, and the official announcement was made in Air Ministry weekly orders (AMWO) in late October 1919.[96] Air Commodore Lambe became the first head of the new branch; the succession of this post since the inaugural appointment is shown in Appendix I.

In addition to stores duties at RAF units, it was intended that officers of the new branch would also form the greater part of the officer personnel of Stores depots, aeroplane repair depots, and the DofE at the Air Ministry. It is interesting to note, however, that the AMWO made it quite clear that the higher commands of those depots and the higher appointments in the Directorate of Equipment would be filled by officers on the RAF general list, except where senior stores officers 'have shown themselves by outstanding merit to be specially fitted for command of a depot'. It was the intention at that time to recruit officers of the Stores Branch from those who had been commissioned from the ranks and that the branch would form a separate list (with separate scales of pay and pension and terms of service) from the general list

Above: The officers of No. 1 Stores Depot, Kidbrooke, 1921. This view of an evening dinner gives an idea of the number of officers at a typical depot of the time. (*Author's collection*)

Right: Air Commodore Charles Lambe. (*Author's collection*)

of the RAF. To reinforce this, the order clearly stipulated that stores officers would not be required to fly. Even so, the medical standards required of stores officers were still fairly stringent and required that they 'labour under no constitutional or mental disease or weakness, imperfection or disability which might interfere with the efficient discharge of their duties in any climate in peace or war'.[97]

Rates of pay and conditions of service for the new branch were published in June 1920 with flying officers earning nineteen shillings a day, flight lieutenants one pound and three shillings a day, squadron leaders one pound and ten shillings a day, and wing commanders one pound and fifteen shillings a day; at 2017 prices, these sums represent the buying power of roughly £20, £25, £33, and £39 per day respectively. These rates of pay, representing a range for the ranks indicated of between six and ten pounds per week, were above what the average civilian worker might expect in the inter-war years (between two and three pounds a week excluding his food, accommodation, and clothing).[98] Retirement ages were different for each rank with flying officers and flight lieutenants retiring at the age of forty-five, squadron leaders at fifty, and wing commanders at fifty-five. The new branch (excluding group captains and above) consisted of 245 officers; 203 had been selected for permanent commissions and forty-two for short service commissions.[99] The Stores Branch first appeared in the *Air Force List* of February 1921. The entry, shown as the Stores List, details those officers who had been re-seconded to the new branch and shows a distinguished range of names, many of whom had been decorated for gallantry or exemplary service. Indeed, there is one VC, one DCM, four Military Crosses (MC), three DCMs, and one Military Medal (MM). Holders of appointments to the Order of the British Empire were even more prolific with fourteen Officers (OBE) and seventeen Members (MBE).[100]

Although not on the formative list of Stores Branch officers, Charles Edward Cullen joined very shortly after and appears in the November 1921 Air Force List as 'Flying Officer (Stores)', but with a seniority date in that rank of 20 July 1920. Cullen is a good example of the breadth of experience the branch was blessed with in those early days. Born in Dover in 1882, he joined the RE as a bugler in 1896 and, by 1910, was a corporal at the Balloon School. He served in the Second Boer War and was present at the Siege of Ladysmith. With its formation in 1912, he transferred to the RFC and became one of its founder members with a service number of twelve. Cullen subsequently went to France in 1914 with No. 2 Squadron in the rank of flight sergeant and was mentioned in Sir John French's despatches of 19 October 1914; Cullen's was the first name in the very first list of RFC mentions during the First World War. Promoted to sergeant major in March 1915, Cullen was eventually commissioned as a second lieutenant in the RFC in October 1917, becoming an Equipment officer with No. 59 Squadron. He was clearly quite a man and was again mentioned in despatches while with the squadron in July 1919. Following his transfer to the RAF Stores Branch, Cullen went on to serve at the Air Pilotage School (Cadre) at Andover. Although he retired from the service at the age of forty-five in 1927, he remained with the Stores Branch as a flight lieutenant (retired) and was one of the many retired officers who formed a key part of the branch during the inter-war years. Cullen served throughout the Second World War, working in the Equipment Section at the Reception Depot, RAF West Drayton.[101]

Towards the end of 1923, the conditions of entry to the Stores Branch were revised and it was decided that stores duties in the future would only be filled by officers on permanent commissions. Vacancies in the branch were to be considered on a twice-yearly basis and filled by existing air force officers who had applied to transfer from their existing branch; on the whole, these were general duties (GD) officers who had become permanently unfit for flying duties or officers holding short service commissions in the GD or accountant branches. Selections were restricted to officers not above the rank of flying officer.[102] By 1927, the number of applications from within the service was not sufficient to meet vacancies in the Branch, and the source of applicants was widened to include civilians.[103]

The growth of the RAF Stores Branch was quite slow up to 1935. From a starting position of approximately 245 officers in 1920, the number climbed very slowly to 319 officers by 1935—an increase of only seventy-four officers over a fifteen-year period. Despite this relatively small number, they had certainly made their presence felt and stores officers were serving on the staff of all the HQ units in the UK and overseas, as well as on each flying squadron and training establishment. With the RAF providing pilots to serve on board Royal Navy aircraft carriers from about 1923 onwards, a Stores Branch officer (usually a flight lieutenant) was also provided as part of this commitment. In 1930, a Stores Branch officer was serving in the RAF's HQ element on each of the four carriers that were active at that time (HMS *Eagle*, HMS *Hermes*, HMS *Courageous*, and HMS *Glorious*). The inter-war period also saw the development of the Branch's first professional qualification with the creation of the explosives specialisation in February 1927. The names of officers so qualified were prefixed by a bold letter 'X' in the Air Force List and were defined as 'qualified to take charge of magazines and explosives'. In 1930, the RAF introduced a policy of promoting warrant officers class one to commissioned rank, with Stores being the first branch in the Service to do so; this policy was extended to the GD Branch in 1933, with the Accountant Branch following suit in 1934.

By 1928, with the RAF in its tenth year of operation, the Air Council directed that an enquiry be undertaken into requirements for officers in the RAF.[104] The Stores Branch completed its review by the first half of 1930 with the results announced in the AMWOs of July 1930.[105] This fresh look at the Branch's officer requirements introduced significant change and established what was referred to as a 'cardinal point of policy'; this provided:

> A nucleus of officers of high administrative capacity and wide experience capable not only of the efficient administration of the complicated materiel of the service in time of peace but also of the adaptation of the peace organisation to meet the varying needs of war.[106]

The review identified that this nucleus would be formed of men who made the Branch their permanent career and, while in junior ranks, would need to be given ample opportunity to gain wide experience within different types of unit. It was also observed that such a career would need to be sufficiently favourable to attract good quality and well-educated men. With these requirements as a baseline, the review came to the conclusion that the new vision could not be realised if the constitution remained as it was. In keeping with a general principle established for the GD Branch, the new solution adopted was broadly a half-and-half mixture; just over one half (mainly the more senior ranks and positions) would be made up of officers who did not make the Branch their permanent career, while the remainder would be made up by employing men who did make Stores work their permanent career. These were to be drawn from three main sources: firstly, employing a limited number of warrant officer (WO) storekeepers in junior staff posts at HQ; secondly, allocating a large number of junior officer posts at home and some overseas to be filled by retired officers under civilian terms of service drawn primarily from retired officers of any branch of the RAF, as well as from the Royal Navy and the Army; and thirdly, a new scheme was to be introduced whereby a limited number of commissions in the Stores Branch would be offered to WOs of any trade.[107] The commissioning of WOs proved to be a successful and fruitful source of officers for the Branch (especially during the years of the Second World War), although the intake was initially limited to five per year.[108] Indeed, during the period 1 September 1939 to 1 September 1945, commissioned WOs accounted for an average of 25 per cent of the total number of Equipment Branch officers serving on permanent commissions.

The RAF Stores Trade

In the early years of the RAF, the range of trades in which airmen were employed was broadly similar to what had been established in the RFC; these reflected the technology of the aircraft that the service was operating at the time, with a diverse set of specific skills such as propeller maker, blacksmith, and coppersmith. Initially, there were five Trade Groups in the new RAF, of which I to III were all Technical, Group IV was Administrative, and Group V was Non-Technical; the latter was unskilled and the lowest paid of the Trade Groups. Stores workers were employed in the trade of Clerk (Stores) (Trade Group IV) with additional support provided by airmen of the aircrafthand (ACH) (GD) trade in Group V.[109] Although the RFC had a trade of storeman and this transferred across to the RAF in the Muster Roll of April 1918, the trade inexplicably disappears from the RAF Trade Structure of 1919.[110, 111] The fact that the trade appears in statistical summaries suggests that the omission is most likely the result of an editorial oversight in the published trade structures. The lowest adult rank of aircraftman second class in the Stores Trade earned three shillings and six pence per day; his equivalent rank in Trade Group I was paid four shillings per day; pay included free food, uniform, and accommodation.[112] By 1934, the number of trades had been simplified, enabling a reduction from sixty-one in 1919 to thirty-three, but still classified within five Trade Groups.[113]

The nature of stores work was driven by two basic requirements. Firstly, the need for accounting, a factor which dominated many of the procedures that had been consolidated within the RAF's Instructions for Store Accounting and Store Keeping (AP 830). The purpose of accounting, according to the regulations, was that the process constituted a record of past transactions and provided data for the estimation of future requirements (part of the provisioning process). What the regulations do not make clear is that an accurate record of stock held was not just an administrative imperative, it was critical in supporting RAF operations; if demands for equipment were to be met quickly, it was essential that the Stores organisation knew what stock it held and where it was located. Secondly, there was also a basic principle within the regulations that stipulated that 'the work of the accounting section should be distinct from the physical store work and should not be under the store holder'. This was an important point in that individuals responsible for the accounting of equipment (Store Accounting) did not have access to the stock itself, and those responsible for the physical handling of stock (Store Keeping) did not have access to the stock account; this made pilfering all the more difficult as differences in the stock account and stock on the shelf could not be easily adjusted and would be detectable during random stock checks or stocktaking.[114]

In practice, this general requirement was achieved by separate work places for each area, overseen by an accountant officer and a Stores officer; the paper stores accounts were progressively transferred to the day-to-day responsibility of accountant officers between 1920 and 1921.[115] This division of responsibility remained until late 1939, when responsibility for the accounting function was transferred from the accountant officer to the Equipment officer, primarily due to the fact that stock accounting was being duplicated in both areas. From the formation of the RAF in 1918, unit stores were manned by a combination of airmen of the Clerk (Stores) trade (Trade Group IV), with assistance being provided by ACH (GD) (Trade Group V).[116] This remained the case until October 1920 when a new trade of storekeeper was introduced in Trade Group III.[117] Following the renaming of the officers' specialist branch from Stores to Equipment in 1936, the trade of Storekeeper followed suit and was renamed Equipment assistant in April 1937, but transferred to Trade Group IV.[118]

The clerical support for stores work was provided by the Trade of Clerk (Stores), who provided the accounting function under the direction of the accountant officer although the title changed to just 'clerk' in July 1921; airmen in this newly named trade were thereafter allocated for specific duties such as pay accounting, stores accounting and medical duties.[119] Although the reason is not given in Air Ministry records, sub-classifications for clerks were reintroduced in June 1924 and saw the introduction of the trade of Clerk (Store Accounting); the other two were Clerk (Pay Accounting) and Clerk (GD).[120] This arrangement endured until April

1935 when it was merged with the trade of Clerk (Pay Accounting) to become the single trade of Clerk (Accounting); the reason for this amalgamation is not evident from the Air Ministry announcement, but it is likely that such a move was part of the ongoing simplification of the RAF's trade structure.[121] One particular point of note is that, prior to 1923, non-commissioned personnel were referred to using the army convention of other ranks. This was changed to airmen (along with airwomen when the Women's Auxiliary Air Force (WAAF) was later introduced) from January 1923 onwards.[122]

At this point in the logistics story, acknowledgement must be made of the significant contribution made by a part of the uniformed workforce, which, as an organisation, was to disappear from the picture and not re-emerge until 1938. A significant number of women in the WAAC had played a major part in the RFC's Logistics organisation during the First World War. With the creation of the RAF in April 1918, there was still perceived to be a need for a dedicated female auxiliary organisation and a Women's Royal Air Force (WRAF) was formed.[123] At the peak of the WRAF, airwomen were employed in over fifty trades, each of these a component of four main categories: Category 'A': Clerks and Storewomen; Category 'B': Household; Category 'C': Technical; and Category 'D': Non-Technical. The logistics organisation was heavily dependent on women in Category 'A' with a significant proportion being employed at the Stores depots. By all accounts, they were integrated into virtually all aspects of depot activity from clerical work through to heavy, manual work. Given the important role that the then WRAF was playing in logistics at the time, it is somewhat surprising that the organisation was disbanded on 1 April 1920, only two years after its formation. Women in uniform would again play an important part in RAF Logistics, but not until 1939 with the formation of the Women's Auxiliary Air Force.

WRAF personnel on the march, 1919. (*Crown Copyright—Air Historical Branch MoD*)

Civilian Stores Organisation

Civilians were and always have been an important part of RAF Logistics. At unit level, the RAF had employed civilians in a variety of roles, predominantly in administrative tasks. One of the earliest specialist roles they played was instituted in June 1925 through the introduction of a civilian storekeeper grade and filling the post of a station warden (along with a clerk), at a specific number of RAF stations. These individuals were responsible for a range of domestic services such as the supply of utilities (solid fuel, electricity, gas, and water), administering building repairs, the monthly inspection of barrack furniture (and repair where required), and the storage, issue, and receipt of barrack equipment. These tasks were not key to the military task of the unit but, nonetheless, were providing essential living requirements for the personnel stationed on RAF units. The significance of this initiative was that it initially released fifty-six RAF logistic tradesmen from non-directly military tasks for employment elsewhere.[124] The station warden role remains a civilian post on RAF stations to the present day. Normally under the leadership of uniformed RAF officers, the chief attribute of the civilian workforce was their continuity of experience, with some of them spending their entire civil service career moving up the promotion ladder at a single location. Of course, there were difficulties from time to time with trades union matters, which did not apply to uniformed staff; these could usually be dealt with swiftly and fairly by the Whitley Council set up at each largely civilian-manned unit.[125]

Logistics Management in the Air Ministry

With the reconstitution of the Air Council in January 1919, CGE and his department, the DofE, moved under the responsibility of the Chief of the Air Staff (CAS). At this time, however, the responsibilities that could be broadly classified as logistics in nature were under the control of two separate directorates: the DofE responsible for aircraft designs, engines, and spares and the Directorate of Aircraft Supplies (manned almost entirely by civilians), which was under the department of the Director-General of Supply and Research; in 1922, this latter organisation was renamed the Department of the Air Member for Supply & Research (AMSR). To rationalise this divided responsibility for logistics, the DofE was transferred to AMSR's charge in 1924. During 1924, a number of important changes were made at the Air Ministry; among these was a move of the DofE from CAS Department to the Department of the Air Member for Supply and Research (AMSR). By 1930, the former Directorate of Aircraft Supplies had become a deputy directorate (renamed to deputy directorate of Stores) alongside a deputy directorate of Equipment, both under the DofE.[126]

By this time, the DofE consisted of three deputy directorates (DD), responsible for Equipment, Stores, and Repair and Maintenance respectively; the directorate was headed by an air commodore (now titled the Director General of Equipment (DGE)), with each of the deputy directorates managed by a group captain. This structure lasted until 1934 when AMSR's department was divided into two new organisations: the Department of the Air Member for Research and Development and the Air Member for Supply and Organisation (AMSO). The DofE found a new home within AMSO's area and was restructured, still maintaining three DDs, but losing responsibility for Repair and Maintenance. This new structure now consisted of the DD Equipment (Aircraft), DD Equipment (General), and DD Equipment (Supply and Movement).[127]

The role of the DofE at this time was the operational control of Equipment organisations across the service, equipment accounting policy, logistic planning, managing scales of equipment, the coordination of equipment issues (especially those for priority requirements), and the provisioning of spares.[128] The total size of the directorate at this time was approximately 206 personnel. Surviving manpower records for this area of the Air Ministry are inconsistent in the level of detail between military and non-military personnel, but the proposals for change submitted to the Treasury indicates that around 80 per cent of the DofE in the mid-1930s were civilians.[129]

Mobilisation Planning

The final and perhaps most critical development in the period leading up to the expansion programme in 1934 was the planning work for future mobilisation in the event of another conflict. The early post-First World War years had seen the RAF operating from largely static bases, both at home and overseas. It was also a period that saw the rapid demobilisation of the newly formed service to a peacetime footing and there was little need to develop a logistical support capability for expeditionary warfare. This position was made quite clear by the British Government on 15 August 1919, stating that: 'it should be assumed, for forming revised estimates that the British Empire will not be engaged in any great war during the next ten years and that no Expeditionary Force is required for this purpose.'[130]

This policy, known as the 'Ten Year Rule' (the assumption that there would be no major war within the next ten years), was further extended in 1925 and was the Government's prime means of limiting defence expenditure. The effect of this is evident from the Air Estimates of 1922 to 1929, which increased from £15,542,000 to £16,960,000: a rise of barely one and a half million pounds over seven years.[131] Notwithstanding the financial limitations on the physical growth of the RAF, its logistic doctrine continued to develop. The experience of the RFC during the German spring offensive of 1918 had clearly demonstrated the requirement for some form of mobile logistics and the resupply convoys devised by Brooke-Popham had proved to be highly successful, bridging the gap between the limited equipment holdings of squadrons and the Stores depots. It was, however, a temporary measure intended to meet a short-term need. Resupply convoys did not initially become a standing part of the RAF's logistic ORBAT, although the principle surfaced again in the late 1920s as part of in-depth thinking on the requirements of army co-operation, and was eventually incorporated as a clearly defined capability in logistics doctrine. This was a highly significant and far-sighted development and one which was to prove crucial in many of the overseas campaigns during the Second World War.

The catalyst for detailed development on RAF/Army co-operation can be largely attributed to a paper that Squadron Leader (later Marshal of the RAF Sir) John Slessor prepared for the Royal United Services Institute Journal in 1927.[132] As part of its initial pre-publication clearance through the Air Ministry, much comment was generated, not least of which was from CAS, who emphasised the point regarding the need for mobility of RAF squadrons and the importance of minimizing the amount of support equipment that they were required to carry.[133] In the ensuing discussions, a basic planning assumption gradually developed that held that squadron establishments of personnel, vehicles, and stores for a future RAF Expeditionary Force would need to be kept to the bare minimum if unhindered mobility was to be achieved.[134] Much of the squadron-owned transport was required to move ground support equipment, and sufficient personnel to cover the period until sustained resupply could be achieved from a supply depot. There was limited space for spares and these needed to be reduced to those required for immediate operating needs. This left the question of how to resupply flying squadrons at forward operating locations. Similar to the concept of the First World War resupply convoys, the idea of Air Stores Parks (ASP) emerged.[135] As part of the planning work that led to the introduction of the RAF's first *War Manual* in June 1928, the concept of a standard maintenance organisation was introduced, which included: a port detachment to 'arrange for and facilitate the clearance of RAF materiel from the dock area'; an aircraft depot consisting of a Stores Section and a Repair Section; and an Air Stores Park that was 'solely a stores distributing and collecting unit and is mobile'.[136] As far as equipment stocks were concerned, deployed flying squadrons would hold only three days' worth of spares, with resupply being carried out by the mobile ASPs, each holding one month's stock and situated within a twenty-five to forty mile radius of up to six deployed flying squadrons. The non-mobile aircraft depots, which would hold up to six months' spares, were situated behind the ASPs.[137]

The first inclusion of such parks in detailed operational planning was as part of a structure intended for RAF contingents to accompany an Army expeditionary force overseas; this plan was structured around the despatch of up to four Army contingents ('A' to 'D'), with an RAF contingent accompanying each. All four of the RAF contingents were allocated an ASP (Nos 1 to 4), with the aircraft depot and a port detachment assigned to just contingent 'A'.[138] The plan was scalable in that contingent 'A' was intended for immediate despatch, with contingents 'B', 'C', and 'D' deploying six weeks, four months, and six months afterwards respectively, as circumstances required. At this time, the four ASPs named in the plan were not actually formed and were intended to be established and equipped when the mobilisation plan was activated.[139] It was, however, quite clear where the ASP's vehicles were to come from and who was responsible for loading them. In the case of No. 1 ASP, for example, the majority of the prime-mover vehicles and various trailers were earmarked from RAF Kenley, with Nos 1, 3, and 4 SDs responsible for their loading when required.[140] To provide a convenient *aide memoire*, the Air Ministry issued a pocket book for use by personnel on operations or exercises when the normal range of publications and manuals would not be available. It covered an extensive range of topics including organisation for war, liaison with the Army and Navy, movement, supply and maintenance, and medical matters. Its pages are packed with valuable and useful data ranging from how to troubleshoot aero and MT engine problems through to how many hours a day a camel needs to feed.[141]

Logistics by the Mid-1930s

By late 1918, the newly formed RAF had benefitted from the experience of the RFC in that it had inherited practices and procedures that had been tried and tested under four years of actual war. Additionally, many of its personnel had served in the RFC and RNAS and brought with them valuable experience that would help shape the new service as it entered the relative peace of the 1920s and 1930s.

Four key points stand out from this formative period up to 1934; these were to prove particularly significant during the remainder of the 1930s and through until the end of the Second World War itself. First, the formation of a specialist discipline in the form of the RAF Stores Branch and Trades provided a clear professional focus for Logistics, which was to prove vital during the Second World War when sustaining air power became considerably more demanding and logistics required careful consideration in campaign and operational planning. This clarity of purpose was strengthened by the fact that the responsibilities of the RAF Stores officer in 1920 no longer included the engineering duties of the RFC's Equipment officer. Second, the RFC had identified and developed a clear supply chain structure, which consisted of the manufacturing base (industry) at one end, depots as an intermediate accumulation point for onward distribution of equipment to users and a stores section on the majority of units to manage equipment requirements on behalf of the actual users. These three components formed the basis for the RAF's supply chain for the future. The third point was the work, which had been done on mobilisation planning and the important concept of additional elements required to support expeditionary operations: port detachments and Air Stores Parks. These would later prove to be a key part of logistics doctrine during the Second World War. The fourth point was the availability of spares. It was already becoming clear in the period up to 1934 that aircraft were increasingly complex structures and the multitude of types from numerous manufacturers required careful management to ensure that sufficient spare parts were always available. This was a recurring theme during the forthcoming expansion programme and throughout the Second World War.

2

Biplanes to Monoplanes: 1934–1939

At the beginning of 1934, the RAF entered a period of transformation that was to prepare it for the Second World War. Before the RAF launched its expansion programme though, the Italian invasion of Abyssinia in October 1935 (hereafter referred to as the Abyssinian Crisis) prompted, not just a reinforcement of RAF bases in the Suez Canal region (which Italy needed as a supply route to its forces in Abyssinia), but also a timely review of RAF mobilisation planning. It was the growing threat from the military expansion of Nazi Germany that then led to the substantial re-equipment programme for the RAF. This was a time when aircraft construction underwent a significant transformation, from the largely wood and linen covered biplanes, to stressed skin, metal monoplanes. This chapter examines the six years from 1934 to 1939 and explains how RAF Logistics was transformed from a discipline supporting air power in an imperial context to one that was largely ready to support highly mobile warfare on a global scale.

The Abyssinian Crisis

The Abyssinian Crisis developed in August 1935 as a result of the growing threat of Italian naval, military, and air forces to British interests in Egypt; it led to the decision to reinforce the RAF stations in Aden, Egypt, Gibraltar, Malta, and Palestine with a mixture of aircraft types from eleven British-based squadrons.[1] A mobilisation plan had been in place since 1927, but proved to be unsuitable for this type of deployment as the concept of operations was based on deploying a previously agreed force, to a specific timetable, and to fit in with the Army's mobilisation programme; the RAF's response required an arrangement that was 'as elastic as possible'. To address the new requirement, AMSO instructed the RAF's Director of Organisation to form a mobilisation committee; this was formally constituted on 13 September 1935, with its inaugural meeting held shortly after on 16 September 1935.[2] The initial plan was for the deployment of a main reinforcing field force with HQ elements, a base area element, a port detachment, and an ASP to support eleven squadrons, as well as a more mobile component, known as 'Q' Force, consisting of a further two squadrons and supporting elements.

Logistically speaking, this first real test of mobilisation planning was not a success. The report on the overall experience by HQ RAF Middle East in October 1936 makes it quite clear that the planners had fundamentally underestimated the extent to which the reinforcement would impose on the existing administrative and maintenance organisations in the Middle East, which was estimated to be in the region of a four-fold increase.[3] A particular concern expressed was that an ASP had not been pre-formed in Britain, and the Middle East Command had to form its own ASP (No. 3) to meet this shortfall from its own already limited resources. This park proved to be a critical resource in resupplying flying squadrons operating in the Western Desert over the lengthy and extremely vulnerable lines of communication from the RAF depots at Aboukir and Mersa Matruh.[4] Concern was also expressed regarding the provision of additional experienced uniformed stores officers, a situation that was largely attributed to the Air Ministry's policy at the time of employing a significant number of civilian stores officers.[5]

The RAF Middle East Command's report on the 1935–1936 emergency is a rich source of lessons learned on what could be considered the first real exercise of the mobilisation planning that took place during the period 1927 to 1930. The committee's immediate priority was to deploy the reinforcements for the Abyssinian Crisis; however, by the time the last of the deployed squadrons had returned to Britain in late September 1936, its work was refocused on the RAF's mobilisation requirements for a European campaign; these preparations eventually underpinned the RAF's deployment to France in 1939. Planning for this began in earnest in April 1938 with the formation of a largely Army-led team in the War Office called General Staff (Plans). Having studied various Cabinet and General Staff papers, the planning team proposed a number of priorities, the first of which was the despatch of an air striking force to France and its maintenance in the field. In due course, this concept became known as the Western or 'W' Plan.[6]

The Expansion Programme, 1934–1938

The threat from Germany became increasingly clear following her withdrawal from the Disarmament Conference for a second time in November 1933 and also from the League of Nations; this marked the point at which Hitler no longer concealed his aspirations for rearmament. The threat from Nazi Germany took some time to be taken seriously, with a significant degree of ambivalence among many British politicians. Prime Minister Baldwin, however, summed up the Government's new stance as far as the RAF was concerned in March 1934 when he stated that 'this Government will see to it that in air strength and air power this country will no longer be in a position of any inferiority to any country within striking distance of our shores'.[7] The realisation of this vision, however, would take until the outbreak of the Second World War to even come close to fruition.

In 1936, the RAF, following the resolution of the Abyssinian Crisis, turned to addressing the threat posed by Germany. After much deliberation in political circles as to the requirement and scale of rearmament, the British Government embarked upon a series of eight expansion schemes between 1934 and 1938, although it took until March 1942 for the final scheme to become fully effective.[8] After Germany revealed the foundation of its new air force—the Luftwaffe—in March 1935, the whole process gained greater momentum, with a marked increase in the number of squadrons and aircraft on the RAF home establishment.[9]

British aircraft design had changed very little from the closing stages of the First World War. The Air Ministry account of the RAF's expansion describes how, in 1934, it was 'a force of wooden biplanes' and 'a world of types which are now but memories and which pilots and air crews of the present day would regard almost as museum pieces, as prehistoric survivals of the era of the Wrights and Farmans'.[10] The expansion of the Service was a critical turning point and consisted of a series of schemes that not only substantially increased the numbers of aircraft, but significantly updated their design. By 1939, it had become a 'force of metal monoplanes'.[11] The transition from largely wood to metal aircraft construction represented a significant change for Britain's aircraft industry, not just in technology, but also in cost.

The expansion schemes introduced a diverse range of aircraft types, from bombers and fighters through to torpedo-bombers, reconnaissance (landplanes and flying boats), and army co-operation. The first of the schemes (scheme 'A') was approved in July 1934, with some of the further schemes being directly attributed to specific concerns or events. For example: scheme 'C' in May 1935 followed Sir John Simon's and Anthony Eden's visit to Hitler in Berlin and Göring's claim of Luftwaffe parity; scheme 'F' in February 1936 came as a result of further German expansion and the Abyssinian crisis; scheme 'L' happened in April 1938 after the Austrian *Anschluss*; and scheme 'M' came in November 1938, after Munich (the first 'all-heavy' aircraft programme).[12] The overall expansion programme in terms of the planned (and approved) increase in the total number of squadrons and aircraft, from July 1934 through to November 1938, is summarised in Table 1.

Scheme	Dates		Home Based		Overseas Based	
	Approved	Effective	Squadrons	Aircraft	Squadrons	Aircraft
A	18 July 1934	31 Mar 1939	84	960	27	292
C	21 May 1935	31 Mar 1937	123	1,512	27	292
F	25 Feb 1936	31 Mar 1939	124	1,738	37	468
H	24 Feb 1937	31 Mar 1939	145	2,422	27	348
J	22 Dec 1937	summer 1941	158	2,387	45	644
K	14 Mar 1938	31 Mar 1941	145	2,305	37	468
L	27 Apr 1938	31 Mar 1940	171	4,138	39	490
M	7 Nov 1938	31 Mar 1942	163	2,549	49	636

Table 1
The approved aircraft expansion schemes, 1934–1938.[13]

By 1 October 1938, the expansion schemes had substantially increased the numbers of squadrons and aircraft. A paper submitted to the Cabinet on 25 October 1938 by the Secretary of State for Air, Sir Kingsley Wood, declared that the first line aircraft strength of the RAF then consisted of: twenty-nine fighter squadrons with 406 aircraft; thirty-one medium bomber squadrons with 372 aircraft and ten heavy bomber squadrons with 120 aircraft.[14] Commensurate with the expansion schemes was a need for a significant increase in manufacturing output. The existing industrial base was able to meet the demands of schemes 'A' and 'C', but scheme 'F' was another matter altogether and the existing manufacturing firms could not tackle the requirement unaided. Consequently, it was decided to introduce what became known as 'shadow factories'.

Based on the large motorcar producers in the Coventry and Birmingham areas, these factories were established on sites close to their parent works and were initially set up to produce airframes and engines; additional plants were set up to produce propellers, carburettors, and magnetos. The companies originally selected for this scheme were Austin, Daimler, Rootes, Rover, Singer, Standard, and Wolseley. However, Singer and Wolseley dropped out of the programme before it started; their places were soon filled by the Bristol Aeroplane Company and the Austin Motor Company.[15] This extensive expansion activity was met with a corresponding increase in Air Expenditure, which rose from £27,496,000 in 1935 to a peak of £133,800,000 in 1938; the data for the years 1935 to 1939 is shown in Figure 1.

Much of the published literature that comments on the expansion schemes focus predominantly on the aircraft production and modernisation success story, with little, if any, wider illustration of the other changes that were required to strengthen the efficiency and effectiveness of the RAF.[17] One of the earliest changes concerned organisation; this enabled a fundamental improvement from the logistics perspective. The RAF's home command structure in the period up until 1935 was largely geographical in nature and the RAF as a whole was simply divided into 'home' and 'overseas'. The home element was classed as the Air Defence of Great Britain and was sub-divided into eight components: Western Area; Central Area; Fighting Area; No. 1 Air Defence Group; Inland Area; Coastal Area; RAF Cranwell; and RAF Halton. The overseas element was sub-divided into six components: RAF Middle East; British Forces in Iraq; RAF India; RAF Mediterranean; Aden Command; and RAF Far East.[18] The significance of this is that functions such as logistics (below Air Ministry level) were without a single controlling specialist authority. This led to logistic units being placed within inappropriate formations; the four Stores depots, for example, were under the command of the Inland Area formation as part of No. 21 Group from 1932 to 1933, then under the direct command of HQ Inland Area from 1934 to 1935, before a further transfer to the command of No. 24 (Training) Group in 1936. The Stores depots (still within No. 24 (Training) Group) came under the newly-formed Training Command in 1937.[19] The diverse range of aircraft types and supporting activities introduced through the expansion process led to a major reorganisation in the RAF command

Part of the aero engine assembly line at a typical expansion scheme 'shadow factory' in 1937. (*Author's collection*)

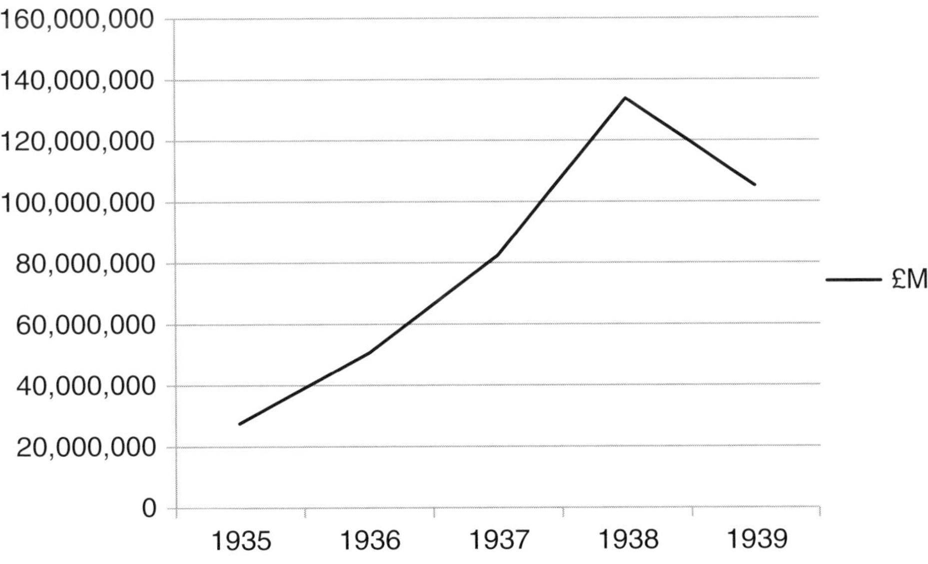

Figure 1: Air Expenditure for financial years 1935 to 1939.

structure in 1936 with, initially, the introduction of four new commands comprising Bomber, Coastal, Fighter, and Training; three further commands were introduced in 1938 to include Maintenance, Balloon, and Reserve.[20] This reorganisation established a clear focus for activities on a functional rather than a geographical basis.

Change of Name: Stores to Equipment

Another notable change at this time was in terminology. With the expansion programme's emphasis on modernisation and re-equipment, the term 'Stores', which had been in use since 1919 as the name of the RAF's Branch and Trade, along with the prefix to the depot titles, had become dated; many working within the discipline felt that it inadequately covered their responsibilities that, by then, included a much wider range of functions such as movements, transportation, POL, and explosives. Consequently, the RAF Stores Branch was renamed the Equipment Branch in November 1936.[21] Shortly afterwards, on 2 February 1937, the Stores depots were renamed equipment depots. A further change followed a year later, in 1938, when all Maintenance Command depots, irrespective of their functions, were redesignated as maintenance units (MU).[22]

Maintenance Command

Despite Trenchard's view that there would be a requirement for repair depots in the UK, by the beginning of 1938, there was no RAF repair depot or properly planned system of repair.[23] This was later resolved by the expansion and development of the Home Aircraft Depot at Henlow in Bedfordshire, closely followed by the development of similar facilities at RAF stations St Athan in South Wales and Sealand near Chester. The expansion programme, however, saw a significant increase in the number of RAF MUs and the accumulation of war reserve equipment stocks on an unprecedented scale. Amid this growth, it became apparent that a single focus was needed for logistics and engineering in the form of a Maintenance Command. This had been recognised in September 1937 when the Director of Organisation submitted a note to the Air Council, suggesting that a dedicated command should be formed to control the RAF's growing maintenance organisation.[24] The director highlighted the fact that the existing units concerned with maintenance were controlled and administered by the DofE, while their domestic administration was taken care of by the AOC-in-Chief (AOC-in-C), Training Command; consequently, the DofE was in effect working as an executive AOC over units with functions that were quite remote from him in addition to a prime responsibility for an Air Ministry department.[25] The proposal to form the new command was submitted to and approved at an expansion progress meeting with the Secretary of State for Air on 21 September 1937. The Command HQ was formed initially within the DofE at the Air Ministry on 1 April 1938, but was later moved to RAF Andover in August 1938 and then to nearby Amport by the outbreak of the Second World War.

Broadly speaking, the new command's responsibilities were twofold. Firstly, it was to be responsible for controlling and coordinating all the RAF's maintenance services. Secondly, and the more sizeable task, it was responsible for the planning and organisation required for the receipt, storage, repair and distribution of the RAF's equipment in both peace and war. To provide a more manageable structure for the myriad technical and logistical activities that came within its responsibility, it was divided into four groups: No. 40 Group (responsible for the storage of equipment and the maintenance of reserve MT vehicles); No. 41 Group (responsible for the receipt, storage, maintenance and delivery by air of all aircraft); No. 42 Group (responsible for explosives and fuels); and No. 43 Group (responsible for repair and salvage). Broadly speaking, Nos 41 and 43 Groups were predominantly responsible for engineering activities, with Nos 40 and 42 Groups responsible for supply and storage matters.[26] Given the scope of logistics as defined earlier, this book will only consider the development and operation of Nos 40 and 42 Groups.[27]

As far as the holdings of equipment stocks were concerned, these were held on what was known as a 'universal' basis (as distinct from 'dispersed'), with each depot holding a complete range and serving as a distributing centre for consumer units within a specified geographical area.[28] A document held in the MOD's AHB (RAF) archive, which appears to be of post-Second World War origin, imaginatively describes the Maintenance Command and Group structure as 'resembling that of a combination of iron-mongers, petrol stations, service garages and other chain store businesses—with the Command HQ staff as the Board of Directors'.[29] Both Nos 40 and 42 Groups formed their HQs initially at Andover; however, by August 1939, they had moved them to Abingdon and Burghfield Common (near Reading) respectively.

The AOC Maintenance Command was directly responsible for the policy that governed how stocks of equipment and supplies would be held and distributed. He was also responsible for mobilisation plans and war readiness. As early as August 1938, this latter responsibility was already acknowledging the need to prepare for disruption caused by acts of war and included planning for the dispersal of stocks, the diversion of lines of supply if and when required, the supply of labour, and railway rolling stock. It was also specifically required that readiness plans for war were to be tested by 'frequent exercises in packing, distribution and mobilisation, in which the co-operation of other Commands will be necessary'.[30] The one area where HQ Maintenance Command retained overall control was the movement of stores and supplies as this was deemed to be more effective and economical than establishing identical coordinating functions within each of the Group HQs. Moreover, there was also a need for close co-operation with the Command HQ planning staff, the Air Ministry, the Board of Trade, and other Government departments.[31] The Air Ministry remained responsible for general equipment policy, determining war

The Maintenance Command badge, May 1939. (*Crown Copyright—Air Historical Branch MoD*)

equipment schedules, contract arrangements and provisioning of equipment; it was acknowledged at the time that the latter task might be transferred to the command in the future.[32] The command's badge, a raven (traditionally symbolic of providence) in the centre of the standard RAF badge format with the motto of 'service', was approved by His Majesty King George VI on 7 September 1939.[33]

Equipment Supply, 40 Group

The formation of Maintenance Command was critical to the successful outcome of the expansion programme. Greater numbers of aircraft, with increasing complexity, significantly expanded the size and range of the RAF spares inventory, a fact that would demand a far greater number of depots than the four already in existence in 1934. The growing size of the inventory is illustrated by the number of aircraft types. In February 1935, this was thirty-five (including mark variants); by the outbreak of war in September 1939, the number had increased to sixty-nine (including mark variants). Moreover, during the same period, the number of aircraft manufacturing companies had increased from fourteen to twenty-one.[34] The growth in the number of equipment MUs started with the Air Estimates of 1937–38 and 1938–39, in which proposals were included to construct five new depots within No. 40 Group at Carlisle, Quedgeley, Hartlebury, Heywood, and Stafford.[35] These new sites were significantly larger than the existing MUs. The depots in No. 40 Group, for example, each had a total floor space of 854,000 square feet, as compared with the 729,000 and 447,000 square feet of the pre-1934 depots at Ruislip and Milton respectively.[36]

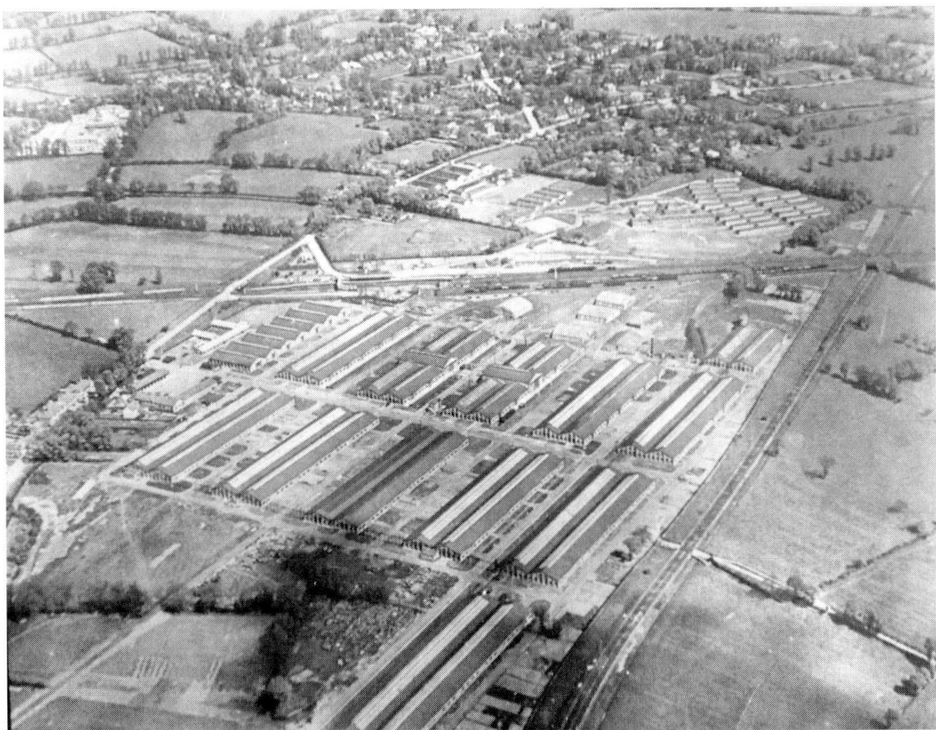

Aerial view of No. 3 MU Milton. This view shows quite clearly how tightly packed the buildings were on the pre-expansion scheme depots. (*Author's collection*)

The size of the new units is well-illustrated by Hartlebury, which covered an area of 350 acres. It provided covered storage of approximately 1.25 million square feet, later increasing to 1.5 million square feet. Railway lines were laid to certain sites along with marshalling sidings capable of holding up to 100 trucks.[37] The estimated cost of the five new MUs ranged from £1,330,000 to £1,450,000 each.[38] Not all of them were built on green field sites; the site at Quedgeley, for example, had been the National Shell Filling Factory No. 5 during the First World War.[39] Each of the new units consisted of a HQ site with six well-dispersed sub-sites. The HQ site consisted of offices, officers' mess and living accommodation, general engineering block, fabric repair block, carpenters' shop, timber store, and transportation block, together with ancillary buildings. The sub-sites consisted of between three and five large storage sheds along with a range of miscellaneous facilities such as wardens' offices, canteens, and sanitary blocks.[40]

In parallel with this significant building programme, there remained anxiety within the Air Ministry planning staff regarding vulnerability of the depots to enemy action. From as early as 1934, there was some concern that Germany was beginning to acquire the capability to mount an air attack on the UK.[41] The fear was not unfounded; the range of German bombers based in north-western Germany enabled them to reach industrial areas in the north-east of England and the Midlands. This risk influenced the design of the new depots from the outset. Sub-sites enabled stock to be dispersed over a slightly wider area, thereby minimising the complete loss of stock held at one location, although single-site stockholding was still largely the case with the four pre-1934 Stores depots. The storage sheds on the sites were built to three standards. The highest standard sheds were fully protected with walls and roofs of concrete capable of withstanding small incendiary bombs and splinters; these buildings were designed for the storage of essential stores, which were difficult to replace and were flammable. The middle standard known as semi-protected was used to house essential stores that were difficult to replace but were of a non-flammable nature. The lowest standard, known as non-protected, were for non-vital stores that were easy to replace.[42]

Despite the ability to disperse stock throughout individual depot sites, the Air Ministry remained concerned about a significant weakness. Each of the equipment MUs was responsible for a specific range of equipment in the RAF inventory. For example, the depot at Ruislip was entirely responsible for aero-engines; the loss of this single depot alone would have had catastrophic effects on the supply of aero engines to the RAF.[43] Stock needed to be dispersed between the depots to mitigate the risk of such a loss. The answer was straightforward and the depots were re-developed into universal equipment depots (UED) where each would hold stocks of spares for the RAF's complete range of aircraft and ground equipment, from a simple nut and bolt to a complete aircraft engine. The redistribution of stock between the equipment MUs commenced in May 1939 and involved a prodigious amount of work. It was not just a question of the physical movement of equipment; much reconfiguration of physical storage and materials-handling facilities was required to accommodate a much wider range of stock. Another change was a move away from each depot having an RAF-wide responsibility to one of a defined geographical boundary. Essentially, each of the UEDs became responsible for the supply of equipment to all of the RAF units in an area spanning west to east across Britain and was organised so that they could take on the workload of the depot to its north and south if there was any disruption due to air attack or sabotage (see Figure 2).[44] Delivery of equipment to RAF stations from the equipment MUs was made by road, rail, or by post, depending on the urgency of need with an overall aim of achieving this within forty-eight hours.[45]

Although the decentralisation of equipment holdings by virtue of the UED concept, improved physical security and resulted in a faster speed of supply to RAF units, it presented a fresh challenge with regards to maintaining an overall record of the stock held. This was further complicated by the fact that the dispersal of stock to the UEDs in May 1939 had been done in haste and, for some time after, no exact stock record figure existed. Once the position stabilised, the challenge was how to ensure that fresh stock of a given item was not provisioned when there was already ample stock available at the other MUs. To address this, a master provisioning office was set up at each of the depots with responsibility for the provisioning of all equipment within given ranges for all depots; the operation of these offices and the complexity of provisioning is examined in more detail in Chapter Nine.

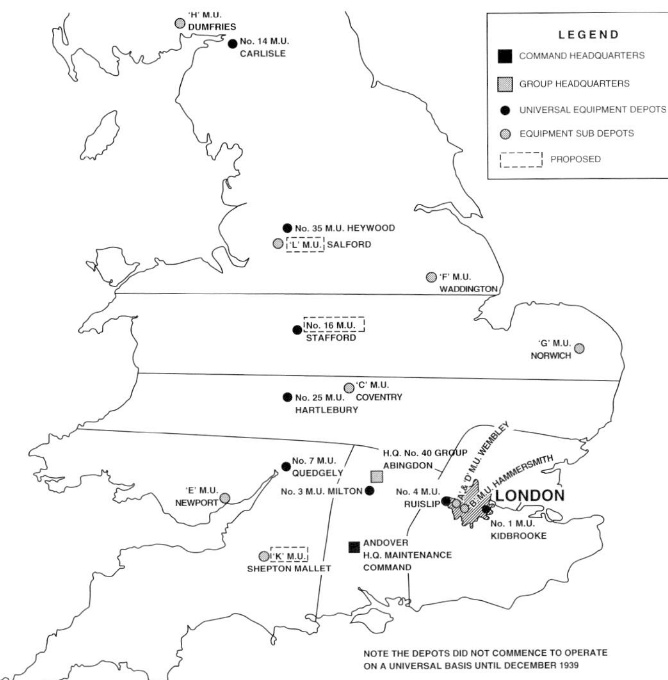

Figure 2: Universal equipment depots and supply areas, 3 September 1939.

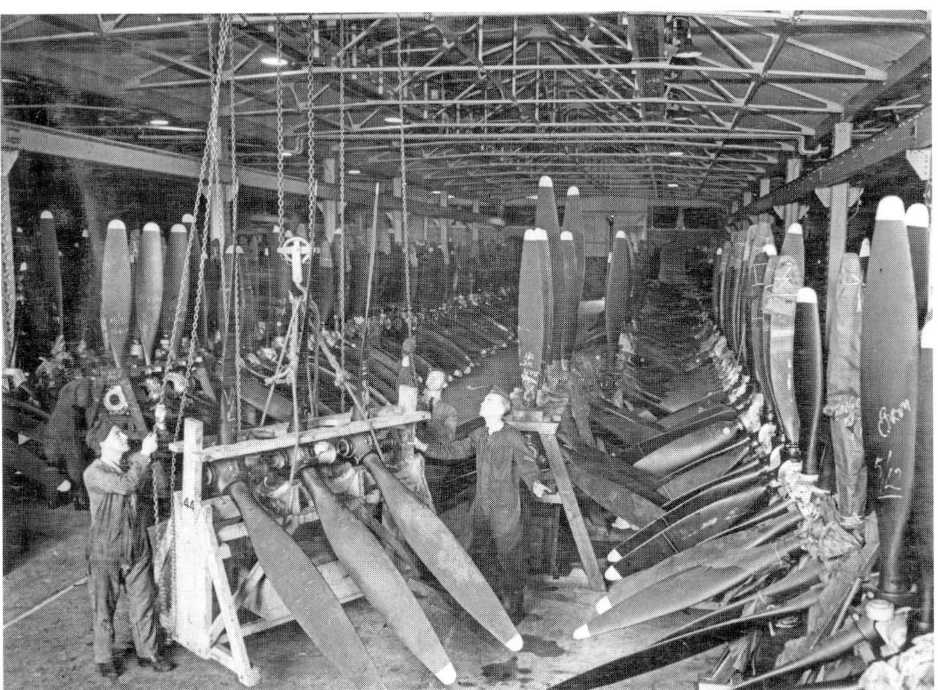

Aircraft propeller storage at an equipment MU. Note the specially made wooden storage cradles. (*Crown Copyright—Air Historical Branch MoD*)

POL Supply, 42 Group

As with many other aspects of RAF Logistics in the inter-war period, little had changed in the arrangements for providing aviation POL that was coordinated by the Air Ministry. Aviation fuel requirements in peacetime were approximately 6,000 tons per month, a figure which was only marginally greater than the turnover of just one of the larger RAF stations towards the end of the Second World War.[47] Most of the requirements were met by standing contracts with the petroleum supplying companies in the UK, through their supply depots. There was also a contractual commitment with the Air Ministry to maintain a standing reserve of about 8,000 tons that, on April 1937 estimates, represented about ten days' war consumption. Experience after the outbreak of the Second World War would show that this in fact represented less than one day's supply at peak consumption. Apart from this limited reserve, there were only the comparatively small stocks held by the few RAF stations then in existence.[48]

The expansion programme brought a whole new challenge in terms of increased fuel requirements for the growing, and projected, numbers of aircraft entering service with the RAF. The engines of the new generation of aircraft used considerably more fuel than their predecessors. The rotary-engined Avro 504 from the First World War, for example, used some six to nine gallons of fuel per hour, the Gloster Gladiator biplane fighter of the late 1930s used approximately thirty-five gallons per hour, while the Supermarine Spitfire used sixty gallons per hour.[49] Estimating the fuel requirement was not an easy task and was made all the more difficult by the uncertain nature of the opening stages of a possible war and its later development. Early estimates suggested that the initial monthly requirement was likely to be in the region of 43,000 tons, increasing to about 70,000 and possibly 100,000 tons. In the opening stages of the war, there were 100 RAF flying stations to be supplied. By the end of the war, this number had dramatically increased to about 600 stations, forty of which were each consuming 3,000 tons or more per month.[50] Volume was but one factor, and the nature of the fuel itself soon proved to be just as critical. The octane ratings of some of the earlier fuels (mainly 77 and 87 octane) limited the maximum performance of aero engines.[51] However, the significant performance improvement that came with the introduction of 100-octane fuel in 1939 raised demand for this grade. Substantial stocks first arrived in the UK from the Dutch West Indies in June of that year.[52] By the end of the war, the total number of grades of aviation fuel had increased to six with eight different grades of oil.[53]

One of the immediate challenges was to build-up reserves of fuel and oil, which was to become an important area of development within the expansion programme. The first step came in July 1936 when the Air Council, in conjunction with the Oil Board, agreed to set a reserve figure for aviation fuel of three months' consumption (approximately 90,000 tons), which would be held in the existing oil companies' storage facilities.[54] It was also agreed that a similar reserve arrangement should be made for lubricating oil, in the region of 6,000 tons. It is clear from surviving records that there was a very close working relationship between the Air Ministry and the oil companies to the extent that the companies even offered to build the additional tankage required at certain of their West Country installations. As a result of the Robinson Committee report on the ownership of new manufacturing capacity for rearmament, the additional storage was built at Air Ministry expense, although it was maintained and operated by the companies. Any spare capacity was acquired and disused tankage belonging to the Anglo-American Oil Company at Brixham was hired, providing capacity for a further 14,400 tons.[55] By August 1936, and with a clearer picture emerging of Germany's military position, the Committee of Imperial Defence directed that sufficient reserves of POL should be built up to meet the requirements for the first six months of a possible war with Germany. Consequently, the Air Ministry's reserve increased to 290,000 tons of aviation fuel and 19,500 tons of lubricating oil.[56] This was a significant uplift and there was a need to take a much wider look at the infrastructure required for storage and distribution. It was decided early on that the construction of the new installations would best be done by the oil companies, in light of their technical and engineering expertise. Moreover, given the fact that the companies were to operate the depots on the Air Ministry's behalf, it made sense for them to plan and design the works to suit their own methods of operating. Overall, the work was shared between the four main companies based, as far as possible, on the proportion of fuel that they were supplying in 1937.[57] Of the new reserve total, 80,000 tons were already within the oil companies' existing storage, leaving 210,000 tons requiring new installations.[58]

In selecting the sites, there were three influencing factors. Firstly, there was the question of supply chain design. As a basic planning assumption, it was agreed that the bulk of the fuel would be held in main reserve depots that, in turn, would supply smaller depots that would act as distribution centres for specific groups of RAF stations. The main depots were sited as closely as possible to the oil companies' existing refineries or depots so that incoming supplies could be off-loaded directly from ocean tankers and then moved by rail to the distribution depots. Secondly, there was the question of strategic and defence requirements. Geographically, the main reserve depots were situated to the west of an imaginary line drawn between Edinburgh and Southampton. The fuel distribution depots, however, were located to the east of this line, closer to the location of the main operational flying stations. In view of the varying degree of risk, the level of protection afforded to the installations varied, with the main depots designed to provide protection from a direct hit by a 4-lb incendiary bomb and the distribution depots able to withstand direct hit from a 25-lb incendiary or high explosive (HE) bomb.[59] The third area was transport, which proved to be quite a challenge. The method of supply to the main reserve depots was from ocean tanker, so close proximity to adequate dock facilities was essential. In practice, it proved difficult to find sufficient locations with facilities for input by rail; river barge or pipeline were therefore also selected. Additionally, as onward movement from the reserve depots was to be by rail, the sites also had to be suitable for the construction of rail links with main lines. The distribution depots, therefore, had to be suitable for reception of fuel by rail, but also for delivery to flying stations by road.[60] In 1938, the reserve of fuel had been increased to 410,000 tons of aviation fuel (eight months' requirements) along with 26,000 tons of lubricating oil; by the end of 1938, these reserves had been virtually doubled to 800,000 tons and 50,000 tons respectively.[61] The decision to make this significant increase was largely based on the assumption that America would remain neutral in the event of war. By the beginning of the war, significant progress had been made with fuel installation construction, despite the stringent siting requirements. In terms of overall numbers, the Air Ministry had in place a total of twenty-nine depots handling and distributing aviation fuel, while the Petroleum Board had sixty-six. By the end of 1944, these figures had increased to seventy-eight and seventy-two respectively.[62] This construction programme, along with the close working relationship that had been established between the Air Ministry and the Petroleum Board, enabled an effective fuel and oil supply system to be established by the outbreak of war in September 1939.[63]

Munitions Supply, 42 Group

One of the other logistical issues that surfaced by the end of the 1930s was the increased carrying capacity of new bomber aircraft. For example, the last of the biplane heavy bombers, the Heyford Mk III of 1935 could carry a bomb load of 1,500 pounds (for a return journey of 749 miles).

By 1939, the Wellington Mk 1A bomber was able to carry three times the Heyford's bomb load nearly twice as far (4,500 pounds for a return journey of 1,200 miles).[64] During the 1920s and up until the commencement of the expansion programme in 1934, all demands for the supply of ammunition and explosives for units in the UK was the sole responsibility of No. 2 Stores Depot at Altrincham in Cheshire (now part of Greater Manchester). Even from the early days of the pre-war build-up, it soon became quite clear that this limited and centralised arrangement would prove to be inadequate. The main driving factor for change was the growing range of munitions in the RAF's arsenal and the planned increase in the carrying capacity of individual bomber aircraft; the size of this fleet alone was planned to increase from 316 aircraft in March 1934 to 1,360 as part of scheme 'M' by early 1942.[65] The first proposals for an expansion in the RAF's munitions storage facilities were submitted to and approved by the Treasury in November 1936 and, included the requirement to construct new storage facilities for an anticipated six-months' war demand of 98,000 tons of HE and incendiary bombs; this calculation was based on existing aircraft being able to each carry 1,250 lb, with an expectation that, with the introduction to service of a new type of heavy bomber, the payload would increase to 3,000 lb. By March 1938, the approved authorized reserve storage had been adjusted to 82,000 tons of HE and 16,000 tons of incendiaries.[66]

Aircraft bomb storage, India or Iraq during the early 1930s. Note the Westland Wapiti in the background. (*Author's collection*)

Wellington waiting for its bomb load. (*Crown Copyright—Air Historical Branch MoD*)

Munitions storage up to the mid-1930s had been on a relatively small-scale and detailed work was required to examine the practical difficulties of more widespread development of new sites to consider issues such as safety distances, dispersal, strategic locations, handling, and distribution of stocks. Of these, one of the most difficult was the requirement for economical and safe storage within the limits of existing armament safety regulations laid down by the Explosives Storage and Transportation Committee. The hazardous nature of these stores required quite demanding protective measures to be taken, not just in terms of protecting the local population from the effects of accidental explosion, but also reducing the effects of a chain reaction between adjacent stocks at a storage location in the event of a detonation.

At the heart of the revised planning for munitions storage and distribution was the basic premise that the new units that would hold the main reserve stocks of HE bombs, incendiaries, bomb components, small arms ammunition, pyrotechnics and bomb filling materials would be regionalised in three sections of the country covering Northern and Southern England and the Midlands.[67] Each of the units was to be stocked using the universal principle, which No. 40 Group had introduced with deliveries to them made by rail, direct from the ordnance factories. It was from this broad concept that the RAF's requirement for five new ammunition depots (AD) emerged. To afford a high level of protection, both from aerial attack and from aerial reconnaissance, it was decided that underground storage would be the most suitable and that disused mines or quarry workings would be the ideal locations. In 1937, a survey commenced with over 100 potential sites being examined, following the advice of the Geological Museum, the mines department, and various mining companies. Many of those considered were completely unsuitable for a number of reasons including: limited size, wet conditions, insufficient overhead cover for defensive protection, the proximity of existing active workings, and poor access or proximity to rail transport. By the end of 1937, suitable sites had been selected to meet the requirements of the three regional areas and in March 1938 approval had been granted for these to be developed. In March 1938, the first four sites (a development of No. 2 MU Altrincham and new sites at No. 11 MU Chilmark in Wiltshire, No. 21 MU Fauld in Staffordshire, and No. 28 MU Harpur Hill in Derbyshire) were given approval for construction, with the fifth (No. 31 MU Llanberis in North Wales) in August 1939.[68] Similar to the equipment MUs, the ADs were located west of an imaginary line drawn approximately from Edinburgh to Southampton to minimise the risk from enemy bombing.

The first of the new ADs to be completed was No. 21 MU Fauld, which was located in a disused gypsum mine in Staffordshire. The extent of the undertaking was considerable. The preparation of the site alone necessitated the clearance and removal of material required for eventual back-fill, levelling of floors and the strengthening and the lining of roofs with additional support columns in areas of weakness. The design also included standard gauge railway sidings with a capacity for 100 wagons.

At the main rail off-load point about a mile away from the mine, a narrow-gauge railway was built, which was used to move consignments to the underground storage area in trucks pulled by diesel locomotives. Within the underground areas, electric battery-powered locomotives were used for haulage. The bulk and weight of munitions (especially aircraft bombs) made road transport quite impractical for transporting any sizeable quantity; some individual bomb weights rose substantially from 500 lb in 1936 to 22,000 lb in 1944 and the use of the UK's rail network became a crucial component of explosives distribution (see Chapter Seven). Overall, the cost of the construction, both under and over ground, amounted to £635,000. Fauld also housed a master provisioning office for the maintenance of stock records of ammunition and explosives at all the ADs. Demands from overseas theatres were also handled by this office, which would route the demand to the depot holding the largest stock of the item in question. Soon after the completion of Fauld, No. 11 MU at Chilmark was completed and opened in March 1939. By the outbreak of war in September 1939, of the five planned ADs, Altrincham, Fauld, and Chilmark had been built and Harpur Hill was under construction. In addition, a small arms ammunition (SAA) sub-store had been established at Ruislip.

While the inter-war practice of munition deliveries direct to RAF units from the then main depot at Altrincham had sufficed, the anticipated increase in the number of bomber stations led to concern that a continuance of direct delivery, even from the increased number of ADs would become unmanageable. To mitigate this, above ground air ammunition parks (AAP) were also authorised for construction and to be located at what was called the 'centre of gravity', approximately equidistant between bomber stations. It was intended that stocks would be moved by rail from the ADs to the AAPs, each of which would hold seven days' stock in addition to the four days' holdings on each station. Stocks would be held in uncovered compounds and, as the AAPs would not be required until war itself, it was accepted that safety distances could be considerably reduced from peacetime standards. By the outbreak of war, four of the seven planned AAPs had been formed (No. 91 MU at Southburn in East Yorkshire, No. 92 MU at Brafferton in North Yorkshire, No. 93 MU at Swinderby in Lincolnshire, and No. 94 MU at Barnham in Norfolk).

Chemical Weapons

A topic that remains particularly controversial today is that of chemical weapons. Against a backdrop of widespread public indignation regarding Saddam Hussein's 'weapons of mass destruction', however, it is easy to forget that chemical weapons have been a feature of the British weapons arsenal ever since they first used chlorine gas at the Battle of Loos in September 1915. It was not until the 1920s that the RAF, in conjunction with the Chemical Warfare Experimental Station at Porton Down, carried out smoke screen laying experiments using a modified Vickers Vimy aircraft;

at this time, smoke was regarded as a form of chemical warfare. Notwithstanding the use of smoke for concealment of ground forces, it was also recognised that airborne spraying might prove a useful means of delivering disabling or lethal gas. Due to a number of practical issues, however, the tests were not as effective as hoped and, by the early 1930s, the RAF was of the view that smoke screen laying was best carried out by artillery. By the mid-1930s, with the military build-up of Nazi Germany, the possibility of an enemy gas attack had become a serious concern and so began the introduction of a number of gas defence measures, including the issue of anti-gas clothing and the formation of the RAF Anti-Gas School at Uxbridge in April 1937. The British Government, though, only intended to use chemical weapons in retaliation, following first use by an enemy.[69] After the outbreak of the Second World War, the government made this chillingly clear in an instruction from the War Cabinet to the Air Ministry:

> Should the enemy initiate chemical warfare, HM Government intends to retaliate in kind with unrestricted heavy-scale bombing against centres of German population best calculated to bring about the collapse of German morale.[70]

In the early stages of the war, it was intended that Vickers Wellington, Westland Lysander, Fairey Battle, and Bristol Blenheim aircraft would be used to deliver phosgene or mustard gas, by bombs or spray tanks. Later, the Boston light bomber became the main aircraft for spray delivery although the Mustang, Typhoon, Bermuda, and Vengeance were earmarked for such use if required. Bomb sizes varied depending on the type of gas, ranging from 30 lb up to 1,000 lb with air and ground burst options. What is not widely known is that when the advanced air striking force went to France to support the British Expeditionary Force, stocks of phosgene and mustard gas bombs were taken to the Continent as a precaution in case of German attack. However, with the German breakthrough on the Western Front in May 1940, it became vital that these munitions were recovered to the UK as a matter of urgency and the gas bombs became priority cargo during the evacuation from France.[71] The bombs were returned via Fowey in south Cornwall, then by rail to Buxton in Derbyshire, where they were inspected and stored at nearby 28 MU Harpur Hill. By the time the stocks had returned from France, a sub-site of No. 94 MU Barnham in Norfolk had been designated for chemical weapons storage, followed by similar but underground storage facilities at Nos 80 MU at Escrick in North Yorkshire, 93 MU at Norton Disney in Lincolnshire, and 95 MU at Lords Bridge in Cambridgeshire. Chemical weapons presented a number of handling, transport, and storage risks due to their proneness to leakage; this was progressively reduced by improved manufacturing and rigorous inspection at the manufacturing plants. As these weapons were not used operationally during the war, they remained in storage for a number of years and presented their own challenges when surplus munitions were disposed of in the early post-Second World War years.

Logistic Architecture: Buildings and Infrastructure on RAF Stations

A less obvious feature of the expansion programme that had an impact on logistics was buildings and infrastructure. With the expansion period came a dramatic increase in the number of RAF stations; in 1934, there were fifty-two RAF airfields in the UK; this had increased to eighty-nine by 1938. The rate of construction was rapid with seven stations constructed in 1935–36, eight in 1936–37, and six in 1937–38.[72] Prior to the expansion period, most purpose-built main stores buildings on RAF units were of a similar design, consisting of two rectangular shaped buildings, situated side-by-side, with a pitched gable-ended roof on each; one of the buildings usually had a double door receipt and despatch point with its floor opening out at lorry-bed level to facilitate the loading of equipment.

The opportunity was taken to introduce a new style of building and, in 1934, the first of these appeared under Drawing Number 2056/34.[73] Of brick construction, the stores complex was an 'E' shape when viewed from above and was approximately 125 feet wide by 103 feet deep with a steel-framed roof and gable ends. In addition to the standard facilities for items such as general spares and clothing, improved facilities were incorporated for the storage of aircraft engines and fabric. Careful consideration was also given to space requirements for the handling of equipment and the overall design permitted a logical flow from equipment receipt into storage and through to issue.[74] In 1935, a revision to this basic design was produced (Drawing Number 4287/35), which was almost identical in floor-plan but was built of concrete with a flat roof and had steel-framed trestles either side of the central fabric store to support

The main stores building at Hendon photographed in 2016. (*Author's collection*)

The expansion scheme main stores building at RAF Digby, pictured in 1983. (*N. Dabin*)

steel clad doors; this overall design was intended to add improved protection from incendiary bombs. The fabric store was later to become more commonly known as the aerofoil store in which large airframe components such as tailplanes, wings, and large control surfaces (such as ailerons and flaps) were kept.[75]

There were a number of other purpose-built logistics buildings on RAF stations including oil and lubricant stores (one of the earliest variants was built to Plan 329/26) and pyrotechnic stores (to Plans 2847/38 and 5488/42); the latter served as a forward holding from explosives storage areas to store ready-to-use items such as flares.[76]

Fine Tuning of Logistics: The Work of the Jones Committee 1938–1939

The final significant change that 'fine-tuned' the logistics process and organisation for war came about as part of a review of existing RAF administrative procedures that was commissioned by the Air Council in June 1938.[77] The RAF's logistic procedures, both store-keeping and stores-accounting (which had been introduced in the early 1920s) were then nearly twenty years old and had been designed for a much smaller air force. The complexity, technology, and sheer size of the new service needed a system that would be flexible enough to meet the needs of a rapidly changing RAF. The review was carried out by what was known as the Jones Committee, named after its Chairman, Brigadier-General (retired) H. A. Jones of the Imperial Tobacco Company.[78] The terms of reference for the review were as follows:

> To examine and report on the present system of administration in the Royal Air Force at Home in the light of the requirements of operational and general efficiency in peace and war, readiness for war, and economy, and to make recommendations.[79]

In broad terms, there were three aims to the review: firstly, to ease the burden of administration on station, squadron and flight commanders so that they could concentrate on their operational and training responsibilities; secondly, to reduce paperwork to the essential; and thirdly, to adopt a standard method of administration that would fit both peacetime and wartime requirements. Of particular note is that the committee's composition included members from civilian organisations (London Passenger Transport Board, General Post Office, and chartered accountants), a feature that suggests that the Air Ministry was alive to the benefit that could be gained by embracing commercial experience. The committee started work in December 1938 and, after twenty-four full meetings, submitted its final report on 2 August 1939. The work of the committee was comprehensive and covered a wide range of administrative functions including administrative training, administrative control by the Air Ministry, administrative control by commands, groups and stations, the system of assessing and accounting for airmen's pay, equipment accounting, personnel administration, and the inspection and maintenance of equipment.[80]

One of the main issues of concern raised by the committee was the serious shortage of equipment, especially engine and airframe spares. This was particularly evident in the local repair organisation where shortages of spares were holding up repair and maintenance work in station workshops. The committee was quite clear though, that the shortages were not due to provisioning or distribution (i.e. the logistics organisation itself) but with production. The answer to this problem was not easy, but it was recommended that equipment inspectors or liaison officers (at squadron leader level) would make a significant difference. Essentially, these officers were 'trouble-shooters' and would visit units to investigate problems that had been reported and track them through the chain of command until the source of the problem had been identified. This could involve following through the process from the equipment MUs, command and group staffs, and branches of the DofE.[81]

Although the shortages were not directly attributed to weaknesses within the DofE, the committee did examine the equipment requisitioning procedure in detail and commented on what might be referred to today as widespread 'red tape', which was adding little value to the overall process. Essentially, all requisitions were being passed to the finance staff for detailed scrutiny and the process was, in effect, a complete duplication of the calculations already made by the Equipment Branches. Moreover, this verification was being applied to straightforward requisitions for low value items. The committee recommended that the solution would be for the finance staffs to be co-located with the Equipment Branches so that they could be continually aware of the policy changes involved and could discuss the more significant issues, face-to-face, as they arose. Such a close involvement would also enable them to target those requisitions that needed closer scrutiny. Allied with this, it was recommended that benefit would be achieved if the Contracts Division was also co-located with the Equipment Division.[82] The bureaucracy involved would probably have been bearable prior to 1935, but the sheer scale of the procurement activity from the beginning of the expansion programme needed a much 'smarter' way of doing business. In the contemporary terminology of the Ministry of Defence, this was truly the forerunner of what would later be termed multi-disciplinary working.[83]

The committee also set in train the beginnings of de-centralised purchasing and provisioning. As will be deduced from the previous paragraphs, virtually all this activity was carried out at the Air Ministry by the DofE. The only real procurement outside of this was the local purchase order (LPO) process, which had been delegated to the COs of maintenance units, albeit with a limit of £25 per single purchase. The committee observed that, within the Air Ministry, there were urgent demands for equipment, which were delaying work at units, which could actually be met by using LPO but were outside the current financial limit. The answer to this was quite simple, and it was recommended that the LPO powers of COs at the maintenance units be increased to £100.[84]

The committee next turned its attention to activity at command, group, and station level. The organisational structure of the RAF had been redefined in 1935 to include commands and, within these, groups. These, in turn, were responsible for a given range of RAF stations. However, with the increase in commands (and a corresponding increase in groups) in 1936 and the rapidly increasing number of stations, command and control were becoming more difficult. As far as logistics were concerned, the committee observed that virtually all the coordination was being carried out at command level. With the wide geographical distribution of the units under their control, it was virtually impossible for command Equipment staff to even visit all the units let alone exercise sufficient supervision. The latter was particularly important, as many Equipment officers were inexperienced. As a result, the committee recommended that Equipment officers should be established at all group HQs.[85]

At station level, the changes were more wide ranging. The committee quickly recognised that while there was careful regulation and coordination of the supply process from the point at which equipment was ordered from industry down to its eventual arrival at the main stores of an RAF station, there was a general lack of coordination and control at the point where it was issued, invariably a squadron. Essentially, there was no dedicated expertise to look after the logistics interests of each squadron. Consequently, each of the flights and technical sections within squadrons were acting independently when it came to demanding and returning equipment. Moreover, much of this work was being carried out by misemploying technical non-commissioned officers. Given the problems that were being experienced with equipment shortages, this clearly needed addressing. The committee recommended that an Equipment Section should be established in each squadron, consisting of an Equipment Branch flying officer, a corporal, and two or more Equipment assistants, depending on the size of the squadron.[86] The new sections would be responsible for all the equipment work of the squadron, demanding and receiving all items required

RAF Kai Tak, Hong Kong, pictured in 1936. The Equipment section is at the right-hand corner of the black hanger. (*H. D. French*)

both for maintenance and for flight stocks within 'lock-ups' as they became known; the latter was a sub-store of ready-use items (such as wheels and tyres, sparking plugs, and aircraft general spares), which experience had shown had to be kept on-hand for quick replacement in aircraft. To maintain the mobility of flights, their respective equipment was kept in dedicated storage 'bins' and equipment in day-to-day use such as opened tins of paint would be kept by flights in their own hangars.[87] While these changes to squadrons might appear purely functional and making better use of the right tradesmen, there was a more important underlying achievement. The committee stated 'the organisation which we recommend would have the great advantage of making each squadron independently mobile in war' and there would be a 'responsible member of the Equipment service in each squadron who would supervise all the equipment administration of the squadron if it were moved to another station or to a satellite landing ground'.[88] The recommendation was not just a theoretical aspiration of an Air Ministry strategist, but was based on actual operating experience during the Abyssinian Crisis of 1935 when Equipment officers had been attached to each deployed flying squadron. There were difficulties in finding suitable officers for the task as the posts did not of course then exist. Moreover, the officers appointed were not familiar with the equipment or the squadron personnel; with the workload at its greatest, it was not the best of times for an Equipment officer to master these basics. A permanently appointed officer could build up this expertise and knowledge over a period of time, thereby making it much easier for him to respond during times of crisis.[89] The committee concluded their recommendation by stating that 'we consider therefore that the establishment of squadron equipment sections is essential both for the efficiency and economy in peace and for operational and administrative efficiency in war'.[90] Little did they know that this principle would be put to the test for real in a matter of months from the report's publication, with the RAF's Advanced Air Striking Force deploying to France shortly after the declaration of war.

There was also a significant change to logistic accounting concepts that, in time, would bring a more cost-effective and logical approach. From the very early days of the RAF, one of the prime concerns of logistic accounting had been the question of propriety and safeguarding the 'public purse' from loss or improper use of stores or equipment. This had led to the complicated situation of both the Equipment officer and the accountant officer having a shared role in maintaining the stores stock record. The committee recognised that the system in place had become over-complicated and involved a much larger amount of work than systems in use elsewhere to meet similar requirements. Indeed, they commented in their report:

> Any unprejudiced person with some experience of public and commercial accounting practice would be left with the impression that there are certain features of the system at present in use which involve an expenditure of effort which is out of all proportion to the needs of the situation.[91]

The real difficulty here was the division of responsibility for accounting between the Equipment officer on the one hand and the accountant officer on the other. The result of this arrangement was that the overall stores record of items held in stock was being kept in duplicate. Each movement of stock was being recorded from the transaction voucher in two separate records: tally cards were kept in the Equipment Section as a record for storekeeping personnel, especially for use by them in framing provisioning demands and the other was the main stock ledger held in the Accounts Section; these records were maintained by two separate groups of people in two separate places. It took little persuasion that this needed to change so it was recommended that, in the place of the two sets of records, only one stock record should be maintained; this was to be completed by the Equipment officer.[92] Various safeguards were put in place to ensure propriety, including the requirement that the records were kept separate from the physical stock and from those personnel actually handling it. There were many other recommendations regarding changes of accounting practice from issues of fuel to visiting aircraft through to the airmen's record of kit. They are too numerous to discuss in any detail here but, suffice to say, they all contributed to a much-needed overhaul of logistics administration. In this respect, the recommendations of the Jones Committee were far-reaching and formed an important part of the expansion programme.

The Equipment Branch and Trade in the 1930s

Despite the overseas commitment throughout the inter-war years, the overall numbers of personnel employed in the stores discipline remained fairly constant. Indeed, as far as the numbers of officers were concerned, the size of the Stores Branch barely exceeded the 300 mark by the beginning of the expansion programme. However, with the significant increase in RAF Stations and MUs, the numbers of Stores or Equipment officers began to increase quite dramatically; by the end of 1938, the branch had increased in size to 452 and by the end of 1939, it had soared to 1,017.

The policy of employing retired officers, while initially a valuable source of experience, soon appeared at odds with the new type of officer that the expansion scheme identified as being required for war. Retired officers were employed both at home and overseas on a pay scale of just over £200 plus a civil service bonus; this was particularly attractive to those demobilised from regular service following the First World War who wished to remain working in a military environment.[93] From the RAF's perspective, a retired officer was cheaper to employ than a regular officer; a flight lieutenant, for example, was paid just over £442 per annum.[94] The numbers concerned were not insignificant and, in 1936, of the forty-two RAF stations that had Equipment officers on their personnel establishments, 48 per cent were retired military officers filling for civilian stores officer appointments, albeit above the average age.[95]

The changing nature of the RAF, which started to emerge from the beginning of the expansion programme, brought new challenges for the Stores Branch. The introduction of new and more complex aircraft types began to expand dramatically the size of the RAF's inventory; this required careful management to ensure that stock was available in the right place and at the right time. This professional challenge, coupled with the opening of new RAF stations and Stores depots, required more Stores officers to manage the supply chain. The most expedient means of achieving this was to increase the use of civilian stores officers as a temporary substitution for posts that were eventually intended for filling by a regular officer.

By early 1938, with the branch having become the Equipment Branch, there were 170 of these substitution officers throughout the service, in addition to the civilian stores officers already employed.[96] The fact that the majority of these men were ex-military enabled them to be accepted within the Stores organisation without any notable resentment from their RAF colleagues. However, the policy came under criticism just after the Abyssinian Crisis in 1936 when the Air Ministry was unable to provide additional uniformed Equipment officers as part of the British reinforcement in the Middle East.[97]

In parallel with a wider review of RAF administrative procedures, which was commissioned by the Air Council in June 1938, the composition of the Equipment Branch was subject to a dedicated review and part of this was to find the best means of achieving an additional 840 Equipment officers that had been identified as being required under expansion scheme 'L'.[98] In the course of the review, it became clear that the population of Equipment Branch civilian Stores officers was an issue of significant concern in three respects. Firstly, the number of available retired officers was by this time beginning to dry up, mainly on account of their age. Secondly, the practical demands of the expansion programme were by then quite clear. Although the commanders-in-chief of the RAF's functional commands commented that the civilian Stores officers had fared favourably, they had reservations regarding their longer-term suitability. Indeed, the Commander-in-Chief (C-in-C) of Bomber Command commented:

> Increased strain is approached when Equipment Sections are asked to work for prolonged periods under conditions prevailing in expansion e.g. shortage of personnel, constant changes of equipment, moves of units and general lack of experience in subordinate personnel.[99]

Thirdly, and perhaps the most significant concern, the growing threat of war was prompting the need for officers who were young and fit enough to meet the demands of modern warfare. The review made the observation that the existing position was considered to be 'no longer safe or sound':

> The majority of them, owing to their having reached the age when their energy tended to flag, were not only unsatisfactory in peace but would be quite unfitted for the increased responsibilities which would fall upon them in war.[100]

This perceived vulnerability was of particular concern to the DGE, Air Vice-Marshal A. G. Garrod, who believed that his organisation would 'break down in war unless sufficient regular Equipment Branch officers were provided'. In particular, he believed:

> Regular officers needed to be available to meet the requirements of any Continental or overseas contingent proposal; that Equipment Branch posts on operational stations in the UK should be filled entirely by regular officers in peace and by at least one regular officer in war and that no civilianized Equipment post should be established at any RAF station that has less than two regular Equipment officers in addition to the civilianised post.[101]

The outcome of various meetings to discuss this issue was the introduction of a policy that effectively put a stop to any further recruitment of retired officers and which stated that an increased effort would be made to replace a substantial proportion of civilian Stores Officers with regular officers, with operational stations as a priority. There was still a place for retired officers (mainly within the Air Ministry and at certain equipment MUs), but the total population was to be limited to a maximum of seventy-five. The proposal was submitted to and approved by the Treasury in late June 1938; despite the arguments that had been articulated regarding preparedness for war, the Treasury approved the measure 'with some reluctance' and were of the opinion that 'retired officers will in many instances be particularly well-equipped for the class of duties to be performed and, as at present advised, they can find no reason why the employment of such officers should not continue to be the normal policy of the Air Council'.[102] It was a stipulation of the approval that the additional provision for war requirements was to be made via the RAF Volunteer Reserve (RAFVR), which had been formed in August 1936 primarily for pilots, but was expanded to include Equipment officers in January 1938, in light of the Air Ministry's need to meet the forecast increase in requirement. The impact of this on retired officers was quite dramatic and required the termination of 120 such appointments by the middle of 1939.[103] Perhaps their day had come, but the Air Force Lists show that many of these officers had been with the Branch since the very beginning and must have formed a mainstay of experience during the uncertainties faced by the Branch during the expansion programme. Credit must be given for the part that they played in getting the branch to where it was by the outbreak of war in 1939.

The replacement of retired officers on units, however, took time to address. Even by January 1939, there was still a significant reliance on them, a position exacerbated by yet more RAF stations having opened during the expansion programme; of the seventy-four stations then operating, the proportion of retired Equipment officers then employed had risen to 56 per cent.[104] There is little evidence to show how this position changed after 1939, but the increase in newly commissioned Equipment Branch officers appearing in the Air Force List from 1940 to 1945 suggests that the proportion of retired officers in the Branch would have reduced to the required level relatively quickly.

In May 1939, the Air Council also decided to introduce an Equipment Branch in the Auxiliary Air Force that had originally been formed in 1924 was intended solely for home defence.[105] There were also a small number of Equipment officers in the RAF reserve of officers. By the outbreak of war in September 1939, the RAF Logistics organisation could call on 722 officers in its main Equipment Branch, with a further total of 322 officers in the Equipment Branches of the Auxiliary Air Force, Volunteer Reserve, and the Reserve of Officers.[106]

Recruitment and training also went hand in glove with this expansion of manpower and the Branch and Trade soon began to draw on a wide range of expertise from civilian life. One of the many who were eager to sign up in 1938 was Donald Hills (later Air Vice-Marshal). At that time, the advertisement for people entering the Equipment Branch required individuals to have a professional qualification and to have worked for a firm of repute for a period of not less than five years. As it happened, the young Donald Hills had worked for the Bank of New Zealand in London since 1933 and by 1938, when he had completed the requisite five years, he had also achieved the certificate of the Associate of Institute of Bankers. In September 1938, fully qualified and with five years in a firm of repute, he reported for interview at the Air Ministry in London. There were about four or five officers on the board and the interview lasted half an hour. At the end of the interview, he was instructed to go off and have a medical examination, which declared him fit. Towards the end of the year, he heard that he had been accepted for a short service commission for four years in the Equipment Branch and was to report to RAF Kidbrooke on the 23 January 1939. Donald Hills duly reported on 23 January 1939 and was commissioned as a pilot officer on probation into the Equipment Branch the very same day, drawing 'the glorious salary of ten shillings per day'.[107] Greater detail on training at this time for both officers and airmen is covered in Chapter Eleven.

At the same time, a number of officers were being commissioned into the RAFVR. Many of them came from the Bank of England; they certainly all came from London, many from the City of London, and they all did some training on one or two nights a week. These officers were generally older than those on the short service commissions and, on the whole, had much more business experience. They were commissioned into the Equipment Branch on various dates from the end of 1938 into 1939. Prior to the end of 1938, there had been an intake of about twelve officers a year into the Branch, and they had received six months' training at RAF Cranwell. Initially, a number also transferred from other branches, mainly from the GD Branch; these were young pilots who, for one reason or another, had lost their medical category or who had been injured in accidents. Donald Hills remembered his first few weeks at Kidbrooke with affection:

> I had no uniform at that time, neither did any of us. A whole bevy of military tailors descended on the place and it wasn't very long before we were all resplendent in Pilot Officers' uniforms. We had quite a large Mess at Kidbrooke at that time—it was hutted from the First World War, but it was quite large and the students had a large room at one end and the staff, which of course included the staff of the depot, had an ante-room down at the other end and I think we all shared the same dining room. Of course there were no bars in those days, you pressed a bell in the anteroom and a steward brought you a drink and you signed a book for it. Life was very pleasant.[108]

Of particular note at this time was that all the direct entrants to the Branch were commissioned into the RAFVR; this stemmed from a decision in October 1937 that, on the outbreak of war, new entrants to the RAF should be enlisted into the RAFVR for the duration of the emergency. This is well-illustrated by the officer manning position at the outbreak of war where there were 722 officers in the Branch with a total of a further 322 officers in the Equipment Branches of the Auxiliary Air Force, RAFVR, and RAF Reserve of Officers.[109]

The Equipment trade also had an overhaul and the previous titles of Clerk (Stores Accounts) and Storekeeper were replaced by the single trade of Equipment assistant in Trade Group IV at the end of 1936; this was introduced at the same time as the officers' change of branch title to Equipment.

Civilians also continued to play their part in logistics during the inter-war period where the greatest concentration was to be found at the equipment depots. In the pre-war period, most of the Stores depots were manned by civilian personnel who were relatively free to come and go within the constraints of their contracts of employment. It was inevitable that, as part of the wider consideration regarding manpower during the expansion programme, the manning of the new depots in a period of emergency or actual war needed addressing, especially the issue of an almost complete dependence on a civilian workforce. These units were acknowledged as being a critical component of the RAF's supply chain. They were the vital storage and distribution link between the manufacturing output of industry and RAF consumers; any disruption in this process by industrial or other action by civilian staff was perceived as having serious consequences. Preliminary estimates were that, at the equipment MUs, this increase in workload was likely to be some seven to eight times the peacetime rate and at the ammunition depots even greater.[110] In terms of manpower numbers, it was estimated that over the next two to three years, some 10,000 additional civilian employees would be required.[111]

The Air Ministry had been grappling with this issue for some time prior to 1937 and had started to formulate options to mitigate the risk. While the early records of this issue avoid any direct reference, the general tenor of the various documents is one of a general uncertainty as to the loyalty that could be expected from the civilian workforce on the outbreak of war and a fear of the impact of specific activities such as disaffection, sabotage or industrial action.[112] There appears to be no mention in Air Ministry correspondence at this time regarding any unease among the civilian workforce regarding the risks from enemy bombing. The RAF was effectively looking towards a means of securing the provision of civilian labour and then being able to transfer manpower as required to meet service needs. Overall, four options emerged from the ongoing debate; these were eventually incorporated into a short summary paper by AMSO.[113] The first option considered was the complete manning of all the MUs by military staff, which would afford the greatest mitigation, but was soon discounted on the grounds of cost and the large numbers of military staff required. The second option was for the partial manning of the MUs by military personnel, but it was considered that mixed establishments had a number of disadvantages, not least of which was that the 'moral influence' of a small proportion of military was likely to be negligible. The third option was to man the MUs with reservists who had completed a period of regular service and could be given a long service reserve engagement. It soon became apparent, however, that there were insufficient men within the reserve to meet the requirement and that it would be unlikely that authorisation would be given for extending reserve commitments, let alone the potential financial impact. The fourth option, and one that had been considered as early as 1935, was to actually ask existing civilian employees if they would accept, voluntarily, an obligation of reserve service in the event of war or declared emergency. AMSO was clearly concerned about this risk as one of his early comments shows:

> I consider that its importance is so great in relation to the efficiency of the Royal Air Force immediately before war and during war, that a somewhat detailed statement should be placed before the Air Council.[114]

In a memorandum following the eighth progress meeting considering this issue, AMSO expanded on his earlier view:

> Without in any way casting doubt on the patriotism of the average civilian employee, I consider that the consequences of a breakdown of the maintenance organisation during the critical days immediately before and on the outbreak of war are so grave that the Royal Air Force cannot be left dependent upon the loyal fulfilment of the moral obligation of such a large number of persons to remain at their posts of duty on the outbreak of an emergency. The position of the Royal Air Force is different from the other Services, and little or no time for preparation may be available before the outbreak of war. It is therefore necessary that, for the Royal Air Force, there should exist a means of securing immediately the hold over their civilian employees that the other services may be satisfied to secure by the introduction of special legislation when war breaks out.[115]

These comments are one of very few made by a senior RAF officer who was not a logistician, yet acknowledge how critical a specific component of the supply chain was to the employment of air power. By this stage, the civilian manpower estimates had begun to mature and it was forecast that on the completion of expansion scheme 'L', the total civilian staff of the MUs would be in the order of 20,000 of whom only about 2,500 were in established grades, the balance of about 17,500 representing various industrial grades employed on a weekly basis. The final paper was prepared for AMSO's consideration and onward transmission in January 1939 but the drafting staff officer suggested:

> You may, however, wish to withhold its reference to the Air Council for the time being in view of the discussion at recent Progress Meetings when S of S [Secretary of State]. said that he felt it would be much better to include civilians employed by the Air Ministry in the Schedule of Reserved Occupations than to ask them to join the Reserve.[116]

The issue was eventually discussed in conference by the Ministry of Labour and the Schedule of Reserved Occupations was amended in favour of Air Ministry demands.[117] The expansion schemes brought a significant increase in civilian manpower requirements and saw close co-operation between the Air Ministry and the Ministry of Labour. In February 1939, the Air Ministry estimated that it would require an additional 905 storekeeping grades with 793 required at various types of MUs and 112 at RAF units.[118] In the event, few if any cases of disloyalty came to notice.

Logistics Management in the Air Ministry

By 1936, the substantial increase in workload that had come about from the expansion schemes was beginning to place great strains on the DofE. This was most acutely experienced within the areas responsible for aircraft, aero engines, MT, and the Stores depots. Consequently, this led to two further changes to the directorate before the outbreak of war in 1939. The first was in July 1936 and, *inter alia*, sought to strengthen the directorate for possible war. Enhancements to some of its branches included new responsibilities for producing maintenance plans for specific theatres of war; the preparation of unit equipment tables listed every item of equipment in the RAF's vocabulary of stores to be provided for each unit in accordance with plans and agreed rates of consumption and working out the organisation of various units from depots to squadrons in the field. There was also a particularly important remit, which was the production of mobilisation plans and arranging exercises to test unit capability and readiness.[119] Overall, the approved increase to the DofE amounted to seventy-seven additional personnel and increased the size of the DofE by some 37 per cent.[120]

The second change was in 1938, by which time the expansion programme had led to an even greater increase in the volume of work within the DofE. In his letter to the Treasury seeking approval for a further reorganisation and an increase in the numbers of staff, the DGE proposed an increase in the number of branches working specifically on aircraft and their equipment to eight and the formation of a fourth DDE. It was not just the introduction and quantities of new aircraft that led to workload increases. The area responsible for MT had experienced a similar exponential rise in workload. The RAF had a total vehicle fleet size of just 2,000 in 1935; this had risen fivefold to 10,000 by 1937 with a notable increase in the variety of specialised types to around 187, the latter of which now included winches for barrage balloons and associated vehicles for their operation. The number of vehicles held in reserve had also risen in a similar timeframe from just a few hundred in the early 1930s to over 5,000. As with aircraft, this all required contracts with manufacturing companies, the total number of such arrangements having risen from just a few in the early 1930s to ninety contracts by 1938.[121] The large proposed increase of 40,000 personnel, to swell the ever-growing size of the RAF, also had a direct impact on the logistics support required, with additional clothing, equipment, and furnishings for the domestic and work accommodation being built at units.

These were but a few of the many increased demands that the expansion schemes had placed on RAF Logistics. The overall result was that the DGE had not only to reorganise his directorate to meet this challenge, but also had to seek approval for a further increase of sixty-eight personnel. This was subsequently endorsed by the Treasury and promulgated in September 1938. This increase also saw the rank of DGE upgraded to air vice-marshal and the additional post of an air commodore.[122]

In addition to the DofE, the expansion programme also saw a much wider growth in the size of the Air Ministry. As part of this, the government had acquired Berkeley Square House in London. Situated on the east side of Berkeley Square, by early 1939, this building housed most of the staff of the DofE. Their stay in London was brief and the directorate was soon moved out of London as part of the government's evacuation plans; work on the whole idea of evacuation had started as early as 1931, when the Imperial Defence Sub-Committee had set up an 'Evacuation Sub-Committee'. As part of this, plans had evolved to move the seat of government out of the capital for fear of air attack; a key part of this was the intention also to move out various ministries and disperse them throughout the country. Consequently, shortly after the outbreak of war in September 1939, the majority of staff in the DofE (those within DofE 1 and DofE 2) relocated to Harrogate in the North Riding of Yorkshire.[123]

RAF Logistics on the Eve of the Second World War

The Abyssinian Crisis in 1935 had led to an important fresh look at mobilisation planning and ensured that the lessons learned from this experience were factored into the RAF's involvement in the Western Plan, which was key to its deployment to France in 1939. The expansion programme itself from 1934 led to many changes in RAF Logistics, not least of which was the significant change it had undergone in terms of structure and procedures. It was in much better shape to meet the forthcoming war and had become a more integral part of the RAF's support structure. The formation of Maintenance Command—with Nos 40 and 42 Groups providing specialist management for equipment, POL, and munitions—provided a much clearer responsibility for stores and supplies. The fine-tuning of logistics that took place through the work of the Jones Committee helped to optimise the management of the RAF's supply chain; it took a fresh look at how logistics was organised and administered as well as making many forward-thinking changes. While the organisation's procedures had been updated to meet what was seen as a totally new requirement from a massively expanded Air Force, it was largely untested in action. Indeed, even on the outbreak of war in September 1939, many of the changes were yet to settle down and be proven. The next and most challenging chapter in the history of RAF Logistics was about to be written.

3

The Second World War: 1939–1945

From Britain's declaration of war in September 1939, through until Japan's unconditional surrender on 2 September 1945, the RAF's Logistics organisation reached its zenith in terms of size and breadth of responsibility. The total number of aircraft operated by the RAF had risen from 3,555 in September 1939 to 55,469 in May 1945.[1] The number of its personnel had risen from 175,692 to 1,130,460 in a similar timeframe.[2] The RAF's global presence became widespread, with units eventually operating across Europe as far afield as North Africa, the Mediterranean, India, and the rest of the Middle East and Far East. The demands on logistics were significantly different from the inter-war years. To deliver air power on this almost global scale required an extensive and efficient logistics infrastructure, the development of that had come a long way during the expansion programme. It was also a period when senior military commanders and planners had started to acknowledge the critical significance of logistics, not simply as a discipline but as a military function. Indeed, the American General Dwight D. Eisenhower is reputed to have commented that 'you will not find it difficult to prove that battles, campaigns, and even wars have been won or lost primarily because of logistics'.[3] This chapter examines how RAF Logistics was organised and operated during the Second World War.

Wartime Command and Control

As the pre-war expansion programme unfolded, the Air Ministry and the RAF recognised that the key to managing logistics in any likely conflict would be effective command and control. The Air Ministry's DofE and Maintenance Command were at the heart of this; however, as the RAF's presence increased in overseas theatres, smaller equipment coordinating offices were established in the HQ elements of the commands and groups that were formed overseas.

The Air Ministry

Within the UK, the DofE was to undergo one more major organisational review and change to prepare it for the demands of wartime equipment management. During 1939, with a much clearer view of the impact of the expansion programme and an initial estimate of what additional workload a war might bring, the size and role of the directorate underwent a major review with the aim of strengthening it for war.[4] The relocation of most of the DofE's staff to Yorkshire had resulted in a number of administrative difficulties, not least of which was that use of the national telephone system, which was very much restricted to priority war-related communication. This led to much of the routine work having to be conducted in writing, which increased the time taken to conduct daily business. Time spent travelling between London and Harrogate also proved particularly time consuming for the director whose attention was divided between the two locations. The review's recommendations were approved in April 1940 and resulted in a reorganisation of the DofE, with staffing level increases amounting to 941 across thirty-five branches. The title of the director was also changed to deputy director-general (DDGE) to reflect the size of his responsibility and to bring it in line with the hierarchy within the Directorate of Maintenance, where Lord Nuffield was the Director-General and his direct subordinate the Deputy Director-General.[5] Archival sources do not record if the 1940 reorganisation resolved the practical and communication difficulties of the London and Harrogate basing, but greater numbers of staff would most certainly have helped address the workload increases.

Maintenance Command

The HQ element of Maintenance Command, which had been formed in 1938, remained at RAF Amport (near Andover, Hampshire) throughout the war, but the progressive growth in the number of its units led to increasing command and control difficulties. The number of units in No. 40 Group, for example, doubled in size from fifteen in September 1939 to thirty by December 1941.[6] The geographical dispersal of these units, coupled with the challenges of wartime communication and facilities for travel, made it increasingly difficult for the group commander to maintain regular contact with his units. It was a similar picture for the other groups of the command. For No. 40 Group HQ, an element of its responsibility was decentralised through introducing what were known as universal equipment wings (UEW) in June 1941, each of which was responsible for a specified number of MUs in a defined area. The respective Wing HQs were located at the now six UEDs (Nos 3, 7, 14, 16, 25, and 35 MUs). Two further wings were formed: No. 65 based on 65 MU at Handforth in Cheshire, and No. 55 at Derby, which was responsible for the barrack and clothing depots.[7] Operating experience during 1942 and 1943 showed that the UEW structure was still unwieldy and in August 1944 the number of wings was reduced to three: No. 55 Wing with its HQ in the Municipal Buildings at Derby; No. 56 Wing with its HQ at RAF Annan in Scotland; and No. 57 Wing with its HQ at Molton House at Milton near Oxford.[8] The devolved command and control structure of the UEWs remained in place for the rest of the war and enabled Maintenance Command to exercise a more pragmatic approach to its wider responsibilities. In terms of personnel, No. 40 Group grew to be a sizeable organisation and, by the end of 1944, it was just under 45,000 strong. Of this total, 25,320 or in the region of 56 per cent were civilians.

One part of the supply chain that was quickly recognised as being of concern was the reliance on an almost total civilian manning of the MUs. This was obviated by including the civilian posts in the schedule of reserved occupations. The significant point here, however, was the high-level recognition of the critical role of civilians in this part of the RAF supply chain. The group's reliance on civilian employees was particularly evident at Nos 3, 7, 14, 25, and 35 MUs. Nos 16 and 61 MUs, however, were predominantly service-manned; in the case of No. 16 MU Stafford, there were only twenty-five civilians out of a total unit strength of 4,688 people. It is not clear why the latter policy was pursued; however, post-war, it is believed it was due to a combination of needing a pool of uniformed equippers in this country on which to be able to draw for manning overseas depots and to ameliorate the unlikely but possible threat of civil service strike action.

The command and control situation for No. 42 Group, with its HQ at Burghfield Common near Reading, proved to be more straightforward than that experienced by No. 40 Group. On the whole, this was due to the smaller number of units that it had to control. During the war, the number of 42 Group units in the UK storing and distributing munitions was roughly half the number of units controlled by 40 Group and did not necessitate the introduction of a lower-level wing structure. Moreover, the supply of fuel, which was direct from commercial depots to units, did not require an intermediate 42 Group depot structure.[9]

Another development at this time was the innovative concept of utilising the experience of senior civilian industrialists. Shortly after the expanded DofE was approved in 1940, the Secretary of State for Air, Sir Kingsley Wood, commented to AMSO that, as several senior positions in the Quartermaster General's Department at the War Office were filled by civilians with extensive industrial experience, at least one of DDGE's deputy directors should be a civilian businessman. This proposal was not well received by the director who argued that such an appointment would not be good for the morale of the Equipment Branch and that someone brought in from outside could not possibly have the breadth of experience required unless he had served in at least one of the lower positions in the directorate. This concept never came to fruition as Sir Samuel Hoare replaced Sir Kingsley Wood in early April 1940 and his suggestion went with him. This should not be seen as resisting exposure to wider experience and the official history of the RAF's Maintenance organisation shows that, from its formation in 1938, its HQ staff had studied industrial practice. For example, railway general managers were consulted on railway issues (including the layout of sidings and branch lines); the petrol chiefs with regard to the fuel depots; the automobile association for road routing; Harrods for quick delivery service; and Selfridges for post order business and office systems, to name but a few.[10] As with the RAF's approach to its earlier review of administration through the Jones Committee in 1938, this collaboration further illustrates just how alive the Air Ministry was to harnessing the benefits of wider commercial practice.

Logistics on RAF Units

During the early part of 1939, the pace of life at RAF units had begun to increase quite considerably and additional manpower became a pressing need. To meet the requirement for more Equipment officers, a number of training courses running at that time were cut short in order that urgently needed officers could be deployed to front-line flying stations. Pilot Officer Donald Hills started his professional training course at RAF Kidbrooke in January 1939. Having settled in for what was intended to be a six-month course, he, and a number of colleagues who had done well in the early course examinations, were advised towards the end of March 1939 that they were to be posted. Despite the urgency, there was still a degree of democracy in the process and Pilot Officer Hills was able to opt for a posting to RAF Tangmere in Sussex, conveniently close to his home in the adjoining county of Kent.

As a predominantly fighter station, Tangmere was one of the more active units at this time and was home to Nos 1 and 43 Squadrons of Fighter Command, both of which had been recently re-equipped with the Hawker Hurricane Mk 1. The station was also the base of No. 217 Squadron of Coastal Command, operating the twin-engined Avro Anson Mk 1. In contrast to the station's up-to-date aircraft complement, Tangmere's Equipment Section was not so modern and had been run by civilian stores officers. Pilot Officer Hills replaced a retired Royal Navy commander, while a flying officer (commissioned from the rank of WO in 1933) replaced a retired Army colonel. Both of these men had shaped things to suit their own pace of life as Donald Hills recalled 'these two retired officers had run the supply and equipment section stores for an active flying station for many years and very largely at their convenience'.[11]

In addition to the more obvious aspects of rearmament such as aircraft and weapons, the Expansion Programme had a much wider impact on RAF bases, placing significant demands on logistics. The building programme, for example, was extensive and Tangmere had its fair share, including a number of new barrack blocks and an enlarged Sergeants' Mess. The need for the latter was primarily due to the fact that the air gunners flying in the Avro Ansons of No. 217 Squadron (largely aircraftsmen up until that time), suddenly became sergeants, thereby significantly increasing the living-in population of the mess. All these buildings, in whatever shape or form, needed furnishing and it was not always a process over which station Equipment Sections had much control. Donald Hills recalled how one evening an unexpected and very large convoy of vehicles arrived with the furniture for a number of new barrack blocks. The buildings had not yet been handed over to the

RAF by the building contractors so the keys were unavailable. With nowhere else to store the furniture, the then very junior Pilot Officer Hills used his initiative and broke one of the barrack block windows in order that the main door could be opened and the furniture offloaded and stored inside. Despite the fact that there were no alternatives, military discipline was slow to recognize such initiative and Pilot Officer Hills found himself before the station adjutant the next morning, in trouble for breaking the window. As part of the preparations for war, all sorts of equipment literally flooded into Tangmere over the days following this incident, including personal anti-gas equipment and steel helmets, for the ever-growing war establishment of the station.

If there was an urgent need for officers, then there was an even greater need for airmen. Many of these, however, found their way into the equipment discipline by a less direct route than the officers who were usually directly commissioned into a main professional branch from the outset. Robert Stamp had joined the RAFVR in April 1939 after the Munich Crisis and had been as good as 'forced' to sign on as an ACH (GD) in Trade Group V by what he described as 'a smooth-talking wing commander' at the Air Ministry in London. Robert attended RAF Hornchurch on Sundays for training and ground defence duties on Lewis guns. He was mobilised on 24 August 1939 and sent to RAF Biggin Hill in Kent where, among other diversions such as guard duties, he found himself assigned to the main stores responsible for issuing petrol and the filling of the flying squadron fuel tankers—all this still as a relatively inexperienced airman. Robert later re-mustered to the equipment trade after serving in France in 1940.[12]

A stock check being carried out in an Equipment section, 1942. (*IWM*)

The logistic needs of RAF stations, at home and overseas, were met by their Equipment Sections; these regulated the ebb and flow of stores and supplies between the equipment MUs and the front line flying squadrons. Their role was critical and ranged from providing literally mountains of clothing at basic training units, to the extensive needs of a front-line Bomber Command unit. At many locations in the UK, the war was a distant thing, but the Battle of Britain in 1940 brought the hazards of war much closer to home. The experiences of Norman Morss provide an insight to this critical period of the war. He joined the RAFVR in June 1939 and, having failed selection for aircrew due to defective colour vision, was initially enlisted in the photographic trade. On being called-up in late August, he found himself working in the Equipment Section at RAF Northolt. After spending six weeks unloading ammunition trucks at Hillingdon Railway Station, Norman was advised that it would be in his best interests to formally re-muster to the Equipment trade with the incentive that if he did, he would have an early advancement from the training rank of aircraftman 2 (AC2) to AC1, thus doubling his pay from two to four shillings a day. By the time of the intensive phase of the Battle of Britain in September 1940, Norman was a substantive leading aircraftman (LAC).

While the courageous exploits of the fighter pilots, described by Winston Churchill as the 'Few', were at the forefront of the battle, there were of course countless numbers of ground crews who worked tirelessly to keep the fighters in the air. Their task was ably supported by the equippers who provided a vast range of items, from aircraft spares to maintaining the almost continual flow of fuel and munitions. Norman Morss recalled how on at least one occasion, Northolt appeared to be the only aerodrome in No. 11 Group Fighter Command with undamaged runways where the returning fighters could land, mainly due to the fact that the station had largely escaped any major daylight bombing when RAF Biggin Hill, Manston, Hornchurch, North Weald, and others had been temporarily put out of action. This put an enormous strain on the Equipment Section as they had to deal with more fighters than usual and found that their additional reserve of spares was very quickly needed to enable the aircraft to fly off again. The reserve of spares that Norman refers to was not officially held stock and was probably due to the station's senior Equipment officer (SEO) locally amending the pre-war stock levels in light of operational experience. This unofficial 'buffer' stock appears to have been quite commonplace at Fighter Command units at the time and the practice soon came to the attention of No. 11 Group HQ at RAF Stanmore Park that implemented a series of 'snap' inspections at its units. Norman's account of one such visit to RAF Northolt illustrates just how determined SEOs were to retain their extra stock:

> The SEO instructed us all in the Airframe and Engine section to seek the co-operation of the squadrons for transport to ferry items such as airscrews, wing tips, mainplanes, undercarriages and tyres for Hurricanes and Spitfires out to the many flight dispersal areas so that, when the party from Command arrived,

> what we were holding in the Equipment buildings appeared reasonable and corresponded with the prescribed minimum/maximum stock levels. The party, from memory, consisted of the AOC himself, Sir Hugh Dowding, accompanied by his *aide-de-camp* and two or three senior Staff Equipment Officers. After their inspection, they left presumably reasonably happy that we were not guilty of any hoarding.

Norman Morss was posted from Northolt in July 1942 and went on to serve in Kenya and then Northern Italy in 1944 as part of No. 40 ASP, and then No. 208 Tactical Reconnaissance Squadron. He was eventually commissioned and left the RAF in 1946.[13]

Wartime Equipment Supply, 40 Group

By the end of 1940, the work to achieve No. 40 Group's universal supply system had been completed, with the seventh and final UED at Stafford (No. 16 MU) opened on 1 December 1939. Despite the logic of the universal supply concept, the reasoning behind it was not always supported. One such dissenter in the early stages of the war was Sir Arthur Harris when he was AOC No. 5 Group. A far-sighted commander, he was keen to ensure that his ground support organisation was as effective as possible, thereby letting his aircrews get on with the flying. As far as Logistics was concerned, he had asked for a dedicated depot to be set up within his group to handle purely Handley Page Hampden aircraft spares; No. 5 Group was the sole operational user of the aircraft at the time. Understandably, he saw the need as quite simple with a dedicated, aircraft-specific depot receiving spares direct from manufacturers. However, when he heard that a new MU was being set up near Manchester for this purpose, he was not impressed, saying 'it is fundamentally wrong, even stupid, to make a triangle out of a line of supply when a direct line is all that is necessary'. He went on to add that 'minutes, let alone hours, days or weeks, will count when the war really starts'. His view made sense, albeit from the perspective of just one group commander and his specific aircraft needs; it also showed that some senior commanders took logistics seriously.[14] His request was never implemented and the UED structure that evolved was viewed as adequate to meet his needs. Moreover, if exceptions had been made for one aircraft type, there was then the risk that other commanders would make similar demands, a position that would progressively undermine the UED concept.

With the organisational changes addressed, attention turned to increasing the effectiveness and efficiency of the new depots. In early January 1940, AOC No. 40 Group, in conjunction with his depot commanders, agreed that the UEDs would work towards achieving a performance standard in three key areas. Firstly, it was acknowledged that equipment needed to be received and brought to account quickly, and that this should be done within seventy-two hours. Secondly, to ensure a speedy issue time to demanding units, it was agreed that issues, other than those for which a specific time instruction had been given, would be made within forty-eight hours. Thirdly, it was agreed that a forty-eight-hour despatch service would be maintained to all RAF stations. To achieve these targets, a standardised way of working for all UEDs was soon implemented with changes to personnel establishments and administration adjusted accordingly.[15] This commitment to a defined level of service was important in two respects. First, bringing equipment to account quickly enabled an accurate picture of logistic capability to be maintained; this was particularly important in terms of assessing, from a planning perspective, whether or not operational aspirations could be met and sustained. Secondly, the speedy despatch of equipment from the depots ensured that front line units could be replenished quickly in the event of unexpectedly high levels of consumption. This was, of course, entirely dependent on industry manufacturing sufficient stock in the first place.

A commitment to providing a defined level of service was one of the more straightforward of the issues facing Maintenance Command at this time. The availability of physical storage space was soon to prove more problematic. At the outbreak of war, planning staff in the Air Ministry had little idea of how long the war would last, nor how many stations the RAF would build, both at home and overseas. The growth, even in the first year of war, soon showed that the RAF's stockholding policy, based on the UEDs serving the six geographical areas in Britain, would not be adequate in the longer term and a range of new storage units began to evolve. A combination of an equipment provisioning programme, in support of the expansion scheme, and an evolving view of the RAF's war materiel needs led to a substantial in-flow of equipment delivered off war contracts, all of which had to be receipted and placed in an appropriate storage location. Given this, and the fact that not all the UEDs and their sub-depots were completed, the rate of equipment receipt outpaced No. 40 Group's capacity to store it.

An early indication of the magnitude of this problem came at a conference held at HQ Maintenance Command on 19 January 1940 when the Air Ministry representative advised that the group should be looking towards holding nine months' worth of stock; in terms of storage space, it was estimated that this amounted to some 9.5 million square feet. When the available storage space was mapped to this planning requirement, two problems emerged. First, the total floor-space available across all the UEDs and other storage when their respective building programmes was complete, only amounted to 8 million square feet; it was agreed that the only way this shortfall of 1.5 million square feet against the planning requirement could be met was by the creation of an additional UED. The second problem was that, of the 8-million-square-feet capacity of the existing depot infrastructure, not all of it was yet available; construction of several of the storage sheds at Heywood and Quedgeley was not finished and none of the sheds at Stafford was yet in use.[16] To

Aircraft propellers being unloaded from a *Queen Mary* trailer. (*IWM*)

compound this problem, the storage of MT vehicles began to present a similar challenge. A similar review was urgently required for 12,800 assorted vehicles in addition to the normal reserves. It was estimated, however, that, when work had been completed on the MT sites at Stafford and Heywood, space would still only be available for 5,350 vehicles, under half the storage capacity required. With the rate of receipt of vehicles estimated to be in the region of 1,000 per month from 1 February 1940, the problem would not diminish.[17] By March 1940, the shortage of storage space in No. 40 Group had started to present a significant problem with congestion occurring at the UEDs and the various sub-depots. At the Wembley and Hammersmith sub-depots, for example, substantial stocks of anti-gas clothing were leading to overcrowding, while at the UEDs some 200,000 square feet of space had been misappropriated for furniture storage.[18] Various temporary arrangements were made such as storage in the open air where possible and the Society of Motor Traders was also approached to seek their assistance in storing RAF vehicles at trade garages.[19]

The actual and projected growth of the RAF led to continuing concern from planning staffs in No. 40 Group as to whether the storage capacity was keeping pace; early estimates envisaged that the expansion was likely to be in the region of 228 new squadrons by June 1942—a 100 per cent increase in front line strength.[20] Along with the increase in numbers of squadrons came the increased range of spares that were required to be held for new aircraft types, particularly those of American origin. To meet this, and taking into account building work that was already underway, it was estimated that a 50 per cent increase in storage space would be required in 40 Group by June 1942.[21] One of the first measures to be taken was to remove the much lower priority ranges of barrack and clothing equipment from the UEDs and to relocate them in dedicated barrack and clothing depots (BCD), six of which had been formed by the end of 1940.[22] The creation of the BCDs relieved part of the storage space problem, but the more pressing issue was the increasing demand load being placed directly on the UEDs. By the end of 1940, there were approximately 478 RAF stations, each making demands separately on an item-by-item basis.[23] This piecemeal way of dealing with equipment demands placed an enormous strain on the logistic system, with each demand requiring its own paperwork, manually picking from stock, packing and then despatch to the demanding unit; it was estimated that ten separate demands for just one item, took almost ten times longer to process than one demand for ten times the quantity.[24] The solution to this problem was to create intermediate depots, or holding parks, forward and much closer to the operational units. Known as equipment parks (EP), these units relieved stockholding pressures and reduced some of the workload at the UEDs by holding forward three months maximum and two months minimum levels of aircraft stores. These new units maintained their holdings (on a similar basis to the UEDs) by submitting demands on their parent UEDs and directly met the equipment demands from the RAF units within their respective areas. Initially, two parks were formed in June 1941 (on a trial basis) at Perth and Inverness; by the end of the war, a total of fifteen EPs had been established. The benefit of the parks was felt not just in terms of creating additional space and reducing workload at the UEDs; they also enabled a greater proportion of equipment to be dispersed, a concern that had gained increasing prominence following the Luftwaffe's attacks on British cities and industrial infrastructure during late 1940 and early 1941.[25]

Although the introduction of the BCDs and EPs did much to relieve the pressure on the UEDs, the relentless flow of equipment into RAF storage continued apace well into 1942. Time precluded the building of a further UED, which was estimated to take at least two years; a further measure was therefore introduced in the first half of 1942 with the creation of a new type of depot, initially known as equipment dispersal depots (EDD), but renamed ground equipment depots (GED) in June 1942.[26] Four of these were initially constructed, each of 250,000 square feet capacity. It was originally intended that they would primarily be a form of bulk holding unit feeding the UEDs, but they soon evolved into a specialist stockholding unit in their own right, holding a wide range of non-airborne equipment such as machine tools, spares for MT and marine craft, general hardware, paints, and metals.[27] A total of seven GEDs were eventually established and served the same geographical areas for their respective range of equipment as the UEDs. By June 1942, the progressive removal of the non-airborne ranges of equipment from the UEDs into the newly formed ground equipment depots, led to them being renamed aircraft equipment depots (AED), a designation they retained for the duration of the war.[28]

In addition to the main equipment storage depots, further specialist depots were also built to receive and store MT vehicles and marine craft. From September 1939 until May 1945, the number of equipment storage units (excluding those for MT and marine craft) more than quadrupled. This overall development of the main 40 Group units is detailed by year in Table 2.

Unit Type	Sept. 1939	Dec. 1940	Dec. 1941	Dec. 1942	Dec. 1943	Dec. 1944	May 1945
Universal Equipment Depots	5	6	7	-	-	-	-
Aircraft Equipment Depots	-	-	-	7	7	7	7
Barrack and Clothing Depots	3	6	5	6	6	6	6
Equipment Parks	-	-	7	15	15	15	15
Ground Equipment Depots	-	-	-	6	7	7	7
Totals	8	12	19	34	34	34	34

Table 2: Growth of No. 40 Group Equipment Storage Units in the UK: 1939 to May 1945 [29]

The provision of sufficient storage space remained a problem throughout the war and the official Air Ministry history recounts a complex and diverse range of solutions to this problem, from new-build sites and hirings through to the use of redundant balloon centres and RAF units at the end of 1944.[30] The quest to squeeze

RAF equipment assistants with various airframe components. (*Crown Copyright—Air Historical Branch MoD*)

the most out of available space also gave rise to some imaginative and enterprising uses as former LAC, Mr L. B. Birch, then an MT driver (later re-mustered to the Equipment Trade) at No. 16 MU Stafford recalled:

> During one visit to No. 6 Site, whilst awaiting to be unloaded, I noticed an airman going into an opening between some large cartons and upon further inspection was surprised to find a space inside these cartons being used as an area fitted with a table and cobbler's last for the purpose of repairing officers' and airmen's shoes![31]

An exact figure for the growth is difficult to determine, primarily due to the lack of comprehensive and comparable statistics for all the 40 Group units. However, of the figures available, the general picture shows that the group managed to approximately double its storage space in square feet between 1941 and the end of 1944, by which time the main storage units had amassed over 22.5 million square feet of storage space.[32]

One aspect that is not commented on in any detail in the Air Ministry's historical accounts of the Second World War is the physical security of the depots. While limited use had been made of underground storage during the First World War, the growth, capability and range of the Luftwaffe's bomber aircraft in the period leading up to the Second World War significantly increased the risk of air attack on the RAF's logistics infrastructure in the UK.[33] Early on in the war, the Air Ministry was particularly concerned that a significant proportion of No. 40 Group's in-use storage space was situated in industrial target areas; of the 8.5 million square feet in use, approximately 1.5 million were located in the areas of London, Newport (Monmouthshire), Sheffield, and Manchester.[34] The perceived risk to the depots from enemy air attack had become a concern as early as the autumn of 1938. The ORB of No. 14 MU Carlisle, for example, recorded that 'on this date, as a result of the Czecho-Slovakia [*sic.*]–German crisis, No. 14 Maintenance Unit was opened. Had the crisis resulted in war, it was anticipated that there would have been a bombardment of the existing RAF Maintenance Units at a very early stage'.[35]

As already explained in the previous chapter, the Air Ministry had implemented a number of measures to improve survival from enemy air attack, ranging from geographical locations to site-layout and building design. Further dispersal measures were implemented in the autumn of 1940 to divide stocks of important items between sheds and sites to reduce further the risk of complete loss of stock in the event of an air attack.[36] Camouflage also had a role to play, and the MUs were subject to the RAF's general camouflage policy, which was developed by the Air Ministry in 1938 and remained in use throughout the war until it was discontinued in 1944. The application of camouflage was not universally applied across logistic sites, although buildings were generally painted using a colour mix of brown, green, and black paint, similar to the schemes on the upper surfaces of wartime aircraft, along with camouflage 'scrim' netting to disguise items stored outside.

Identifying how the RAF went about its stock protection measures is relatively straightforward. Assessing the effectiveness of the measures is more complex. The first real test of the measures in the UK came with the Blitz during late 1940 and early 1941. As part of a wider enemy air raid on Coventry during the night of 14–15 November 1940, some 3 per cent of No. 40 Group's storage space was lost when 'C' MU at Coventry (predominantly barrack stores) was hit.[37] While there was not an immediate Air Ministry reaction, the attack did precipitate many of the engineering firms in the Midlands to seek dispersed factory accommodation, including Rover (whose Helen Street works had been severely damaged during the raid). Some six months later, the Ministry of Aircraft Production encouraged Rover to consider relocating their component production to an underground facility at Drakelow near Kidderminster. Rover was not entirely enthusiastic about this proposal, primarily due to the disruption to production that would inevitably occur through relocation of plant and machinery. Lengthy negotiations between the Ministry of Aircraft Production and Rover, along with the reduction in the intensity of the German bombing campaign by the end of 1942, meant this initiative made little progress and only half the Rover component production capability was relocated to Drakelow. Drakelow was used by the RAF and some 82,500 square feet was utilised by No. 40 Group for aircraft components in 1942.[38]

Such was the level of confidence in the protective measures that had been incorporated into the design of the RAF's depots that the Air Ministry Directorate General of Works saw no reason to establish any department or office to monitor damage from air attack: 'efforts were naturally concentrated on repair and rehabilitation'.[39] This assumption proved to be reasonably well founded as by the end of the war a relatively low number of attacks or direct threats had actually been experienced (see Table 3).

MU	Location	Recorded Air Raid Alerts	Actual Attacks/Direct Threat
1	Kidbrooke (S.E. London)	13	10 attacks in 1940 3 attacks in 1941 (Blitz related) 4 attacks in 1944 including 2 direct hits from V1 flying bombs.
3	Milton (Oxfordshire)	89	1 attack in 1940
4	Ruislip ((Middlesex)	151	1 attack in 1940
7	Quedgeley (Gloucestershire)	132	
14	Carlisle (Cumbria)	1	
16	Stafford (Staffordshire)	6	1 enemy aircraft incursion
25	Hartlebury(Worcestershire)	10	
35	Heywood (Lancashire)	26	2 attacks in 1940

Table 3: Enemy air raid alerts/attacks causing damage or a threat to the RAF's UEDs, 1940 to 1944.[40]

The greatest number of actual attacks occurred at No. 1 MU Kidbrooke in South East London, more as a result of its proximity to the heart of the City of London rather than as a specific target. It is clear that the RAF's supply chain was not subject to any concerted or sustained effort by the Luftwaffe to destroy or disrupt it, excluding, of course, the targeting of British industrial sites during the German night offensive from November 1940 through to May 1941.[41] The Luftwaffe, however, was well aware of the location of the RAF's key logistic sites through active intelligence gathering.[42] Given the significance of the depots in terms of their role in sustaining RAF air power, the question which arises is why they were not selected as specific targets for intensive or sustained attack. The answer lies not in the doctrine of German air intelligence, which clearly acknowledged the significance of logistical targets.[43] The most likely explanation is three-fold. Firstly, the Germans had been more interested in tactical military intelligence at this time, rather than the more strategic picture of the British war economy.[44] The second factor was poor intelligence practice. While the information gathered as part of the German planning for an invasion of Britain (Study Blue) and the subsequent accumulation of photographic reconnaissance data provided a relatively comprehensive assessment of target detail, this was not used effectively by the Luftwaffe's own intelligence department that, surprisingly, was headed only by a major.[45] Overall, there does not appear to have been recognition that there were links between aircraft manufacturing companies, the RAF depots and RAF flying units—a supply chain perspective.

It was not just complete aircraft that industry was manufacturing and supplying to the RAF, but a host of spare parts and materials, as well as tools, test equipment, and various ancillary items to enable activities such as battle damage repair and maintenance to be conducted. Enemy targeting of industrial plants was an understandable priority but, given that aircraft spares were being accumulated in great numbers at the UEDs and that these units were the main distributors to RAF flying units, serious targeting of these units at an early stage of the Battle of Britain would have had a significant impact on unit activity. The intelligence data gathered failed to recognise that large amounts of mission critical equipment and spares were effectively being funnelled in to just eight UEDs. The third issue, and perhaps the most influential, was the ultimate decision-making. In this respect, Herman Göring and his Chief of the Air Staff, Hans Jeschonnek, had much to answer for and contributed to a regime of unsystematic target selection.[46]

No. 40 Group's wartime achievement was impressive by any standards and, at its peak in 1944, the staggering total of 2,299,000 tons (dead weight, both receipts and issues) were been handled in that year alone. However, impressive as they might be, the figures alone tell little of the commitment and sheer hard work of the many thousands of people (service and civilian) who manned the Group's depots and associated units in the UK. On the cessation of hostilities in 1945, the number of 40 Group MUs and sub-units had risen from twelve on its formation to 159; they were operated by 72,400 officers, airmen, and WAAFs as well as 48,650 civilians, male and female. The commitment that was expected of these people was well summed up by the AOC of No. 40 Group in his foreword to a set of notes produced for his most junior Equipment assistants and storekeepers in March 1944:

> You belong to the organisation whose job it is to supply the Royal Air Force (and other authorised customers) all over the world with the equipment they need for their work. If your work is well and quickly done the RAF will have the equipment it needs to do its job, and we know how well it does it. We must: Keep them flying. This means: The right part, in the right place at the right time.
>
> Our aim must always be to supply the needs of the RAF without delay and to despatch the equipment so that it arrives promptly and in perfect condition. I hope these notes will help you in your part of this worthy task.[47]

Wartime POL Supply, 42 Group

During the pre-war period, much time and effort had been invested in fuel storage, tank design, and construction, which was to reap considerable benefit when it came to resisting damage from enemy action during the Second World War. A decision was taken as early as 1937 to form a special Technical Sub-Committee of the Oil Board to oversee all aspects of tank design. Headed by the Secretary of Mines, the Board consisted of representatives from the Oil Board, petroleum companies, service departments, and the Home Office. The Board had a fair amount of executive authority as no construction could proceed without their approval. In parallel with this, the Air Ministry Works Directorate was formulating design principles to afford the best possible protection from air attack as well as carrying out full scale trials on the effects of explosion and penetrations to tankage.

As far as tank design was concerned, four types were developed, three of which met the needs of the main reserve depots with the fourth providing the mainstay of the distribution depots. The three types of tank at the reserve depots took account of the geographical opportunities and limitations of the selected sites. The standard and most successful of these tanks was known as the C2. An above-ground tank, this was essentially a vertical steel cylinder with a 4,000 tons capacity. To provide protection it was surrounded by concrete with a flat roof and then covered with an earth mound, some two and a half feet in thickness with the sides forming a natural slope. To minimise the effect of fire or explosion from adjacent tanks, a separation distance of 100 feet between the walls of tanks was mandatory. This tank was so successful that out of the 1,444,200 tons of specially constructed main reserve storage, 983,000 tons were kept in C2 tankage. For areas where it was impracticable to construct these, such as where there was a high water table or where space was restricted, a reduced standard of protection was used in the form of two and a half feet concrete walls and a concrete roof covering, though the separation distance was still maintained at 100 feet.[48]

Similar to the siting of explosives storage, investigations were also carried out into the possibility of completely underground storage. The original work tended towards constructing horizontally driven tunnels with a steel lining or tanks inside. However, cost, safety, and constructional problems made this impractical and attention then turned to locating tankage at the bottom of a suitable cutting, open pit, or similar feature, building a concrete arch support over them and then back-filling with earth to provide the required overhead protection. The D2 tank was designed for this use. The first of these installations was built at Micheldever on the Southern Railway where there was a wide and deep railway cutting in chalk. Work commenced in early 1938, and it was ready for use by the outbreak of war the following year. The finished installation for aviation fuel consisted of twenty-eight cylindrical tanks that were one hundred feet long and twenty feet in diameter, with two similar tanks for holding lubricating oil. Following the success of this construction, similar facilities were built at Buxton and Much Wenlock in large, disused, open, stone quarries. The last of the storage tank designs was for the distribution depots, the majority of which were in the east coast areas. Given their location and greater vulnerability to enemy action, these tanks were afforded much greater protection. The D1 tank, as it became known, was an underground rectangular steel tank of 250 or 500 tons capacity, with a minimum of 10 feet of earth cover above. This tank was also highly successful and some twenty original distribution depots were equipped with this type of tankage.[49]

Apart from the bulk storage of fuel, arrangements were also made in 1937 for the manufacture and filling of suitable tin containers, known as 'packed stocks'. This requirement would prove to be an important tactical 'enabler' during many of the campaigns during the Second World War as it meant fuel could be maintained until bulk tank storage or pipeline supply could be introduced in theatre. A container, similar to the pre-war four-gallon tin used in the Middle East and India, was adopted as standard. Joint schemes were set up in conjunction with the Army, who also had a substantial need for packed fuel stocks for their mechanised forces; tin-making and filling factories were set up at Stanlow and Ardrossan, each adjacent to a ready supply of fuel from a Shell Refining and Marketing Co. Ltd refinery. In 1940, it was decided to create separate dumps of packed stocks in suitable locations as an emergency operational reserve. Overall, there were forty-six of these dumps, storing a total of 120,000 tons of fuel.[50]

Fuel by Pipeline

Of all the supplies required to meet the needs of air power, fuel was one of the most difficult in terms of movement from refineries to the point of use, largely due to weight and volume. The inter-war years, with the financial constraints on the growth of the RAF, offered little opportunity or pressing need for any change to the

The utility of the jerrycan, Normandy, 1944. (*Crown Copyright—Air Historical Branch MoD*)

largely road and rail based movement of fuel. On flying units, fuel was supplied to aircraft on the flight line by bowser or by fuel can. Evidence does exist, however, to show that the relatively small grass airfield at RAF Halton in Buckinghamshire was using one of the earliest fuel hydrant systems in the UK, which enabled fuel to be piped from the on-site bulk petrol storage tanks to a dispense point in the flight line area.[51] The UK's first oil pipeline was constructed in the Second World War, initially to address the problem of supplying the London region from the west coast. Constructed in 1941 by the Ministry of Fuel and Power, the pipeline was first laid between Avonmouth and Walton-on-Thames. A branch line from this route was added in June 1942, connecting Aldermaston with the oil ports each side of Southampton Water at Hamble and Fawley.

The growing demands for aviation fuel by the RAF and US Army Air Force (USAAF) bomber stations in the East Midlands and East Anglia soon placed enormous demands on the rail and road supply in these areas where most of the bases were served by road tanker from the various petroleum storage depots (PSD) throughout the country. The PSDs were resupplied from the petroleum company storage installations by canal barge, rail and sea. To ease this situation, an important and significant extension was made. By the end of May 1943, a pipeline circuit had been completed that linked the existing pipeline from Avonmouth, north to Stanlow (Ellesmere Port), then east to Misterton near Doncaster, then south via Sandy in Bedfordshire to join the original Avonmouth–Walton line at Aldermaston. With the Air Ministry's decision to hold some of its bulk stocks of aviation fuel at Thames

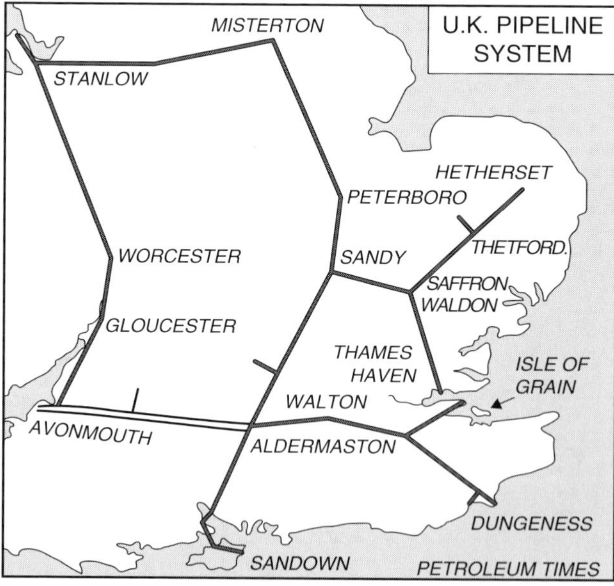

Above: Fuel being received from a tanker on an RAF unit, 1942. (*IWM*)

Left: Figure 3: The UK oil pipeline system, 1944.

Haven, a link was made from here to Hethersett near Norwich in East Anglia with a connection across to the main pipeline circuit at Sandy. With the requirements to link-in with the pipeline underwater transport of oil, or PLUTO as it became more commonly known, to the Continent for Operation Overlord, a south-east extension was developed that connected Dungeness and Thames Haven through to Walton-on-Thames. By 1944, the UK oil pipeline system connected five major estuaries, to forty of the PSDs, twenty-four RAF stations in East Anglia and to RAF Scampton in Lincolnshire (see Figure 2). In 1944 alone, some 4,400,000 tons of petroleum products were moved by the UK Pipeline System.[52]

Pipelines also played a key part in the logistics operation in North Africa and by 1943 these had linked the protected bulk fuel storage in the Suez Canal Zone to Ghamara in Cairo to a 6,000-ton storage facility from which two nearby airfields were supplied. Pipelines were also built in Iraq during the Second World War to connect the refineries at Abadan in Iran, to the RAF airfields at Shaiba and Habbaniya.[54] The RAF's use of the cross-Channel, underwater pipeline PLUTO during Operation Overlord is commented on later in this chapter.

Wartime Munitions Supply, 42 Group

As the war progressed, the need for munitions of all types grew rapidly and this led to a significant growth in the holdings of the No. 42 Group depots. With the introduction of the Lancaster in 1941, a typical munitions payload was some 14,000 pounds albeit by then comprising much heavier bombs ranging from 1,500 lb to 8,000 lb.[55] By the end of the war, the RAF's range of bombs was extensive with numerous types ranging from general purpose bombs to anti-submarine weapons, depth charges, and incendiaries. The size and shape of these weapons led to the need for new bomb trolleys that were used both at the explosives depots and at airfields for transporting bombs from storage sites to the aircraft; throughout the war, eleven types of trolley were introduced.[56] Prior to 1939, the RAF's inventory of ammunition was predominantly .303-inch with five types in service by the outbreak of war. Over the years of the war up until the end of 1945, a further thirty types of ammunition were introduced consisting of five more of .303-inch rounds, four of .5-inch rounds, twelve of 20 mm, and nine of 40 mm. In addition, there were also ten new types of American-designed ammunition introduced including .30-inch, .5-inch, and 20 mm. The advent of aircraft-launched rockets saw four types of cordite-powered rocket motors. Perhaps the greatest increase of types on the explosives inventory was pyrotechnics. Between the beginning of 1941 and the middle of 1945, seventy-six different varieties were introduced to service including (*inter alia*) fuses, rockets, cartridges, and flares.[57]

A substantial expansion in munitions holdings occurred as a result of the preparations for the invasion of NW Europe. In February 1943, for example, the total holdings of HE and incendiaries amounted to some 192,486 tons but, just one year later, this figure had grown to 275,000 tons. Even more dramatic, the turnover from the beginning of the war through to December 1940 was 350,000 tons but by 1943, this had tripled to 1,059,696 tons and, by 1944, had reached 3,068,127 tons—almost a ten-fold increase.[58] Accompanying this growth was a corresponding increase in the number of depots, although nowhere near as extensive and diverse as that seen in No. 40 Group.

At the start of the war, the main explosives storage facilities were the ADs; to the four that were in place in 1938–39, a fifth was added at Llanberis (No. 31 MU) in North Wales and was operational in May 1941. Forward of these were the AAPs that, as described in the Maintenance Command official history, were the 'retail shops' in the supply chain, constructed at carefully selected locations before the war within the geographical areas of the operational bomber stations. Despite its apparent simplicity, this supply chain up until 1941 had nine stages of handling within the Group. Given the projected significant increase in the requirement for bombs between 1943 and 1945, it became clear that a more flexible and rapid distribution system would be needed.

Consequently, what became known as the forward ammunition depot scheme was introduced in late 1941–early 1942, a concept which was similar to the 40 Group equipment park idea. All the existing AAPs became forward ammunition depots

Typical underground bomb storage at an RAF ammunition depot. (*Crown Copyright—Air Historical Branch MoD*)

(FAD), each with a storage capacity for 10,000 to 20,000 tons of HE and looking after fifteen to twenty-five heavy bomber squadrons, operating from ten to fifteen airfields situated within a radius of twenty-five miles of each FAD. The depots in the forward area were particularly important to the bomber stations as each unit's bomb storage area, on average, could hold only 200 tons. A number of the FADs had sub or 'satellite' sites (many of which had been constructed in early 1940). In the early years of the war, these acted as a form of reserve holding and held duplicate stocks to the parent unit; as the danger of enemy air attack lessened, these satellites were absorbed into the general storage plans of the parent unit and provided much-needed extra capacity as the bomber offensive commitments grew. Many utilised open storage on standings in woodlands and along the verges of minor roads (known as 'brigaded areas', which then had to be closed to the public) supervised by 'X'-qualified Equipment officers.

Interestingly, most of the satellites were built using the units' own labour. The AAP designation was retained; however, for a much smaller size of units that were situated in outlying areas looking after the comparatively smaller and infrequent needs of Fighter and Coastal Command stations. To cater for any potential breakdown in the forward supply programme, reserve ammunition depots (RAD) were also created, each with a capacity for 20,000 to 40,000 tons of HE. The revised scheme worked well although the numerous designations became somewhat confusing and before long the new RADs became ADs and the FADs and AAPs both became AAPs. Despite the name changes, the functions of the various units remained the same.

The development and growth of a typical AAP is well-illustrated by No. 100 MU, RAF South Witham. This unit was one of three AAPs in Lincolnshire that looked after the bomber stations in the county and was opened in March 1942. Its location, in keeping with its sister units, was carefully chosen. Some twelve miles south of Grantham and adjacent to the Great North Road (today's A1), the unit took its name from the nearby village of South Witham (just to the west of the road) with the unit itself growing up in and around the site of Morkery Wood (on the other side of the road). The wood, comprising some 550 acres, provided an ideal storage area for explosives with the dense foliage providing good natural camouflage and also a form of containment that could soak up the effects of blast and shrapnel in the event of accidents. The administrative and domestic needs of the MU were located in and around the nearby Stocken Hall, utilising as much existing infrastructure as possible; even the Hall's stables were put to use, providing a new home for the MU's workshops and armoury. The site was also very close to the railhead of South Witham on the London, Midland, and Scottish Railway so an additional siding was constructed on the north side of South Witham station to cope with the unit's additional traffic. By June 1943, this was fully operational with its own RAF transportation office. As the war progressed, the MU's storage facilities were expanded and nearby roads were pressed into service for the outside storage of both HE bombs and incendiaries in the vicinity of Stretton Road and Moor Lane; security picket posts were sited to control access. In Stretton Road, HE bombs were neatly stacked along the verge, at thirty-six feet intervals. The turnover of explosives for this one unit alone virtually doubled from 37,440 tons in 1942 to just over 70,000 by the end of 1944; the unit's personnel strength rising from just ninety-five in 1942 to a peak of 261 in March 1945.[59]

Major Incidents, 42 Group Depots

The location of explosives storage proved to be extremely effective in avoiding air attacks of which none were reported on any of the Group's storage depots in the official history of Maintenance Command. However, a very close call came in the early hours of 19 November 1942, not from the enemy, but from a severely flak-damaged Royal Canadian Air Force Halifax BII bomber aircraft of No. 158 Squadron based at RAF Rufforth, which crashed within the confines of No. 100 MU South Witham. The aircraft had been hit when homeward bound from Turin. The pilot managed to coax the aircraft back to the UK but he and his crew were forced to abandon the aircraft over what was believed to be open ground. The aircraft came down in Morkery Wood and hit the ground only thirty yards from a stack of HE bombs. Despite bursting into flames, the aircraft only damaged some trees and the fire was successfully extinguished by airmen who were on duty in the area.[60]

The Group experienced two other incidents, however, which were considerably more significant, but not as a result of enemy action. The first of these occurred on Sunday, 25 January 1942, at No. 31 MU Llanberis in North Wales. Formed in May 1941, the unit was an underground main reserve depot designed to hold 18,000 tons of HE bombs along with surface buildings to store tail units, fuses, and other ancillary items. Constructed in an old slate quarry, MU consisted of two-storey concrete storage galleries with a curved concrete roof. On top of this, some twenty-five feet of quarried slate waste was dumped to provide both protection and concealment. The weight of the top fill eventually proved to be too great and led to the collapse of the roof, blocking the main entrance as well as the railway siding. The fall buried or prevented access to some 14,277 tons of explosives, bombs, depth charges and TNT; this was a significant stock-holding at the time, representing almost 15 per cent of the total stocks of that range of explosives held at ADs in the UK at that time. Thankfully, there was no loss of life despite the fact that twenty-two airmen and one civilian were working in the tunnel at the time. The collapse led to an urgent enquiry, with resultant inspections of similar depots revealing that a number of cracks had started to develop in the tunnels at Harpur Hill. Remedial action was taken quickly by No. 42 Group and, by arranging for all overseas issues to be made from Harpur Hill, the galleries were quickly emptied and emergency repairs carried out.[61]

The most significant and disastrous incident took place at No. 21 MU Fauld in Staffordshire on 27 November 1944. The 450,000 square feet site at Fauld was located in a disused gypsum mine and had been purchased by the Air Ministry in 1937. Its proximity to a nearby farm, a plaster works and a still-working underground gypsum mine, was to have tragic consequences for many others, as well as for those of the MU. The mine itself, some ninety-feet underground, was an ideal location for an explosives store, and consisted of a whole series of underground caverns. Pillars of uncut stone supported the roof, to which had been added a reinforcement of 2.5 feet of concrete; from there to ground surface was the topsoil. The depot at Fauld was not just a storage facility; it also carried out the repair and refurbishment of bombs that had been jettisoned from aircraft in an emergency and which had been recovered for reuse. Of particular significance is that many of these still had had their detonators fitted, thereby making them all the more sensitive. This refurbishment work was carried out underground, alongside weapons in store awaiting issue.

There are a number of accounts of the explosion, but the evidence given at the subsequent enquiry by a survivor (an armourer who had just been leaving the caverns at the time) provides an indication of the most likely explanation. He recalled hearing a much smaller explosion just before the main one; he also remembered just having seen a colleague using a brass chisel to remove a broken detonator on one of the returned bombs. From this, it seems likely that the underground maintenance work on one of these recovered bombs led to an initial explosion, which, in turn, set off a 'chain' detonation of nearby stocks. The resulting blast at just after 11 a.m. that November morning was quite staggering and was the largest non-nuclear explosion of the entire war. It was estimated that between 3,500 and 4000 tons of bombs exploded, generating a mushroom cloud some fifty-yards wide. When the dust had settled, all that remained was a crater a quarter of a mile across and three hundred feet deep. Seventy people were killed, including twenty-six men in the underground caverns and five farm workers. The animals of Upper Castle Hayes Farm perished (as did the farm itself); five men in the adjacent working mine died of carbon monoxide poisoning. The blast also led to the breakage of the thirty-foot high wall of the six-million-gallon reservoir above the working mine, the resulting torrent of water and mud bursting on to the surface buildings killing another twenty-seven. Among the dead of the MU staff were six ex-POW Italians, by then known as 'co-operators' as Italy had been out of the war for six months. Eighteen bodies were never recovered. Not surprisingly, the rescue operation was extremely hazardous, a fact not helped by the water from the reservoir, underground pockets of gas, and an estimated 10,000 tons of rubble.[62]

The efforts of many rescue workers were heroic. The rescue and recovery operation took three months and led to twenty-four awards for bravery. Of these, eight went to members of No. 21 MU including three George Medals, one MBE (Military Division), two BEMs (Military Division), one BEM (Civil Division), and one Commendation for Brave Conduct.[63] Shortly after the disaster, a relief fund was

The crater left by the Fauld explosion in 1944. (*Author's collection*)

established and remained in operation until 1959. In addition, in 1990, a memorial was erected in nearby Hanbury Church, near the site of the explosion. Consisting of a stone of fine white granite, it lists the names of the seventy people who lost their lives; the crater remains the last resting place of those whose bodies were never found. Given that six Italians lost their lives, it was perhaps fitting that the memorial stone was provided as a gift organised by the Commandant of the Italian Air Force Supply Depot at Novara, a 'sister' depot of No. 16 MU RAF Stafford.

The Equipment Branch and Trade throughout the War

The number of RAF Equipment Branch officers rose markedly during the war years, mainly as a result of the increasing numbers of operational theatres and rose from approximately 1,430 in June 1940 to 4,733 in September 1945. While the requirement for Equipment officers was largely driven by achieving sufficient numbers, the position for airmen was more complex. At the start of the war, there was just the single airman trade of Equipment assistant and they were required in ever-increasing numbers. The physical way in which logistics operated, however, saw the need to increase the number and type of trades involved. The substantial increase in the volume of equipment flowing into the equipment depots as a result of the expansion programme was accompanied by a similar growth in the issues of equipment to RAF units, all of which brought with it a requirement to manually process large volumes of paperwork such as requisitions, invoices, and issue vouchers. This was largely a clerical task and the Air Ministry therefore decided to reintroduce the old pre-war trade of Clerk (Equipment Accounting) as part of Trade Group IV in September 1940. Numbers employed within this trade were never sizeable when compared to the eventual population of Equipment assistants and the approved establishment rose from just 2,202 in June 1941 to a wartime peak of 5,103 in October 1944.[64]

It was not just the increase in the volume of equipment being handled by the RAF's supply chain that led to an increased demand for personnel. The growth in the number of RAF units and formations was just as demanding. Most, if not all, flying stations had an Equipment Section on site, each of which was manned by about fifty personnel.[65] In the UK, there were only fifty-two airfields in 1934, but this had risen to eighty-nine by 1938, with a further 389 constructed between 1939 and 1945.[66] The number of units overseas also increased significantly as a result of the campaigns in North Africa, the Middle East, Italy, and North-West Europe, all of which saw substantial numbers of new squadrons, specialist units and operating bases established. Within No. 40 Group, where the greatest proportion of equipment personnel was concentrated, the number of units performing a logistics-related function rose from just ten in February 1939, to twenty-three in December 1940, then to a wartime peak of forty-two units in December 1944.[67] The proportion of other ranks employed at the 40 Group units rose to 18,696 by 31 December 1944, representing some 41 per cent of the work force.[68] This increase in the number of units led to the need for a sizeable population of Equipment assistants with the approved establishment figure (RAF and WAAF combined) rising from 13,011 in June 1941 to a peak of 31,068 in August 1945.[69]

While receiving and issuing equipment was a relatively straightforward operation (largely governed by standard processes), the means by which equipment was first acquired (the provisioning process) was less straightforward and required considerably more analysis of stock consumption and the forecasting of future requirements; this all needed dedicated manpower to meet the growing size of the task. The requirement to control large volumes of stock at multiple locations, which had led to the introduction of the master provisioning offices in late 1939, also generated a requirement for substantial numbers of clerks to carry out this manually-intensive work. This led to the formation of the trade of Clerk (Provisioning) within Trade Group IV in October 1942. The nature of their duties was limited to processing great volumes of paperwork, essential in order that equipment was re-ordered when required and brought to account when it was received. Initially, these clerks were employed at the MUs and RAF stations but, by December 1943, the Air Ministry decided that the provisioning clerks would only be employed at the MUs and that there was sufficient expertise on RAF stations for the lower-level part of the procurement operation to be performed by the local Clerks (Equipment Accounting).[70]

With the formation of the WAAF in June 1939, women began to join the ranks of the RAF's equipment organisation. The primary purpose of the WAAF was as a substitution, thereby freeing up men for front-line duty; the extent of this on units was limited to no more than 66.6 per cent. At the equipment depots, where there was a requirement to move a greater number of heavy items on a regular basis, the substitution level was drastically reduced to 20 per cent.[71] As the war progressed, opportunities for the employment of airwomen in RAF Logistics broadened beyond the Equipment assistant trade, which was the sole opportunity for women in this specialization at the outbreak of war, to include the trades of Clerk (Equipment Accounting) in September 1940 and Clerk (Provisioning) in October 1942.[72] The one area that made little use of airwomen though was the movements specialisation, largely due to the physical nature of the work involved. Although the trade of Clerk (GD) (Movements) Control had been introduced for men in 1942, it was not until nearly two years later in July 1944 that women began to be employed in this trade, and then only in relatively small numbers.[73] Airwomen were paid considerably less than their male counterparts, irrespective of whether they were carrying out identical duties, a practice which was in line with the government's pre-war policy of sex differentiation, where women who were public employees could not normally earn more than 80 per cent of a similarly qualified man doing the same job; this policy was applied to women in the armed forces, though women were only awarded two thirds of men's rate of pay.[74] Another differential between men and women at this time was liability for overseas service, with airwomen employed only in the UK until May 1944 when the first draft proceeded to the Mediterranean theatre, followed by subsequent drafts to the Far East in October 1944. Following the invasion of the Continent in 1944, growing numbers of Airwomen joined the Supreme HQ Allied Expeditionary Force and 2nd Tactical Air Force (2TAF) as part of those formations as they advanced through France, Belgium and into Germany. The WAAF Logistics trades formed part of these drafts but all were volunteers.[75]

There was no immediate opportunity for employment of females as Equipment officers on the formation of the WAAF and it was not until April 1941 that the employment of WAAF officers for equipment work was considered. The DDGE's view at the time was that only junior posts in certain commands were suitable but he was opposed to female Equipment officers being employed on operational stations as they would have to accompany squadrons if they were required to go overseas. The substitution rate for female officers was therefore capped at 50 per cent.[76] There was a limiting factor in this move in that, as these WAAF officers would be required to complete the explosives course, which included being taught about the effects of gas and chemical weapons, they would need to be volunteers.[77] In due course, the numbers grew and, by 1 July 1943, there were 280 WAAF Equipment officers serving; by October 1945, this figure had increased to 438.[78] Opportunities for WAAF Equipment officers to serve overseas arose slightly earlier than for Equipment assistants, with the first officer joining the RAF Delegation in Washington, USA probably in late 1943 or early 1944. Alongside Equipment assistants, female Equipment officers were also posted to the Far East from June

WAAF driver refuelling her vehicle. (*Crown Copyright—Air Historical Branch MoD*)

1944 onwards and also as part of Supreme HQ Allied Expeditionary Force and 2TAF as part of those formations as they advanced through France, Belgium, and into Germany.[79] The WAAF made a significant contribution to the RAF's logistic effort, let alone the service as a whole; their employment allowed the RAF to divert large numbers of men to other combatant duties, especially overseas.

Broadly speaking, while airwomen integrated well within a predominantly all-male environment, the perception regarding officers was quite different. It appears not to have been a question of ability but the acceptance by men of being placed under the direct authority of women. Commissioned rank, even at the most junior level, brought with it a command responsibility for those working under their charge. For men and especially civilians, the acceptance of a female superior proved to be difficult. It was an attitude that, despite the needs of unity in time of war, actually impeded the extent to which female Equipment officers were employed throughout the RAF's supply chain; this effectively reduced the numbers of male Equipment officers who could have been released for more urgent duties elsewhere. It was not just a conceptual difficulty as the visual presence of a female officer also appears to have had an impact. An anecdotal example of this is provided by the experience of Hilda Rothnie who joined the WAAF in November 1941 aged twenty-two, completing her basic training at RAF Bridgnorth and then Equipment Trade training at Bridlington. Following this, she was posted to No. 7 Air Gunners School at RAF Stormy Down, primarily working in the airframe storage section but also in the clothing and rations areas. After reaching the rank of corporal, she was selected for commissioning and attended the Officer Training Unit at Grange-Over-Sands in October 1942. Following Equipment officer training at Loughborough, she was commissioned as an acting section officer and posted to No. 14 Balloon Centre, then to No. 951 Balloon Squadron at RAF Barnwood as the first woman to be in charge of a Station Equipment Section. When touring her various outlying storage sites, it was not unknown for her to be greeted by 'Christ, it's a woman' when she appeared in battledress.[80]

RAF Logistics also utilised personnel from overseas within its equipment organisation and drew personnel from five of the dominions, twenty-five of the colonies, and from eight European allied nations (Norwegians and Yugoslavs also served with the RAF but as part of their own native air forces).[81] The numbers, however, were relatively small and it could be argued that the employment of personnel from the dominions and allied nations was perhaps more of a political gesture than any earnest contribution towards Equipment Branch and trade manning. Despite the small numbers, it was acknowledged by the Air Ministry that there were benefits such as high motivation and that those from the Air Forces of Allied nations were in many cases already trained and therefore familiar with service discipline. Personnel from Canada and Poland (both officers and airmen) made a very specific contribution in terms of expeditionary logistic capability as part of the ASPs. Two parks were formed, consisting entirely of Canadian and Polish personnel—No. 406 (Canadian) in July 1943 and No. 408 (Polish) in September 1943.

With such a broad range of trades and sources of people for logistics, training was crucial and an extensive training organisation was developed from what had been put in place in the 1930s. This is covered in more detail in Chapter Eleven.

Logistics and the Main Campaigns

The number of overseas campaigns, their duration, and their complexity during the Second World War makes this area a substantial narrative in its own right. It is not possible in a book such as this, which covers such a broad time span, to do this complete justice, but comment does need to be made on the logistical aspects of the main campaigns in which the RAF took part.

France and the Low Countries: September 1939–June 1940

Elements of the RAF deployed to France in support of the British Expeditionary Force in September 1939. As far as the RAF's contribution was concerned, two distinct formations were to be created, each with quite separate responsibilities. Firstly, the Advanced Air Striking Force (AASF) was intended to be a bomber force only, made up of squadrons from Bomber Command and based in France because of the comparatively short range of their aircraft. The second formation was known as the Air Component of the Field Force and was designed to be a completely integral part of the British Expeditionary Force (BEF) with the aim of providing air reconnaissance and protection for ground forces. Both formations were eventually to come under the control of British Air Forces in France (BAFF) at the end of December 1939 commanded by Air Marshal Sir Arthur Barratt. The period from October 1939 through to 9 May 1940 was relatively static. However, on 10 May 1940, the Germans began their offensive with a surprise invasion of Belgium and the Netherlands, both neutral countries. With the Netherlands surrendering five days later, the Allies moved their key forces into Belgium ready to meet the expected German advance.

The overall logistical support concept for the RAF squadrons that deployed to France was based on the maintenance concept in the RAF's 1928 *War Manual*. The use of ASPs was a key part of this, with three each allocated to the AASF and to the Air Component. [82] Additional units were also assigned for supply and transport, salvage and movements control. There was also much reliance on the Army, which, broadly speaking, was responsible for transporting its own and RAF supplies to sea ports and rail heads on the Continent, with the RAF then responsible for collection from these destinations. A base depot (No. 21 Aircraft Depot) was established at Nantes with its own port detachment to receive shipments of equipment from Britain; its location had been carefully selected as the location for the base area as the city was a major port situated on the River Loire, near the Bay of Biscay. In addition to a repair capability for tasks requiring up to 400 man-hours of work, the depot was responsible for the issue of repaired engines and airframes and holding equipment for the RAF in France. The depot's deployment to France and initial setting-up did not go smoothly, mainly due to shortages of equipment and personnel, and it took until the end of January 1940 to bring stock holdings up to the required levels.[83]

A number of the flying squadrons that deployed to France were allocated their own Equipment officer as part of their official war establishment. With No. 1 Squadron at Tangmere being assigned to the RAF component, its Equipment officer, Pilot Officer Donald Hills, found himself re-assigned to this squadron as its new Equipment officer just as the mobilisation commenced. In addition to the squadron adjutant (a pilot by training) and a doctor, the Equipment officer was the only other ground branch officer on the squadron at this time. With the orders to mobilize, much had to be done in very short order and, like the in-flow of equipment to Tangmere as a station, vast quantities began to flood in to No. 1 Squadron; the coordination of this was largely the responsibility of the squadron's Equipment officer. In addition to stores and supplies, large numbers of vehicles (in the region of sixty to seventy) began to arrive, ranging from mobile workshops and field kitchens to the squadron commander's staff car, communication and radio vehicles, and aircraft refuellers. There was also an extensive range of domestic type equipment including fold-flat tables, chairs, tentage, and paliasses; the latter were for sleeping on and were akin to a very rough form of mattress-case, but intended to be stuffed with straw or the like. There was then no such thing as a military issue sleeping bag, such as the one that later generations of servicemen were to be issued with. It is also worth noting that, of the new wartime establishment of the squadron (around four hundred people), approximately half had been recalled from the reserve.

Both the AASF and the RAF component deployed to France very quickly with the advance party of the AASF departing at dawn on 2 September, with much of its ground crew, equipment, and spares travelling by civil aircraft. The RAF component's departure occurred a few days later. The deployment of both did not go smoothly with numerous problems experienced ranging from a lack of suitable accommodation to a shortage of transport. The plans put in place before the war relied very much on the assistance of the French authorities; it transpired that they were largely unprepared for the arrival of so many personnel. All in all, it was not a satisfactory state of affairs, but much was learned that would be improved upon during later campaigns in the war. The saving grace for many of the squadrons was the resourcefulness of their Equipment officers and it was in this respect that Pilot Officer Hills made his mark with No. 1 Squadron (the first of the fighter squadrons to arrive in France) following the arrival of its advance party at Octeville (just north of Le Havre) on 5 September 1939, just two days after Britain's declaration of war on Germany. Donald Hills' reminiscences provide an insight into the many challenges that were faced. He takes up the story on Monday, 4 September 1939:

> The advance party consisted of a Flying Officer Palmer (a pilot), in fact I think he came from Detroit and myself, about forty or so men and some equipment, no vehicles strangely enough. Round about mid-day on 4 September a train pulled up on a railway line near RAF Tangmere, on the line not at a station. We went up to the train and clambered aboard and away we went to Southampton. We got on board a ferry which was in the process of being repainted white to grey and that night we sailed across to Le Havre. The next morning we disembarked and with some French vehicles which had been provided for us we were taken along the coast northwards to a brand new airfield which had just been constructed called Octeville.[84]

The airfield (now the site of Le Havre-Octeville Airport) consisted solely of a concrete runway that went right up to the edge of a sea-facing cliff. Apart from that, there was nothing else there at all. However, an adjacent small grass airfield, housing a private aero club with a small hangar for its fleet of four or five civilian-owned aircraft, provided some shelter; the advance party set up its camp in and around this area. One of the first problems that arose was that there was no drinkable water on either of the two airfields; this issue became one of Pilot Officer Hills' early priorities:

> I had to do something about this. I needed barrels and the only place I could think of to get these was at a brewery. So off I went to the brewery to buy a barrel. They

wouldn't sell me a barrel, except a barrel full of beer so I bought a barrel full of beer. It was the very first purchase I made and I took it back to the little airfield. We managed to get the beer out of the barrel and we thereafter had a container to go and get water in if we could persuade the French to let us have a vehicle.

Feeding arrangements were woefully inadequate, and it was fortunate that the advance party had brought with them forty-eight-hour rations from Tangmere. However, these were soon consumed and a new source of supply was urgently needed. The advance party heard that a British supply depot was being set up at Yvetot, some 15.5 miles inland from Le Havre. The ever-resourceful Equipment officer was soon on the case:

With help from the French, I got hold of a 1920s vintage lorry with solid tyres which did about 20 kph flat out! So I went off with one of the airmen to find Yvetot where we discovered the Royal Army Service Corps had set up a depot and we found some food. On the way back this lorry ran out of petrol and it took us about twelve hours to get back to Yvetot for some fuel and back again to Octeville—but at least we had some rations.

The deployment experiences of the squadrons varied, but the common denominator was the failure of the road convoys to arrive before the rail parties, despite the fact that most of these had been despatched five days beforehand; much of this had been caused by the not surprising congestion at the ports of Brest and Cherbourg. It was fortunate that the RAF's deployment to France was unopposed by the enemy and the shortcomings (albeit some of them highly uncomfortable for the personnel affected), were largely resolved with no more than a time penalty. Lessons would be learned and these would prove vital for later expeditionary operations, most of which would be under enemy fire.

The logistical requirement at this time was extensive and demanding, with support being required for a deployed force, with twelve squadrons operating from seven different airfields. The ASPs supporting these units operated on a geographical basis, looking after the squadrons within their respective areas, with distribution of stores and supplies carried out by Supply and Transport Sections, which were attached to each of the parks. As far as POL was concerned, the pre-war plans had intended that POL would be drawn directly by the squadrons from railheads. In practice, though, it was soon realised that to maintain continuity of supply and to guard against any breakdown in the supply chain, it was necessary to form reserve dumps; most of these were located forward of the railheads and in the rear of the airfields and were positioned next to the ASPs. This turned out to be a very heavy commitment on the Supply and Transport Sections that had not actually been established with the manpower and vehicles to meet the commitment. Additionally, forward air ammunition parks were formed; each of these held two weeks' supply of all explosives required by the units they served and delivered stock to the squadrons to replace what had been consumed.

Life for Equipment officers on the flying squadrons was often problematical and their duties included a diverse range of responsibilities. They were responsible for catering and, even during wartime, this involved arranging a whole host of contracts with local suppliers for the supply of fresh foods such as bread, vegetables and water. One of the more unusual but important local contracts placed by the squadron's Equipment officer while they were operating at Vassincourt (fifty miles east of Reims) included an arrangement with a local bath house at Bar-le-Duc to enable the airmen to take a weekly bath. If the officer's experience was one of variety, an airman's experience was even more so, as was experienced by ACH (GD) Robert Stamp who joined the BEF during late August–early September 1939. On arrival in France, Robert found himself working as part of a labour force on various supply and fuel dumps, digging trenches for the Army, guard duties at electricity sub-stations and with the Royal Army Ordnance Corps (RAOC) maintaining ammunition stocks. Towards the end of 1939, Robert was moved to 'A' Flight of No. 150 Squadron, then operating Fairey Battles as part of the AASF at Écury-sur-Coole near the River Marne, approximately ninety miles west of Paris. Although destined for ground defence duties manning one of the Lewis gun posts, Robert's pre-war civilian experience as the storekeeper for a builder's merchant was soon recognised and he found himself appointed as the 'A' Flight storekeeper. After acquainting himself with RAF storekeeping procedures through studying the flight's copy of the AP830 equipment regulations, he was re-mustered 'in the field' as an Equipment assistant. Even though his trade was now far more specific than that of an ACH GD, the demands of field service still necessitated turning his hand to whatever was required. Indeed, he found himself on the one hand, digging latrines, and on the other helping to start aircraft and 'bombing-up' the Fairey Battles with 250-lb bombs. Robert remained with the rear party of 'A' Flight, prior to being evacuated from Brest later in the campaign.

One notable issue with RAF Logistics, from the outset of the campaign through until the BEF's eventual withdrawal from France in May–June 1940, was the provision of adequate road transport. The establishment of MT for both the AASF and the Air Component was largely governed by the overall defensive concept of the campaign, which envisaged that a high level of mobility would not therefore be required. Some of the early basing decisions for the AASF soon caused problems when it was decided to locate only one squadron on each airfield. This led to significant overstretch, especially for domestic vehicles, as the distance between billets and airfields was often quite considerable. Attempts were made to alleviate this by locally purchasing a number of Renault vans and the import of some additional buses, but the difficulties persisted. The whole provision of adequate MT was reviewed in early 1940 by the Air Ministry. The transport problems took an inordinate amount of time to resolve and it was not until early April 1940 that a revised scheme was introduced, which introduced MT pools in the Air Component on a group, wing, and HQ basis.

Within the AASF, three MT pools were to be introduced for explosives, fuels, and general use under HQ AASF control to serve their bomber squadrons but with a completely self-contained mobility capability for No. 67 (Fighter) Wing. The requirement was one thing but the actual process of physically acquiring the vehicles and associated personnel turned out to be a painfully slow exercise. Even by the middle of April 1940, the RAF in France was some 1,000 vehicles short against the new establishment, much of which was due to contractors failing to deliver on time and a number of vehicles being redirected to other urgent requirements. Despite direct engagement by the AOC-in-C AASF with the Air Ministry, the final agreed MT establishment for BAFF actually rendered it only semi- rather than fully-mobile. When the German offensive opened, BAFF was still some 600 vehicles short against even the semi-mobile establishment. To have embarked on such a major change (certainly to one based on the pooling of vehicles) to a critical component of force mobility was a risky, if not highly questionable, policy. In the final reckoning, the impact on operational capability was significant. Perhaps the most telling impact of the whole saga was that, in self-preservation, the AASF was forced to borrow transport from the French and to reduce the number of its operational bomber squadrons from ten to six. In the forthcoming weeks, both the AASF and the Air Component needed every vehicle they could lay their hands on.

The actual attack came much further south through the Ardennes, an area considered to be almost impassable and therefore with relatively weak defences. The rapid advance of the German ground forces very quickly threatened BAFF and plans were formulated as early as 13 May for a complete withdrawal; within a matter of days, the HQs and units of both the AASF and the Air Component were on the move to the South and West as the enemy advanced. As the withdrawal progressed, the ASPs were in an almost constant state of turmoil as they endeavoured to keep the supply chain intact between the base area and the squadrons. By this stage of the campaign, No. 1 Squadron had experienced a series of moves and, on the opening of the offensive, had just relocated to Berry-au-Bac, just south of Reims to provide close cover for the Fairey Battle squadrons based in this area. From here, the squadron started their withdrawal eastwards on 16 May, relocating to a further five airfields before eventually reaching Nantes on 14 June. Although this was a chaotic period for the squadrons, the supply organisation worked hard to ensure that their needs were met as Donald Hills later recalled:

> I suppose someone from the supply point of view at the headquarters' staff must have done a jolly good job because every time we got to a new field there was always fuel, always fuel. Food and oxygen and things like this I used to have to scavenge for a bit. But fuel just came and .303 ammunition which was all we wanted; that just appeared as magic so the staff must have done their job extremely

> well. We were always short of transport. We moved at night and we got mixed up with refugees, and horse-drawn artillery and everything you could think of.

Having reached Nantes, the majority of No. 1 Squadron's ground crew moved south to La Rochelle; at midnight on 17 June 1940, two officers (one of these being Pilot Officer Hills) and forty-two men departed France on board two coal boats. The journey on these boats was far from comfortable as Donald Hills described:

> They had come from Newport in Monmouthshire. The coal hadn't been unloaded and I think there were about 3,000 people on each of these boats which normally had a crew of about ten so the facilities on board were pretty basic. I got a bunk somewhere in a pretty scruffy little cabin It took us three days to get to Newport.[85]

The changing tactical situation, which saw British forces withdraw and eventually evacuated from the Continent, placed No. 21 Aircraft Depot at significant risk and some 800 tons of its equipment were evacuated to the UK as a result of the pace of the German offensive. Despite the considerable efforts to evacuate equipment, a great deal was still lost during the withdrawal. Much of the Air Component's equipment was lost by enemy interception and there was no time or capacity to ship much of the AASF's equipment that reached the western ports at the end of the campaign. The loss of aircraft (from all causes) was also high and amounted to nearly one thousand between 10 May and 20 June 1940. At the end of the campaign and following the evacuation to the UK, the AOC Maintenance Command estimated that the RAF had lost in France (excluding aircraft and equipment in squadrons and smaller units in the forward area) the equivalent of four complete ASPs, or stock to the value of about £1 million.[86] For his work as No. 1 Squadron's Equipment officer during the campaign in France, Donald Hills was awarded the MBE in the 1941 New Year's Honours List.

North Africa: 1940–1943

The threat to British forces in North Africa emerged in June 1940 when Italian forces in Libya crossed into Egypt and occupied Sidi Barrani. From then on, the ebb and flow of the campaign in North Africa developed in what can be considered as four distinct phases: the initial incursion into Egypt by the Italians and their subsequent pursuit back into Libya by Allied forces between September to 1940 abd early February 1941; the arrival of German forces under the command of Rommel and their advance well into Egypt from the middle of February 1941 to the Battle of El Alamein in late October 1941; the counteroffensive by the British from early November 1942 that saw Rommel's forces pushed-back into Tunisia; and finally, the Allied invasion of North Africa in November 1942 that enabled the Allies to attack the remaining German and Italian forces in North Africa from the east and west and their eventual defeat by May 1943.[87]

The RAF's logistical footprint in Egypt on the outbreak of war was relatively small, consisting of No. 101 MU at Aboukir (north east of Alexandria) and No. 102 MU at Abu Sueir (further east towards the Suez Canal area). An additional equipment depot was also formed at Kasfareet (relatively close to Abu Sueir) and commenced operating as No. 107 MU in December 1940. Concern soon began to grow regarding the vulnerability of the depot at Aboukir to air attack and sabotage. This led to a move of them to the Canal area and the spares holdings and equipment personnel were moved back to Abu Sueir. By November 1941, there were at least twelve MUs and miscellaneous units operating in the Nile Delta area providing engineering and logistic services.[88] The supply chain for the RAF in North Africa was challenging to say the least. Its manufacturing and supply base was some 2,000 miles away and even further for stores, supplies and aircraft originating from the USA. At the start of the war and up to early 1940, resupply was largely by sea and dependent upon shipping through the Mediterranean to Alexandria or Suez. With Italy entering the war in June 1940 and the growing U-boat menace, the situation changed dramatically with the Mediterranean route becoming considerably more hazardous. Of the various options considered, the best trade-off in terms of safety and utilisation of shipping space was what became known as the West African Reinforcement Route, via Takoradi on the then Gold Coast of Africa (now Sekondi-Takoradi in Ghana). Takoradi was barely halfway to the RAF in Egypt and a further journey of over 2,000 miles covering vast expanses of uninhabited jungle, and wilderness with unpredictable weather further complicated the picture. Essentially, crated aircraft were landed by sea at Takoradi where they were then assembled and flown by ferry crews right across the breadth of Africa to Egypt.

The ASPs quickly proved their worth during the first phase of the North African campaign, supporting RAF flying squadrons that participated in General Wavell's opening offensive against the Italians who, in September 1940, had advanced some sixty miles from Cyrenaica into Egypt.[89] To reinforce the RAF already in the Western Desert, a number of squadrons and flights were relocated from Aden, Sudan, Alexandria, and the Canal area, thus enabling the RAF to muster what amounted to the equivalent of ten squadrons to support the British Army in their offensive against the Italians, which commenced on 9 December 1940.[90] Although this number of squadrons should have been supported by at least three ASPs, there was only one ASP in North Africa at the time (No. 31 ASP, which had been formed in November 1939) and this, along with repair and salvage units and a supply and transport column (S&TC), provided the support throughout the offensive. These columns provided a centralised pool of load-carrying vehicles for the movement of POL, small arms ammunition and bombs from air ammunition parks and to assist in the moves of transportable units. It was a difficult period for the ASP as they had very little transport, a resource which was essential for their intended purpose. This became so acute that the heavy vehicles required for moving fuel and explosives often had to be augmented by resources from the supporting S&TC and, in some cases, even by squadron MT. At one stage, No. 31 ASP became non-mobile at El Adem due to vehicles being purloined for other purposes so it was fortunate that the British advance was relatively swift, reaching El Agheila in Libya by 9 February 1941, covering a distance just short of 700 miles.[91]

Despite the initial British success, their fortunes in North Africa changed for the worse on 14 February 1941 with the arrival of *Generalleutnant* Rommel in Cyrenaica; German land and air forces arrived in Tripoli two days later. With the exception of the Operation Crusader battles in early January 1942, during which the British managed to push the Germans back westwards to El Aghelia in Libya, Rommel turned this around and progressively drove the British eastwards to El Alamein in Egypt by the end of June 1942; unchecked, this situation would have allowed the Germans eventually to reach the heart of the British command and control network, along with its logistics and maintenance activity in the Nile Delta area.[92] The arrival of Rommel and his Africa Corps in North Africa in February 1941 signalled a marked change in the way the war was progressing in North Africa. By the middle of the year, Axis forces had intensified their attacks on Allied bases. During July and the early part of August 1941, No. 102 MU at Abu Sueir was attacked systematically. The loss of spares was not as great as it might have been and after the first 'serious' air raid, the depot managed to evacuate most of its valuable plant and stocks—a feat accomplished within the remarkable timescale of just three days. The attack on Abu Sueir was a timely reminder to the logistics organisation that the pre-war layout of a conventional depot consisting of tightly packed buildings, usually in an isolated position out in the desert, was highly vulnerable and too inflexible to meet the needs of a war whose boundaries were constantly moving.

The loss of Abu Sueir prompted urgent action to find an alternative location and one was found south of Cairo at the Tura caves in the Mokhattam Hills. This site was one of the more intriguing and its development tells us much of the ingenuity and sheer effort that went into their operation. The RAF had established an ammunition and petrol depot at El Ma`sara el-Mahatta with a sub-site at the Tura caves (approximately ten miles south of Cairo) as early as October 1938. By the outbreak of war, the unit was operating as No. 101 MU. The Tura caves area had an interesting past and had been created by the ancient Egyptians when quarrying stone to build the pyramids. It was therefore a site of historical interest and the RAF had to seek permission from the Egyptian Department of Antiquities to take over the caves for their use. The Tura caves complex offered an ideal and secure site and its suitability was considered as part of a visit by a number of officers from HQ Middle East in August 1941. There was little doubt regarding its suitability and within a matter of days an Equipment officer (Squadron Leader Boston), two junior officers, and nine other ranks arrived on detachment to No. 101 MU, charged with forming what was to become No. 111 MU, known to many who served there as 'treble one'.

History often repeats itself and some 2,000 locals, with numerous donkeys and camels, were employed on clearing the caves—a scene that would not have been too dissimilar from the quarrying, which took place there during the time of the pharaohs. In time, the floors were concreted, the walls whitewashed, power and running water installed, and a comprehensive aircraft depot (predominantly for engine repair and overhaul) was constructed, along with what would become a sizeable universal equipment holding unit (EHU). A number of the caves at Tura were extensive. Indeed, one of the largest, which was used for propeller storage, soon earned the not unsurprising name of the 'cathedral'. A fair amount of the equipment salvaged from the bombed-out No. 102 MU, much of it having been literally been picked out of the debris, was soon relocated to the new MU; this transfer became a sizeable task in its own right. At about the same time as Squadron Leader Boston's party arrived, so too did some thirty-five rail truck loads (the first batch of many to come) of this salvaged equipment into the Cement Company's sidings at Tura el-Asmant railway station. With five lorries borrowed from Helwan, an ongoing transfer operation began between the station and the caves. The unit grew steadily in uniformed strength from fifty in November 1941 to a peak of 1,355 in February 1943. Locally engaged civilian personnel were a sizeable component of the workforce and reached 2,000 in 1944. The logistic operation was a major part of the real estate with the EHU occupying approximately 75 per cent of the cave complex. Despite greatly improved security, storage conditions were less than ideal. Climatic conditions caused serious damage in March 1943 when a violent rainstorm inundated the valley, totally ruining stores and supplies stored in the open valley bed.

Times of hardship often bring out the best in people and the duration of the RAF's occupation of the Tura caves was no exception. By the end of the war, and despite the long hours and difficult working conditions, the MU was running an extensive range of social and sporting activities for what little spare time its people must have had. Its Autumn Annual published in 1945 described an impressive range of activities from dancing classes to arts and crafts and from motor cycling to water polo. The unit was also famed for a male voice choir that, by the end of the war, had given over a hundred concerts all over the local area. Many of those working at Tura were also particularly resourceful individuals in a professional sense, one of these being Norman Henry. Norman was a corporal Equipment assistant who worked at the MU from 1941 to 1942, having joined up and completed his training at RAF Cranwell in late 1939. A good friend of his was a fitter in the engine repair shop, which was one of a number of engineering sections at Tura.

Norman recalled how his friend used to complain that work was often held up for lack of spares. During their many conversations on this topic, they soon realised that, incredibly, the stores section next door did not actually do anything about this and merely supplied what they could from stock, and there matters rested. Before the war, Norman had done some buying and materials-chasing in a light engineering works and so took it on himself to write to the CO, describing the situation as he saw it and saying that a business with a repair shop as large as No. 3 ERS would support it with a section devoted to acquiring its stores and supplies.

A week or two passed, apparently with his Equipment assistant colleagues chiding him with comments such as 'corporals will be telling generals how to win the war next!'. He was eventually sent for by the CO who informed him that a Technical Requirements Estimating Section (TRES) was to be formed consisting of Norman as the corporal in charge and two leading aircraftmen. Eventually, the TRES was allocated its own cave and, in Norman's own words, 'acquired a useful assortment of spares, including some carburettor float needles so rare that we actually supplied Imperial Airways with a few'. Norman's resourcefulness also led to the TRES being granted its own priority identifier for spares demand signals. After a prolonged spell of supply difficulties, he arranged for a batch of signals to be sent out prefixed 'aircraft on ground'. Apparently, they got away with this for a short while until someone (presumably at the Cairo MPO) challenged them, pointing out that, as No. 111 MU did not have a landing ground, they could not possibly have any aircraft to be grounded. They might have been rumbled, but as a concession, they were granted a special signals prefix of their own: PHU (production held up). His commitment and resourcefulness say much for the calibre of many of the people working at such units during the war years.[93]

The risk of enemy action resurfaced in June 1942, with the Allied withdrawal to El Alamein following the fall of Tobruk. The proximity of the MUs to the rapidly advancing Axis forces became a growing concern, a position that RAF Logistics had also experienced in France during 1940. Consequently, it was necessary to disperse No. 111 MU's equipment further afield and 50 per cent of the stock holdings were transferred to Ramleh and Khartoum. The dispersal of stock from Tura was but one part of a much bigger exercise to evacuate equipment from the threat of the Axis advance, much of it being sent to Khartoum in the Sudan. This was a substantial task and took some three weeks, with personnel averaging between an eighteen and twenty-hour working day.

At Khartoum, the wagons were unloaded, the equipment was repacked into boxes, then dispersed in nearby cotton fields.[94] Robert Stamp, then an RAFVR corporal Equipment assistant, was posted to No. 104 MU at Khartoum at the time and was heavily involved in this evacuation. Robert recalls how the operation was carried out in 'much haste and confusion' with much of the equipment being 'thrown into railway wagons in the Suez area then transhipped down the Nile and put back on to railway wagons to Khartoum'. At Khartoum, the wagons were unloaded and the equipment was re-packed into boxes and crates but with a contents list affixed to each box to facilitate easy identification. In many cases, certain ranges of equipment were grouped in special pack-ups with a specific codename, the two main ones being codenamed 'Cooler' and 'Koko'. When an item was called for, the box had to be recalled and the item extracted. Following Montgomery's decisive victory at the Second Battle of El Alamein in October–November 1942 and the resultant retreat of the Axis forces, the crisis subsided. Gradually, many of the units and equipment holdings in the Sudan retraced their steps north to Egypt and Palestine.

Throughout this period, aircraft of the Desert Air Force operated from a large number of temporary air strips, many of which were known simply as landing grounds (LG), a significant number of which were identified by a number, rather than a name. In the Western Desert area alone, there were some seventy of these air strips.[95] As the number of squadrons in the Desert Air Force increased, more ASPs were required and between May 1941 and July 1942, a further six parks were formed.[96] Of these, the experience of No. 40 ASP provides one of the clearest and most detailed pictures of the challenges that these units faced and their critical significance to deployed air power.

Formed at Padgate, Cheshire in the UK during November 1941, the park embarked for Egypt on 10 November 1941, eventually disembarking at Port Tewfik on 9 January 1942. Initially operating from Burj Al Arab in the coastal area south west of Alexandria, the park was given responsibility for the supply of equipment for all fighter aircraft types that were operating from temporary LGs in the forward area of the Western Desert.[97] The arrival of No. 40 ASP coincided with the German advance to El Alamein, a position that the British Eighth Army found itself desperately trying to hold at the end of June 1942. In early June, the forward section of the park was still operating west of El Alamein at Gambut, some forty miles to the east of Tobruk. Although not in direct contact with the enemy, the park's operational area still placed it at high risk of attack from the Luftwaffe supporting the advancing German Africa Corps. From as early as 21 March 1942, the park had been at a state of high readiness with a general warning from RAF Middle East Command that

'Cooler' and 'Koko' equipment packs being unloaded in Sudan, 1942. (*R. A. Stamp*)

a German paratrooper attack was likely. While that threat did not materialise, the advance section of the park was subjected to strafing by Messerschmitt Bf 109 fighters and bombing between 5 and 10 June 1942, although with no casualties and little damage to the park's equipment. The rate of enemy advance led to the park being progressively withdrawn to the east from the middle of June 1942; through at least five short notice moves, No. 40 ASP was relocated to LG 100 at Wadi Natrun on 24 July 1942, some 70 miles south west of Alexandria.[98]

There are three points of particular note regarding the capability of No. 40 ASP at this time. First, all of its personnel were subject to continual training by their officers and NCOs in the use of weaponry such as the Lee Enfield rifle, Lewis machine gun, Thompson sub-machine gun, and hand grenades; the use of these arms was part of ground defence skills that were more common to the Army's infantry than RAF airmen. Apart from this, these tradesmen received no other battlefield training. In the open desert and operating far from well-defended positions, such ground units had to be self-supporting and able to defend themselves in the not unlikely event that their positions might be over-run by the advancing enemy. The second, and particularly significant point, is that the park had quickly improved its mobility. In its early days, the ASP's vehicles were primarily load-carrying in nature with equipment just loaded onto the floors of their trucks and trailers; this was invariably unloaded into tented storage when they arrived at new locations. This proved to be time-consuming when it came to moving site and throughout July and August 1942, the park's carpenters (wisely included as part of its personnel establishment) fitted many of the vehicles with wooden storage racks and bins, thus enabling the vehicles to remain loaded at all times, greatly reducing the time taken to strike camp. A particular success story for the carpenters was the difference they made to the number of complete aircraft propellers that the park could carry on its vehicles. Prior to this, only three could be carried on a three-ton truck and due to their size and shape, proved to be an extremely awkward load. The carpenters' design and construction of a special storage stand tripled the number of propellers that could be carried. They also modified the unit's low-loader articulated trailers to enable the park to carry up to eight fighter aircraft wings. The third point of note concerns camouflage. Throughout July, work was carried out constantly to improve the concealment of vehicles, trailers, and tentage by the acquisition of additional camouflage netting and the application of sand-coloured paint that went some way towards reducing the conspicuousness of the park when it was camped in open desert conditions. Such was the difference this work and operating experience made that the park was able to record in its operational record book 'practice in moving has greatly improved unit's mobility. Unit may now be said to be truly 100 per cent mobile'. By the end of August 1942, No. 40 ASP was supporting seventeen fighter squadrons and twelve ancillary units operating in the Western Desert. It was estimated (and later proved to be accurate) that the park could move at two hours' notice without any disruption to the service it provided, either before moving or on arrival at a new location.[99]

The critical role that the ASP played in the support of deployed air power is particularly well-illustrated by its contribution to the advance of the Eighth Army westwards after the Battle of El Alamein, which saw Montgomery's pursuit of the retreating German Africa Corps from El Alamein at the beginning of November 1942, through Libya and back into Tunisia by mid-February 1943.[100] The planning for the ASP's role in this phase of the campaign (Operation Buster) began on 5 October 1942 with the park's CO attending a conference during which it was confirmed that his unit was to support what would be known as 'A' Force, comprising No. 211 Group and its offensive fighter wings, No. 239 Wing, No. 244 Wing, No. 285 Wing, and a number of ancillary units; the park's role was to move with these units in the advance and supply them *en route*. A new section was also formed within the ASP to supply American fighter types in No. 239 Wing and also to carry photographic equipment for the aircraft of No. 285 Wing. A liaison officer from the USAAF was attached to the park to assist with the American spares commitment. From this point on, No. 40 ASP was placed on one hour's notice to move. Just a day later the Park relocated to LG 92 near Amriya on the outskirts of Alexandria and began preparing for the forthcoming offensive, which would begin with the Battle of El Alamein; in the period up to the beginning of the battle on 24 October 1942, 40 ASP made in excess of 3,000 issues of equipment and received some 120 tons of equipment from the storage MUs in the Nile Delta area. By 20 October 1942, the Park was fully prepared to support 'A' Force for the start of the RAF offensive in Operation Buster.[101]

The Battle of El Alamein began at 9.30 p.m. on 24 October 1942 and the period up until 4 November 1942, just after the point at which the Eighth Army managed to break out from El Alamein, provides a clear example of just how critical the role of the park was in supporting the participating RAF aircraft. Among the demands that No. 40 ASP received in this period, 147 were for AOG spares, each of which was causing an aircraft to be grounded and unable to operate in the battle.[102] Of these, the park was able to satisfy 132 (90 per cent) of the AOG demands directly from the stock it was carrying, with the remainder shortly thereafter. After the Eighth Army had broken out from El Alamein in early November 1942, the advance proceeded apace through Libya, eventually driving Rommel's Africa Corps back to the Mareth line in Tunisia on 24 February 1943, having taken Tripoli on 23 January.[103] During this advance, the park moved progressively westwards, supporting its nominated squadrons and units, relocating to new sites on at least fifteen occasions.[104] As the line of communication from the supporting MUs in the Nile Delta area to the east began to lengthen, resupply to the continually advancing ASPs moving to the west became a growing problem and was largely reliant on air transport provided by No. 216 (Transport) Squadron; by early January 1943, No. 40 ASP was located at Nofaliya in Libya, some 650 miles west of El Alamein.[105] Air resupply was a difficult task as, to make the best possible use of aircraft carrying space, consignments for No. 40 ASP often had to be collected from nearby landing grounds because their freight had been aggregated with another unit's consignment. The reliance on air transport and the growing problems associated with freight space prioritisation came to a head at the end of December 1942 when the CO of No. 40 ASP had to engage with Air Officer Administration (AOA), Air HQ Western Desert, due to his quota of entitlement to air freight being reduced to just AOG spares. The remainder was being transported by road but that was taking fourteen days; by the time these reached the ASP, many more of the spares demands had become AOG requirements. The AOA was fully sympathetic to the plight of the ASP and agreed for a liaison officer to be appointed; they then worked directly with the MU and air movement staff to achieve an increased movement of spares by air beyond just the AOG requirements.[106] This liaison role was not an easy one and relied on needs being judged by operational experience.

By 8 January 1943, with the lines of communication increasing even further, the difficulties of air supply re-surfaced and led to an agreement with Air HQ Western Desert and No. 216 Squadron that one aircraft per day would be dedicated to No. 40 ASP freight. The reliance on air transport had become more pronounced due to the fact that the army would not allocate freight space on the railways for RAF equipment except POL, ammunition, explosives, and bombs.[107] Resupply for the RAF eased considerably on 17 April when the park started to receive consignments by sea through the port at Tripoli. With the fall of Tunis on 7 May, the campaign in North Africa approached its end with the surrender of the Germans and Italians by 12 May. The ASPs played a key part in enabling the fighter and fighter-bomber squadrons to keep pace with the advance of ground forces throughout this time. It was, however, more difficult for the bomber squadrons that were more dependent on elements of the Army's supply system to move their greater munitions and fuel requirements; this, according to the official history saw the Army 'stretched to its utmost limits' and 'came along more slowly'.[108] The ability to support expeditionary operations centred, as originally planned, on mobility, a point alluded to by the wartime author Philip Guedalla who observed that 'Desert life, it seemed, had taught the RAF to be nomadic'.[109]

The Invasion of North Africa: Operation Torch

The advance from the east was complemented by the Anglo-American landings to the west in French North Africa (Morocco and Algeria) took place in November 1942, codenamed Operation Torch. Under the direction of General Eisenhower, the Torch planners set up what was known as HQ 333 in Norfolk House, St James' Square in London. Despite its basing in the UK, the organisation and methods employed by the HQ were those of the US Army, albeit the staff consisted of both British and American officers. One of the RAF Equipment Branch officers on the planning team at Norfolk House was a recently promoted Wing Commander, Jack Maggs. An Oxford history graduate, Jack Maggs was commissioned into the Branch on 2 January 1939. Not only did he have a notable war record but he went on to give distinguished service in the post-war RAF, retiring in 1969 as an air vice-marshal. Throughout his time in uniform, he was affectionately known as 'Bishop', a nickname earned during his Equipment officer's course at RAF Halton in early 1939. At his course's first formal dinner night, and in the absence of a *padre*, Jack Maggs was called upon to say Grace. Not aware that he was literally just required to say 'Thank God' and sit down, he intoned the whole of the St John's College Grace in Latin, much to the astonishment of the assembled diners. In contrast to peacetime expectations, many officers reached senior rank very quickly. Jack Maggs was no exception, achieving the rank of acting wing commander in just over two years from joining the service. By April 1942, he was in London on the staff of the Assistant Chief of the Air Staff. After working on a number of top secret planning tasks, he was moved to the Operation Torch team when it was set up in the summer of that year. Wing Commander Maggs went on to participate in the operation itself, landing in North Africa on D+2 and then went on to form part of the Eastern Air HQ when it was established in Algiers.

The Torch landings were a significant change for the RAF in that their ground personnel, which were required to support aircraft operating from captured airfields and temporary airstrips after the landings, had to go ashore as part of the amphibious operation. This was quite different from France in 1939 where the RAF was able to disembark through ports and without enemy opposition. Given that the operation was the first large-scale amphibious operation to be mounted by Anglo-American forces, it is not surprising that its planning was not just a technical challenge but one of complex coordination between the British Army and the Royal Navy, the United States Army and Navy, and an air element drawn from the RAF, the Fleet Air Arm, the United States Naval Air Force, and the USAAF. From the British perspective, little had been done in the inter-war period to develop inter-service working, although an Inter-Services Training and Development Centre was established at Fort Cumberland near Portsmouth in 1938, followed by the formation of a Directorate of Combined Operations in mid-1940.[110]

In the early days of planning, the majority of amphibious assaults were intended to be of a 'hit and run' nature, rather than substantial and sustained amphibious invasions requiring the establishment and build-up of a bridgehead. As such, there had been little if any need for involvement of RAF's logistics. As combined operations planning began to develop in the late summer of 1940, attention began to be focused on developing a more detailed approach to beach maintenance, the term that was by then being used for controlling disembarkation and support activities on open beaches. This whole concept was seen as an interim measure only, as it was assumed that any sustained logistical activity would be provided through the early capture of a port. A key planning assumption that emerged from this work, was that any new beach maintenance organisation would need to be able to support a much larger force for a considerable period of time.[111] It was not, however, until early 1942 that this early work began to take shape with the Army Council's announcement that it would form a permanent organisation to undertake overseas operations, to be known as the Expeditionary Force.[112]

In February 1942, it was agreed that all formal beach training would be carried out at the Combined Training Centre at Dundonald in Scotland where personnel of all three services would be required to live together so as to foster the team spirit that was so critical to a beach organisation. Notwithstanding these developments, the RAF had a limited role in the concept of beach maintenance, with a beach party consisting of just one beach liaison officer and three airmen included in the overall Beach Group organisation, to supervise the disembarkation of RAF personnel and the unloading of RAF stores.[113] The growing urgency to develop an improved and formalised beach maintenance organisation was brought sharply into focus in August 1942 with the disastrous Dieppe landings where, among the many lessons learned, a requirement for well-trained and efficient beach parties was clearly identified.[114]

By September 1942, development work was mature enough for HQ Combined Operations to make a more clearly defined reference in their doctrine, stating that 'the units normally working in the Beach Maintenance Area are referred to as the Beach Brick'.[115] Essentially, a 'Beach Brick' consisted of a number of 'Beach Groups' (numbered consecutively), each of which was designed to support the landing of a battalion group. When required, an RAF beach party would be included, although the main disembarkation of RAF personnel and their equipment would be carried out by the Army. Given this limited involvement at this stage of the war, the RAF intended to man its beach party commitment from its existing embarkation units (EU) (see Chapter Eight). These units, however, had originally been intended only to look after the movement of personnel and stores through ports, and on railways and roads; they were not trained to be used in a front-line capacity and had not undergone wider training to enable them to survive and operate under combat conditions.[116] It was thus that for Operation Torch, the RAF used three of its EUs (Nos 59–61), each of which was around thirty personnel in size.

The RAF's concept of operations for logistics during the landings there and after was almost identical to that used in France during early 1940 and not dissimilar from that in the Western Desert. Flying squadrons were allocated to one of six wings and were required to be as self-contained as possible, deploying with their stock of war equipment and a maintenance reserve of seven days' stock. Each of the wings was supported by an ASP, six of which (Nos 131–136) were formed for the operation. The parks held thirty days' stock with a further thirty days' worth of equipment being delivered to each ASP fourteen days after landing. For the longer term, a RAF base maintenance unit (No. 351 MU), holding ninety days' worth of equipment for all RAF units, would deploy at a later date. In common with other operations, the Army was responsible for landing, holding. and distributing all POL and munitions. The ASPs supported RAF aircraft, which began to operate from captured enemy airfields during the advance towards Tunisia from the west after the landings.[117] As these airfields would need to be put to operational use as quickly as possible following their capture, any RAF formation moving in would need to be self-sufficient and capable of defending the airfield without reliance on the Army, whose priority would be to continue the advance. The problem was all the more complex, given the range of tradesmen, equipment, and supplies required to support modern aircraft. Until the end of 1941, the RAF did not have such a deployable maintenance organisation within its logistic ORBAT.

Due to some far-sighted planning, the answer came at the end of January 1942, when the Director of Organisation at the Air Ministry approved the formation of the RAF Servicing Commando Units (SCU). Despite the use of the term commando in the title, the SCUs were not intended to fight for airfields but to occupy them as soon as the Army had moved on and to prepare for receiving and supporting aircraft, prior to the arrival of the squadron ground crews and their equipment. The SCUs would then move on to another forward airfield, leaving the squadrons to be supported by their own ground crews, with supply support coming from their allocated ASP and No. 351 MU in the longer term.

The RAF base at Gibraltar was used for the amassing of aircraft, many of which were brought in by sea and packed in crates. Additional tankage for aviation fuel was also constructed on the airfield for reserve stocks. As far as equipment preparation was concerned, the Air Ministry produced a series of schedules that were passed to the relevant equipment MUs, which were then responsible for assembling the items into deployable packs. Given the other operational commitments at that time, it is perhaps not surprising that many depots reported shortages of up to 72 per cent against the schedules. Apparently, to improve security, each of the packs was given what was known as a field unit serial number, albeit the code used to decipher these numbers was given such a limited distribution as to cause significant problems and it actually led to much equipment getting lost.

The Torch landings commenced at dawn on 8 November 1942 and went generally well. The first RAF ground personnel, which included Nos 59 and 60 EUs, landed along with the assault troops. The landings at Algiers were very lightly opposed and it was here that the RAF set up its Advanced Wing HQ near the beach; it was also where the EUs would operate. Following this, the priority was the occupation and provision of aircraft support services at the aerodrome of Maison Blanche. The EUs very quickly experienced the practical difficulties that landing heavy equipment on a beach could present when trying to get their first vehicle ashore onto what was meant to be a hard beach and finding that it immediately sank up to its axles in soft sand. Although metal tracking had been included as part of the invasion equipment, it had not been landed with the initial assault equipment and much manhandling was necessary to get the vehicles safely from the landing craft to the cliff top. Difficulties and delays with the disembarkation of equipment was a major factor affecting the landing operations as one particular incident illustrates, involving the resupply of aviation fuel to the flying squadrons at Maison Blanche. The request from the aerodrome was received by No. 59 EU at dusk on 8 November, and the fuel was essential to keep fighter aircraft in the air. The sea conditions were still poor and the sole landing craft carrying the fuel ashore was swung violently by the breakers on the beach, which made it extremely difficult for off-loading. There was also a foot of water in the craft when it arrived at the shoreline and heavy seas continued to break over it as the EU staff battled with the off-loading. With all the tins of fuel ashore, the men of the unit formed a 'human chain' to manhandle cases up the hill to a point where they could be loaded onto an American lorry. Unfortunately, the American driver got lost during the night journey to the aerodrome and did not reach his destination until 5 a.m. the next day. When unloaded, there was only just enough fuel to get the fighters of the three squadrons airborne. The resupply operation was critical as the fighters were a key part of countering an enemy air attack on Algiers, only hours later at 9.30 a.m., when they destroyed twelve of the thirty attacking aircraft.

Unsurprisingly, this first experience revealed a number of challenges that such landings could present for beach maintenance personnel. In the docks at Algiers, the EUs soon found that their numbers were woefully inadequate for the sheer size and tempo of unloading and the delivery of equipment to forward units was hampered by insufficient vehicles and drivers who had travelled separately and were often disembarked at different ports. Further forward in the supply chain, a lack of sufficient RAF Movements personnel led to a reliance on Army personnel at rail heads who, without any information on the RAF Field Unit Serial Numbers, were unable to forward the consignment to the correct destination. Such was the confusion that arose from this that much of the equipment off-loaded from the first

Equipment and vehicles being unloaded on the beach, North Africa, 1942. (*Crown Copyright—Air Historical Branch MoD*)

convoys out of the ports did not reach the correct units for a number of weeks. The seven days' spares holdings of the flying squadrons also proved to be inadequate to keep aircraft serviceable as nearly two weeks elapsed from the time their ASPs landed, found suitable accommodation, collected their equipment, and were ready to start making issues of equipment.

Between 10 and 19 November 1942, the First Army moved eastwards, making its first real contact with Axis troops on 16 November; by that date, five airfields had been captured for RAF use. Throughout the period that the British First Army attempted to reach Tunis, the RAF built up its logistic organisation, with the base equipment depot (No. 351 MU) arriving on 23 November 1942. Concurrent with the First Army's advance eastwards, Montgomery's Eighth Army was advancing westwards, pursuing Rommel's retreating forces. However, as Operation Torch had not included landings and the occupation of Tunisia in its first phase, there remained some 400 miles for the Allies to advance to secure Tunis. This shortfall in the plan gave valuable time to the enemy and enabled Field Marshal Kesselring to pour in German troops by air from Sicily to Tunisia, forming a defensive perimeter to cover Rommel's retreat from the east. Consequently, the enemy's rapid reinforcement of Tunisia effectively halted Allied operations in Tunisia by early December 1942. By January 1943, a regrouping of Allied armies in North Africa was decided upon and, as part of this, no further advance of the First Army took place until about the middle of March 1943.

The pause in operations enabled the RAF to make much needed changes to its supply chain. Essentially, the extended lines of communication between the main military base at Algiers and the most forward of the captured aerodromes in Tunisia were leading to a number of difficulties. Not only was the distance significant (in the region of 350 miles), but the various means of reaching the forward area (road, rail, and sea) had to be shared with the British First Army and the Twelfth US Air Force. This was further compounded by the fact that the extremely difficult terrain restricted use of road transport to and from the forward area. Up until the invasion of North Africa, the base area for operations in the Western Desert had been in the Nile Delta area of Egypt. With the RAF moving further westwards supporting Montgomery's campaign, coupled with those squadrons operating in support of the First Army's advance eastwards, the line of communication to the Nile Delta had stretched considerably and needed an urgent reappraisal. The capture of Tripoli in January 1943 provided an ideal opportunity and location to build up a more substantial base support area and a number of industrial sites were taken over on which to base technical support facilities. To maximise this opportunity, elements from existing units in the Levant, Palestine, and Egypt transferred to the area, merging with the recently relocated No. 113 MU. To provide much needed additional capacity for aircraft repairs, No. 3 Middle East Repair Unit was transferred in from Egypt to become No. 159 MU. With the ever-expanding supply needs of these two new MUs as well as the need to meet the resupply of the squadrons through the ASPs, a main equipment unit (No. 114 MU) was set up 28 miles from Tripoli at

Zawia at the beginning of March 1943. Extensive use was also made of S&TCs (Nos 4, 5, 6, and 10) along with MT companies (Nos 51 and 52) to move freight between ports, railheads, and the MUs. The wider development of both of these unit types is covered in Chapter Seven.

The beginning of the end for Axis forces in North Africa came on the night of 20–21 March 1943, when the Eighth Army opened its attack on what was known as the Mareth Line. As a result of various advances by the British First and Eighth Armies, along with the US II Corps, the enemy continued to retreat, losing most of his forward airfields by 7 April. By 7 May, Tunis was captured and a week later all organised enemy resistance in the Cap Bon peninsula ended. Thus, after six months of ebb and flow fighting, Africa was finally cleared of all Axis forces. This operation showed that, even with relatively light enemy opposition during the assault phase, the follow-on landing of equipment and combat supplies did not proceed as planned; it was difficult to bring loads ashore at the right place, at the right time, and in the right order.[118]

The key point that emerged though was that the EUs were too small to cope with the task and that the RAF needed to develop its beach maintenance capability, especially with further large-scale amphibious operations on the agenda. It was thus that the RAF decided in early 1943 to form specialist RAF Beach Units, although its approach to this was somewhat complicated. Three specific groups were formed: in the UK, Middle East, and North Africa. The five units formed in the UK (Nos 68–70 and 76–77) were known as Beach Units; the six units formed in the Middle East were known as Beach Bricks (RAF Component) (Nos 31–36) and for North Africa, three auxiliary embarkation units (AEU) (Nos 1 –3).[119] As far as possible, personnel were all volunteers and, due to the arduous nature of the work, had to be of a strong physique and meet the fitness standards required for combined operations training. They were kitted out with Army khaki battledress, but retained RAF blue headdress when not wearing steel helmets. As far as possible, the COs of the RAF Beach Units and their sections were drawn from the RAF Equipment Branch, with movements experience.[120] Each unit had quite a broad responsibility, which included controlling the landing of RAF personnel, vehicles, and stores; their assembly on shore and despatch to forward areas; to establish small dumps of supplies and stores; to provide labour, traffic control, and provost services; and to salvage and repair 'drowned' vehicles.[121]

The War in Asia

India and Ceylon

The RAF had been in India throughout the inter-war period and its presence here had become relatively well-established, with the majority of its stations located in the north-west of the country. Operationally, the RAF here was controlled from HQ India Command in the country's capital city of New Delhi, with No. 1

Group at Peshawar responsible for India and No. 222 Group at Colombo in Ceylon responsible for the island and bases in the Indian Ocean. Before the war, the entire India Command was looked after by a single depot at Karachi, which had an equipment section and a provisioning office. The entry of Japan into the war, following its attack on Pearl Harbour in December 1941, triggered significant change in India for the RAF and led to a build-up of its units, an expansion that saw the number of groups increase to seven by the middle of 1942. Of these, No. 226 (Maintenance) Group at Karachi was the focus for logistics. By the beginning of 1943, the logistic footprint had expanded significantly and was operating on a regional basis with a static UED in each of six areas. This was a similar concept to that which had already been established in the UK and each depot supplied ASPs in its respective area; by the beginning of April 1943, most of these parks had been re-designated as semi-mobile equipment parks. This variation on the original support concept was viewed as providing a more flexible means of meeting the needs of the forward units although it was not adopted elsewhere. Some twenty-one parks operated in this theatre with the majority numbered in the 70, 80, and 90 series.[122] No. 91 ASP, which largely operated in Bengal, moved the furthest east of the ASPs and in March 1946 was sent to Japan as part of the forces of occupation and was the 'first complete UK unit of all three services to arrive on Japanese soil'.[123] In Bengal and the eastern forward areas, support was provided by a combination of equipment parks and ASPs that were capable of a leap-frog progression in the event of a rapid advance by the air forces.

As far as aviation fuel was concerned for India, high octane products were shipped in from Abadan in Iran, via the main ports, while supplies of lower octane fuel came from in-country refineries located at Digboi (situated in northern Assam) and Rawalpindi (situated on the North-West Frontier). The supply of explosives was tied in with the Army, whose arsenals or ordnance depots held the RAF's central holdings of common stock. These central holdings were distributed to advanced ordnance depots, which, in turn, supplied ordnance field depots that replenished the RAF stations in their respective areas. The RAF holding at the Army depots was usually controlled by the command or group HQ in whose area they were located. Wherever possible, Equipment officers who were explosives or 'X' qualified were attached to the various Army holding units. In due course, the RAF stock holding element of the various Army depots became known as 'X' MUs. This brought a new status to the resident RAF Equipment officer who became the OC 'X' MU, although the overall command of the ammunition depot remained with an Army officer.

By the end of 1943, logistics in India, Ceylon, Assam, and Burma were controlled by two maintenance groups in the east and west of the area, each of which had quite different challenges. The reason for this difference was not just that one of them was closer to the growing threat from Japanese invasion, but largely one of topography. The region covered by No. 226 (Maintenance) Group included Ceylon and India up to the Brahmaputra river. Here the ground communications were reasonably good and there were no major land or water barriers to prevent an extensive base maintenance organisation being built up. The lines of communication were therefore relatively straightforward with full use being made of road, rail and inland waterways. The region to the east of the river was a different matter altogether. Here, No. 230 (Maintenance) Group was faced with land communications that were described as so bad as to be almost non-existent. Their condition was one thing, but their mere existence came and went as most of the roads, due to their proximity to rivers, disappeared under flood waters during the monsoon season. To cap it all, the railways in Assam suffered from the handicap of frequent changes in gauge. The contrast in two regions could hardly be greater. As a result of the terrain and conditions that prevailed in the eastern region, air transport came into its own and became the vital lifeline to supply the needs of the forthcoming campaign in Burma (see Chapter Seven). Indeed, from the Battle of Imphal in April 1944 through to the capture of Rangoon in May 1945, both the Army and the RAF had to be resupplied by air.

Ceylon was more self-contained with a single ASP (No. 89) based at Colombo; it was responsible for equipment, with Army personnel at No. 338 MU (X) supplying explosives and fuel. There was also a small RAF Movements Unit based at Colombo, which worked in liaison with the Army for sea and rail transport and with No. 89 ASP for road transport; air movements were handled in conjunction with RAF India, HQ No. 222 Group and, later, with Supreme HQ in Kandy. Squadron Leader (later Wing Commander) C. S. W. Harte, an Equipment officer commissioned in September 1938, arrived to command No. 89 ASP in October 1943; post-war memories of his time there provide an insight into how the unit operated. As with many such overseas locations, the park was housed in temporary commandeered accommodation with large stocks housed in six sites in Colombo, most of which were tea warehouses and therefore ideally suited to the requirement, albeit for a totally different commodity. Although the park was static, it had a large MT section that not only delivered stores to RAF stations on the island, but also served as general carriers, assisting the Navy and the Army when required. Not long after Squadron Leader Harte's arrival in Ceylon, the ASP was renamed No. 89 Equipment Park, presumably because it was mainly static. However, with the British forces in India successfully halting the Japanese advance and gradually beginning to push southwards through Burma, the park reverted to ASP, presumably in anticipation of an eventual advance by the RAF in Ceylon to Malaya and beyond, when No. 89 ASP would most likely have moved forward to support the operational squadrons of No. 222 Group. The surrender of Japan after the atomic bombs were dropped, of course, made this unnecessary. The administrative arrangements for the Park were quite unusual as Wing Commander Harte related:

> All units in Ceylon were administered by 222 Group, which was the only survivor of the RAF's Far East Command, and theoretically independent of India. We

were, for example, paid by the British Government, whereas in India the Indian Government paid us. This could make a difference: on my return to the UK in 1945 my income tax for 1943–44 was reassessed because I had 'legally' changed my employer and I had to pay more than £100 extra. That was a lot of money in those days.[124]

Singapore

The RAF's relatively short stay in wartime Singapore was dramatically cut short by the island's capture by Japanese forces in February 1942. The RAF's logistic organisation was inextricably caught up in this and, while many managed to escape as part of the evacuation, a number of officers and men were taken prisoner and experienced harsh treatment by their Japanese captors. The RAF had been in Singapore since the 1920s and, by 1934, their station at Seletar was home to two torpedo-bomber squadrons and two flying boat squadrons. The pre-war expansion programme had led to a significant build-up of the RAF's overseas squadrons, which led to a corresponding increase in the support infrastructure with a sizeable aircraft depot developing at Seletar along with a general engineering section at Kuala Lumpur; by June 1941, the depot at Seletar became No. 151 MU and the facility at Kuala Lumpur became No. 153 MU. Here too, the UED concept was utilised with such depots included at both of these MUs.

The build-up of equipment stocks soon led to acute congestion at Seletar; to alleviate this, a further UED was opened in August 1941 as No. 152 MU at Bukit Panjang (western part of Singapore Island). For explosives storage, two AAPs were established towards the end of 1941 at Seletar with a dump at Batak Quarry.[125]

With the entry of Japan into the war following the attack on Pearl Harbour on 7 December 1941, the threat of invasion became a very real possibility. Indeed, the very day after Pearl Harbour, the Japanese launched their first attack on Seletar. Shortly after this, and following the Japanese invasion of Malaya, the salvage of equipment from airfields in that area began, the majority of it finding its way back to the Armament Park at Seletar. The Japanese advance through Malaya also saw the need to evacuate No. 153 MU at Kuala Lumpur; this was completed by 9 January 1942. It was clear that the Japanese would continue their advance south but, as no effective defences had been put in place to resist an invasion of Singapore from the north, it became inevitable that an evacuation from the island would be required.[126] Preliminary arrangements had been made as early as 5 January 1942 to move men and equipment further south to Sumatra; however, a shortage of shipping meant that by 18 January, they were still waiting to leave the island. On 21 January, orders were issued for two-thirds of the personnel from Nos 151 and 152 MUs to evacuate to Batavia on Java, with the remainder of the two units being formed into a Repair and Salvage Unit; an ASP (believed to be No. 41) was formed on 25 January 1942 to look after the needs of the fighter force remaining in Singapore. The range of stores for the ASP had been dispersed from 151 MU's stock and segregated in a hangar at Seletar. Nowhere was safe, and even the spares storage hangar was riddled with shrapnel from a bombing raid just after the date of the ASP's order to form.[127]

The formation and leadership of the ASP fell to an Equipment officer, Squadron Leader (later Group Captain) J. H. Nancarrow. There are very few written personal accounts by members of the supply organisation that covers this period and theatre; it is therefore fortunate, if not quite remarkable, that details of Nancarrow's experiences survive. He had originally written a report of his activities but was taken prisoner by the Japanese on Java. Fearing that the discovery of anything official by his captors would not be in his best interests, his original report was destroyed. On release from captivity as a POW, Nancarrow rewrote his report from memory for his personal archives and later presented a copy to the RAF Supply Branch in 1992, with a wish that it should be made available to young supply officers to illustrate progress made over fifty years.

By 31 January 1942, further orders were received from Air HQ to move the equipment, uncased and unlisted, to a cane factory on the Bukit Timah Road and RAF Station Bukit Panjang. The hangar at Seletar was finally cleared of the ASP spares on 6 February 1942, an operation made all the more difficult due to the station being under shellfire from the advancing Japanese forces. A few days later, the position had become desperate following the invasion of Singapore by the Japanese during the night of 8–9 February. Fortunately, the spares at the cane factory had been cased and delivered to the port by the afternoon of 10 February. The spares at Bukit Panjang did not fare so well and, with the advance of enemy forces, had to be destroyed on site by the unit's CO, Squadron Leader Aylwin. The remaining spares from the cane factory and the remaining ASP personnel just managed to leave Singapore on 10 February, arriving at Batavia on Java during the afternoon of 14 February. Many of the remaining MU personnel were not so fortunate and were taken into captivity and interned in a POW Camp at Surabaya.[128]

The Invasion of Sicily and Mainland Italy

Operation Husky was the codename for the Allied operation to invade the island of Sicily in July 1943. The successful capture of the island was important to the longer-term plans for invading mainland Italy in that Sicily provided an important stepping stone from North Africa. An Anglo-American venture, the plan was for a US western task force to rendezvous with the British Eighth Army, south west of Malta on D-1 for pre-dawn landings. The operation was conducted in three phases, the first of which was the highly important achievement of both sea and air superiority. The second phase was simultaneous landings by US and UK forces on the south-east corner of the island. The third and final phase was the establishment of a firm base from which to capture specific ports and airfields. Many of the planning staff from the North African landings found themselves involved with this operation, including Wing Commander

Jack Maggs who was posted to HQ Mediterranean Allied Air Forces in Algiers, working under Group Captain Douglas Jackman; similar to Maggs, he was also to have a distinguished RAF career and went on to become the Equipment Branch's only officer to reach the rank of air marshal; he was appointed DGE in 1955 and knighted in 1959, not long after he became AOC-in-C Maintenance Command. As a group captain, Douglas Jackman was one of very few RAF officers to receive awards from the Greek Government for his part, while working at HQ Middle East, in the planning of the British expedition to aid Greece following the Italian invasion in October 1940 (see Jackman's entry in the honours and awards list at Appendix II).[129]

A significant bonus for the Allies with Operation Husky was the position and availability of the island of Malta; up until the eastern air task force was set up in Sicily, the better part of it was based on Malta under the command of the AOC of the island. Preparations for the use of Malta as part of Operation Husky had started in January 1943 with the priority being to build up stores and supplies, from what had been virtual starvation level during the Siege of Malta between 1940 and the Autumn of 1942, to a level that would support a force that finally reached some thirty-five squadrons working at maximum effort.

As with all such operational planning, the work was top secret and Maggs became part of what was known as Force 141, which was set up by General Eisenhower and Air Marshal Sir Arthur Tedder to prepare and submit plans for the invasion of Sicily. Assembling in early February 1943 in a requisitioned school in Bouzaréah, a suburb of Algiers, the UK planning component was truly a joint Service outfit with representatives from the Navy, Army and Air Force. Following so closely on the heels of the North African landings, Force 141 was not working from scratch. Not only was there a re-employment of planning staff, but a number of lessons learned from Operation Torch were addressed in the planning for Operation Husky. From the logistics perspective, as mentioned earlier, the one key aspect that had not worked well during the North African landings was beach maintenance.

The earliest involvement of RAF Logistics was as part of the assault phase with the early landing of the RAF components of Nos 31–35 Beach Bricks supporting 13 Corps and Nos 68 and 69 RAF Beach Units supporting 30 Corps and Nos 1–3 AEUs. At D+14, No. 40 ASP was scheduled to be convoyed in from Tripoli with twenty-eight days' pack-up for five Kittyhawks and five and a half Spitfire squadrons. In a separate convoy from North West Africa, No. 135 ASP was also due in with twenty-eight days' pack-up for nine Spitfire squadrons and one Beaufighter squadron. The reinforcements for both 40 and 135 ASPs, with additional spares pack-ups, were planned for D+28. The steady state maintenance support of all air forces on Sicily was planned to revert to UK provision by D+42.

The operation commenced at 2.45 a.m. on 10 July 1943 and the landings generally went as scheduled, albeit with a heavy swell on the beaches. The ORB for the RAF Component of No. 31 Beach Brick provides a good example of the pace experienced by a typical RAF beach unit. Their account commences on board ship and describes how the first RAF units went ashore in a landing craft assault at about 9 a.m., by which time the shelling had stopped and there was very little small arms fire. Improvisation was clearly important and 'runners' had to be used to call forward troops below deck to their disembarkation points on deck as the method using the ship's tannoy system had to be abandoned. Once ashore, the RAF Component succeeded in establishing an MT assembly area, POL and explosives dumps and a personnel marshalling area all by 11.45 a.m.; it was a close-run thing as the first RAF equipment started coming ashore at 12 p.m. The volume of supplies built up by D+2 was substantial and by late afternoon on 12 July, 7,708 gallons of aviation fuel in cans or drums had been accumulated, with some 1¼ tons of explosives being discharged over the beaches. During this time, the unit was also subjected to a number of enemy air raids.

From 12 to 25 July, the RAF component of 31 Beach Brick worked continually on the beach, receiving and recording landed supplies and equipment and moving them to the appropriate dumps or onward to those units requiring issues elsewhere in the beach head. By D+15, their work on the beach came to an end with no further landings of equipment or supplies to handle and their various dumps cleared of stock. The RAF component of No. 31 Beach Brick went on to undertake embarkation duties as part of the Allies' move into the toe of Italy. Although No. 40 ASP was not due to land until D+14, the flexibility offered to the operation by the use of Malta enabled an advanced component of the unit to land on D+3 over the beaches on

Fuel drums being loaded on the beach, Sicily, 1943. (*Author's collection*)

Cape Passero, near Pachino, enabling them quickly to set up operations on the nearby airfield. The main party of No. 40 ASP disembarked through Syracuse docks about five days afterwards. No. 135 ASP arrived about a week later than planned (on D+19) at Syracuse from Tunis, moving forward to Lentini to support No. 322 Wing.

Following his work on the Operation Husky planning staff, Wing Commander Maggs was assigned to be an RAF liaison officer with the US XII Air Support Command and to accompany the US Army and US Air Force's planned landings opposite the Gela and Comiso airfields on the southern coast sector. The Eighth Army's and Desert Air Force's planned landings were to be on the South East to capture Pachino airfield and to advance into the interior beyond, with North African Tactical Air Force in support of the Eighth Army advance into Catania. He embarked in an American landing ship infantry assault on D+1 after a very stormy crossing during which most on board suffered from sea sickness. His week at Comiso airfield was an eventful one in many respects, not least as his timely intervention possibly saved a casualty evacuation Dakota aircraft from being shot down. As soon as the airfield had been made operational, a flight of about six USAF Dakota aircraft flew in on a mission that was to return the wounded to Tunisia. The CO of the flight had promised to take Wing Commander Maggs with them, and he was duly invited to attend the short pre-take-off briefing. Rather alarmingly, the flight only had one map of the local area between them, and the CO briefed the pilots that they should take off and circle over an airfield called Agrigento, approximately fifty miles down Sicily's southern coast. Having thus formed up, the plan was that the CO would lead the flight back to Tunis using the single map for navigation. The only problem with this plan, as Jack Maggs pointed out, was that Agrigento was the last Southern Sicily airfield remaining in German hands and was therefore heavily defended by Axis anti-aircraft guns. Needless to say, the CO stopped the briefing at once and a revised flight plan was formulated. In his memoirs, Jack Maggs stated 'I claim credit for saving six USAF Dakota aircraft, full of evacuated sick and wounded from being shot down, not least as I would have been one of them!'

Once Sicily had been successfully captured and steady state operations achieved, a new RAF MU (No. 118) was formed at Catania in early November 1943. In addition to its engineering function, the MU was also responsible for supplying all forms of RAF equipment (except POL and explosives) to RAF units and squadrons.

Having secured Sicily, the first steps in the general invasion of mainland Italy were taken on 3 September 1943 with Montgomery's Eighth Army's crossing of the Strait of Messina as part of Operation Baytown; this operation saw the participation of Nos 31–35 Beach Bricks (RAF Component). The main invasion took place on 9 September 1943 with the First British Airborne Division landing at Taranto in Operation Slapstick and the US Fifth Army landings in the area of the Gulf of Salerno (consisting of the British X Corps and the US VI Corps) in Operation Avalanche. Of these three operations, it was the Operation Avalanche landings at Salerno that would require the main effort of RAF Logistics in support of air operations, with units and personnel going ashore as part of the British X Corps landings, north of the river Sele, on three beach areas codenamed Uncle, Sugar, and Roger; beach maintenance across these was provided by the RAF Component of No. 35 Beach Group, Nos 81 and 82 RAF Beach Units (operating with No. 12 Beach Group) and Nos 68 and 69 RAF Beach Units (operating with No. 3 Beach Group). Once the Beach Units had paved the way, they were followed by the Servicing Commandos and the advanced elements of the ASPs to provide support for the flying squadrons, which would gradually operate from newly-captured airfields. As the tactical situation allowed, the main parties of the ASPs would then move in, followed by the main parties of the flying squadrons, which would then take on the support of their respective aircraft. Sicily and Malta were the key bases for mounting the invasion of mainland Italy and, by the time the invasion had started, Sicily alone was holding enough supplies to maintain the entire Tactical Air Force for at least two weeks of intensive effort.

Operation Avalanche is particularly significant for RAF Logistics in that it is the first and only occasion that an Equipment Branch officer has been awarded the Distinguished Service Order (DSO). The recipient, Wing Commander Rowland George, was a remarkable man in many respects. A graduate of Lincoln College, Oxford, George had been a keen rower, winning a gold medal in the Coxless Fours at the 1932 Olympic Games in Los Angeles. Joining the RAFVR in 1939, he specialised in explosives and as an acting squadron leader, was awarded the OBE for his part in Operation Torch, where he commanded one of the RAF units responsible for unloading and dispensing supplies to the First Army and RAF squadrons. Little did he imagine when rowing his way to success in the Olympic Games that just over ten years later, he would be distinguishing himself again in an amphibious venture. The first waves of the British forces landed under fire on the beaches at 3.30 a.m. on 10 September; among them were the advance elements of the RAF Beach Units. Wing Commander George, in his role as a liaison officer with one of the American units, had embarked as the only RAF officer onboard a Landing Craft Infantry (LCI) along with a detachment of British Light Infantry. He landed on the beaches at about 5 a.m.; his recollections provide an idea of just what it was like:

> Gradually we drew nearer to the black line of the shore as the night wore on and at last a rather fitful green light and then an amber one appeared on the shore. 'Get your chaps ready, we are going in!' announced the skipper to the major and we were all keyed to intense excitement. The soldiers were in full battle array with only such kit as they could carry in their webbing, but I, with my less warlike role to play had a kit bag, a large envelope of official papers and two haversacks, not to mention such odd items as a water bottle. The craft lurched to a standstill on a small sandbank some ten yards from the brink of the seas and in a few seconds the major was in the water followed by his men. I waited until last but could not delay longer as it was vital that the precious ship should not remain in so vulnerable a position a second more than was necessary. Had it not been quite so dark, I must

> have been a joyous sight with my revolver hung round my neck, a kit bag on one shoulder and a haversack on the other and one strung high on my back and my papers stuffed into the tunic of my battledress – obviously every inch not a soldier! As I slipped awkwardly into the water (but the right end up notwithstanding), the sailor at the bottom of the gangway shouted 'All clear,' there was an answering call of 'Good luck' from the Bridge, the ships engines whirled into activity and she slid into the darkness with her share of the job beautifully done.[130]

It was some hours before George was able to meet up with any RAF personnel and he spent many uncomfortable moments taking cover from enemy shell and small arms fire. During the first two weeks ashore, the ground held was so narrow that gun batteries, supply dumps, camp hospitals, and tanks were all mixed up together. This close-knit community could prove somewhat unnerving as George recalled:

> One quickly got used to driving along a road with guns in the adjoining fields blazing away in full action firing over one's head and on one or two occasions, I was on the wrong side of tanks making free use of their big guns. I always hoped that they would know that I was on their side, which fortunately proved to be the case!

The majority of the RAF Beach Units landed at about midday on D-day and most had established their main transit areas and dump sites just before nightfall. By all accounts, they performed well and in the first two weeks following the landings, the northern beaches handled some 136 units, comprising 7,164 men and 1,290 vehicles. The advance parties of Nos 135 and 136 ASPs landed on 12 September and 2 October respectively, with their main parties following on during the following months. The logistic arrangements worked well with resupply coming in by sea and air from the Middle East.

Throughout this period, George was continually active in his liaison role and spent much time visiting the various sections of the RAF Beach Units at their dispersed locations. It was during one of these visits that he had a very close call that proved to be a highlight to what was later seen as an extraordinary commitment to duty and coolness under fire, resulting in the award of his DSO. It was in the early hours of one morning while camped in an apple orchard that George and his men were on the receiving end of two bombs jettisoned from a low flying enemy aircraft, after it had been fired upon by Allied anti-aircraft fire. The resulting blast wounded George's driver, despatch rider, and batman, as well as himself. When safe to do so, George borrowed a truck from the Americans and drove all three of the wounded men to an RAF mobile field hospital a mile away. The account written by George is modest regarding the part he played, dismissing his own wounding during the bomb-dropping incident: 'I escaped scot-free except for a small cut in my knee which Doc insisted on examining and stitching.' The citation for his DSO is more illuminating:

> Wing Commander George, the senior movements staff officer, was responsible for the smooth and efficient working of the supply system from the beaches to the airfields during the assault landings at Salerno. He landed with the first assault troops on the beaches in the early morning of the 10 September 1943. Thereafter, he was under fire, both on the beaches and while travelling between the various supply dumps and airfields, until the enemy had been forced to retreat sufficiently to allow the airfields to be occupied by units of the Tactical Air Force. Wing Commander George was wounded when his tented camp was hit by two enemy bombs; he did not, however, allow this to interfere with his personal supervision of the work of unloading and distributing the urgently required supplies. Throughout the operation Wing Commander George displayed great gallantry and his example and coolness while under fire were an inspiration to those under his command and contributed largely to the success of the operation.[131]

Rowland George went on to become the CO of the County of Suffolk Fighter Control Unit in the Royal Auxiliary Air Force from 1948 to 1951 and took early retirement in 1959. He died on 9 September 1997, aged ninety-two.

As originally planned, No. 114 MU became the main logistics depot on the Italian mainland, initially operating from the port of Naples and later was the RAF's key supply depot in theatre for the rest of the Italian campaign. Not all equipment could be provided by the MU and RAF units became quite adept at seeking out additional vehicles to meet their needs. The recently commissioned Equipment Officer Norman Morss joined No. 40 ASP at Tresimino, Northern Italy in July 1944 to find the unit as follows:

> Making good use of three 'requisitioned' Italian civilian coaches, one as the Officers' Mess, one for the Sergeants and the other for stores. These were obtained from an Italian POW camp (probably in Tunis) to provide extra carrying capacity for 40 ASP when it moved into Italy.

Despite the show of initiative and resourcefulness, the military authorities were not so understanding as Norman described:

> As the desert Air Force (as we called ourselves then) moved forward in support of the advancing 8th Army, the Officers' Mess coach and Sergeants' Mess coach were filled to capacity with Spitfire tyres and other variously small aircraft components and we were well prepared when the Military police at the frequent road barriers reminded us that 'purloined' civilian goods could not be kept and had to be abandoned at their barrier. They were promptly informed that these vehicles were essential to give us the extra carrying capacity, they could check for themselves what they were carrying, and if we could not retain them, maintenance of the

airworthiness of the Spitfires would suffer for the 8th Army as the RAF would thus be unable to provide the necessary air support! Needless to add, we were allowed to proceed and the three coaches were still in use by 40 ASP at Klagenfurt in mid-1945 after the armistice.[132]

With the Italian campaign under way, there was no longer a requirement for so many RAF beach units and by December 1943 all six Beach Bricks (RAF Component) and the three AEUs were disbanded.[133] With the invasion of North West Europe (Operation Overlord) now the main planning priority, attention turned to reorganising the remaining beach units into a coherent logistic ORBAT to support the planned landings in Normandy.

The Invasion of North West Europe: Operation Overlord

The Allied decision to invade mainland Europe was taken at the Quebec Conference in August 1943 and was given the codename Operation Overlord. The intention was for a large-scale invasion to take place in the spring of 1944 but, rather than landing in the Pas-de-Calais area as expected by the Germans, the chosen location was Normandy, which was less heavily fortified and would give the Allies a greater

The Officers' Mess coach used by 40 ASP, Italy, 1944. (*N. Morss*)

chance of surprise. In due course, five beaches were selected for the landings covering some fifty miles of channel coastline, between the Cotentin Peninsula on the western edge and Le Havre on the eastern. The Americans would land on the westerly beaches codenamed Utah and Omaha, the Canadians on Juno, and the British on Gold and Sword to the east. In short, this would enable the Allies to establish a firm bridgehead on the Continent, followed by a breakout and then a rapid advance towards the German frontier. The air support for the Operation was covered by the formation of the Allied Expeditionary Air Force (AEAF) commanded by Air Marshal Sir Trafford Leigh-Mallory, consisting of the 2TAF (comprising Nos 2, 83, 84, and 85 Groups), No. 38 Group, No. 46 Group, Air Defence of Great Britain (formerly Fighter Command), and the US IX Air Force.

The RAF Logistics concept of operations for Overlord followed largely the same principle that had been developed from earlier seaborne invasions such as Torch, Husky, and Avalanche. In keeping with the operational doctrine already developed for beach maintenance, the first echelons of the forward maintenance organisation were the RAF Beach Units that would be landed early in the operation and would facilitate the disembarkation of the remainder of the RAF's forward units and, later, the base maintenance organisation. By the beginning of 1944, the various Beach Units required for the European theatre had been rationalised to form Nos 1, 2, 3, and 4 Beach Units. By the end of April 1944, all five beach units had been renamed Beach Squadrons, each consisting of two flights. The need for a comprehensive beach maintenance organisation was critical to the success of Operation Overlord as the plan did not anticipate the capture of the first major port until D+17 at the very earliest. Thus, the beaches were crucial, not only to the landing of men and machines, but also to the resupply operation. By the beginning of 1944, Nos 1, 2, 3, and 4 RAF Beach Units were all back in the UK and participated in a series of training exercises in readiness for Overlord. The Beach Units had been created under Technical Training Command but came under the operational control of the Air Ministry's Director of Movements; these were later transferred to the command of 2TAF on 1 February 1944 when it was confirmed that all four were likely to be committed to Operation Overlord, with No. 3 RAF Beach Squadron held in reserve at RAF Old Sarum. Their work was critical to the RAF's involvement in the operation with much of it involving the manhandling of supplies from landing craft to beach supply dumps and the marshalling of men and vehicles prior to them moving off the beach area. At the beginning of April 1944, authority was granted for RAF Beach Squadron personnel to wear war service dress (blue) and fly the RAF Ensign while on the Continent. Additionally, authority was granted by HQ Combined Operations in March 1944 for RAF Beach Unit personnel to wear the Combined Operations Badge on the upper sleeve of their battledress.

Following D-Day, a series of advanced LGs were established on the Continent to enable the maintenance of air superiority for the eventual breakout from the bridgehead; the RAF administrative plan for Overlord envisaged the development of twenty-five airfields by D+40.[134] These airfields were initially occupied by the RAF

Servicing Commandos and then, when they moved on, were replaced by an airfield HQs to control the location, but supported by an ASP. In total, eight parks took part in the operation (Nos 34, 401, 402, 404, 406 (RCAF), 408 (Polish), 414, and 418).[135] Much thought had gone into the design of the ASPs with the range and level of stockholdings determined after months of research involving visits to operational units, discussions with technical and equipment staff, analysis of consumption data, and identifying high turnover items for particular aircraft types. Perhaps the most significant development from a deployment perspective was the ASPs' structure. Each park had a HQ and consisted of a series of consecutively numbered, self-contained vehicles. All drivers had to be storekeepers as well as stores accountants and all records were maintained in manuscript ledger form, one per vehicle. By 1944, most of the vehicles were three-tonners although there were a few 25-cwt prime movers and trailers. All movements were by convoy, with the vehicles being kept in their numerical order in case any spares were required on the move. Should this happen (as was often the case), a despatch rider would be sent down the convoy and the appropriate vehicle pulled out of the line so the spares required could be issued. The ASPs formed for the European theatre trained hard, an important part of which was acclimatizing them for what was to come in Normandy. Mr R. C. Gorddard, an ex-RAF officer who served with No. 401 ASP, described how his unit acclimatised themselves for what was to come in Normandy:

> From the winter of 1942 right up to the landing in Normandy, the unit was under canvas. This was considered to be good training for the operations which lay ahead and it was not until 18 September 1944, at Eindhoven in Holland, that covered accommodation was taken up.[136]

To hold the substantial stocks of fuel and munitions that would be required, four Aviation Fuel and Ammunition Parks were established and their role was to stockpile these commodities after they were landed over the beaches. Bulk POL was delivered directly to airfields by the Army. In-theatre delivery of RAF stocks of packed POL, ammunition, stores, and supplies from the beachheads was the responsibility of the Army, but only to agreed points within a distance of forty miles from RAF units. The movement from those points to the units themselves was the responsibility of the S&TCs.

There were three key planning challenges for RAF Logistics in Operation Overlord. First, the main mounting base for the operation had to be the UK. Given its unprecedented scale, the build-up prior to the invasion required an enormous concentration of men, supplies and equipment into a relatively small geographical area. This required a substantial support infrastructure, much of which would not form any part of the invasion force but would provide a vital springboard for its successful launch. Second, there was the question of where and how the enormous volume of men, machines and equipment could be disembarked on the other side

No. 401 ASP in the field, 1944. (*R. C. Gorddard*)

of the Channel. As there were no sizeable ports in the selected invasion area and the capture of such a facility was not envisaged until D+17 at the earliest, it was planned that two artificial harbours would be constructed in the UK and towed across the Channel to Normandy. Codename 'Mulberry', one would be installed in the American sector just off Omaha beach (Mulberry 'A') and the other in the British sector at Arromanches (Mulberry 'B'). However, that process would take time and the British alone planned to continue to land supplies via the beaches until as late as D+30. The British therefore needed a robust beach maintenance organisation until the Mulberries were operational. Third was how to support RAF formations once they were ashore in the early days during and immediately following the assault phase. With priority for shipping space going to combat arm formations, there was little room available for supplies and so-called non-operational personnel.

Consequently, the early establishment of a Base Maintenance Group on the Continent was out of the question so the RAF force, on arrival ashore, would need to be largely self-sufficient. This required a stand-alone, forward maintenance organisation that could provide the required support until a more permanent base structure could be established in-theatre. The need for such a base maintenance organisation had been considered for some time prior to Overlord but it was not until 8 January 1944 that the HQ of No. 85 (Base) Group was formed. The Group had an operational, as well as a support role, deploying a static fighter defence organisation in the early part of the operation (in advance of its main deployment) to provide protection for 2TAF's base area.

As far as the Group's units were concerned, most of them had already been formed or were in the process of forming-up by the time the group as a whole was established. Overall, the Group was designed to be capable of moving in echelons, thereby providing the flexibility to move support units into any additional ports that might be taken as the operation progressed. Until airstrips and a port were established on the Continent, resupply by air or sea from the UK was not possible and it was therefore essential that a form of mini-equipment supply depot was established in the Continental Base Area as soon as possible. It was approved in mid-September 1943 that this need would be met by an FEU with a spares stock holding of one month's requirement for all RAF units in-theatre. Five EU were also formed to look after the embarkation and disembarkation of RAF personnel and supplies at ports, both in the UK and eventually on the Continent. In the early stages of the operation, their work was largely limited to embarkation from UK ports, with the RAF Beach Squadrons meeting the requirement in Normandy across the open beaches. The RAF's EUs took on the task in Normandy once the Mulberry Harbour was in place and other ports as they were captured after the landings. The overall RAF Logistics ORBAT for Operation Overlord is detailed in Table 4.

Formation	Beach Squadrons	Air Stores Parks	Supply and Transport Columns	Aviation Fuel and Ammunition Parks	Embarkation Units
2 TAF	1, 2 and 4	Nil	Nil	Nil	Nil
2 Group		414	314 (6 companies)	423 (HQ + 2 ammo and POL sections)	Nil
83 Group		401 404 406 (RCAF)	309 (8 companies)	407 (HQ + 5 ammo and POL sections)	Nil
84 Group		402 408 (Polish) 418	312 (8 companies)	422 (HQ + 5 ammo and POL sections)	Nil
85 Group		34	313 (6 companies)	424 (HQ + 2 ammo and POL sections)	85, 86, 87, 89 and 93

Table 4: RAF Logistics ORBAT for Operation Overlord, 1944

One of the many challenges with assembling RAF units in the UK was being able to move units into holding areas and then on to points of embarkation at exactly the right time; it was essential that tight movement control was enforced. For the RAF, this was exercised by RAF Movement Control, with overall tri-service coordination of movement resting with the Combined HQ at Portsmouth through two movement organisations: a build-up control organisation (BUCO) responsible for day-to-day supervision of the initial build-up, phasing-in of units, and the allocations of ships and craft to the various users and a turn-round control organisation (TURCO), which was a naval organisation responsible for the turn-round of ships and craft. Movement instructions were issued to units detailing how and when they were to move, a process that was basically the same for all forces participating in the operation.

Each unit started from what was known as its tactical location that, in the case of the RAF, was usually its parent unit or where it had been temporarily based. The next stage was to a concentration area where units would spend around forty-eight hours, usually about five days before the planned landing date in France; the RAF's area was at RAF Old Sarum, outside Salisbury. Those RAF units due to land on D-Day or D+1 proceeded through one of the other military concentration areas with a target arrival date there of about D-8. The second stage was to a marshalling area where units were assembled into a load for eventual embarkation on a specific type of ship or craft. It was a very precise process with units moving into the marshalling area in suitably sized convoys. The convoy commander of each was required to despatch an officer to the marshalling area's regulating post one hour before its scheduled arrival time to report full details of the convoy in advance of its arrival. Once in the area, the marshalling began with an officer or NCO appointed in charge of each party. An OC Troops was appointed for each ship or craft and he remained in command until disembarkation in France. Formations would spend about eighteen to thirty-six hours in the marshalling areas. The third and final stage was the embarkation area where vehicles and personnel were called forward for loading on to ships or craft. These were in very close proximity to the marshalling areas and, for the purposes of Overlord, there were five main embarkation areas sited on the south coast. By way of example, area 'A' was centred on the city of Portsmouth with two embarkation areas, each of which was located either side of the coastal entrance to the harbour itself. To feed in to these, there were four marshalling sub-areas, stretching in a broad arc around the city from Hamble to the north-west across to Emsworth on the eastern side of the city. The marshalling sub-areas were well-chosen, all aligned with railway lines with each area having a designated de-training station.

Road movement was carefully regulated, with the main routes designated as either one or two-way roads across the area. To provide room for flexibility, a waterproofing requirement was extended to all those vehicles that would be disembarking on the Continent until D+42. Consequently, all vehicles had to be waterproofed for wading up to a depth of 3 feet 9 inches. This was a complicated and lengthy process that had to cater for many vehicle types. The process was carried out in three stages, each of which was completed in the concentration, marshalling and embarkation areas respectively. On completion of the waterproofing, vehicles were driven through a water-filled 'wading pit' to test the thoroughness of the work. At the completion of each stage, vehicles were annotated on the offside wing with a small coloured paint mark (blue, yellow and red respectively for each of the stages). This was a simple and effective system and no vehicle was permitted to be loaded on a ship or vessel unless it bore all three marks.

The seaborne element of Operation Overlord was launched on 6 June 1944 and, according to plan, a high degree of air superiority was achieved over the bridgehead. The first RAF personnel to land were those of the three RAF Beach Squadrons. Notwithstanding the support role they were to fulfil, these squadrons landed as part of the assault phase and its personnel were exposed to very similar, if not identical risks and conditions as the combat troops. The first elements of No. 1 Beach Squadron (No. 101 Beach Flight) for example, came ashore on Sword Beach (Queen Roger Sector), between Ouistreham and Lion-sur-Mer at 9.25 a.m. Although this was nearly three hours after the landings first commenced at 6.30 a.m., there was still strong enemy opposition with heavy shell and mortar fire as well as a myriad of small arms fire; the arrival of the Flight's commander, Squadron Leader J. N. Dobbin MC, a little later at 11.15 a.m. was equally hazardous when his landing craft was hit by enemy fire just below the water line, as it touched down on the beach. No. 2 RAF Beach Squadron was assigned to Juno beach (Mike and Nan sectors). One of the first members of the Squadron to land was Ted Inge who was the 'X' NCO responsible for setting up an explosives dump a mile or so inland from the landing beach. Ted had joined the Squadron from No. 3 Embarkation Unit on Merseyside and his account of coming ashore says much of the Squadron's experience:

> I was the only RAF type on my LSI. All the remainder were Canadian assault troops and the only person I knew was a Major who apparently had been at Anzio. He was to do for the army what I was to do for the RAF i.e. set up an explosives dump. The landing was not too bad. I had experienced worse on practice landings. When I got ashore the Canadians were still milling around in Courseulles. It was no place for us with just two S&W .380 (revolvers) between us. So I brewed up and the major left me to recce, only to return hours later pushing a cycle with the news that he was setting off for his site. I decided that I would stay the night in the grounds of some chateau and push on in the morning light. The rest of my squadron were to have a terrible time being kept off shore for three or four days. Priority being given to fighting troops. I have no idea what time I actually landed but I was scheduled for D Day plus two hours and have always thought that I must have been one of the first of RAF ground staff to land in France. However it would seem that in all probability that honour could go to the boys in No 1 Beach Squadron. We collected two Croix de Guerre and I was lucky in the draw for Oak Leaves.[137]

This squadron, like the others, made a significant contribution to the landings; from D-Day through to 6 September 1944 when it was disbanded, No. 2 RAF Beach Squadron handled 20,650 tons of RAF stores, 30,728 RAF personnel, and 8,644 RAF MT vehicles across its area of responsibility. No. 4 RAF Beach Squadron was assigned to Gold beach but arrived somewhat later as they had been assigned to be part of force 'L', the follow-up force on D-Day, but after a short wait offshore, most of the Squadron was ashore just after dark. The four beach squadrons were disbanded in August 1944, with many of their number absorbed into the RAF embarkation units that were operating in the Mulberry Harbour complex at Arromanches. The first of the eight ASPs (No. 401 ASP) landed at Arromanches on 19 June 1944, within a day of the British Mulberry Harbour outer anchorage first opening for the reception of vehicles and stores.[138] The remaining seven ASPs landed in France between 21 June 1944 and late October 1944.[139]

As the bridgehead in Normandy enlarged and became more secure, the Allies were able to develop what was known as the rear maintenance area (RMA), which provided a more permanent location for logistics, maintenance, and administrative facilities in support of the forthcoming breakout from Normandy. The British RMA was substantial and its layout resembled a spider's web, with numerous depots and bases radiating from the town of Bayeux, south-west of Arromanches. In many ways, the whole of the surrounding countryside resembled an enormous retail park. Within this boundary, the RAF had four main depot areas, three of which were in the vicinity of Creully with a fourth established later in the campaign just outside Caen.

The first phase of the Mulberry harbours provided a simple barrier (codenamed Gooseberry) using scuttled ships and concrete caissons as breakwaters. This was in place by 11 June. In due course, the Mulberries evolved into two sizeable port complexes with unloading platforms on the shoreward side of the breakwaters, connected to the land by floating roadways. A major setback occurred on 19 June when one of the greatest storms to hit the Normandy area for many years raged for three days. Despite the substantial damage, Mulberry 'B' at Arromanches was recovered and put back into action.

Mulberry 'A', in the American sector, was not so fortunate. Although it could have been repaired within about two weeks the expectation that Cherbourg was about to fall led to Mulberry 'A' being abandoned. The need for the RAF Beach Squadrons declined dramatically, as loading and unloading activity switched to Mulberry 'B'. The RAF muscle power for this was provided by personnel from the RAF EUs and, by 15 August 1944, all three of the RAF Beach Squadrons that had participated in Overlord had been officially disbanded, with many of their personnel being absorbed into the EUs.

Despite attempts by the Army and the use of a substantial volume of both strategic and tactical air power, the heavy concentration and fighting strength of the enemy in the area of Caen, effectively prevented a breakout within the planned timescale.

RAF Beach Squadron personnel unloading fuel jerrycans, Normandy, 1944. (*Crown Copyright—Air Historical Branch MoD*)

Inland from the beaches, Normandy, 1944. This shot shows the control which was necessary for road movements in the bridgehead area. Note the signpost with directions to various RAF supply dumps. (*Crown Copyright—Air Historical Branch MoD*)

The Mulberry harbour at Arromanches, 1944. (*Crown Copyright—Air Historical Branch MoD*)

This meant that the RAF could not acquire the urgently needed airfields so it was necessary to increase the number (above those planned) for the area of Ouistreham-Caen-Bayeux-Arromanches. The disembarkation and build-up of the RAF in the bridgehead was equally rapid and, by D+3, 2,615 vehicles and 11,202 men had been landed; by 20 June, a total of 3,200 vehicles and 13,000 men had been disembarked. As the landing grounds and airfields were established, it became possible to start moving the squadrons in 2TAF from their advance landing grounds in Southern England to Normandy; this started in earnest on D+4. The movement plans for this operation worked extremely well and enabled the squadrons to continue operating during the daytime. Each of the wings was divided into three parties consisting of a main, airlift and rear party. The main party travelled by sea and were established at the new site in Normandy before the wing was moved. While the main party was in transit (around ten to twelve days including packing-up, concentration, marshalling, ship-borne time, landing and onward transit), the wings and squadrons moved to one of three 'backer-up' stations in the UK and carried on operating from that location until the advance party in Normandy signalled to say that they were ready to receive the aircraft. The operational squadrons then flew to Normandy, accompanied by the airlift party in Dakota aircraft; the airlift requirement for a typical wing of four squadrons was approximately ten to twelve complete aircraft loads. A small rear party followed by sea after the airlift party had flown to Normandy.

Notwithstanding the high quality of airfield construction, an unexpected environmental factor soon emerged, which was to provide a challenge for engineering and logistics. The soil on which the airfields had been built contained a very high proportion of abrasive silica dust, the ingestion of which significantly reduced the life of engines, especially those types not fitted with air filters. As an interim measure, oil or sea water was pumped on to the main aircraft operating surfaces and warming-up times were reduced to a minimum. The dust problem, however, required all Typhoon aircraft to be returned to the UK to be fitted with dust deflectors, which overcame about 80 per cent of the problems. Notwithstanding this, sixty-six aircraft engines removed from aircraft were found to be beyond RAF repair as a direct result of dust damage. In time, it was found that the laying of large hessian strips on the airfields proved particularly effective.

By 20 June, 2TAF had six landing grounds in use and the build-up of equipment and supplies in Normandy had become massive; some 3,000 tons of fuel were in dumps and at certain airfields along with 2,500 gallons of oil and 500,000 rounds of ammunition. An earlier shortage of bombs had been addressed by the urgent despatch from the UK of five special ships each carrying 350 tons of bombs as well as thirty Dakota aircraft loads, each carrying two and a half tons of 500-lb bombs.

The supply of aviation and ground fuel for the RAF was a critical part of the logistic operation. A basic pipeline system for transporting some aviation fuel had already been established within parts of the UK, but the RAF did not participate in the development of PLUTO that supplied ground fuel from the UK to British forces in France.[140] This resulted from a planning requirement identified in the preparation for the invasion of North West Europe (Operation Overlord) in which a clear need emerged for an efficient and uninterrupted tri-service supply of MT fuel

Spitfires and Typhoons in Normandy, 1944. This shot shows the problems with dust clouds on the temporary airstrips. (*Crown Copyright—Air Historical Branch MoD*)

for units operating on the Continent after the landings. This pipeline, however, was of little operational value to the RAF as aviation fuel, with its more stringent quality requirements, it was transported across the English Channel by ocean tanker and then by a ship-to-shore pipeline at Port-en-Bessin near Arromanches and then via an on-shore pipeline to storage installations in the RMA.[141]

Following the capture of the first port at Cherbourg on 27 June by the Americans, subsequent action succeeded in the Allies securing the entire Cotentin Peninsula down as far as Lessay and then east through Saint-Lô, to the far end of the Sword beach area to the east.[142] The breakout from the Normandy bridgehead came in late July 1944 with the British advancing through Belgium, Holland, and then into Germany, with the ASPs keeping pace with the flying squadrons as they moved forward.

As experienced in the North African campaign, operations along extended lines of communication became particularly difficult, more so as the distance from the source of supply in the Normandy bridgehead increased.[143] Air resupply to the forward airfields became essential in order that the ASPs could be restocked as they advanced. The RAF Logistics organisation had passed its supreme test with flying colours as the official history records:

> The organisation for the Supply of the Royal Air Force with reserve aircraft, aviation petrol, bombs, ammunition, technical stores, etc., functioned well. At no time in the campaign were operational units prevented from carrying out sorties due to lack of the necessary supplies.[144]

The Breakout from Normandy and the Advance into Germany

The breakout from Normandy brought a new challenge in the form of meeting the needs of the advancing airfields and units over an increasingly lengthened line of communication. Initially, the advancing forces were resupplied by road and rail from the RMA but, as the lines extended, it soon became necessary to open supplementary ports through which to discharge men, machinery, equipment, and supplies. However, continued enemy opposition in the Channel ports area made this difficult; it soon became clear that the capture of the port at Antwerp was an urgent operational necessity, although it was not successfully captured until 4 September 1944.[145] The problem was that Antwerp is some eighty miles inland and connected to the North Sea by the River Scheldt; land on either side of the river remained occupied by the enemy with the German Sixteenth Army (bypassed by Montgomery on his advance) effectively controlling access to the port from the sea. It was not until the end of November 1944, following further operations to clear the enemy, that the port of Antwerp became usable by the Allies.[146] Notwithstanding this, the area around Antwerp was soon developed into an advanced logistical base, which

Refuelling a Spitfire by hand, Normandy, 1944. (*Crown Copyright—Air Historical Branch MoD*)

No. 401 ASP in the field, Normandy, 1944. (*R. C. Gorddard*)

enabled a sizeable component of the Normandy RMA (including much of the No. 85 (Base) Group stock) to move forward. This was particularly important for the air component as, up until this point, stores and supplies (especially POL, explosives, and large airframe spares) for the ASPs that were supporting the advancing RAF units in northern France, Belgium, and Holland were still being disembarked in Normandy and moved-on by road. The new logistical base at Antwerp enabled holdings of equipment and supplies to be accumulated in quantity much closer to the advancing RAF squadrons. With the eventual opening of the port, the need for road movement from Normandy rapidly diminished.

The first few months of 1945 were a period of building up reserve stocks to support the forthcoming spring campaign. A target date of 1 March had been set by RAF planners as the point by which the deployed RAF was required to be at its maximum strength in aircraft and crews, as well as having adequate supplies and reserves. The target was achieved by the beginning of the offensive and the move forward did not cause any undue problems for RAF Logistics, with existing bases being able to support operations up to the crossing of the Rhine. The problem from there on was how the advancing forces could be supported through an area where the railway infrastructure was completely wrecked and there was limited bridging over the River Rhine itself. There was still little hope of opening any further ports and Antwerp remained the main harbour until Bremen could be captured.

Inside of a No. 401 ASP stores tent, Normandy, 1944. (*R. C. Gorddard*)

Indeed, the Twenty-First Army Group decided that they would be looking towards Hamburg as their next advanced base. For its requirements, the RAF concentrated stocks of equipment and supplies in the area of Goch, a position on the main line of communication and as close to the River Rhine as was possible; by the time of the crossing of the river, the RAF had concentrated sufficient supplies to maintain any advance that Nos 83 and 84 Group might be required to undertake.[147]

The Conclusion of the War

Events moved swiftly during the closing months of the war in Europe. The German commanders in Italy surrendered on 29 April, in Berlin on 2 May, and the armies in north-west Germany on 4 May. The final unconditional surrender of all German forces was signed on 7 May 1945. The end of the war also brought about the release of many thousands of British, Dominion and Colonial prisoners-of-war; at least 150,000 were flown back to the UK, an operation coordinated by RAF Movements staff attached to Fighter Command. In the UK, RAF Movements Officers were based at the receiving airfields to ensure their arrival went smoothly; the moving on of these men was contributed to by detachments from the RAF MT Companies who transported them to reception camps and then to railheads for their final journey home. The campaign, from the landings in Normandy to the final German surrender, had taken just under a year and a key lesson for the RAF throughout this period was the vital importance of mobility and movements to the supply chain. In this respect, the capability of the ASPs was highly significant. Three other Beach Units were formed before the end of the war. No. 5 RAF Beach Unit was formed in November 1943 and took part in the assault landings in the South of France in August 1944 (Operation Dragoon).[148] A small RAF Beach Unit, No. 6, was formed in South East Asia late in 1944, participating in the landings in Malaya (Operation Zipper) in early September 1945.[149] The seventh and final RAF Beach Squadron was formed in Bombay on 1 August 1945 as an additional unit for South East Asia.

In early 1945, the attention of the RAF's manpower planners began to shift to the demand for tradesmen for the war against Japan. This was a significant commitment and it was estimated that it would be necessary to re-muster (with additional training where needed) some 96,000 airmen; over 30,000 would have to be drawn from surplus airmen in other trades. The first steps towards this came in May 1945 when a first batch of approximately 5,000 airmen was selected from specified trades including a requirement for 1,000 Equipment assistants. This need (and the associated Tiger Force) was cut short by the dropping of the atomic bombs on the Japanese cities of Hiroshima and Nagasaki in August 1945.

Logistics at the End of the Second World War

With the pre-war expansion scheme having transformed RAF Logistics, the war itself required RAF Logistics to sustain the employment of air power for some six years. It was also a time during which it needed great flexibility. Sustainment was an enormous challenge and required the development of substantial numbers of MUs and other units to receive, store, and issue the vast quantities of stores, supplies, POL, and munitions that were the life blood of air power. The supply chain required an extensive movements organisation; this too evolved from a relatively rudimentary capability in 1939 to a highly capable operation in 1945 by which time air transport had become a more significant component. The highly uncertain nature of war required considerable flexibility and RAF Logistics continually adjusted its operations to meet changing needs. The maintenance of mobility and achieving logistical reach were key and the many units that were formed to do this, such as the ASPs and the Beach Squadrons, were highly successful. The requirements for such units had diminished by the end of the war and it would be over fifty years before their significance would re-emerge in the post-Cold War period. The use of the atomic bombs in 1945, however, set the scene for a very different post-war period.

4

The Cold War Years: 1946–1989

Demobilisation, Downsizing, and Disarmament

The immediate post-war period brought a number of new challenges for RAF Logistics, but there were three in particular that demanded considerable time and effort up until the mid-1950s. Firstly, there was the pressing need to demobilise a substantial proportion of the RAF's personnel from wartime service; secondly, the disposal of vast amounts of surplus equipment and munitions; and thirdly, the disarmament of the defeated German Third Reich and Imperial Japan.

The release of RAF personnel was more of an administrative rather than a logistical challenge, with the issue of civilian clothing and the disposal of returned service apparel the preoccupation of equippers working within the five predominantly civilian-manned demobilisation centres. The task was a sizeable undertaking though; in the four-year period from 1944 to 1948, the service reduced by roughly two-thirds from a wartime peak of just over a million men and women to 315,000. While a large number of these people were based in the UK, many had to be repatriated from overseas; as of 1 September 1945, there were 783,639 men and women stationed at home and 291,448 overseas.[1]

Many who had been conscripted for wartime service welcomed a return to civilian life, but there were some for whom a career in the post-war Air Force was an attractive proposition. Among these was a significant number of former aircrew who, with the substantial run-down of the RAF's aircraft fleet, needed to look elsewhere for a service career; the Equipment Branch and Trade proved to be a popular choice. It was quite common to see pilot's 'wings' and other aircrew badges adorning many an equipper's uniform for a number of years after the war. One such officer, who transferred to the Equipment Branch in 1949 after being grounded due to high-tone deafness through wartime operational flying as a fighter pilot, was Flight Lieutenant (later Air Vice-Marshal) Harry Gill. He went on to have a highly successful career in the Equipment, then Supply Branches, culminating in his appointment as the Director General of Supply in 1976. On his retirement from the service in 1979, he loaned the Branch his RAF officer's sword, which is awarded annually to an officer of the Branch who has brought the most benefit to the RAF through the performance of their duties.

Air Commodore Harry Gill. (*Crown Copyright—Air Historical Branch MoD*)

Flying Officer (later Air Commodore) Charles Clarke also transferred to the Equipment Branch in 1945, having served as a bomb aimer with No. 619 Squadron on Lancasters. He was shot down in February 1944 and spent the rest of the war at Stalag Luft III in Poland during the period of *The Great Escape*. Both men were stalwart supporters of their new Branch and were regular supporters of the annual branch dinner. There were, of course, many like them, and the Branch and trade benefitted enormously from their backgrounds.

The more difficult issue perhaps, certainly in terms of sheer scale, was what to do with the vast quantities of equipment and supplies that had accumulated throughout the RAF's supply chain. The cessation of hostilities and the significant reduction in the size of the RAF required considerably less materiel to keep it functioning. Enormous stockpiles had been accumulated at the various depots, much of it having been delivered directly from manufacturers and not even issued to units by the time the war had ended. For the main equipment depots, much of the disposal activity was carried out in-house, with specific sites being set aside specifically for this purpose and items disposed of by auction. In May 1947 for example, No. 14 MU Carlisle was using its storage sub-site at Sandysike for disposals; the auctions held there during late 1947 and early 1948 alone required some 68,000 square feet of floor space for the auction 'lots', with the first four local sales realising £160,000, just over £3.5 million in today's money.[2] In addition to what was at the depots, large amounts of surplus equipment was held at RAF units and other temporary storage areas; to tackle this, nine equipment disposal depots (EDD) were formed, while six MUs were re-designated for disposal work between June 1945 and January 1946.[3]

Within Germany, three EDDs were formed (Nos 431–433), similar in function to their UK counterparts. The work of each varied and some tended to specialise in specific types of equipment. No. 433 EDD, for example, was formed at Stade in February 1947; it mainly handled MT vehicles, radios, and radar equipment. The depot had an extensive range of workshops in which vehicles and equipment destined for other users could be inspected, serviced, or repaired. The turnover was sizeable. In July 1947 alone, the depot handled some 100 tons of surplus radio equipment. Its MT disposal park had between 100 and 200 vehicles of various types on its forecourt at any one time. Every effort was made to put MT to good use, including by organisations other than the RAF. In July 1947, for example, the depot passed eighteen vehicles to the Belgian Air Force and sixteen to the Malcolm Clubs.[4] With their task complete, all of the EDDs in the UK and Germany were closed by the end of 1948.

There was also a requirement to dispose of surplus munitions. Two explosives disposal units (EDU) were formed between late 1945 and mid-1946 (Nos 275 and 277 MUs) and their work proved to be sizeable and hazardous. The manufacture and consumption of explosives throughout the war had been enormous; deliveries of weapons from Ministry of Production factories between 1939 and 1945 amounted to 3,801,900 tons. Having considered its future needs, the RAF estimated that it had some 500,000 tons of bombs that were surplus to requirement in the UK alone. There were three means of disposal available: explosives could be dismantled back at the manufacturers and components recycled if this could be done safely; they could be demolished or burnt at disposal sites; or they could be dumped at sea.[5] Given the sheer tonnage of these surplus explosives and the hazards involved, it was evident that deep-sea dumping was by far the most efficient and safest means of disposal.

The first of the EDUs to be formed was No. 275 MU in November 1945 at Cairnryan on the east bank of Loch Ryan, approximately five miles north of Stranraer in West Scotland. A military port had been established there during the Second World War as part of a scheme to provide reserve locations in the event that any of the ports on the east or south coast of the UK were put out of action through enemy attack. It soon became necessary to augment this unit and in late August 1946, HQ No. 42 Group, Maintenance Command announced that a detachment from the MU would be established at the port of Silloth on the Solway Firth in Cumbria, west of Carlisle. This detachment was relatively small, consisting of two Equipment Branch officers and approximately thirty airmen of various trades, but working under the overall supervision of No. 616 Water Transport Company of the Royal Army Service Corps; much of the loading of the coasters used for the deep-sea dumping, however, was carried out by personnel from the Ministry of War Transport or dockers from the Silloth port authority.[6]

The first Equipment officer in charge of the No. 275 MU detachment at Silloth was Flying Officer Ray Drean, who took up post on 30 August 1946. His personal papers contain a number of original documents from the period that illustrate the hazardous nature of the disposal work and just how makeshift many of the procedures were. Perhaps the most hazardous cargo to be handled was phosgene gas canisters. The first RAF load to be dumped at sea was carried out in mid-September 1946 from the coaster, RASCV *Sir Evelyn Wood*. In his report to the CO of No. 275 MU, the officer in charge recounted how two canisters unexpectedly floated to the surface when they were thrown overboard. Clearly, these had to be dealt with. When all ships involved had been moved upwind and personnel had donned gas masks, 'rifle fire was opened up on the bombs, from approx. 100 yards'. It took some effort to damage these bombs sufficiently; 'the first bomb received ten hits, and then quietly sank; the second required thirty hits before sinking'. Even before loading on the coasters, handling these bombs could prove highly problematical. While loading the coaster *Malplaquet* on 18 September 1946, one of the civilian workers drew the attention of the officer in charge to the fact that there was a leaking bomb in the hold of the ship. Having donned gas masks, along with two dockers, he descended into the hold; with the help of the loading crane, they extracted the culprit bomb to the quay side. The leaking nose cap was sealed by the liberal application of red lead paint and then a cloth pad soaked in caustic soda.[7]

The dumping operation from both Cairnryan and Silloth was sizeable, although the surviving records for the RAF are somewhat patchy. By the end of September 1946, 180,221 tons of Army and RAF explosives had been disposed of; by the end of 1949, the RAF had dumped some 137,767 tons. Work continued up to 1956 when the last of the surplus 4,000-lb, 8,000-lb, and 12,000-lb bombs had been disposed of; by that stage, at least a further 47,500 tons of explosives had been dumped since 1950. Although the RAF had withdrawn from Cairnryan and Silloth by 1957, the military port (under Army operation) continued until 1960.[8] With their hazardous but important task completed, both Nos 275 and 277 MUs had been disbanded by the early 1950s.

As the stocks of equipment began to reduce, there was a corresponding need to reduce the number of equipment and munitions depots. The first to close in any great number were the equipment parks (including mobile units) and the barrack and clothing depots; the last of these had ceased operation by the middle of June 1947. Within roughly the same timeframe, nearly half of the conventional explosives depots and related parks had also closed.

The third of the post-war challenges was the disarmament of the German and Japanese Armed Forces. For Germany, the way this would be handled was discussed towards the end of the war with the four Allies agreeing that they would each be responsible for disarmament work within their respective zones of occupation. The British approach was that the Royal Navy, the Army, and RAF would each be responsible for their equivalent service. Thus, the RAF was charged with dismantling the Luftwaffe, the German anti-aircraft forces, and Germany's military aviation industry.[9] As early as August 1944, the Air Ministry had authorised the formation of an Air Disarmament HQ, initially within HQ 2TAF, then transferring to HQ British Air Forces of Occupation (BAFO) Germany in July 1945. From the outset, the Equipment Branch and Trade was heavily involved. Indeed, out of the

130 senior RAF officers filling key appointments in the disarmament organisation, a quarter of these were equippers.[10]

The task itself, codenamed Operation Eclipse, fell to three of the four groups within 2TAF: No. 2 Group was responsible for the Westphalia and Rhine provinces; No. 83 Group for Schleswig Holstein and Denmark; and No. 84 Group for Hanover Province and Berlin. The HQ element directly supervised activity in Belgium, Holland, Denmark, and Norway.[11] Within the groups, the practical task of searching for, identifying, and reporting enemy war materiel rested with dedicated Air Disarmament Wings.[12] While much of the captured materiel was destroyed (especially munitions), every opportunity was taken, not just to recycle, but to examine items of particular technical interest. The disposal of the most important materiel was controlled by the Air Intelligence Branch of HQ SHAEF (Air) with its Technical Intelligence 2 section headed-up by an Equipment Branch wing commander. The amount of equipment subject to such detailed study was considerable; during the period December 1944 to December 1946, 2,582 tons were despatched from Germany. In many cases, only samples were returned to the UK for provisional analysis and this led to the formation of a German Air Force equipment centre within No. 40 Group, Maintenance Command (originally at Chessington, then Stanmore Park) to handle this materiel on arrival in the UK.[13]

In all of this, there was a key role for the equipment organisation and its expertise in stock accounting, storage, and movements was much in demand. Initially, much of the captured materiel was accumulated on the Continent in what were known as Luftwaffe materiel concentration depots, usually located on the sites of former enemy equipment depots. Of the many equippers who found themselves working within this environment was Sergeant Robert Stamp, who joined No. 8502 Air

War-surplus vehicles awaiting disposal, RAF Altona, Germany, 1949. (*B. J. Sullivan*)

Disarmament Wing at Wülfrath within the North Rhineland area in May–June 1945. Of his many reminiscences, Robert recalled that much of his time was spent in accumulating vast quantities of scrap aluminium and handing it over to the Allied Control Commission who were then selling much of it back to German manufacturers for the more peaceful purpose of producing domestic items such as cooking pans and utensils.[14] The accounting and transportation need grew to such a level that air disarmament disposal parks (ADDP) had to be formed within three RAF Groups. These were based at: No. 437 at Massen for No. 2 Group; No. 440 at Bergedorf for No. 83 Group; and No. 438 at Delmenhorst for No. 84 Group. Each of these parks, commanded by an Equipment Branch wing commander, accumulated enemy equipment and ensured it was correctly identified before disposing of it to the UK, to other RAF users in Germany, or to other Allied nations.[15] It was not just the military who benefited from this wholesale recycling. Operation Medico, for example, was the shipment of some 1,029 tons of ex-Luftwaffe technical equipment to the British Government sponsored College of Aeronautics at Cranfield in the UK.[16] On completion of the disposal operation in December 1946, 4,810 aircraft and 12,800 spare engines had been captured, while 220,000 tons of bombs and munitions had been disposed of, along with 195,000,000 rounds of ammunition.[17]

A similar task faced the Allies in the Far East, although archival records are not as detailed from the logistics perspective. The unconditional surrender of Japan precluded the need for an invasion of the Japanese homeland; attention therefore turned to planning for occupation. The situation facing the Allies, though, was quite different from that experienced in Germany. Although the US Army Air Force had managed to attack targets in Japan from February 1945 onwards, destroying some thirty-two square miles of urban areas, there was nowhere near the same level of widespread destruction as in Germany.[18] On the day of surrender, the Japanese Emperor was still on the throne and his government and military commanders were still in place. Moreover, there were also sizeable numbers of Japanese Imperial forces, amounting to just under seven million, with just over two and a half million within Japan itself. The greater part of the country was occupied by American forces who arrived on 3 September 1945, while the British Commonwealth's contribution (known as the British Commonwealth Occupation Force (BCOF)) arrived six months later, on 5 March 1946, and was allocated the south west end of the island of Honshu, including the smaller island of Shikoku; this was an area of approximately 20,000 square miles and contained about 10 to 15 million people of the country's total population of around 80 million.[19] The RAF's contribution to the British Commonwealth Air Forces in Japan (BCAIR) was found by two Spitfire squadrons, Nos 11 and 17, both of which were stationed at Miho and No. 1315 communications flight operating from Iwakuni, a location that also became BCOF's airport of entry to Japan.

For arrivals by sea, the port at Kure was utilised with the RAF's 106 embarkation unit formed here on 1 March 1946 to handle the arrival of British forces into the BCOF area. One of the British units to arrive in Japan was No. 91 ASP, which had embarked on the SS *Esperance Bay* at Singapore at the beginning of March 1946, arriving at Kure ten days later. The park established itself at the Teijin Seiki factory, Iwakuni, thirty-two miles from Hiroshima. Although their role was to provide support for the RAF flying units at Miho and Iwakuni, the park also prepared domestic and working accommodation for the RAF element of BCOF when it arrived in the country. The park was the last RAF unit to be closed down in Japan, on 31 March 1948.[20]

As with Germany, RAF Equippers played a significant part in the occupation and disarmament, although a lack of surviving archival sources makes it hard to outline their role in any detail. What is clear is that BCOF was faced with a sizeable disposal challenge as a disposal section, manned by some 230 personnel posts, was set up within HQ BCOF in July 1946; by the end of that month, search teams had already identified 300 locations of military interest such as bases, depots, installations, and store facilities. The immediate priority was seeking out the stocks of lethal weapons, ammunition, and explosives, vast quantities of which had been built up in anticipation of an Allied invasion; much of it had been hidden in caves and underground chambers. In the BCOF area alone, some 225,000 tons of explosives, ammunition, bombs, and mines were located. For this, dumping at sea proved to be the most practical and safest means of disposal and, by 31 July 1946, 20,000 tons had been disposed offshore. The Japanese had also accumulated substantial quantities of toxic chemical munitions of which there were some 17,000 tons located on seven sites. Deep sea dumping was by far the safest method for disposing of these highly hazardous munitions, the bulk of which was loaded on two old American landing ship tank vessels and scuttled in deep water south east of Shikoku island.[21]

Modernising RAF Logistics: The Binbrook Study

Despite the cutting-edge technology of nuclear weaponry in the 1950s, the RAF's organisation for logistics on its units remained very much as it had been during the war years without the technical sophistication of twenty-first century supply chain operations; the movement of equipment required sheer physical effort without the convenience of mechanical handling aids, such as fork lift trucks or automated conveyor belts; stock control required pen and paper, along with a plethora of clerks, an environment devoid of computerised stock control systems, or even electronic calculators. Prior to the Second World War, the master equipment account (known as the main stock ledger) was kept by the station accountant officer; the idea was to reduce the opportunity for fraud by separating responsibility for keeping the books from physical stocks of equipment, which were the responsibility of the SEO. The main stock ledger was considered as the formal account and required by statute. The Equipment Section maintained what were known as 'tally cards'; these served as the Equipment officer's record of his stock, as well as for the purposes of provisioning. As part of the review of RAF administration that took place in 1939, the examining committee observed that this equipment accounting practice was not just a duplication of stock records, but also working practices; issue and receipt vouchers for equipment had to be actioned to both the main stock ledger and the tally cards. As a result of this review, the main stock ledger was transferred back to the Equipment officer as a single stock record, but was to be kept separate from the physical stock holding and the stores staff handling receipts and issues.[22]

On most RAF station Equipment sections, the main stock ledger became the responsibility of what was known as the Equipment Provisioning and Accounting Section (EPAS), which was usually commanded by an experienced flight lieutenant of the Equipment Branch. The section consisted of perhaps a dozen or more desks, manned by clerks (equipment accounting), each of whom had a stack of huge brass-bound loose-leaf ledgers for the range of equipment for which they were responsible, and each individual reference number had its own page. Every one of these pages had to have an 'establishment' figure on it, set by the officer-in-charge of EPAS every three months. The accounting clerks had to compare the establishment figure with the balance in stock and if necessary, raise a stock demand to top-up the station's holdings; each of these demands, often hundreds of them every day, had to be signed by an officer and much of this fell to the junior Equipment officer. It was not practicable to check each demand thoroughly and it was largely a matter of knowing from the handwriting whether the clerk who had prepared it was reliable or not, thus there were inevitably errors. The demands then went off by post, to the appropriate master provisioning office, and it was not unusual for some demands to get lost in this paper-based process. This process was known generically as primary accounting.

For items held forward of the Equipment Section, hand-written inventories were maintained by the secondary accounting clerks who kept a duplicate record of each inventory in their own ledgers. An individual needing permanent use of a small tool or whatever, would sign for it on a loan card from his squadron or flight inventory holder. The inventory, hand-written on sheets of pre-printed paper and 'bound' with file-tags inside a green outer folder, listed the class 'A' and 'B' stores used by that squadron and was subject to annual independent checks. The inventory record was duplicated within EPAS in massive 'articles in use' ledgers, each comprising perhaps 250 individual handwritten sheets often several inches thick.

In the warehousing areas or stockholding groups as they were known, a stock record in the form of bin cards was maintained and these recorded not only how much stock was on hand but also where it was located. These cards were maintained by the storemen, who were not always as meticulous as the EPAS clerks and their records were often barely legible and not always accurate. In theory, bin stock cards and the EPAS master record were never supposed to meet but often the only way of sorting out discrepancies was to take the bin cards into EPAS and compare the two. In this way, taken with his equally physically large stock records, the SEO theoretically had visibility of all the class 'A' and 'B' (further accountable) stores on any given RAF station.

EPAS at RAF St Eval, Cornwall, 1955. (*Crown Copyright—Air Historical Branch MoD*)

In these early days before computers, stock control was a cumbersome process, further delayed by a slow delivery chain (mainly rail and sea transport, rather than road or air) with many opportunities for loss or error. One such opportunity, often remembered with amusement by many ex-RAF equippers and suppliers, is the denomination of quantity (DofQ) category. All items in the inventory had a DofQ rating. Often, this was 'each' for single items, but a number of items were supplied in quantities such as by weight, length, sets, or numerical batches. Air Commodore Mike Allisstone recalls an incident when he was in charge of barrack stores at RAF Khormaksar, when the *Padre* came to see him seeking help in refurbishing the station church. While the *Padre* understood some of the finer points of equipment supply, he did not understand how to measure the chancel for new carpeting. Mike went along to help, and they decided that 20 yards of blue Wilton carpet would be required and the necessary demand was despatched to the UK. Several months later, twenty rolls (rather than yards) of this carpet arrived in barrack stores. As it would have been highly uneconomical to send the surplus back, first the station commander's residence and very soon afterwards every senior officer's married quarters on the station became resplendent with beautiful blue Wilton carpet.

As computerised stock control was introduced and developed, better decisions could be made on procuring and allocating stock, and the service-wide inventory could be managed much more accurately and economically. It became much less labour-intensive to monitor consumption, set establishments, provision stock, meet the equipment accounting requirements, and produce scales of equipment needed for particular tasks. The drudgery was eventually removed and stock visibility was greatly improved. Such was life for the equippers in the late 1940s and throughout the 1950s.

Although little could be done to modernise the administrative process until the advent of automatic data processing in the early 1960s, work was started just after the war to examine the operational process of logistics on RAF stations. In 1946, the first of a series of studies that continued over the next ten years was undertaken into the organisation and structure of RAF units. Throughout the war years, flying units in particular had grown more complex and station commanders had become over-involved in the much lower-level detail of their unit's operation. These organisational studies were conducted at the Bomber Command stations of Tuddenham in Suffolk and Binbrook in Lincolnshire. It was the work at Binbrook, however, that led to a fundamental change in station organisation throughout the RAF, with the introduction of the three 'wing' structure of technical, administrative, and operations, each commanded by a wing commander and directly responsible to the station commander for their area of expertise. The studies also examined more specific areas of unit organisation and in January 1956, the Equipment Section at RAF Binbrook was so targeted; that study brought about fundamental and widespread change for the organisation of RAF Logistics.[23]

At the start of the study, using work study techniques, the examining team went to great lengths to ensure that the section being examined was operating strictly in accordance with the correct accounting procedures and that its turnover of supplies represented normal stock replenishment that was not skewed by any abnormally high accumulations of stock. The final report reflected three key themes: organisation, physical layout, and supply activity. In terms of organisation, the report confirmed that the existing organisation of Equipment Sections, based on what they saw at Binbrook, was generally fit for purpose with just a minor reduction in overall numbers of personnel.[24] Despite the fact that the Technical Wing on the unit was its prime customer, the Equipment Section was located within the Administrative Wing, although the SEO did have the right of direct access to the station commander and could by-pass the OC Administrative Wing *in extremis*. At the heart of this unusual arrangement was a somewhat adversarial relationship between the technical and equipment disciplines. The engineers, who were often quite keen to shift any blame for technical shortcomings onto a lack of spares when possible, were keen to have the equippers under direct command so that they could (and perhaps improperly) directly influence spares' levels and stock holdings.[25] The equippers felt that this could compromise their professional integrity and resisted the idea tooth and nail.

It was the physical layout of Equipment Sections that benefitted the most from the work study methodology, especially in terms of how and where work was carried out and the physical flow of activity. The existing main store building (some 12,000 square feet) was usually a conglomeration of small storage rooms and offices separated by relatively narrow corridors and built to a 1930s standard design. This included an aerofoil store, originally designed for small biplane components, which was fronted by massive reinforced steel doors that were virtually useless for anything else. At the heart of the building was a tiny open courtyard, adjacent to which were the offices of the senior staff. This configuration resulted in nearly 20 per cent of the building not being directly used. Moreover, the receipt and despatch (R&D) section and its goods inward area was separated from the storage areas by corridors, resulting in equipment having to be manually manoeuvred during the issues and receipts process from one side of the building to the other, often through administrative areas. The recommendations regarding the ergonomics of the Equipment Section were well ahead of their time and sought logically to match the flow of work with the physical layout of the building. In essence, it recommended that the ideal main stores building should be divided into two parts with the main storage area (clothing, technical, and barrack groups) merged into one largely open plan environment, free of corridors and dividing walls, with the R&D section at one end; this allowed equipment to flow into and out of the storage area without passing through any of the administrative areas. The other part of the building was seen as a two-tier structure of offices containing the squadron management, EPAS, and customer service counters for clothing and barrack issues. The layout of the expansion scheme and wartime-constructed stores buildings did not readily lend itself to such a complete redesign but, wherever possible, the general principles were gradually incorporated throughout the RAF. In later years, these new principles were factored into new-build facilities. The report also led to two other key changes in logistics practice: the wider adoption of temperature allowance charts enabling the more accurate measurement of bulk fuel volume, taking into account the expansion and contraction of liquids due to temperature variation, and the introduction of a forward delivery service that enabled demanded equipment to be delivered directly from centrally-held stocks to consumers as and when it was required.[26]

The outcome of the Binbrook study led to a new and standardised organisational structure for Equipment Sections. The EPAS Section eventually became the supply control and accounting flight, with specialist stockholding groups in the form of: technical supply flight; domestic supply flight; and, on some units, an electronic supply flight. The new structure was widely known as the Binbrook model and remained an organisational feature of RAF Equipment/Supply Squadrons until the late 1990s. The introduction to service of new aircraft and the phasing out of old, also changed the physical storage requirement. On a number of units, the former wartime-built Equipment Sections and their similar vintage storage media, no longer met the needs of the types and volumes of equipment that had to be held. Many an SEO was faced with the requirement to find room for extra stock in his already 'bulging' technical supply flight or to withdraw his overflow stockholdings from one of the aircraft hangars so that the unit engineers could use the space. On some units, larger scale developments in unit infrastructure saw the need to relocate an Equipment Section/Supply Squadron and the often very welcome opportunity of a new-build complex (courtesy of the Ministry of Works up until 1970 when much of the estate management function was taken on by the Property Service Agency).

As with RAF stations in general, Equipment Sections and Supply Squadrons were inspected on an annual basis as part of their respective AOC's inspection regime. These were usually preceded by a pre-AOC's inspection of the various professional disciplines on units. Logistics was inevitably examined in detail by a small team from the respective Command HQ. These inspections were always thorough, ranging from a check of orders and procedures, a check of stock and invariably a review of how effectively repairable items were being managed. The results formed part of a pre-inspection briefing pack for the AOC when he visited the unit. These were always a significant day in the life of RAF units, invariably preceded by much cleaning and painting to ensure the best possible impression was presented. The day itself consisted of a formal parade, usually followed by the AOC visiting as many squadrons and flights as could be squeezed into the day. By the 1990s, formal parades were gradually phased out of the inspection process and the previous two-part system became known as the annual formal inspection. With the introduction of BS5750-based quality standards in 1994, quality inspections led by Group HQs and tri-service quality inspections for locations such as Cyprus and the Falklands became commonplace.

An Iron Curtain Descends

Although Britain and her allies had been united with the Soviet Union in waging war against a common enemy, there was a surprising amount of mistrust between them. This led to a very fragile relationship and one that was further complicated by the balance of power, in that the United States had developed, and used, the atomic bomb. Although the Soviets had massive conventional forces, Stalin was particularly conscious of America's nuclear advantage and this factor was a major influence with the Soviets' pre-occupation with their perceived vulnerability. As far as the geographical boundaries of post-war Germany were concerned, the former allies of Britain, America, France, and the Soviet Union divided Germany, and Berlin itself, into four zones. Each of the nations controlled one zone and one sector of Berlin. This placed the former Third Reich capital in an odd position as virtually an 'island' in the Soviet zone of Germany that was accessed from the west by three air corridors, the military railway trains, and controlled road access. There were significant differences too in how Britain, America, and France on the one hand, and the Soviet Union on the other, saw Germany's re-emergence in the new world order. The west believed that a new and strong Germany would enable democracy to flourish after the years of Nazi dictatorship. They also believed that

Europe needed a relatively robust Germany so that their economies would prosper. To enable their administration to work more effectively, the British, Americans, and French amalgamated their zones into one unit and introduced a new currency, the Deutschmark. The Soviet Union saw things quite differently and wanted to keep Germany as weak as possible to ensure that they could never again attack the Soviets. They also saw Germany as an additional resource and took whatever they needed for their own use from their zones. Their priority was quite clearly the rebuilding of the Soviet Union at Germany's expense.

This difference in approach was particularly evident in the subsequent economic growth and Stalin grew particularly concerned that the German inhabitants of the Soviet-controlled sectors could see the developing prosperity in the other zones. It was particularly pronounced in Berlin where the relative prosperity of the British, American, and French zones was most evident. In Stalin's eyes, the Allied presence in Berlin was a major cause for concern; quite simply, he needed to gain total control of the city. The balance of power was not in his favour; however, there was a factor that Stalin was quick to exploit. Although the air corridors into Berlin had been defined in a written agreement, rights of access by surface means (road, rail, and water) had not been included. Stalin capitalised on this omission and in June 1948, he closed all rail links, canals, and roads that entered West Berlin through the Soviet sector. This effectively cut off the Allied surface supply routes to the city so the only way to resupply their sectors was by air. Thus began a stand-off that was to last some eleven months, and lead to the Berlin Airlift, until the Soviets finally lifted the blockade in May 1949; the RAF's logistical involvement in this operation is covered in more detail in Chapter Seven. From a broader viewpoint, this time was described by Winston Churchill in a speech at Westminster College, Fulton, Missouri in March 1946, when he commented that 'from Stettin in the Baltic to Trieste in the Adriatic, an Iron Curtain has descended across the Continent'.[27] The Cold War had begun.

North Atlantic Treaty Organisation

It was against this backdrop that the North Atlantic Treaty Organisation (NATO) was formed in 1948. In joining the new alliance, the UK agreed to accept the logistical implications of the defensive strategy that was set out by NATO's Military Committee (MC) under its directive MC14/1 in December 1952.[28] The central tenet of this approach was the belief that the only means of deterring the Warsaw Pact from attacking the West was to maintain a posture of massive nuclear retaliation in the event of any incursion into NATO territory. This was generally known as the 'tripwire' response, a philosophy that was largely based on the assumption that there would be a brief conventional war, leading to a substantial nuclear exchange, and was formally incorporated within MC 14/2 in May 1957.[29] Its impact on the RAF's supply chain was minimal when compared with Second World War operations as it did not require any significant stocks of war consumables such as spares, fuel, and munitions; on the whole, these would be held well forward on operational units, with any other reserves being moved forward quickly after the outbreak of hostilities.[30]

By January 1968, this posture had changed radically to one of 'flexible' response whereby any Warsaw Pact aggression would be matched by a corresponding level of force, without the rapid escalation to nuclear exchange. From a logistical perspective, this changed the commitment significantly and required, for example, considerably more conventional weapons and greater stocks of consumables to support a more protracted period of conventional warfare. There was, of course, a financial impact to this change in that supporting potentially lengthier operations would be considerably more expensive. The alliance went on to agree stockpile planning guidance that required member states, initially, to maintain stocks for up to thirty days of conventional fighting; thereafter, nations were expected to build up sustaining stocks, theoretically sufficient to maintain the front line in battle until continuous resupply from industrial production could be established.

In the early days of NATO, overall strategy was focussed on countering a Soviet attack in the central region of Europe (Germany), with an assumption that the alliance's northern and southern flanks were unlikely to be attacked in any force.[31] The requirement to defend these was revised in 1960 when NATO formed the Allied Command Europe (ACE) Mobile Force, with air and land components (AMF (A) and AMF (L)) that could be despatched at short notice to any part of ACE, but particularly its flanks; the UK's contribution to this was found from within the UK Mobile Force (UKMF). The adoption of this strategy demanded a much wider view of planning, a task which occupied much of the time of the logistics staffs within the MOD and at HQ Air Support Command (HQ ASC) at Upavon in the early 1970s.

One of the logistics officers involved in this work was Squadron Leader (later Group Captain) David Packman, who arrived at the HQ in August 1970. He recalled that these were still early days for the new philosophy and the UK-based RAF was still in the process of determining what it would need if deployed to NATO's flanks, from Norway and Denmark in the north to Greece and Turkey in the south. There was also a long-overdue realisation within the RAF that, if a war was to be fought successfully, it would be necessary to work closely with the Army so this relationship was strengthened by establishing good working relations with UK Land Forces at Wilton. David's role, jointly with the air and engineering staffs at Upavon, was to work out what ground equipment, fuel and administrative facilities would be required to sustain elements of the RAF when deployed to NATO's flanks and to establish the extent to which host nations on the NATO flanks could assist with this. This involved many overseas visits, the outcome of which, in broad terms, was that there would be relatively little difficulty in waging war in the north but that, if the RAF was to give a good account of itself in Turkey and Greece, a great deal of pre-positioning of equipment would be needed as little was likely to be forthcoming in the way of host nation support. David highlighted how the implications of the change in NATO's strategy to flexible response was not as well understood at working level within the RAF as it might have been. Certainly, other than for the harrier and support helicopter (SH) forces, the concept of operating away from fixed RAF bases came as something of a culture shock to many RAF people. This being the case, the Logistics planners, backed wholeheartedly by the senior air staff officer and air officers engineering and administration, set up a two-day seminar for all officers at the HQ during which the subject of NATO flank operations was addressed.

A convenient venue for the seminar was found at the Joint Warfare Establishment, which was close to Upavon at RAF Old Sarum on the northern outskirts of Salisbury. Apparently, the permanent staffs here were taken aback that the RAF should be taking life so seriously. Of particular significance was the fact that the seminar was also attended by staff officers from HQ UKLF and from HQ Maintenance Command at Andover. At the same time, as the new philosophy was being developed, the concept of NATO-wide paper-based exercises, such as Wintex, was coming to the fore. A large amount of effort went into deciding how the RAF as a whole would be involved and what roles the AMF (A) and (L) and UKMF (Air) would play. Planners were also required to devise realistic exercise incidents that would test preparedness for war.[32]

The V-Force

The British Government's commitment to building nuclear weapons was made quite clear in October 1945 by a group of senior ministers known as the Gen 75 Committee; this gave rise to the requirement for a very different type of aircraft that could carry such a bomb and led to the introduction of three new-generation jet aircraft, collectively known as the V-Force.[33] The first to enter service was the Vickers Valiant B.1 in February 1955, which remained with Bomber Command until 1965 when it was removed from service due to stress-induced metal fatigue in the aircraft's main wing spars. The second of the trio to enter operational service was the Avro Vulcan B.1 in May 1956 and this remained in service in later marks until December 1982, having seen active service in the Falklands conflict.

The third of the V bomber aircraft was the Handley Page Victor B.1 that entered service in November 1957; its V-Force role was shorter-lived than the Valiant and Vulcan but, from 1965 the Victor was re-roled as an airborne tanker, a role in which it proved highly successful. It was the V-Force that was initially charged with maintaining Britain's strategic nuclear deterrent until this role was taken up by the Royal Navy's submarine launched the Polaris missile in 1969. The main British nuclear arsenal throughout this period included the Blue Danube free-fall atomic bomb (1953–1962), the Yellow Sun thermo-nuclear weapon (1959–1966), the first British tactical nuclear weapon Red Beard (1962–1969), the Blue Steel stand-off

Avro Vulcans. (*Crown Copyright—Air Historical Branch MoD*)

missile (1963–1970) and, finally, the last of these weapons to remain in RAF service, the tactical nuclear weapon WE.177 (1966–1998).[34]

V-Force operations brought the equippers into very close contact with the cutting edge of the nuclear deterrent and saw the Equipment Branch entrusted with the command of the two entirely Service-manned nuclear weapons depots within Maintenance Command (Nos 92 and 94 MUs). The site at No. 94 MU Barnham had been developed from a Second World War ammunition depot near Thetford in Norfolk. The unit was commanded by a wing commander of the Equipment Branch, with a squadron leader (Equipment) as his second-in-command, an armaments squadron leader with an electrical engineering deputy and a MT officer, and a RAF Police flight lieutenant with several flying officer and warrant officer deputies. There was also a Secretarial Branch pilot officer who acted as adjutant. In addition, there were a number of flying officer/flight lieutenant equippers whose duties included stock control officer, officer in charge of the storage site, the area fuels officer, and the unit Equipment officer, while two or three others acted as convoy commanders when nuclear weapons were moved by road. In total, there were approximately 100 NCOs and airmen.

Flying Officer (later Air Commodore) Mike Allisstone, an Equipment Branch officer who had graduated from Cranwell in 1954, completed the conventional explosives specialist course at RAF Calshot in 1959, before being posted to RAF Barnham. Prior to arriving at the unit, he had also completed nuclear familiarisation training at RAF Wittering so that he had a basic understanding of what the weapons looked like, how they worked and the risks of fire, explosion, and the various radioactive hazards that could ensue in the event of an accident while in storage or in transit. Mike Allisstone was posted initially as a convoy commander, which involved sitting for hours at a time in a modified Morris J2 van with local radio communications, in charge of several six-wheeled Leyland Hippo load-carriers and a number of RAF Police motor-cyclists, plus a specially-designed fire and technical safety vehicle with an RAF armaments specialist aboard. Much of their work was carried out between Barnham and various royal ordnance factories, especially Burghfield near Reading, the Atomic Weapons Research Establishment at Aldermaston, and various other suppliers and manufacturers of weapon components. Deliveries took them out from Barnham to the Special Storage Areas (SSA) at the more southerly V-Force stations such as Honington, Wittering, and Cottesmore.

Barnham's sister depot, No. 92 MU at RAF Faldingworth, near Lincoln, looked after the Bomber Command units in the north. Most stocks of RAF nuclear weapons were held forward in the special storage areas and were rotated through the depots for periodic servicing; depot stocks were apparently intended mainly for second strike sorties. In the early 1960s, Barnham held stocks of the nominal 10,000-lb Blue Danube free-fall atomic bomb; these were gradually superseded by the physically much smaller nominal 2,000-lb Red Beard fission weapon. Both of these bombs had spherical implosion main charges in the centre section of the weapon, each sphere being made up of a number of shaped explosive lenses that fitted tightly together to form a large ball. These shaped charges were detonated simultaneously from the periphery of the sphere and were designed to focus their shockwaves inwards towards its hollow centre, into which a small spherical core of uranium U235 was inserted shortly before take-off, thus radioactively arming the weapon. The implosion compressed the uranium core into a dense super-critical mass, which resulted in a chain reaction, or 'fission', the instant release of a huge amount of heat and other radiation, and hence the requisite nuclear explosion. The U235 cores were removable and stored separately in individual below-ground, double-combination safes to which no one person had sole access. Each core was kept inside a drum lined with heavy metal, just about portable (always with an escort), and special precautions were taken not to allow one core to come within a certain distance of another, again to avoid any risk of a nuclear chain reaction. The cores were normally transported by road, in separate convoys from the weapons, which meant that any hijackers would not get away with a completely viable nuclear bomb. The cores were in substantial shock-proof containers that were fixed to the floor of the load-carrying vehicle and designed to survive the most severe accident imaginable. If convoys had explosive components or radioactive cores aboard and thunderstorms threatened, they were required to find the nearest parking area and to pull in until the squall had passed. This was not always easy, as there were often three Hippos, sandwiched between the two J2s and the safety van, plus four police motorcycles, and most lay-bys were too small. On one occasion, recalled Air Commodore Allisstone, a storm beat them to it:

> There was increasing lightning and a lot of noise, and then one exceptionally vivid flash hit a lamp-post right alongside one of the still-mobile Hippos just ahead of

me, followed immediately by the biggest thunderclap I have ever encountered. The load-carrier swerved into the middle of the road and stopped almost dead in its tracks and so did the rest of the convoy, narrowly avoiding a shunt in the process. As the RAF Police closed the carriage-ways in both directions, I leapt out of my J2 and went round to the Hippo where the driver was sitting transfixed and completely dumb-struck. We lifted him out of the cab, stiff as a board and still in the sitting position, and we laid him as gently as we could on the floor of my van. We then put a relief driver in his place and got the convoy moving again as quickly as possible. It eventually transpired that our victim, having seen the flash and heard the enormous explosion just to his rear, was convinced that the load he was carrying had blown up and that he was dead! It took him several days to recover.[3]

From a wider logistic perspective, there were two aspects of V-Force operations that led to new procedures and responsibilities. The first came about largely as a result of the quick reaction alert concept introduced in February 1962 that required one aircraft from each V-Force squadron to be on constant armed standby and capable of taking off within four minutes.[36] Spares availability to keep these aircraft serviceable was vital and the Logistics organisation adopted a completely new approach to the initial provisioning of spares for the V-Force, purchasing some two and a half times as much equipment as they normally did for the introduction to service of a new aircraft type.[37] Despite this generous approach to provisioning, there were still a number of items that, due to their high value or long manufacturing lead-times, remained in short supply. This required careful management and each of the Equipment Sections on the RAF's V-Force stations had a small section (cell) that managed specific high priority spares demands, the lack of which was grounding a V-bomber. The system, Valiant/Victor/Vulcan on Ground (VOG) was a variation of the existing highest priority AOG designation and was closely managed by a dedicated VOG cell, which worked in close co-operation with the unit's Engineering Operations section. Any activity connected with the VOG requirement was afforded top priority and the outer packaging of such spares was always clearly marked so that they did not languish in the supply chain. After the demise of the V-Force, the concept remained a key part of logistic operations and the priority cell (as it later became known) remained a feature of most flying station Equipment Sections/Supply Squadrons.

The second aspect of V-Force operations requiring a logistics input was mobility. In the early years of the force, the RAF relied on physical dispersal of aircraft to afford protection from enemy attack. Indeed, in addition to the V-Force main operating bases, there were thirty-six dispersal airfields in the late 1950s, although by 1962 this had reduced to twenty-six. The force was kept at the height of operational readiness and regular exercises formed a key part of this: Exercise Mick practised alert and arming procedures without actually dispersing the aircraft; Exercise Kinsman was a squadron dispersal exercise; Exercise May Flight tested all aspects of Bomber Command's dispersal and readiness plans; and the interestingly named

Avro Vulcan on detachment to RAF Wyton, 1982. (*Author's collection*)

Exercise Micky Finn was a no-notice dispersal that could be called at any time, day or night.[39] This all required very careful coordination in terms of support, calling for engineering operations to work closely with the Equipment Squadron.

To provide movements support, most of the V-Force units were established with a Mobility Supply Flight (MSF). These were responsible for supporting the station's aircraft when they deployed to bases outside the UK and providing unit level specialist support for surface and air movements and the liaison with specialist movements organisations such as the Mobile Air Movements Squadrons. The MSFs also maintained a fly away pack (FAP), an assortment of sturdy storage containers, which a pre-agreed range of critical and high turnover spares were kept, alongside of other bulkier items such as wheels, tyres and avionic items in their own special-to-contents containers—all ready to go almost anywhere at the drop of a hat. The content of FAPs was always tightly controlled and the use of any item, when not deployed, usually required the express permission of the SEO.

The RAF in Germany

Following victory in Europe in May 1945, British forces became one of the occupying powers, an arrangement that was formalised for the RAF by the formation of the British Air Force of Occupation (BAFO) on 15 July 1945, with its HQ at Bad Eilsen.

Its initial strength was sixty-eight squadrons within twenty wings and four groups spread across twenty operational airfields in Germany and the low-countries. Its task was support to the British Army of the Rhine and air policing of the British zone of occupation. In line with the rapid reduction in the RAF's size, BAFO's front line strength of thirty-four squadrons at the end of 1945 was dramatically reduced to only ten by 1947. By the beginning of 1951, it had become clear that there was no longer any need for a force of occupation and BAFO reverted to the wartime title of 2TAF, with its HQ relocating to Rheindahlen.

By the early 1950s, the Cold War had really started to deepen. Growing tension between the east and the west saw the start of an extensive programme of NATO-funded airfield construction. In addition to the reuse of a number of former Luftwaffe airfields, such as Gütersloh, new bases opened: Wildenrath in January 1952, Geilenkirchen in March 1953, Brüggen in July 1953, and Laarbruch by the end of 1954.[40] This group was known as the 'clutch' stations. A significant development from a logistics perspective was that aviation fuel storage on the clutch stations was linked to the already extensive NATO central European pipeline system; a rail link was also established to provide a back-up means of delivery, not just for fuel supplies, but also for stores and munitions. A RAF hospital was opened at Wegberg near Mönchengladbach in 1953 to provide specialist medical facilities for the RAF in the Lower Rhineland area. Throughout the earlier years of the Cold War, the RAF became dependant on well-prepared operating bases (both main and forward), a concept that in later years was often to be referred to as the 'citadel' strategy.[41]

The 1957 White Paper on Defence, however, had a significant impact on the size and shape of the RAF and placed an increasing emphasis on missile forces with a correspondingly limited role for fighter aircraft and the requisite support infrastructure. From an operational perspective, this stance saw a much greater emphasis on the early use of nuclear weapons; this had a significant effect on 2TAF, which was to lose its ground attack and fighter capability, leaving a more limited role of nuclear strike and reconnaissance. The effect on the numbers of squadrons within the force was dramatic and saw it reduce by two-thirds from thirty-six in 1956 to only twelve in 1961. This downsizing, accompanied by the return of a number of bases to the emerging post-war German Air Force, saw 2TAF renamed RAF Germany (as a command) on 1 January 1959.

Although the number of stations and aircraft reduced in the 1950s and 60s, the capability and complexity increased exponentially. The new Command re-equipped a number of times over the coming years, the more notable introductions being the Lightning in 1965; the Harrier and Phantom in 1970; the Buccaneer in 1971; the Jaguar in 1975; and the Tornado in 1983. By the end of the 1980s, RAF Germany comprised eight squadrons of Tornados (based at Brüggen and Laarbruch), two squadrons of Phantoms (based at Wildenrath), two squadrons of Harriers, and a squadron each of Pumas and Chinooks (based at Gütersloh). The RAF Regiment also had a sizeable presence within the Command with its Rapier surface to air missile unit and field squadrons. No. 230 Squadron Pumas replaced No. 18 Wessex at Gütersloh in 1980, with No. 18 returning with Chinooks in 1983. Wider support requirements also embraced No. 60 Squadron at Wildenrath, whose Percival Pembroke C.1 aircraft were replaced by Hawker Siddeley Andovers in 1987.[42]

NATO Evaluation: TACEVAL

Throughout the RAF, operational readiness was taken seriously and units were subject to what were known as tactical evaluations (TACEVAL). These assessments were conducted against agreed criteria and by teams of NATO staff officers who reported the results to SACEUR. There were two types of evaluation. The counter surprise evaluation was conducted under secure, no-notice arrangements. For most station staff, the first they were aware of these was through a unit recall following the station siren sounding; the second type was the formal alert evaluation, which was preceded by realistic warning and escalated from a peace to war footing by means of progressive levels of intelligence summaries. The evaluations were wide ranging and each station or unit was evaluated and rated under four areas: alert posture and reaction; mission effectiveness; support functions; and ability to survive. Each of these areas was considered for resources and performance and ratings of one, two, three, or four were given, with one where the expected standard was exceeded and four where there were serious limitations or deficiencies. Each of the areas was sub-divided into items and sub-items, with most being graded excellent, satisfactory, marginal, or unsatisfactory.

Readiness for operations, as well as exercises, was as important to supply squadrons as it was to flying squadrons. Indeed, although logistics was generally evaluated under the support heading, it invariably had a direct input in to the other headings and was thus an important contributor to the overall assessment. Both the NATO and Strike Command evaluation teams usually had RAF logistic specialists within their number and little would escape their attention. Areas of interest would invariably include the availability of up-to-date recall plans for personnel (including those on leave or detached duty); that operating procedures included comprehensive instructions for transition-to-war (TTW); the allocation and control of manpower; logistic control displays in operations centres (known as 'tote' boards) used by logistic staff to manage key resources; stocks of war consumables (including unit war reserves); and the dispersal of vital stocks of equipment around the unit to minimise loss in the event of an enemy attack. The loss of a bulk fuel installation (or parts of its pipework) and areas within the unit's explosive storage area were a favourite exercise scenario input from the Directing Staff. Group Captain Andrew Humphries recalled his experience of a V-force TACEVAL when, as a young pilot officer, he was OC Movements and Fuels at RAF Scampton from 1971–1972:

> I was sitting in my office around midnight. Seeing the Group Supply Officer and OC S&M Sqn (Sqn Ldr D. I. Dawson) go past my door on their way to the R&D Section, I dashed after them. They stood with hands behind backs staring out into the night on the raised cargo handling floor. After a pause, the inspecting officer said 'an enemy aircraft has just flown over and dispensed poisonous gas'. OC S&M looked at me which made me jump. Thinking fast I ordered the 2 airmen working in the vicinity to drag all the stores into the building and to pull down the roller shutter doors. SAC Flack, a hulking man who boxed heavyweight for the station, hauled on a large, black and yellow striped container by its convenient red handle. It promptly exploded with loud hisses, wheezes and squeals into a self-inflating, twelve-man life-raft. Keeping his cool, Ian Dawson turned to his companion and said 'sandwiches and coffee in my office?' And they both turned and sauntered off into the blacked-out building leaving me to my embarrassment.[43]

Less intensive evaluations were also carried by HQ Strike Command (STC) and HQ RAF Germany (RAFG). MAXEVALs were a full-blown practice for a TACEVAL and a MINEVAL (usually at the behest of station commanders) was a limited test for a specific aspect of operational readiness. The drive for operational effectiveness was relentless and could be reflected in officers' annual staff reports.[44]

The 'Hardened' Operating Environment

The invasion of Czechoslovakia by Warsaw Pact forces in August 1968 and the crushing of the Prague Spring led to a significant deterioration in east-west relations and brought the threat from Eastern Europe into much sharper focus. In the Government White Paper of 1970, it was announced that RAF Germany would be the subject of a programme of measures designed to protect aircraft on the ground as part of the European defence improvement programme.[45] Thus, what was known as the 'hardening' of many RAF bases commenced, with the aim of improving survivability from enemy attack. This was a time-consuming process; the work at RAF Laarbruch, for example, was still ongoing when the author was stationed there in the early 1980s. When complete, the hardened infrastructure at each unit enabled each flying squadron to operate from its own dispersed site (usually situated on the periphery of the station) with a network of taxiways providing access to the main runway. At each of these sites, protection of aircraft on the ground was provided through the construction of hardened aircraft shelters.

Supporting facilities in the form of hardened personnel briefing facilities, personnel shelters and fuel bowser sheds were also constructed. The nerve centre of the station's command and control function was a hardened combat operations centre (COC) that housed, not just the key operational staffs, but also other important functions such as logistics (see below) and the coordination of ground defences; the COC was invariably sited away from the dispersed squadron sites. During TTW or exercises such as TACEVAL, the unit's Supply Squadron would activate and man a logistics cell within the COC, usually situated alongside the engineering operations desk; both had a significant influence on unit flying activity. The logistics cell was responsible for all operational aspects of supply work, such as the progression of priority equipment demands, issues of equipment, and the control of fuel and explosives. The latter two often demanded particular attention and the logistics cell was required to keep a close eye on overall stocks to ensure operational needs were met and that any damage from enemy attack on the unit's storage infrastructure was quickly assessed and dealt with.

The availability of sufficient aviation fuel had a direct effect on flying operations, but the careful management of weapons required much closer control. It was not just the main conventional munition such as a 1,000-lb bomb, for example, that required accounting for. Many of the weapons employed by the Tornado aircraft could be configured for different mission types with specific bomb tail units, fuses and other attachments, which were known as ancillaries. The loss of any or all these ancillaries, limited the mission profiles that the aircraft could fly; the stock of fuel, weapons, and ancillaries was reported on a regular basis to HQ RAFG in a standard signal message format known as the logistics report or LOGREP. This enabled a command-wide view of critical 'war fighting' assets to be maintained.

Although designed for war, most of the hardened buildings were used for their assigned role on a day-to-day basis, thereby minimising set-up time in the event of hostilities. One particular element of the hardening programme that brought a major change in the way logistics did its business was the introduction of hardened equipment shelters (HES); these were an important facility on each of the dispersed squadron sites. Essentially, the HES was a concrete squadron store with heavy blast-proof doors, without any windows, tightly packed with high density racking and usually with an upper or mezzanine floor, which maximised use of available space. Each was run on a shift system by a sergeant or corporal supplier with two senor aircraftmen (SAC). The HES team demanded and progressed the delivery of equipment for its squadron, maintained a stock of consumable stores, controlled the issue of all tools and test equipment, and maintained stocks of high-turnover spares.[46] An important part of their task was progressing the return of unserviceable equipment so that this could be fed back into the repair process, either at the second, third, or fourth line.[47] Despite its close integration into squadron operations, the HES Supply staffs were always on the personnel establishment of and under the command of the unit's OC Supply Squadron who also retained full visibility of stock levels.[48]

The HES was not just a flying squadron facility. It was also used as a storage point for the dispersal of critical stocks of aircraft electronic and mechanical equipment from the main Supply storage buildings on the unit.[49] The mezzanine floor was usually used for this purpose with shelving closely mirroring that of the unit's electronic or mechanical supply group storage environments; the shelving for avionic equipment, for example, was lined with anti-static rubber matting to prevent electro-static damage and enclosed with protective polythene sheeting to minimise the ingress of dust and moisture.

Stock dispersal brought a number of challenges, not least of which was stock control. Prior to dispersal, equipment was held in single locations. With the advent of the HES, equipment could be stored at multiple locations. In the early days of HES operations, the ICL 4-72 supply computer system offered little functionality in this respect and Supply Squadrons (usually in their electronic supply groups) reverted to basics by relying heavily on what was known as the T-card system where a T-shaped card (one for each uniquely serial numbered item) was located in a special wall-mounted rack in horizontal slots that could be set up to hold cards by area such as those in main stock, in a HES, or elsewhere such as a unit repair workshop or off-unit. The T-card system was also a commonly used system in the supply squadron priority progression cell (PPC), a small but important section that managed high priority and AOG demands. Although not particularly sophisticated, the cards were a highly visible means of viewing and managing stock and remained popular for many years until they were largely replaced by a computer based system known as 'demand progression' (DEMPROG). The advent of the Unit Supply ADP System (USAS) in December 1984 brought a much-needed means of managing stock at dispersed locations; the practical benefits of USAS in this respect are described in greater detail in Chapter Ten.

Support in the Field: Harrier Operations

Notwithstanding the preoccupation with the hardening of airfields and the focus on operating from fixed bases, the introduction to service in Germany of the Harrier aircraft demanded yet another approach to support. The VSTOL capability of this aircraft enabled it to deploy into the field and to operate from short road strips or from fields almost anywhere. In January 1970, RAF Logistics therefore faced a new challenge—how to support a significant force of fixed-wing combat aircraft in the field, away from established infrastructure and close to the front line. Such a task had not been undertaken by the RAF in any major fashion since the rapid forward deployments of tactical air forces in the Second World War. Squadron Leader (later Air Vice-Marshal) R. C. Allerton was posted to HQ RAF Germany to oversee the development of field logistics for the RAF Germany Harrier Wing. The task was considerable—to prepare, maintain, deploy, store, conceal, deliver, and, if necessary, redeploy the POL, weapons, spares, and field equipment for thirty-six Harriers to logistics parks and forward-operating sites in the woods somewhere in the forward battle area. It was thus that a tactical supply flight was formed. The formation and early development of this unit is examined in more detail as one of the more specialised perspectives in Chapter Six.

Interior of a HES at RAF Laarbruch. The large Perspex covered board at centre was used to book out aircraft test equipment. (*Crown Copyright—Air Historical Branch MoD*)

Harrier at a deployed operating location in Germany. (*Author's collection*)

Equipment Depots in Germany

As far as RAF equipment depots in Germany were concerned, these had largely evolved from the ASPs that had accompanied the groups within 2TAF as the Allies advanced into the heart of Germany after D-Day.[50] As the need for mobility diminished, No. 431 Equipment Park (EP) was formed on the site of the former Reemtsma cigarette factory at Altona, Hamburg in late August 1945. In April 1946, the park was renamed No. 431 Equipment Depot (ED), becoming a general equipment park (GEP) in April 1953. In its earlier guise, the unit had been the main supply depot for the RAF in Germany and Holland and played a key part in providing equipment for the Berlin Airlift. The location of many RAF units at this time was invariably the result of where they (or their predecessors) had ended up on the cessation of hostilities in 1945. The deterioration of relations between the east and west in the late 1940s and early 1950s though, led to greater scrutiny of unit locations, especially their vulnerability to attack from Warsaw Pact forces. Consequently, the GEP was moved west of the Rhine to RAF Brüggen in September 1953. The more generic title of this unit reflected the fact that it was divided into three main components: the equipment park itself and Nos 401 and 402 ASPs. The ASPs had been disbanded in 1945 and 1946 respectively but had been reformed on 1 July 1950 to provide deployed supply support for 2TAF. With the decline in mobility that resulted from the Defence White Paper of 1957, the parks were disbanded in April 1958 and 1961 respectively, the last such units to remain in RAF service.[51] The GEP was staffed by six officers, three warrant officers, approximately seventy RAF personnel and augmented by up to 120 local civilians who were part of the uniformed German Service Organisation. Geographically, the Park was similar to a British MU with a HQ site (housing the CO, adjutant, chief Equipment officer, and local procurement officer) and three dispersed sites, each controlled by an Equipment Branch junior officer.

The new site at Brüggen initially proved to be on the small side, with approximately thirty-six wooden huts into which were literally crammed every conceivable type of spares from Mercedes and Volkswagen vehicle parts to RAF and WRAF clothing. Life was still hard for much of Germany's post-war population at this time and pilfering of stock was a constant problem. The unit's first adjutant, Flight Lieutenant Frank Noble, recalled how MT spares were particularly attractive for sale on the black market, as too were WRAF nylon stocking (although, as he related, not the standard issue elasticated knickers).[52] In due course, the park became a more permanent fixture of RAF Germany and was renamed as 431 MU in October 1960; the unit remained the focal point for a wide range of supply and engineering activities for the command until it was disbanded in March 1993, following a decision taken in the Options for Change defence review of 1991. One other supply related MU was formed in Germany at Duren in 1954 as an explosives depot (No. 398 MU), closing in 1964 when it was handed back to the German Air Force.[53] The storage and supply of explosives in Germany was subsequently catered for by the Army's base ammunition depots at

Bracht and Klinikum Bad. The RAF, however, stored its stocks of 1,000-lb bombs at Bracht; these were on the stock charge of OC Supply Squadron No. 431 MU.

Logistics in the Middle and Far East

Up until the mid-1960s, Britain had endeavoured to play its part as a major world power, but economic challenges at home forced a major rethink, leading to changes that were to have a far-reaching impact on air transport and the associated air movement commitment. The catalyst for change came in late 1964 when Denis Healey, the Secretary of State for Defence, initiated a defence review, set against the economic backdrop of a crisis over the British Sterling currency. One of the notable outcomes of this review was the cancellation of the Tactical Strike Reconnaissance 2 (TSR2) aircraft in April 1965. It was, however, the announcement in July 1967 that Britain would withdraw from East of Suez by the mid-1970s that signalled a marked change in the need for long range air transport. The timescale for this withdrawal was revised by the government in January the following year, resulting in a large-scale withdrawal from east of Suez by the end of 1971 and leading to a concentration on Europe.[54] In due course, British forces were withdrawn from Malaysia, Singapore, and the Persian Gulf; the Far East Air Force was disbanded in November 1971 with a complete withdrawal from the Persian Gulf just a month later. British forces remained longer in Cyprus, Hong Kong, and Malta, with a withdrawal from Malta in 1979 and Hong Kong in 1997.[55]

Spitfires over the Suez Canal, 1947. (*Crown Copyright—Air Historical Branch MoD*)

Development of the UK Equipment Depots

As the number of overseas commitments and aircraft types in service reduced, it became possible to reduce further the holdings of spares and then to close more of the UK storage depots. The differentiation between air and ground equipment depots, which had come about in early 1942, was no longer necessary and the latter had all been closed by the end of 1957. Attention then turned to the main equipment depots. The first of the original pre-war depots, No. 1 MU Kidbrooke, closed in early 1947 followed by the depots at Milton, Ruislip, and Handforth (Nos 3, 4, and 61 MUs) by the end of 1959. The depots at Heywood (No. 35 MU) and Hartlebury (No. 25 MU) closed in 1967 and 1977 respectively. One of the early post-war changes was that, given the nature of the threat of attack, there was little need for stock to be dispersed between all the depots and it was accepted that stock could be dispersed on a two-point holding basis; certain equipment was exempted even from this so that one depot held the entire stock. By the end of the 1950s, it was accepted that most ranges of equipment could be safely held in single-point holdings. Thereafter, Quedgeley, Carlisle, and Stafford (Nos 7, 14, and 16 MUs) became the main equipment depots for RAF Logistics; although they remained MUs, each was re-designated as an equipment supply depot (ESD) in December 1963. A specialist depot for the storage and supply of compressed gasses was established as No. 279 MU at RAF Cardington in Bedfordshire in 1948, subsequently combining with No. 244 MU (the Air Ministry gas factory) at Cardington to reform as No. 217 MU in 1955.

A further rationalisation came about in the mid-1960s when the MOD implemented a scheme whereby each of the services became responsible for supplying specific ranges of equipment to all three. For the RAF, this led to No. 7 MU Quedgeley becoming responsible for tri-service defence accommodation stores, Carlisle for American-sourced aviation spares, and Stafford for other sourced aviation spares and equipment requiring calibration. This of course required much movement of stock between the depots as well as the relocation of stock from closing units; this is well-illustrated by the relocation of machine tools from Quedgeley to Carlisle in May 1965, which amounted to 200 tons, while the closure of No. 35 MU Heywood saw 258 tons of Anson aircraft spares moved to Carlisle in July and August 1965.[56] At Quedgeley, the exercise was not finally completed until 1979. Adoption of commercial warehousing techniques enabled greater quantities of equipment to be held at the depots and a high-density storage shed was created at each of the depots, intended to hold the high-turnover items. These buildings were located next to the receipt and transportation points, thereby significantly reducing the internal transportation requirement and greatly speeding up the whole process.

In the case of No. 16 MU Stafford, one of the sheds from the original depot design was reconfigured to a high-density store for rapid turnover items, the concept being subsequently expanded with the construction of a purpose-built density activity complex, housing freight receipt and distribution within the same building; it was opened by AMSO in April 1977. Renamed the Supply and Distribution Activity Complex (SADAC) in the 1990s, this building became the hub of the entire depot operation and was driven by the computer process. Instead of tall storage racks built at ground level, the new buildings had several internal floors connected by lifts and, later, conveyor belts. Larger items were located on pallet racking accessed by high-reach forklift trucks. As well as making greater use of the height of storage warehouses, the introduction of modern mechanical handling aids also enabled the aisle gaps to be reduced from eighteen feet to less than half that distance thereby enabling more racking to be installed.

The following years saw the government preoccupied with driving down costs. One initiative that left a legacy that pervades defence today was contractorisation. The concept came to No. 7 MU Quedgeley in September 1984 when the defence accommodation stores element of the depot was largely contractorised; this saw some 60 per cent of the work on the unit being undertaken by a contractor made up of RCA and Securicor (subsequently becoming SERCO in 1987). In March 1991, the depot won back the contract through an MOD 'In House' bid; this arrangement remained in place up until the unit closed in 1995, with Quedgeley holding the unique position within the RAF and indeed the public sector of being the only organisation to have regained work previously contracted out.[57]

Development of the Munitions Depots

The focus on the nuclear deterrent also enabled a further reduction in the number of conventional munition depots and related parks. From mid-1938 until just after the war, some thirty-three different types of explosive storage unit had been constructed as part of the RAF's complex munitions supply chain. By the mid-1950s, virtually all of these had been closed leaving RAF Faldingworth (No. 92 MU) in Lincolnshire and RAF Barnham (No. 94 MU) in Norfolk catering for the nuclear storage requirement, with RAF stations Altrincham and Chilmark (Nos 2 and 11 MUs) handling conventional explosives; Altrincham closed as an explosives depot in late 1957, leaving Chilmark as RAF's sole ammunition supply depot.

The day-to-day life of supply staff officers in the RAF's explosives supply management branch when it was at MOD Harrogate (SM32 (RAF)) was never dull, as experienced by Squadron Leader David Sefton during the mid-1980s. David was involved in a disposal programme for obsolete Red Top and Firestreak missiles, which were carried by the Lightning, an aircraft then going out of service. Both missiles contained precious metals, which could be reclaimed. Consequently, a scrap contractor visited RAF Binbrook and took one of each (explosives removed) away in his van. As it turned out it was too difficult to recover the precious metals and the missiles were simply scrapped. At a scrap yard by the A1 and the main railway line near Newark, the dealer mounted a Firestreak and Red Top over his gate to complement a Lightning in the yard. An eagle-eyed RAF policeman from RAF Newton thought he had a coup as the relevant technical publication stated that both missiles were classified secret; he was most disappointed to find the publication was decades out of date and there was nothing awry.[58]

Storage and Materials Handling

The Binbrook study in 1946 had made it clear that economy and efficiency could be gained by paying greater attention to building layout and design. It was against this backdrop that in 1969, RAF Support Command formed what was known as the Storage and Materials Handling Advisory Team (SMHAT). Initially consisting of a Supply Branch squadron leader and a retired wing commander of the Engineering Branch, this team could be tasked to advise on storage and materials handling issues and, after a detailed on-site survey would produce a report with recommendations and copies of data and illustrations of their suggestions. Detailed costs were also included, sometimes realising longer term savings, sometimes not, but always leading to essential improvements. The Team provided much needed advice and the work led to significant savings. During the first half of the 1970s, for example, SMHAT realised savings in the region of £2.8 million alone.[59] The Team remained

A well laid-out domestic supply flight, RAF Wildenrath, Germany, 1978.
(*Crown Copyright—Air Historical Branch MoD*)

a valuable and much respected in-house capability for many years until the Government's pursuit of public organisation privatisations in the late 1980s saw the gradual demise of the requirement for SMHAT as their expertise became part of the services provided by industry in more comprehensive building and installation contracts. These early enhancements, along with the developments in computerised stock control in the 1960s, placed the capability of RAF Logistics well ahead of many of its civilian counterparts in the field for many years to come.

Change of Name: Equipment to Supply

With the substantial reduction in the size of the RAF following the Second World War, it was inevitable that the organisational structure of the Service should come under review. One of the earliest areas to be examined was the number of professional branches for officers. The first such review was carried out by the Babington committee in 1945 that considered, but eventually rejected, a proposal to amalgamate the Equipment and Secretarial Branches; the range and scope of duties of each was considered too wide to affect a successful merger. The number of branches was reconsidered in 1948 through the work of the Post-War Manning Committee, which had been tasked with improving the career prospects for Secretarial Branch officers. By 1949, this Committee was seriously considering the amalgamation of the Equipment and Secretarial branches and not for the last time but, this never came to fruition; it was believed on this occasion that an amalgamation would harm the Equipment Branch, but not resolve the career prospect issue for the Secretarial Branch. An alternative proposal was considered for a merger with the Technical Branch but, this too, was not taken forward.

Having survived what was seen as a threat from possible amalgamation, the Equipment Branch was subject to change regarding its name. As with the concerns regarding the inadequacy of the term 'stores' back in the 1920s, similar views began to surface in the early 1960s regarding the term 'equipment'. One such view, prompted by the content of an Equipment Branch recruiting advertisement at the time, was that it 'still conjures up nuts and bolts on shelves and in bins; packaging; issuing stores over the counter; and so on—important though unglamorous sides of our work'. Moreover, 'No mention is made of explosives, petroleum, special fuels and compressed gasses; embarkation units and other surface and air movement duties; MT and global supply of everything the Royal Air Force requires in peace and war'. Thus, an ongoing debate began.

By April 1968, the general discontent with the name had become widespread with many officers of the branch feeling that the name was indeed inappropriate for its activities, as well as not being helpful in attracting young people to join the specialisation. As a result, DGE (RAF) produced a paper that was submitted to AMSO. The paper makes interesting reading and contains a number of paragraphs that say much about how the Branch had developed. In the section describing the Branch's historical background, DGE (RAF) related:

> During the 1939–1945 War, it was found that Equipment Officers were particularly well suited by training and experience to undertake a wider range of duties than those of Supply and they filled many Administrative posts throughout the Royal Air Force. During the same period, there was a great expansion in the Movements organisation, partly brought about by the large increase in Air Movement. For the first time, too, the RAF gained experience in the conduct of large scale operations under various conditions of mobility. Out of all this emerged the concept of a 'logistician' and the name began to be associated in the Royal Air Force with Equipment Officers. Their involvement through supply and movements, with every aspect of operations and maintenance made them particularly good co-ordinators of logistics requirements and led, to-day, to the word 'logistics' being closely identified with the role and activities of the Equipment Branch.[60]

There were three main objections to the use of the word 'equipment'. Firstly, and perhaps a little tongue in cheek, was that it was a noun and could not properly describe a function. Indeed, DGE (RAF) cited that the service, for example, had Directors of Engineering, Manning, and Training and, in that vein, he ought to be more properly described as the Director-General of Equipping. The second reason was the term's inadequate description of the Branch's responsibilities, which had moved on a great deal from those of the 1920s and 1930s. One of the most notable omissions was Movements, which was employing one fifth of all officers in the Branch at that time. The third was that 'the description of the Branch fails to indicate the responsibility its officers have for advising the Air Staff on the logistics feasibility of operational plans and for making the preparations necessary to support these plans'. The two options proposed by DGE (RAF) were the Logistics Branch or Supply Branch. His reasoning behind Logistics was quite extensive, culminating in the observation that 'Logistics, which began by being a comprehensive word embracing all activities concerned with the maintenance of forces has now acquired a popular meaning which pretty well coincides with the functions of the Equipment Branch'. Interestingly, the alternative of a Supply Branch was viewed as less appropriate. Although it was seen as a more embracing term than 'equipment', DGE stated:

> The word Supply does not adequately cover Movements duties and certainly not Catering. Additionally, it does not embrace that part of an Equipment Officer's duties which require him to advise the Air Staff on the logistics feasibility of operational plans. It is, therefore, also inadequate.[61]

The final paper was submitted to AMSO in August 1968, but its consideration was placed on hold pending the outcome of the report of Air Vice-Marshal Hodgkinson's

Committee on the officer structure of the RAF. Just over a year later, DGE (RAF) was advised that the Committee's recommendation to the Air Force Board had been agreed that the title of the Equipment Branch should be changed to 'Supply'. Thus, in 1970, the Equipment Branch was renamed Supply. By the end of 1972, there were some 8,553 uniformed Supply personnel serving in the RAF, a figure that represented 7.7 per cent of the RAF's total uniformed manpower strength.[62] With the change of name from Equipment to Supply, the old Equipment Sections became Supply Squadrons, most of which had a standard structure consisting of a Technical Supply Flight, a Domestic Supply Flight for Clothing and Accommodation stores, and a Supply Control and Accounting Flight (previously known as EPAS). A number of units also had MSFs to support flying squadron deployments.

Logistics Management in the Air Ministry and the Ministry of Defence

For just short of twenty years after the Second World War, DDGE's organisation (still under AMSO) remained the focus for logistics management in the Air Ministry. It was however, gradually reduced in size as the post-war RAF reduced and the title of its director reverted to the pre-war DGE. In 1964, the five Departments of State then responsible for various parts of Defence merged into a single Ministry of Defence (MOD). This led to widespread reorganisation but, suffice it to say, DGE still remained within AMSO's department under CAS. With the renaming of Equipment to Supply in 1970, the post of DGE became the Director General of Supply (RAF) (DGS(RAF)), along with an accompanying renaming of his area of responsibility. Throughout the 1970s and 1980s, DGS' area remained largely the same (give or take some minor changes) with seven directorates, each headed up by a one-star officer (or equivalent). Of note is that DGS(RAF) was also responsible for the Defence Codification Authority (DCA) and the Directorate of Catering (DCat).[63]

Review of Support in the 1970s

In March 1972, the Air Force Board established a Support Organisation Project Team that was tasked with carrying out a fundamental review of all aspects of support and to recommend an organisation that would serve the frontline efficiently and economically for the longer term. The most significant outcome was, *inter alia*, the formation of RAF Support Command, which effectively renamed Maintenance Command and absorbed No. 90 (Signals) Group. The new command's role was widened further in June 1977 when it absorbed the responsibilities of Training Command on its disbandment. Thus, by the mid-1970s, the RAF's command structure had contracted to the three components of RAF Germany, Support Command, and Strike Command.

While RAF Germany and Strike Command each had a Supply staff component at their respective HQ, Support Command was functionally responsible for the depots, which in 1977 had reduced to the five remaining Equipment and Ammunition Supply Depots at Quedgeley, Chilmark, Hartlebury, Carlisle, and Stafford. By this time the RAF's inventory was almost 1.25 million line items, with some three million transactions a year and approximately 150,000 tons of equipment being moved to various units around the world.[64]

RAF Mobility in the 1970s: First and Second Level Support

Although much of the RAF's main effort was refocused in Europe during the 1960s, a general capability was still required to meet commitments in dependent territories, should they arise. As part of this, the RAF was expected to be able to redeploy, either within the UK or overseas, up to 75 per cent of the UK-based air forces to established bases and up to 40 per cent to non-established bases.[65] The Air Staff guidelines for mobility in the post-1971 period postulated a worst case scenario involving three major bases (forward mounting, tactical, and maritime) and two minor bases (two forward air strips).[66] The loss of certain established overseas bases though, notably those located in Libya, Tunisia, and Aden, along with locations that would be relinquished leading up to the British withdrawal from east of Suez in 1971, had led to a growing concern as to how support could be provided to deployed flying squadrons. During the 1960s, the tactical element of the RAF had spent much of its time operating from temporary overseas operating bases in support of the Army and air mobility was key to this. The helicopters procured under the Anglo-French collaborative agreement and the Hawker Siddeley Harrier GR1, both of which were expected to enter service in the early 1970s, assumed great importance and were expected to operate from 'bare' bases.

The logistical planning for this challenge was started in late 1966 by Equipment plans (RAF), a small team within the MoD Air Force Department headed by a wing commander and comprising three squadron leaders. Their main task was to propose support solutions to emerging and future operational scenarios. The planning of supply support for air mobility was allocated to Squadron Leader (later Group Captain) Dewi Edwards who was joined in 1967 by Squadron Leader (later Group Captain) John Craven-Griffiths. At the time, support for aircraft detachments away from their parent base had been catered for by MSFs, operating a deployed FAP. This approach was intended to provide specific-to-type support for detached squadrons, but only for small numbers of aircraft and for a short duration (measured in weeks rather than months). What was not clear was how supply support could be provided for aircraft and personnel operating from 'bare' bases for lengthier periods of time. The conclusion reached was that a self-supporting professional logistics unit was required, which was trained and equipped to operate in potentially hostile climatic, geographic and environmentally-challenging conditions. Although the ASPs of the Second World War had provided a similar capability, these had all been disbanded by this time and thus the development of a fresh approach to the challenge needed widespread support if it was to gain Air Force Board approval. An ideal opportunity came in 1968 as part of an equipment plans presentation to the advanced supply course, then a five-day course held in London for selected Equipment Branch squadron leaders. It was perhaps not the most orthodox way to expose emerging thinking, but the course was used to provide an ideal window of opportunity to air the idea, given that it consisted of presentations often delivered by one and two-star officers, on the future of the RAF and the developing role of the Equipment Branch. During his presentation to the course on air mobility, the head of equipment plans took the bold step of proposing the creation of a Tactical Supply Wing, which could be located at No. 16 MU RAF Stafford and manned by a combination of full and part-time service personnel, with the latter drawn from the regular establishment of the MU. The outcome was not as had been hoped for and gained neither the support of the Director of Equipment Policy, nor the course members; the existing MSF and FAP system of support, which had been developed as part of V-Force operations, was still seen as fit for purpose.

Equipment plans continued to develop the idea and worked hard to gain wider support for it within the Air Mobility and Air Staff Departments of the MoD. A key change to the original concept, and one that made a significant difference to such a unit's flexibility, was that the responsibilities were expanded to include aircraft refuelling. A revised planning paper was prepared to await an opportune moment for resubmission; this came with a change in the appointment of a new Director of Equipment Policy (RAF), Air Commodore Donald Hills, who gave his enthusiastic support to the project. Following Air Force Board approval, the concept of a two-level support organisation was formalised in the RAF Supply Policy Statement (RAF Mobility in the 1970s), which was issued in August 1969. The first level was for reinforcing adequate established bases, while the second level was intended to augment inadequate or non-established bases. The requirement for MSFs became much wider and Supply Squadrons on units with a deployable role were required to maintain such a flight, commanded by an air movements qualified junior officer. When not deployed, the flights were required to maintain their FAPs at high readiness to ensure that deployment tables were maintained and that an ongoing training programme was carried out.

The second level of support required development of a new capability in the form of a Tactical Supply Wing (TSW). This wing had the most demanding task, providing support at locations where only the most basic of facilities were available. The wing was also required to provide fuel in the field where either local resources were inadequate or required reinforcing.[67] The wider development and history of TSW is a longer story in its own right and is therefore considered as one of the more specialised perspectives in Part Two, Chapter Six.

The two-level concept of support introduced at the beginning of the 1970s was to remain a highly effective approach to deployed operations for many years until the evolution of the more complex Air Operations Logistics Doctrine and the Air Logistic Concept of Operations in the late 1990s; this saw units such as TSW classified as Air Combat Service Support Units amid a wider range of newly developed deployable support organisations.

The Branch and Trade

The airman's trade structure had a very different evolution. The war years saw it change to meet the needs of the moment, with little eye on the future in terms of a career structure for the longer term. This was addressed, however, in 1951 when the previous and very generic Equipment assistant trade was replaced and started to use the term supplier; this was nearly twenty years before the officer's branch became Supply. By the late 1950s, the trade had become a complex structure with five categories of storeman and four types of clerk up to and including the rank of corporal. From there on, there were two career paths up to the rank of warrant officer: Supplier I and Supplier II; the latter was for technically qualified (and ranked accordingly) tradesmen.

A storeman issues equipment for a Canberra of 31 Squadron, RAF Laarbruch, 1958. (*Crown Copyright—Air Historical Branch MoD*)

Movements at this time was still part of the mainstream supply trade.[68] The introduction of a separate Movements trade in 1971 and the introduction of the Supply ADP system led to a complete review of the trade structure, which had become unwieldy, over-complex, and did not reflect the responsibilities of the trade in the 1970s. The formation of the movements trades (although strictly speaking still within TG 18) had introduced the roles of movements operator in the aircraftman ranks, and movements controller for senior airmen and NCOs.[69] The overhaul of the main Supply trade occurred a year later and saw the trades of supplier accounting and supplier material introduced for aircraftmen and progression, following further training, into a career stream as a supplier general up to the rank of warrant officer.[70]

The structure for the Supply trade saw a further modification in 1974 when the trade of Supplier II was introduced for aircraftmen and then, after a promotion examination and an education test, conversion to Supplier I; this facilitated a career path up to the rank of warrant officer. By the late 1970s, a level of discontent had started to grow regarding the Supplier I and II trade structure, not least of which was the perceived lack of formal training beyond the rank of SAC, a shortfall in experience of those seeking to transfer to Supplier I and a numerical imbalance between the two levels gave rise to a trade review in January 1980, the findings of which were published in December that year. The result was that a new trade of Supplier was introduced in April 1982. The training concerns were addressed by a new and longer basic training course being introduced. Following this, LACs were required to complete a trade ability test at a later date on their first unit and achieve a requisite length of service before promotion to SAC. A new course (further training one) was introduced for all SACs selected for promotion to corporal and a trade management training course for those later selected for promotion to sergeant. The trade qualification for promotion was also in addition to the RAF's wider requirements for the two-part education test and general service training.

Civilians in Logistics

One of the many personnel issues that emerged during the closing stages of the war was the continuing employment of civilians in the RAF. The task fell to a specially convened group called the committee on the future employment of civilians in the RAF. The units of Maintenance Command were already employing substantial numbers of civilians and it was not surprising that this area should attract specific attention. Set against an overall requirement in the UK to support a force of 163 squadrons, the study considered (*inter alia*) the AEDs, one equipment park (EP), two ASP, and eight ammunition depots (AD). Of these, it was the AEDs that were considered prime candidates for civilianisation. The study confirmed what had already developed in practice—that the maximum possible number of civilians should be employed in the AEDs, as long as the needs of trooping, mobility, training, and mobilisation were safeguarded. It was for this reason that the EPs, ASPs, and ADs had largely remained service manned. The study also recommended that, as far as possible, units should be entirely civilian or service manned rather than mixed; later experience was to show, however, that mixed manning did in fact work perfectly well. The study also highlighted the view that civilian manned units should be located close to populous centres to provide a sizeable source of labour; later RAF contractorisation initiatives at some of the more remote units found contractors struggling to recruit suitably qualified local labour in the numbers they required. The study considered civilianization at Command and Group HQ as well as on RAF units, with the view that sizeable numbers of Equipment assistants were in scope; indeed, just over 2,500 posts from aircraftsman to flight sergeant were considered.[71] At No. 16 MU Stafford, for example, the strength in August 1950 was eighty-five officers and 2,469 airmen. By the mid-1960s, the balance had changed significantly and the figure was 829 servicemen (all ranks) and 1,202 civilians.[72]

The late 1960s also saw the widespread adoption of emerging scientific approaches to work measurement and improved management techniques. Perhaps the most influential in terms of its impact on civilian staff, particularly those at the MUs, were the management productivity schemes. At the time, RAF Maintenance Command had been conscious for some time that it needed to reduce its operating costs; in the early 1970s personnel accounted for some 80 per cent of the Command's running costs. The general aim of the schemes was to reduce labour costs by increasing productivity but still maintaining the expected level of customer service. The project was a significant undertaking for the Command and was aimed at saving 7,500 civilian industrial employees at eleven supply and engineering units. The Command formed a team of management services staff for the project and these assisted units in carrying out was called method study whereby the best way of doing a job was determined along with work measurement to ascertain how long each job should take at a standard rate of performance. Each scheme was made up of a natural work group of people such as a flight or squadron and their work rate was carefully monitored. The schemes were essentially a 'carrot and stick' initiative that encouraged greater productivity by the payment of a bonus to staff, equal to a third of their basic pay, when working at what was termed the incentive rate. Experience at the time in industry had shown that work-measured schemes could lead to increases in productivity of around 70 per cent and, providing that remained constant, numbers of personnel could be reduced by about 40 per cent. The first of these was introduced at No. 14 MU Carlisle for civilian industrial grades in the high-density store in August 1972. As the schemes became more widespread, it became clear that the efficiencies in working that they introduced would bring about the loss of jobs, a thorny issue which was to generate much heated debate between the trade unions and management. Widespread adoption of the schemes at Carlisle led to the loss of just over 600 jobs in the 1970s alone.[73] A similar picture emerged at Quedgeley where, in the early 1970s, the savings amounted to a reduction of 400 industrial grade civilian posts and a saving of in excess of £0.5 million per year.[74] By 1978, the schemes had managed to reduce manning levels at the equipment supply depots by some 46 per cent.[75]

Notwithstanding the numbers or proportions employed throughout the RAF's supply chain, civilians continued to be an important part of its logistics workforce. They had valuable experience, often as a result of being on the same unit and working area for many years. They were quite rightly acknowledged as providing continuity in environments where most servicemen were subject to posting on a regular basis. Many ground branch officers, for example, were posted every two to three years. Most civilians, through remaining in post for much longer, built up more extensive experience in specific areas over many years. This was particularly noticeable within the supply management branches at Harrogate where the extensive knowledge of equipment types and their management challenges acquired by equipment range managers was greatly valued. Many civilians had also served in the Armed Forces and it was not unusual at Harrogate, for example, to come across many who had been wartime aircrew and decorated with flying gallantry awards. The employment of civilians though, did bring different staff management requirements. In the majority of cases, civilians throughout the RAF were usually civil servants with specialised grades in the industrial and non-industrial groupings such as the stores officer as well as executive grades. On most RAF units, the administrative wing had a civilian administration officer who looked after civil service administration and was a highly-valued advisor to military staff on the finer points of their terms and conditions of service. On larger units, the civilian administration officer role was carried out by what was known as the civilian assistant and accountant who was the senior civil servant on the unit. Most depots were heavily unionised environments and industrial relations required careful handling, especially during the many changes that took place during the Cold War years. This fine balance was managed through what were known as Whitley Council committee meetings, which had to be held between management and the unions and were chaired by COs.

Small Wars and Insurgencies

Although Central Europe occupied centre stage for the RAF during the Cold war years, RAF Logistics still had a much wider remit further afield, supporting air power in what are often referred to as small wars and insurgencies. The twenty-year period following the end of the Second World War saw the RAF involved in operations in Malaya (1948–1960); Kenya (1952–1956); Korea (1950–1953); Suez (1956); Cyprus (1956–1960); SE Asia (1963–1966); and the Radfan (1964).[76] With the exception of Korea, the RAF was able to operate from already established bases, a fact that made logistics a relatively straightforward affair.

Argosy of No. 215 Squadron dropping fuel to a jungle security post during Operation Firedog, Malaya, 1955. (*Crown Copyright—Air Historical Branch MoD*)

The Falklands Conflict: Operation Corporate

Argentina's occupation of the Falkland Islands in April 1982 and the dispatch of the British Task Force once again posed an enormous challenge for RAF Logistics. Operation Corporate, as it was known, was a supply chain over what was probably the longest single line of communication the RAF has ever had to maintain. Ascension Island, a tiny volcanic speck in the South Atlantic 4,000 miles from the UK and a similar distance from the Falkland Islands, was pivotal in the operation to retake the Islands and in the post-war restoration of British rule. Part of the British Overseas Territory of Saint Helena, Ascension, and Tristan da Cunha, Ascension Island had undergone two brief periods of military usefulness prior to the Falklands War: firstly, as a forward base to forestall any French effort to liberate Napoleon Bonaparte from his exile on St Helena; secondly, as a staging post for transatlantic deployments of aircraft during the Second World War, for which purpose the Americans had built a long runway that, in 1982, proved invaluable for heavily-laden RAF transport and tanker aircraft. By then, it was essentially American-run, if not owned, and a base for NASA space event monitoring. The British presence was entirely civilian, in the shape of Cable and Wireless, BBC, and GCHQ. Other than its single runway, the airfield had only limited infrastructure, not least in terms of fuel handling and storage, maintenance facilities and personnel support and accommodation. Equally significant from a logistics standpoint, the island had no onshore port. All supplies had to be transferred by boat from ships offshore and craned onto a small jetty. Aviation and ground fuel was pumped from ocean tankers a couple of miles offshore through a floating hose onto the jetty and then by pipeline to a small storage depot a few miles from the airfield. The few aircraft using Wideawake Airfield, named after the local sooty terns or wideawakes, were fuelled by bowsers from the depot. There was little spare infrastructure available for the massive influx of British forces in April 1982 and precious little protection from the subtropical and maritime elements.

The island was a critical staging point for the UK Task Force as it gave the Royal Navy the opportunity to load on board anything that had been forgotten or that was not ready on sailing from the UK. These items were flown to Ascension Island by RAF transport aircraft, augmented by Victor tankers and various aircraft arriving to stay or joining ships. The air transport operation soon developed into what became the largest since the Berlin Airlift of 1948–1949. A British Forces support unit was established on the Island and commanded by a Royal Navy Captain until after the Argentinian surrender. One of the early priorities was fuel storage as it was quite clear that the existing aviation fuel capacity would be completely inadequate to meet the needs of the huge air effort required. The Army's REs deployed emergency fuels handling equipment and rapidly constructed a pipeline complete with booster pumps between the fuel depot and the airfield, where they also installed a large fuel farm of eight 30,000-gallon pillow tanks that was up and running for the first transfer of fuel on 11 May 1982. The RAF despatched a fleet of aircraft refuellers and the POL operations room in the Directorate of Supply Policy and Logistics Plans (RAF) during the late 1970s, arranged for an ocean tanker loaded with aviation fuel to stand permanently offshore. The aviation fuel operation was jointly managed by the RAOC (ship-to-fuel farm) and RAF in the shape of a TSW detachment. The fuel operation, critical to the success of the air-bridge and offensive air activity, was a remarkable and enduring success during Operation Corporate and post-war recovery and reconstruction. The weak link—the floating ship-to-shore pipeline—was severed on several occasions by Atlantic rollers up to 40 feet high that frequently crashed onshore, with sufficient force on one occasion to wash a 20-ton Coles crane off the jetty into the sea. It is testimony to the combined efforts of the local US authorities, the Army, and the RAF that the massive and diverse air operations were never curtailed for want of fuel and was a classic example of inter-agency co-operation and logistical excellence. Operation of the airfield installation was eventually handed-over to the TSW detachment, which successfully ran it for the remainder of the campaign, including providing fuel for the Operation Black Buck bombing raid on Stanley airfield.

The TSW detachment, commanded by logistics officers drawn from outside the wing and reinforced from stations other than RAF Stafford, also assumed responsibility for common user supply activities on the island and supported the various MSF elements deployed by the AAR, AT, AD, and MP detachments, many of them with their own fly away packs of spares. Concurrently with the supply operation, an air movements detachment based on the UK Mobile Air Movements Squadron (UK MAMS) (this unit is described in more detail in Chapter Seven) was also established and did a fine job handling the cargo and passenger traffic, which was particularly challenging once the airbridge was established after the war. The RAF's logistics operation on Ascension Island was overseen by a logistics co-ordination officer, which was invariably the OC TSW detachment. All in all, the logistics support arrangement that was put in place at Ascension was exactly as intended by the two levels of support which the review of RAF mobility had put in place in 1969.

Despite, or perhaps because of, its intensity, the operation was not without its lighter side. On one occasion, a supply management branch invited RAF Ascension Island, three degrees south of the equator, to submit its return of snow-clearance equipment. On another, a staff officer from RAF Support Command challenged a demand for 3,000 bed sheets; when informed that these were for the MV *Norland* to replace those damaged and soiled by repatriating Argentinian POWs, he simply declared 'no scale, no entitlement' and could not be persuaded that the war and its aftermath required extraordinary measures and a modicum of flexibility from Logistics staff. The call on equipment from the Supply depots seemed never-ending and they supplied stores to no fewer than thirty-eight ships in the first six weeks of the operation. Movements personnel at Lyneham and Brize Norton worked around the clock to keep supplies moving; among the most unusual items received for delivery were half a ton of strawberries and cream donated by a Norfolk farmer and a mobile laundry. Shortly after the war, while emergency repairs were made to the Port Stanley runway, C-130s operated a 'snatch squad', which flew non-stop to the Falklands and back to airdrop mail and collect it by means of a hook trailing from the aircraft—a tricky and hazardous operation. The discovery of a cow's skull in one of the first mailbags to be opened on Ascension Island caused the RAF station commander to send a serious and heartfelt complaint to the Army commander in the Falkland Islands, who responded with a sincere apology and a promise to send the rest of the cow in the next consignment.[77]

One of the significant difficulties that logistics had to contend with was communication with the UK. Initially, the standard signals network was used but this proved to be too slow and the existence of a satellite link made the installation of a Supply computer system (ICL 4-72) a possibility; this was up and running by mid-May, with the connection and subsequent maintenance of this owing much to the hard work of the Tactical Communications Wing. Although quite primitive by later standards of communication, the supply computer had what was known as an 'Asterisk P' messaging facility, which allowed five lines of text to be sent. This was invaluable for the MSFs who were each allocated a specific transmission time by HQ STC and one VDU printer allocated for transmission and likewise for receipt in the

The first RAF C-130 Hercules lands at Port Stanley after the Argentinian surrender in 1982. (*Crown Copyright—Air Historical Branch MoD*)

UK. While the MSFs looked after the special-to-type equipment of the aircraft they were supporting, common user items came under the responsibility of TSW and were demanded from RAF Lyneham as the parent accounting unit. As the operation progressed, the RAF Supply Section on Ascension became manned twenty-four hours, seven days a week, and was organised very much along the traditional lines of the Binbrook model with even a small clothing store.[78] Even after the surrender of Argentinian forces on the Falklands, Wideawake Airfield remained very busy with resupply flights.

After the successful return of the task force to the UK and the departure of the remaining Royal Navy and Army personnel, TSW was heavily involved in the transition of the RAF detachment at Wideawake Airfield into RAF Ascension Island. Squadron Leader Robin Springett handed over command in July 1982 to Squadron Leader (later Group Captain) Alan Matthews, who became the first OC Supply Squadron at RAF Ascension Island.

The Falklands War from a logistics perspective was notable in that it was arguably the first sizeable expeditionary operation in which the RAF had participated since the Second World War. While the front-line units and their achievements have quite rightly attracted the historian's pen, comment also needs to be made about the extensive effort that was made much further back in the supply chain. Apart from TSW and the various MSFs that had, by their very nature, become highly mobile and self-contained, a lot of equipment and supplies still needed to be provided at very short notice from the equipment supply depots, various RAF units, and from numerous supplying companies. In some cases, even the civilian police became involved as evidenced by the staff of the SM 7(RAF) branch who called on the services of the Stirlingshire Police to find a local firm's manager to 'have him dragged from his bed early one Sunday morning to provide some 2,000 locking pins securely located in his factory, but urgently required at Ascension Island—the items were despatched within hours'.[79] All of this effort required close co-operation between the supply management staff at Harrogate and Carlisle, the MOD Finance Branches, RAF engineering authorities, MOD (PE), and the manufacturing company. The accommodation stores depot at Quedgeley along with the largely technical stores depots at Carlisle and Stafford experienced a substantial increase in workload. Indeed, in the first six weeks of the operation they supplied equipment to some thirty-eight ships. This of course had a knock-on effect for the Movements organisation. This saw additional RAF Supply personnel working in the joint service movement control centres controlling the loading of ships at the various ports involved in the operation along with the MT resources of No. 2 MT Squadron, the London Movements Unit, together with Nos 14, 16, and 431 MUs with the inter-connecting priority freight distribution system's schedule being stepped up to a twice-daily, seven-days-a-week operation.[80] Such was the wider effort involved that, in addition to the awards made to TSW and UK MAMS personnel, two MBEs were awarded to officers working at MOD Harrogate, a BEM to a corporal from RAF Odiham and thirty-five various commendations to service and civilian supply personnel at a number of depots and units.[81]

With the end of the hostilities in mid-June 1982, the RAF established a small airfield, just under four miles from Port Stanley harbour on the Falkland Islands. At the end of June, OC TSW, Wing Commander Mike Barham had arrived on the island to join the staff of the Land Force Commander Major-General Moore. He was joined two weeks later by an advance party from RAF Stafford headed by Wing Commander Bill Girdwood, who was to become the first OC Supply and Movements Wing at RAF Stanley. Amid the chaos left over from the Argentinian occupation, this small party established the beginnings of a supply complex in tented accommodation. By mid to late August 1982, a Supply computer link had also been established with the UK. Although the Argentinian occupation had been thwarted, there remained a likelihood that they might make a further attempt in the future—a risk that saw a growing need for strengthened air defences on the Falkland Islands. Given this, the limited size of the airfield at Stanley was not suitable for such a growing commitment and a new base, RAF Mount Pleasant was built and opened some thirty miles south-west of Stanley in 1985. The supply and movements organisation relocated here, the manning of which remains a UK out-of-area (non-NATO) detachment commitment to this day.

The RAF has also maintained a standing detachment at Wideawake Airfield on Ascension Island since the Falkland conflict and remains an important airhead for travel to the islands. Flying Officer (later Squadron Leader) Nigel Dabin was detached there for six-months as OC Stockholding Flight in 1984.

Accommodation at the time was still quite basic, consisting mainly of tents and other temporary buildings.

The management of aviation fuel stocks was always of paramount importance and the main reserve stock was held offshore in a moored tanker, the MV *Maersk Ascension*. To maintain its seagoing capability, the ship would sail around the island once every three months, before returning to its moorings; the captain invariably invited some of the detached RAF staff on board for this welcome break from the day-to-day routine. When required, fuel was pumped ashore from the tanker to an American PSD at Catherine Point; from here, a resident British Army RE detachment pumped the fuel to pillow tanks at the airfield, a distance of about 5 miles or so.

Nigel related how this process proved to be a rather curious mixture of units of measure for the fuel. On board ship, it was accounted for in cubic metres, the US depot used US gallons, the Army's REs pumped using Imperial Gallons, while the RAF accounted for the fuel at the airfield in litres and their aircrew customers worked in kilograms or pounds of fuel. Quality was of course important and Nigel recalled how he was approached one day by a very concerned member of his staff with a fuel sample that was green in colour. Fearing that it was contaminated, the batch was segregated and a sample sent back to the UK for priority testing. It turned out that all was well and the unusual colour was a characteristic of the Venezuelan crude oil it had been distilled from.

Towards a Thaw: The Reunification of Germany and a Brave New World

When Mikhail Gorbachev became General Secretary of the Communist Party of the Soviet Union in 1985, he set in train a dual programme of *glasnost* (openness) and *perestroika* (restructuring), both of which led to major changes in not just internal affairs but international relations. By the end of the decade, and into the early 1990s, this programme had swept away many communist governments from power, a change which effectively brought a close to the Cold War. As part of this, the former East and West Germanys were reunified into a single German state in 1990, following the dramatic fall of the Berlin Wall in 1989. This all saw a particularly welcome end to the brinkmanship that had endured since the end of the Second World War. For RAF Logistics planners though, this moved their assumptions from the known to the unknown. The known had been the largely predictable 'citadel' philosophy of the Cold War years, the unknown was a question of probability—where would the next conflict emerge and what support for air power would be required?

5

Towards the Future: 1990–2014

At the beginning of the 1990s, the responsibility for Logistics within the RAF rested with what had become the Supply Branch and Trades. This name, however, was set to change, as was its broader responsibility as part of a Defence supply chain, following the 1998 Strategic Defence Review. At the beginning of the 1990s though, defence was trying to adjust to the planning uncertainties that had arisen following the end of the Cold War, symbolically marked by the fall of the Berlin Wall in November 1989. At that time, much of the RAF's Logistics policy and planning remained focused on the support of operations within Europe and on the NATO flanks; the development of support for expeditionary operations was less of a priority. Much time, effort, and money had been invested in accumulating munitions, fuels and materiel to meet the minimum NATO stockpiling requirement for a thirty-day conventional war. This was all to change as the forthcoming decade saw defence beginning to embrace the quite different requirements of expeditionary warfare. Change was also to come about through a growing pressure on the defence budget as the RAF, along with the other services, reduced in size and the extent of supply chain costs became the subject of ever growing scrutiny.

Adjusting to a New Future: *Options for Change* and Frontline First

The so-called peace dividend realised by the end of the Cold War saw the UK Government taking early stock of the new geopolitical situation and in July 1990 published the results of its defence review, *Options for Change*. At the heart of this study was the recognition that a Soviet invasion of Western Europe was no longer likely; defence capability needed to be realigned to this reduced threat. For the RAF, this heralded the beginning of a significant reduction in the size of RAF Germany with the closure of two out of four RAF bases and the withdrawal of six RAF squadrons.[1]

The first RAF bases to close were Wildenrath in March 1992, with Gütersloh handed over to the British Army a year later in March 1993. The command itself

(RAFG) was disbanded in March 1993, with control of the RAF's remaining units falling to the newly constituted HQ No. 2 Group at Rheindahlen. With further reductions in the RAF's presence in Germany, HQ No. 2 Group was disbanded in March 1996, with control passing to HQ No. 1 Group at RAF High Wycombe in the UK. The last of the 'clutch' stations, Laarbruch and Brüggen, were closed in 1999 and 2002 respectively. The final RAF station to be handed back to the German authorities was the hospital at Wegberg in September 2010, although by then, it had actually been part of the Army's UK Support Command rather than an RAF unit.

In July 1994, the UK Government announced the results of a further review, *Front Line First: The Defence Costs Study*. Although critics proclaimed this as a Treasury-driven exercise, the Government was adamant that it was preserving the front line, but was mainly targeting support areas. The report made the point that the MOD and other HQs were too large, too top heavy, and too bureaucratic. Consequently, the number of MOD civil servants was reduced by 7 per cent (7,100 staff) and, along with cuts to the other services, the RAF was to be reduced by 5 per cent, a cut amounting to 7,500 uniformed personnel. Additionally, it was announced that three RAF flying bases were to be closed (Finningley, Laarbruch, and Scampton). It was not all bad news as the review confirmed that 142 Tornado GR1s were to be upgraded to GR4 standard and that there was an intent to spend £300 million on laser-guided bombs and laser designators. It was also outlined that there was an intention to form a Defence Clothing and Textile Agency (DCTA) on a single site (eventually located at Bicester); in time, this would reduce the RAF's involvement in its own clothing and textiles supply management as the new agency would have tri-service control.[2]

Organisational Structure of the RAF and its Logistics in the Post-Cold War Period

At the beginning of the 1990s, there were just three RAF Commands—Strike Command, Support Command, and RAF Germany. By the middle of 1993, RAF Germany had been reduced to Group status. The overall lead for Logistics still remained with DGS (RAF) within AMSO's area in the Air Force department, now part of the unified MOD. Wider efforts, however, to integrate the higher-level organisation of supply and engineering led to a complex series of changes to the DGS organisation over the next ten years or so. These are too involved and detailed for this part of the logistics story and have therefore been included for completeness in Part Two, Chapter Nine (Development of Collaborative Working). Within Strike and Support Commands, logistics came under the remit of an Air Commodore Supply and Movements. The RAF's Supply Control Centre was well-established at RAF Stanbridge, a unit that also had a responsibility for the Joint Service Air Trooping Centre at Hendon.

The number of equipment supply depots came under further scrutiny as Options for Change also called for a reduced RAF front-line and proportionate savings in support costs. In July 1992, HQ RAF Support Command (HQ RAFSC) established a working group to review the functions of the depots; this work led to the closure of both Quedgeley and Carlisle by the end of September 1996.[3] No. 11 MU Chilmark was also closed in 1995 and the RAF's storage and supply of munitions was met by the defence munitions sites at Kineton in Warwickshire and Glen Douglas in Scotland. The Defence Munitions organisation was absorbed into the Defence Storage and Distribution Agency in 2003 that, in turn, became part of Joint Support Chain Services in 2010. Within the RAF, the finer points of explosives management were the responsibility of what was known as the armament role office at HQ STC, a mixed team of both engineering and logistic specialists. They, in turn, interacted with the MOD level specialist offices. The RAF's compressed gas cylinder filling and maintenance depot at No. 217 MU Cardington remained in operation until its closure in April 2000. No. 16 MU Stafford was to remain the RAF's last ESD in operation until it too closed on 31 March 2006 after sixty-seven years of operation. From here on, the issue of equipment to the RAF from depot sources was made by the tri-service Defence Storage and Distribution Agency, mainly from its two sizeable units at Bicester and Donnington.[4] Further rationalisation to the organisational structure came in 1994 as a result of the Government's 'Prospect' study in 1991; this led to the disbandment of Support Command and the formation of Logistics Command on 1 April 1994, along with a new Personnel and Training Command.

The First Gulf War 1990–1991: Operation Granby

Given that the focus of logistical planning during the 1980s had been largely centred on a potential conflict in Europe, it was ironic that the Middle East was to be the location of the largest combined and joint operation for the UK since the Second World War. The Saddam Hussein-led Iraqi invasion of Kuwait on 2 August 1990 precipitated what turned out to be just short of a twenty-year presence in this region for the UK. The invasion and subsequent occupation of Kuwait by Iraqi forces resulted from Iraq's claim that Kuwait had been stealing oil from a shared oil field; this hostile act was widely condemned by the major world powers, especially the member nations of NATO.

Following Iraq's non-compliance with the subsequent UN resolutions that imposed economic sanctions and a final ultimatum to withdraw its forces, the United States launched Operation Desert Shield on 7 August; this was essentially the build-up of coalition forces in Saudi Arabia to prevent a risk of a similar invasion. Two days later, Britain announced that it too would participate in the coalition and by 11 August 1990, British aircraft began to arrive in theatre. In a nutshell, the Gulf War itself lasted from August 1990 to February 1991. The air campaign began on 17 January 1991, closely followed by the ground war, which commenced on 24 February. The conflict itself was relatively short. US President George Bush announced a ceasefire and that Kuwait had been liberated on 28 February with Iraq accepting terms of the ceasefire from the UN Security Council on 3 March 1991. One of the most significant points was that, by and large, conflict requiring a coalition intervention was not expected at this time in the Middle East. This was not just a challenge for the physical employment of air power but particularly for the associated logistics. The 'unknown' nature of what has been colloquially referred to as the First Gulf War was summed up by its Joint Commander, Air Chief Marshal Sir Patrick Hine, who described the operation as follows:

> A totally unforeseen deployment for which no Joint Tactical Plan existed. Neither had there been any previous thought given to the deployment of a BAOR formation Out of Area, into a theatre at the end of extended lines of communication and on to hostile terrain.[5]

Although the main campaign went under the American name of Operation Desert Storm, the British component used the codename 'Granby'. Broadly speaking, the initial deployment of RAF aircraft to the Gulf saw six main operating bases used during the campaign: Dharan (Saudi Arabia) hosted the Tornado GR1, GR1A, and the F3; Muharraq (Bahrain) hosted the Tornado GR1, VC10 K2 tankers, Victor tankers, and Buccaneers; Riyadh (Saudi Arabia) acted as the military air transport 'gateway' to the Gulf region, as well as the main base for C130 Hercules in-theatre tactical transports; Seeb (Oman) hosted the Nimrod MR2; Thumrait (Oman) hosted Jaguars and VC10 K3 tankers; and Al Jubail (Saudi Arabia) was the main operating base for Puma and Chinook helicopters. As the campaign unfolded, the Tornado GR1s from Muharraq relocated to an additional operating base at Tabuk (Saudi Arabia), the VC10 K3s moved from Thumrait to Seeb, and the VC10 K2s relocated from Muharraq to Riyadh (see Figure 4).

The key to providing logistical support for this broad pattern of operating locations was the widespread deployment of supply personnel from their parent bases to the Gulf region, many of which accompanied their respective squadrons when they deployed. The expertise of TSW was crucial with regards to the supply of fuel; their part in Operation Granby is covered in Chapter Six. One of the issues that quickly became evident when the crisis broke was the extent of uncertainty surrounding the likely employment of air power. Questions such as how many and what types of aircraft, where might they be deployed, what rates of effort would they experience, and what facilities could be made available by a potential host nation were typical and became the subject of frantic planning activity in HQ STC's Primary War HQ at High Wycombe in Buckinghamshire. Within this, the logistics co-ordination centre was soon working on a twenty-four-hour-a-day footing,

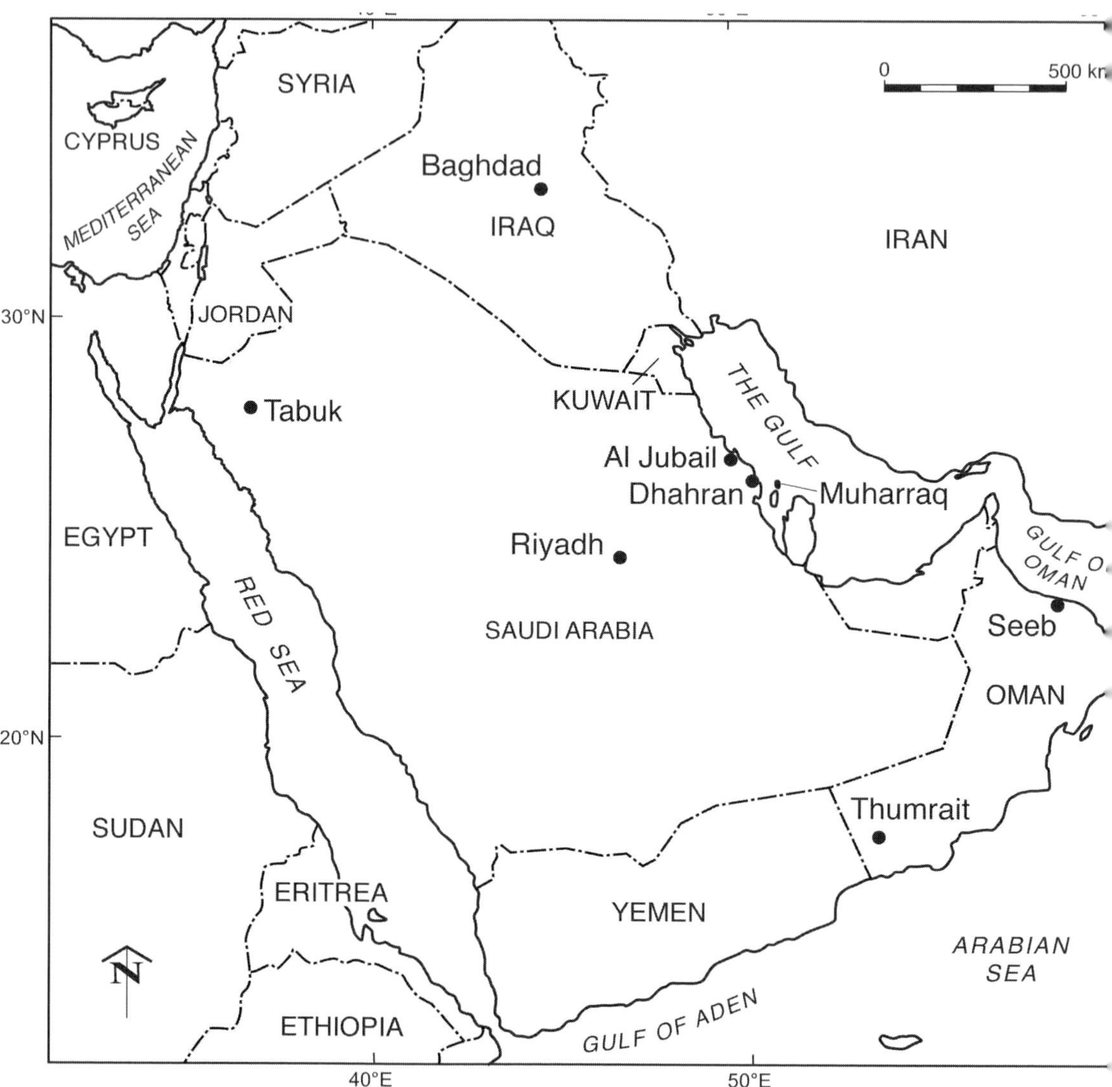

Figure 4: RAF operating bases in the Gulf region during Operation Granby, 1990–1991.

trying to grapple with the finer points of the logistics challenge. Uppermost in their minds was the geographical problems of a supply chain that would extend some 3,000 miles by air and 6,300 miles by sea.

During the Cold War, when there had been many exercises, stations were generally well-prepared for their likely war roles. By the early 1990s, and with the exception of the Harrier, Jaguar, and Support Helicopter forces, there was little experience of operating away from main bases. Indeed, there had been no experience of deployed operating for extended periods since Operation Corporate in 1982. Consequently, there were very few members of the RAF supply organisation at this time who had such experience.[6]

One of the finer details was the availability of logistic resources. With the primary focus up to this point having been on NATO operations in its central region, spares, POL, and munitions had been provisioned and stockpiled for a probable thirty-day war in a European theatre against a NATO planning requirement, not for an out-of-area operation in the quite different terrain and climate of the Middle East. Although tensions between the east and west had eased considerably by this time, the NATO commitment still remained a significant part of British defence policy. With the decision to deploy Tornado aircraft to the Gulf region, one particular concern was the availability of spares for fly away packs (FAP). Both the GR1 (GR1A) and F3 variants were deployed to the Gulf, having first entered RAF operational service in 1983 and 1987 respectively.

Given the Cold War pedigree of the aircraft, their logistic support had largely evolved to meet the non-mobile requirements of fixed-base operations. As such, FAPs for the GR1 aircraft had not been established for the aircraft and the spares required on overseas training exercises such as Maple Flag in Canada and Red Flag in the United States were met by what were known as 'peacetime training packs', which were usually assembled from the aircraft's parent unit stock holdings for the occasion and then dismantled again on completion. With the support of the Central Servicing Development Establishment at Swanton Morley to provide data on ranging and scaling, three FAPs were rapidly assembled for the GR1 aircraft, drawing components from Strike Command and RAF Germany units, along with spares from the British Aerospace production line and the German and Italian Air Forces, through the mutual supply support arrangement.[7]

It was not just aircraft spares that were required as similar challenges were encountered with ground support equipment. In the case of the Tornado, much of its ground equipment had been designed to be used in hardened aircraft shelters on main bases and they were not easily air portable. The Mk 11 hydraulic rigs and 48 KVA generators, for example, required the use of wooden planking as a track-way into the cargo hold of the C-130 Hercules to prevent damage to the aircraft flooring and large wooden blocks were placed underneath axles to act as load 'spreaders' when they were tied-down with restraint chains and strops. This all required additional time, work, and coordination in the movement process. Fortunately, much development work had been carried out on these workarounds by the Joint Air Transport Establishment in the early 1980s when Nos 15 and 16 Squadrons from RAF Laarbruch first started to take these aircraft on training exercises to Canada, Sardinia, and the United States.

The challenge of preparing the deployed support package for Tornado aircraft is well-illustrated by the experience of Squadron Leader (later Air Commodore) Les O'Dea who had been in command of the Supply and Movements Squadron at RAF Laarbruch in Germany since the summer of 1990. At the time, Laarbruch was home to four Tornado Squadrons (Nos 2, 15, 16, and 20) and two RAF Regiment Squadrons (Nos 1 and 26). Les had perhaps more operational experience than a typical OC Supply Squadron at the time. He had previously been the staff officer in HQ RAF Germany with responsibilities for the Harrier and Support Helicopter forces, was a qualified NATO tactical evaluator and had also served a tour at RAF Coltishall with the Jaguar Force. He recalled the hectic preparations at Laarbruch when the crisis broke:

> When Iraq invaded Kuwait, I was on leave and remember remarking that it would have little impact on me as 'the Tornado is not a deployable aircraft'. Of course, we had Fly Away Packs (FAPs) to support Red Flag and other such deployments,

No. 48 KVA generator used by the Tornado. (*Crown Copyright—Air Historical Branch MoD*)

> but there was no plan to forward deploy the Tornado and we had certainly not exercised such a scenario nor can I recall there ever being even a contingency plan for such an option. Against this background, one might imagine the frantic preparations once it became clear that the Tornado would be deployed to the Middle East. Unfortunately for the Engineering and Supply preparations, there was no early decision about which squadrons would be deployed. There was natural competition from squadrons at RAF Lossiemouth, RAF Marham and RAF Brüggen as well as RAF Laarbruch to be involved. With critical spares in short supply, everybody was holding on to what they had and it was essential to monitor demand very carefully. FAPs had to be brought up to full stock but everybody was chasing the same shortfalls and this situation did not resolve itself until there was finally some clarity of which squadrons would be deployed. In the end, it was decided that all four squadrons from RAF Laarbruch would deploy so we could assume a priority and prepare. The pace was frantic as both RAF Regiment squadrons were to deploy as well. The whole of the Station was working very hard indeed but the two-man Movements Section, led by the then Sgt (later Squadron Leader) Ken Felton had an enormous task on their hands. Needless to say, through supply art, sheer hard graft and occasional subterfuge, all was prepared and all of RAF Laabruch's operational forces were deployed to various locations in the Gulf. I deployed in November 1990 with the bulk of the RAF Laarbruch personnel to Bahrain where there were already Jaguars and VC 10s based alongside the Tornado.[8]

During the first few months in theatre, the lack of deployment experience started to become clear, particularly from the HQ. Understanding and taking in to account the geography of the region was one of the many issues that surfaced as Les recalled:

> People may well remember the sheer scale of the main Sea Port of Entry at Al Jubail in Saudi Arabia, but that Bahrain was an island and a different country from Saudi Arabia, seemed to pass the HQ Staff in Riyadh by. Consequently, critical supplies for Bahrain were routed through Al Jubail rather than through Bahrain's own Khalifa Bin Salman port. Picture the response when OC Supply stands up at the morning ops brief and tells the aircrew that they would have to keep their drop tanks when in combat because we didn't have any; despite repeated pleas they had been delivered to Saudi Arabia and the process of finding them among the chaos that was Al Jubail and then sorting the administrative procedures for export/import meant we would run out of spare tanks.

The logistical requirements of the desert operating environment led to significant shortfalls in a wide range of equipment types. The fact that there was a phased RAF deployment to the Gulf region of aircraft and support organisations was a saving grace in that it gave much needed time to assemble equipment and spares from a wide range of sources. This called for not just imaginative and flexible thinking, but close co-operation between many organisations. This co-operation was not just a front-line unit need; as the campaign unfolded, it became clear that significant efforts were made across the whole of the supply chain from industry at one end, though the equipment depots and parent RAF units, all the way to the deployed operating bases in the Gulf region. In parallel with this, various logistic organisations within the MOD and at the Command and Group HQ played their part in the planning and decision-making process. Although the deployment phase and ongoing support was not easy by any means, it was much to the credit of RAF Logistics that it was able to make such a drastic adjustment to its supply chain operation in such short order.[9]

The sheer scale of the operation required the movement of substantial volumes of freight, the lion's share of which was moved by sea through the Saudi Arabian port of Al Jubail. The air movement component of the lines of communication relied heavily on RAF Akrotiri in Cyprus as a staging post for flights into Saudi Arabia, and the volume of work saw the need to utilise additional air movements support from No. 4624 (County of Oxford) Squadron Royal Auxiliary Air Force (RAuxAF) and RAF Wildenrath's Movements Squadron. The more specific movements activity, especially the role of the UK MAMS, is commented on in Chapter Seven. It must be said that the task came close to overwhelming the RAF's air movements organisation, a problem that was not helped by the fact that there were serious shortages of freight-handling equipment, particularly at RAF Brize Norton and Lyneham; much of the existing equipment was old and had poor serviceability. This led to extra equipment having to be hired in and specialist items required as the TriStar, for example, had to be flown to the Gulf in chartered Antonov An-124 heavy-lift aircraft. The scale of the task was also manpower 'hungry' with a shortage of movers at some of the key locations; however, this was eased considerably following the call-up of RAF Movements reservists.[10]

A particular challenge during the campaign was one of knowledge—more specifically the ability to know where an item or consignment was as it moved through the supply chain to the Gulf region. While RAF Logistics was able to identify broadly where a consignment was in the air line of communication, it was not possible to achieve total asset visibility for the complete supply chain. With the bulk of items moving by sea, and with most consignments loaded into shipping containers, this proved to be a major issue. The problem was compounded by the fact that large numbers of shipping containers were arriving in theatre and that supply staff at HQ and in-theatre levels had no information technology support that could show what had arrived and in which containers items were located. This led to frustrated consignees who, unable to ascertain the exact location of their demanded equipment, re-demanded the items that could not be located quickly. This duplication proved to be a significant handicap and led to a number of projects that would provide a more robust consignment tracking capability for RAF Logistics.[11]

A particular area that proved to be a steep learning curve for logistics was munitions. As with the wider planning, most of the data concerning stock levels and weapon types was based on the mainly Europe-centric theatre and a possible conflict with the forces of the Warsaw Pact. The outload of weapons to the Gulf was a major undertaking, which involved stocks from both RAF Germany and from the UK where No. 11 MU RAF Chilmark was heavily involved in preparing and transporting weapons to ports and airheads, often at very short notice. The changing nature of the air war and the tactics employed, also proved a significant challenge. The switch from using free-fall 1,000-lb high explosive bombs to the precision laser-guided bombs resulted in urgent procurement of considerably more laser guidance kits, which were attached to the standard high explosive bomb.[12]

While fuel for the RAF's support helicopter force was catered for mainly by TSW, fuel at the main operating bases for fixed wing aircraft became a concern of the senior deployed RAF supply officer. At Muharraq, for example, Les O'Dea found that it was a task that required much careful and often imaginative management:

> We were also told to ensure we had seven days' reserves of fuel at sustained rates stored on base. Given that, by that stage, we had Tornados, Jaguars, Buccaneers, Victor tankers and transiting Air Transport, seven days' worth of fuel would have covered much of the airfield and adjoining land. I had our storage capability surveyed (we had on-airfield storage tanks, a refinery within 4 miles and a robust international airport hydrant refuelling system) for vulnerability by the Specialist Technical Royal Engineer experts who concluded that we only had one key vulnerable point and that, in the worst case, it would take them thirty-six hours to restore pipeline refuelling if that was damaged. Despite making my case to the HQ, it was decided that they knew better and that we were to adhere to the instruction for seven days' worth of fuel to be stored. Luckily, I had an excellent OC Engineering Wing who asked what I wanted to do when I explained the problem and was happy to support me when I said I would turn a 'Nelsonian Blind Eye' and be economical with the truth on the daily Assessment Reports by reporting a regular build-up of stocks to the required level while in fact only keeping seventy-two hours (100 per cent redundancy) emergency fuel on the ground. On the post-conflict staff visit, I was asked where all the fuel was and told them what I had actually done and then showed them just how much redundancy we did have which was met with a shrug of the shoulders.[13]

While Operation Granby was highly successful, with air power playing a key part, it took much innovation, commitment, and sheer hard work to make air logistics work. There were two key points that emerged from the operation. Firstly, the size of the transport of personnel and materiel to the Gulf was substantial; the quantity carried by air alone amounted to some 46,000 people and 46,000 tons of freight. This outload, along with the recovery operation, required the use of almost all the

RAF's transport fleet (2,300 sorties in total) as well as the charter of 490 flights at an additional cost of £69 million.[14] While it was acknowledged that the MOD could never economically justify the ideal air transport fleet size and that chartering of aircraft would invariably remain as an option for meeting unexpected shortfalls, a lack of heavy lift aircraft was a constraint on air movements. It would take until the Strategic Defence Review in 1998 before this would be addressed by the leasing (initially) of Boeing C-17 Globemaster III aircraft from the United States.

The second point was that of adequate IT services. There was a growing need for a tri-service stock control system to overcome the inability to track consignments in the supply chain. Again, this shortfall took time to resolve and it was not until 1997 that the RAF adopted the Army's Visibility in Transit Asset Logging System (VITAL). The wider story of developments in this respect is covered in more detail in Chapter Ten. The broader issue of a lack of operational logistics experience, at both the strategic and tactical levels would improve exponentially as the years following Operation Granby would soon show.

Mobility and Deployed Support Study 1993

The experience of the First Gulf War, which had exposed many shortcomings in the logistic capability of the post-Cold War RAF, prompted a number of urgent reviews of defence capability. For RAF Logistics, the mobility and deployed support study (MDSS) led by Air Vice-Marshal David Saunders (who had been the RAF's Director of Engineering Policy and then became AO Engineering and Supply at HQ STC) was launched in 1993 and led to a number of important outcomes that would enhance the development of logistic support for expeditionary operations. The broader backdrop to developments at this time was the need to improve readiness and deployment of British forces that would be committed to the emerging NATO Response Force doctrine. The outcome of MDSS would provide important logistic enablers for the RAF's role in the British Joint Rapid Reaction Force, which would later emerge from the UK Government's Strategic Defence Review in 1998.

There were five key elements that emerged from MDSS. Firstly, the concept of host nation support was formally introduced into the planning lexicon, which was a mechanism by which the provision of a range of services and commodities would be agreed with a host nation, thereby reducing stockpiles and minimising airlift requirements.[15] The second element was modules, a term applied to a grouping of equipment and personnel that could be used to tailor the build-up and level of support at a deployed operating base. The third was express chain management (see Chapter Nine for more detail), a technique that enabled various parts of the supply chain to be accelerated or 'making it sweat' as some rather imaginatively referred to it. The fourth element was the wider development of second level support units; this term had first been coined in the review of RAF Mobility for the 1970s conducted in

1969, although then only including the Tactical Supply Wing. The fifth element of the study was logistics command and control and reporting. Central to this theme was the development of a deployable version of the RAF's Unit Supply ADP System (known as DUSAS) that, coupled with use of the Army's consignment tracking system VITAL, would provide a more effective logistics command, control, and reporting capability.

The Iraq 'No-Fly' Zone Commitment, 1992–2003

Shortly after the conclusion of the Gulf War, the Kurds of Northern Iraq, heartened by the success of the campaign, tried to overthrow Iraqi President Saddam Hussein. Their failure to do so resulted in the Iraqi Army retaliating, forcing the Kurds to move *en masse* into the mountainous region of south-east Turkey. The United Nations' response—encouraging the Kurds to return to their homeland—was to create a secure area in Northern Iraq where they would be safe from the attentions of Saddam's army. This resulted in Operation Provide Comfort, in which thirteen countries contributed air and ground forces to help establish and maintain the safe haven for the Kurds in September 1991. Following the withdrawal of the ground forces, a no-fly zone was established north of the 36°N parallel in Iraq and enforced by an American-led combined task force based at Incirlik Air Base, near Adana in southern Turkey. This coalition became Operation Northern Watch in January 1997, with the British contribution of Tornado GR1s, Jaguars, Harriers, and VC10 tankers, operating under the codename of Warden. In time, the British aircraft operating from Incirlik reduced to detachments of Jaguars from RAF Coltishall and VC10 tankers from RAF Brize Norton. A tour of duty at Incirlik, usually between four and six months in duration, remained a popular out-of-area detachment for the RAF and presented a number of interesting experiences for logistics personnel up until its conclusion in May 2003; a tour here normally qualified individuals for the General Service Medal 1962 with the clasp 'Air Operations Iraq'. In addition to those deployed to provide supply support for the deployed RAF aircraft, a Supply Branch squadron leader, and a Trade Group 18 (Supply) sergeant and corporal were established as part of the American-commanded deputy directorate of Logistics (DDC4) on the staff of the American commanding general. The supply tradesmen had the often-problematical task of facilitating the clearance of inbound and outbound British freight through Turkish customs, while the squadron leader operated as effectively the US logistics director's chief of staff, managing American Army and Air Force personnel, in addition to the two British staff. This detachment was typical of the many operational environments, which RAF Logistics personnel found themselves in at this time and their background and training enabled them to make valuable contributions in many areas.

At Incirlik, despite the hospitality of the Turkish authorities, there was still a requirement to comply with the various legal requirements of their national customs procedures. Inaccurate paperwork was often at the heart of problems in this respect and non-complying American and British consignments of equipment had been 'impounded' by the Turkish authorities at Incirlik for a number of years after the start of the operation and locked-away in a small warehouse building on the airfield. Various DDC4s had tried to negotiate the release of this impounded equipment, but their collective efforts remained unsuccessful until 2001 when the author and his American colleague Major Jeff Decker USAF, both nearing the end of their tours of duty at Incirlik, capitalised on a change of heart by the Turkish authorities and helped release some $2 million worth of impounded equipment. The general euphoria was short-lived on the opening of the warehouse. Under the detritus left by nesting birds and layers of dust, much of the equipment turned out to be obsolete, with the Americans whimsically suggesting that many of their items, which turned out to be for F-111 and B-52 aircraft, would be more useful if they were re-consigned to the Smithsonian National Air and Space Museum in Washington DC.

A no-fly zone (south of the 33°N parallel) was also established in Southern Iraq in August 1992, following a similar threat to the Kurds by the Shia population in this region known as the 'Marsh Arabs'. Under the overall control of Operation Southern Watch, the British contribution under the codename Jural operated from Al Kharj in Saudi Arabia (Tornado GR1, later F3) and Ali Al Salem in Kuwait (Tornado GR1, later GR4). By early 2001, British forces operating in the Gulf region were amalgamated under the generic Operation Resinate, and sub-divided into 'north' for the former Operation Warden and 'south' for the former Operation Jural. The northern and southern no-fly zone operations ceased with the commencement of the Second Gulf War (Operation Telic) in 2003.

Conflict in the Balkans: Bosnia Herzegovina

The dissolution of the Soviet Union in December 1991 led to the emergence of fifteen independent states. Freedom from the yoke of Communism brought with it instability as some of the post-Soviet states sought to re-establish themselves and long supressed disputes re-emerged. On 15 October 1991, Bosnia-Herzegovina took its first steps towards independence from the Republic of Yugoslavia by adopting a memorandum of sovereignty. This was followed in December 1991 by the president seeking formal European community recognition of Bosnia-Herzegovina as a state in its own right. The move was boycotted by Serbia who asserted that this memorandum was illegal; the following day, its assembly of people voted to declare the region a Serbian Republic. On the whole, the Serbs rejected independence while the Croats and Muslims supported it. Consequently, the Serbs established themselves in areas they believed to be Serbian, as did the Croats in the western part of the Republic and the Muslims in a number of smaller areas in the interior. The international recognition of Bosnia-Herzegovina was followed by an outbreak of violence. This went on to become a bloody civil war that pitched the Bosnian Croats and Muslims against the Bosnian Serbs.

The international response to this escalation of violence saw the deployment of a UN Protection Force (UNPROFOR) to the region in the autumn of 1992 to provide humanitarian support; this role subsequently expanded to include a monitoring role for the various ceasefire agreements. The RAF was involved in five separate but related operations in connection with Bosnia-Herzegovina between 1992 and 2000. The first, Operation Cheshire, took place between July 1992 and January 1996 in support of the UN's relief operation in providing food and medical supplies to the besieged towns in Bosnia, especially the capital, Sarajevo. The operation involved RAF movements personnel working as an essential part of the air transport contribution, which delivered some 26,577 tons of supplies in 1,977 sorties. The conflict in the region took a whole new turn in early 1993 when the ethnic Serbs in Bosnia increased their attacks on the Muslim Slavs in what amounted to ethnic cleansing. In response, the UN implemented an economic blockade of Serbia-Montenegro and a no-fly zone over Bosnia-Herzegovina.

The RAF's participation in this was through Operation Deny Flight and saw Tornado F3s deployed to Gioia del Colle in Italy, a Sentry E-3D to Aviano in Italy, and VC10 tankers to Palermo in Sicily; logistic support at these deployed operating bases was provided by supply personnel from home bases. Chinooks and Pumas were also deployed to Split in Croatia and supported there by TSW (see Chapter Six). This operation was particularly intensive in terms of aircraft flying hours, with the Tornado F3s notching-up some 3,000 sorties by the time of their withdrawal from theatre in February 1996. The rejection of the Vance-Owen peace plan by the Bosnian Serbs in May 1993 was followed by the UN creating six 'safe havens' for the Muslims fleeing the Serbian aggression but the UN deployed forces, which were acting in a peacekeeping role, were unable to contain the Serb attacks. This led to an appeal to NATO for their intervention, a new phase of involvement for the RAF that saw them deploy Jaguar aircraft to Gioia del Colle in July 1993 as part of Operation Deliberate Force. The escalation of hostilities in 1995 saw both Harrier GR7s and Jaguar GR1s carrying out 326 sorties as part of NATO attacks on Serb targets. Following the Dayton Agreement at the end of 1995, NATO put in place its Implementation Force (IFOR) with the policing of the no-fly zone conducted under Operation Decisive Edge, with RAF Harriers participating. By December 1996, IFOR became the Stabilisation Force (SFOR) and the air operation component became Operation Deliberate Guard. The relative stability in the region saw a progressive reduction in the RAF's aircraft contribution; by 2000, the last aircraft, the E-3D Sentry, had returned to the UK.[16]

Aside from the direct support of RAF aircraft, RAF Supply personnel were detached as part of UNPROFOR, the NATO forces IFOR and SFOR, and the enduring European Union Force (EUFOR (Althea)) presence in the region from December 2004. A regular detachment for supply and logistics officers was at the

IFOR/SFOR/EUFOR multinational HQ site at Camp Butmir on the outskirts of Sarajevo and at the British Forces (BRITFOR) HQ at Banja Luka. Such detachments not only brought valuable RAF Logistics expertise to the region, but also enabled supply and logistics officers and tradesmen to gain new experiences. The author, for example, served in the logistics directorate of HQ SFOR at Sarajevo in 2002 (Operation Palatine). His tour here saw him involved a number of unusual projects for an RAF supply officer such as the recovery of former Serb armoured vehicles for use as targets on the NATO firing range and the handover of former NATO sites at the Croatian port of Ploče and at Split, back to Croatian hands.

The Strategic Defence Review 1998

While the *Options for Change* and *Frontline First* Defence reviews had adjusted the size of the armed forces following the demise of the Cold War, the outcome of the Strategic Defence Review in 1998 (SDR 98) was quite different. Of the three reviews since 1990, SDR 98 was the most significant as far as RAF Logistics was concerned. The results, announced in July 1998, consisted of a number of key decisions that, it was claimed, would enhance the armed forces. It also signalled a change in the way in which Britain's armed forces would be employed:

> Our armed forces are Britain's insurance against a huge variety of risks. They need to be flexible, highly capable, mobile and responsive, i.e. they need to be prepared for expeditionary operations. In the words of the Secretary of State, 'In the post-Cold War world, we must be prepared to go to the crisis, rather than have the crisis come to us.'[17]

This was a clear signal that British Defence posture had moved on from the Cold War culture to one of developing, maintaining and employing fully-deployable forces world-wide. This would turn out to be not just a practical challenge that required different resources, but a significant shift in support philosophy that would have an impact on the mindsets of people at all levels. Strategically, the Government declared that British armed forces should be able to respond to a major international crisis on a similar scale to Operation Granby, as well as having the ability to mount two lesser-scale operations overseas, although these would not necessarily involve combat operations or last longer than six-months. Specifically, though, there were four specific outcomes that directly affected RAF Logistics.

The first was the announcement that a Defence Logistics Organisation (DLO) (later renamed Defence Equipment and Support (DE&S)) was to be formed, which would subsume the existing single-service logistics management structures; this would see the end of the RAF's Support management branches at MOD Harrogate and their absorption into a new, integrated project team (IPT) structure, eventually moving to new purpose-built premises at RAF Wyton in Cambridgeshire. As part of this change, a new four-star post of Chief of Defence Logistics was established who became responsible for the totality (end-to-end) of the MOD's logistic process. The second outcome was the decision to lease four C-17 Globemaster III aircraft, re-establishing the much-needed strategic lift capability that the RAF had lost in the 1970s. The third outcome resulted from the decision to form a Joint Helicopter Command (JHC), which eventually led to the TSW transferring from RAF Strike Command to JHC in 1999. The finer detail of this change is covered in more detail in Chapter Six. The fourth outcome was that a new 'single, defence-wide, storage and distribution Defence Agency [would be formed] in the early years of the next century'.[18] This change was intended to replace the existing single-Service storage and distribution arrangements and led to the transfer of No. 16 MU RAF Stafford to the new agency in April 1999.

The change saw the title of No. 16 MU disappearing and the unit being renamed Defence Storage and Distribution Centre (DSDC) Stafford; in April 2002, this became DSDC (North). It was also announced the Royal Navy's Sea Harrier fleet was to merge with the RAF's Harrier GR7s to form a new 'Joint Force Harrier'. While the number of RAF frontline aircraft was to be reduced by thirty-six aircraft, the Government did re-affirm its commitment to the Eurofighter project.

With the formation of the DLO there was no longer a need for the single Service logistics formations and RAF Logistics Command was therefore disbanded at the end of October 1999; much of it was absorbed into the new tri-service organisation. This was a watershed for the RAF and removed much of its direct control over how its logistics were conducted. It was thus that from April 2000, HQ STC became the focus for RAF Logistics, eventually becoming responsible for policy, planning and execution. Following the RAF's process and organisation review in 2007, both Strike Command and Personnel and Training Command were co-located at High Wycombe and merged into a new single formation known as Air Command.

Conflict in the Balkans: Kosovo

While the Dayton Agreement brought an end to the conflict in Bosnia and Croatia, unrest had been developing to the south east of the Balkans in the region of Kosovo, a province which had been within the Yugoslav federation since 1946. Although Serbia had tolerated its autonomous status and enjoyed a degree of self-government since 1974, this privilege was subsequently withdrawn by the Serbian President Slobodan Milosevic in 1989. In July 1990, ethnic Albanian leaders declared independence from Serbia, an action which precipitated the dissolution of the Kosovo Government by Serbia.

During the period 1993 to 1997, ethnic tension and unrest escalated; by mid-1998, open conflict had developed between the Serbian police and the separatist Kosovo

Liberation Army (KLA). In turn, this led to a brutal suppression by Serbian forces with many Kosovo Albanian civilians being driven from their homes. In September 1998, NATO issued an unsuccessful ultimatum to President Milosevic to stop the crackdown on Kosovo Albanians; following the failure of internationally brokered peace talks in March 1999, NATO launched air strikes, which lasted for seventy-eight days until Serbia yielded.

The UK's contribution to the campaign was initially as part of the NATO air strikes (Operation Allied Force with the UK working under Operation Engadine), a period during which RAF and Royal Navy aircraft flew just over 1,000 strike sorties, a figure which represented 10 per cent of all strike sorties. Additionally, the RAF's air transport force was heavily tasked with deployment and resupply missions for, not just deployed RAF formations, but also in support of the UK's contribution to the eventual deployment of land forces in Macedonia and Kosovo (Operation Agricola). The airlift commitment showed yet again the shortfall of heavy lift capability that had just been flagged-up in SDR 98 and a number of air charter arrangements had to be put in place to help met the need. Besides the participation of Tornado GR1 aircraft from RAF Brüggen in Germany, the RAF's deployment turned out to be a complex affair and was largely influenced by what locations could be made available by Italy under Host Nation arrangements. This involved RAF aircraft operating from five different operating locations: E3D AWACS aircraft at Aviano; VC10s and TriStars at Ancona; Tornado GR1 at Solenzara in Corsica; E3D AWACS at Pratica Di Mare; and Harrier GR7 and Canberra PR9s at Gioia del Colle.[19] These locations all saw logistics personnel deploying from the aircraft parent bases, along with augmentation where required from across the RAF. The number of operating locations also posed a challenge for RAF's supply chain although its adoption of the asset tracking system, VITAL, made this a much easier task to manage than during Operation Granby some eight years earlier.

Serbia agreed to withdraw its troops from Kosovo and the UN established a Kosovo Peace Implementation Force (KFOR), which led to the arrival of NATO forces in the province in June 1999.[20] The ongoing KFOR operation in the country saw a number of RAF Logistics personnel involved in both national, UN, and NATO appointments through until much of the force started to be scaled down in 2008 and responsibilities gradually handed back to the Kosovo Police.

Expeditionary Logistics Wing

Following the end of the Cold War, the British Government gradually adopted a more interventionist approach to its foreign policy. While it had become clear to military planners that the UK's Armed Forces would become more involved in expeditionary operations, it was not until SDR 98 that greater significance was attached to this, which led to a more proactive approach to be taken towards developing the required capabilities.[21] By this time, the lessons learned from Operation Granby in 1991 and the analysis carried out during the MDSS in 1993 had provided a much clearer understanding of where the shortfalls were in logistic capability.

The rationale behind the decision to transfer TSW to JHC had emerged from wider discussions at HQ STC during the lead-up to the review, much of it led in the early stages by Wing Commander Mike Barcroft. While TSW had already developed a mature support capability for deployed rotary wing aircraft, there was no equivalent for supporting deployed fixed wing aircraft. By this time the organisation of TSW was considered suboptimal, with half of it responsible for providing fuel in the field (by now, just to the Joint Helicopter Force and some UK-based allies) and its 'non-cadre' squadron responsible, at least on paper, for deployed supply support; the latter was always contentious, with the Supply Squadron staff from the flying stations considering, with some justification, that they should support their deployed forces, while the non-cadre element of TSW was formed and authorised for this role. Work to address these issues was taken forward by two former OC TSWs (Group Captains Andy Spinks and Neil Cromarty) at HQ STC in early 1999. The outcome of their deliberations was that the opportunity should also be taken to form a new and separate wing, which they called the Expeditionary Logistics Wing (ELW), for supporting deployed RAF fixed wing forces. Following further staff work, this concept was approved and funded, with the new wing being formed at RAF Stafford in October 1999 under the command of Wing Commander Guy Selby.[22]

The wing's initial structure consisted of three squadrons. The first of these was the Training and Support Squadron (TSS); it was a new formation and established to develop and manage the RAF's deployable supply capability. The other two, No. 2 MT Flight and Mobile Engineering Support Flight (MESF), already existed at Stafford as part of TSW and No. 16 MU's Engineering Wing respectively. No. 2 MT Flight was then commanded by a RAF warrant officer and had formed part of the otherwise civilian manned depot MT Squadron. In the immediate aftermath of SDR 98, both the Station Commander and OC TSW became concerned that, as No. 16 MU was absorbed into the newly formed Defence Storage and Distribution Agency (DSDA), there was a risk that the civilian MT Squadron would transfer into the new agency, leaving No. 2 MT Flight isolated from military command and control and therefore in real danger of being civilianised and possibly disbanded. As the SDR had set defence on the new path of expeditionary operations, it had become clear that the RAF would need a deployable road transport capability and that No. 2 MT Flight was the kernel of such an organisation. It was thus that No. 2 MT Flight was transferred to TSW in August 1998 and work started to develop it into a fully operational military MT squadron under the command of its new OC, Squadron Leader Nigel Stevens. The decision to transfer TSW to the new JHC placed the ownership of the MT capability at risk once more; it was thus that the decision was taken to transfer this to ELW in October 1999 with its squadron status being reinstated at about the same time. The history and development of this specialist transport capability is covered in more detail in Chapter Seven.

The ownership of MESF on the other hand, which was responsible for the RAF's deployable engineering facilities, such as portable aircraft hangars and various types of airfield operating equipment, appeared more secure as DSDA did not want to take over the pure engineering elements of the RAF Engineering Wing. Consequently, MESF became No. 5001 (Expeditionary Airfield Facilities) Squadron, also in 1999 when it joined ELW. The wider development and history of ELW is covered in more detail in Chapter Six.

Air Combat Service Support Units

The RAF has had deployable support units in its logistic ORBAT since 1935 when the first ASP was formed. As commented on elsewhere in this book, a number of other specialist units have been formed, some for a limited duration and for specific campaigns, some enduring to the present day. The review of RAF mobility conducted in the late 1960s introduced the concept of first and second level support, with RAF unit MSFs and the TSW fulfilling these roles respectively. Although mobile air movement squadrons had been formed some ten years earlier, and were well practiced in providing deployed air movement support, these were not then formally classed as a second level support unit; their history and wider development is covered in more detail in Part Two, Chapter Seven. Following the MDSS in 1993, the attention of logistical planning staff began to focus on the wider development of second level support units and a need to introduce a collective term that reflected their role in supporting a deployable RAF. Much of this work can be attributed to Wing Commander (later Air Commodore) Andy Spinks in the mid-1990s, when he was an Air Plans desk officer. At that time, RAF planning assumptions were the core of the funded elements of the RAF. While specific aircraft types and numbers were listed for the approved and funded military tasks, logistic support elements, which would undoubtedly be required on most deployments, were not included in the RAF's listing for long-term funding. Single-handedly, and initially against the views of his aircrew-dominated Air Plans colleagues, Andy got the formed logistic units inserted into all relevant planning assumptions so that the funding for their existence was thereafter secured. In the initial revision to the planning assumptions, TSW, No. 2 MT Squadron, and UKMAMS were listed as essential logistic force elements for specific military tasks.

In 1999, and as part of wider work to reorganize deployable logistic support units into a more coherent structure, Group Captain Andy Spinks and Group Captain Neil Cromarty, both then at HQ STC (DACOS A4 Operations and DACOS A4 Support respectively) agreed that the term Air Combat Support Units (ACSU) would be an ideal descriptor. This was duly adopted and initially included TSW,

No. 2 MT Squadron, UK MAMS, No. 4624 (County of Oxford) Squadron RAuxAF (a Movements unit based at RAF Lyneham), and the Mobile Catering Support Unit (MCSU), which was then at RAF Benson. ACSUs later became Air Combat Service Support Units (ACSSU) in deference to the Army, where direct support such as that provided by the Royal Artillery and RE, is regarded as a combat arm, whereas logistics in the Army is termed service support.

Following the formation of ELW (No. 85 (EL) Wing from 2003) in 1999, No. 5001 (Expeditionary Airfield Facilities) Squadron was added to the RAF's logistic ACSSUs, followed by No. 1 Expeditionary Logistics Squadron in 2007 after its development and renaming from the original TSS. The RAF also restructured its non-aircraft engineering ACCSUs in 2007 by forming No. 42 (Expeditionary Support (ES)) Wing; as part of this reorganisation, No. 5001 Squadron transferred to the new Wing from 85 (EL) Wing.[24] A new ACSSU was also formed the same year and named the Joint Aircraft Recovery and Transport Squadron (JARTS), becoming part of 85 (EL) Wing.[23]

By 2014, the A4 Force through its ACSSUs was able to establish a comprehensive range of essential infrastructure and services at deployed operating bases wherever they might be required. The engineering services of No. 42 (ES) Wing, working in conjunction with the Army's 12 (Air Support) Group RE, could install a number of essential services such as hangars and other temporary buildings, portable aircraft arrestor gear for runways and air conditioning for technical facilities. The wing's armament related squadrons were able to clear any unexploded munitions and to establish temporary explosive storage areas. The comprehensive movements expertise of No. 1 AMW enabled them to set up a deployable air terminal as well as building any temporary freight handling facilities and providing the necessary air cargo handling equipment. The core squadrons of No. 85 (EL) Squadron were then able to establish a range of support services, from air and sea port cargo clearance to supply and catering services. The wing was also able to establish domestic accommodation, laundry, and welfare facilities for deployed personnel.[25]

In the fifteen years since a return to more expeditionary type warfare was announced in SDR 98, RAF Logistics has come a long way in developing its deployable capability. The A4 Force has a much greater range of specific capabilities than can be detailed here but, suffice to say, is now exceptionally well placed to support RAF expeditionary operations. The development of deployable RAF logistic support units since 1935 is shown in Table 5.

Logistics Reserve Capability

By 2014, the RAuxAF was providing an important contribution to RAF Logistics. In addition to No. 4624 Squadron, six other Auxiliary squadrons had a number of logistics personnel on their establishment: No. 501 (County of Gloucester) at RAF

Brize Norton (now part of 85 (EL) Wing and the A4 Force); No. 502 (Ulster) at Aldergrove in Northern Ireland; No. 504 (County of Nottingham) at RAF Wittering (now part of 85 (EL) Wing and the A4 Force); No. 606 (Chiltern) at RAF Benson (supporting the helicopter force); No. 611 (West Lancashire) at RAF Woodvale; and No. 614 (County of Glamorgan) in Cardiff. Between them, they are able to provide an important reserve capability of drivers, chefs, and suppliers.

Unit	Approximate Dates	Remarks
Air Stores Parks	1935–1961	
Supply and Transport Columns	1939–1950	
MT Companies/Squadrons	1940–to date	Only No. 2 MT Squadron remains operational, now within 85 (EL) Wing
Embarkation Units	1941–1955	
Mobile Air Movements Squadrons	1958–to date	Became No. 1 Air Mobility Wing in 2006
Tactical Supply Wing	1970–to date	Became part of JHC in 1999
No. 4624 Squadron RAuxAF	1982–to date	Auxiliary Movements unit
No. 3 Mobile Catering Squadron	1975–to date	Formerly MCSU at RAF Benson. Transferred to 85 (EL) Wing in 2003
No. 1 Expeditionary Logistics Squadron	2007–to date	Constituted as a new squadron in 85 (EL) Wing in 2007
Joint Aircraft Recovery & Transport Squadron	2007–to date	Part of 85 (EL) Wing
No. 504 Squadron RAuxAF	2013–to date	Part of 85 (EL) Wing
No. 501 Squadron RAuxAF	2014–to date	Part of 85 (EL) Wing. Re-roled to logistics support in 2014

Table 5: Development of deployable RAF Logistic Support units/ACSSUs since 1935.

A Home for Deployed Logistics: The A4 'Hub'

As part of the wider efforts to rationalise defence real estate and to provide a clearer focus for units committed to expeditionary air operations, a review of the basing requirements for these and other types of units was conducted in 2003–2004. The outcome from the rather lengthy titled *STC* [Strike Command] *Air Combat Service Support Unit, Air Surveillance and Control Systems and Minor Unit Basing Review* was that the opportunity should be taken to relocate most of the logistic ACSSUs to RAF Wittering by 2006. Additional space was to be freed-up here following the announcement in the Strategic Defence and Security Review in 2010 that the Joint Force Harrier would be withdrawn from service at the end of that year and moved to nearby RAF Cottesmore. It was thus that in 2006, No. 85 (Expeditionary Logistics) Wing relocated to Wittering from Stafford. Not all ACSSUs moved to Wittering. UK MAMS, which became No. 1 Air Mobility Wing (AMW) in November 2006, rightly remained with the air transport force at RAF Lyneham. The fuel-centric TSW, which was part of JHC, remained at RAF Stafford as it was required to provide a strategically located helicopter landing site (with rotors-turning refuelling) halfway between the main rotary wing bases of Benson, Odiham, and Middle Wallop, and the exercise areas in northern England and Scotland. Of the Auxiliary squadrons, only No. 504 is based at RAF Wittering, with Nos 4624 and 501 located at RAF Brize Norton. The various adjustments that had been made by the end of 2014 had re-balanced the A4 Force along logistic and engineering lines to provide optimal support to RAF Wittering and to both the Air and Joint Force Logistic components on operations.[26]

This was to be a change of identity for RAF Wittering, from its better-known role as 'Home of the Harrier', to become the RAF's logistic (or A4) 'Hub' in 2006. The change in role of the station was marked by the station commander appointment becoming a Supply (later Logistics) Branch post in November 2006, with Group Captain Ro Atherton becoming the first female incumbent in the unit's history; this was a career opportunity that had been lost with the closures of RAF Carlisle and Stafford. This post also carried the responsibility of the A4 Force commander although this was later changed to A4 Force elements commander when the RAF created one-star level force commanders. This geographical command responsibility required a dedicated coordinating function and on 1 April 2007 an A4 Force HQ was established at RAF Wittering to provide this key role.[27] By 2014, the wing commander-led HQ was configured to undertake a number of functions expected of such an organisation including coordination of effort, planning, training, assurance, advocacy, and acting as the A4 Force interface with external agencies.

Expeditionary Air Wings

One final requirement that needed to be addressed by the RAF for supporting expeditionary air operations was command and control at deployed operating bases. Even at relatively well-established forward locations, experience since the First Gulf War in 1991, and even during the Cold War during exercises, had shown that many required a degree of preparation and additional infrastructure before they were suitable for hosting RAF deployed aircraft. Indeed, some could require up to thirty days preparation before the arrival of deploying forces.[28] This work required coordination in-theatre through some form of command and control function. It was thus that on 1 April 2006, following ministerial endorsement, the RAF introduced Expeditionary Air Wings (EAWs). These were intended to be permanent formations brought together from various pre-identified sources throughout the RAF when required. The EAWs were established at nine Main

Operating Bases in the UK, with their station commanders also holding the dual responsibility of EAW force commander.[29] The initial concept was that two EAWs were to be held at readiness for deployment and would form the core command and control function, as well as support staff at a deployed operating base; this would provide a basic support infrastructure for the reception of further force elements such as the ACSSUs.[30]

A further five wings were formed at overseas deployed operating bases with No. 901 EAW at Al Udeid, No. 902 EAW at Seeb (later Musannah), No. 903 EAW at Basra in Iraq (later Camp Bastion in Afghanistan), No. 904 EAW at Kandahar in Afghanistan, and No. 905 EAW in the Falkland Islands, South Atlantic. A further wing, No. 906, was formed at Al Minhad in the United Arab Emirates. Given the number of wings operating in the Middle East, a higher coordinating HQ in the form of No. 83 Expeditionary Air Group was established at the UK Air Component HQ in Al Udeid.[31] The RAF's numbering of these EAWs carried forward identities from the Second World War, with a number of the UK units based on wings in 2TAF and the overseas EAW numbering based on tactical wings formed in India in 1944.

The Purple Dawn: The Joint Supply Chain

The disbandment of RAF Logistics Command as a result of SDR 98 marked the point from which more logistics functions and organisations became a tri-service or joint responsibility, a relationship that has been colloquially referred to as a purple environment (as opposed to the dark blue, khaki, and light blue of the three services). In reality, there had always been some form of interaction between the supply chains of the three services. The creation of the DLO—followed by the formation of new organisations such as DCTA, DSDA, and the Defence Fuels Group to name but a few—quite quickly began to establish this approach. As this new landscape unfolded, the single services progressively relinquished much of their supply chain management responsibilities; the various bodies and functions that emerged were staffed by a mixture of personnel from the three services and the civil service.

One of the important points from an 'end-to-end' study carried out in 2004 was the need for defence to adopt a more holistic approach to supply chain management; in broad terms, this concept covered what was colloquially known as the 'factory to foxhole' (or cockpit in the case of the RAF) continuum, which stretched from industry at one end, through the new integrated project teams in the DLO who managed much of the acquisition, support and engineering process, across the strategic link to operational theatres known as the 'coupling bridge', to the end user at the front line. It was thus that with this 'purple dawn', a new Joint Supply Chain began to develop. The day-to-day control of activity across the chain was vested in the Defence Supply Chain Operations and Movements organisation based at Andover, an organisation that had evolved from the Defence Transport and Movements Agency.[32] In the words of the manual that was produced to provide corporate governance for this new arrangement, the front line commands (of which RAF Strike Command was one) became 'customers of the JSC', while providing 'much of the manpower and resources required to establish and run the JSC'.[33]

This time also saw the first real efforts to converge all three single-service supply regulations into one publication, the first iteration of which became Joint Service Publication (JSP) 336 in 2004. In 2006, the supply regulations and supportability engineering regulations were merged into a new JSP 886 with the result becoming the Defence Logistic Support Chain Manual. The rationalisation of the various regulations was a lengthy and time-consuming process and even by 2012 was just 65 per cent complete. The convergence work continued until 2014 when a Government decision was made to reduce the number of JSPs and to digitize those that were still required. The JSP 886 was chosen as the 'flagship' for this work and the regulations became a series of policy statements, each of which was supported by process 'maps'; all of these are now part of the Defence Logistics Framework and accessed on-line through a defence 'gateway'. It was thus that after some eighty years' service the RAF's AP830, which had been introduced in 1921, was finally subsumed into the new world of Joint Supply Chain governance.

The RAF and Joint Logistics

In the years following the First Gulf War, the UK became much better at deployed operations, helped considerably by its experience in support of the Balkans conflict. While the planning for and coordination of activity during the Falklands War of 1982 had emphasised a need for improved coordination between the three Services, it was the First Gulf War and the emergent work to strengthen the UK's ability to plan, coordinate, and conduct expeditionary operations, which led to the MOD establishing a Permanent Joint Headquarters (PJHQ) at Northwood in Middlesex on 1 April 1996. For the first time, this co-located planning, operational, intelligence, and logistics staffs on a permanent basis. The new organisation included elements of a quickly deployable Joint Force Headquarters (JFHQ), which could be deployed to operational theatres and was able to exercise command of the rapid deployment of front-line forces. As would be expected, the new HQ was staffed by personnel from all three services along with MOD civil servants. Among these, RAF Logistics officers and tradesmen soon formed a growing part in the logistics division as well as a number of other related areas.

Another significant change at this time was the move to what was known as 'componency'. Britain, quite quickly, had to re-learn the lessons from the Second World War about how important joint operations are and, with the formation of PJHQ, the five components of joint operations were established: land, maritime, air, logistics, and special forces. Over time, this gave the RAF Logistics community some difficulty as the Army believed they should provide the logistic component in joint operations. The requirement for a HQ for a Joint Force Logistics Component (JFLogC) that would coordinate the various logistic force elements on joint operations, had become quite clear following Operation Granby in 1991. Based around an Army Logistic Brigade with augmentees from the RN and RAF, the first JFLogC HQ was deployed on Exercise Saif Sareea II in Oman during September–October 2001, for the initial operations against the Taliban in Afghanistan as part of Operation Veritas in 2001 and to Iraq as part of Operation TELIC in 2003.

The Army felt strongly that any JFLogC HQ should be based around one of its Logistic Brigades; however, this was opposed by both the RAF and the RN. As part of the development discussions, the Army did offer that the post of Deputy Commander 104 Logistics Brigade could be an RAF appointment or even, in extremis, command of the Brigade. However, experience during this time indicated that a standing (rather than as and when needed) JFLogC HQ was required and this was duly formed at PJHQ in 2005, initially of some twenty-five staff from the three services. The new style HQ was held at five days-notice to deploy and was intended to be one of the first elements to establish itself in a theatre and invariably the last to leave. Its role was key in the command and control of the various stages in theatre logistics support, from the initial reception and staging of forces, through ongoing support, to eventual recovery to the UK.

The JFLogC deployed to Afghanistan in late 2005 with an RAF Logistics officer, Air Commodore Graham Howard, taking command in July 2007 for a six-month tour.[34] In time, what was the JFLogC HQ took on more responsibility across the Afghanistan and Middle East theatres and was retitled HQ Joint Force Support; the commander was also Deputy Commander British Forces. The HQ Joint Force Support was based at Kandahar until 2009 when it became clear a move was needed to co-locate the HQ with the majority of the enabling force elements at Camp Bastion, further south in Helmand Province.

The JFLogC/Joint Force Support HQ was rotated every six-months with the Army's three Logistics Brigades (101, 102, and 104) and the PJHQ JFLogC providing four of the core staffs. The rotation plan required a fifth HQ that, on two occasions, was an entirely augmented HQ generated from scratch, trained, deployed, and then disbanded. An RAF logistician filled either the deputy or commander post for each rotation and RAF logisticians filled many key posts. RAF Logistics acquitted itself well throughout this process and continued to provide a number of personnel up until the eventual withdrawal from Afghanistan in 2014. The post of commander of Joint Force Support was also filled by two more senior RAF Logistics officers, Air Commodores Les O'Dea in 2009 and John Bessell in 2014. The distinguished service of both officers in Afghanistan was recognised by the award of the Queen's Commendation for Valuable Service (QCVS).

While the capability and operation of the new joint structure continued to develop, most of the various Government defence reviews implemented after

Options for Change in 1990 focused their attention on the size and capability of the armed services. Although the SDSR of 2010 addressed which Armed Forces would be required over the next decade, it had not tackled the wider problem of how defence itself was structured and managed. It was thus that in August 2010, the defence secretary launched a defence reform study headed by Lord Levene.[35] Amid the fifty-three recommendations of the report, which was published in June 2011, it was announced that a four-star led Joint Forces Command would be formed to 'strengthen the focus on joint enablers and on joint warfare development'. Essentially, the new command achieved initial operating capability in April 2012 and brought together PJHQ (including the Joint Force HQ and Joint Force Logistics Component) into an overarching organisation along with a number of other joint formations, which then existed.[36] It was becoming clear that logistics, hitherto regarded as a purely supportive function, was at last being recognised as essential to the front line.

An important requirement of coordinating the input of the single services to joint operations was the ability of the new PJHQ to be able to interact with the respective command, operations, and planning departments of the three services. For the RAF, this 'conduit' was through HQ STC (Air Command from 2007) at High Wycombe. Broadly speaking, an operational tasking from the MOD would be passed to PJHQ, which, for the air requirement, would be relayed to Strike Command's Operations Centre. Following this, an RAF contingency action group (CAG) would be convened at which all the main disciplines would be represented, including a representative from the Logistics Support Centre (LSC).[37]

The LSC became the linchpin of operational logistics planning and coordination. By 2004, the centre was headed up by a then Supply Branch wing commander with five main sections, which enabled it to address development and exercises, along with the main life cycle elements of operations from tasking, through the mounting process to longer-term sustainment. This work was complex and the myriad logistic options (or modules as they were known following the MDSS in 1993) from what became a sizeable master list, required IT support for the LSC to cope with the almost endless permutations. This support was provided by the highly successful software package known as the modularised support force packaging information technology system (MSFITS). The software tool, which became the RAF's main deployment planning aid, enabled the LSC and other users to very quickly identify the personnel and equipment required to meet a specific deployment requirement. These were then incorporated into what was known as a force element table, which would specify all the elements required for a deployed operating base, along with further work to determine their desired order of arrival. Once approval for this package had been granted by the Strike Command CAG, tasking signals were then issued to the respective units or formations and the deployment process was then initiated.[38]

Cutting the Coat to Suit the Cloth: Defence Reviews after SDR 98

Close on the heels of SDR 98 came the Government's White Paper, *Delivering Security in a Changing World*. Published in December 2003, this review announced a series of cuts to core equipment and numbers of personnel, along with the scaling-back of a number of future capital procurement projects. The review also made an adjustment to the SDR 98 strategic commitment with a new defence posture that would expect the armed forces to support three simultaneous small to medium scale operations, and, at longer notice, to conduct a large-scale operation (such as Operation Telic in Iraq), while running a concurrent small-scale operation. The RAF was to be reduced in numbers by a further 7,000 men and its Jaguar force of some forty-one aircraft was to be withdrawn from service, along with the closure of their home base RAF Coltishall in Norfolk. The review also announced a reduction in the procurement numbers of the Nimrod MRA programme, along with fleet reductions of the Nimrod MR2, Tornado F3, Puma helicopters, and Rapier missile launchers. The Typhoon purchase was confirmed although the 'Tranche 2' contract was delayed until December 2004. It was also announced that the four C-17 Globemaster III aircraft leased as part of SDR 1998 would be purchased along with an additional aircraft, bringing the RAF's heavy lift fleet total to five aircraft.[39]

The final review in the period that this book covers came in 2010 in the *Strategic Defence and Security Review*. While this aimed to provide an updated security policy, the review was set against a pressing need for the Government to address the MOD's £38 billion overspend in its procurement budget. The outcome saw a further reduction of 7,000 RAF personnel, the early retirement of the Harrier GR7/GR9, the abrupt termination of the £3.2 billion Nimrod MRA project (due in part to technical difficulties), and a reduction in the number of Chinook helicopters that were then on order. Although it was announced that the Hercules C-130J fleet would be retired ten years earlier than planned in 2022, it was confirmed that the Future Strategic Tanker Aircraft procurement would still go ahead to replace the VC10 and TriStar. A further strengthening of the RAF's air transport capability was announced by the confirmation to purchase twenty-two Airbus A400M aircraft. A key announcement was that the RAF's future fast-jet fleet would be based on the Typhoon and Lockheed Martin F-35 Lightning II aircraft.[40]

All-in-all, it was a complex picture. While SDR 98 was largely concerned with a return to expeditionary operations and the associated enablers to support them, following reviews have tried to grapple with the often diametrically opposed requirements of addressing emerging security threats on the one hand, with the ever-pressing need to reduce costs on the other. The manpower reductions to the RAF, which amounted to 21,500, proved to be particularly difficult for its personnel managers. The challenge from the defence reviews by 2010 was having to do more with less. Experience would show that cutting the coat to suit the cloth was, and continues to be, highly problematical.

The Second Gulf War, 2003: Operation Telic

Iraq was yet again to feature in expeditionary operations in late 2002. Following growing concern regarding their apparent possession of weapons of mass destruction, plus continual difficulties with the access of UN weapons inspection teams, the UN passed Security Council Resolution 1441 in November 2002, which declared that Iraq had not complied with previous resolutions, set out new requirements, and that serious consequences would result from further non-compliance. Iraq's failure to comply with the resolution saw the UK, through Operation Telic, join a US led-coalition that commenced military operations on 20 March 2003. This was to be the largest military operation since Operation Granby in 1991, with the main deployment from the UK and Germany taking place in January 2003; the air component alone comprised 115 fixed-wing aircraft and 100 helicopters.[41] The deploying force was of a similar size to that assembled for Operation Granby, but was deployed in half the time. Of particular note is that the operation took place against a background of UK commitments in the Balkans, Sierra Leone, Afghanistan, and Northern Ireland. The RAF had an advantage at this time as it already had aircraft and personnel in the Gulf region as part of its involvement in the no-fly zone operations over Iraq.

As the campaign unfolded, a further 100 aircraft were deployed along with a further 7,000 personnel. The air campaign that began on 21 March 2003 saw the RAF fly 2,519 sorties with the majority of the munitions used being precision-guided or 'smart' weapons. A wide range of aircraft were employed: Tornado F3s and GR4s; Harrier GR7s; VC10s and TriStar tankers for air-to-air refuelling; Nimrods and Canberras for reconnaissance; the Sentry E3-D for airborne early warning; Hercules and C-17s for air transport; and Chinook and Puma helicopters. This resulted in a complex support programme. Combat operations officially ended on 1 May 2003.[42]

The National Audit Office's report on the campaign highlighted the significance (and success) of a number of tri-service organisations that had been formed in the wake of SDR 98. Of particular note was the benefit of a having a CDL who was responsible for the totality of the MOD's logistics process. To reinforce this, an additional post of assistant chief of the defence staff (logistic operations) was established in the MOD central staffs to provide a senior and independent logistics focus within the MOD operational planning team. Within the DLO, the formation of a logistics operations centre based at Andover provided an important role in coordinating the movement of consignments to theatre.[43] The lease of the four C-17 Globemaster III aircraft made a substantial contribution and, along with other air transport, deployed about half of the personnel involved. Despite the enhancement to the RAF's heavy lift capability, commercial air charter was still required, the cost of which alone amounted to £53.5 million. This raised an interesting issue in that the balance of MOD ownership of lift assets and the reliance on commercial aircraft would need to be kept under review.[44] This campaign also witnessed the employment for the first time of urgent operational requirements, a process by which normal procurement procedures were bypassed in order to introduce urgently required equipment to operational service more rapidly. The difficulty here was that much of the equipment was not NATO codified and thus incapable of control through MOD stock control systems.

The UK maintained a military presence in Iraq until the last of its forces were finally withdrawn in May 2011. Unlike Operation Granby in 1991, the campaign in Iraq saw coalition forces occupy the main cities and towns of the country, primarily due to a concern that the conflict could lead to a humanitarian crisis resulting from a large-scale refugee problem and a significant disruption to essential services. Moreover, the country had suffered many years of neglect under the rule of Saddam Hussein. The RAF therefore maintained an operational presence in Iraq, mainly at Basra Airport, but also at Baghdad and Balad. Wider afield, its logisticians also served in Saudi Arabia and the United Arab Emirates during the initial phase of the operation, and then also in Bahrain, Kuwait, and Qatar. There were also TSW personnel in theatre and their involvement with the operation is covered in Chapter Six.

Life at these operating bases proved to be particularly hazardous in the years following the campaign but notably so in 2007 when, following the success of Operation Sinbad, which had endeavoured to stabilise Basra for handover to Iraqi Government forces, insurgents effectively laid siege to Basra and its airport.

Squadron Leader Andy Marshall was on his third Operation Telic tour in 2007–2008 as the senior air movements officer (SAMO) at Basra. Andy had a mixed team working for him, including personnel from the Army's 24 Regiment Royal Logistic Corps (RLC). He also had the additional role of being responsible for all the movements

Cargo loading in Iraq during Operation Telic. (*A. Marshall*)

detachments in-theatre including Kuwait, Baghdad, Talil, and Ballad. At Basra, he was also the VIP 'meeter and greeter' and dealt with many interesting people and activities. Andy recalled just how much the level of personal danger had increased:

> Unlike my previous tour when I could count the number of IDF [indirect fire] attacks with my fingers and toes, this time it was worse, although not as bad as the summer previously. In total there were 71 attacks with 263 rockets launched against us, causing a number of casualties and death on the base. One of those was Sergeant Baz Barwood who was an MT driver. He was a good colleague and his death was a very sad event. In addition to IDF, the ground situation also was more dangerous; you could not walk by yourself any more due to threat of kidnap and you were permanently armed.

Flight Lieutenant Tom Cousins was also serving here on his first operational deployment to Basra Air Station in early February 2007, when the vehicle park at Trenchard Lines was subjected to repeated rocket attacks and a number of vehicles were destroyed. No. 903 EAW's MT SNCO, Sergeant Duane 'Baz' Barwood, was first on the scene and ensured there were no casualties before carrying out post-attack recovery activities. No. 903 EAW MT Section worked tirelessly over the next few days to repair vehicles to ensure that operational tasking could be completed. For their actions during this period, No. 903 EAW MT and MTMS were awarded an AOC 83 EAG commendation. Indirect fire attacks during this period were relentless and, on 29 February 2008, Sergeant Barwood was tragically killed in another rocket attack on Trenchard Lines. Tom Cousins described him as 'an incredible SNCO who led his team with conviction, dedication and humour. He was respected and liked equally by those who worked for him and those whom he worked for'. His loss was tragic and, as a fitting tribute, the main road at RAF Brize Norton has now been named Barwood Avenue in Baz's honour.

Afghanistan, 2006–2014: Operation Herrick

The terrorist attack on the World Trade Centre in New York and the Pentagon in Washington on 11 September 2001 and the United States' subsequent assertion that Afghanistan was harbouring al-Qaeda terrorists saw British forces deploy to Afghanistan in support of American operations seeking to drive the ruling Taliban regime from power.[45] In 2006, the UK deployed its forces to the south of Afghanistan in support of NATO as part of Stage Three operations; Stage Two had seen movement into the north and the west of the country, and Stage Four would go on to cover a similar movement into the east.[46] In due course, the RAF's commitment to the campaign in Afghanistan (Operation Herrick) would be centred at Kandahar Airfield and at Camp Bastion in Helmand Province.

The decision to join the campaign in Afghanistan presented a number of new and significant challenges for RAF Logistics. Perhaps the most demanding was that the commitment was in addition to the campaign of combat operations in Iraq. Supporting two major theatres of operation at once presented many issues, ranging from greater demands on spares and supplies to managing a more complex supply chain from the UK. With Afghanistan being a landlocked country, establishing and maintaining lines of communication was problematic.

The air line of communication from the UK for freight and personnel staged through RAF Akrotiri in Cyprus on the outbound leg to Kandahar in Afghanistan; requirements for Camp Bastion in Helmand were moved on by C-130 tactical transport. For the return leg to the UK, aircraft were routed through Minhad in the United Arab Emirates and Incirlik in Turkey. Freight moved by sea was routed through Pakistan and then overland (utilising a commercial contract) to Kandahar and Camp Bastion. The land route into Afghanistan was particularly hazardous due to the difficult terrain, harsh climate, and the omnipresent risk of insurgent attacks. The amount of personnel and freight moved through these lines of communication was considerable. From January 2006 to May 2009, for example, 186,000 personnel and 64,260 tons of freight were sent to Afghanistan.[47] The logistics issue that arose from this was as a result of tasking the air transport fleet. In May 2009, this consisted of sixty-nine aircraft but the age of these aircraft, their usage, and the hazardous environment in which they were operating led to significant numbers being out of service for maintenance work and modifications; in the case of the TriStar, VC10, and C130K, availability was reduced by as much as 50 per cent.[48]

The RAF's role in the campaign, similar to its involvement with Iraq, was two-fold. First, the maintenance of the air line of communication. This was an enduring commitment from the early days of the campaign to the final withdrawal from the country in October 2014. It was a campaign that stretched the RAF's air transport fleet and movements organisation to the limit. The air-bridge was also a critical enabler of the largely biannual mass changeover of the Army's corps and regiments after their tour of duty. The airbridge was also the only means by which personnel could return home for their rest and recuperation. A particularly sad but important duty that the movements' organisation was heavily involved in was the repatriation to RAF Lyneham of those killed in action during the campaign. The second aspect was the RAF's role in the campaign itself and the deployment of its aircraft to theatre. In the later stages of the campaign, rotary wing aircraft were very much the focus. At Camp Bastion, the logistic support of aircraft was the responsibility of a tri-service Aviation Support Group, which, by 2010, was supporting Chinook, Apache, Sea King, Lynx, and Merlin helicopters. TSW also had a standing detachment at Camp Bastion.

Logistics Arrives, 2009

In late 2008, the then head of branch, Air Vice-Marshal Matt Wiles, canvassed the senior officers of the Supply Branch for their views on making a bid to rename the branch to 'logistics'. Similar to the reasons behind the renaming of the Equipment Branch to Supply in 1979, there had been a ground swell of support for such a move for quite a while. The need for a further change of name was important as the term logistics was becoming more widely recognised and the branch believed that a change would not only strengthen its identity, but also improve recruitment and retention. The name was also more relevant in the joint service area where the Royal Navy had renamed their Supply and Secretariat Branch to Logistics in 2004 and the Army had formed the RLC much earlier in 1993. The name change was officially approved in 2009 and was marked by a launch event held at RAF Halton. Of particular note was that this was not just a change of name but also a merger of both the former Supply and Administration (Catering) Branches. The change saw a widespread renaming of various organisations, although many of the former Supply Squadrons had started to rename themselves as Logistics Squadrons in the early 2000s.

In tandem with this work, Group Captain Steve Harpum was successful in securing a new badge for the Branch. His initial enquiries had revealed that there was not a tradition in the RAF of officer branches having a badge, with the exception of the RAF Regiment and Police, which were both deemed as being a corps and not a branch. The precedent had just been set, however, as the RAF Dental Branch had just succeeded with such a request. It was found that re-using and amending an existing, but disused badge was more straightforward and could be approved by the appropriate Herald at the College of Arms rather than a lengthier process that required Her Majesty the Queen's final approval. It was agreed that the most appropriate choice would be the old RAF Logistics Command badge, with its wording amended to 'Logistics Branch'. The motto, *sustentamus ut bellent* (we sustain that they might fight), was retained as it continued to reflect the branch's role in sustaining air power.

The new identity for the branch also prompted a renewed interest in its wider heritage and ethos and a RAF Logistics tie was designed, consisting of three equal stripes of blue, red, and gold. The inspiration for colours can be traced back to the very early days of logistics support to military aviation. The blue and gold stripes reflect the colours from the blazon of the village of St Omer in France, where the very first aircraft park was established in October 1914. The red stripe represents the ingenuity of those very early air logisticians who had to support the demands of a new and rapidly evolving military capability. The colour is taken from the truck that was requisitioned from Maples department store and used to support No. 5 Squadron RFC; the truck bore this brilliant scarlet livery throughout the war. Having established a heritage back to the very early days of air logistics, the same colours still resonate today. The blue and red stripes echo the flash displayed on the tailfin of all Royal Air Force aircraft. The use of sky blue rather than the darker shade reflects the subdued markings carried by the operational fleet, with the darker red reflecting the flash on the non-operational fleet. This juxtaposition emphasises the role of the Logistics Branch and Trades in enabling air operations both at home and when deployed. The gold stripe is perhaps the most important; it represents the golden thread of logistics that runs throughout the Royal Air Force, and its role to 'sustain that they may fight', the motto on the Branch badge.

In 2009, the then head of branch, Air Vice-Marshal Matt Wiles, formally opened the RAF Logistics Heritage Centre at RAF Halton. A project that began in 2005 and was headed by the author (as Branch and Trade Historian), the centre is in the Supply and Movements Training Wing at RAF Halton. Run by a small team of volunteers, it consists of a number of displays, showing the past and present of RAF Logistics.

Operations over Libya, 2011: Operation Ellamy

The Arab Spring movement that brought about the overthrow of the rulers of Egypt and Tunisia also encouraged a similar revolt by the people of Libya against the rule of Muammar Gaddafi in February 2011. The brutal response by pro-Gaddafi forces to rebel activity in Western Libya led to international condemnation and was seen as violating international law. On 17 March 2011, the UN Security Council passed Resolution 1973, which sanctioned a No-Fly Zone and the protection of civilians in Libya. This authorised a NATO operation (Unified Protector); this began on 19 March 2011 with French aircraft being the first to enter Libyan airspace. The ensuing campaign, which saw a critical role for NATO air forces, was a crucial factor in the ultimate success of the revolution, which effectively came to an end on 20 October 2011 with the capture and death of Gaddafi in the city of Sirte.

The rate at which the civil war in Libya progressed left little time for NATO planning and operations began literally within hours of the UN resolution being signed. This was particularly the case for the UK, with the RAF receiving direction to mount its contribution under the codename Operation Ellamy as early as the afternoon of 18 March 2011. The first of its aircraft to be committed to the operation were airborne the following day. For command and control, a Joint Force Air Component HQ was set up at RAF Akrotiri in Cyprus on 21 March, along with No.906 EAW initially supporting Sentry, Nimrod, Sentinel, and VC10 tankers; the Sentry and VC10 aircraft subsequently moved on to operate from Trapani in Sicily. No. 907 EAW established its base on 21 March at Gioia del Colle in Italy, a location that was to host RAF Typhoon and Tornado GR4 aircraft. Additionally, Tornado GR4s and TriStar tankers also took part but operated from their bases in the UK.

The initial part of the operation proved to be real headache for RAF Logistics as the exceptionally short notice deployment of aircraft left no time for the normal PJHQ to HQ AIR tasking process and the planning/tasking-cycle work through the LSC at HQ STC. The problem was also not helped by the fact that, as a result of various manpower reductions and re-focussing of military posts within NATO, the RAF no longer had a staff presence in the NATO HQ (AFSOUTH) at Naples in Italy, which was heavily involved in the wider planning; representation here would have enabled a much earlier understanding of the logistics implication for the UK of NATO's overall plans. It was thus that many of the RAF unit Logistics staffs involved in the deployment phase of Operation Ellamy received direct tasking phone calls rather than through the more usual routing through the chain of command. Staff in the LSC and the A4 Force HQ at RAF Wittering worked with ACSSU staff to ensure that overall control was maintained and that there were no 'back-door' taskings. Indeed, staff at all levels showed great pragmatism, flexibility, and commitment amid all this planning uncertainty. It was yet another example of where logistics, despite the widespread dependence on information technology, still required a fusion of people, common sense, and basic communication skills. The resulting load out of equipment by air to the forward operating bases required a mix of some seventeen C-130 and C-17 aircraft.[49] The size of this outload was less than it might have been, due to the fact that Tornados were due to deploy to Nancy Air Base in France as part of Exercise Southern Mistral. The equipment was on a 2 MT Squadron convoy of twenty vehicles that was already *en route* to France when operations over Libya began. The convoy was diverted with its important load to help set up Gioia del Colle, which was to become the deployed operating base for the RAF Tornado and Typhoon aircraft. No. 2MT Squadron was to continue with a role in the operation, providing a vital road resupply service to RAF units in Italy. Logistical support to units deployed on the operation was coordinated through what were known as logistics focal points for various services and squadrons in the UK.

One of the logistics officers heavily involved in the operation from the outset was Wing Commander Rob Sutton who was working as OC Force Generation Wing in the A4 Force HQ at RAF Wittering when the crisis broke. Rob deployed to Trapani in May 2011 for a four-month deployment as the detachment commander. Prior to his arrival, the force elements there had operated as two separate detachments with No. 8 Squadron from RAF Waddington providing Sentry aircraft as part of the NATO AEW Force operating from the well-found NAEW Forward Operating Base already established at Trapani, and No. 101 Squadron operating its VC-10 aircraft from the ITAF flight line. The two detachment commanders here had operated autonomously and the posts were filled by aircrew squadron leaders who took on these additional responsibilities, but without any formal integration into the EAW structure.

The situation was complicated because RAF flying regulations mandate the maximum number of flying hours aircrew can undertake during specified periods of time and all aircrew members were operating at far higher rates of effort than on routine operations.[50] As such, they were being rotated between operational detachments and peacetime locations every three to four weeks in order to maximise their utility across the fleet. Rob Sutton's arrival provided much needed continuity in the post. Rob recalled how the detachment, much of which was accommodated in nearby hotels, was dependent on food being provided under Sicilian host nation arrangements. While this might appear to have been a popular gastronomic arrangement, food hygiene was difficult to maintain and personnel were soon craving the nourishing, wholesome, traditional, and plentiful fare that field catering had provided for decades. It was not long before a detachment from the RAF's No. 3 Mobile Catering Squadron was assigned to the detachment, and they provided excellent support throughout the operation.

One of the many logistical challenges to supporting RAF aircraft on an island in the eastern Mediterranean was the provision of aviation fuel. For various reasons, this could not be provided through host nation arrangements and had to be sourced by the Defence Fuels Group back in the UK. Delivery to the island was by ocean tanker and then from a receipt point near the mooring jetty by pipeline to the on-base fuel storage installation. As with all aviation fuel, quality control was critical and the whole fuels management task was overseen by a dedicated RAF Logistics fuels specialist, Flight Lieutenant Vinnie Jackson. Wing Commander Rob Sutton eventually handed over command of the detachment to another Logistics officer, Wing Commander Rob Williams, in August 2011; Williams remained at Trapani until the end of the operation in October 2011. There was little respite for Rob Sutton who was deployed again, this time to the EUFOR HQ at Sarajevo in Bosnia-Herzegovina as the chief of the Logistics Infrastructure and CIS Branch. His commitment was marked by a much-deserved OBE in the Operational Honours and Awards List of 2013.

A sad footnote to the logistics of Operation Ellamy was the death of SAC James Smart, a driver with No. 2 MT Squadron, who was tragically killed in a road traffic accident. He had been part of the convoy that had been destined for Nancy Air Base as part of Exercise Southern Mistral and was re-tasked to go to Gioia de Colle. He had remained there for some time, undertaking general driving duties; however, when he returned to RAF Wittering, he quickly volunteered for the next available convoy bound for Italy. It was on this convoy that he was involved in a fatal accident and his untimely death was a great loss to the detachment and was felt by many, especially those from his parent base at RAF Wittering. It is fitting that RAF Wittering, in his memory, instigated the Smart Award, which is made to the outstanding airman of the year from the A4 Force.

Syria and Iraq, 2013–2014: Operations Luminous and Shader

While the first part of this book draws to a close following the British withdrawal from Afghanistan in 2014, instability in the Middle East has provided a curtain call. It will not be the last operational commitment, but it is a timely reminder that logistics continues to be a crucial enabler in the sustainment of air power. In 2013, concern had grown that the escalating violence in Syria was posing a real threat that might destabilise neighbouring nations. In August 2013, Typhoons of XI Squadron, Sentry E-3Ds of No. 8 Squadron; and a route support C-130 Hercules operating under the aegis of No. 121 EAW was deployed to RAF Akrotiri in support of Operation Luminous, which was the RAF's contribution to the air defence of Cyprus during the Syrian chemical weapons crisis.

This proved to be a timely reminder of the strategic significance of Cyprus, especially in the logistics line of communications. The base at RAF Akrotiri had been built in the mid-1950s to relieve pressure on RAF Nicosia following the withdrawal of British forces from the Canal Zone in Egypt. By the 1990s, the logistics and engineering functions at Akrotiri were being catered for by the Cyprus Logistics Unit and the Cyprus Maintenance Unit; both formations became part of the Cyprus Service Support Unit in 2001 within the base's Operations Wing.

By late 2012, it had become clear that the command responsibilities within the two-wing organisation of RAF Akrotiri (Operations and Base Support Wings) were out of balance. Operations Wing by that time was responsible for seven squadrons and over 700 personnel, leaving little spare capacity at wing commander level to address some of the station's longer-term concerns. The problem had been exacerbated by the fact that the station commander post had reverted to an aircrew appointment having been tied to the Logistics Branch since 2008; this had resulted in a lack of senior logistics experience above the rank of squadron leader. It was thus that in June 2013, a Logistics Wing was formed at Akrotiri under the initial command of Wing Commander Jamie Cameron who became responsible for a Joint Logistics Squadron, a Joint Movements Squadron, and a quality continuous improvement team. This re-established a clear focus for logistics at this key RAF airbase, enabling the new wing to concentrate on the inflow of personnel and equipment for emerging commitments, while allowing the Operations Wing to focus on the operation itself. This proved to be particularly timely for Operation Luminous as a number of specialist support units were hosted by Akrotiri and their seamless integration proved to be a notable success. Operation Luminous was wound down in November 2013.[51]

British participation in the military intervention against the Islamic State of Iraq and the Levant through Operation Shader, which began in August 2014, again saw RAF Akrotiri become a vital forward operating base for RAF aircraft when supporting the Iraqi Government; the new structure at Akrotiri again facilitated a much more focused approach to logistical support for deployed squadrons and their supporting staffs. Logistics Wing supported the Tornado GR4, C-130 Hercules, and Voyager air-to-air refuelling aircraft of No. 140 EAW. Operation Shader commenced with humanitarian aid being dropped to civilians trapped on Mount Sinjar in Northern Iraq directly from RAF Akrotiri, supported by Logistics Wing, No. 47 Air Despatch Squadron RLC, and the Department for International Development. The UK parliamentary vote in September 2014 to permit UK airstrikes against IS enabled No. 140 EAW to launch Tornado GR4 and Voyager refueller aircraft in support of coalition forces. Logistics Wing at Akrotiri played a key role in maintaining the air and sea bridges, airfield support transport activity, refuelling, and broader logistics command and control.

The Branch and Trade in the Nineties and Noughties

While much of the logistics story has focused on the more high-profile aspects of sustaining airpower on overseas operations, the Branch and Trade, by way of their breadth of experience and expertise, filled logistic appointments across the MOD, the joint environment, and within NATO and the UN. A number of opportunities arose over time, which has seen logisticians filling high profile appointments such as Military Assistant to the Under Secretary of State for Defence and the defence *attaché* in Paris, to name but a few. These are but two examples from a much wider range, which, alas, are too numerous to discuss in any detail here. Within the RAF, some unusual opportunities also arose that called for logistic skills. One of the more unique postings was the Supply team on the Battle of Britain Memorial Flight Trade Group 18. Based at RAF Coningsby since 1976, the Supply Trade has provided an NCO, SAC, and MOD civil servant for this support commitment to a fleet, which includes the piston-engined Lancaster, Hurricane, Spitfire, Dakota, and Chipmunk aircraft. The Supply Trade, by and large, remained much the same throughout this period. By the early 2000s, though, the RAF started to use the generic term 'Logistics Trades' to encompass Trade Group 18 (Supply and Movements), Trade Group 19 (Chefs and Caterers), and Trade Group 6 (MT Drivers).

A New Future

The end of the Cold War had seen RAF Logistics having to adjust to a whole new era, much of which was involved with developing a deployable capability to meet the needs of expeditionary warfare. In this respect, the progressive evolution of the A4 Force was a significant achievement, with the development of an extensive range of ACSSUs that now enables the RAF, in conjunction with its EAWs, to deploy at short notice overseas and to start flying from 'bare-base' locations. Since the first Gulf War in 1991, there has been no shortage of opportunities for the Branch and Trades to gain operational experience, although the concurrent commitments in Iraq and Afghanistan, between them, occupied much time, attention and commitment of resources. The SDR of 1998 not only brought the concept of expeditionary operations back into much sharper focus but was also the point from which the RAF's approach to logistics became part of a Defence approach. As such, many of its capabilities began to be subsumed into tri-service operations, along with contractor support packages playing a much greater part in its logistic support. The withdrawal from Afghanistan, which was symbolically marked by British troops leaving Camp Bastion in Helmand Province on 26 October 2014, brought to an end a thirteen-year campaign, which had seen 453 troops killed fighting the Taliban insurgency. This point in the book also brings to a close this first part of the history of RAF Logistics. Part Two now examines in more detail the specialist areas of tactical and expeditionary logistics, movements, the post-war management of POL, managing the supply chain, information technology, before finishing with training, and education. Part Three concludes the overall work by drawing some broad observations on the Logistics journey.

PART II

Perspectives

6

Tactical and Expeditionary Logistics

In Chapters Four and Five, reference was made to the formation of three tactical and expeditionary formations. The largely Cold War role of the RAF Germany Harrier Force required support in the field to meet its operating needs and this gave rise to the Tactical Supply Flight (TacSF), which was formed in 1970 at RAF Gütersloh in the former West Germany. At about the same time, the Tactical Supply Wing (TSW) was formed in the UK. Although originally intended as the RAF's main second level support organisation with wider logistic capability, its core expertise soon became the field refuelling of rotary wing aircraft. The increased significance of expeditionary operations following SDR 98, led to the formation of ELW in 1999, along with the transfer of TSW to the then newly formed JHC; this point also enabled a much clearer division of supply responsibility between rotary and fixed wing aircraft. This chapter examines the development of these three organisations in more detail.

RAF Germany: Tactical Supply Flight[1]

Following the initial work by Squadron Leader R. C. Allerton at HQ RAF Germany on determining how a significant force of fixed-wing combat aircraft could be supported in the field, away from established infrastructure and close to the front line, approval was granted to establish a TacSF at RAF Gütersloh. Noting the enormity of the responsibility and the far-reaching consequences for NATO's operational capabilities, the RAF posted a first-tourist, Pilot Officer (later Group Captain) Alan Matthews, fresh from the RAF College, to RAF Wildenrath to set up the first TacSF; he was armed with little more than a copy of *Flight* magazine containing an article about the revolutionary capabilities of the VSTOL Harrier and a picture of the jet taking off vertically with a full weapons load. Alan's team consisted of just twelve NCOs and airmen, all of whom were expected to be HGV drivers in addition to their main trade of Supply and Movements. The arrival of the aircraft of Nos 3, 4, and 20 Squadrons in the first few months of 1970 was matched by the arrival of scores of 10,000-gallon pillow tanks and associated pumps, pipes and filters, air portable fuel containers (APFC), thousands of FAP items, tons of field equipment, and several vehicles for the TacSF to operate with. Meanwhile, hundreds of tons of weapons and munitions filled the station's bomb dump and the local No. 431 MU storage facility at the Army's Base Ammunition and Petroleum Depot at Bracht. The learning curve in these early days was steep, incident-packed, and sometimes painful. For example, early deployments of fuel pillow tanks involved simply laying them on the ground until it was discovered that safety and German environmental laws required the tanks to be protected by earth 'bund' walls that were lined and every last drop of waste fuel had to be recovered. This further increased the pressures on the few suppliers and MT drivers available for the multitude of tasks.

In the early days of the Harrier Force, much emphasis was placed on security and secrecy for the development and deployment of this revolutionary and unique operating capability. It was therefore much to Alan Matthews's consternation when, driving the leading three-ton truck of the first ever off-base deployment on the autobahn somewhere near Hanover, he glanced down to see alongside a gleaming Russian limousine containing a senior Soviet Army officer grinning up at him and saluting, with a 'we know what you're doing' look; the Soviet Military Mission in West Germany (known as SOXMIS) was well aware of what was going on. Much was gleaned from the British Army in terms of field skills, camouflage, off-road driving and working in rough terrain. The Army, in the shape of the Harrier Support Signals Regiment, Field Engineer Squadron and nearby logistic units, were well endowed with men, equipment, vehicles, ammunition and expertise and were very keen to help the boys in blue. Not everyone in the RAF though was so keen to become green as well as blue. On one occasion, a fully armed and dangerous TacSF detachment arrived on a site to be greeted by an engineering warrant officer with the words 'Who do you think you are, bloody commandos?'

Despite the early teething problems, the RAF Germany Harrier Force, including its unique logistic support package, was declared operational in 1971 and went on to serve as a key component of NATO air forces for more than twenty years. Much of the credit for the success of the logistics operation rests with the handful of Supply NCOs and airmen who served in the early years of the flight, when the available expertise and resources were often in short supply. Their enthusiasm and determination to overcome any obstacle shone through—a tribute to the flexibility and multiple skills of Trade Group 18.

The Harrier Wing moved to RAF Gütersloh in 1977, a move that saw TacSF becoming part of the RAF Gütersloh Logistics Squadron, a dedicated tactical unit formed in May 1983. The squadron was separate from the main Supply and Movements Squadrons on the unit, which provided the traditional range of services for the base itself. The Logistics Squadron was made up of two flights (TacSF and Operations and Training Flight) along with two logistic planning officers (one for each of the Harrier and Support Helicopter Forces). The TacSF was the real hub of the squadron and was further sub-divided into three sections looking after fuel, FAPs, and mobility. The Squadron was manned by a main cadre of officers and tradesmen reinforced by non-cadre personnel drawn from the RAF Gütersloh Supply and Movements Squadron for exercises and for war should it occur; this was a similar system to that employed by TSW at No. 16 MU RAF Stafford who drew their non-cadre personnel from the main depot.

By the 1980s, the RAF Germany Harrier Force had become highly experienced in its war role, which required it to deploy to pre-surveyed field sites; to accommodate its aircraft, they required up to six sites with two standby locations for emergency relocation.[2] The preparation of the sites was carried out by the Army's RE, who established camouflage 'hides' for the aircraft and laid steel matting as temporary taxiways. In wartime, the sites would be between ten and sixty miles behind the forward edge of the battle area, thereby minimising the transit time to the operational area. In a five-hour period of sustained operations, the Harrier was able to fly ten short sorties as opposed to the more heavily-armed Tornados or Jaguars in the far west of Germany, which were only able to complete half the number of missions during the same time span.[3] Command of the sites rested with a Forward Wing Operations Centre (FWOC) where the RAF Gütersloh station commander was based, having become the Harrier force commander.[4]

The Logistics Squadron provided a team of about eight suppliers for each flying site, whose job it was to set up and maintain a fuel farm of 10,000-gallon pillow-tanks supplying a local hydrant-line system to a number of Harrier 'hides'. They also controlled the supply of ground fuels and maintained a first line FAP. In close proximity to the flying sites were logistics parks, usually one per three flying sites; the parks held reserve stocks of war consumables, a main fuel farm (replenished each night from RAF Gütersloh) and a second line FAP. The command and control of the deployed supply operation was exercised through the force logistics officer (OC Logistics Squadron) and a team of logistic controllers, co-located with the force engineer in the FWOC.[5]

The logistical support of helicopters was more straightforward. For the Pumas of No. 230 Squadron in the light support role, a single supplier was provided for each flying site with a SNCO, Junior NCO (JNCO), and two airmen on a support site. The work of these was limited to operating a FAP and the issue of ground fuels. Wherever possible, the supply of aviation fuel was kept mobile in 4,000 or 5,000-gallon tankers with 1,000-gallon tankers used as the pumping station. The much thirstier Chinooks operated by No. 18 Squadron in the medium support role required a different approach and utilised a combination of mobile and static reserves of fuel; the mobile fuel supply was available at flying sites while the static supply was located in pillow tanks elsewhere. It was standard operating procedure for both the Puma and Chinook to be refuelled with engines running and rotors turning to reduce the turnaround time and to get the aircraft back in the air as quickly as possible; this practice was known as 'hot' refuelling. This capability was

A camouflaged Harrier, Germany, 1980. (*Crown Copyright—Air Historical Branch MoD*)

unique to the RAF Logistics organisation and, honed during the Cold War, paid dividends in subsequent highly mobile conflicts. Although the Logistics Squadron never had to deploy in anger, they had a demanding exercise commitment by any standard—three to four Harrier Force deployments per year, as well as numerous helicopter exercises, Army exercises and various command post exercises, with the latter exercising the command and control elements without physically deploying into the field.

Both of the Harrier squadrons based at Gütersloh were relocated to RAF Laarbruch in November 1992 before eventually returning to RAF Cottesmore in the UK in mid-May 1999. The Pumas and Chinooks also left Gütersloh in 1992. No. 18 Squadron moved to Laarbruch in December and No. 230 Squadron was disbanded but reformed again at RAF Aldergrove in April 1992. The RAF eventually withdrew from Gütersloh in 1993, at which point its Logistics Squadron was also disbanded.

The Tactical Supply Wing[6]

Following its formal approval as a new second level support organisation in 1969, work proceeded apace to set up the new wing at No. 16 MU RAF Stafford; however, this took some time to accomplish, especially the appointment of its first OC. In the event, Squadron Leader (soon to become Wing Commander) John Craven-Griffiths became the first OC of the Wing. Prior to taking up command, he was sent to Singapore in early 1970 as OC RMA for Exercise Bersatu Padu, a deployment that provided valuable experience of the challenges of supporting a complex mix of units and aircraft on a deployed operation. The exercise ran for three-months, involving five nations, and was designed to simulate operating from Singapore without any form of permanent support infrastructure.

Based at RAF Changi with deployments to Duggan and Malacca, the RMA operating area consisted of an unused dispersal, with two offices and several huts on its perimeter. The RMA was responsible for the logistical support of four aircraft types during the exercise: C130 Hercules from the RAF and the Royal Australian Air Force; Bristol Freighters from New Zealand; Wessex helicopters from RAF Odiham; and, for a short period, an RAF Phantom Squadron operating from RAF Seletar. Deployed personnel came from the UK, the Malaysian Armed Forces, the Singapore Armed Forces (SAF), Singapore Police, a detachment of Gurkhas, and fifteen teams from the UK and Far East MAMS. The Army provided a major as a second-in-command of the RMA, a captain who was responsible for movements, and a lieutenant as an adjutant. A movements-qualified Equipment Branch squadron leader was seconded from HQ Far East Air Force. Due to a lack of any form of portable refuelling equipment, the tactical refuelling of aircraft was not included in the exercise and this task was carried out from fixed installations at Changi and Seletar. The exercise, nevertheless, proved to be a valuable training opportunity for all involved and highlighted the practical difficulties of providing support, much of it improvised, from a simulated bare base.

In September 1970, the now Wing Commander Craven-Griffiths returned to No. 16 MU to start work in earnest as OC TSW. One of the first priorities was to establish a Wing HQ, which was set up in a former barrack block; there were no telephones or office furniture and the HQ staff consisted of just one corporal for administrative duties. Storage areas and training accommodation were located in a nearby, unheated storage shed with a leaking roof and full of empty packing cases. It was widely rumoured that these premises had been allocated on the basis that the new Wing was to operate from 'bare' bases and that they should therefore operate at Stafford under the same conditions. From the outset, and to meet the peaks and troughs of operational tasking, it had was agreed that the Wing would be manned by a mix of permanent staff (known as cadre), supplemented by part-time staff (known as non-cadre), which could be drawn from Supply Branch and Trade personnel on the strength of the MU at Stafford.

To some extent, the terms cadre and non-cadre were misnomers in the early days. Only a few personnel were actually posted to TSW. These included: four Equipment Branch officers and eight Trade Group 18 (Supply) Senior NCOs and airmen, along with six Engineering NCOs and tradesmen, plus a corporal for administration. Initially, the tasking of cadre personnel was at the discretion of OC TSW, while participation of non-cadre personnel was agreed with the MU's OC Supply Wing and OC Support Wing, and subsequently endorsed by the station commander. It is generally believed that this was the main reason for basing the wing at this location, although there were strong views at the time for locating it elsewhere; Stafford did not have an airfield and it was a long way from the wing's principal mounting bases. It was also felt that morale would be enhanced by its personnel being more closely involved with the operational RAF, rather than working within the warehousing and distribution-focused atmosphere of the depot. In the event, experience showed that the right decision was made.

The early days of TSW were not easy, and some of its early members felt that their presence at No. 16 MU was at best tolerated and at worst opposed. There was also opposition from many NCOs and airmen of the depot who had secure and comfortable jobs as they had no intention of 'playing soldiers' by living in tents and working in the field. A great deal of effort was therefore made by all ranks on the wing to forge good working relationship at all levels. This soon paid-off and attitudes began to change once the wing began to assemble a 'critical mass' of trained personnel.

One of the early imperatives was to ensure that the Wing had a clearly defined role. At this stage, TSW had only a draft statement of unit policy (SUP), the document that defined not just an organisation's status but also laid down the chain of command and control, the war roles, and peacetime tasking level; the latter was particularly important with regard to the level of commitment expected of non-cadre personnel from the MU. The document also set out the composition and skills required by the various teams that were to make up the wing. The statement was particularly important in terms of defining precisely who did what and, in particular, the chain of command that stemmed from the Director of Supply Policy (RAF) staff and in stipulating the limits of responsibility towards TSW of the MOD, HQ STC, HQ ASC, and No. 16 MU Stafford. The statement also referred to the relevant joint theatre plans, operation orders, and the detailed role of TSW in given circumstances together with the wing's concept of operations. Aided by the planning staff at HQ No. 38 Group, the wing managed to identify detailed roles, along with the men and equipment required to support Wessex, Puma, and Harrier aircraft in the field. This work took up much of 1976 and the first part of 1977. Under the direction of a cadre officer, Flight Lieutenant John Furney, the lessons learned from Exercise Bersatu Padu were to feature quite prominently in the early days of the wing and OC TSW spent much time during the early part of his command visiting the Army Strategic Command, HQ ASC, and HQ Maintenance Command to discuss the post-exercise report.

Joint service doctrine at this time was moving towards a single-fuel policy, which required all military vehicles engaged in or supporting combat to be capable of using kerosene in the form of AVTUR F-34 in place of diesel (see also Chapter Eight). Out-of-area planning foresaw the emergency supply of fuel over a beach from an off-shore tanker, followed by pumping it to an airfield. If that fuel was kerosene, and aviation standards of fuel handling were met, the fuel could be blended with fuel system icing inhibitor to become F-35 for aviation use, or used directly in vehicles and ground equipment. To meet this task, the Army's RE had established a team of fuels specialists and acquired Emergency Fuels Handling Equipment (EFHE), which enabled them to build a six-inch diameter pipeline over several miles from a beachhead to an airfield. Powerful pumps were incorporated to deliver the fuel. Once up and running, the pumping operation would pass to the Army's RAOC from the beachhead to the point of Army use, but also to an airfield perimeter; from where responsibility for storing, handling, blending and issuing the fuel to aircraft would pass to the RAF. This was a ready-made task for the fuels handling part of TSW.

It was under this doctrine that one of the very first taskings of the wing came about. A team of six airmen headed by Corporal Jim Coleman was detached to Inverness in Scotland to operate EFHE in an exercise designed to prove that an emergency pipeline could take aviation fuel from an off-shore tanker in floating Dracone Barges (large flexible watertight tubes full of fuel that could be towed behind a tug) just off a beachhead and deliver it twenty miles or so inland to a simulated non-established base. The small detachment, however, was ill-equipped for this task and was not familiar with the equipment as it had been laid by the Army over a number of weeks without any involvement of TSW tradesmen. The team also had only limited basic equipment for field deployment. Their only personal equipment were a few combat jackets and trousers; they had no tents, field equipment, vehicles, or side arms, nor had they any form of specialist training, let alone any idea of the task ahead. During the weeks before deployment, some items of equipment were borrowed from a nearby Army barracks, including additional combat clothing, a long wheel base Land Rover, and some tents. Thus equipped, the first TSW detachment deployed to Scotland. Although the wing coped with the task, the deployment to Inverness showed just how much work and training was needed to get them operational.

The wing soon began to grow in size and capability, with much work undertaken to accumulate the right resources and ensure they were in the right place. There were a few anomalies though that required adjustment in these early days. Once such issue was that a Mobile Fuels Handling Squadron (MFHS) had been located at RAF Colerne in Wiltshire under the command of Flight Lieutenant (later Squadron Leader) Roger Cresswell. The reason for this was that the unit had aviation fuel on base, a spare bulk fuel installation (BFI), and was close to RAF Lyneham, the likely mounting base. Colerne also had spare hangar space, which was not available at Stafford. Fuels training for wing personnel was initially undertaken at Colerne, although vehicles and equipment had to be split between the two locations, and no economies of scale were possible at a time when everything was in short supply. The command, control, and training of the detached airmen proved problematic, and it soon became apparent that fuels handling would become the key to TSW's future. Thus, efforts were made to identify and convert suitable accommodation at Stafford to house the MFHS, with them relocated by early 1972.

The complement of officers soon began to grow and the arrival of Flight Lieutenant (later Group Captain) Robin Springett and Flying Officer (later Wing Commander)

VOLUNTEERS FOR DUTY WITH TACTICAL SUPPLY WING

Vacancies in TSW are normally filled by volunteers. If you think you are good enough to serve with us you can apply under the terms of AP3392 Vol 2 Leaflet 1551.

Unfortunately, we cannot accept you if you:
Are on PWR.
Are already screened under the Key Personnel Scheme.
Have a MES below A4 G1 Z1 CP2.
Are over 40 (Sgts and below).
Are in UK and have less than 3 years to serve.
Are overseas and will have less than 3 years to serve when you return to UK.

Don't bother to volunteer if you:
Are unfit and not prepared to get fit.
Are not prepared to get dirty, cold and tired and still smile.
Don't like the smell of aviation fuel.
Are not prepared to spend a fair amount of time away from home comforts in exotic places like Salisbury Plain, Sennybridge and Northern Ireland.

You'll be more welcome if:
You can drive (especially HGV).
You don't smoke.

Still interested?

If you are still interested, before you fill in the application form, call the Wing WO on RAF Stafford ext 6018.

Here are some shots of the Wing in action on a recent exercise.

Recruiting advert for TSW. (*Crown Copyright—Air Historical Branch MoD*)

Brett Morrell enabled important work to begin, such as the substantial task of identifying individuals from the MU staff at Stafford who could join the Wing as non-cadre members and arrange basic training courses. The selection of non-cadre officers proved to be an easy task as there were now many enthusiastic volunteers. Leading the way was Squadron Leader (later Wing Commander) Mike Liddiard, who took up the non-cadre post of the second in command.

While the sourcing of manpower gathered pace, the availability of equipment proved to be more problematical and required much goodwill from across the RAF. A physical trawl of airfields resulted in several Coventry Victor portable fuel pumps being acquired, about twenty air portable fuel containers (APFC) and a number of portable 10,000-gallon tanks. These could be rolled and folded into a valise, which together with an accompanying valise of pipes and valves were easily transported and could be used to construct emergency BFIs (EBFI). Tentage proved particularly difficult, a fact not helped by the wing's equipment scales at the time allowing only twelve tents for the entire wing. This challenge was rather cannily overcome by demanding canvas and various structural components as replacement parts, thereby enabling additional tents to be assembled while scales were argued over.

The MT fleet was also an important resource that needed to be expanded and soon four 'Eager Beaver' rough terrain fork lift trucks and a number of four-ton Bedford 4×4 trucks were borrowed from the Army. A small fleet of Land Rovers was also built-up using vehicles from a small reserve held by Air Support Command for air portability trials. None of these, however, had been adapted for winter operating conditions; this soon became an urgent requirement for the wing as its capability was beginning to attract the attention of the planners responsible for exercises in Norway, as part of the UK's commitment to the defence of NATO's northern flank (acting as a component of the NATO ACE Mobile Force (Land and Air)).[7] In terms of technical accommodation at RAF Stafford, the leaking shed initially occupied by the wing was repaired and additional acceptable storage facilities were allocated by the MU and Nicholson block, the wing's HQ, was extensively modified, including the conversion of two rooms into an armoury.

Training was an important task and good relations were quickly established with the helicopter flying training school at nearby RAF Shawbury. This was an important resource that enabled personnel to be trained in helicopter handling and refuelling. Similar relationships were also established with other units: RAF Cosford for radio operating; RAF Wittering for the refuelling of Harriers; RAF Odiham for helicopter handling and refuelling; and RAF Lyneham for air cargo loading and lashing training and the Army's Staffordshire Regiment allowed the wing to use their weapons firing range. In-house training first concentrated on physical fitness for all members of the wing, both cadre and non-cadre. This started every morning for those on base at 8 a.m. with a cross-country run and circuit training in the gymnasium or swimming. An initial problem to be overcome was the use of Trade Group 18 (Supply) airmen for duties around aircraft, particularly for aircraft refuelling. The actual connection of the earth and refuelling line to an aircraft or helicopter had always been done by aircraft tradesmen, and what amounted to a trade union dispute threatened to de-rail the entire TSW role in refuelling. This was eventually overcome when the Air Officer Engineering at HQ ASC offered training for suitable Supply tradesmen in the safety aspects of aircraft refuelling.

Being able to operate under field conditions was a key part of training new entrants to the Wing and they spent several days under canvas as part of their initial induction. A substantial proportion of the Equipment Branch and Trade at this time was used to working from purpose-built buildings on established airfields and accommodated in messes or barrack blocks. Field living was something that many had not experienced since their basic training and it was often the first time they had both worked and slept in these conditions. The physical work of laying-out and assembling refuelling points was invariably quite demanding, a task often accompanied by the equally physical requirement to dig slit trenches and latrines. Exercises formed an important part of the training regime and often consisted of setting-up radio links on high ground, preparing under-slung loads for helicopters, small arms shooting, refuelling techniques and operating rough-terrain fork-lift trucks. Any individual unable to adapt to these conditions was returned to their previous section or unit; the rejection rate was encouragingly low. Despite this intensity, training was not without its lighter moments. The digging of slit trenches during one such exercise led to a visit from the local constabulary, following reports from concerned locals who had reported what they thought was the burying of bodies.

Digging a slit trench. (*Crown Copyright—Air Historical Branch MoD*)

Above: Tornado fly away pack, Decimomannu, Sardinia, 1984. (*Author's collection*)

Below: *Aide memoire* for nuclear, biological, and chemical warfare hazards on the internal wall of a HAS, RAF Laarbruch. (*Author's collection*)

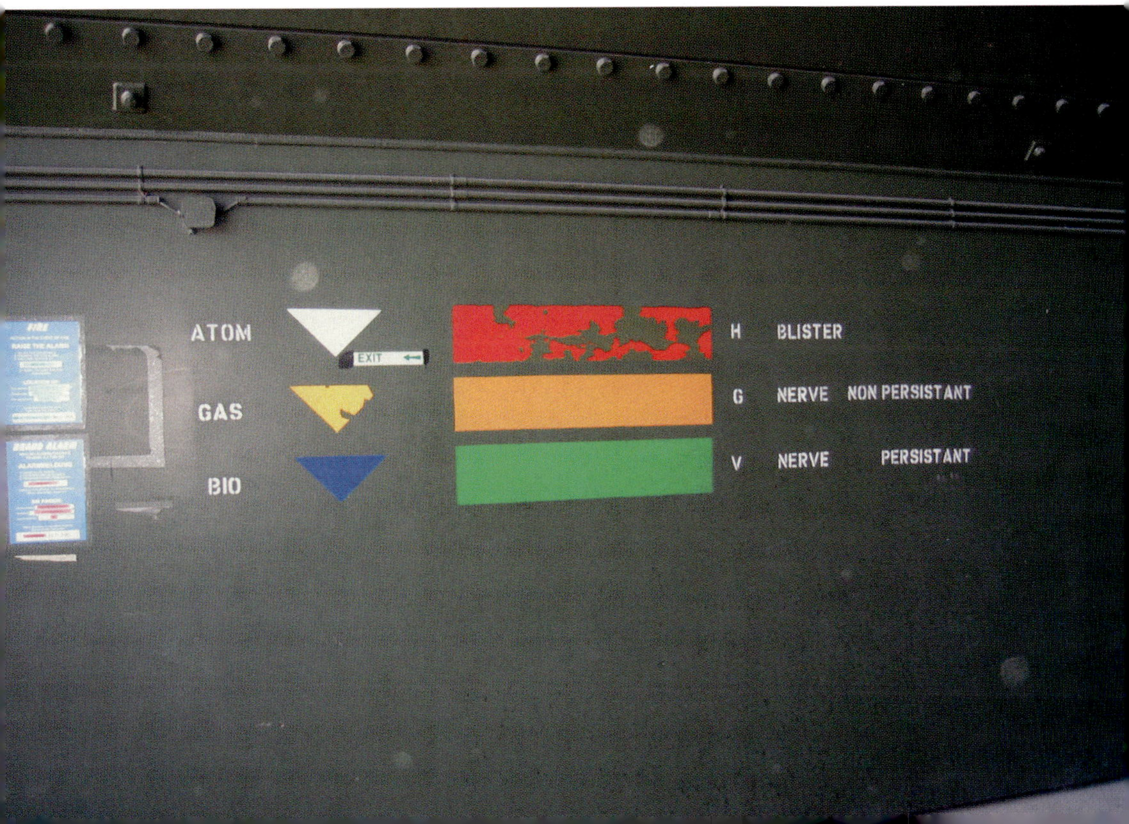

Above: HAS at RAF Laarbruch, pictured in 2008. (*Author's collection*)

Below: HES at RAF Laarbruch, pictured in 2008. (*Author's collection*)

Above: Interior of the SADAC at No. 16MU Stafford in 1993. (*Crown Copyright—Air Historical Branch MoD*)

Below: The RAF Supply Section on Ascension Island pictured in May 1984. (*N. Dabin*)

Above: Ascension Island anchorage pictured in August 1984. (*N. Dabin*)

Below: Gulf War aircraft (*front to rear*: Tornado, Victor, and Buccaneer). (*Crown Copyright—Air Historical Branch MoD*)

Above: HQ SFOR at Camp Butmir, Sarajevo, 2002. The different national flags illustrate the number of nations serving in the HQ at the time. (*Author's collection*)

Below: Aerial view of Ploče, Croatia, 2002. (*Author's collection*)

Above: Aerial view of the SADAC at No. 16 MU Stafford in 2002. (*Crown Copyright—Air Historical Branch MoD*)

Below: ELW training exercise. (*Crown Copyright—Air Historical Branch MoD*)

Above: Auxiliary 'movers' preparing a cargo load at Kandahar, Afghanistan. (*A. Marshall*)

Below: The A4 'Hub', RAF Wittering. (*Crown Copyright—Air Historical Branch MoD*)

Above: Camp Bastion, Afghanistan, 2010. (*Crown Copyright—Air Historical Branch MoD*)

Below: Chinook moving supplies in Iraq. (*Crown Copyright—Air Historical Branch MoD*)

Above: Basra Airport, Iraq, 2006. (*E. Stephens*)

Below: The hazards of the desert: a dust storm approaching Camp Bastion, Afghanistan, 2010. (*Crown Copyright—Air Historical Branch MoD*)

Above: Cargo hold of the C-17 Globemaster. (*Crown Copyright—Air Historical Branch MoD*)

Below: Storage area of the Aviation Support Group, Camp Bastion, Afghanistan, 2010. (*Author's collection*)

Above: Commemorative cake made for the merger of RAF Supply and Catering to Logistics, 2009. (*Crown Copyright—Air Historical Branch MoD*)

Right: The Logistics Branch badge. (*Crown Copyright—Air Historical Branch MoD*)

Puma approaching a refuelling point, Exercise Hardfall, 1985. (*N. Dabin*)

Above: TSW refuelling a Chinook in the Balkans. (*Crown Copyright—Air Historical Branch MoD*)

Below: TSW unloading fuel farm 'pillow' tanks during Operation Telic, Iraq, 2003. (*Crown Copyright—Air Historical Branch MoD*)

Above: Rough terrain container handler in use, Camp Fox, 2003. (*D. Lester-Powell*)

Below: A welcome meal: No. 3 MCS food servery in the field. (*Crown Copyright—Air Historical Branch MoD*)

Above: No. 3 MCS camp at Hainault during the 2012 Olympics. (*Crown Copyright—Air Historical Branch MoD*)

Below: Loading IFOR equipment at RAF Bruggen, Germany, 1995. (*Crown Copyright—Air Historical Branch MoD*)

Unloading armoured vehicle from a Hercules. (*Crown Copyright—Air Historical Branch MoD*)

The hard work paid off and TSW declared itself as having achieved a limited operational capability in April 1971. Very soon, the planning staffs at HQ Land, Wilton were encouraged to include the fledgling TSW in exercises and contingency plans for joint operations, although there were risks in including a relatively unknown support unit into these. Fortunately for the wing, one of the RAF contingency planning officers at Wilton at this time was Squadron Leader Mike Slade, who had commanded the UK MAMS teams during Exercise Bersatu Padu and he was able to initiate many of the tasks that were to be so important for the future of TSW. These ranged from deployments in Norway in mid-winter, supporting Harriers, to one in the Caribbean with No. 230 Squadron Puma helicopters supporting the Royal Navy and Royal Marines on anti-drug patrols.

Before the formation of the wing, helicopter refuelling in the field had been carried with the aircraft's engine shut down and using either small tactical bowsers, occasionally an APFC and pump, or 45-gallon drums of fuel and an electric fuel pump plugged into the helicopter batteries. As such, refuelling could often take up to twenty minutes, making the aircraft very vulnerable in operational situations. The wing was aware of rotors turning refuelling, which occasionally took place on RAF main bases, or by the Royal Navy on board ship, but the technique had not been developed for field deployments. It was clear that the wider use of the technique could prove to be a significant operational benefit for RAF support helicopters, at a time that the Westland/ Aérospatiale Puma was replacing the Westland Wessex, and the Boeing Vertol Chinook was on the horizon, both providing improved battlefield mobility. With such an enhanced capability, quick refuelling turn-round would become essential. At the time, only one refuelling line could be connected to the fuel source. If more lines could be connected then more aircraft could be refuelled at any one time—a step change in field refuelling. The means to do this were pioneered by the wing's fuels team led by Sergeant Mick Humphrey, which came up with a design for a splitter-box that would allow up to three lines to be connected to a single pump. A drawing was made and RAF St Athan was tasked to manufacture a prototype. The result proved the concept and the design was further enhanced by the addition of a fourth connection. The design was soon officially approved by the appropriate RAF Engineering Authority and the splitter boxes were rapidly introduced to service for TSW and the RAF Germany Harrier Force. Although up to four aircraft could be refuelled at once, the wings existing Coventry Victor pumps were not really up to the job, and work was started to provide a replacement. A design of a more robust diesel powered portable pump was agreed by engineering and provisioning staffs, and an urgent operational requirement contract was placed with Hamworthy Engineering in Poole. Within eighteen months, the wing had pioneered the deployment of a rotors turning refuelling capability within the forward area of the battlefield, thus enabling helicopters to spend more time on their operational tasks. The splitter box and the new Hamworthy pump enabled the unprecedented sight of up to twenty support helicopters being refuelled simultaneously in the field during Exercise Sky Warrior (see below).[8]

Developments during the 1970s

In January 1972, TSW was declared fully operational. The tempo of activity gradually increased as the performance of the wing in its early deployments began to be noticed by the operators and planners. In 1972, two events clearly demonstrated their versatility. The first was a major exercise Sky Warrior, which involved all helicopter types from the RAF and the Army, plus ground forces and was staged at Otterburn in North East England. It was during this exercise that the first airborne deployment into the forward area of the battlefield was rehearsed. This in effect increased the on-station time for all helicopters over the battlefield by more than twenty minutes. The second event was one where the Wing also gained valuable experience in a humanitarian support role, deploying to Nepal in 1973 as part of Operation Khana Cascade. Here, it supported Hercules aircraft on famine relief missions and, subsequently, in transporting more than 34,000 war refugees in both directions between Pakistan and Bangladesh as part of Operation Lucan.[9] By 1973, the wing had also established itself as a key logistics enabler for three aspects of the UK's contribution to NATO operations: refuelling of helicopters as part of AMF(L) and UKMF(L), together with refuelling of Harrier, aircraft assigned to support SACEUR's Strategic Reserve (Air) (SSR(A)).

By the mid-1970s, TSW had revolutionised the way in which aircraft were refuelled in the field. The use of 10,000 and 30,000-gallon flexible pillow tanks,

Hercules at low Level, Operation Khana Cascade, Nepal, 1973.
(*Crown Copyright—Air Historical Branch MoD*)

400-gallon APFCs, and small fast portable pumping and filtering equipment enabled supplies of fuel to be positioned in the field where the operating aircraft required them. Perhaps more significantly, refuelling times had been drastically reduced. The Puma helicopter, for example, could take on 1,300 lb of fuel in an average time of around 109 seconds; such a rate could enable nine of these aircraft to be refuelled and cleared from a site within ten to twelve minutes. Moreover, the wing itself could undertake a tactical move in extremely short order, thus affording it the added strength of being able to maintain tactical mobility. Puma operations illustrated this capability well: in a deployment some 80 km forward from a main helicopter base, the wing was able to commence refuelling for a mixed force of thirty-six aircraft within two hours of arrival. The task was completed in a mere ninety minutes. This forward deployment reduced the distance that the Pumas would have had to fly for fuel by 200 km.[10]

Northern Ireland

In mid-1973, TSW was given warning for a deployment to Northern Ireland as part of Operation Banner. An initial reconnaissance was carried out and personnel first began to deploy in late 1973. Initially, operation was with a single team of one corporal and five airmen, working with a single pump and APFCs (later a 10,000-gallon flexible tank) from a single location. During 1974, the wing's presence in-country increased to three locations, all operating with flexible tanks, and some capability for forward deployment with an APFC and pump. By 1975, the wing had established permanent detachments at Castle Dillon (near Armagh), Bessbrook Mill (between Newry and Crossmaglen) and at St Angelo (Enniskillen). These sites provided refuelling for RAF and Army Air Corps helicopters operating over what was known as 'bandit country'. Operations at Bessbrook were in a particularly hostile part of South Armagh and the deployed personnel found themselves in constant danger although none was ever injured, despite the helicopter landing-pad being targeted by IRA mortars. The nature of aircraft refuelling itself could present a hazard and in 1985, SAC Peter Donkin was awarded an AOC's commendation for his part in identifying and extinguishing an aircraft fire during a refuelling operation. The landing site here was always particularly busy and refuelling was a round-the-clock operation. The work was demanding (mentally and physically) and a six-week tour was invariably accompanied by a well-deserved one-week stand-down. While refuelling was an important service, the relatively simple refuelling of two or three types of helicopter presented limited training value to the wing. The true value of the detachments was highlighted by the Wing's OC at the time:

> The way in which the duties undertaken served to bring out the best in the airmen and NCOs. They matured mentally in just the right way and became

> true professionals proud of doing their job well and determined to bring about improvements in techniques wherever possible. In two years only one airman seriously complained about going back to Ulster for a subsequent tour.[11]

It is also worthy of note that two TSW airmen were awarded the Queen's Commendation for Bravery during operations in Northern Ireland: SAC A. J. S. Holsgrove in 1993 for rescuing aircrew from a crash at Bessbrook Mill and Corporal A. M. Bennett in 2003 for bravery in extracting a trapped crew member following the crash-landing of a Puma helicopter at Ballykelly, County Londonderry, in January 2002.[12] By 2004, there were twenty-two TSW personnel deployed at five security force operating bases that operated twenty-four hours a day, 365 days a year. The wing detachments were to remain in Ulster until the peace process was concluded. It is widely believed that TSW was one of the longest continuously serving units in Northern Ireland during Operation Banner.

Belize

In 1975, the second Belize crisis broke. Formerly British Honduras, this colony in Central America, which had long been threatened by neighbouring Guatemala, was the subject of renewed aggression with a massing of Guatemalan troops on the border following unsuccessful negotiations. In October 1975, three Puma helicopters of No. 33 Squadron were deployed to Belize Airport by Short Belfasts of No. 53 Squadron. Additionally, six Harrier GR 1A aircraft of No. 1 (Fighter) Squadron joined the Pumas in early November. At the same time, a detachment from TSW deployed via RAF Brize Norton and RAF Lyneham in early November and quickly established itself alongside the support helicopter detachment at Belize Airport. The main task from then on, and up until 1979, was supplying fuel to Harrier aircraft located in hides around the perimeter of the airport and to helicopters at the forward operating locations at Punta Gorda, Salamanca, and Holdfast. Flight Lieutenant Roger Maunder led the initial deployment, followed by Flight Lieutenant John Furney until it was decided that Flying Officer (later Air Commodore) Peter Whalley should do a four to six-month period as detachment commander. Up to that point, the wing's role was largely confined to the provision of aviation fuel; however, that changed on Peter Whalley's arrival. Operating from an office with two army majors, he also maintained a watching brief over the two MSF detachments. Moreover, as the SAMO he also was the *de facto* head of the deployed UK MAMS team (headed by Flight Sergeant Mervyn Cork) for every air transport offload and onload. Finally, and possibly of considerable relevance, to ensure the security of fuel supply, he took over responsibility for the two large static fuel tanks from Shell Oil Company.

Operations in Belize for TSW were significant as it was probably the first time, albeit in very embryonic form, that the wing started on the road to becoming the full Supply Support organisation envisaged by E. Plans (RAF) in 1968. When No. 1 (Fighter) Squadron aircraft were replaced with RAF Germany Harriers in 1977, support was to be provided by the RAF Gütersloh TacSF under the command of Flying Officer (later Group Captain) Chris Markey, who also encompassed all supply functions beyond fuel support under one organisational banner. Although Belize, like Ulster, afforded good practical operational experience, albeit on a static rather than a mobile basis, it did result in a significant increase in the length of time personnel spent away from home at a time when this was most unusual for airmen who were not serving at RAF Odiham or RAF Wittering. Although the anticipated invasion did not materialise, British forces remained in Belize under the guise of BRITFORBEL until 1994 when both the Pumas and Harriers departed the theatre.[13]

The Falklands Conflict: Operation Corporate

The invasion of the Falkland Islands by Argentina in 1982 saw the wing deploy yet again on active operations. In April 1982, elements of the wing deployed with Task Force 317 to the South Atlantic. They were charged with two main tasks: firstly, with the coordination of supply support at Ascension Island, and secondly, following the successful recapture of the Falklands, TSW was tasked with supporting aircraft based on the Islands. The story of TSW's wider role in supporting Ascension Island has been described in Chapter Four.

Although the wing lost equipment when the Atlantic Conveyor was sunk on 25 May, it was able to establish a forward arming and refuelling point at Port San Carlos, supporting both aircraft and ground forces attacking Port Stanley.[14] In all, 131 personnel out of a total strength of 180 deployed to the South Atlantic Theatre, both during the conflict and for the following four months; of these, six received honours and awards, including one British Empire Medal and five commendations from the Task Force Commander. In addition, thirty-four TSW personnel were awarded the South Atlantic campaign medal.[15]

Commitment to NATO: Support of the UK Mobile Force

Notwithstanding the various operational one-off tasks during its early years, the main task of the Wing was to support the UK's Harrier and support helicopter (SH) aircraft assigned to reinforce NATO. A significant proportion of the wing was committed to the UK Mobile Force (UKMF), which would deploy with the RAF component as part of the First Infantry Brigade during transition to war.[16] The support of both AMF (L) and the SSR (A) brought with it a commitment to deploy to either the Arctic Circle or Turkey and Greece; training for this role had started as early as 1976, with the Wing's first real involvement in TACEVAL when elements deployed to Denmark with No. 1 (Fighter) Squadron. At this time, TSW was the only unit in NATO that operated a hot refuelling service.

By 1983, the standard policy for refuelling the mix of Pumas and Chinooks of the SH Force was to use semi-static, collapsible pillow tanks for rotors turning refuelling, complemented by the smaller but more mobile APFCs. The greater fuel consumption of the Chinooks required additional fuel tankers (trucks tanker fuel (TTF)) as the main means of fuel re-supply, as opposed to the use of standard aircraft refuellers. While this combination met the needs of refuelling, the primary focus of the pillow tank configuration presented two limitations: set-up time and mobility. The establishment of a main refuelling area (MRA) could take up to five hours, including assembly, filling, concealment, and the construction of 'bund' walls, which were required both to contain any spillage and also to provide a measure of protection from blast and splinter damage in the event of enemy action. All of this was a sizeable footprint, taking time and considerable effort if it needed to be relocated at short notice. A more flexible approach that could meet the uncertain and highly changeable nature of the modern battlefield was required.

Although the TTF seemed ideally suited in terms of bulk fuel carrying capacity, it had been designed for the Army, purely as a fuel tanker to carry a range of ground and aviation fuels; as such, it had no pump or fuel filter and had six-inch diameter bottom-tank connectors for gravity offload. The Wing came up with an innovative solution to this limitation in the form of a trailer-mounted fuel pump and filter unit, known as the tactical aircraft refuelling trailer (TART). This was designed and built by TSW to be air-portable and used as an interface between the TTF and aircraft. The TART proved to be a highly effective solution and the trailer could be towed behind a four-ton truck or Land Rover. This was a significant step forward in the Wing's capability and enabled the concept of a highly mobile tactical refuelling area (TRA) to be developed; this used a combination of the TTF, tactical bowser, vehicle mounted APFC, and TART. This configuration also brought further flexibility in that the TTF could replenish both the APFCs and the tactical bowser by cross-connection. If required, this also permitted two Chinooks to be refuelled simultaneously.

The TART, nevertheless, had a long and difficult gestation. It was top-heavy and had less mobility than the 1,000-gallon tactical bowser, which was based on a Bedford MK chassis. After several years of development, however, the TART was eventually introduced to service, and it provided a good alternative for small-scale FARPs. That said, TRAs were increasingly required to provide increasingly large volumes of fuel to support Chinook flying, and so moves were made to replace the ageing tactical bowsers with newer air-transportable fuel delivery vehicles (AFDV) to help increase the availability of fuel carried on wheels. These became the preferred fuel delivery method, but the TART remained a valuable back-up and offered an air-portable option.

The TRA could also provide a much prompter service than the MRAs; the latter could take a minimum of two hours to provide a rotors-turning service (providing fuel was sourced from a trusted location and tested with a portable petroleum test kit), while a TRA with its own fuel could provide the same service within five minutes of an aircraft's arrival on site (in that it had tested fuel readily available in tactical bowsers and could simply refuel aircraft using the bowser's integral hoses). This capability could be enhanced to deliver multi-aircraft operations in less than half an hour by laying out hydrants and using the bulk fuel from the TTFs. The development of the TRA concept was a major step forward and enabled greater speed and flexibility in TSW's support of the UKMF.[17] The significant developments in rotors turning refuelling, especially for the Chinook, led to TSW being awarded, in 1985, the Wilkinson Battle of Britain Memorial Sword for 'enhanced operational effectiveness of the Support Helicopter Force'—the first and only award to a non-flying unit.[18]

The Tactical Supply 'Triangle'

Personnel employed on tactical supply duties acquired a wide range of specialist skills, from working with helicopters through to advanced field and driving skills, arctic survival and fuels handling. Among these was a chemical laboratory assistant qualification that enabled airmen to operate portable petroleum test kits and ensure that any fuel received from host nations or the NATO pipeline system was of an acceptable standard. All of these skills meant that the RAF personnel management staffs at RAF Innsworth had a tendency to post TSW-trained personnel in a 'triangular' circuit from Stafford to Gütersloh, with Ascension Island and the Falklands in between. While this built up a specialist cadre and reinforced their field and fuels handling skills, it did little to enhance the wider career opportunities of individuals. In the late 1980s, significant efforts were made to break this cycle, but there were still notable characters who made many repeat appearances on the Wing in a number of ranks. Of particular note is Bob McBey, who, at some time, served in every non-commissioned RAF rank in Trade Group 18 on the wing.

Flight Safety

Working in such close proximity to aircraft and interacting with onboard fuel systems brought with it an ever-present responsibility for flight safety for TSW. In 1986, three airmen from the Wing were recognised for their contribution to aircraft safety in two separate incidents. The first involved SAC Alan McGee, who, just before commencing the rotors turning refuel of a Wessex helicopter, noticed fuel leaking from the underside of the aircraft. After McGee informed the crew, the aircraft engine was shut down and engineering assistance summoned. On investigation, it was found that the leak was from the starboard engine fuel flow divider that was situated immediately under the engine combustion chamber; the leak could easily have led to a serious aircraft fire. For his vigilance, McGee was awarded a 'well done' certificate by the RAF's flight safety organisation.

The second incident involved SACs Peter Donkin and Kevin O'Rourke, both of whom were the duty refuelling crew when a Lynx helicopter returned to their forward landing site. The helicopter had suffered major damage to its undercarriage skids to such an extent that it was unable to attempt a landing at the site. The pilot declared an emergency and requested that the aircraft be refuelled while it was still in the hover. This was a difficult task and required Donkin to climb into the aircraft's cabin to operate the standby refuel and defuel switch as the normal control is inaccessible with the aircraft's rotors turning. O'Rourke had the difficult task of connecting the pressure refuelling line to the hovering aircraft. The swift action in unusual (if not unprecedented) circumstances by both airmen enabled the aircraft to be successfully refuelled and safely recovered to its home base. Both airmen were awarded 'good show' certificates by the AOC 1 Group for their actions.[19]

Peter Donkin was to distinguish himself again the following year in February 1987 when he was part of a TSW detachment supporting No. 33 Squadron during Exercise Hardfall in Norway. On moving back from a Puma helicopter on which he had just completed rotors turning refuelling, he noticed a slight spray coming from under the starboard edge of the upper sliding cowling. He attracted the attention of the aircraft's captain and the aircraft's engine was shut down. Further investigation

APFC, pump and filter unit combination in use during Operation Maralinga, Australia, 1987. (*Crown Copyright—Air Historical Branch MoD*)

found that the spray was hydraulic fluid leaking under pressure from a faulty filler cap. Had this leak not been detected, it was highly likely that the aircraft's hydraulic system would have become depleted of fluid resulting in the aircraft having to make a forced landing; an emergency landing site in the mountainous terrain of Norway is often difficult to find and the subsequent recovery of such aircraft would have been a time-consuming process. For his alertness and quick-witted action, Donkin was awarded what would be his second 'good show' certificate by AOC 1 Group.[20]

An unusual commitment for the Wing came in mid-1987 when they sent a small detachment to South Australia to provide refuelling support for two Wessex Helicopters of No. 28 Squadron, which carried out an airborne survey of the nuclear weapon test sites at Maralinga and Emu. The survey was to ascertain the extent and effect of any residual contamination that had endured from the UK's nuclear weapon trials, which took place at these locations between 1953 and 1963.

The First Gulf War: Operation Granby

While the continued support of operations in Northern Ireland maintained TSW's operational edge, it was nearly ten years before the Wing was again involved in active operations, following the Iraqi invasion of Kuwait in August 1990. At the time, TSW was participating in Exercise Windmill East in Cyprus, a tactical training exercise and their first experience of hot weather training since its formation. On 9 August, preparations were made to deploy the first forty of the eventual 160-man detachment. The initial deployment of twenty men departed RAF Akrotiri for Dhahran in Saudi Arabia to support the Tornado F3s of No. 29 (Fighter) Squadron. The task at Dhahran soon turned out to be much larger than had been anticipated and the volume of inbound freight increased to such an extent that TSW had to provide both a twenty-four-hour airhead clearance team and assistance to the UKMAMS detachment. In late September, a two-man team consisting of Squadron Leader (later Group Captain) Don Belmore and Sergeant (later Warrant Officer) Mick Johnson was redeployed from Dhahran to Tabuk in North West Saudi Arabia (just south of the Jordan–Iraq border) to establish similar support for RAF Tornado GR1 and GR1A aircraft. This was a particularly demanding task at a remote location, some fourteen hours' drive from a source of aviation fuel and the nearest sea port of Yanbu. This small team remained at Tabuk until November, working eighteen to twenty-hour days, performing most of the tasks of a small RAF station The TSW detachment remained here until it moved north in support of the UK Support Helicopter Force Middle East (UKSHFME) in mid-December 1990.

By mid-August 1990, an additional fifteen-man detachment had deployed to Thumrait in Oman to support RAF Jaguars and to provide refuelling to transport aircraft during the initial outload. As the Coltishall Jaguar Wing was organised as a mobile force, the station's Supply and Movements Squadron was able to provide all the required supply support, thus enabling the TSW team to be quickly redeployed to Muharraq in Bahrain to support Tornado GR1s; these aircraft were later joined by Tornado GR1As, the Jaguars from Thumrait, and Victor tankers. The detachment installed EBFI equipment to increase and disperse fuel reserves and remained a key part of the supply team until they redeployed to Jubail, a large petrochemical city in the North East of Saudi Arabia (mid-way between Bahrain and Kuwait) in December to support the UKSHFME under command of the then OC TSW Wing Commander (later Group Captain) David Bernard.[21]

It was not just in theatre that TSW was kept occupied. Back on Cyprus, the remaining elements of the Wing, which had deployed on Exercise Windmill East, provided a welcome reinforcement at RAF Akrotiri, which, by this time, had become a forward mounting base (FMB) for any further deployments. The Wing not only established EBFI equipment here but also assisted with providing twenty-four-hour cover for the resident fuels and supply organisations. The Wing also provided much needed assistance to the air movements organisation as the numbers of transport aircraft being handled by the station began to increase rapidly. The Wing's reinforcement of Akrotiri came to an end in mid-December 1990, when the remaining personnel on Cyprus moved to the Gulf to support the UKSHFME.[22]

By early January 1991, the size of the helicopter force in theatre had risen to nineteen Pumas, twelve Chinooks, and twelve Royal Navy Sea King aircraft, all operating from Jubail. The helicopters were dispersed to three separate areas: the Pumas to a Royal Saudi Naval Force base, the Chinooks to the Old Port Barrack,s and the Sea Kings to the main Royal Saudi Naval base. The Wing's bulk fuel stocks were established at Jubail on two sites at 32 General Hospital and the Old Port Barracks and at Abu Hadriyah, some eighty kilometres north, which was built up in anticipation of the eventual move of the ground forces into Kuwait.[23] Contrary to expectations, the coalition forces did not embark on a full-frontal attack into Kuwait, but positioned themselves for an outflanking move to the North West. Many TSW personnel had been in the theatre since August and the opportunity was taken to change over personnel during the first few days of January, including OC TSW, who was replaced by Wing Commander Robin Springett, ex-TSW and then working on the Al-Yamamah (Saudi Arabia) project for the MOD. By 10 January, and with the 15 January UN deadline for the Iraqi withdrawal from Kuwait approaching, the SH Force was aware that it was required to move north-west to the area of Wadi Al-Batin.[24] This saw the Pumas and Sea Kings establishing their main operating base at King Khalid Military City (approximately 80 kilometres south of Hafar Al-Batin), with the Chinooks' MOB being constructed in the desert about 100 kilometres east. FOBs were later established west of Hafar Al-Batin and the deployment of the SH Force was completed by 23 January.

Aviation fuel was provided by Saudi Arabia under host nation arrangements. By January 1991, the only secure source came from the ARAMCO refinery in Dammam; however, the fuel had to be collected by road vehicle. The total quantity of fuel required for each day of helicopter flying by the SH force was based on a figure known as the maximum daily off-take (MDO), a figure which was determined by multiplying aircraft numbers, the expected flying hours, and consumption per hour. This translated into an estimated requirement for the SH force commander of five times the MDO, which was required to be held as far forward as possible. This saw three bulk fuel farms established in the forward staging areas around Al Qaysumah; two of these each held two MDO with the remainder held at a location elsewhere.[25]

Apart from aviation fuel, TSW also provided a wider supply service with common user equipment sourced from Army stocks through No. 62 Ordnance Company at Jubail. Failing this, the RAF was able to purchase items from the local economy. In the early days of the campaign, all aviation supplies were obtained from nominated parent bases, using signal messages via a local communication centre. By the end of January 1991, however, three RAF Supply computer terminals were installed in Logistics Operations in the RMA at Jubail, one each for RAF Odiham, RNAS Yeovilton, and the Army Air Corps base at Middle Wallop. These provided a significant advantage in that Supply staffs were then afforded 'global' visibility of stock and could demand items directly from UK units. Inbound equipment was moved from the RAF distribution point in the Old Barracks at Jubail to a forward drop point, and then on-moved to detachments.

By 1 February 1991, Priority One air freight was taking on average three days from receipt of the demand in the UK to receipt of the equipment in theatre. It was taking just two or three days to be cleared from the airhead and moved forward by road although airlift was used when available.[26] Just prior to the commencement of the ground campaign, the helicopter main operating base and the SH Force HQ moved to Log Base Bravo, an assembly point north-west of Hafar Al-Batin. In due course, TSW established a large fuel farm at this location, with multiple refuelling points. A resupply drop point was also co-located with the Chinooks. It was thus that TSW was prepared to move forward into Iraq alongside the medical forward dressing stations. The TSW commander at the time, Wing Commander Robin Springett, commented:

> These men, Suppliers and MTDs [MT drivers], who would drive and operate fuel tankers in hostile territory, were armed with SA 80 rifles, and equipped with hand-held Satnav terminals (called Magellan) to enable pinpoint desert navigation. With the exception of some RAF Regt personnel, they were to be the most forward RAF tradesmen in the land battle. They crossed into Iraq and then Kuwait, right behind the fighting troops. Their task was to refuel any helicopters inserted to recover casualties.[27]

The wing refuelled not only the largest helicopter forces assembled by the UK, but also the helicopters of coalition partners on an *ad hoc* basis. Working closely with the First Armoured Division and carrying the fuel that would be essential for the helicopters,

TSW followed the British armoured forces as they breached the Iraqi defences on 25 February 1991, with convoys of fuel for the helicopters. Within four days, elements of TSW were in Northern Kuwait and were among the first British units to enter Kuwait City. An additional three tactical refuelling teams followed on into Iraq within twelve hours of the initial breach. The Wing entered the city from the north down the Basra Road to a location at Doha just west of the city to support RN Sea Kings, continuing to do so until 30 April 1991. As a result of the relatively light number of casualties in the ground campaign, the work of the SHF became concerned mainly with the movement of enemy prisoners of war; this led to a requirement for large quantities of fuel to be held forward at the concentration points where prisoners were consolidated before being transported on to larger compounds.[28] Initially, TSW established a single tank farm in Iraq, but such was the pace of the coalition advance that this soon necessitated the use of road tanker stocks only, and all the way into Kuwait. By the time that the Coalition's objective had been achieved and its forces had recovered from Iraq back into Kuwait, TSW found itself controlling some 250 men and 180 vehicles. The latter included some forty fuel bowsers. In terms of refuelling hardware, the Wing was operating a total of nine refuelling and bulk fuel storage sites.[29] It had also established itself at seven locations in Cyprus, Oman, the United Arab Emirates, and Bahrain, as well as twenty-one locations in Saudi Arabia, Iraq, and Kuwait—and all within just nine months.[30] Following the redeployment from the Gulf in May 1991, TSW was redeployed to support the Royal Marines engaged in Operation Haven, which was the operation in the north of Iraq to protect the Kurds who had fled from Saddam Hussein's army.

The TSW Parachute Cadre

In the late 1980s, largely through the individual efforts of Flight Lieutenant David Natrass, TSW developed a good relationship with No. 23 Special Air Service Regiment (Reserve) based in Kingstanding, Birmingham, and provided them with support during exercises. The Wing's value to the limited number of special forces (SF) rotary wing aircraft was immediately realised, and they were soon to find themselves supporting larger multi-national exercises. The need to provide rapid reaction fuel support, both for UK operations and in support of activity beyond the forward line of own troops, had become clearly identified and this new-found role for the wing was soon to be written into SF doctrine. This in turn generated a need for a capability that could deliver fuel beyond enemy lines and with equipment and men that were able to operate independently without a road-bridge. By 1992, using SF funding and, more importantly, given the Directorate of Special Forces' willingness to embrace innovation, TSW was authorised to have eighteen parachute-qualified posts on its establishment, which would deploy and support an air dropped/despatched forward aircraft refuelling point (ADFARP). This was a self-contained unit, based on a medium stressed platform (already then in use to air drop Land Rovers, artillery and ammunition). It was made up of two APFCs, a pump unit, filter, and one pressure/open line and was capable of delivering just less than 4,000 litres of aviation fuel. In about 1995 the means of air-dropping the ADFARP was converted from the old 'standard' military parachute to the low-level parachute, deployed via a static line from the C-130 Hercules. At that time, the main alternative was the square steerable parachute used by the SF and others for whom accuracy of landing was important.

Among the first volunteers to be parachute trained included the then OC TSW, Wing Commander (later Air Commodore) Andy Spinks. By 2005, the wing had been authorised to establish eighteen low-level qualified and eighteen static line qualified parachutists, and, with the exception of No. 2 Squadron RAF Regiment, this remains the only formal unit-level operational parachute role within the RAF.[31] The parachute capability enables a refuelling point to be dropped behind enemy lines, with operators inserted when required by helicopter or parachute to activate the site and refuel helicopters *en route* to and from deep penetration missions. This role was exercised on several occasions, a typical example being Exercise Windmill East in 1993, when TSW was allotted its own C130 Hercules aircraft to drop twelve of its parachutists direct from the UK onto the salt lake close to RAF Akrotiri in Cyprus. All twelve landed successfully on the hard surface, and deployed to their exercise location on the former Bloodhound missile site near Episkopi. Less than twenty-four hours later, the parachutists returned to UK on the same C-130 aircraft, this time dropping after a low-level pass onto a grass airfield near their home base at Stafford. A capability to refuel helicopters with hoses run out from the rear of a C-130 (air landed aircraft refuelling point) was also developed and exercised to support operations where a short landing strip was available. The capability was nearly used in anger in 1994 in Bosnia to supply fuel to the enclave at Zepa where Ukrainian UN forces had run out of fuel.

Support to Strike: Granting of the TSW Official Badge

Although TSW had used an unofficial form of badge for a number of years, it was not until March 1992 that Her Majesty the Queen was invited to approve an official version. The badge follows the standard RAF design of a circular component, with the Queen's crown above and a scroll below with the motto 'Support to Strike'. At the centre of the badge is a Peregrine Falcon hovering over a three-arched bridge representing the three RAF commands in place at the time: Strike Command, Support Command, and RAF Germany.[32]

Operations in the Balkans: Former Yugoslavia

As part of its commitment to UNPROFOR operations in the former Yugoslavia at the beginning of 1993, the UK deployed four Sea King helicopters of No. 845

Naval Air Squadron to Split, a coastal town north west of Dubrovnik in Croatia.[33] The helicopters were intended to provide a casualty evacuation capability for the deployed British Army battalion, in addition to other support tasks for UNPROFOR. The Naval Air Squadron had deployed its own first-line refuelling capability but this was to prove inadequate for enabling the Sea Kings to achieve their full operating range; this capability was therefore augmented by a TSW detachment in February 1993. The initial deployment planning was carried out by MOD Petroleum Plans (RAF) who, in the first instance, had arranged for the pre-positioning of Tactical Fuels Handling Equipment (TFHE), comprising 13,600-litre airfield refuellers and 20,000-litre all-wheel drive (AWD) fuel vehicles, which were all painted in UN white. Until this point, the Sea Kings had obtained their fuel on a repayment basis from Split airport but this arrangement was soon superseded by a local contract arrangement for bulk aviation fuel from the Croatian Government-owned company INA-Industrija nafte, d. d., at Split airport. The Wing soon established a refuelling facility here, with four airfield refuellers providing second-line storage, a facility which improved responsiveness to the Royal Navy's day-to-day flying in the Split area. The AWDs were used to provide fuel to forward operating bases, a service which soon saw round-trips of over 500 kilometres over treacherous mountain roads to meet single aircraft refuels.[34] Eventually, permission was given for the Royal Navy to position 8,000 litre tactical bowsers at Kiseljak, a location which was also the base for UNPROFOR's HQ Bosnia Command (HQ BHC) and to where an RAF Supply officer was detached. This location had become a principal forward base and, together with the Royal Navy, Norwegian, and French mobile air operations teams were also co-located there.

As the refuelling task increased, the detachment was reinforced by six additional TSW personnel to assist with AWD fuel resupply between Kiseljak and Split. Additionally, a TSW officer was established as the combat fuels officer in the HQ British Forces in Split. Unfortunately, one of the main supply routes between Split and Kiseljak (via Mostar and Sarajevo) was to be denied on 9 November 1993, following the destruction of the Old Bridge across the River Drina at Mostar by Bosnian Croat forces. This resulted in the Wing having to use an alternative route that had been created by the British Army's RE, to access northern Bosnia, which linked Tomislavgrad (known to the Wing's airmen as 'TSG') with Prozor Lake. This route, known as the 'trail', was only suitable for medium mobility vehicles and effectively limited movement of aviation fuel to carriage by the AWDs only. The refuelling facilities at Kiseljak were eventually supplemented by American and French pillow tanks. This necessitated a revision to the fuels support plan which saw the introduction of what were to become known as the loop routes, one for the north and another for the south. The northern loop moved fuel to Kiseljak, normally from Split, but it could draw stock from Tomislavgrad if necessary, and the southern loop linked Split to Tomislavgrad. By mid-1995, TSW became responsible for running the bulk aviation storage at Tomislavgrad and, a short distance away, a

TRA close to the Lipa checkpoint, the *de facto* border between Croatia and Bosnia-Herzegovina. Operations in Bosnia at this time were extremely hazardous for the Wing, and their convoys were often caught in the cross-fire between the various factions, particularly when transiting a town called Gornji Vakuf-Uskoplje; this was not made any easier by occasional incidents of local children stoning vehicles as they passed through other towns and villages.[35]

In June 1995, Bosnian-Serb forces had managed to overrun the Bosnian-Muslim enclaves. This led to an Anglo-French initiative, which saw 24 Airmobile Brigade deploying as part of a Rapid Reaction Force to the Port of Ploče in Croatia. This deployment saw a marked change in the UNPROFOR posture, where revised rules of engagement enabled NATO to undertake a close air support operation in September 1995 and the deployment of 105-mm light guns of the Royal Artillery (together with similar French units and a Dutch mortar company) on Mount Igman overlooking Sarajevo, in order to facilitate access to the town and to displace Serb heavy weapons from the surrounding hills. The Rapid Reaction Force hub at Ploče soon grew into a

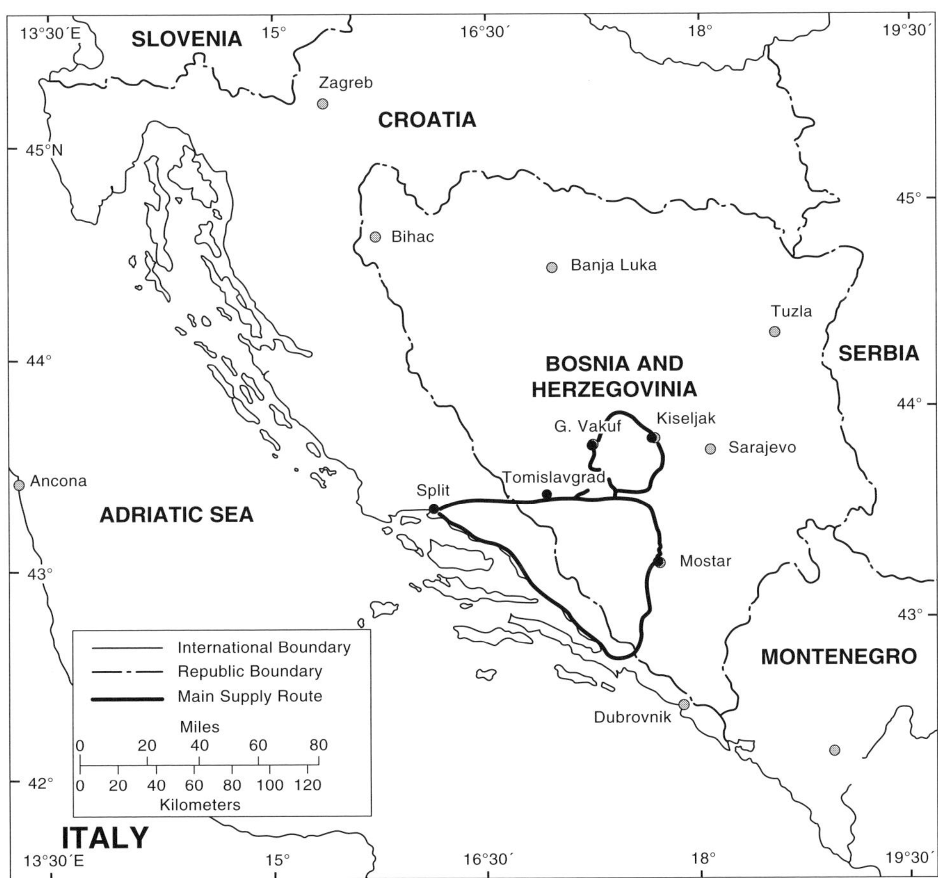

Map of Bosnia and Herzegovina.

sizeable operating base with some 4,500 British personnel based there together with thirty-nine helicopters, which included Chinooks, Pumas, Lynx, and Gazelles. The TSW detachment here established a bulk fuel installation, which turned out to be the largest such installation established by TSW to date and surpassed anything it had set up in the Middle East during Operation Granby. This installation was used mainly as a storage facility to resupply sites in Bosnia and also served a more immediate need by providing aviation fuel for the bowsers at Ploče itself. By the beginning of November 1995, the majority of the Rapid Reaction Force had returned to the UK and the reduction in operations saw the requirement for the BFI and its supporting detachment diminish considerably; the Ploče installation was dismantled by a team of seven in just over a week. Following the General Framework Agreement for Peace in Bosnia and Herzegovina (popularly known as the Dayton Agreement), formally signed in Paris on 14 December 1995, peacekeeping duties passed to the NATO-led Implementation Force (IFOR).[36] This new arrangement saw the region divided into three sectors controlled by British, American and French forces. TSW eventually found itself responsible for six refuelling sites located at Split, Lipa, Ćoralići, Šipovo, Gornji Vakuf-Uskoplje, and Banja Luka; the sites at Ploče and Kiseljak were eventually closed down.[37]

The Wing distinguished itself yet again on operations with SAC Christopher Hopkin awarded the Queen's Commendation for Bravery in September 1997 for protecting a NATO aircraft from a flailing fuel hose after the connector separated from the hose during a rotors turning operation at Banja Luka. TSW's detachment in former Yugoslavia finally withdrew in 2006 after a sustained deployment of over thirteen years.[38]

Operations in the Balkans: Kosovo

The conflict that developed in Kosovo in 1999 and the beginning of the NATO air strikes against Serbia saw a team of eleven TSW personnel led by Squadron Leader (later Wing Commander) Clive Watson deployed to Macedonia with the SH force in April 1999 to refuel a small detachment of Puma helicopters at Petrovec. With the deployment of 5 Airborne Brigade and additional aircraft from the UK SH force, TSW deployed a larger team in June 1999, enabling a second refuelling site to be established at Petrovec. The Wing also established an MRA at Skopje airfield following the arrival of further Chinook and Puma helicopters. Having established an MRA in Macedonia, TSW supported 5 Airborne Brigade's entry into Kosovo and set up a TRA at Lipljan, working alongside 1 Royal Gurkha Rifles. The MRA at Skopje was gradually dismantled and by early August 1999, all but five TSW personnel at the Lipljan site had returned to the UK. During this time, the Wing provided an important role in supporting RAF, NATO, and non-governmental helicopters operating in Kosovo. Indeed, during the period between 7 June and 23 July 1999, TSW issued nearly 1,500 cubic metres of fuel to British, American, Canadian, French, Italian, German, Belgian, and UN helicopters.[39]

Impact of the Strategic Defence Review 1998

The analysis carried out as part of SDR98 noted that all three services were operating battlefield helicopters to support ground forces; these included the Sea Kings of the Royal Navy, the Lynx and Gazelle of the Army Air Corps, and the Chinook, Puma, and Wessex of the RAF. The review also noted that operating experience in Northern Ireland, Bosnia, and the Gulf had clearly shown the 'unique contribution of battlefield helicopters throughout the conflict spectrum' but that it was evident that 'there are frequently too few of them to meet the collective demands they face'. To optimise the command and control of these important aircraft, consideration had been given to transferring all the battlefield helicopters to a single service but it was felt that this would be 'outweighed by the damaging impact it would have on ethos, morale and operational effectiveness'.[40] This led to the decision to create the JHC, under Army operational command, which would be responsible for training, standards, doctrinal development, and support to operations. The new command was formed at Wilton on 1 October 1999. Having developed a core capability for the tactical refuelling of helicopters, it made sense for TSW to become part of the new organisation; the command and control of TSW therefore transferred from RAF Strike Command to the new JHC in 1999.

The Defence review's recommendation that a DSDA should be formed to rationalise Defence storage and distribution, also led to further changes in TSW's structure. Given that No. 16 MU was a prime candidate to be transferred into the new agency and that it could very well close as part of the storage capacity reduction exercise, the Wing started to increase the proportion of its cadre or full-time manning; this reduced the wing's dependency on non-cadre personnel, which had hitherto been drawn from the uniformed personnel of the RAF depot. The loss of the non-cadre personnel had started before the review and resulted from the civilianisation of airmen posts in the depot as it became part of DSDA.

The most significant change though was linked with the formation of ELW. By the end of the Gulf War, it had become clear that many RAF Strike Command Supply and Movements Squadrons, especially their MSFs, had become highly capable in terms of supporting operations. This prompted a review of TSW's role and it became clear that the Wing needed to move away from providing general supply support and consolidate its position as a premier refuelling organisation. Additionally, the Harrier GR3 was replaced by the more capable, but less mobile GR5 and GR7 and this saw the re-equipped Harrier squadrons become more static and the SSR(A) role was, at least as far as TSW's involvement, no longer exercised. Given this, TSW sub-units that were not specifically tasked with providing support to helicopter operations, but did provide logistics support to the broader RAF, were separated and transferred to ELW on its formation in October 1999. This led to the emergence of a separate fixed wing aircraft fuel support capability, deployed supply support enablers, and an organisation that could provide logistics command and control on operations. This then enabled TSW to concentrate more on its niche helicopter refuelling role.

African Adventures: Mozambique and Sierra Leone

In February 2000, not long after its return from Kosovo, elements of the Wing deployed on Operation Barwoood, the UK's contribution to an international humanitarian aid operation in response to severe flooding in Mozambique. This was the worst flooding that the country had experienced in nearly fifty years, during which 699 people died and hundreds of thousands were displaced from their homes. Over forty-nine countries and thirty international non-governmental organisations provided humanitarian assistance. The RAF deployed four Pumas to assist with rescue operations in the southern part of the country, working alongside aircraft from the South African Defence Forces (SADF), which operated from Maputo, its capital city, in the far south of the country. The SADF helicopters were transiting some eighty miles to the rescue operating area, and then returning to refuel at Maputo. Prior to TSW's arrival, SADF aircraft had to close down to refuel and this was delaying their turn-round time. After just forty-eight hours, the TSW team had established refuelling points and were able to provide rotors turning refuelling for all nations participating in the relief operation. By the middle of March, the situation had improved considerably, leading to the decision to end the operation.

The year 2000 also saw elements of TSW deploying to the African continent, but this time in support of UK operations in Sierra Leone following nearly eight years of civil war. The country had experienced a turbulent history since its independence from Britain in 1961 marked by a number of actual and attempted military coups and led by a series of authoritarian, corrupt civilian governments and a military junta. Moreover, the country had descended into civil war in 1991, finally coming to an end with a return to civilian rule under President Kabbah in early 1996. The peace was to be short lived following yet another military coup in 1997 and the establishment of a military junta, which was only to be ousted in the subsequent year with the support of the Economic Community of West African States Monitoring Group (ECOMOG) forces that saw the reinstatement of the democratically-elected government, under President Kabbah, who had been in exile in neighbouring Guinea. However, in early 1999, rebels supporting the Revolutionary United Front seized parts of the capital city Freetown, a move which eventually left some 5,000 dead and substantial damage to the city. It was at this point that the UK Government first began to get involved in Sierra Leone, following an evacuation of UK entitled non-combatant personnel, with the deployment of an operational liaison and reconnaissance team and maritime forces to afford support to both President Kabbah and the Nigerian-led ECOMOG forces. Following a peace agreement which was negotiated in July 1999, UN forces were deployed to the country towards the end of the year to police the agreement and to oversee a programme of disarmament, demobilisation and reintegration of the rebels into society. However, the situation continued to deteriorate and in April–May 2000, UN forces in the east of the country came under attack. In order to support British interests, the UK Government deployed forces to Sierra Leone yet again, this time under Operation Palliser to evacuate British citizens and to help secure Freetown's Lungi International Airport for the UN.[41] This eventually saw their mandate extended to take offensive action to defeat the rebels and to restore order to the country. This was successfully met. As part of this operation, TSW deployed to the airport in May 2000. Tasked with rotors turning refuelling of Chinook, Sea King, and Lynx aircraft, the Wing played a key part in enabling aircraft to undertake high readiness sorties in support of SF and the First Parachute Regiment battle group. The evacuation had largely been completed by 12 May and the Operation was progressively scaled down.

The Second Gulf War: Operation Telic

In February 2003, eighty-seven TSW personnel augmented by eight personnel from No. 606 Squadron RAuxAF, plus assorted vehicles and TFHE deployed to Ali-Al Salem Air Base in Kuwait to provide rotors turning refuelling in support of coalition helicopters operating in Iraq. A further twenty to twenty-three personnel were allocated to Task Forces 7 and 14 (Special Forces roles). For a period of time prior to deploying, all TSW personnel worked extended dayshifts preparing over eighty vehicles for transportation to the Gulf region by sea. Every vehicle was loaded, unloaded and reloaded until it complied with the many regulations governing the carriage of dangerous goods.[42] All vehicles were then driven down in convoy to Marchwood military port near Southampton for embarkation. From the end of January 2003 through to the end of February 2003, TSW and RAuxAF personnel were deployed in stages from Stafford by coach via the Joint Air Mounting Centre at South Cerney, and then flown from RAF Brize Norton to Ali Al Salem Air Base.

On 19 February 2003, the main party consisting of fifty-eight personnel departed from Stafford for Ali-Al Salem. These were followed by a further sixteen personnel on 22 February 2003 with the final group consisting of one regular TSW and eight Auxiliaries departing on 28 February 2003. From 20 February through to 18 March 2003, TSW spent its time planning and preparing to meet its proposed commitment of one MRA and two TRAs. During this time, all the vehicles were collected from the docks, driven to the vehicle paint shop and sprayed in desert camouflage colour. They were then prepared for crossing over the border, with the addition of extra food and water, along with the attachment of camouflage netting. TSW personnel undertook a number of secondment and support roles While based at Ali-Al Salem, notably dispatching a team of fourteen personnel to assist 3 Commando Brigade during their preparation and deployment to the Al Faw Peninsular. On 19 March 2003, the MRA and elements of the second TRA moved in convoy with No. 51 Squadron RAF Regiment (Force Protection) to Abdali Farms; this was the assembly point prior to crossing the border. TSW spent three nights in 'shell scrapes' before going across the border to occupy the objective of Safwan airfield. At Safwan, the MRA established eight refuelling points which were able to provide rotors turning refuelling capabilities to the two resident medevac Pumas and any other coalition helicopters.

While at Safwan, eight members of the TRA were dispatched to Shaibah airbase to support seven Lynx helicopters. At the beginning of April 2003, a further nine personnel were dispatched to Al Amarah to support elements of 16 Air Assault Brigade and helicopters of the Army Air Corps. This second party formed parts of a Second Tank Regiment convoy and were escorted along the banks of the Tigris to their destination. The middle of April 2003 saw thirty personnel of the MRA re-deploy to Basra International Airport where they operated four refuelling points initially from low mobility tankers then 136-cubic-metre tanks with the arrival of the remainder of the personnel who had been left at Safwan. By May 2003, the main TSW detachment was based at Basra airport supporting the Joint Helicopter Force, with a forward refuelling point further north. At the height of the operation, TSW had around ninety-three personnel (eighty-five regulars and eight Auxiliaries) deployed to the Gulf Tasking and had worked with a number of different aircraft types including Chinooks, Pumas, and Sea Kings, although they were also refuelling American Apache and Cobra aircraft.[43]

Developments Following Operation Telic

Operations in Africa, the Balkans, and the Middle East enabled the Wing to develop its concept of operations and organisation; much of this work was underpinned by lessons learned from operating under actual combat conditions. By 2005, the Wing's mission had become quite specific 'to provide aviation fuel support to deployed battlefield helicopters'.[44] The Wing by now had divided into two component squadrons. The service delivery element was provided by the Tactical Fuels Squadron (TFS), whose prime task was to supply aviation fuel using MRAs, FRPs, and TRAs, in conjunction with the ability to use its parachute-trained personnel for insertion behind enemy lines or to access remote areas. The physical delivery of fuel was usually by tankers and TFHE, a key component of which was the pillow tank, each of which could hold some 136 cubic metres of aviation fuel. The logistic support for the TFS was provided by a HQ Squadron with a wide range of services including maintenance of MT and ground support equipment, mobility, training, force protection, administration and providing additional personnel when required. Overall, this combination provided TSW with a flexible structure, which enabled it to refuel SH on the battlefield, taking fuel from source behind Third Line, to the front line, and also behind enemy lines using its own parachute capability.[45]

A significant addition to TSW's tanker fleet came in 2005 with the introduction of the heavy wheeled tanker vehicle produced by the American company Oshkosh Defence Inc. Consisting of a tractor unit and a wheeled tanker, the inclusion of independent suspension, all-wheel drive and rear steering significantly improved the Wing's ability to transport fuel over rough terrain to remote locations and away from un-metalled roads.[46] The Wing initially received fifty eight of these vehicles, comprising a mixture of the close support tanker with a capacity of 20,000 litres and the tactical aircraft refueller with a smaller capacity of 15,000 litres and replacing the Wing's existing DAF 4,000 litre Tac-B bowser. While this increased the off-road carrying capacity of the Wing by just over 70 per cent, it also required an increase in the number of Trade Group 6 MT drivers on the Wing's personnel establishment; previously, the Tac-B bowser could be driven by Trade Group 18 Supply tradesmen.[47]

Operations in Afghanistan

In November 2001, TSW deployed to Oman as part of Operation Oracle, providing rotors turning refuelling for both UK and American SF aircraft, as well as multinational aircraft. The main commitment in the region came in 2006 as part of the major deployment by the Joint Helicopter Force (Afghanistan) (JHF (A)) in early April 2006, consisting of eight AH-64 Apache, four Lynx, and six CH-47 Chinook aircraft. This force was split between Kandahar Airfield (KAF) and Camp Bastion in the south of the country. The JHF (A) Main HQ, the bulk of its engineering facilities and approximately half the aircraft were based at KAF, with a forward HQ and FARP teams located at Bastion. By 20 April 2006, TSW had established a two-point refuelling facility at Bastion, some two days ahead of schedule. Much time in the first few weeks in theatre was taken up with moving equipment and vehicles from KAF to Bastion.

The 24-ton Oshkosh tankers proved particularly difficult to move and a local heavy lift contractor was used to move them by road, a task not made any easier by attacks from Taliban insurgents. Conditions at Bastion at this time were particularly harsh; the helicopter refuelling site was a patch of gravel with two large mats for the aircraft to land on and the whole area was surrounded by dust some 30 cm deep.[48] TSW were not required to carry out refuelling at forward locations although the detachment was required to drive a replacement Oshkosh tractor unit from KAF to Bastion to replace a unit destroyed by the Taliban in the original deployment to theatre. The journey was particularly hazardous, requiring two TSW airmen to drive the unit along one of the 'most infamous roads in the world, with stretches known as 'IED [improvised explosives device] Alley'. The detachment commander, Flight Lieutenant Jon Smith, related how such situations made him 'see why leadership skills are so important. IOT [Initial Officer Training] doesn't teach you what to say to two airmen who are about to drive out into a war zone and I probably made them laugh with my attempts at a "rousing speech"; but the experience certainly taught me that there is still a lot to learn about leadership'.[49]

The TSW detachment HQ at Camp Bastion, Afghanistan, 2010. (*Author's collection*)

TSW 'pillow' tank installation at Camp Bastion, Afghanistan, 2010. (*Author's collection*)

Developments since the Commencement of Operation Herrick

By 2009, TSW had evolved into a highly capable and specialised organisation. It remained the only such unit that could provide rotors turning refuelling to battlefield helicopters at First and Second Line and beyond. While the Army Air Corps and Commando Helicopter Force were able to refuel their battlefield helicopters at First Line, they were only able to do so from tactical aircraft refuellers. However, in doing so, they also required support from the fuel support sections of the Commando Logistics Regiment and 13 Air Assault Support Regiment of the RLC for bulk stocks of fuel and resupply at second line. The advantage that TSW had achieved was that it was able to provide a more coherent capability by achieving this as a single unit, thereby delivering greater operational effect. As such, TSW became JHC's main port of call for battlefield helicopter refuelling.[50] The ability to deliver such a service required myriad skills. By 2009, the Wing's size was around 211 personnel drawn from some ten RAF trade groups. Irrespective of trade, all deployable personnel were qualified to carry out rotors turning refuelling, carry out quality checks and operate aircraft refuelling vehicles. The quality of fuel remained paramount and, as a consequence, a number of the Wing's officers are required to be graduates of the tri-service officer's petroleum course at West Moors. Additionally, a number of its NCOs were qualified as chemical laboratory assistants; this qualified them to operate portable petroleum test kits, which enabled greater testing and analysis of fuel while in the field.[51]

One fact of life that had not changed for the Wing was the constant liability for deployed operations. Indeed, in 2009, its commitments included Afghanistan, Iraq, the Falkland Islands, an eight-month standing detachment in Kenya, together with a four-month exercise commitment in Norway. With the bulk of Operation Telic having been scaled down by 2009, TSW's main effort was with Operation Herrick in Afghanistan supporting the rotary wing aircraft of the Joint Aviation Group. Much of this work was at Camp Bastion but also in the more hostile environment outside of the base at forward refuelling points, combat logistic patrols, and in forward operating bases. As the Afghanistan effort also began to reduce leading up to the British withdrawal in 2014, the wing was able to rebalance its resources in support of its wider JHC commitments. Among these was the ongoing presence in Kenya supporting the British Army Training Unit and at the remote helicopter landing site at Fox Bay, West Falklands to name but a few. The wing was also actively involved during 2010–2011, with the ongoing work to develop a new Joint Operational Fuel System, which will provide a new generation of deployed fuels capability. They also provided invaluable test support to the DE&S Battlefield Utilities Project Team, which was also running a programme to replace the trusty APFCs. More broadly, the wing continues to fine-tune its readiness to support worldwide contingency operations, a process in which training and exercises remains important.

Expeditionary Logistics Wing

Following the formation of ELW at RAF Stafford in 1999, one of the early priorities was to harmonise the disparate group of three squadrons (Training and Support Squadron (TSS), No. 2MT Squadron, and No. 5001 Squadron), which made up its new structure. Each of these operated under different concepts of operations and had little in common. While No. 2 MT Squadron and No. 5001 Squadron were reasonably well structured, TSS, elements of which had transferred from TSW and RAF Stafford, required closer attention and included a mixture of training and supply service functions; the training element was bolstered by adding the training elements from Nos 2 MT Squadron and 5001 Squadron.[52] The original case to support the formation of the wing highlighted the requirement for an ELW HQ element that would also have a role in providing trained and exercised air logistic battle staff to augment either Nos 101 or 102 Logistic Brigades in the creation of a JFLogC HQ. A HQ element was also an essential requirement in providing a degree of control across the three squadrons of the new ELW. The creation of a new Wing HQ was initially achieved by releasing the required staff by re-organising the Deployed Supply Group (DSG) Plans element of TSS, which had transferred to the Wing from TSW on its formation. The HQ element was further enhanced with the arrival of Squadron Leader Rod Duguid as the first Chief of Staff/Second-in-Command in November 2002.

Many of the early challenges faced in setting up the new wing were similar to those encountered during the formative years of TSW such as finding suitable accommodation and establishing standard operating procedures. It was recognised that in order to take the Wing forward as a cohesive organisation, it needed a collective identity and an *esprit de corps* engendered among its 400 or more personnel, similar to that enjoyed by TSW personnel. Under the leadership of Wing Commander (later Group Captain) David Lester-Powell who took command of the Wing in August 2002, work was started, which resulted in a proposal that ELW should be renamed 85 (Expeditionary Logistics (EL)) Wing, a concept that carried forward the identity of 85 (Base) Group, which had provided expeditionary logistics support to the RAF Air Component of 2TAF during Operation Overlord in 1944 (see Chapter Three). The new title was approved by the Air Force Board on 29 January 2003.[53]

The Second Gulf War, 2003: Operation Telic

The start of the conflict in Iraq in 2003 saw HQ STC immediately tasking the HQ element of 85 (EL) Wing to join HQ No. 102 Logistic Brigade in Gütersloh, Germany. Here, it became involved with operational logistics planning for two weeks, prior to departing for Ali Al Salem Air Base in Kuwait, before moving on to Camp Arifjan in Southern Kuwait, where it established itself with the JFLogC HQ. Of significance, the RAF was to provide the component's Deputy Commander, Group Captain Chris Markey, a former TSW officer, who brought with him a wealth of operational logistics experience. At Camp Arifjan, the HQ was co-located with the American 377 Theatre Support Command, which was then responsible for the reception and onward movement of the Combined Joint Force to its deployed locations (a process known as reception, staging, and onward movement (RSOM) in defense logistics terminology). The 85 Wing HQ staff found themselves performing a range of tasks within the HQ, but they were principally engaged as J4 air logistics staff with responsibility for providing oversight of and coordinating support to the air component's RSOM, specifically for the new Harrier and Tornado GR4 deployed operating bases at Ahmed al Jaber in Kuwait and Al Udeid in Qatar. The wing staff also found themselves involved with wider planning work, the most significant of which was working with the British Embassy staff to draw up contingency plans for the evacuation of British citizens and other UK entitled persons from Kuwait. A full mission rehearsal for this plan was also successfully conducted with the support of No. 1 Squadron RAF Regiment from Ali Al Salem Air Base, which had been assigned to provide the necessary force protection.

At the same time that the wing HQ deployed, so too did the vehicles of No. 2 MT Squadron on the very first ship to depart for theatre. A total of fourteen general service tankers, seventy 40-foot flatbed vehicles, and three curtain-sided trailers, as well as a host of land rovers and other support vehicles were deployed, including No. 2 MT Squadron's own MT Maintenance Section (MTMS) Light Aid Detachment. Once in theatre, the squadron was not only able to make a significant contribution to the load of this and other Army units, but importantly to help with receiving equipment and weapons for the Harrier deployed operating base at Ahmed Al Jaber.

The Logistic Component was to consist of three transport regiments/units: Nos 7 and 10, with No. 8 Joint Logistics Transport Group (JLTG). Once in the theatre, the decision was quickly and sensibly made to pool the transport assets of the three units by capability to respond to tasks as they arose. This resulted in all-liquid carrying vehicles being placed under the command of No. 7 Transport Regiment, all tactical mobility cargo vehicles falling under No. 10 Transport Regiment, and low mobility/commercial vehicles being congregated within No. 8 JTLG. This saw No. 2 MT Squadron vehicles being subdivided between the three formations.

One of the challenges that came to light during actual war fighting operations was the difference in the respective RAF and Army cultures and attitudes towards taking risk and, hence, what might be expected of RAF personnel. The RAF SNCOs within No. 2 MT Squadron were understandably concerned that the squadron might be tasked to perform something for which it was neither properly equipped or trained. This concern came into sharp focus following the squadron's first major task at the onset of operations during which it was tasked to move No. 34 Field Hospital (requiring the movement of some 500 ISO shipping containers) into

Shaibah airfield in Iraq only forty-eight hours after coalition forces had started to move forward. The squadron arrived during the middle of an artillery barrage and counter-barrage, a sobering experience for all involved who had to spend the night taking cover under their vehicles. Remarkably, on one occasion, an elderly Iraqi gentleman noticing that the RAF were 'back in town' approached, one of the squadron NCOs and explained that he used to be the NAAFI manager and, presenting his identity card from that time, asked if he could have his old job back.

The concerns over the type of tasking, including those of command and control, were nevertheless to be allayed to some extent when an opportunity arose for 85 Wing HQ to reconstitute itself and to take under command No. 2 MT Squadron, the JLTG (which then became known as the Military Civil Transport Group (MCTG)) and, indeed, where appropriate, other RAF elements operating 'outside the wire', which included those of Tactical Armament Squadron working within the rear explosive storage area at Camp Fox. This opportunity came as a result of No. 8 Transport Regiment HQ staff having to return to the UK to take receipt of its new heavy equipment tank transporters with which it was being re-equipped. The deputy commander JFLogC, Group Captain Chris Markey, recommended to Brigadier Shaun Cowlam, the Logistic Component commander that No. 85 Wing HQ staff should take up the baton from No. 8 Regiment, a recommendation that was readily agreed. Group Captain Markey then sought support of both the Air Component HQ and HQ STC for this novel proposal, which was duly given. Accordingly, 85 (EL) Wing relieved No. 8 Transport Regiment HQ on 18 April 2003, an immensely proud moment for all those concerned.

The challenge was to build up and equip the deployed Wing HQ at very short notice and to ensure that it was capable not only of interfacing with its Component HQ but also with conducting business with its sister units. The core HQ structure was, nevertheless, swiftly established with Squadron Leader (later Wing Commander) Rod Duguid reassuming his role as 2IC, Flight Lieutenant Simon Watkins becoming wing adjutant, Warrant Officer Peter Bond (the wing warrant officer, and a TSW and 2 MT Squadron veteran) as wing operations officer, and Flight Sergeant Paul Giles as the wing regimental quartermaster sergeant. HQ communications were also enhanced by the reapportionment of a small, but extremely effective, Tactical Communications Wing (TCW) detachment from the Logistic Component, which importantly provided the Wing with what was considered as the best command 'net' of any unit within the Component. Both Warrant Officer Bond and Flight Sergeant Giles also used their powers of negotiation, persuasion, and occasional subterfuge to gather together various assets, including vehicles and other items of equipment from across the Logistic Component and the RAF deployed operating bases at Ali Al Salem and Ahmed Al Jaber. The largest, and probably the most welcome addition to the inventory, apparently 'gifted' by the US Marine Corps, was a 'reefer' refrigeration container, which proved indispensable in keeping the Wing's stock of bottled water chilled given the intense summer heat, which regularly exceeded 40°C.

The Wing received widespread support from a whole host of organisations as it embarked on its new endeavour, including its sister Army Regiments within the Logistic Component, particularly No. 6 Supply Regiment and No. 7 Transport Regiment, who willingly provided advice and guidance, even on basic things such as how to operate as a transport HQ in the field and provided copies of standing operating instructions. Back home in the UK, HQ STC also ensured that the wing was manned and equipped to meet its task. Of particular note was the support received from the LSC under Wing Commander (later Group Captain) Adrian Maddox, whose contribution to supporting the Air Component as a whole was to be later recognised with the well-deserved award of an OBE in December 2003.

In addition to the resources of No. 2 MT Squadron, 85 (EL) Wing also inherited some thirty-five passenger coaches, four ISO container baggage vehicles, and responsibility for up to 170 assorted cars and pickups, as well as a collection of host nation supplied forty-foot vehicles driven by an eclectic mix of host nation and third country national drivers from Kenya, Nepal, Pakistan, and various Arab countries, as well as Territorial Army drivers and Regular NCOs from No. 8 Transport Regiment who acted as their escorts. In due course, all of the Regular Army NCOs were replaced by those of the RAF. The concept of mixed irregular drivers had been used by the Army in Germany in the 1950s and 1960s using largely displaced Yugoslavs, but the MCTG was much more diverse. For force protection considerations, the Group was confined to operating mainly in Kuwait and just inside the Iraqi border given the questionable condition and serviceability of many of their cargo vehicles and, consequently, the relatively slow speeds at which they moved. Following some very clear direction by the component commander on the importance of passenger safety, however, MCTG's passenger vehicles were to be replaced by a fleet of brand new air-conditioned fifty-five-seater coaches hired from Saudi Arabia. Much of the success of the MCTG was due to the flexibility, agility and the considerable patience of its RAF command team of NCOs managed by Warrant Officer Stewart McKenna (later to become No. 2 MT Squadron Warrant Officer) and led by Squadron Leader Chris Sendell, who was transferred from Al Udeid.

The re-brigading of transport assets under No. 85 (EL) Wing eventually saw the return (under command of the core of No. 2 MT Squadron) of the general service fuel tankers from No. 7 Regiment, which were needed for the dedicated resupply of aviation fuel to the airhead at Basra. In addition, the detachment of Tactical Armament Squadron personnel at Camp Fox, who were running the RAF sector of the joint rear explosives storage area, was transferred under command of No. 85 (EL) Wing from No. 6 Supply Regiment RLC. At one point, in order to perform a specific task, the Wing even had a troop of Army demountable rack offloading palletised system (DROPS) vehicles placed temporarily under command which had been transferred from No. 10 Transport Regiment. The new arrangement proved to be a highly successful means of brigading RAF sub-units and other RAF force elements, even those temporarily visiting theatre, which had to operate 'outside the wire'. It afforded them the requisite command and control to permit the safe freedom of manoeuvre, in the semi and non-benign environments, within and between the rear and forward support areas, in order to sustain the RAF deployed operating bases in Kuwait.[54] Additionally, the Wing provided capabilities offering unique operational benefit to the wider Joint arena, carrying out significant missions into Iraq. These included a substantial movement of fuel forward to the American V Corps near Nasiriyah, where its advance had stalled due to a combination of bad weather and lack of fuel. Perhaps the Wing's finest moments, and particularly those of No. 2 MT Squadron, were the successful, but potentially hazardous, deployment of the 16 Air Assault Brigade battle group to Al Amarah and the prestigious task to deliver the 'flat-pack' British Embassy to Baghdad immediately after it was liberated, at a time when Fedayeen forces were still disrupting the main surface lines of communication. Also worthy of mention was the outstanding leadership shown by No. 2 MT Squadron's Flight Sergeant, Derek Burgess, who was tasked with transporting, within a very tight timeframe, a number of airfield fire crash vehicles from Kuwait to Basra airport in time to cover the arrival of the aircraft conveying US Presidential Envoy Paul Bremer to Iraq. The squadron was to prove extremely effective at quickly delivering large numbers of ISO containers by including within its convoys a low loader to carry a Rough Terrain Container Handler (RTCH) vehicle. An experienced RTCH driver could rapidly offload a complete convoy of containers within a very short period of time as was demonstrated time and again. The contribution of No. 2 MT Squadron to Operation Telic was significant, with its OC, Squadron Leader Axel Jinadu, being awarded the QCVS.

At the beginning of June 2003, by which time stabilisation operations had become firmly established, the three Logistic Component Transport units started to withdraw from theatre, with 7 Transport Regiment assets absorbing those of No. 10 Transport Regiment, in preparation for them both to be relieved by No. 27 Transport Regiment. A number of 85 Wing HQ staff, led by Squadron Leader Duguid, transferred to their Regimental HQ, located at Camp Coyote in Northern Kuwait, close to the border with Iraq, in order to oversee the redeployment of No. 2 MT Squadron vehicles by sea before recovering back themselves to the UK the following month. It is remarkable that despite the length of time spent in harm's way, especially those operating with No. 2 MT Squadron, no individual on the Wing was lost either to enemy action or an accident.

Exercise African Shield, 2003

There was little respite for the wing as in November 2003, its Wing HQ deployed for three weeks on Exercise African Shield, a PJHQ command post exercise at Snake Valley Air Force Base, near Pretoria in South Africa. The objective of the exercise, which involved up to 850 personnel, was to build trust and understanding between South African and British forces in the conduct of peace support operations. Neither Nos 101 nor 102

Logistic Brigade HQ staff were available to form the core of a JFLogC HQ and so 85 Wing stepped into the breach. The Wing's OC, Wing Commander David Lester-Powell, became the Component Chief of Staff working to Group Captain Tony Davenport as Commander, with Group Captain Chris Markey acting as a mentor. The Wing Warrant Officer, Peter Bond, looked after the more practical daily functioning of the HQ.

The HQ staff of just over sixty personnel was drawn from the South African Military Health Service, from students (some of one-star rank) from a variety of nations at the South African National Defence College and from UK individual augmentees of all three services. Although this eclectic mix brought its challenges, especially in getting them to operate effectively as a coherent HQ staff, a number of UK staff were Operation Telic veterans and able to bring their collective experience to bear. Although this task was to prove more difficult than had been anticipated, the exercise proved immensely beneficial for developing the 85 Wing HQ staff's understanding of planning and executing joint operations. They were then able to put this experience to good use for an 85 Wing-led ACSSU training exercise in 2004 (Exercise Bright Raven), back in the UK at the Nesscliffe Training Area in Shropshire and later in 2007 when the Wing conducted its most ambitious exercise, Raven's Wing in Germany.

Operations in Afghanistan

Various elements of No. 85 (EL) Wing were involved in Operation Herrick at various stages, especially No. 3 MCS and No. 2 MT Squadron. The latter was tasked to support the operation in 2004, initially located at Kandahar Airfield. The ensuing years saw the squadron's responsibilities and involvement on this operation encompass additional permanent embedded detachments at Camp Bastion and also at Kabul.

Service: Granting of the 85 (Expeditionary Logistics) Wing Official Badge

The only draw-back with using the 85 (Base) Group identity from the Second World War was that this unit had never been granted a unit badge, nor was there any evidence of one even having been proposed. The foyer of the RAF Stafford Officers' Mess held the key where, adorning the wall, hung the badge of the now defunct RAF Maintenance Command. During a discussion on the subject with the Wing's OC, the Station Commander at the time, Group Captain Neil Cromarty, suggested that the former Command's emblem, 'the Raven of Providence', together with its motto, 'Service', would make an excellent identity for the new Wing. Following Air Force Board approval, a new badge, based on the Maintenance Command components and motto, was granted in 2005 and later presented at the RAF Wittering Annual Formal Inspection that same year.

Developments Since Operation Telic

The end of the combat phase of Operation in Telic in 2003 also saw a number of significant developments for No. 85 (EL) Wing. The ACSSU and Minor Unit Basing Study, which was conducted during 2003–2004, led to the Wing relocating to RAF Wittering during the period August 2005 through until April 2006.[55] This move was accompanied by a series of other changes to the core structure of the wing, much of the rationale for which had emerged from its experience during Operation Telic; these were all implemented to improve the Wing's ability to conduct subsequent deployed operations.

The overall size of No. 2 MT Squadron was reviewed with the intent to reduce it to more manageable proportions, in terms of span of control, following its growth prior to and during Operation Telic to some 261 personnel. The more detailed operation of No. 2 MT Squadron is covered as a more in-depth analysis of Movements in Chapter Seven.

A much welcome addition to the Wing's structure was the Mobile Catering Support Unit (MCSU), which relocated to RAF Stafford from RAF Benson in the spring of 2003. While at Benson, the SH force viewed (and valued) MCSU as one of their assets and there was a risk that it could have become part of JHC as this

No. 2 MT Squadron driver training at RAF Wittering. (*Crown Copyright—Air Historical Branch MoD*)

command developed, hence its move to become part of No. 85 (EL) Wing and its retention as an RAF ACSSU. In April 2008, MCSU was amalgamated with the RAF Wittering Catering Flight to form No. 3 Mobile Catering Squadron (MCS). In practice, this did not work as the breadth of responsibility was too wide, from its operational focus on the one hand to catering services for personnel based at RAF Wittering on the other. Coupled with this was the imminent introduction of the RAF's contractorised catering arrangement for its units (Catering, Retail, and Leisure); this too would not sit comfortably with the ACSSU nature of the MCS. Consequently, the RAF Wittering Catering Flight was separated from No. 3 MCS in April 2011 so that the latter could focus solely on support to operations and exercises.[56]

Its reputation is second to none and the squadron provides essential catering facilities for both exercises and operations. Such commitments can be extensive. On Exercise Saif Sareea II in 2000, for example, the former MCSU was feeding some 1,500 people at the Thumrait operating location alone. A notable commitment was for the Olympic Games held in the UK during 2012 where, after the military were brought in after the problems with the security company G4S, the squadron was involved with feeding personnel at two sites on the outskirts of London. On the Hainault site, the consumers of their meals amounted to around 3,500 people. A number of its personnel are highly accomplished chefs and many take part in national and international culinary competitions.

The year 2007, though, was one of a number of changes for the A4 Force, which would rebalance the RAF's ACSSUs along logistic and engineering lines and to provide more efficient support to the A4 'Hub' at RAF Wittering. As outlined in Chapter Five, the creation of No. 42 (ES) saw No. 5001 Sqn transfer to the new Wing and 85 (EL) Wing gaining the newly formed JARTS, although this squadron was physically based at MOD St Athan in South Wales and Gosport in Hampshire.

One of the more complex developments, though, was the original TSS. The precise composition of this squadron since 1999 is difficult to track, although by 2004 had started to gain better shape from its earlier days. By 2007, this had become No. 1 Expeditionary Logistics Squadron (ELS). By 2014, the squadron was configured to maintain a short-notice readiness to deploy capability to provide a number of key capabilities, which would enable the early establishment of logistic services at forward operating bases. The squadron provides the RAF's only deployable fixed wing refuelling capability through its fuel support teams. These are able to rapidly build and operate a primary BFI (PBFI) or alternatively, deploy to operate on existing Host Nation maintained fuel installations. Fuel support team personnel were deployed on Operation Shader to assist with the surge of fuel operations at RAF Akrotiri by building and operating a PBFI; during an eight-month period supporting this task, they issued 100 million litres of aviation fuel.

The Squadron also maintains a Deployable Supply Group (DSG), which provides a range of inventory management functions, to establish an early logistics squadron

No. 1 ELS carrying out refuelling training. (*Crown Copyright—Air Historical Branch MoD*)

type service at the onset of an operation prior to being augmented by an EAW. The capability that DSG provides is important as it also enables the RAF to ensure that early materiel accounting procedures are implemented to meet National Audit Office requirements. The squadron also has port clearance liaison teams to expedite high-value aviation spares from sea ports to airheads. Finally, No. 1 ELS is the custodian of the RAF's deployable supply account (each of which has a unique unit identity number or UIN) and its accounts closure team is responsible for ensuring that the UINs supply accounts are in good order before they are closed at the end of an operation. Their work could be quite lengthy and involved as their experience at the end of Operation Herrick in 2014 showed. After a nine-month investigation of the RAF's redeployed inventory, the result of their reconciliation work had reduced any loss to just 0.3 per cent of the overall stock value. By 2014, No. 85 (EL) Wing comprised four regular ACSSUs: No. 1 ELS, No. 2MT Sqn, No. 3 MCS, and JARTS, along with a small Wing Headquarters to co-ordinate operations, plans and administrative activity at the home base. By this time, two RAuxAF squadrons—501 (County of Gloucester) and 504 (County of Nottingham)—came under command of No. 85 (EL) Wing in a logistics support capacity delivering Supply, MT, and Catering functions.

7

Movements

Irrespective of where the RAF has operated from, the ability to transport equipment and personnel has remained a sizeable and challenging task. This has not been a wholly introspective capability; RAF Logistics has also been a service provider in this respect, not just to the Royal Navy and the Army but, from time-to-time, to other Government departments as well. This wide ranging sub-discipline within RAF Logistics has been generically referred to as Movements, an activity that can be said to concern everything connected with moving personnel and freight from one place to another, including the control of that process. In more prosaic terms, the Movements network has often been referred to as the 'arteries through which the precious lifeblood of warfare flows'.[1] The Movements capability, however, is not just a haulage function. It also enabled mobility, a concept which was identified as one of the five characteristics that were seen as having the 'largest influence on the strategy and tactics of air warfare' as early as the beginning of the Second World War.[2] Aircraft, by their very nature, are highly mobile, but their ground support services require a range of transportation should they be required to relocate during operations away from main bases. Movements also enabled logistical reach, a characteristic very closely related to mobility and enabled the RAF's supply chain to be extended, often over many thousands of miles. This capability developed significantly during the Second World War as the RAF became involved in numerous operations away from established bases such as the invasions of North Africa, Italy, and Normandy.

The Movements discipline has come a long way during the lifetime of the RAF, with perhaps the growth of air transport since 1945 being one of the most significant. Many of the RAF's Logistics personnel have been drawn to the air movements specialization as a career path, invariably lured by the opportunity of working in close proximity to aircraft and their operational environment. This, however, has often drawn the spotlight away from the work surrounding the use of other means of transportation. Indeed, in the thirty-seven years from the formation of the RAF, up until the demise of sea trooping in 1955, surface movement by road, rail and sea were the main means of getting things from one place to another. With this in mind, it is appropriate that the opening pages in this chapter begin on the ground.

Movements by Road

From its early days, RAF Logistics has relied on a whole host of MT vehicles, not just to conduct its business on RAF bases but also to support the many aspects of active operations in overseas campaigns. The extent of this has already been illustrated in earlier chapters. The depots too also relied on a wide range of vehicles, many of them for specialist heavy lift. The detailed development of vehicles in the RAF has already been written about in detail elsewhere and it is not therefore necessary to cover this ground again.[3] There are two areas that do warrant examination, though: freight distribution and the formation and development of the MT companies.

Freight Distribution

Up until the mid-1920s, freight distribution to and from the RAF's Stores depots within the UK was carried out mainly by rail, with consignees collecting freight from their nearest railhead using their own transport. It was Britain's first and only general industrial strike in May 1926, called by the Trades Union Congress in support of striking coal miners, which prompted the RAF to establish its own freight distribution service by road. As all national transport services were suspended during the nine-day strike, the RAF Stores depots used their MT to form a road convoy system to deliver stores to RAF stations in the UK. In the case of No. 3 Stores Depot at Milton in Berkshire, three flight lieutenants were attached to the unit as officers in charge of road convoys, which consisted of anything up to twenty lorries and trailers that departed from the depot night and day. Over 210 tons of stores were despatched by road during the first week and vehicles notched up nearly 20,000 miles before the end of the strike. The scheme was curtailed when the national railways started operating again but the experience showed that stores could be delivered and collected more cheaply by road than rail and the Air Ministry therefore implemented a three-month trial of the concept under normal operating conditions. The results showed that movement by road was some 50 per cent cheaper than by rail and the Air Ministry therefore decided that it would make sense for certain groups of RAF stations to be supplied by road. The impact on depot activity was considerable as the scheme developed. By the end of financial year 1931–1932, for example, the distance covered by depot transport at Milton on convoy and duty journeys was just over 90,000 miles.[4]

This arrangement, though, was relatively small scale in the overall freight distribution operation, and rail still carried the lion's share of stores and supplies throughout the rest of the 1930s, during the Second World War, and for much of the 1950s. With the introduction of the V-bomber force in the late 1950s and the introduction of the QRA concept for the aircraft of Bomber Command in February 1962, RAF Logistics needed a responsive road distribution system to move spares

Leyland lorry in 1920. (*Author's collection*)

and equipment that were urgently required for any grounded V-Force aircraft. This saw the introduction of the priority freight distribution system (PFDS), or *Early Bird* as it was more affectionately known and was initially set-up to deliver priority one consignments from No. 16 MU Stafford. The availability of much improved vehicles and the ability to redistribute assets across the RAF, which had been enabled by the introduction of automatic data processing saw the PFDS develop significantly.

By the early 1970s, the other ESDs were feeding-in consignments to Stafford for wider movement via PFDS; the Army depots at Chilwell and Donnington also became an integral part of the network. With the advent of larger vehicles, the service was able to expand its service and in 1980 was able to handle lower priority freight on a fill-up basis, as well as delivering RAF-provisioned equipment to the Royal Navy and the Army. The system quickly evolved into a comprehensive network across the UK and provided an almost continuous delivery service; there were two departures per day from Stafford, six days per week, fifty-two weeks per year. Not all units were served directly and drop-offs were made at main distribution points with smaller consignees collecting their respective consignments. The PFDS was not just a delivery operation and every opportunity was made to utilize spare capacity on return journeys, an arrangement that was formalized as the vehicle back-loading scheme in September 1980. This not only enabled units to return equipment to the depots (for return to stock or repair), but also enabled them to dispatch equipment on priority demand to other units. During the period September 1980 to April 1982, approximately 5,066 tons had been back-loaded. This was estimated to have saved the RAF £350,000 in commercial transport costs.[5] The service could also move priority freight from airheads that were on the PFDS network, as well as forming a regional collection service for spares that had been placed on order with industry.[6]

By 1982, PFDS consisted of twenty-six vehicles and forty drivers, operating eleven primary routes and six secondary (feeder) routes. The routes of the network were linked via thirteen major distribution centres (MDC), serving 116 units in the UK.[7] By this time, there were also routes operated by National Carriers Ltd (NCL) as a dedicated contract to units in Scotland and the West Country from Nos 14 and 7 MU respectively. The service was a great success, as witnessed by the substantial increase in throughput. In the period 1980–1982, the tonnage passing through the ESDs increased from a monthly average of 500 tons to well over 1000 tons, with approximately 470 tons per month attributed to routine freight transfer. It was estimated that if the volume of routine freight had been moved by commercial means it would have cost the service in the region of £830,000.[8] The RAF's PFDS remained in operation until the service became part of the tri-service operation when DSDA was formed following SDR 98.

The movement of freight to overseas units could not be catered for on the daily basis that PFDS operated and this need was catered for by aggregating loads, with less frequent departures from the UK. The early 1970s saw the development of a scheduled container service to a number of the RAF's major overseas units. The first of these was introduced in 1974 from Quedgeley to RAF Germany and known as QUECON; by 1977, the service had moved to No. 16 MU Stafford, becoming known as STACON. Similarly, No. 14 MU Carlisle hosted CARCON, a service to Northern Ireland. The end of the 1970s saw a container service to RAF Wildenrath in Germany (WILCON), Cyprus (CYPCON), and Malta (MALCON).[9] Before the closure of Stafford in 2006, the management of TORCON was transferred to the International Procurement Organisation at DLO Wyton and FRUCON to the Jaguar/Canberra integrated project team, also at Wyton.[10]

The MT Companies and Squadrons

One shortfall in the RAF's road transport capability that became increasingly apparent from the late 1920s and into the pre-Second World War Expansion Programme was that there were no specialist MT units that could be tasked for *ad hoc* requirements that were beyond the capacity or capability of unit resources. The geographical footprint of the RAF in the UK during the early 1930s was still (by later comparison) quite limited. The RAF's ORBAT for 1932, for example, consisted of approximately fifty main operating locations (flying and non-flying bases) and just four Stores depots; the majority of these locations were connected to the country's rail network and therefore well served in terms of transport links.[11] The 1930s expansion programme brought about not just large volumes of stores that needed to be distributed throughout the country, but a significant increase in the size of individual pieces of equipment that needed to be moved, especially from the depots to specialist repair units. This broadening of activity away from a unit focus, placed an increasing demand on MT resources and it soon became clear that the RAF required a specialist road transport capability that was able to move larger volumes and sizes of cargo. This requirement came sharply into focus in 1940 amid the fears of a growing threat of invasion to the UK by Nazi Germany. Although Hitler did not issue his directive for his forces to begin planning for an invasion until 16 July 1940, the German invasion of the Low Countries and France, which began on 10 May 1940, left little doubt that England would be next. As far as the RAF was concerned, detailed plans were evolved for the roles of Fighter, Bomber, and Coastal Commands in the event of an invasion, much of which involved the movement of their squadrons to new airfields. The move of complete squadrons was but one requirement of the overall plan. It was also acknowledged that in the event of an invasion, the RAF operational commands would need to use as many aircraft as possible and the re-deployment of aircraft used in training roles within Flying Training and Technical Training Commands would need to be included. In the case of Bomber Command, Operation Banquet set out the requirement for fourteen of its bomber stations to receive a total of 169 additional aircraft from training units.[12] The respective AOC-in-Cs of Bomber, Fighter and Coastal Commands were formally alerted of the need for detailed planning by the Deputy Chief of the Air Staff (Air Vice-Marshal Douglas) on 24 June 1940 who commented:

> In view of the possibility of an attempted invasion of this country, I am directed to draw your attention to the necessity to maintain in operation from alternative locations squadrons whose aerodromes, especially in the vicinity of the coast, may be subject to a local threat by enemy land forces.[13]

Douglas suggested that planning should not assume the wholesale evacuation of stations but the detachment of aircraft to alternative locations and it was acknowledged that 'the bulk of personnel should remain to defend the [parent] station and deny its use to the enemy'. As far as the logistics of this was concerned, Douglas added that 'in order to move the essential minimum maintenance detachments to enable the squadrons to continue in operation from alternative aerodromes, local transport should be earmarked and, if necessary, requisitioned'.[14] This was an underestimate of the size of the task and would have placed an inordinate strain on all concerned. Moreover, it was not clear from where 'requisitioned' vehicles would be obtained. Earlier discussions, though, had considered this requirement in more detail through the work of the Expansion and Re-Equipment Policy Committee that, largely as a result of discussion involving a much wider range of specialists (including the Air Ministry's DofE), had endorsed the proposal to form 'M.T. companies to provide centrally controlled pools of M.T., which could be used to move the operational squadrons of Bomber, Fighter and Coastal Commands from place to place to meet operational requirements'.[15] Initially, it was intended to form three MT companies: one company to be located in the area between the Tyne and Flamborough Head, with two companies further south between the Wash and Newhaven. The vehicle establishment of these units reflected not just the requirement to move equipment, but also personnel and were therefore initially established with thirty-two buses and eighty lorries. Each company was divided into four sections, each of which was designed to move one flying squadron.[16] Thus, on 16 July 1940, Nos 1, 2, and 3 Companies were officially formed at Darlington, Cambridge, and West Malling respectively. All three companies were placed under the operational control of the Air Ministry's DofE but administratively supported by No. 40 Group, Maintenance Command.[17]

The planned German invasion of the UK never came, although the Luftwaffe's failed attempt at achieving air superiority during the Battle of Britain did lead to a number of attacks on RAF airfields and resulted in some flying squadrons having to be relocated; between 12 August and 6 September 1940, there were sixty significant attacks on RAF airfields, the majority of these borne by No. 11 Group in south-east England.[18] The details of the MT company involvement in these squadron moves are difficult to assess due to an inconsistent level of detail in their respective ORBs. The most detailed record, although still lacking some tasking information, is that of No. 2 MT Company, which carried out three squadron moves in No. 11 Group during October 1940, along with the transportation of explosives consignments between No. 42 Group depots.[19] The number of squadron moves carried out by No. 2 MT Company the following year (1941) was quite different with some sixty-five moves.[20] Despite this increase, the resources of the MT companies came under close scrutiny as part of the RAF's ongoing commitment to wartime economy. By the end of 1941, with the risk of invasion having passed, it was timely for the road transport resources of the three MT companies to be re-assessed and their establishments were halved.[21] The opportunity was also taken to consider wider vehicle utilisation (especially on return journeys where vehicles were often empty) and a series of collection centres were nominated at specific MUs within Maintenance Command to enable inter-depot transfers to take place, much of which involved the movement of repairable equipment.[22]

A further five MT companies were formed in the first half of 1941, but with quite different responsibilities. No. 4 MT Company, although still under the control of the Air Ministry, was established to act as a transport pool for the Ministry of Aircraft Production and was based at St John's Wood (London). Nos 5, 6, and 7 were established at the ports of Liverpool, Glasgow, and Hull (moved later to Cardiff) and much of their work involved the clearance of crated aircraft, aero engines and associated equipment, as well as urgently required machine tools flowing in to these West Coast ports from the USA. These companies were also involved with the export of aid to Russia. Initially, this was shipped by the northern route to Murmansk but, by May 1943, a southern route via the Mediterranean and Persia was utilised. In total, some 4,500 aircraft, 800 vehicles, and 7,000 tons were dispatched. The movement of equipment consignments to British ports took careful coordination as much of it came from the various Stores depots across the country; most of the road moves were carried out using RAF vehicles of the MT companies, although there was some augmentation by civilian vehicles. The last of the companies to be formed in the UK was No. 8 at Colerne in Wiltshire in December 1941 and was responsible for road movement in the west and south west of the country. A further company, No. 9, was formed at Reykjavik in Iceland in December 1943 and supported eight different RAF squadrons based in Iceland, operating a wide range of aircraft including the Liberator, Catalina, Ventura, Hudson, Anson, Fortress, Warwick, and Hurricane.[23] Following Operation Overlord in June 1944, the RAF MT Companies provided urgently needed heavy lift transport when the Germans launched their V1 flying bomb attacks against the UK. As a response to this onslaught, balloon squadrons and RAF Regiment Anti-Aircraft (AA) squadrons, in conjunction with the Army's AA Command, formed a protective screen around London. The companies, along with vehicles obtained from the Ministry of War Transport Road Haulage Organisation, played a vital part in moving many of these units to where they were needed.[24]

Overseas campaigns also demonstrated the need for a specialist MT capability. The ebb and flow of the campaigns in North Africa led to the RAF's Desert Air Force having to remain highly mobile, and two more MT Companies (Nos 51 and 52) were formed in Egypt during 1942, with a third in Algeria (No. 53) in May 1944. The work of the two MT companies based in Egypt was quite different as the early days of No. 51 MT Company illustrates. The unit was formed in April 1942 at Heliopolis and was initially tasked with daily distribution runs in the Nile Delta area, many of which were to and from the sea ports. With Rommel's capture of Tobruk on 20 June, the Company became heavily involved in the frantic efforts to stem the enemy's advance into Egypt and was reinforced by a further forty Thornycroft trucks. The unit was divided into convoy sized units with two main tasks in support of the RAF: firstly, deliveries in the area of Cairo–Suez–Port Said–Alexandria and back to Cairo and, secondly, providing long distance convoys to the Western Desert–Lebanon–Syria and collecting stores from the docks for all points.[25] The unit's significant role in the direct support of air power is illustrated by the role it played in supporting the RAF's Desert Air Force, following the German capture of Tobruk on 20 June 1942 and the subsequent advance to El Alamein, which saw the British Army in retreat with the RAF mounting maximum bombing rear-guard actions against the advancing enemy.[26] The MT Company's ORB entry for 25 June opens with the comment: 'The big day, a total of sixty vehicles, leaving only one unserviceable in the camp, went out on urgent work'. Much of this tasking was moving vital munitions and aviation fuel for the Desert Air Force. In June 1942 alone, it moved 2,767 tons and covered some 50,000 miles. The high intensity operations lasted until the end of July when the threat to Egypt from Rommel's Africa Corps had diminished. Although it was not until May 1943 that organised German resistance ceased in Tunisia, the year still saw a significant effort with the unit covering 1,700,136 miles and carrying 119,864 tons.[27] The overseas requirement for specialist MT support brought about the formation of three more MT companies overseas before the end of the war: two were established in Italy in July 1944 (No. 54) and April 1945 (No. 58) and one in India and Burma in November 1944 (No. 57); the work of these units was similar in nature to those in North Africa.[28]

While the MT Companies were largely established to meet specific taskings that could not be met by unit resources, or for commitments that did not sit clearly with one unit or another, the RAF's logistic ORBAT for specific campaigns used a variation on the MT Company concept and involved S&TCs. As already referred to, these transported POL and munitions directly to units, along with delivering stores and supplies from semi-static depots to the mobile ASPs. The first three of these units were specifically formed for the campaign in France as part of the AASF in France during 1939–1940 (Nos 1 to 3). A further twenty-one S&TCs were formed: twelve in the Middle East and North Africa to support the campaigns in the Western Desert and the invasion of North Africa; four in Sicily and Italy to support the respective invasions; and five for the invasion of North West Europe in 1944.[29] The majority of the S&TCs were progressively disbanded between the end of the war and the late 1950s.

Post-war, three MT Companies remained in operation (renamed MT Squadrons between 1952 and 1954): No. 2 in the UK; No. 51 in Egypt, which remained operational until 1956 following the British withdrawal from the Suez Canal zone; and No. 317 at RAF Bruggen in Germany, which had been formed from No. 317 S&TC and was finally disbanded in 1962. The longest serving, No. 2 MT Squadron, remains operational in today's RAF as part of No. 85 (EL) Wing at RAF Wittering. From its original base in Cambridge where it was formed in 1940, it moved home a number of times: to RAF Stow-cum-Quay in 1945, RAF Leicester East in 1946, RAF Warton in 1947, RAF Bicester in 1949, RAF Lichfield in 1954, RAF Stafford in 1958, and to its current base at RAF Wittering in 2006. The squadron was granted its unit badge in April 1957, at the centre of which was an elephant carrying a golden log denoting the value of loads entrusted to it. Its Latin motto translates as 'Wherever you may wish to carry something'.

In May 1992, the Squadron was disbanded as part of the UK Government's Options for Change review, but its vehicles and personnel were reformed as No. 2 MT Flight as part of No. 16 MU RAF Stafford's MT Squadron. In the period up to the end of the Cold War, the unit went on to achieve some impressive results as the RAF's own international heavy road haulage capability, supporting the operations in Northern Ireland, the Falkland Islands, and Bosnia. From about the mid-1950s until 1981, the Squadron also operated a HGV Driving School. During the First Gulf War (Operation Granby), the flight was subject to particularly intense tasking and during the period August 1990 to July 1991, it moved 20,600 tons of freight over 1,274,200 miles.

By 1997, the flight consisted of forty-five personnel, with a fleet of thirty-eight Seddon Atkinson tractor units and forty-seven specialist trailers of various types. While the bulk of the personnel were MT drivers, the flight was commanded by a Trade Group 18 (Movements Controller) warrant officer and included two Movement JNCOs. The flight at this time was under the functional control of HQ STC (Logistics Mobility) and was classified as a second level support unit. Its remit as such was very broad and, in addition to the movement of surface freight, it was also responsible for supporting RAF operations and exercises; providing a reconnaissance capability for wide or outsize loads; providing diplomatic clearances for loads that needed to cross international frontiers; and providing transport support to the Nuclear Accident Response Organisation.[30]

A regular part of its container movement commitment was in support of the Anglo–French and Tornado multi-national aircraft programmes. As part of this, the squadron's vehicles operated the FRUCON service to Bordeaux in France and the TORCON service to the German and Italian depots at Erding and Novarra. Much of this work involved long and hard hours, with many of the drivers spending between 180 to 200 days per year away from home.[31] Following the formation of DSDA following SDR 98, there was a risk that the RAF might lose its specialist MT capability to the new agency so No. 2 MT Squadron was temporarily transferred to TSW at Stafford; it then became part of ELW on its formation in 1999, with its squadron status being reinstated on 10 August 1998. In 1999, the squadron supported RAF operations in Kosovo, with much of it deploying to Corsica where they operated the line of communication from the port at Bastia to the French Air Force base at Sari-Solenzara, supporting RAF Tornados when they deployed forward from RAF Brüggen in Germany. A welcome change for the squadron at this time was in November 1999, when SAC drivers were reintroduced to the squadron and then in 2002 the first LACs began to be posted in.

Following the first Gulf War (Operation Granby), the flight supported RAF detachments that took part in the enforcement of the Northern and Southern Iraq No-Fly Zones (Operations Resinate North and South) before seeing action again in 2003 as part of the second Gulf War (Operation Telic); it was one of the first RAF surface-based units into Iraq. The squadron initially deployed 126 personnel and 100 vehicles to the Middle East and operated further forward in hostile territory than any other RAF ground based unit. In addition to transporting large quantities of freight, it provided support to the Joint Logistics Component well beyond the Iraq–Kuwaiti border to within two kilometers of the front line.

In addition to transporting aircraft spares, armoured vehicles, and ground support equipment, it also assisted with the deployment of a field hospital from Kuwait to the Basra area. This was no small undertaking and consisted of 151 lorry loads, carrying just over 3,000 tons of equipment and covering a total of 57,380 miles in the process. A squadron detachment also operated a fleet of fourteen 32,000 litre fuel tankers, which supported the Joint Helicopter Force, various Army

No. 2 MT Squadron vehicles on the move from RAF Wittering. (*Crown Copyright—Air Historical Branch MoD*)

units, and the Royal Marines. By April 2003, the squadron had covered some 187,462 miles while transporting 21,344 tons of freight; this alone was roughly equivalent to 1,341 Hercules aircraft loads. The squadron's involvement with the operation ended in 2006.

The conflict in Afghanistan also saw the squadron involved in Operation Veritas during 2001 and subsequent operations in Afghanistan as well as the more unusual tasking of supporting the Armed Forces involvement in the UK firemen's dispute during 2002 and 2003 (Operation Fresco). One of the more recent and particularly notable achievements of the Squadron was its involvement in Operation Ellamy, the UK's participation in the military intervention in Libya from March to October 2011. This required the Squadron to transport a wide range of equipment and supplies to No. 906 Expeditionary Air Wing at Gioia del Colle in southern Italy, which was supporting RAF Typhoon and Tornado aircraft involved in policing the no-fly zone over Libya. This was a sizeable undertaking for the MT Squadron and it maintained a freight sustainment surface line of communication capability through France and Italy during combat operations; this consisted of an eight-day return journey from its base at RAF Wittering, during which its vehicles were escorted through Italy by the Italian police. The Squadron played a leading role in opening the airheads at Gioia del Colle and Trapani and was heavily involved in the closure of the military airheads once hostilities ceased in Libya. From March until November 2011, in support of Operation Ellamy, 2 MT Sqn drove 1,089,634 miles and moved 7,100 tons of freight equating to the approximate movement of 767 C-130 aircraft loads.[32]

In March 2012, the Squadron took a lead role in the military's Operation Escalin response to the UK fuel strikes and co-ordinated the placement of over 150 Trade Group 6 MT drivers around the UK, as well as training drivers from the British Army. From July until September 2012, the Squadron supplied fifty personnel to provide both logistics and security support for the entirety of the military support of the Olympic Games while also maintaining its full out-of-area commitment and European exercise commitments. The Squadron is a highly respected and much sought-after tri-service freight movements specialist and continues to provide support for world-wide operations, as well as support for exercises throughout the UK and Europe.

Movements by Rail

The use of railways had been an important part of the military effort during the First World War, both at home and overseas. On the Continent alone, the British had laid some 800 miles of railway throughout the course of the war.[33] The early 1920s, however, were not an easy time for the railways, with growing competition from many of the newly-established road haulage companies, many of which were run by ex-servicemen who had learned to drive in the forces and had purchased ex-military vehicles.[34] Despite this competition, the railways still provided the only way to move large, heavy volumes of freight around the country, especially to and from the RAF's Stores depots. Indeed, before the rail company amalgamation in 1923, thirteen different companies were involved with moving RAF stores.[35] By the mid-1930s, the Air Ministry had significantly increased its ownership of rolling stock and was operating twenty-two of its own locomotives, a figure which was to rise to a peak of 112 during the Second World War.[36]

The pre-Second World War expansion schemes, which brought with them a growing number of airfields and associated infrastructure, generated a similar increase in the need for links with the nation's railways. The five depots at Quedgeley, Carlisle, Stafford, Hartlebury, and Heywood, which were constructed in 1938 and 1939, were all built with rail links to their dispersed sites.[37] Similarly, the ammunition depots at Chilmark, Fauld, and Harpur Hill were all established close to main railway lines.[38] The line into the depot at Chilmark, established in 1937, developed into probably the most extensive internal rail network, with two and a half miles of standard gauge and more than nine miles of two foot gauge tracks for the three main sites.[39] For general work above ground, diesel engines were utilised, While battery electric locomotives were used in the underground tunnels. Rail links were also a vital feature of the many air ammunition parks that were built to serve the British bomber bases as these were the only practical way of transporting heavy munitions from the ordnance factories to the storage sites.[40]

It was not just munitions that were best moved by rail. The sheer bulk of aviation and ground fuel was also ideally suited to rail transport. In 1938, the decision was taken by the Air Ministry to divert 75 per cent of UK petroleum imports to west coast ports to minimise the risk of air attack. With most of the RAF's airfields being sited towards the east coast, this fuel had to be transported cross-country, and rail was then clearly the best way to move the large volumes that were being imported. The decision was not without additional cost so the Air Ministry purchased 300 extra tank wagons to cope with this; however, they were operated for them by the railway companies.[41]

In 1939, most of the RAF units and their equipment that deployed to France as part of the expeditionary force travelled to their ports of embarkation by train, similar to their BEF predecessors in 1914. The proximity to rail links on the Continent was quite different, and many units found that their forward operating bases were nowhere near a local railway station that could receive inbound supplies. They therefore had to rely heavily on road transport from the ports; these, along with the base depots, were controlled by the Army and the RAF was responsible for moving its own equipment and supplies for up to forty miles from the railheads.

The use of the railways proved to be just as valuable in the UK following the Battle of France and, in the eight days following the evacuation from France in June 1940, 620 trains carrying 300,000 troops were run; all of this was without any prior knowledge of what numbers would arrive at seven ports in south-east England and was coordinated almost entirely by telephone.[42] Surviving wartime statistics for the movement of goods by rail in Britain do not show figures pertinent to RAF usage. However, the rail companies estimated that in 1943, approximately 140,000,000 wagon loads of traffic had been despatched by rail since the beginning of the war.[43] Rail formed an important part of the RAF's transport network in the UK for the rest of the war, enabling large volumes of bulky and heavy goods to be shipped, which proved particularly valuable for the RAF's MUs.

The official histories do not include detailed figures for the Air Ministry and RAF usage of rail, but the ORBs of the depots do provide some indication. During 1942, for example, approximately 50 per cent of the freight turnover (tons) at No. 25 MU Hartlebury was carried by rail.[44] Perhaps the most significant value of rail transport for the RAF though was for the movement of bulk fuel and munitions. Until the construction of a government fuel pipeline in 1941, which connected the west coast ports to the operational airfield areas of the east of England, movement of fuel by rail was the only means of transporting the substantial quantities required. The size of the requirement is well-illustrated by the example of the 1,000 bomber raids, the first of which the RAF carried out in May 1942. For one raid alone, the aircraft fuel requirement was just over two and half million gallons, all transported by twenty-five train loads in a total of 650 tank cars.[45] Even after the construction of the pipeline system, rail transport remained a vital and more flexible link in the fuel supply chain and continued to be used to move fuel from pipeline terminal depots in the east of England to the operational flying units.[46]

Rail movement was not without its risks and the civilians of the rail operating companies shared many of the hazards that were inherent in moving large volumes of fuel and munitions across the country's rail network. On 1 June 1944, two railwaymen (driver and fireman) by the names of Benjamin Gimbert and James Nightall were crewing a train of fifty-one trucks loaded with 500-lb bombs destined for East Anglia. As they approached Soham station in Cambridgeshire at 1.25 a.m., they became aware that the first truck in their load had caught fire from an overheated axle box. The men stopped the train, uncoupled the rest of the trucks, and towed away the blazing truck so that it was clear of the station. The truck with its load of forty bombs on board exploded just the other side of the station, killing Nightall and seriously injuring Gimbert. The station signalman was also fatally injured, dying twelve hours later. The explosion left a massive crater some 20 feet deep and 66 feet wide, which obliterated the entire station complex at Soham, leaving over six hundred buildings damaged in the local area. Both men were awarded the George Cross for their gallantry.

Post-war, the demobilisation of large numbers of personnel returning from overseas kept rail traffic particularly busy and railway transport officers (RTO) were positioned at the main UK railway stations to act as a liaison between the services and the railway companies; many of the RAF provided RTOs were Equipment officers. Although most of the RTO offices were run jointly by the three services, the RAF's Directorate of Movements was solely responsible for maintaining offices at the nine London terminus stations and at forty-five provincial stations. It was not just people that were on the move at this time: large quantities of equipment were being back-loaded to the equipment depots and many thousands of unused bombs were being returned to the ammunition depots from the forward holding locations, many of them destined for further movement to ports for eventual dumping at sea.

One of the more interesting overseas railway ventures was on the island of Masirah, just off the coast of Oman in the Indian Ocean where there had been an RAF base since 1935. The only way to get bulk supplies to the island was by ship, but the cargo from these could not be landed between May and October due to the rough seas during the southwest monsoon. Supplies for these six months had to be stockpiled on the island, including drummed fuel, munitions, and food, and were dispersed around the airfield. The problem was moving large amounts of stores from the coastal landing point to the dispersal sites. To meet this need, a narrow-gauge railway was laid amounting to seven miles of track over which two locomotives and twelve wagons were to operate. By the end of the war, the size of the railway had grown to twelve miles of track and was serving thirty-five dispersed sites, including fuel and bomb dumps and stores compounds. The offload of fuel, usually transported in 45-gallon drums, was not easy. Air Commodore Gerry Pengelly was stationed as a young officer

Steam tank locomotive *Aldwyth* pictured at Kidbrooke in the 1950s. (*Author's collection*)

at RAF Khormaksar during 1955–1957, and was responsible for fuel stocks at the three route stations of Ryan, Salalah, and Masirah. He recalled that, at that time, resupply of fuel was by ships chartered by Shell, but these were unable to proceed inside the reef off-shore at Masirah. The ever-resourceful Movements staff solved this by throwing the drums of fuel overboard and then floating them ashore on the tide before they were plucked from the sea and then moved to the storage area by rail.[47]

From 1956 onwards, Masirah hosted a number of detachments of bomber and fighter aircraft involved in various campaigns and exercises. A notable example during 1958 was in response to a rebellion in Oman where Shackletons from Nos 37 and 244 Squadrons flew a number of bombing missions from the island; the majority of the 1,000-lb bombs used were delivered to the aircraft dispersals using the Masirah railway. In 1961, a construction programme to modernize the airfield included a pipeline from the anchorage to storage tanks. This took away one of the main purposes of the railway and it was closed, albeit it remained as part of the station's recreational amenities until it was finally shut down in 1977 when the Sultan of Oman's Air Force took over the airfield from the RAF.

The rail infrastructure at RAF Chilmark went on to have an active life post-war and was linked by a spur from the main London to Exeter line at Dinton into Ham Cross where incoming freight was transferred to the narrow-gauge railway for movement throughout the 350-acre site.[48] The post-war closure of many of the depots brought a gradual decline in the RAF's dedicated use of railways, but perhaps the greatest reduction came as a result of the increased use of road transport. The lines at RAF Stafford and RAF Quedgeley closed in 1976, with Carlisle's following eight years later in 1984. The rail infrastructure at the depots not only served a functional purpose but also provided light relief in the visit programmes for senior officers and civilian dignitaries who were often invited to drive the engine. The last of the RAF lines to go came with the closure of RAF Chilmark in 1994.

While the RAF's close relationship with rail transport diminished in the post war years, it still remained a valuable means of movement, especially in the UK. In April 1963, British Rail set up an experimental service that transported packages using its passenger rail network. The Red Star service, as it was named, evolved into an excellent system that used scheduled trains rather than dedicated freight services, thus providing a much greater choice of timings. For many years, the service was one of the fastest (and most economical) means of transporting packages long distance throughout the UK. Indeed, many unit supply squadrons used the service to deliver AOG and other high priority consignments to other units when they had been subject to issue order requests (via the Supply IT system) and the required delivery time could not be met by PFDS. The growing availability and door-to-door service offered by road transport companies in the 1990s led to this method of priority movement becoming road-based, and Red Star was replaced with the use of couriers to move priority items.

Movements by Water

With such an extensive network of road and rail routes within the UK, there was little need for the transport of equipment and supplies by sea on the home front. The main role for water-borne transport was for moving personnel, stores, and supplies to overseas theatres of operation. This was achieved through the extensive use of merchant shipping for routine movement or directly embarked on naval vessels when landing as part of amphibious operations such as the invasions of North Africa, Sicily, Italy, and Normandy. The RAF did have marine craft, but these were used primarily for air-sea rescue duties and supporting amphibious aircraft such as the Catalina and Sunderland.[49]

Embarkation Units

There was no tri-service organisation in the period up to and during the Second World War to work with ships in port so the RAF established its own specialist capability in the guise of embarkation offices, embarkation staff or port detachments, all of which had a very similar role. This miscellany of units were renamed embarkation units (EU) during the autumn and winter of 1941–1942. By the end of the war, nearly fifty EUs had been formed at home and overseas, most of which were based in or around sea ports. In the very early days of the war, the role of the UK units was not just to support the feed-in of freight and RAF passengers to the troopships, but also to assist the other services. One such example was assisting the Royal Navy, which did not have any facilities for embarking aircraft onto their carriers while in port; this work was carried out by the EUs, in conjunction with the RAF MT companies on the Mersey and the Clyde. A posting to an EU seems to have been popular one, although one calling for much hard work, an experience related by Mr Jack Hall, who qualified as a RAF Equipment assistant in 1941. After an initial posting to No. 16 MU Stafford, he joined No. 28 EU at Workington in Cumberland, a unit whose HQ was based in the famous Liver Building in Liverpool. Jack related how training was invariably carried out on the job and that they normally worked shifts of eight hours on and eight off but, when a ship needed to be loaded without a break, they could work thirty-six hours or more. By all accounts, they were a hardy breed:

> [They] glorified in being scruffy and [were] tough enough to do it. One time in Manchester, after going there for a couple of days and staying a fortnight in civvy digs, our landladies were ashamed of us and made us go to work in their husbands' shirts etc. while they did our washing.[50]

The EUs became an important part of the Movements organisation and were used with great success overseas to provide a loading and unloading capability at captured

Embarkation unit personnel unloading supplies on the Mulberry Harbour, Normandy 1944. (*Crown Copyright—Air Historical Branch MoD*)

ports. Following the work of the RAF Beach Squadrons in the opening stages of Operation Overlord, the RAF EUs took on the role of unloading RAF supplies and personnel through the Mulberry Harbour at Arromanches. The EUs lasted until the demise of sea trooping in 1955 with many of them becoming Movements units and later air movement squadrons to meet the growing Movements support required for the rapidly developing air transport fleet.

Troopships

The EUs were also involved in the staffing of British troopships, one of the more unusual Movements responsibilities that endured up until just after 1955. Not only was there a significant number of RAF personnel arriving in the UK during the war, but also a sizeable number embarking for overseas, many of whom were trainee aircrew departing for and returning from overseas training in countries such as Canada, Australia, New Zealand, and South Africa as part of the Commonwealth Air Training Plan. The sheer number of personnel on the move by sea brought with it a requirement for the RAF to contribute to the staffing of the troopships that were then the only means of moving large numbers of personnel over long distances. On the whole, and where possible, if more than 50 per cent of the troops to be shipped were Army, then the permanent staff on board were drawn from that Service; if, however, that percentage was in favour of the RAF, then the permanent staff were drawn from the ranks of the EUs. Three of what were known as the 'monster' class troopships, including the *Queen Elizabeth*, had permanent RAF commandants.

There was a significant amount of work involved in the administration of troopship loading. The planning of a passenger load was based around each deck being divided into a number of tables called messes, each consisting of about twelve men. Once the overall load had been worked out, the EU staff then produced a boarding ticket for each passenger on the nominal roll; these would be very specific and showed the ship and convoy number, along with mess and seat number. The tickets were an important part of the process and were sent to the relevant transit camp so that road convoys or rail movements could be organised to enable the men to be dispatched and received at the dockside in boarding ticket order. Little was left to chance and guides were positioned throughout the ship during boarding, with a military policeman (MP) at the top and bottom of gangways to keep order. There was an added incentive for troops to cooperate, with embarkation staff exchanging individuals' pay books for boarding cards. The MPs regulated the flow of those embarking, twelve at a time to each of the allocated mess numbers. The personal kit of officers was brought on board by nominated baggage parties who then carried it to the respective cabins. To make sure these men returned on board, their personal headdress was handed to the MP at the top of the gangway and only handed back when they had returned on board. The significance of this was that

Troopship *Empire Pride*. (*D. Barnes*)

anyone remaining in the docks or pier head without headdress would have been immediately apparent.[51]

Movement of Explosives: The Mobile Explosives Team

In the post-Second World War period, the movement of explosives became more tightly regulated. Due to weight and safety considerations, the movement of explosives out of the UK by sea remained (as it had throughout the war years) the only practical method of transportation for these potentially hazardous cargoes. Such movement through civilian ports required insurance cover, which was provided by HM Government indemnity and required strict compliance with a whole range of UK legislation (both military and civilian), covering standards of transport and handling equipment, and training personnel in all aspects of the movements of explosives. To ensure compliance with this legislation, there was a requirement for a military representative to be present at ports through which explosives were being moved to protect the government's indemnity. This appointment was known as the authorised explosives representative (AER) and was a task shared by the three services; the Royal Navy covered their own moves, while the Army supervised movements through ports in Scotland and the east and south coasts of Britain. The RAF was responsible for moves through ports on the west coast from South Wales up to northern Cumbria. The RAF was additionally responsible for providing AER cover during all United States Visiting Forces movements, irrespective of the ports that were used for imports or exports.

The RAF's AER role was vested in what was known as the mobile explosives team. Based at No. 11 MU RAF Chilmark in Wiltshire, the team was made up of a Supply Branch junior officer, two explosives qualified sergeants of Trade Group 18 (Supply) and a civilian stores officer Grade 'C'. The team was functionally tasked by HQ RAFSC through the Command Transport and Movements officer; this appointment also had the responsibility for the protection and issue of government indemnity.[52] Following the closure of Chilmark, the AER duty became a responsibility of the RAF's armament role office at HQ Strike (later Air) Command.

Inland Waterways

It was not just the sea that provided a highway for Logistics. The RAF also used inland waterways for a short period during the war years. Although the use of inland waterways and canals in the UK can be traced back to the days of Roman occupation, canals began to be developed continuously from the second half of the sixteenth century.[53] The period of significant growth was from the late eighteenth century onwards when an inland waterway network developed, which linked many of the country's rivers, playing a significant part in the transportation requirements of the industrial revolution. At the peak of its growth, there were some 4,000 miles of inland waterways in England.[54] The growth of the railways, however, saw a progressive decline in the significance and usage of the canals. The inland waterways in Britain had been of relatively small value during the First World War. Pre-Second World War thinking by the Committee of Imperial Defence had considered them:

> Instead of being a second means of inland transport they had become a bad third. Since canals were expected to carry only a small volume of traffic compared with rail and road in a future war, no special measures for war-time control were favoured.[55]

Notwithstanding, the Air Ministry did consider the use of inland waterways as an alternative means of transport and a series of experiments were conducted between January and April 1942. Set against an overall aim of saving on road transport as well as relieving the load on the railways, it was believed that the inland waterways could offer an alternative means of transport that could be used in the event of disruption by enemy action. The concept was not seen as being of value to the growing number of RAF units, but as a means of shipping manufactured goods from contractors (mainly from contracts placed by the Air Ministry and Ministry of Aircraft Production) in the large industrial areas of London, Birmingham, and Manchester, a role that was very similar to that played by the inland waterways during the industrial revolution.[56] Following the trial, three canal clearing depots (CCD) were established at Paddington, Birmingham, and Manchester, located within 10 to 25 miles of the contractors that they served; the flow of goods to the CCDs was controlled by the RAF's Master Provision Offices. During 1942 alone, some 14,983 tons was shipped by the CCDs.[57]

Despite what appeared to be a promising start, the scheme was short-lived. Not surprisingly, the transit time (by comparison with road and rail) was lengthy, often running into many weeks. This was not just as a result of the relatively slow speed of the barges but because of the numerous locks that had to be negotiated. Additionally, collections to and from the CCDs had to be carried out by road, which led to a large expenditure on fuel, conflicting with one of the Government's principles: to conserve petrol.[58] With such lengthy transit times, the various Ministries became increasingly reluctant to divert their cargo from road and rail and this progressively led to the termination of the scheme by the end of October 1944. The three CCDs were disbanded at the beginning of November 1944. Although the scheme was not a great success, some 61,419 tons of equipment were moved via the canals. It was estimated that the closure of the scheme placed an additional fourteen trucks per day on the national railway system or an additional two trucks per day into each of the AEDs.[59]

Movements by Air

The relative infancy of aircraft design and development during the First World War had precluded their use for the practical transport of personnel and equipment in any sizeable volume. The inter-war years saw a very slow development in any form of air transport and it was not until the later stages of the Second World War that the RAF achieved an effective and sizeable capability in this respect. Post-war, the design and development of much larger jet-engined transport aircraft saw air movements become a more viable capability.

The Cold War years, though, especially after the withdrawal of British forces from east of Suez in 1971, saw less significance for air transport and it was the First Gulf War in 1990–1991, which brought into focus the significance of both strategic and tactical air transport. The SDR of 1998 acknowledged that expeditionary operations would become a more common feature of Defence commitments in the future and identified the need to regain lost airlift capability. Air transport not only remains a critical force enabler for Defence, but also a vital element in maintaining the RAF's supply chain.

Early Developments in Air Delivery

Arguably, the first use of military fixed wing aircraft to air deliver stores and supplies was by the RFC and RNAS during the First World War, both of which were involved in dropping supplies to the British Sixth Division at Kut Al Amara in Mesopotamia, which had become surrounded by Turkish forces. During the period 17 to 29 April 1916, the end of which saw the garrison in Kut having to surrender to the Turkish forces, 19,000 lb of supplies (mainly food) were dropped in 140 sorties.[60] This was, however, a temporary measure to meet an urgent need and largely used modified bomb-dropping apparatus under the aircraft's lower wings to release supplies contained in sacks. It was also at about this time that the RFC is believed to have dropped supplies of small arms ammunition by air to ground forces for the first time. The task fell to No. 9 Squadron, operating RE8 aircraft with modified bomb racks, which could hold two boxes, each holding 2,000 rounds of .303 ammunition (with an attached parachute); the containers were released by the aircraft's observer using a cable release mechanism. To indicate where the main drops were required, ground troops marked the required point with a white 'N'; specific machine gun posts were able to seek specific drops at their location by displaying a white 'V'. The technique proved highly successful and on 4 July 1918, during the advance of the Fourth Australian Division, ninety-three boxes of ammunition containing 111,600 rounds of ammunition were dropped with the loss of just two R.E.8s.[61] Further air dropping of supplies continued through to the end of the war, with the nature of stores dropped being extended to include signal flares, barbed wire, and food.

Inter-War Development of RAF Air Transport

In the early post-First World War years, the air transport needs of the RAF in the UK and overseas were quite different. The RAF's presence in Iraq and Afghanistan, with large distances between its bases and inhospitable terrain, saw a very clear need for air transport.[62] From its introduction to service in 1922, the Vickers Vernon aircraft was used extensively in the Middle East, enabling the movement of a significant volume of spares to be undertaken; this was well beyond what could realistically be carried by much smaller, two-seat aircraft.[63] In due course, the Vernon was replaced by two further Vickers aircraft of similar design: the Victoria in 1926 and the Valentia in 1934. These aircraft were almost exclusively operated by 70 and 216 Squadrons who, by the-mid 1920s, were the RAF's sole air transport operators in the Middle East.[64] The introduction of the Victoria and Valentia almost doubled the troop-carrying capacity of the Vernon, with a substantially increased operating range of 800 miles.[65]

Air transport support in India during the inter-war years had been on a much smaller scale, primarily due to the RAF's operations and basing being predominantly focused on the North-West Frontier region of the country.[66] A Heavy Transport Flight was formed at Lahore in March 1929, operating the Handley Page Clive troop carrier aircraft, a modified version of the Hinaidi bomber.[67] The unit was re-designated the Bomber Transport Flight in July 1932 and by the outbreak of war

Vickers Victoria. (*Author's collection*)

had been absorbed into No. 31 (Bomber Transport) Squadron operating the Vickers Valentia at Lahore.[68]

Although the introduction of new types of aircraft from 1926 onwards brought an evolutionary improvement in air transport, the broader contribution to RAF Logistics capability was still relatively small. The aircraft's limited carrying capacity meant that it would still take a large number of them to move the ground personnel of a flying squadron, let alone the panoply of spares and equipment, much of which would have been too bulky to have been accommodated in interiors that were primarily designed to accommodate passengers. As far as the Army was concerned, one aircraft alone could not even move a complete platoon. Geographically, the aircraft were almost entirely based in the Middle East and India; there was little requirement for such a capability in the UK where distances between bases was much shorter, terrain and climate more moderate, and where there was a better developed road and rail infrastructure. Thus, by the beginning of the expansion programme in 1934, the RAF had developed an air transport capability that reflected the geographical needs of its foreign policy at the time, rather than one which would support operational doctrine for future warfare. Moreover, its role was largely to effect inter-base transport, rather than providing a wider capability for expeditionary warfare. The requirement for Army support and how the RAF might be involved in a major campaign, particularly in Europe, was not high on the planning agenda.[69] Unless future conflict occurred in the Middle East, the RAF elsewhere was largely dependent on surface methods of transport such as road, rail, and sea.

Air Transport during the Second World War

By the outbreak of war in September 1939, the RAF had just three air transport squadrons operating solely the Vickers Valentia aircraft overseas: No. 70 Squadron at Helwan in Egypt, with a detachment at Habbaniya in Iraq; No. 216 Squadron at Heliopolis in Egypt; and No. 31 Squadron at Lahore in India.[70] The number of squadrons committed to air transport changed in 1940, a year that saw No. 267 Squadron established at Heliopolis operating a mixture of transport aircraft and No. 70 Squadron changing its role to a bomber squadron with the Vickers Wellington in September 1940. Two further squadrons joined the air transport fleet in the Middle East: No. 117 Squadron operating the Bristol Bombay at Khartoum in the Sudan from April 1941 and No. 173 Squadron operating a mixture of aircraft at Heliopolis from July 1942.[71] By September 1942, Nos 117, 173, 267, and 216 Squadrons were brought under the control of No. 216 Group in the Middle East Theatre Group, much of which supported the Eighth Army in North Africa.[72]

Air transport resources in India were strengthened by the newly formed No. 353 Squadron operating Lockheed Hudsons at Dum Dum in June 1942, with a detachment from No. 216 Squadron at Karachi and Agartala also operating Hudsons in November 1942. These squadrons came under the control of No. 29 Group in December 1943.[73] The value to logistics is more difficult to assess in this theatre due to the limited level of detail in squadron ORBs. The role of No. 31 Squadron, however, is particularly notable, with it flying in supplies and reinforcements, along with evacuating the wounded, in support of ground forces after the Japanese advance into Burma in 1942. The squadron was also actively involved in supply dropping to the Chindit Special Forces expeditions in Burma during 1943 and 1944.[74]

The development of air transport in the European theatre of war got off to a much slower start. In September 1939, there were just two air transport units in the UK: No. 24 Squadron based at Hendon and No. 1680 Flight at Doncaster, both of which were controlled by RAF Fighter Command.[75] No. 24 Squadron had been at Hendon since July 1933 and was a disparate collection of aircraft, many of which were from the civilian airlines; its role had limited logistical value and was largely confined to transporting VIPs and mail for the Services. The role of 1680 Flight, however, was more significant. The RAF's eclectic mix of transport aircraft at this time had come about through a pre-war enabling measure known as the 'Dormant Contract', which had earmarked sixty-eight transport aircraft from thirteen civil operators. Many of these aircraft were allotted to specific RAF stations just before the outbreak of war; this proved to be a timely and important source of additional aircraft, not just for No. 24 Squadron, but also for No. 1680 Flight. The same day, the British Government also introduced the *Air Navigation (Restriction in Time of War) Order 1939*, which placed most civil airfields in the UK under military control.

At the beginning of September 1939, the aircraft of a number of private air transport companies were relocated to airports at Bristol, Exeter, Coventry, and

Poole. The administration of these wartime measures was carried out by the National Air Communications (NAC) organisation, a new statutory department that was established within the Air Ministry. By the end of March 1940, most of the work of NAC was taken over by the RAF, with the exception of wartime regular scheduled air services within the UK and to some overseas destinations. The RAF takeover included some 150 aircraft being impressed into military service.[76] This influx of aircraft, *inter alia*, resulted in the status of 1680 Flight being upgraded and it became No. 271 Squadron on 26 March 1940. The formation of No. 271 Squadron broadened its operational responsibility from just Fighter Command to include taskings from Bomber and Training Commands. These included a liability for the movement to, and support of, squadrons deployed to France along with the movement of bomber and fighter squadrons in the UK when required.[77] Along with a number of chartered civilian aircraft controlled through NAC, No. 271 Squadron had an active part in the campaign in France during 1939–1940 and was actively involved in numerous flights to, from, and within France, conveying stores and personnel for the RAF's squadrons on the continent.[78] The use of air transport during this campaign proved to be highly significant, a point made in a despatch by the commander of British Air Forces, France (Air Marshal Barratt) who commented that 'the importance of having an adequate number of transport aircraft available was emphasised on numerous occasions'. Barratt also observed that 'more aircraft and a large transport organisation would have been invaluable'.[79]

The Squadron also performed valuable work during the Battle of Britain, with the movement of combat squadrons between airfields. At the height of the battle, the transport aircraft of No. 271 Squadron carried out some thirty-four taskings for Fighter Command, much of which involved moves of complete squadrons.[80] These taskings were in addition to the work of the first three of the RAF's MT companies, which had been formed in July 1940 for this very purpose. The squadron remained in the UK throughout the war, eventually becoming part of No. 46 Group and playing an important part in Operation Overlord in 1944.

There were two significant changes in command and control that enabled a more focused approach to air transport. The first of these came on 5 August 1941 when one of the branches within the Air Ministry's DDGE was renamed the deputy directorate of Movements (DD Movements) and transferred to the control of the Directorate-General of Organisation (DGO). The new directorate was similar in structure to its predecessor, but with a strengthened planning/policy function and the notable addition of a section responsible for the import of American aircraft to the UK.[81] The DD Movements' organisation was upgraded to directorate status (still within DGO's area) on 23 May 1942.[82]

The second and more significant change for the RAF came on 25 March 1943 with the formation of RAF Transport Command. This placed transport aircraft resources under the command and control of a single RAF Command that was responsible for 'the organisation and control of strategic air routes, for all overseas ferrying, for reinforcement moves of squadrons to and between overseas theatres, and for air movement of freight and personnel'.[83] By early 1944, the transport assets and related activity of the RAF were, broadly speaking, overseen by five groups and one wing. Within Transport Command, Nos 44 and 45 Groups were responsible for ferry services and Atlantic transport, with No. 46 Group responsible for transport aircraft units in the UK. Overseas units were covered by No. 216 Group (within Mediterranean Allied Air Forces) for the Middle East, No. 229 Group (within Air Command South East Asia) for India, and No. 114 Wing (within Mediterranean Allied Air Forces) for West Africa. As part of the preparations for Operation Overlord, No. 38 Group was formed in October 1943 with its transport squadrons assigned to the AEAF.[84] By and large, the significant expansion of RAF air transport capability can be attributed to the purchase of large numbers of the Douglas C-47 Dakota from the USA under the Lend-Lease Agreement. Unlike many of the RAF's earlier aircraft used for transport duties, the C-47 Dakota was produced with larger cargo doors and strengthened floors. This, coupled with its ability to operate from rough terrain airstrips made, it an ideal aircraft for general purpose transport.[85]

Thus, by the beginning of 1944, the RAF had developed a much stronger air transport capability, although this had been achieved largely through the needs for the invasion of Europe through Operation Overlord. The wider air transport activities (mainly delivery of airborne forces and their equipment) connected with Overlord and other airborne operations that took place in Europe up until the end of the war are well covered in other works and there is little more that can be added as

Casualty evacuation by air, Normandy, 1944. (*Crown Copyright—Air Historical Branch MoD*)

far as this book is concerned. What has not been given as much recognition though is that RAF transport aircraft of No. 46 Group also made a much wider contribution to the logistical support of both 2TAF and Twenty-First Army Group through what was known as supply-by-air.[86] Within this, the overall control and tasking of all scheduled and emergency airlifts was carried out by the Combined Air Transport Operations room at the HQ of the C-in-C AEAF at Stanmore, just outside London, with an Air Freight Control Centre at Poulton, close to the main 46 Group airfields in Wiltshire (Broadwell, Down Ampney, and Blakehill Farm). Poulton received freight from both the Army and RAF and ensured that it was prepared for air transport before moving it to the nominated departure airfield.[87] The first air-landed supplies were flown into France (Bazenville, near Bayeaux) by No. 271 Squadron on 13 June 1944 (D+7). Following this, the first dedicated transport aircraft airstrip in France (Creully, near Bayeaux) was established on 6 July 1944. The size of the RAF's air supply operation into Normandy was substantial and included a diverse range of freight, ranging from munitions and fuel to medical stores and vehicles. By the end of August 1944, No. 46 Group had carried some 2,636 long tons of freight plus 8,815 passengers to the Continent and evacuated 22,814 casualties to Britain.[88]

One of the more critical contributions made by RAF Logistics during the campaign was in direct support of the British Army as it advanced north-east through France, Belgium, and into Holland during August and September 1944. There was a significant logistical issue here in that the source of supply for the advancing Army was still in Normandy, much of which was coming in through the Mulberry harbour at Arromanches. Although the famous American 'Red Ball Express' vehicle convoy system did its best to keep pace with the advancing British and American armies, the resupply lines of communication grew ever longer. Indeed, even by early September 1944, RAF transport aircraft of the Allied Air Force assisted with 'rushing petrol, ammunition and rations to the armies in France and Belgium in order to keep them fighting and they had become entirely dependent upon air supply'.[89]

Of all the resupply needs, vehicle fuel became one of the most urgent. The withdrawal of No. 46 Group aircraft from re-supply operations and commitment to the airborne operation in Holland during the period 1–25 September (Operation Market Garden) posed an unwelcome threat to the support of the advancing ground forces. This saw the direct intervention from Eisenhower, who requested (through AEAF) a temporary daily assignment of seventy RAF Bomber Command aircraft to supply fuel by air for the Twenty-First Army group. The task was carried out by Halifax aircraft of No. 4 Group Bomber Command in late September 1944 operating mainly from RAF Pocklington and RAF Elvington near York to airfields near Brussels.[90] Such was the significance of the air transport contribution that it warranted specific comment in the post-campaign despatch by the Air C-in-C AEAF, Air Chief Marshal Sir Trafford Leigh-Mallory:

> The principal lesson so far from the campaign is that the tactical use of air transport to supply a rapidly advancing army can be of decisive importance, and that the limiting factor in its employment is not so much the availability of suitable aircraft as the availability of sufficient landing strips in the forward area and adequate loading and re-loading arrangements at the terminus.[91]

One of the theatres of war where air supply really came into its own was in the inhospitable terrain of Burma where the Dakota aircraft of No. 31 Squadron played a critical role. Indeed, during July 1943 alone, the squadron flew 286 supply-dropping sorties to Army units in and around Falam, delivering 784 tons of supplies with just fifteen available aircraft.[92] Nearby India was the focus for a notable Transport Command air trooping operation in late 1944, when significant numbers of personnel were flown in by air for eventual redeployment as part of the war against Japan; this carried on until March 1946.

The 'movers' of the war years experienced a host of challenges that were very similar to those faced in the twenty first century. Of these, passenger expectation is perhaps an area where the greatest frustration often occurred, a challenge not too dissimilar from today. An ex-RAFVR Movements officer, who served at Air HQ Iraq, RAF Habbaniya, recalls part of the closing paragraph of a notice that was prominently displayed in the station Movements office:

Dakota wet take-off, 1944. (*Crown Copyright—Air Historical Branch MoD*)

> Curiously enough we like this job. Odder still, we get a kick out of giving you a good journey. But there is still a war on. You cannot always go on the most comfortable train. You cannot always take 4 tons of kit when moving by air![93]

The Immediate Post-War Period

The early post-war period found the Movements organisation heavily tasked as the UK Services returned to a peacetime footing. Many men and women were returning to the UK for demobilisation, among which were large numbers of liberated prisoners of war. To hasten their return home, a number of aircraft from Coastal and Bomber Commands were temporarily transferred in to Transport Command to provide additional aircraft for the task. The return to peacetime activity saw Transport Command maintaining trunk routes across the globe and throughout 1946 and 1947 scheduled flights were operated to the Middle East, Singapore, India and Ceylon. Significant air movement operations at this time included the evacuation of UK forces from India resulting from its independence in 1947 and from Palestine when the British Mandate ended there a year later. Other commitments included the deployment of troops and equipment to Korea in 1950–1953, Kenya in 1952, the Suez crisis in 1956, and troop movements to Cyprus in 1957.

The Berlin Airlift 1948–1949

One of the more notable post-war operations involving a substantial air movements commitment was the Berlin Airlift of 1948–1949. This came about as a result of the Soviets trying to make the Western Allies' position in Berlin, which was essentially an island within the Soviet zone of occupation in East Germany, untenable by cutting its surface resupply routes. Determined to thwart this attempt to starve West Berlin into submission, the Allies set up an airlift for essential supplies. From the outset, it was not envisaged that any form of relief operation would last long and that diplomatic negotiations would soon resolve the issue. However, the latter was not successful and the Berlin airlift, codenamed Operation Plainfare, very quickly turned into a round-the-clock operation, which lasted just short of a year. There were no alternatives to the air-landing of supplies although a number of other unworkable suggestions had been made including air-dropping from bomber aircraft and even airlifting out of the city a sizeable proportion of the population.

Towards the end of June 1948, the RAF's Air Staff estimated that the sixteen aircraft currently based at Wunstorf could lift about seventy-five tons per day into Berlin. With an expected increase of aircraft to forty-eight Dakotas by the end of the month, the estimated carrying capacity was expected to rise to 750 tons by the first few days of July. In the early stages, the Air Ministry planners had set a target of 450 short tons per day increasing to 840 short tons by 7 July (1 short ton = 2,000 lb). The 450 figure was achieved by a fleet, initially, of fifty-four Dakotas (nearly one half of the RAF's Dakota fleet). This was to change later to a reduced Dakota fleet of thirty-two and forty of the larger Avro York aircraft; the latter was capable of lifting up to about 8.25 tons. The 840 target was reached by 14 July, largely as a result of a revised aircraft mix, a significant increase in crews, and an increase in the capacity of the Dakota by stripping out unnecessary safety equipment and reducing the fuel load.[94] Early July saw an important introduction to the fleet with the arrival of two squadrons of Sunderland flying boats, which operated from Finkenwerder (near Hamburg) on the River Elbe, flying into Lake Havel in Berlin. The Sunderlands carried a curious mix of goods including salt, meat, sanitary towels, and cigarettes.[95] With congestion becoming a growing problem at Wunstorf, the Dakotas moved to Lubeck in August, with the Yorks remaining at Wunstorf. By November the newly introduced Handley Page Hastings joined the fleet operating from Schleswigland. August saw a number of civilian freighters joining the airlift under contract and these were mainly based at Fuhlsbüttel from October onwards.

Two eminently sensible principles were established from the outset; these laid the foundations for a 'pull' based supply chain. The first of these was that nothing would be sent by air to Berlin unless it had been asked for. The second was that the city would not request anything that could be supplied from its existing resources, in either original or substitute form. During the airlift, these principles saved an enormous amount of unnecessary tonnage being dispatched. Deliveries in West Germany were made by the German Railways, with Airlift freight receiving track

Sunderland on Lake Havel, Berlin Airlift, 1948. (*Crown Copyright—Air Historical Branch MoD*)

priority. Once at the railheads, the freight became the responsibility of the Allied military who, in turn, moved the consignments on to the airfields. As the airlift progressed, it became more convenient to concentrate specific goods at certain airfields. Once at the airfields, the supplies were checked in and accumulated into stockpiles under the direct control of the HQ Army Air Transport Organisation (HQ AATO); there was a direct link between this HQ and liaison officers in Berlin regarding daily loads so that stocks in Berlin were kept at a steady level. Aircraft loading was carried out by what was known as the Rear Airfield Supply Organisation (RASO) and under the direct control of HQ AATO. This was a complex operation and required much careful coordination. Once the estimated time of arrival of an inbound aircraft was known, a designated parking bay was allocated in advance and the outbound freight for that same aircraft was driven out to the nominated location. At the same time, the refuelling bowsers and technical staff would also converge, ready for the aircraft's arrival. With cargo manifests already produced, the physical loading was carried out by mainly German workers. In one particular case, an RAF York aircraft had difficulty taking off from Wunstorf and struggled to make the flight to Berlin. On landing, it was discovered that the aircraft had been loaded with its own consignment plus that of another Dakota.

In the early stages of the operation, it was found that the standard Transport Command method of documenting freight and passengers was too complicated and a simplified approach was therefore adopted. For each aircraft type, a master weight and balance form was devised, which showed the cargo space divided up into compartments, each showing the maximum weight that could be carried in that particular area. Together with a simplified flight manifest that gave the actual load and weight placed in each of the compartments, this ensured much more rapid and safer loading. The physical loading of the aircraft was mainly a manual process (there was little room for handling aids in the aircraft or at the parking areas) and was surprisingly effective. For example, a consignment of sacked coal or flour could be completely loaded in just fifteen minutes, from the aircraft hold door being opened to the loading vehicle pulling away.

Liquid fuel was more problematical as the use of 45-gallon drums proved inefficient and dangerous. The drums weighed some 365 lb each and were difficult to restrain in the aircraft holds. The solution came from a civilian company, Flight Refuelling Ltd, operating the Lancastrian aircraft (a converted Lancaster bomber) in a rare configuration for the time—as a tanker aircraft. The Lancastrians were later joined by Tudor and Halton tankers. In total, over 92,000 tons of liquid fuel was airlifted by the British during the operation.[96]

On arrival in Berlin, unloading was carried out by German civilian labourers working as part of what was known as the Forward Airfield Supply Organisation. This, again, was run by the Army. Once empty, the hold of the aircraft was swept clean. Nothing was wasted; spilt coal dust was re-bagged and any spilt flour was similarly handled but destined for animal feed. From Gatow, most of the food

Food awaiting shipment to Berlin, 1948. (*Crown Copyright—Air Historical Branch MoD*)

and coal consignments were driven to a loading jetty at Lake Havel for onward movement by barge. With such a large involvement of German civilians, security was always tight but crime was reported as low throughout the operation, although a snap search of an off-going shift (approximately 1,000 people) at Gatow discovered some 36 kg of sugar, 28 kg of butter, 4.5 kg of milk powder, 5.5 kg of coal, and a number of tins of meat.[97]

Of all the nations taking part in the Airlift, the turn around time of British aircraft was the longest as the UK was the only one that back-loaded cargo from Berlin. Although both the RASO and the Forward Airfield Supply Organisation in Berlin were largely Army-manned, the back-loading component (including a significant passenger handling responsibility) was carried out by the RAF air movements organisation. In terms of goods, this averaged 350 tons per day for most of the Airlift. From a scratch start, the supply chain evolved into a well-disciplined and highly effective process.

To enable the aircraft to keep up such an intensive flying rate, it was critical that the support infrastructure was on top line. It is not surprising that the Airlift had a significant impact on Transport Command's resources, and a number of early problems were experienced due to participating aircraft (with the exception of a few Dakotas) not being part of BAFO's normal aircraft establishment. Consequently, at the outset, there were no pre-stocked holdings of special-to-type equipment or spares. As far as the spares were concerned, squadrons initially brought these with them, but the range and scale soon proved to be inadequate. Aircraft (particularly the engines) were subjected to an abnormal amount of strain with the repeated number of landings and take-offs; this led to a much greater unserviceability rate than expected. On top of this, the supply of spares in the UK was limited, either by obsolescence (Dakotas and Yorks) or because of the limited operating experience of new types (Hastings).

In the early stages of the Airlift, a number of Equipment officers were deployed from the UK to support activity at the despatching airfields, in many cases at very short notice. The real 'hub' of the UK support operation was RAF Honington where Transport Command had its major servicing centre. It was here in August 1948 that a specialist unit known as Operation Plumber was set up. Consisting of six Dakotas and crews, the unit was responsible for collecting spares within the UK and then flying them direct to the British airlift units in West Germany. Their achievements were impressive by any standard; each month, they flew some 60,000 miles and carried between 400 and 500 tons of spares.[98] As far as basic or standard unit equipment was concerned, this was supplied from No. 431 Equipment Depot, RAF Altona. This unit had begun life as an ASP at the end of the Second World War and had settled near Hamburg in a former cigarette factory at Bahrenfeld. Brian Sullivan, a former AC1 wireless operator who served at the depot during the Airlift, recalled how 'the Equipment Branch as represented by No. 431 ED coped magnificently throughout the Airlift period with no breakdown in the operation or interruption through lack of spares or equipment'. The impact of the operation on the depot is well-illustrated by the volume of signals traffic that the unit handled. Prior to the Airlift period, Brian remembers how the unit was a relatively 'quiet supply unit serving a dormant occupation air force'; at that time, the total traffic consisted of about eight or nine signals in and out each day with the office opening at 9 a.m. and closing at 5 p.m. The Airlift saw this increase to around 100 to 150 signals per day, with the office on a three-watch, twenty-four-hour operation.[99]

Realising that they could not win this first trial of strength in the Cold War, the Russians lifted the blockade on 12 May 1949. By this date, the British had made a substantial contribution to the overall operation. The RAF had flown into Berlin just under 542,000 tons of supplies, which represented 23 per cent of the overall total for the Airlift. The back-loading achievement from Berlin was just as impressive as nearly 36,000 tons were exported and 131,436 passengers were handled. This came at a price as eighteen RAF and twenty-one civilians were killed in various accidents during the operation.[100] The lessons learned section in the official report on the operation is surprisingly short as far as logistics is concerned but it does acknowledge that 'A system of supply by air [to Berlin while it remained isolated in East Germany] is a vital necessity'.[101]

Yorks at RAF Gatow, Berlin Airlift, 1948. (*Crown Copyright—Air Historical Branch MoD*)

The Development of Post-War Air Transport

In the post-war period up to the mid-1950s, the Douglas Dakota, Avro York, Handley Page Hastings, and the Vickers Valetta were the mainstays of Transport Command's fleet for about ten years. Although both the York and Hastings had ranges in excess of 1,500 miles, the maximum number of passengers that could be carried by any of the aircraft types in service at this time was just fifty (Hastings), thus limiting any long-range deployment of sizeable numbers of British troops.

These aircraft in their transport role went out of service: the Dakota and York by the end of the 1940s and then the Valetta and Hastings by 1968. They were gradually replaced from 1956 with the introduction of the Blackburn Beverley heavy tactical freighter, and the RAF's first jet transport, the de Havilland Comet C2. Over the next six years the Command's fleet was expanded to include the turbo prop Bristol Britannia C1 in 1960, followed by the Hawker Siddeley Argosy C.1 and Comet C4 in 1962. The introduction of these aircraft not only strengthened the RAF's tactical transport capability, but the Comet and Britannia provided a much-needed long range, strategic capability; these aircraft could carry in the region of 100 passengers over two to three thousand miles. For the support of major crises, Defence policy at the time envisaged that the air transport fleet would be supplemented by the use of civil aircraft, particularly those already under charter such as in the air trooping service.

The increase in airlift capability at this time was significant. During the Suez Crisis of 1956, the RAF's entire air transport fleet was able to move 2,400

Beverley with troops and cargo, 1959. (*Crown Copyright—Air Historical Branch MoD*)

passengers or 375 tons in one single lift. Some six years later in 1962, that capability had increased substantially to 5,600 passengers and over 1,000 tons of freight. Given that the movement of an Army brigade required the transport of 2,600 passengers, 100 trucks and trailers, and 70 tons of freight, this increase was a major step forward in force mobility. By mid-1960, studies into air transport needs had considered, *inter alia*, the adequacy of the existing long-range air transport fleet, which then consisted of the Britannia, Comet C2, and Beverley for heavy freight. Of concern was the need to significantly improve both speed and range, which led to the introduction of the British Aircraft Corporation's VC10 C1 in 1966. This was part of a major re-equipment programme that also saw the introduction of the Short Belfast the same year, which provided a much-needed long range, heavy lift capability that had been identified in 1957 with the Army pressing for a fleet of long range freighters capable of lifting up to fifteen tons over a range of 3,000 miles.[102] In addition, the RAF's tactical capability was augmented by the introduction of the Hawker Siddeley Andover C1 in 1966 and the Lockheed Hercules C1 in 1967.

The need for this growing air transport fleet was firmly underpinned by British Defence policy, which, in 1964, was quite clear about the role that it played, pointing out that 'the long and medium range transport forces enable ground forces to meet sudden troubles wherever they may occur'.[103] The significant contribution that could be made by air transport is illustrated by the RAF's role in the Sarawak confrontation between 1963 and 1966. In the last twenty-one months of that operation, transport

Britannia of No. 99 Squadron over Mount Kilimanjaro, 1960. (*Crown Copyright—Air Historical Branch MoD*)

aircraft and helicopters of the RAF, along with the Royal Australian and Malaysian Air Forces, carried some 31,000 tons of freight and just short of 250,000 men. The RAF capability was not without significant financial cost. During the period 1967–1968, the total cost of RAF transport operations amounted to £140 million with the air transport effort supported by some 27,300 personnel (service and civilian); the lion's share was attributed to the strategic fleet (including tankers), which represented £61 million alone.[104] The cost of the air transport fleet progressively reduced and by the end of the decade was in the region of £98 million with some 23,000 personnel working in support.[105] It was at this time that discussions on a new RAF Command structure were taking place within a much wider review of British Defence policy. As part of this, it was accepted that the strategic and tactical aircraft based in the UK, providing support to all three services, should remain within one command. However, the command's ORBAT had increased to include the Hunter ground attack aircraft in 1962, and later, the Harrier and Phantom. The addition of this offensive support element did not fit with the title of 'transport' and led to a change of name to Air Support Command in August 1967.

Despite the progress that had been made to strengthen air transport resources, UK economic pressures in the mid-1960s led a wide-ranging review of Defence commitments. The announcement in July 1967 that Britain would withdraw from east of Suez by the mid-1970s brought into question the continuing need for long range air transport; the timescale for this was revised by the Government in January the following year for what would be a large-scale withdrawal by the end of 1971. The opportunity was also taken in 1970 for further restructuring work, which led to RAF Brize Norton becoming the main strategic air transport base, with RAF Lyneham becoming the main tactical air transport base.

It was the statement on defence estimates in 1974 that had the greatest impact on air transport as a result of the UK re-focusing its forces on NATO commitments. The outcome was significant, with a declared aim to reduce the fixed wing element by 50 per cent from 115 aircraft to fifty-seven. By the end of 1976, the Argosy, Beverley, Comet, and Andover had all gone out of RAF operational service, leaving only the Hercules, VC10, and Belfast.[106]

Britain's commitment to NATO was emphasised in the statement on defence estimates in 1977, which highlighted that virtually all RAF combat and support aircraft were assigned to the alliance. Reference was also made to the fact that the Belfast heavy transport aircraft had now been withdrawn from service but with compensatory changes made to the VC10s and Hercules, with a programme being continued to extend the in-service life of the latter.[107]

As far as the Hercules was concerned, it was found that it regularly 'bulked out' with cargo but was still capable of carrying much more weight. The decision was therefore taken in 1978 to run a programme that would effectively lengthen thirty C1 aircraft by 15 feet. The C3 as it became had its troop-carrying capacity increased from ninety-two to 128 and an improvement in its load carrying volume of 37 per cent; the first modified aircraft was delivered back to RAF Lyneham in August 1980. Some of the C-130 Mk1s were fitted with Andover fuel tanks and other air-to-air refuelling modifications to become C-130Ks in 1982; these were all C-130 model Ks that retired from service in October 2013. A further variant, the C-130J, was introduced to RAF service in 1999. The C-130J models currently in service are the 'stretched' C4s and the shorter C-130 C5s.

Following experience in the Falklands campaign in 1982 (Operation Corporate), which had emphasised the importance of in-flight refuelling, the Lockheed TriStar was introduced to service in 1983. The previously unplanned need to support the new garrison on the islands required a robust air bridge from the UK; the tanker/passenger/freighter configuration of the TriStar was ideally suited to these tasks. The aircraft started RAF service primarily as a passenger aircraft (C2) with the KC1 and K1 variants subsequently converted into passenger/freight/AAR aircraft. The TriStar was the first wide-bodied type transport to be operated by any NATO air force apart from the United States Air Force.[108] As such, it was not without its challenges and the aircraft's introduction required changes to loading and unloading along with new

Belfast in flight. (*Crown Copyright—Air Historical Branch MoD*)

Belfast and armoured cars. (*Crown Copyright—Air Historical Branch MoD*)

Hercules and palletised load at RAF Lyneham. (*Crown Copyright—Air Historical Branch MoD*)

cargo and baggage handling equipment.[109] As welcome as it was to the RAF's transport fleet, many 'movers' found the TriStar a difficult and time-consuming aircraft to load.

The aircraft's first tasking was to provide the UK–Ascension Island air link and support the Ascension Island to the Falkland Islands sea-link between 1984 and 1986; subsequently, the TriStar supported the whole airbridge route. Two ships had provided the sea link and every two weeks one of them would leave Ascension Island taking personnel down to the Falkland Islands to start their tours. These changeovers (roulements) were able to be carried out quickly due to the carrying capacity of the TriStars. Once on the ground passengers, baggage, freight, and consignments of surface mail were immediately transferred by helicopter to the ship; the return journey brought personnel off the ship for their flight home. This task also saw the first operational use of No. 4624 Movements Squadron RAuxAF (first formed in August 1982), which provided a team to assist the regular RAF Movements personnel.

The SDR 98, with its clear signal of a commitment to expeditionary operations, recognised that there was a serious shortfall in heavy lift capability. This had come about following the retirement of the Belfast in 1976 and the loss of capability had become all too evident during the Falklands conflict in 1982 and the first Gulf War in 1991. The review announced the introduction of the Boeing C-17 Globemaster III in 2001, of which four aircraft were initially leased but then purchased outright, plus a further three acquired by 2007. Two of the RAF's transport stalwarts were retired from service after the C17 became operational: the VC10 in 2013 and the

TriStar in 2014. The RAF's air transport fleet is currently undergoing much needed refreshment with new aircraft, such as the A400M Atlas entering service between 2014 and 2019.

Air Transport Basing and Movements Infrastructure

The withdrawal from east of Suez and the refocusing of Defence effort on Europe started to see an increasing investment in UK air movements infrastructure. The first part of this was the construction of a new passenger terminal at Brize Norton in 1969, followed very shortly by the Gateway House transit hotel to accommodate passengers, which was opened in 1970. The design of the new terminal building incorporated a number of advanced design features that enabled the control, segregation, and flow of inbound and outbound passengers. The infrastructure had been somewhat *ad hoc* up to then. The developments at Brize Norton benefited significantly from similar work some ten years earlier at Lyneham, where the RAF's first specially designed air terminal in the UK had been opened in late 1960. The work at Lyneham had identified benefits in co-locating the Movements load control section with the operations and engineering control organisations, thus enabling a much better interaction between the three areas. With these important developments in place by the beginning of the 1970s, both units were established as key facilitators of air transport operations, both in terms of aircraft and infrastructure. In Cyprus, a new air terminal was also built, which was more conveniently sited than the previous arrangement that was over a mile away from the aircraft parking area.

Route hotel at RAF Lyneham in 1965. (*Author's collection*)

In 2004, following an organisational review at RAF Brize Norton, an Airport of Embarkation Wing was formed. This allowed air movements, MT, fuel, in-flight catering, and contract management functions to be brought together under a single specialist command chain to provide the station and defence community with better focused logistic support for dispatching and receiving military and civilian air transport aircraft.

The RAF's air transport fleet bases were also rationalised in December 2012 when RAF Lyneham closed and its aircraft and personnel transferred to RAF Brize Norton. Lyneham had a long and illustrious history. Opened in 1940, it had become a key base in RAF transport operations. Since the UK's involvement in Iraq and Afghanistan, Lyneham had also played an important role in handling the repatriation of British personnel killed in those theatres, with funeral corteges departing the unit through nearby Royal Wootton Bassett, where crowds lined the streets to pay their respects to the fallen. The important duty of repatriation also involved many RAF Movements personnel. The task, sadly, continued, albeit relocating to Brize Norton.

Air Trooping

In 1955, the decision was taken to end sea-trooping and this signalled the beginnings of a significant growth in RAF Transport Command. From then on, the Government maintained a clear policy that sought to increase the extent of air trooping; as the carrying capacity of Transport Command increased, the number of troopships began to decrease.[110] The task was initially undertaken almost exclusively by charter companies. Indeed, some of the civil air charter companies built up their business on trooping contracts, but gradually Transport Command took over more of the routes, until only regular trooping to North-West Europe remained as a chartered service. The financial saving as a result of the greater use of Service air was marked and reduced the cost from some £7 million in 1967–1968 to just £2 million in 1971–1972.[111]

However, in more recent years, due to the limited number of MOD-owned air transport aircraft, it has made more economical sense for the RAF to make use more use again of charter aircraft (and seat bookings on commercial aircraft) for longer routes such as to the USA, the Falkland Islands, and Cyprus. There remain limitations and due to the requirement for defensive aids systems to counter the threat from ground launched projectiles, military transport aircraft continued to be used for passenger movement to and from operational theatres such as Iraq and Afghanistan.

The greater use of air transport for passenger movement though, required suitable facilities for handling and processing people. The first such premises in the UK was the London Reporting Centre in Goodge Street was opened in 1954 and processed passengers who were scheduled to travel overseas on the long-range air trooping charter flights. After check-in, passengers were taken by coach to the airports at

Blackbushe and Stansted to link up with the respective flights. Following a fire, the London centre was moved to a new location at the Regents Park Barracks in 1955 and renamed the London Assembly Centre. The air trooping scheme between the UK and Germany commenced in October 1960 and was carried out by Silver City Airways from RAF Manston in Kent to RAF Wildenrath and Düsseldorf, with passengers travelling via Victoria Station as the primary reporting point.[112]

Throughout the 1950s, each of the services was responsible for booking and handling its own passengers to and from overseas but it soon became apparent that this was not the best use of resources. Consequently, in 1958, the decision was taken to form a Joint Service Air Trooping Centre (JSATC). Its initial role was the co-ordination, flight planning and passenger handling for the long-range air trooping charter flights. The centre was based at RAF Hendon and consisted of an RAF-run transit accommodation facility and a tri-service manned movement control wing. Tri-service manned movement control detachments were also based at key points throughout London and its airports. The location at Hendon was the obvious choice at the time as the facilities were already in place from the pre-JSATC days.[113] The early years of the centre were not blessed with the most salubrious of accommodation and the initial reporting point was a temporary portacabin outside Euston Station; passengers were then transported by coach to Hendon for flight processing and then on-moved to Blackbushe, Stansted, or Gatwick for charter flights courtesy of Caledonian or Eagle Airways. At the time, the majority of overseas movement of personnel was to Europe and this short-range requirement was ideally suited to the civil air charter operators working from the London airports. Control of the short-range charter operated by Skyways from London Gatwick airport was initially handled by the Joint Service Continental Booking Centre (JSCBC) working from Rochester Row, with passengers reporting directly to the JSCBC representatives at the airport.

Booking also needed rationalisation as by 1969 there were twelve booking offices in the UK, each of which was running its own call-forward system for passengers within its seat allocation on service and charter flights. This was less than ideal and was therefore centralised in 1969 with the formation of the Services Booking Centre (SBC). This led to the various booking centres in the UK progressively relocated to the King's Buildings in Dean Stanley Street, Westminster. By the end of 1971, all of the individual service booking procedures and documentation had been rationalised into one system.[114] In 1970, JSATC took over the short-range trooping from JSCBC but handed over its responsibility for long range flight planning to the SBC. At about this time, Britannia Airways started operating the short-range trooping to and from Europe and check-in for these passengers was carried out at the Phoenix Road and Mableden Place terminals; this remained the case until the check-in was moved to a JSATC office at St Pancras Station where passengers were better placed for travel to Luton Airport.

By 1987, the heart of JSATC was at RAF Hendon and consisted of the Movements Wing HQ and the Airbridge House transit accommodation. The Wing was controlling quite a dispersed organisation, which then included detachments at London

Heathrow and London Gatwick airports; these handled the long-range air trooping to and from Hong Kong. Detachments based at St Pancras and Luton stations served as the reporting point and feeder service for the short-range air trooping service from Luton Airport to and from north-west Europe and Gibraltar. The busiest of the JSATC detachments was Luton, which, on average, was handling 170,000 passengers per year; this included some 3,000 school children travelling between their UK schools and their Service parents overseas during the three main holiday periods each year. The transit accommodation at Airbridge House had a capacity of 240 beds with an average monthly throughput of 3,000 passengers. With the closure of RAF Hendon in 1987, the HQ of JSATC and Airbridge House needed a new home and were moved to a purpose-built facility at RAF Stanbridge in 1988.[115] Airbridge House at Stanbridge closed in the late 1990s when Stansted, and then later Birmingham airports, became the main airports supporting the ever-shrinking trooping service. The role of JSATC then became the civil airport detachment flight (comprising RAF and Army RLC personnel), operating from RAF Northolt under the command of the SAMO. Overseas, following the closure of Gütersloh and Wildenrath, the greatly reduced numbers of trooping flights were handled by an RAF liaison officer at Hanover.

Cargo Control

Up until the mid-1960s, the control of air cargo was very much a single-service affair. This changed in October 1966 when an agreement was reached on a common procedure for the movement of service cargo by air. Initially, the Air Cargo Allocation Centre was established at HQ Transport Command (subsequently Air Support Command) at RAF Upavon, under the control of the Command Air Movements Officer. Its task was to receive airlift bids from the three Services, to challenge them if required and to allocate accepted loads to available airlift capacity. By the early 1970s, much work had also been done on the management of surface movements but it soon became clear that both air and surface cargo management had very much gone their own way. Despite this, there was more synergy between both areas than had been previously acknowledged. This was particularly evident in 1975 when a trial to use training aircraft based at Thorney Island to move low priority surface cargo to Germany met with only limited success. Post-trial evaluation showed that the RAF had 'neither the infrastructure at HQ level nor the necessary climate at working level to accomplish it'.[116] As a result, the emphasis on air was dropped and the management function was changed to the cargo allocation centre, but allied to what was known as the open port system. This was a profound change in operating concept from the previous apply and call forward system. The open port was a terminal (air or surface) into which fully documented cargo was 'free-flowed' by the consignor without prior notification. There were of course exceptions to this and the movement of explosives (because of safety implications) and priority one cargo was still managed by telephone to ensure that the most suitable outlet was used. On the surface side, this involved 'open ports' being set up at No. 14 MU Carlisle and No. 16 MU Stafford, with similar facilities for air cargo being set up at RAF Lyneham and RAF Brize Norton. Wherever possible, cargo was to be moved utilising the PFDS.[117] The key benefits of the open port scheme were to speed up the movement of cargo and to make better use of transport assets. The RAF managed its own cargo movement up until SDR 98 when the freight distribution elements of the three services were brought together under a new Defence Freight Distribution Group.

Movements IT Support

Notwithstanding the many improvements in organisation, the administration of the process was still largely manual and time-consuming. Various studies had been instituted into computerising the process but it was found that the cost of the technology at the time outweighed the benefits that might be realised. This began to change by the mid to late 1970s. In 1979, a series of studies were initiated to consider the viability of an ADP-based reservation system. The outcome was that the Defence Movements Co-ordinating Committee agreed to buy processing time and peripheral equipment as a total system package, based on an existing airline computer.[118] Formulated on the British Airways international passenger reservation system (Maxipars CRS), the system was named the Movements management air reservation system (MMARS) and was unveiled by the RAF's Director of Movements in 1984. Designed to handle 300,000 routine movements per year the system consisted of fifty-two computer terminals in the UK, Germany, Cyprus, Hong Kong, Brunei, and North America.[119] The new MMARS became part of a wider suite known as the air movements information systems (AMIS), an ex-British Airways suite, and included the flight departure system (FDS), services air cargo system (SACS), and air load planning (ALP). The AMIS suite was replaced in 2013 by two 'off-the-shelf' software systems: Air Core for passenger reservations and departure control and the Interim (now integrated) Cargo System (ICS) currently used by the USAF.

Air Movements Squadrons

The air transport task brought with it the need to provide specialist Movements support. The Second World War EUs gradually became Movements Units, with many on the air transport stations and staging posts becoming Air Movement Squadrons. Each of the squadrons was usually commanded by a SAMO who was usually answerable to the unit operations staff. The squadrons had quite a broad remit and were responsible for all Movements activities on the units including loading and off-loading, the documentation and processing of passengers and cargo. At the heart of the operation was the load control section with supporting passenger, cargo, and traffic sections; the latter was viewed by many as the more physically challenging part of the organisation, loading aircraft at any time of day in all weathers and often against short time scales. The passenger and cargo sections made the most of warmer and drier indoor working conditions.

Despite the carefully regulated working practices of loading cargo on transport aircraft, it was often more of an art than science, although flight safety was always paramount. Squadron Leader Andy Marshall recalled working as a 'mover' on Ascension Island in 1984:

> After the Falklands war, Movements' life on Ascension Island settled into a regular if very hectic schedule. In the spirit of jointery, the Army was in charge of the troopships, the Navy ran the helicopters and the RAF manned the Port Unit. Five days a week, a C-130 was despatched to the Falklands—three freighters and two full passenger aircraft. To achieve this required five aircraft at 0600 with engines running—a Victor tanker and a spare, a C-130 tanker and a spare, plus the aircraft destined to reach Stanley—a mere thirteen-hour flight. Not all made it, but thankfully none were lost; they either diverted into Brazil or Uruguay or simply made the round trip without landing, particularly if the Falklands weather was too severe. Freight destined for the South Atlantic flowed into Ascension at a far faster rate than could possibly be shifted South by air. Effectively, the RAF's Standard Priority System ended at Ascension and a daily 'Freight on Hand' message was sent to Stanley by MMARS, who then called-forward what was most urgent. The Cargo Section not only looked after air but also sea freight. With no harbour and high seas, loading and unloading ships was a tricky task. The 'Saints' workers (from St Helena) expertly manned the lighters under extreme conditions. One of the most notable aircraft loads of this period was a replacement periscope for a submarine—the guard ship for the Falklands. This top priority cargo arrived on Ascension by chartered [ex-RAF] heavy-lift Belfast aircraft. In theory, the periscope in its heavy crate was too long to fit in a C-130, but by placing it crosswise, with the head on the floor by the aircrew entrance and the tail jacked up on wooden pallets at the rear the clamshell doors just closed.

Despite the hazards faced by Movements personnel operating in Afghanistan, life there had its lighter moments as recalled by Flight Lieutenant Tom Cousins, who served as the second in command of the Joint Movements Unit (JMU) at Camp Bastion in Helmand Province from November 2011 to May 2012. The JMU was a sub-unit of the Theatre Logistics Group and comprised a Flight from 1 Air Mobility Wing, a Royal Logistics Corps Troop, and RAF and Danish Air Force individual augmentees. In addition to the main hub at Camp Bastion, JMU personnel manned detachments in Kabul and Kandahar. The JMU was responsible for the inter- and intra-theatre movement of freight and personnel. In 2012, the focus switched to effective redeployment and there was a significant increase in tasking. During the offload of a Danish C-130 aircraft, the Camp Bastion airfield was subjected to an indirect fire rocket attack. After carrying out their individual immediate action drills the Movements team lead the evacuation of the aircrew and passengers to safety. The JMU team then carried out airfield post-attack recovery. Flight Lieutenant Cousins also recalled how his unit learned that simple abbreviations have different meanings. At the time, the JMU shared the air terminal and ramp infrastructure with the Americans and received a regular supply of the popular American soft drink Gatorade. Tom hosted a visit from some senior American personnel who he thought went well, until he got a call from the British Brigadier's Military Assistant who wanted to know what he had done to upset the Americans. Tom apologised, but said that he really did not know. It turned out that the Americans thought the JMU were not allowing them access to the facilities that had been predominantly funded with American finances. It turned out that there was a sign on a door that said 'Door US, do not use', which an American colonel interpreted as 'Door: US do not use'. The acronym US (or U/S) is commonly used in military parlance to mean something that is unserviceable. The sign was changed to read 'Door broken: do not use' and all was resolved.

Mobile Air Movements Squadrons

By the late 1950s, British Defence policy acknowledged that it might need to conduct overseas operations in support of political commitments, but in areas where the UK no longer had base facilities; the key to this would be the use of mobile forces. The Defence White Paper of 1957 therefore announced significant improvements in air transport capability, which, between 1955 and 1960, increased carrying capacity by nearly three-fold.[120] Clearly, this required corresponding air movements support, but of a mobile nature. Prior to this, Movements squadrons in the UK had to detach personnel for mobile operations as and when required. Most of these detachments were to Middle East and African airfields where, in many cases, aircraft handling facilities were basic to say the least; the recollections of many who served in such roles at the time recall how improvisation was often the key to success and required 'your wits, cunning and, at times, a liberal helping of good luck'.[121] Consequently, in 1958, mobile air movements teams were created, the first of which was formed in the UK at RAF Abingdon, building on a capability that already existed within the Air Transport Development Unit. Further teams were established in Cyprus, Aden, and Singapore; all were granted squadron status, becoming Mobile Air Movements Squadrons (MAMS) in 1966. The withdrawal from east of Suez announced by the Government a year later, saw the eventual disbandment of the Aden and Singapore squadrons and by 1974, only two teams remained in Cyprus and thirteen teams in UK MAMS, the latter meeting the lion's share of worldwide commitments.[122]

One of the early and major UKMAMS commitments was Exercise Bersatu Padu in 1970. The exercise was a combined Commonwealth exercise in Malaysia and required significant UK air Movements support. This included the Group Air Movements officer and staff of HQ 38 Group, along with six MAMS teams from the UK and FEAF. The UK teams deployed their bulky and heavy handling aids in advance of the exercise by sea, with personnel deploying on 1 June 1970.[123] The deployment phase of the exercise involved the transport of 2,800 passengers and some 900 tons of cargo; in all, ninety-one sorties were flown with the main lift being achieved in just over ten days. Throughout the exercise, 1,400 passengers were flown from the UK in thirty-two sorties along with 150 tons of cargo. The recovery phase of the exercise was substantial in itself and involved 109 sorties carrying a total of 4,000 passengers and 650 tons of freight. All of this was routed through the Air Movements Squadron at RAF Changi in Singapore; the last of the UKMAMS teams recovered to the UK on 3 July 1970.

UKMAMS moved to RAF Lyneham in 1974 and consisted of base and mobile teams; the base element worked a shift system taking care of the loading and unloading of the home-based Hercules squadrons. A typical month's turnover in the mid-1970s would see UKMAMS base teams handle between 800 and 1,000 tons of air cargo.[124] The mobile teams spent much of their time away from base and it was not unusual in the mid-1970s for team members to clock-up over 300 hours flying each year.[125] In the mid-1980s, it was not unusual for a team member to spend in excess of 200 days away on tasks. In 1985, Squadron Leader Andy Marshall, then a young airman 'mover', spent 300 days away (including three months in Ascension and two months on Operation Bushell in Ethiopia). A tour on MAMS has always been a popular one for air movements personnel, with the opportunity for worldwide travel being one of its many attractions. The role of MAMS, however, also brought with it involvement in virtually all of the major conflicts and humanitarian support operations since the 1980s.

The Falklands conflict in 1982 (Operation Corporate) saw UKMAMS live up to its motto of 'Swift to Move'. Within hours of Argentina's invasion of the Islands, three teams were on their way to Ascension Island where they started work on breaking-down incoming loads of cargo into specific allocations for movement by helicopter to ships of the British Task Force, which were in the process of sailing south to the Falklands. Twenty-four hours after the cease-fire in June 1982, UKMAMS personnel loaded and accompanied the very first long-range Hercules that flew into the Falkland Islands. Fifty-four members of UKMAMS were awarded the South Atlantic Medal, with two officers being awarded the Commendation of Commander Task Force 317 (South Atlantic).[126]

A few years later, in November 1984, UKMAMS was heavily involved in the famine relief operations in Ethiopia (Operation Bushel), an operation that saw some 30,000 tons of supplies and equipment air-dropped or air-landed within the country.[127] Three teams deployed to Addis Ababa and were fully operational within a matter of hours. The RAF's role was to fly relief supplies from the airhead at Assab to the feeding centres at Mek'ele and Axum where the relief workers would distribute the aid. The working days proved to be long and hard; the conditions were described by Wing Commander D. J. Blore who related how the UKMAMS teams 'worked upwards of eighteen hours per day in stifling heat to build allocated freight into viable aircraft loads, load the aircraft, travel on the aircraft to the destination and then offload the aircraft before returning for the next shuttle'.[128]

The Gulf War of 1990–1991 (Operation Granby) was a substantial operation for UKMAMS. On 9 August 1990, five full teams were deployed to Akrotiri ready for further movement into theatre; two of these remained on Cyprus to assist the resident air movements squadron handle incoming aircraft, while three teams moved forward to Dharan on 10–11 August. In the theatre, MAMS teams were positioned at Bahrain to help receive the Tornados on 26 August, along with a detachment placed at Seeb in Muscat to receive the RAF Nimrods and VC10 tankers. A need also arose at this time to provide for resupply cargo coming into theatre for the Royal Navy. As the resupply ports were designated as Jebel Ali and Raschid, the airfield at Al Minhad was chosen as the most convenient airhead with UKMAMS providing air movements support. Life was equally as hectic back in the UK, with MAMS providing early support to the deploying Jaguar aircraft from RAF Coltishall. During the UK's deployment phase, UKMAMS provided support to some 320 Hercules sorties from RAF Bruggen in Germany, and the UK stations of Coltishall, Coningsby, Honington, Kinloss, Leuchars, Wittering, and Wyton.

At this stage of the operation, all flights to the Gulf were staging through RAF Akrotiri and MAMS provided much-needed reinforcement to the resident air movements squadron. In late September 1990, the Saudi Arabian base at Tabuk became the main operating base for the Tornados with a MAMS team deployed in support, a key part of which was the off-load of the aircraft's JP233 runway cratering weapons. One of the largest tasks requiring Movements support was the deployment of Seventh Armoured Brigade, much of which was carried out through the airstrip at Jubail. Not only was the base only 125 miles from the Kuwait border, but the runway was also able to accommodate wide-bodied aircraft. Three MAMS teams were eventually positioned at Jubail and, by 28 September, they were up and running at a point that would become a vital location in the resupply chain. In one month alone, MAMS personnel at Jubail handled 11,000 personnel and just under 1.5 million tons of freight.[129] As far as the overall supply chain was concerned, it was decided at this time to set up what was referred to as a 'hub and spoke' concept, with the 'hub' located at King Khalid International Airport at Riyadh (largely operated by UKMAMS) and other airheads in theatre at the end of the 'spokes'. Freight and passengers would flow into the 'hub' from RAF Brize Norton, before being moved on to the final destination. By mid-November 1990, it had become clear that a ground campaign was increasingly likely to dislodge Iraqi forces from Kuwait. In preparation for this, the UK formed the First Armoured Division—further activity that saw a significant increase in the Movements workload at Jubail. The work in theatre was not just a physical challenge but the MOD's increased use of commercial transport saw MAMS working in conjunction with Boeing 707s, the Belfasts, and Guppies of the cargo airline Heavy Lift and the Boeing 747s of Kuwait Airlines that were used as shuttle aircraft.

Throughout the relatively short ground campaign that was to follow, MAMS teams remained heavily committed to the handling of resupply freight. A number of its personnel, however, moved much closer to the action in the battle area to receive freight at two forward operating bases established at Al Qaysumah and Talon; these were rough desert airstrips that were mainly used to resupply the forward elements of First Armoured Division, for casualty evacuation and the air evacuation of enemy prisoners of war. A further two forward bases were established as the Allies advanced into Kuwait. On the cessation of hostilities, the forward bases played a key part in the recovery process and became troop assembly points for the eventual on-move to Jubail or Kuwait International Airport for return to the UK. The last of the MAMS teams left Dharan on the final TriStar out in mid-April 1991, although some remained to support residual Army activity and the tail-end of the process to recover equipment back to the UK. The extent of UKMAMS' involvement in Operation Granby is illustrated by the fact that 107 of its members received the Gulf Medal, eighty-five of whom were awarded the clasp '16 Jan to 28 Feb 1991' for those on active service in liberating Kuwait.[130]

Operationally focused organisations such as UKMAMS can invariably be found in the RAF's ORBAT for virtually all the operations and exercises since Operation Granby, not least of which were Iraq (Operation Telic), the Balkans (Bosnia and Kosovo), and Afghanistan (Operation Herrick), along with operations in Angola, Rwanda, and Sierra Leone. UKMAMS has also provided growing support to the SF community. In November 2006, UKMAMS became No. 1 Air Mobility Wing (AMW) with three component squadrons: a HQ Squadron, 44 MAMS, and 45 MAMS. With the closure of RAF Lyneham, No. 1 AMW moved to a new home at RAF Brize Norton in February 2012 and was re-organised with a single MAMS and an Operational Support Squadron, which was responsible for various detached elements, training, and support. Operational activity continued apace with extensive support being provided to humanitarian operations in the Philippines, West Africa, and Nepal, air operations over Iraq and Syria and the withdrawal of UK combat forces from Afghanistan in 2014.

Auxiliary Air Movements

An RAF review conducted just prior to Operation Corporate in 1982 found that there was a shortfall in trained Movements personnel to support future operations, which led to the first and only RAuxAF dedicated Movements unit, No. 4624 (County of Oxford) Squadron, being formed at RAF Brize Norton on 8 August 1982 under the command of Squadron Leader (later Group Captain) David Bernard. The main purpose of the Squadron was to provide a pool of trained 'movers' to reinforce the regular Movements organisation. Within a year, it had managed to recruit and train enough personnel for three operational flights and to deploy individuals on operations. By 1987, it was declared fully operational and consisted of six constituent flights.

As previously mentioned, their first operational task was a deployment to Ascension Island to support the Falkland Islands sea-link roulements. The first major mobilisation for the squadron though, came in 1991 for the First Gulf War (Operation Granby), with personnel reinforcing the resident air movements squadrons at RAF Brize Norton, RAF Lyneham and RAF Akrotiri in Cyprus, along with UKMAMS and units in Germany. Many of the squadron carried on after hostilities ceased, taking part in recovery work and in Operation Provide Comfort, which provided food, medical, and other supplies to the Kurdish people in Northern Iraq. In recognition of its contribution to the Gulf War, No. 4624 Squadron received a Unit Citation from the Lord Lieutenant of Oxfordshire. While the squadron's OC had been a regular RAF officer since its formation, this changed in April 1993 when the first RAuxAF officer, Wing Commander Richard Mighall, was appointed to command No. 4624 Squadron.

Further recognition for the squadron came in 1997 when its unit badge was dedicated in the Church of the RAF at St Clement Danes in London. The squadron participated in a number of operations in the Balkans: Bosnia (Operation Loadstar in 1996 and Palatine in 1998) and Kosovo (Operations Agricola and Engadine in

Movers of No. 4624 Squadron RAuxAF loading an Apache helicopter into a C-17 Globemaster. (*Crown Copyright—Air Historical Branch MoD*)

1999). This was a particularly busy period with its personnel serving for up to six months on detachment. The second Gulf War in 2003 saw the entire squadron mobilised and reinforcing the Movements squadrons at RAF Brize Norton, RAF Lyneham, RAF Akrotiri, DCTA Bicester and deployments to Iraq at Basra and Umm Qasr. Since the beginning of the new millennium, the squadron has been undertaking out of area Movements support almost continuously and, in addition to Iraq, has been involved in operations in Sierra Leone (Operation Palliser in 2000), Afghanistan (Operations Veritas in 2001, FINGAL in 2002 and Herrick from 2002. The squadron has made a substantial contribution to RAF Logistics since its formations and has truly met the original intent behind its formation. Indeed, in the period February 2003 to May 2012 alone, the squadron has mobilised over 1,000 reservists in support of operations.[131]

The Movements Specialisation and Trade

The specialist nature of Movements duties led to the formation of two new trades during the Second World War. The first of these was the trade of Clerk (GD) (Movements Control), which was introduced as a wartime trade in 1942.[132] These clerks were established for duties in connection with the movement of personnel and freight by road, rail, sea, and inland waterways. The second of the trades came about as a result of the introduction of the EUs, which were initially manned by Equipment assistants and aircraft hands from Trade Group V. The specialist nature of working with shipping soon demanded a dedicated trade and the all-male trade of embarkation assistant was therefore introduced in November 1943.[133] The work of the embarkation assistants was quite different from that of Equipment assistants at RAF flying stations. A short article published in the Royal Air Force Journal in September 1945 on the School of Administrative Trades related how the training course for this trade taught its students 'something about ships, includes the calculation of tonnage, systems of stowage, the various forms relating to stowage, and so on'.[134] To facilitate the easy identification of Movements staff in the often busy and congested embarkation areas, distinguishing armbands in scarlet cloth were introduced for both officers and other ranks as early as 1940; officers had the letters MC with an eagle above a crown, while airmen had the letters MC alone on the armband.[135] Armbands continue to be used in the UK and overseas bases, but rarely in operational theatres.

The growth in air transport towards the end of the Second World War led to a rationalisation of the Movement's trades, with the Clerk (GD) (Movements Control) and embarkation assistant being replaced with the single trade of Clerk (Movements Control), still largely charged with the previous duties, but a further new trade was also created, air movement assistant, exclusively to handle the movement of personnel and freight by air. Both of these trades were part of Trade Group IV.[136]

In the RAF's 1951 Supply Trade Structure, Movements appeared only as an identified specialisation up to the rank of corporal but as Clerk (Surface Movements) and Clerk (Air Movements); the descriptor 'clerk' did not really do justice to the role as both were very much practical jobs, with the latter involved in actually loading aircraft.[137] The underlying philosophy to meeting the air movements requirement was for airmen to be drawn from the Supply Trade Group and to be qualified for employment on Movements duties by formal training at the Air Movements Training School, with a career pattern thereafter that would be balanced between Supply and Movements. While this worked for a number of years it was difficult for personnel to maintain currency on the numerous air transport aircraft types and to maintain up to date experience. Consequently, a separate Movements Trade sub-group was introduced in March 1972 to coincide with the move of the Air Movements Training School from RAF Abingdon to RAF Brize Norton; the main Supply Trade became Trade Group 18a, while Movements became 18b, although this later became Trade Group 18 (Supply) and 18 (Movements). The sub-trades of movements operator and movements controller were introduced at the same time although specialist training evolved over time to meet the needs of ever more complex aircraft such as the C-130 Hercules, TriStar, and C-17 Globemaster III with their more sophisticated loading systems. By the 1990s, the Movements Trades had also been opened up to females, although female officers had been employed on Movements duties for many years before this.

Between 2001 and 2003, a major review of the Movements trades took place stimulated by recognition that the divide between Movements operator and Movements controller was largely historical and had become out-dated. Consequently, just one Movements Trade was formed, replacing the separate Movements operator and Movements controller trades. This change brought with it a through-career training structure, which included new basic movements training and further movements training courses, new trade management training courses and, significantly, introduced an operational performance standard and formalised on-the job training linked to national vocational training accreditations. In 2012, fuelled by a requirement to improve the process for basic Movements training graduates to reach the required operational performance standard, a Movements Conversion Unit was created at RAF Brize Norton. The Logistics (Movements) Trade as it is now known has, since 2001, undergone significant change, coincident with the introduction of new, and increasingly advanced, air transport aircraft.

Tri-Service Movements Management

By the mid-1990s, the management of tri-service Movements had become complex. Responsibility for strategic tasking was split between the Assistant Chief of Defence Staff (Logistics) (ACDS (L)) organisation in MOD London and the Joint Transport and Movements Staff (JTMS) at PJHQ Northwood; between them, these two organisations were responsible for formulating the Strategic Estimate, a process which allowed ministers to make better-informed decisions. At the onset of an operation, the London end of the operation was the starting point, with ACDS (L) and a team from the Defence Movements staffs forming a Movements advisory cell within the Defence Crisis Management Centre. From there, the JTMS translated the Movements requirement into a Movements plan and strategic tasking; this process enabled the Movements organisations at an operational level be tasked, with the Defence Transport and Movements Executive (DTMX) taking care of the surface component and the Air Movements Executive (AME) the tasking of air assets.[138]

It soon became clear that this complex arrangement was far from ideal, a situation exacerbated by the fact that DTMX and the AME were in different chains of command and were within different budgetary structures. Moreover, perhaps the key difficulty was that PJHQ did not have a single point of contact with the operational Movements organisation. This position was formally recognised by SDR 98, which recommended the formation of a single organisation to provide a 'one stop shop' for a range of transport and Movements services for the MOD. Following an eight-month implementation programme, which required a modest two-storey new-build temporary structure on the Andover site and the installation of essential secure communications systems, the Defence Transport and Movements Agency (DTMA) was formed as a Defence agency on 1 April 1999. The agency merged personnel of the Joint Transport and Movements Staff from London and Northwood, and the staff of the Air Movements Executive based at High Wycombe, together with the Army's Defence Transport and Movements Executive already on site at Andover. Additionally, DTMA took on responsibility for the Defence Passenger Reservation Centre (DPRC) and, from 3 October 1999, the Defence Freight Distribution Group (DFDG).[139]

The creation of this single Movements organisation effectively brought together the three single services, one-star led organisations, plus much of the MOD Movements and HQ 38 Group (subsequently No. 2 Group) Air Movements tasking staffs under a single one-star officer; doing this in such a short space of time was remarkable and due entirely to the drive and determination of the implementation team leader, Air Commodore Tim Leaning (a Supply Branch officer). A simple structure of four directorates under the Chief Executive (Operations and Plans, Transport and Surface Movements, Business Support, and Finance) the agency employed 127 military and 310 civilian staff spread from the borders of Scotland to the South Coast of England with the majority employed at Andover. Its mission statement was 'To provide Defence and other authorized users with agreed transport and movements services to meet their world-wide requirements in peace, crisis and war'.

The DTMA was developed to be a key operational Agency within the newly created DLO and sat within the ORBAT of Director General Defence Logistics Support, a member of the DLO Management Board. Operationally focused, the

DTMA was a vital contributor to the deployment, sustainment and recovery of forces on operations and exercises. For support to operations, MOD provided the necessary policy and overall priority for Movements issues. MOD and the resultant PJHQ operational and exercise requirements were passed to DTMA as the single provider and tasking authority of air, sea and surface transport and movements services. However, the DTMA's influence in Defence Logistics was much wider, given its control of routine freight and unaccompanied baggage transportation, coupled with the business and administrative travel of MOD personnel. The grouping of these Movements activities within DTMA provided a multi-modal capability for all operational, exercise and routine transportation and movements business with a controlling influence over DTMA-managed contracts and numerous one-off charters with a value of over £350 million across the MOD and various Government Departments.

The first year following its creation proved to be a baptism of fire. From the word go the DTMA was supporting operations in Kosovo, Iraq, Bosnia, East Timor, and Mozambique while juggling resources in support of a major exercise in Egypt. The use of the newly installed secure video conferencing facility linking the Agency directly with the MOD crisis management cell and PJHQ proved critical and enabled the operations and plans division to be intimately involved in the planning of operations from the very outset.

At the end of the first year, in May 2000, Air Commodore Leaning handed over the reins of Chief Executive to Air Commodore Peter Whalley, who held that appointment for the next three years during which the Agency consolidated its position as the lead organisation for all Movements matters. Major development initiatives at that time included: the introduction of new IT systems for air freight, air passenger, and surface freight tasking; the successful introduction of tasking of C-17 Globemaster III aircraft; the replacement of the freight distribution service's ageing vehicle fleet with a new, fuel efficient lease-hire fleet; the tasking of the newly introduced modern fleet of six large, Joint Rapid Reaction Force chartered roll-on/roll-off ships and the introduction of a single prime contract for the movement and storage of all MOD unaccompanied baggage.

In 2002, in addition to the routine operational and exercise movement coordination, the major effort of the agency was directed towards the final planning and execution of Exercise Saif Sareea II in Oman. During the deployment, transport aircraft moved over 14,000 passengers, and fifteen voyages by sea were undertaken. In addition, 1,900 ISO shipping containers were moved. However, even this extraordinary effort was soon to be diverted by a number of operations, including Operation Bessemer in the Former Yugoslav Republic of Macedonia, and then by operations arising from the events of 11 September 2001. Even those achievements were dwarfed by the massive effort required by the planning, tasking, and co-ordination of air and surface movements associated with the second Gulf War (Operation Telic). The planned move of the agency from its temporary accommodation to the massive DLO new-build on the airfield side of the road at Andover had to be micro-managed to maintain operational and business continuity at such a critical time. So, the preparations for war continued unabated with the CE and his relatively small numbers of operations staff enduring greatly extended working days.

One particular event proved the effectiveness of operational thinking and sheer importance of DTMA and has become a classic subject for operational risk management training. UK troops were commonly expected to enter Iraq by way of the 'northern' route through Turkey. Air and sea-lift assets were being planned against this assumption, including DTMA tendering for a small number of ships for the movement of freight to the far end of the Mediterranean. Immediately prior to Christmas, however, and the opening of the contract bid tenders on Boxing Day, it became apparent that the southern entry route had suddenly become the preferred option necessitating a much longer sea passage through the Suez Canal. This longer sailing time and the ever-closing operational readiness date prevented the use of ships on a double or triple shuttle basis. On opening the tenders, the CE and director of operations and plans were faced with offers for ninety ships against an advertised requirement for only eight. Although no political statement had been made about the change of entry routing, and without any sort of military direction or financial authority, the unilateral (and brave) decision was taken to take all ninety ships on contract. They were engaged and tied up in readiness in ports along the south coast of England. In the event, Prime Minister Tony Blair saved two military careers by making the formal announcement in Parliament on 22 January and all ninety ships were indeed used to move British forces into theatre with our troops arriving on time. Had the contract decision not been taken on Boxing Day, not all the ships would have been available and the contract price would have increased by at least £42 million. To cap it all, because they had stripped the market of available shipping, DTMA was able to sub-lease some of the ships to the Americans.

The original SDR decision to form a unified service transport and movements organisation was proven correct from the outset. The DTMA emerged as a dynamic organisation geared to providing the best possible operational and administrative support to its customers. Further rationalisation took place in October 2005 when DTMA joined with the DLO Operations Centre (DLOC) to form the Defence Supply Chain Operations and Movements (DSCOM). It was at this time that the DFDG (then part of DTMA Freight Operations) was transferred to the Defence Storage and Distribution Agency (DSDA).[140]

Permanent Air Movements Detachments

While most of its overseas units after the Second World War, which were destinations for the RAF's air transport fleet, had an air movements squadron or flight to handle passengers and cargo, the RAF also used locations such as civilian airports and other national air force airfields staging points or temporary operating locations for exercises. For many years, a number of these locations had a Movements qualified RAF liaison officer (RAFLO) to liaise with national authorities and the various on-site service providers for aircraft turn around; much of their work involved arranging airfield support to the aircraft and crew, accommodation for passengers and customs clearance for freight, as well as coordinating host nation support for exercises in their geographical area of responsibility. Until the 1980s, these positions were manned by aircrew, but it was recognised that air movements officers had more appropriate skill sets.

For many years, RAFLO offices have been located in Africa (Nairobi), the USA (Dulles, Las Vegas, and Travis), Canada (Calgary, Gander, and St Johns), Sri Lanka (Colombo), the Middle East (Abu Dhabi, Bahrain, and Dubai), and Germany (Hanover). Originally under the control of No. 2 Group, the RAFLOs came under the command of No. 1 AMW (originally as part of No. 45 MAMS but now within the Operational Support Squadron) on 1 April 2006. Collectively, the six locations now in operation—Sub Saharan Africa: Nairobi; Canada: Calgary; USA (West) and Pacific: Las Vegas; USA (East): Dulles; Middle East: Abu Dhabi; and the RAF Airport Unit at Hanover—are known as Permanent Air Movements Detachments and provide essential support for RAF air transport work and essential support for operations and the UK Defence exercise programme overseas.

The Joint Air Delivery Test and Evaluation Unit

The development of airborne forces and the greater use of transport aircraft towards the end of the Second World War required a coordinated approach to the development of the technology involved in such areas as parachuting, cargo restraint and aerial delivery. Building on the experience of a number of Army specialist organisations in this area, a Joint Air Transport Establishment (JATE) was formed in January 1968 at Old Sarum, near Salisbury in Wiltshire. Following the Defence review of 1974, JATE was moved to RAF Brize Norton where it remains today although renamed the Joint Air Delivery Test and Evaluation Unit. Although a Defence organisation, its work provides an important service to RAF Logistics.

Its air portability section develops new techniques and procedures for the loading and restraint of vehicles and load in fixed and rotary winged aircraft, while an aerial delivery section carries out operational testing and evaluation of aerial delivery systems for a range of items such as vehicles, boats and stores dropped by parachute. Additionally, a helicopter section develops lifting schemes for helicopter underslung loads. RAF air movements personnel have been part of JADTEU's work for many years and their expertise has been instrumental in the work to restrain outsize loads into C-17 aircraft and are heavily involved in similar work for the A400Ms.

Joint Helicopter Support Unit

The introduction of new aircraft types has often had an indirect effect on wider organisation and has invariably led to the need to develop specialist techniques and procedures for their handling and use. This was very much the case with the introduction to RAF service of the Chinook HC1 in December 1980. The internal and underslung load capability of this aircraft, particularly when more than one aircraft was used, was such that the organic helicopter handling expertise within Army field units was insufficient to exploit the sheer magnitude of logistic capability now offered by this aircraft. Consequently, in the first months of 1982, this led to the formation of the two Joint Helicopter Support Units, one for each of the expected two Chinook squadrons being deployed. Both units were commanded by RCT captains with the unit's second-in-command being RAF Movements flying officers with the rest of the manpower being drawn from the Army's Royal Corps of Transport and RAF Movements Trade Group.

RAF Movements personnel had to pass a five-day selection course (run originally by UK MAMS) before they could be considered for a tour on JHSU. After bespoke specialist training was provided for the units' original officers and NCOs by JATE, Flying Officer (later Group Captain) Neil Cromarty and a small joint team designed and delivered a training course for the remainder of the joint service personnel. These soldiers and airmen then reported for duty at the combined units' base—two portacabins in the MT yard of No. 27 Logistic Support Group Regiment RCT at Aldershot. After a few months, a hangar at Farnborough was allocated to the unit, which was to remain their home until JHSU(G) deployed to RAF Gütersloh in early 1983 and JHSU(UK) to RAF Odiham shortly thereafter. The role of JHSU was to offer peacetime helicopter handling training to British Army and RAF field units and in war to select, manage and operate single and multiple-point landing sites, by day and night, for use by Support Helicopter assets, mainly the Chinook.

The JHSU was declared operational on 1 April 1982 and saw action almost immediately during the Falklands conflict of 1982. Flying Officer Neil Cromarty commanded the JHSU detachment on Ascension Island throughout the conflict, serving there from 5 May until July 1982. Having flown to Ascension Island from RAF Lyneham (via Dakar, Senegal), Neil recalled his first impression was 'one of amazement. In this lunar type landscape of volcanic rock and dust, helicopters were buzzing overhead as loads were taken out to various ships'. There were all sorts of cargo to be moved. Neil recounted how, on 6 May for example, they assisted with the lift of 'everything from twelve pallets of ammo (under a Chinook) to single pallets of cabbages and carrots (under a Wessex) or Sea King rotor blades to Pegasus (Harrier) engines'. Members of JHSU also sailed further south on the MV *Norland* and on the MV *Atlantic Conveyor*, which called in at the island on its way to the Falklands. These vessels had been requisitioned by the MOD under the ships taken up from trade (STUFT) arrangement.

Above left: MV *Atlantic Conveyor*, 1982. (*Crown Copyright—Air Historical Branch MoD*)

Above right: JATE underslung load trials with a Chinook and Tornado ground equipment, RAF Laarbruch, Germany, 1985. (*Crown Copyright—Air Historical Branch MoD*)

The ship was a roll-on/roll-off container ship that carried vital supplies and aircraft for the British Task Force, including RN Wessex, RAF Chinooks, and Harrier GR3s. Having left Ascension Island on 7 May, the *Atlantic Conveyor* was later hit by two air-launched Argentinian Exocet missiles and sank on 28 May 1982 with the loss of twelve men. The Harriers had been unloaded at Ascension Island and transferred to HMS *Hermes* and HMS *Invincible*, but the remaining helicopters on board (including three RAF Chinooks except aircraft *Bravo November,* which had flown off earlier) were all lost, along with its cargo. Fortunately, both the JHSU men (Sergeant Johnson and Lance Corporal Sheppard both of the RCT) survived the sinking. Chinook *Bravo November* is now famous for her role in the Falkland campaign but few know that each of her two crews included two JHSU load 'hookers'. For his work with JHSU on Ascension Island during this period, Neil Cromarty was awarded a Commander Task Force 317 Commendation. In acknowledgement of the team effort, Neil did point out that the commendation was for the 'work we did on Ascension'.

Now based at RAF Odiham and part of JHC, the JHSU deploys with helicopter squadrons when required and has been involved in most operations since their formation. While the unit is commanded by an Army (RLC) officer, the second in command is normally a Movements qualified RAF Logistics officer.

8

Post-war Management of POL and Compressed Gasses

As described in Part One, military aircraft required ever-increasing volumes of petroleum, oils, and lubricants, a range that had collectively become known as POL. With the progressive introduction of gas turbine engined aircraft in the mid to late 1940s, the supply of aviation fuel not only became more complex, with an increased number of grades, but the sheer quantity required increased exponentially. This was further complicated by the requirement to maintain fuel supplies for a wide range of piston-engined types already in service. While the gas turbine engine produced a far greater amount of thrust than the piston engine, it used considerably more fuel. The jet fighter of the early 1950s was using almost five times as much fuel as the later marks of the Supermarine Spitfire.[1] The RAF's first front-line jet aircraft, the Gloster Meteor, entered operational service in 1944, closely followed by the de Havilland Vampire in 1946. From then on, the arrival of further jet-engined aircraft was rapid. By 1957, ten more had entered service; by 1969, there were a further three.[2]

In addition to fuel, aircraft also required a range of oils and lubricants, not just for engines, but for other systems such as hydraulics and flying controls. Similarly, there was a requirement for compressed gasses for both air and ground use. MT vehicles also required POL and, of course, the RAF's buildings required heating during the winter months; the latter was still by solid fuel (predominantly coal) for many years after the Second World War until heating oil (furnace fuel oil or FFO) was introduced. The requirement for stringent standards of quality control and safety required additional training for Logistics personnel, many of whom specialised in this field for much of their service career. Often referred to as the lifeblood of air power, sufficient POL of acceptable quality was critical to air operations. This chapter examines the invariably challenging and complex task of managing POL and compressed gasses in the post-Second World War period.

Types and Grades of Aviation Fuel

The development of fuels and lubricants is a continuous and evolutionary process. During peacetime, this is generally related to technical advancements in the design of aero engines where the requirement is for increasing propulsive power to achieve greater aircraft speed and range. The thrust required to move an aircraft varies approximately as to the square of the speed; to double the speed will require four times as much power. Broadly speaking, aviation fuel falls into two types. Aviation gasoline is used in piston engined aircraft, where the fuel is required to enable a rich mixture (a high fuel to air ratio) for higher power during take-off and combat and also a weak mixture to permit economical cruising. The second type is jet fuel for turbine engines, various grades of Kerosene, or even low-grade ('wide cut') gasoline, all of which need to remain pumpable at the very low temperatures encountered at great heights, meet specific quality requirements, burn cleanly, and remain stable at high temperatures.[3]

Fuel for Piston Engines

The early 1950s saw a complex development in the use of aviation gasoline types. At this time, there were four grades in service; these, along with their usage, are shown in Table 6.

Grade	Use
73 AVGAS	A lead-free fuel used in various light aircraft such as the Gipsy Major Series 1 engine fitted to the de Havilland Tiger Moth aircraft. Leaded fuel was particularly unsuitable for piston engine aircraft as it led to fouled spark plugs and corroded exhaust valves.
NLAVGAS	A lead-free fuel used for test running stored engines prior to being put into storage.
91/98 AVGAS	Used for most non-operational aircraft at the time such as the Avro Anson
100/130 AVGAS	The main grade for operational RAF aircraft.

Table 6: Gasoline fuel types in use by the RAF in 1950.

A general shortage of commercial tankage in 1950 led to a reduction in the number of aviation gasolines in use and this was achieved by replacing 73 Grade AVGAS and NLAVGAS with a single lead-free fuel (80 octane), which was used for the Tiger Moth and stored engines. The closure of Abadan in the Persian Gulf, which was the UK's main supply point for all overseas areas, led to a critical shortage of aviation fuels. This resulted in a need for the RAF to review its range of fuels and to economise on the short-supply basic material for aviation gasolines—alkylate, which was a mixture of various iso-octanes, the main petroleum component used in blending the fuel.[4] This rationalisation was short-lived. As a measure to secure the most economical use of alkylate and produce the maximum amount of aviation gasoline to replace the lost Abadan production, the American Petroleum

Administration for Defence issued a directive in November 1951, which, *inter alia*, introduced a requirement that all 80 octane gasoline should be manufactured to include a specified amount of tetra-ethyl lead (TEL), an additive that enabled higher octane ratings to be achieved. This curtailed the use of lower grades of fuel by the RAF and led to the re-introduction of 73 AVGAS and NLAVGAS.

The arrival in RAF Coastal Command service of the American P-2 Neptune maritime patrol aircraft in 1952 required a much higher grade of fuel. Although the RAF did consider the possibility of operating the aircraft on one of its fuels to ease supply difficulties, this proved impracticable. Moreover, the Royal Navy was re-equipped with American carrier aircraft, such as the Skyraider, along with the need to operate with American fleets that, like the Canadians, were using AVGAS 115/145; this led to the RAF opting for that too. There were operational benefits as well. The use of high grade fuel enabled greater power for take-off and combat conditions, characteristics that were particularly important for carrier-borne aircraft. This was not without its problems, however, as the production of the higher-grade fuel meant a production loss of about 30 per cent of aviation spirit due to the greater requirement for alkylate and other high octane blending components. Thus, by the end of 1952, RAF Logistics was provisioning and managing six grades of aviation gasoline (see Table 7)

Grade	Use
73 AVGAS	Retained for use by the de Havilland Tiger Moth aircraft.
NLAVGAS	Retained for test running stored engines prior to being put into storage.
82 AVGAS	For stored engines (TEL added)
91/96 AVGAS	Used for most non-operational aircraft at the time such as the Avro Anson
100/130 AVGAS	The main grade for operational RAF aircraft.
115/145 AVGAS	Introduced for the Neptune aircraft

Table 7: Gasoline fuel types in use by the RAF in late 1952.[5]

Fuel for Jet Engines

While jet engines are more tolerant of different fuel types than piston engines, their fuel systems are more sensitive to the chemical and physical properties of the fuel, especially when exposed to the greater heights and lower temperatures associated with modern high-performance aircraft.[6] The standard aviation jet fuel in the RAF at the end of 1950 was AVTUR (NATO Grade F-34), although by the end of 1952, this was used principally by the Canberra and in overseas theatres. By December 1952, the Royal Navy introduced an aviation kerosene called AVCAT, designed specifically to reduce fire risk in aircraft carriers. At the same time, the oil companies had a glut of low-grade gasoline as a by-product of setting up their refineries to match the huge

American demand for automobile fuel. There was widespread pressure from the oil industry for the aviation world to adopt wide-cut gasoline as a cheap and readily available alternative to kerosene, and the RAF and other air forces thus began to use AVTAG (F-40) quite widely despite its flammability. However, there is a probably apocryphal story of a very senior airline executive offering to stand in the middle of a pool of AVTUR and drop a lighted match in it if his equally senior friend in the oil industry would do the same in a puddle of AVTAG. Whatever the truth of that, AVTUR won the day, for safety reasons and, in 1954 the RAF switched its main grade of aviation turbine fuel to the safer AVTUR. This fuel was initially received at petroleum supply depots (PSDs) as F-35 but was then converted to the F-34 specification by the addition of fuel system icing inhibitor (FSII), which effectively lowers the freezing point of any minute water droplets in the fuel and prevents ice crystals from forming in the fuel at very high level, which could block aircraft fuel filters.[7] The switch from F-40 to F-35 in the UK was done in two phases. Firstly, those RAF stations that were supplied by pipeline from the PSDs reduced their stocks of F-40 and replaced them with F-35. Secondly, the remaining PSDs bridged F-40 to stations by road tanker and then restocked with F-35. The switchover took about seven months to complete.

Road tanker receipt of AVTUR, 1965. (*Crown Copyright—Air Historical Branch MoD*)

The NATO Single Fuel Concept

The move towards using F35 represented a major move within NATO towards the standardisation of military fuels Alliance-wide and an extension of that aim was the NATO Single Fuel Concept whereby all military aircraft and vehicles would use F-34; diesel and MT gasoline would be eliminated. Trials were carried out and proved very successful. In wartime, the concept would greatly simplify resupply. However, the properties of F-34, while similar to diesel, have a detrimental effect on the performance of tactical and non-tactical vehicles without suitably-modified engines; typically, power output is reduced by about 20 per cent. Moreover, diesel contains properties to lubricate vehicle fuel pumps, engines, and seals. US military vehicle engines are required to operate on NATO aviation fuel and are procured on that basis. Vehicles procured by MOD do not have these standards and the British Army has always resisted the adoption of the Single Fuel Concept, although on some operations they have had to accept it.

Fuel Additives

There was a later requirement for AVTUR to contain three additives before it was issued to aircraft: anti-static additive (ASA3) added at the refinery to reduce the risk of a build-up of static electricity when the fuel moves through pipelines, so causing a fire risk; fuel system icing inhibitor (FSII); and Hitec 515 (or Santolene C). The latter two were combined into a single fluid known as AL38 and this effectively converted the pipeline supplied AVTUR F-35 grade to AVTUR F-34. This strict requirement was a particular challenge for UK aircraft on overseas deployments as a number of overseas countries did not use Hitec 515 with their FSII so this required any RAF detachment locally to blend additional AL38 with supplied AVTUR to rectify the deficiency'.[8]

A big problem with the RAF's C-130 Hercules aircraft in the early 1970s was the growth of *Cladosporium resinae*, a fungal growth that develops on any water content in the aircraft's fuel tanks. The problem did not occur in USAF aircraft as they were still using AVTAG. The solution was to inject FSII into bulk fuel stocks. That was fine for refuelling in the UK, but RAF C-130s and Andovers were obtaining fuel overseas, where FSII was not available. The RAF solution was the issue of packed stocks of FSII for overseas flights, usually one jerrycan for a C-130 and five half-gallon sample cans for an Andover.

Shell UK, however, was dubious that pouring FSII into an aircraft tank, rather than injecting it directly to the fuel, would work. On one unfortunate occasion, the air loadmaster for an Andover flight picked up the required jerrycan from the squadron oil store. When refuelling in Oporto, the contents were poured into the wing tanks and, on the flight to Gibraltar, the aircraft fuel gauges malfunctioned. It was later found that the additive was not FSII but a cleaning fluid. The fuel system had to be flushed out before the aircraft could return to base.

POL Management on RAF Units

The sheer size and complexity of the POL management task, along with quality control and health and safety requirements, has invariably required a team of personnel at unit level to take care of receipt, storage, quality, and issue; this has ranged from a dedicated section within the Equipment Section/Supply Squadron's Technical Supply Flight (managed by a SNCO) on smaller units to a flight managed by a junior Equipment/Supply officer on larger units, such as RAF Brize Norton. Their task was diverse, ranging from controlling large volumes of aviation fuel in BFIs dispersed around the unit to a range of liquid ground fuels, such as MT and furnace fuel oil, along with an extensive range of oils, lubricants, and other flammable products, such as paint and solvents, which required segregated storage.

Fuels duties on RAF units in the Far East provided a wide range of challenges as Flight Lieutenant (later Group Captain) Ron Robertson experienced when he served at RAF Tengah in Singapore during the early 1960s as the unit's OC Technical Supply Flight. He was also the fuels officer for No. 20 Squadron (then flying the Hawker Hunter), and also the Far East Air Force mobile fuels officer. In the three years he spent at Tengah, Ron spent about eight months each year deployed to Chaing Mai in Thailand, Brunei, Borneo, and Kuching, mainly with No. 20 Squadron.

During 1960–1963, the Indonesian Communist terrorist campaign took place; in addition, Operation Bibber was mounted to deal with the Communist invasion of Laos. Accordingly, No. 20 Squadron was deployed to Chaing Mai. Although the airfield had been built by the South-East Asia Treaty Organisation, the fuel installation was totally unserviceable. Consequently, five 10,000-gallon pillow tanks were sent to Chaing Mai, reputedly the first such operational use by the RAF. Ron recalled how, during installation of the tanks, he noticed that the attached label read 'for temperate climate use only', but was acutely aware that the temperature at the airfield was 34 degrees centigrade. Resupply of AVTUR was a complex affair involving transport by rail from Bangkok (900 miles), bridged from the railway station by Shell road tanker, transferred to an RAF bowser at the airfield, and then pumped into the pillow tanks. The Shell tanker was not able to connect directly to the pillow tank as its couplings did not match. Moreover, even if they had fitted, there was a two-hour turnaround for the Shell tanker to fill up at Chaing Mai railway station and their base. The tankers would then have to 'settle' the fuel for one hour (to allow any foreign particles to sink to the bottom). Ron was anxious to get the pillow tanks filled so the bowser was used; the settling time for the bowser was ignored. For ten months of the year, it was very hot in Chaing Mai, but in January and February, the nights were fairly cool, often requiring a blanket when sleeping. Following the first cool night, Ron recalled how he went to the pillow tank installation to carry out his usual daily checks and, to his horror, saw a dozen or so King Cobra snakes sleeping on each tank. During the cool nights, the snakes enjoyed the warmth of the tanks as they had been exposed to and retained much of

Fuel farm at RAF Gan. (*Crown Copyright—Air Historical Branch MoD*)

the sunny daytime temperatures. He called out the fire tender crew who managed to get rid of the snakes by hosing them down with water. This became standard practice every morning.[9]

Flight Lieutenant (later Group Captain) David Packman served at RAF Tengah in 1968 prior to being posted to the HQ Far East Air Force, Joint Warfare Branch as the Supply and Movements specialist. His role here was to plan the administrative and logistics aspects of joint Army and RAF exercises in the jungles of Malaysia, including the supply of AVTUR to the local support helicopter squadrons deployed into the field. At this time, the helicopters were refuelled from 45-gallon drums (which were sometimes airdropped into a vaguely-convenient drop zone) using semi-rotary hand-pumps and chamois leather filters. The squadron engineers and aircrew were, rightly, concerned that there should be no particulate contamination of the fuel and, in an attempt to minimise the risk, would not draw off the last five gallons or so from each drum. This meant that considerably more fuel had to be delivered than would otherwise have been the case. It was only after David was able to persuade the squadron commanders to agree to consolidate the dregs and then to have them tested for contaminants in a fuel laboratory that it was accepted that the risk of problems occurring was more in their minds than in reality.[10]

On the whole, operation of fuel tankers or bowsers and the actual refuelling of aircraft (with the exception of situations such as the RAF Germany Harrier Force in the field and helicopter refuelling by TSW) had been carried out by engineering tradesmen. Stock control of the fuel was the responsibility of the POL-qualified Supply tradesman. Apart from the obvious safety requirements and maintaining sufficient stock, the most critical responsibility of RAF Logistics was ensuring quality. Protection from contaminants, especially water, remained a key concern, with various technical aids available to check for this. During fuel receipt and as part of the regular stock check of fuel installations, large dip-sticks or flexible dipping tapes were used with water-detecting paste smeared on the ends. Routine samples of bulk fuel were taken using various sampling devices, which could take small quantities of fuel from the top, middle, or bottom of BFIs. Where fuel was held in metal drums, a simple brass tube known as a 'thief' was used. The drum had a narrow hole at each end. The device was inserted into the drum with the holder's thumb over the other end, which was then removed to allow fuel to flow into the device. Fuel samples were decanted into clean glass sample jars and sent to fuel laboratories for specialist testing. For many years, this facility was maintained at No. 11 MU RAF Chilmark in Wiltshire for units in the UK and overseas, although RAF Germany units were covered by the RAOC Petroleum Laboratory at Munster.[11]

Quality control of packed products such as oils, paints, and adhesives was more straightforward although it required meticulous batch control in storage areas. This was reliant on package labeling showing batch details and shelf-life; in many cases, these items had a finite life and unless a life extension was granted, they could not be used beyond a specified date. The basic principle was that the oldest stock was to be used first to ensure, as far as possible, that products were consumed before their life expiry. Packed stocks were also subject to periodic testing and, along with bulk fuel monitoring, defective stock was subject to recall or quarantining if required.

Clearly, and especially in the case of aviation fuel, the loss of stock could prove to be serious in terms of flying, but it could have its lighter moments. An ex-Supply SNCO based at RAF Tangmere during the 1950s recalled being called out one wet evening by the duty POL crew due to the apparent breakdown of the unit's main fuel installation, which was causing a major hold-up in the night flying programme. The SEO was duly called out and the entire party proceeded to the BFI in question. This was known to be empty, due to cleaning, but the SEO was not prepared to accept this and went over to dip the tanks. By this time, the station commander had joined the gathering. To the amazement of all, the SEO used his cigarette lighter to read the dipstick. Needless to say, everyone dived for cover on the wet ground. The station commander, far from amused, cancelled night flying and in the months to come, never let his SEO forget that night.[12]

Of all the POL range, aviation fuel was perhaps the trickiest when it came to measuring stock in BFIs because, like all fluids, its volume expands and contracts as its temperature changes. The volume of gasoline changes at about four and a half times the rate of water. To compensate for this, the temperature of the fuel is always taken at the time that tanks are dipped and a correction formula applied to the measured quantity to show the volume at a standard temperature. Accounting regulations required BFIs to be dipped daily (usually first thing each morning), not just to ensure that sufficient stock was held, but also to ensure that there was not a leak from the tank itself. Many of the older BFIs, especially those of wartime origin, were buried or semi-buried and, with age, had become subject to corrosion that either allowed fuel to leak out or water or other contaminants to enter. These problems were not uncommon and BFI infrastructure was often the subject of ongoing maintenance work and rebuild programmes. Such losses were not just a quality control or accounting concern; fuel spillage was always taken seriously with particular concern being the risk of fire or environmental damage. Where the possibility of large scale leakage was a risk, especially on BFIs, special 'interceptor' pits were built into the site drainage structure to prevent spilt fuel entering this or soaking into surrounding ground. Units were required to maintain and exercise what was known as a spill plan; this covered a wide range of scenarios from a large-scale spillage on a BFI to smaller scale spills, such as in the vicinity of an MT fuel pump. A key component of this plan was the requirement to maintain a wide range of equipment to help contain spillages, such as sandbags or absorbent granules.

Of the many issues that might just keep an OC Supply Squadron awake at night, a fuel spill was perhaps close to top of the list. Squadron Leader David Sefton (then a young pilot officer) recalled how one Sunday morning he was sitting in the

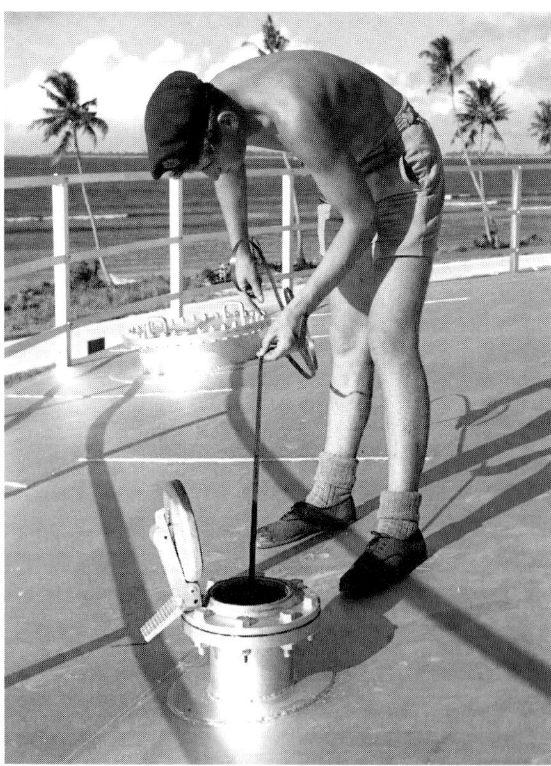

Tank dipping at RAF Gan. (*Crown Copyright—Air Historical Branch MoD*)

Officers' Mess at RAF Thorney Island in the very early 1970s, drinking coffee and reading the newspapers, when a very agitated SAC burst in. He had been accepting a delivery of AVTUR but had miscalculated the free tank space (known as ullage). When David and the SAC reached the tank 'farm', fuel was literally spurting out and, unbelievably, a contractor was still cutting the grass with a petrol mower. Most of the fuel at Thorney Island at that time was stored in pre-war semi-underground tanks. The problem on the island was that the station was barely above sea level and the tanks had an automatic pump to remove water from the tank farm. At this stage, OC Supply Squadron arrived and the growing ensemble set off to 'The Deeps' drainage channel at the top of the island to see what was happening. As it was low tide, the sluices were open and the growing fuel 'slick' was able to pass out to sea. With the Torrey Canyon disaster still fresh in people's minds, the impending crisis, albeit on a much smaller scale, was leading the assembled company to reflect on the longevity of their careers. With the help of the resident Search and Rescue Squadron, a Whirlwind helicopter was launched and it monitored the fuel slick as it meandered down the Thorney Channel and out to sea where it dispersed.[13]

Squadron Leader Bob Little recalled his first posting after training as a boy entrant (aged just seventeen) in 1965 to RAF Syerston in Nottinghamshire, then home to No. 2 Flying Training School, which was equipped with the Jet Provost. His first job was in the POL section and like any new job, there was a lot of on-the-job training. An important part of this was obtaining a certificate of competency, which was a mandatory requirement to operate the unit's BFIs. This certificate was issued by the depot superintendent of the Ministry of Public Building and Works after you had satisfied him that you were sufficiently confident in the operating of the BFI's and had a thorough knowledge of the various valves that required opening and closing during aviation fuel receipts and issues. After just three weeks in post, Bob was directed by his sergeant to undertake a road tanker receipt of furnace fuel oil; this is thick, black oil used to fuel boilers prior to the development of the modern diesel boiler and was usually transported warm to help in its handling. Although excited by the thought of doing a receipt on his own and unsupervised, he did point out that he did not yet have his certificate of competency. His sergeant's response was somewhat dismissive: 'It's black oil, you fool, you don't need a certificate of competency for oil deliveries, only for operation of the more complex aviation fuel BFIs. Just see the boiler man and he will tell you which tank to put it in and the driver will do the rest'. Bob related the situation at the boiler house:

> He found the boiler attendant drinking a large cup of strong tea from a well stained mug and sitting in an old arm chair reading a girlie magazine and really uninterested in anything else, but in answer to my question he told me to put the 3,616 gallons of oil into tank No. 3. On entering the compound I discovered it contained three tanks but they did not appear to be physically numbered. Not wishing to disturb the boiler attendant again, I assumed that the first tank on entering the compound was No. 1 and went on to offload the delivery accordingly.

> All went well and I was back in the office in forty minutes completing the paperwork for the receipt. Job done—I was feeling rather proud of myself.[14]

Three days later, Bob was soon brought down to earth when his warrant officer took him to task, asking which tank he thought he put the fuel delivery in. After a very one-sided conversation, Bob was advised that he had put the fuel into tank No. 1 (not No. 3), which contained 1,000 gallons of tank cleaning detergent. Fortunately for Bob, no disciplinary action was taken against him as the tanks were not clearly labelled. The detergent and water were subsequently drained from the tank, leaving the black oil to be used as normal. Bob's footnote to the experience was that it taught him never to assume and always check.

The Government Pipeline and Storage System

In the post-war years, the UK oil pipeline system, with further additions, became known as the Government Pipeline and Storage System (GPSS). The system was built to provide the country with a secure means of storing and distributing reserve and operational stocks of aviation fuel, mainly for the MOD and USAF, but it did include some pipelines that were connected directly to airfields, which were, or became, commercial airports (including Heathrow, Stansted, and Manchester). The system is essentially an enormous 'ring main', comprising some 1,300 miles of underground pipeline running from Humberside to Merseyside, south to Avonmouth, across to West London, then north through East Anglia back to Humberside. The main pipes are 6 or 10 inches in diameter, while the pipes connecting RAF stations to the main network were usually of 6 or 8 inches in diameter. The MOD (Air) owned PSDs, of which there were forty-four by the early 1990s, remained a key component of the fuel distribution system. By the early 1980s, the day-to-day running of these had been contracted out to the British Pipeline Agency (BPA), later the Oil and Pipelines Agency (OPA). The storage capacity at each of the depots varied from 3,000 cubic-metres to 120,000 cubic-metres with a total storage capacity for both the RAF and USAF exceeding 1 million cubic-metres. Facilities at eight of the PSDs were NATO-funded as were some 100 miles of pipeline. They were administered by HQ RAFSC, a task that included accounting for RAF stocks, approving maintenance work, and carrying out regular inspections. The pipeline between the PSDs was owned by the UK's Department of Energy. By this time, the GPSS had evolved into a sophisticated network, carrying different grades of product from gas oil to motor gasoline (MOGAS) and aviation fuel for both commercial and military use. As far as the RAF was concerned, there were two systems for the supply of bulk fuel to its units: the first method was where an RAF flying unit was connected directly to a PSD, which was dedicated to the supply of AVTUR; the second was where a spur-line was taken from the main multi-product, cross-country Department of Energy lines to a RAF station.

The pipeline was in continuous operation with fuel moved in discrete quantities known as 'parcels' separated by 'plugs' of water; parcels were usually around 2,000 cubic-metres in size and went to various locations throughout the country. The scheduling of these 'parcels' was worked out many weeks in advance in conjunction with three pipeline control centres that looked after RAF requirements, located at Rawcliffe (Humberside), Aldermaston (Reading), and Saffron Walden (Suffolk). The PSDs were considered vulnerable points for home defence and a number of officers had a war role (rarely exercised) as PSD military liaison officer. By the early 1990s, fifteen RAF and nine USAF bases were supplied by the GPSS. Although the movement of fuel 'parcels' along the pipeline appeared to be quite slow (averaging about 1.6 miles per hour), a 2,000 cubic-metres 'parcel' would take in the region of sixteen hours to receive—the equivalent volume by road tanker would take roughly forty hours.[15] The benefit of pipeline movement was not just speed; it remained the most cost effective and secure method when compared to movement by road, rail, or water with the lowest accident rate of all methods of transportation. Of particular significance was that fuel could still be moved irrespective of weather conditions. Pipeline operation was also the most economical in terms of energy consumption.[16] In 1989, the Department of Energy transferred all pipelines and essential infrastructure to the MOD. They had wanted to do this for a number of years but the MOD had stipulated that the DofE first surveyed all the pipelines and paid for any repair work. They initially refused but, with the matter eventually at prime ministerial level, they had to concede.

Squadron Leader (later Group Captain) David Packman served in Depot Supply 3 at HQ RAFSC in the late 1970s where much of his time was spent in planning to the preparedness of ESDs and other logistic support units for war. He also had a responsibility for the RAF's interest in the national fuel pipeline system and the oversight of no fewer than nineteen PSDs throughout England and Scotland. All this was at a time when pipeline supply direct to an increasing number of major airfields was being set up. Farmers and others were relatively tolerant about tracts of countryside being temporarily dug-up to allow pipes to be laid. In particular, there was great relief in northern Scotland when the pipeline from the PSD at Inverness to RAF Lossiemouth; RAF Kinloss was commissioned as the need for daily runs by a large number of road tankers was eliminated. Part of David's planning role required him to devise incidents for inclusion in the biennial WINTEX exercises, NATO exercises held to test the preparedness of staff. Inevitably, PSDs and pipelines figured largely and he recalled often considering if the 'opposition' realised just how dependant the RAF was on these facilities. The PSD at Sawtry was a case in point, being sited alongside the A1 road with a pipeline junction above ground and only a few yards from the carriageway.[17] The manning of the PSDs in times of crisis and war was also of concern and the need for a joint HQ STC/HQ RAFSC Operation Order was seen as a key requirement for the reinforcement of the UK Pipeline and the PSDs. The document was many years in draft and was finally signed off just as the Berlin Wall came down.

For many years after the Second World War, and throughout many of the Cold War years, the RAF maintained a number of regional fuels officers (RFO), usually junior Equipment/Supply officers who provided a much-needed liaison between the Air Ministry/MOD, BPA/OPA, and RAF units. Initially, this function was controlled by HQ No. 42 Group; it was passed to HQ RAFSC, then later to HQ RAF Logistics Command at RAF Brampton. By the 1980s, the organisation was divided into two parts: the northern element with its RFO based at No. 14MU Carlisle and the southern region with its RFO based at Brampton (although its incumbent here also had a wider staff officer role within the command HQ). Each of the RFOs had an assurance and monitoring role for the GPSS in their geographical area. Essentially, they contract monitored and inspected the depot's readiness and compliance with war plans and the arrangements in place to receive reinforcement military manpower in the event of a crisis and transition to war.

The NATO Pipeline System

The growth of NATO in the post-war years brought with it a pressing need to coordinate fuel supply across the alliance, especially via the much-extended national pipelines that had developed. These formed what was known as the NATO Pipeline System (NPS). Begun in the 1950s, this gradually expanded to include nine separate systems of which the UK's GPSS was one.[18] The NPS ran through eleven different host countries and consisted of some 12,000 km of pipeline.[19] Coordination of the NPS was vested in the NATO Pipeline Committee, a body established in 1956. Although a large part of the committee's work was related to the NPS in support of Allied Command Europe and Allied Command Atlantic, it had a wider remit as the senior advisory body in NATO on military petroleum in a wider sense, including fuels, lubricants, associated products, and equipment. One of the key strands of work for this committee was to try and standardise not just POL products, but also the facilities, equipment and procedures for handling POL products right across NATO. This was particularly significant in terms of enabling aircraft from the many NATO air forces to operate with resources from, and using the facilities at, other members' airfields.[20]

Of particular importance to RAF Logistics for its operations in RAF Germany was the Central Europe Pipeline System (CEPS), which served all the RAF's flying units in that country with the exception of RAF Gatow in Berlin. Similar to the GPSS, it was built to provide a secure means of storing and distributing aviation and ground fuels, but specifically for NATO air and land forces operating in the central region. The system was vast with storage depots and pipelines extending across eastern France, the Netherlands, Belgium, Luxembourg, and Germany.[21] In addition to representatives from these national 'hosts', CEPS was managed by the Central Europe Pipeline Operating Agency located at Versailles in France and also included representatives from Canada, the USA, and the Supply Branch in the UK.[22] Commercial fuels were also moved by CEPS to help offset its operating costs, although it was intended for sole military use during the lead up to, and in the event of, war. The network consisted of entry points, off-take facilities and storage capacity connected by pipelines. By 1996, CEPS consisted of some 6,000 km of pipelines (with 200 km of spur lines), sixty-four depots, 116 pump stations, together with twenty-eight refineries and twenty-one national depots connected to the system. The storage capacity of CEPS by this time was substantial, amounting to some 1.3 million cubic-metres of fuel.[23]

Fuel by Sea

The location of a number of RAF units, especially in the days of the Near and Far East Air Force, required fuel to be delivered by sea. This resulted in the need for specialist training for Equipment/Supply personnel in the form of ocean tanker operations. Fuels duties were often a popular choice for junior Equipment/Supply officers and many qualified on what was known as the long fuels course that, for many years, was run at RAF Calshot. One such officer was Flying Officer (later Group Captain) Ron Robertson, who in 1959, following his long fuels course and a two-week ocean tanker operations course at Falmouth, was posted to RAF Gan, an RAF staging post in the Indian Ocean. The fuel depot at Gan was the largest on-base depot in the RAF at the time and his posting was coincident with an MOD decision to increase the war reserves at the location. As they were short of land, the MOD positioned an ocean tanker, the Wave Victor, in the Maldives at the Addu Atoll lagoon. The tanker held some 8,000 tons of AVTUR. The fuel was transferred from the tanker to Gan's fuel jetty by dracone, a sausage-shaped rubber tank with a capacity of 10,000 gallons and towed by a marine craft. Ron recalled how on the first tow from the tanker, a couple of his airmen walked along the dracone on its journey to the jetty. When he observed that its sausage shape attracted a lot of sharks, he soon put an end to the pedestrian activities.

It was not just aviation fuel that was delivered by sea and there was of course a requirement for ground fuels. The remote base of RAF Saxa Vord on the island of Unst in the Shetland Islands in the north of Scotland and home to a radar station was one such location. The station's energy needs, both electricity and heating, were provided from an on-site power house, with the fuel for this being provided by the station's POL section who were responsible for pumping furnace fuel oil from the unit's main BFI on a twice-weekly basis. Fuel replenishment was from the MOD's supply contractor at Grangemouth and delivered to Saxa Vord by BP coastal tanker. The receipt of a fuel consignment, enough for three month's operations, required much preparation, not just administratively, but also ensuring that fuel was cross-pumped between the tanks in the BFI to equalise fuel levels to ensure that the fuel flowed equally into each tank. There was also a requirement for flexible pipelines and couplings to be connected to the permanent valves on the waterside jetty. Once the tanker berthed at the jetty, samples of fuel were taken and the amount of fuel to be transferred agreed. An earthing strip was connected to the ship and the flexible pipeline to minimise the risk from static electricity and then pumping could begin; an RAF fire tender was always in attendance. The whole process was carried out by POL tradesmen who maintained radio communication with the BFI to ensure that the correct valves were open for the receipt. The whole process was usually completed within three hours of the tanker berthing.[24]

The RAF station at Akrotiri in Cyprus had a PSD that was supplied by sea tanker via two hoses in discharges that could last up to fourteen hours. The fuel was then pumped to the airfield by a two-mile long pipeline. Group Captain Andrew Humphries, who was OC Technical Supply Group (which included responsibility for POL, Tech, and DSF) during 1976–1979, recalled how the captains of the BP tankers were always very hospitable; on one occasion, his boss, Squadron Leader Roger Wood, nearly fell out of the boat on the way back to Limassol. Andrew's team also handled the high altitude AVTUR for the American *Olive Harvest* U2 reconnaissance aircraft, which were also based at Akrotiri. This arrived by C-130 Hercules twice per month in 45-gallon drums. The empties were disposed of locally and were much in demand by Cypriot businesses.

Compressed Gasses

Although gaseous oxygen had been carried on some RAF aircraft prior to the Second World War, by 1939, the RAF was beginning to use an increasing range of substances that were technically classed as vapours or gases. Some of these were reduced to the minimum for storage and transportation by compression, liquefaction or solution, usually inside a metal cylinder. In the early post-war period, the RAF was using some eleven types of gases (see Table 8).

Gas	Use
Hydrogen	This had been used for the inflation of barrage balloons during the war, but subsequently for balloons used in the training of airborne forces and those used for meteorological purposes
Liquid Oxygen	Used to produce gaseous oxygen, in aircraft for crews at high altitudes and passenger emergency supplies, and as an oxidiser in rocket motors
Gaseous Oxygen	For breathing in aircraft flying at altitude and for medical purposes;
Compressed Air	For a multitude of engineering maintenance uses and ground testing gun turrets that were still in use in a number of aircraft types
Nitrogen	Used in the latter part of the War for aircraft fuel tank purging
Methyl Chloride and Gas Refrigerant	Used in photographic and radar specialist vehicles;
Propane, Argon and Acetylene	For welding and metal cutting uses;
Butane	For use by Bunsen Burners in medical and dental laboratories

Table 8: Compressed gases in use by the RAF in the early post-war period.

Oxygen cylinders being loaded to a railway wagon, 217 MU Cardington.
(*Crown Copyright—Air Historical Branch MoD*)

These gases presented their own particular challenges, primarily as a result of their nature and the fact that they were stored and transported in pressurised cylinders. Additionally, many were highly flammable or would vigorously support the combustion of other materials; some were inherently unstable under certain conditions, in storage or movement. As such, compressed gas cylinders in any quantity were subject to similar storage conditions as for explosives.[25] The production of most gases for the RAF was carried out at No. 217 MU, RAF Cardington, in Bedfordshire until April 2000 when the unit closed and gases were then directly sourced from commercial companies.[26]

Organisational Responsibility for POL Management

The planning and procurement of POL requirements from the 1920s through to the early 1960s rested largely with one of the Directorates of Equipment in the Air Ministry, and this continued despite the formation of the MOD in 1964, albeit the Directorates of Equipment had become the Directorates of Supply Policy, Supply Systems, and Supply Management (1 and 2) in the early 1970s.

Pre-1939 and throughout the Second World War, responsibility for POL rested with a single branch within the DGE. By the turn of the 1950s, the organisational structure had become more complex. Essentially, the POL management task was divided between two directorates within DGE. The POL forward planning responsibility sat within DofE (D) as part of the DDE Plans office ('E' Plans 4), while the actual provisioning and day-to-day management rested with DofE(C), with offices looking after three key components: the supply of aviation fuels, along with storage and distribution (E19 Branch); standardisation and regulations (E28); and the supply of aviation oils and other POL products (E49). These, in turn, were supported by the finance and contracts staff within the area of the Assistant Under Secretary of State (Supply and Organisation), who was responsible to the Second Permanent Under Secretary for monitoring financial expenditure. The wider links to the planning operation included staff within the Director General of Organisation's staff, who handled an extensive range of inputs from studies and reports, to the specific activities of forecasts and estimates. Not only did this work require close links with the RAF's operational staffs, it also needed particularly good collaboration with the oil industry. This was achieved through the Petroleum Division of the Ministry of Fuel and Power. The oil industry at this time was particularly proactive in the field of planning, a strength on which the Air Ministry's planning and POL provisioning staffs were able to capitalise. Committees that were particularly relevant included: the Overseas Supply AVGAS Committee (set up to deal with supply problems following the Abadan crisis); the Petroleum Industry Advisory Committee; the Petroleum Industry *Ad Hoc* Committee; the Oil Emergency Planning Committee; and the Port Emergency Planning Committee.[27]

With the formation of the Director General of Supply (RAF) in the 1970s, the management of POL became part of the responsibility of the Directorate of Supply Policy (RAF) (later Directorate of Supply Policy and Logistics Plans (RAF)) through its deputy directorate 10(RAF). This remained the arrangement until the reorganisation of AMSO's department in 1989 (following the Government's New Management Strategy) when the responsibility became part of DGSM's organisation and looked after by the Director of Logistics Operations (RAF) through its DD Pet CG (RAF) branch. Throughout this time, the RAF's POL managers remained mostly in London due to the vital importance of having close links with the London-based petroleum industry. It was also important for rapid reaction to contingency planning by the Air Staff in Whitehall.

Provisioning and Supply

Contracts for the supply of aviation POL products were placed on behalf of DGE by the Air Ministry Contracts Branch with various oil companies. Requirements for ground POL were placed through the Army. The five main oil companies who were handling the majority of the RAF's requirements at this time were: Shell Mex and BP, Shell Petroleum, Anglo Iranian Oil Co, Esso Petroleum, and the Regent Oil Co. Ltd. A number of other companies provided speciality products, such as the Ethyl Corporation, which supplied tetra-ethyl-lead (TEL). In order to provide the oil industry with details of the RAF's likely requirements for the various grades of aviation fuel, the Air Ministry produced annual estimates of future consumption, taking into account the existing strength of the force, any planned expansion and the existing (planned) rates of activity. When finalised, the estimates were passed to the finance staffs who checked the cost against the budget allocation and then to the contracts staff for information. These annual estimates were revised at six monthly intervals so that consumption trends could be kept under close observation. At this time, there were no computers to assist in calculating future requirements so the six-monthly review required planning officers to use a planning document known as 'Secret Document 98', which contained predicted rates of effort and a hand-cranked rotary calculator to work out the amounts of fuel required by each type and mark of aircraft at every airfield in the RAF.[28] In addition to annual forecasting, longer term estimates were provided by the Air Ministry to facilitate industry in planning capacity and the use of plant and distribution facilities. These estimates looked ahead for five years and were passed to the Petroleum Division of the Ministry of Fuel and Power, which coordinated requirements for the Royal Navy, Army, and Royal Air Force, and then passed on to the Petroleum Industry Advisory Committee. This link with industry was particularly important from the point of view of planning future refinery output with economic amortization of capital equipment and arranging importation programmes and shipping schedules.

There were of course many more companies involved in the supply of POL so deliveries in this respect were co-ordinated by the master provisioning office (MPO) at No. 21 MU Fauld in Staffordshire. All such demands were made on the regional office of the petroleum company in the area concerned and the company then arranged distribution from the depot under its control. Overseas commands also placed demands through MPO Fauld, who arranged for the barrelling of oils and lubricants at one of the five barrelling depots in the UK and ships for despatch to the main depots overseas.[29] All supplies of oils and lubricants for overseas were packed in 45-gallon drums for piston engine products and jerrycans for turbine related products. These demands were placed to bring stocks up to maximum stock establishments, which varied between fifteen and eighteen months depending on the length of the supply line and the time taken to effect replenishment.[30]

Input to major operations and exercises was a day-to-day fact of life for the MOD's POL staff; such requirements would often tax the most experienced of staff officers. One such occasion, as recalled by David Sefton, was the requirement to evacuate Britons from Rhodesia in 1979. The country, which had been a British colony since 1923, had been troubled by violence and international alienation during its struggle for independence. Throughout, there had been a long guerrilla war between Rhodesian forces and those of the Patriotic Front. The RAF's role was to support the Commonwealth force, which monitored the ceasefire agreement as the precursor to elections for a new government in what was to become Zimbabwe.[31] While working in MOD S Pol 28 Plans 1(RAF), David (then a flight lieutenant) and his boss were initially tasked with planning an operation to evacuate all the 'whites' from the country; the Joint Theatre Plan (JTP) envisaged using the complete RAF Air Transport Fleet and the whole of British Airways for the task. Their first task was to advise where this 'armada' could obtain aviation fuel. Having looked at a world map they came to the conclusion that only Nairobi and Johannesburg would fit the bill. They then spent months proving that their initial idea was the only correct solution. Johannesburg was excluded for political reasons but ambassadors and high commissioners throughout Africa kept putting forward their countries as candidates. The most difficult to refute was the claim that Lagos could be a refuelling point. The MOD's Defence intelligence desk for Sub-Saharan Africa maintained that Nigeria not only produced crude oil, but also had a refinery and plenty of tankage. Their counter argument to this was that the refinery did not produce aviation fuel, the tankage was empty and Nigeria's own aviation fuel came from Venezuela. When the JTP was eventually mounted it was not to evacuate, but to reinforce the country with British troops. It was decided that Nairobi was to be the refuelling point but it needed additional fuel for the operation. The solution was discreetly to deploy an ocean tanker load of AVTUR into Mombasa in advance of the operation as it took some ten days to pump fuel up to Nairobi. The Kenyan Government was kept in ignorance of this until just before the operation. Matters were further complicated by the appointment of Lord Soames who was to become the interim Governor of Rhodesia for the period between the Lancaster House negotiations and that country gaining its independence. The new governor was to be flown in by RAF VC10 but, all across Africa, countries denied permission for overflying rights. In the event, the route for his aircraft was from RAF Brize Norton (utilising AVTUR), via Lajes (refuelled with AVTAG) and Ascension Island (refuelled with AVCAT).[32]

The POL Operations Room

In 1976, the then Group Captain Mike Allisstone was Head of the RAF Fuels organisation (aka Deputy Director of Engineering and Supply Policy 10(RAF)), and he was acutely aware of the crucial importance of POL, especially aviation fuel, to the RAF's ability to sustain its fighting capability. From time to time, he was called upon to brief the operational staffs on the day-to-day availability of fuel during exercises and occasional live operations. He therefore decided to form, within his organisation, a POL operations room, or POLOR, which would be manned in times of crisis by members of his own staff. Arrangements for this were still in their infancy when he left the following year to command No. 7MU Quedgeley, but the concept took root and is now a permanent feature of MOD crisis management. Shortly before he departed, the Head of ESP 28(RAF), Wing Commander Jim Shearer, told him that the Army were fed up with storing the emergency fuel handling equipment on behalf of the RAF. There was little prospect then of British forces storming ashore over enemy beaches; the bulky pipelines were cluttering up one of their depots and

Jim sought his boss's agreement to dispose of it. Mike still cannot quite work out what made him refuse but, six years later, it was the very same kit that was flown out to save the day, as described earlier, during the Falklands War.

A series of tanker driver strikes led to POLOR being activated at the MOD and manned by SNCOs on detachment. AMSO required a daily update, by 11 a.m., of all thirteen grades of fuel from every UK unit. The huge flow of immediate signals severely taxed the MOD Communication Centre and had the HQ Supply staffs looking up the *Confidential Location of Units* publication to find where strange places such as Eddlesborough were. As suppliers, they were normally only used to dealing with self-accounting units and then only with aviation fuels. The strike, however, required them to manage ground fuel problems from isolated units. While not welcome, the strikes did reveal a number of weaknesses that required remedial measures to be put in place. First and foremost was that POL was to be put under ADP control to improve stock visibility. Additionally, approximately thirty road fuel tankers were purchased to give the RAF the ability to redistribute its fuel throughout the UK and shadow contracts were also placed with smaller suppliers to be invoked if the major fuel companies went on strike again. The RAF POLOR concept proved its worth and became the template for what later became a joint Service operations room.

Tri-Service Fuels Management

Notwithstanding the similarity of this work across Defence, each of the three services was responsible for the procurement, storage and distribution of their own POL, although a particular service took the lead for some of these. The RAF, for example, procured aviation fuel for all three services. There had been several attempts to form a tri-service fuels organisation but little progress was made in this respect until the drive for efficiencies began to break down some of the single-service concerns at what they viewed as a potential loss of direct control in this vital area of logistics. The DD Pet CG staff in MOD Main Building had long felt that a more efficient arrangement would be to have a lead service for all fuels, oils, and compressed gases. This was one of the early initiatives of the DLO when it was formed; indeed, it was part of the justification for the merged Logistics organisation. Group Captain (later Air Commodore) Paul Hedges led a study to recommend the formation of what was to become the Defence Fuels Group (DFG); he was the first Director of DFG when it formed on 1 January 2000. The DFG was formed to bring together the fuels staffs from single services into a single, coherent, fuels management organisation acting on behalf of Defence as a whole. The RAF provides the 'spine' of the DFG as it cut across the old deputy directorate of Petroleum and Compressed Gasses (DD Pet CG), which was the only single-service fuels organisation that provided cross-cutting activities for the other services. DD Pet CG had been commanded by Group Captain Paul Hedges who, along with Wing Commander Kevin Thistlethwaite, had been instrumental in creating the case for the DFG. The DFG was duly formed and Group Captain Hedges was promoted to Air Commodore; he became the first Director of the DFG, bedding the newly formed organisation into its brand-new building at RLC West Moors near Bournemouth. He handed over to Air Commodore Andy Spinks in 2003, who was the director until 2007. Command was then handed over to Brigadier Ian Abbott (Late RLC) for a short period, with Group Captain Nigel Arnold as his assistant director of operations, before Air Commodore Sue Armitage-Maddox took over in 2002 at the former Army Petroleum Centre at West Moors in Dorset, where the Army had a school of petroleum (including a training pipeline) and the bulk storage of ground fuels for Army exercises, including the MOD's only jerrycan filling plant.

The DFG became responsible for tri-service fuels, oils, and gases procurement and distribution, some storage, the MOD fuels inspectorate (responsible for monitoring safety standards), and fuel scientists from QinetiQ (who advised on fuels standards and the acceptability or otherwise of contaminated, life-expired, or off-specification fuel and lubricants). The school of petroleum remained at West Moors as an Army training formation but ran the long fuels course for selected officers of the Army and RAF. DFG's fuel storage facilities included the former RN fuel storage facility at Senoko in Singapore, which remains an MOD asset to this day (Senoko and the nearby berth at Sembawang are the main UK contribution to the Five Power Defence Arrangements (FPDA)). The director of DFG also became the MOD's member on the Oil and Pipelines Agency (OPA) Board; OPA is the public corporation charged with running the GPSS in line with MOD requirements. The RAF Commands (later just Air Command) and the RAF flying stations retained responsibility for the fuel storage facilities on stations, with DFG and OPA being responsible for delivery of the product to the station boundary, which in most cases was by pipeline.

DFG also assumed responsibility for bulk fuel supplies to the overseas bases, including Singapore, Cyprus, Gibraltar, and the Falkland Islands. For this purpose, DFG chartered a Maersk-owned multi-product tanker, the *Maersk Rapier*, which picked up DFG-procured fuel in bulk from locations such as Rotterdam and Algeciras (Spain) and shipped it on a planned route to Gibraltar, Cyprus, Ascension Island, and the Falkland Islands. On its returning 'empty' leg, Maersk would arrange appropriate bulk cargoes from the civilian market and this revenue was shared with MOD (DFG) to offset the cost of the charter. Fuel supply to operations was sometimes by the *Maersk Rapier* but, more often than not, procured locally from oil companies in the region. For example, fuel supply for the First and Second Gulf Wars (Operation Granby and Telic) was arranged through friendly nations in the Gulf Region. Offloading the *Maersk Rapier* in Cyprus, Ascension Island, and the Falkland Islands, typically through a single point mooring offshore, with integral fuel pipes running to the onshore fuel facility, was a specialist task, overseen by Supply officers and SNCOs who had completed the Ocean Tanking course. Safe delivery was no mean feat in poor weather in the Falkland Islands or the swells off Ascension Island.

RAF pillow tank BFI, Wideawake Airfield, Ascension Island, 1984. (*N. Dabin*)

The DFG was a huge success initially, and it was enthusiastically embraced by the single-services; its ambit reflected a truly end-to-end responsibility for fuels across the physical supply chain, including responsibility for the manpower of the related depots and the various technical support activities. The amalgamation of the various subject matter experts into this powerful new organisation reaped huge benefits and it became a new template for fuels management, which was adopted by many Allies and partners, most notably the USA. Unfortunately though, despite these initial successes, the nature and extent of the DFG's responsibilities did not sit naturally with what the DLO saw as their core outputs. With the requirement for the DLO to make government-mandated savings to its output costs within the first five years of its formation (known as the strategic goal), it was inevitable that DFG would come under close scrutiny. Over the next decade, the 'one-stop shop' for Defence fuels that DFG had established fell foul of the DLO's relentless quest to achieve its strategic goal. Several reviews of its roles were conducted and, in 2011, the decision to close the DFG was taken. In November 2011, the DFG pulled out of its HQ at West Moors and became part of the newly formed Defence Fuel and Food Services (DF&FS) project team headed up by an RAF Logistics officer, Group Captain Andy Killey. The nature of this new team as far as fuels was concerned, was more acquisition related and was seen to be more aligned with the core outputs of what had then become DE&S. The wider aspects of tri-service fuels policy and doctrine, ownership of the physical supply chain, and fuels technical services (and their related personnel) became part of organisations outside of DE&S. Responsibility for operations, plans, and policy was transferred back to the front-line commands, the fuel handling equipment team was wound up and the petroleum inspectorate was transferred into the Defence Safety and Environment Agency.

This was all an example of where the pursuit of government-mandated, aggressive savings measures and the application of very narrow functional boundaries to emerging Defence organisations did more harm than good. The merger of the DLO with the Defence Procurement Agency in 2007 to form DE&S seemed to further entrench the acquisition boundaries with a growing (and perhaps understandable) lack of understanding of the fuels management function. The practical and operational impact of the DFG's dissolution gradually became clear as the lack of coherence, fragmentation of policy and doctrine setting, lack of a detailed strategy for Defence Fuels and the cessation of all international fuels engagement began to take effect. Concerns were raised by the DF&FS team leader who produced a paper setting out what he felt the problem areas were. The paper was taken very seriously and, in November 2013, Air Vice-Marshal Graham Howard who was the Assistant Chief of Defence Staff (Logistics Operations) in the MOD commissioned a study into what was seen as an unsatisfactory state of affairs. A small study team was formed and given an aggressive timeline to finalise a report with detailed recommendations within three months. The report recommended that a new Defence Strategic Fuels Authority (DSFA) should be formed. The report was ratified by the Defence Logistics Board and, in September 2014, the DSFA formed at MOD Abbeywood. The DSFA was charged with plugging the strategic gaps that had been identified, recovering the ground that had been lost since the DFG closed, creating greater coherence across Defence fuels and re-engaging with NATO, along with international partners and allies.[33]

9
Managing the Supply Chain

By their very nature, armed forces require not just large numbers of people, but a vast and diverse range of materiel. The acquisition and management of this resource is complex and has been continually influenced by a multitude of factors, not least in terms of technical developments, changes in operational usage and ever-increasing complexity. The accumulation of materiel has added to what has generically been referred to as the RAF's inventory (not including complete aircraft and vehicles). This chapter explores how the RAF has acquired its equipment and managed its supply chain, from the origin of the resources, through to the front-line. The size and management of this inventory, though, along with its accompanying processes, has often been the subject of controversy, especially in the post-Second World War period where it has been the subject of ever closer attention as successive governments have grappled with the challenges of balancing the national economy. If the maxim of 'getting the right equipment to the right place at the right time' has long been the driver for military logistics, the focus on 'at the lowest possible cost' gained more significance with the end of the Cold War when the political imperative to cut costs was matched by an increasing ability (through enhanced information technology) to identify and attribute costs. This chapter examines how the RAF acquired its resources and the decision-making techniques it used to do that. It also considers a number of the organisational challenges which arose, the difficulties of maintaining the right size of inventory, and explores some of the collaborative aircraft projects which have become more commonplace since the end of the Cold War.

Change and Complexity

Before considering the more detailed aspects of RAF supply chain management, comment does need to be made about several factors that have made this task all the more difficult—change and complexity. Since its formation in 1918, the RAF has been subject to significant shifts in operational profile and almost continual organisational change. The inter-war years saw the fledgling service finding its feet, with much of its overseas resources largely committed to imperial 'policing'. The expansion programme of the mid to late 1930s saw a transformation of the service as it re-equipped to face the Second World War. This period saw the progressive replacement of largely wooden biplanes with metal, stressed-skin monoplanes.

The change continued apace as the war progressed and the RAF entered a period in which it reached its largest size in terms of numbers of aircraft, equipment and people. Following a substantial run-down in the size of the service, the post-war period or 'Cold War', up until the collapse of the Soviet Union in 1989, was a further period of change with the introduction to service of jet aircraft, along with the RAF playing a key role in NATO's nuclear deterrence. The British withdrawal from east of Suez in 1971 signalled further change; with its once global lines of communication considerably shortened and the UK refocusing its forces on NATO commitments. The 1974 Statement on Defence Estimates set out to halve the numbers of transport aircraft. From 1990, the Middle East, the Balkans, and Afghanistan dominated RAF operations and the requirements of these theatres of operation placed their own demands on the RAF's supply chain. This period also saw RAF Logistics having to contend with the uncertain requirements of a return to expeditionary operations. The British withdrawal from Afghanistan in 2014 is perhaps the latest major milestone in the change process; the future will see RAF Logistics having to adjust its organisation and output to support air power capability which is becoming more aligned to the asymmetric threats from international terrorism. All of this change, to a greater or lesser degree, has presented a continual challenge. Large numbers of differing aircraft types have come and gone, weapon technology has evolved considerably, and overseas basing has demanded the establishment and maintenance of numerous 'tailored' supply chains around the globe. Additionally, and particularly since 1945, there have been eight major government Defence Reviews, from the Defence White Paper of 1957 (the Sandys' Review), through to the Strategic Defence and Security Review of 2010. In parallel with these reviews, there have also been numerous RAF studies and initiatives to try and identify the optimal means of engineering and logistics support.

The second factor, complexity, arose from the number of aircraft types and marks which the RAF operated at any one time and the impact of technology. By October 1918, the newly formed RAF was operating around forty-two aircraft makes and types and some fifty two-engined variants.[1] By 1921, the number of aircraft types had dropped to thirteen, but then gradually increased to thirty-nine in 1935 and to sixty-nine by the outbreak of the Second World War; this figure had barely changed by the end of the war, which saw the RAF operating some sixty-six main types of aircraft. By 1952, this figure had dropped to twenty-nine, and remained in the region of thirty to thirty-two types up until the early 1980s. By 1995, the number had dropped to twenty-four and to nineteen by 2013.[2] It is not just the in-service aircraft and equipment that require logistical support as many of them gradually go out of service, some of which can be over a considerable period of time. The Canberra aircraft, for example, which first entered RAF operational service in 1951, remained part of the RAF's fleet for

Canberras in flight. (*Crown Copyright—Air Historical Branch MoD*)

some fifty-five years in varying numbers until the last three flying Canberra PR9s of No. 39 Squadron were retired from service in 2006.

The significance for logistics is that the number of aircraft and equipment types in service at any one time, including obsolescent types, has led to an enormous inventory having to be maintained to provide the required support. This in-service stock-holding was essential as a counter to the aviation industry's understandable reluctance to guarantee supply support for aircraft flying well after their originally planned life-cycle. The nature of this inventory has been further complicated by the addition of an ever-widening range of manufacturers and new items that were introduced as the result of modifications.

Although there is a vast difference in complexity between the RAF's aircraft in service at the end of the First World War and the Typhoon jet of the twenty first century, they have, individually, remained complex structures. Despite the widely held view that the early biplanes were simple structures of wood, wire, and linen, they were still intricate. The fuselage of the First World War R.E.8 aircraft, for example (excluding the wood itself), consisted of 273 individually referenced items, within which there was a total of some 800 parts including nuts, bolts, washers, rivets, split pins, bracing wires, and various metal jointing plates.[3] As aircraft and aero engine designs developed, they became considerably more complex and required a growing range of on- and off-aircraft components.

A sea change in the complexity of RAF aircraft came with the pre-Second World War expansion programme in the mid-1930s as a number of metal monoplanes began to replace the largely wooden biplanes then in service. By 1938, the expansion schemes had begun to deliver fifteen new types to RAF and Royal Navy service. The range of aircraft armament provides a good example of how complexity had begun to increase at this time The Air Ministry's DofE was managing some twenty-eight types of gun turret, which were becoming a common feature of the new bomber aircraft, such as the Wellington and Manchester (with two and three turrets respectively), as well as smaller aircraft types, such as the Boulton Paul Defiant (with a single turret situated behind the pilot's cockpit).[4]

All of these were complex structures with their own hydraulic and electrical systems in addition to the actual machine gun installations within them. The situation was further complicated by the fact that the range of aircraft came from a supplier base of some sixteen main manufacturers, each of which would have had its own administrative procedures for ordering against specific contracts. An important point when considering the supplier base is that each aircraft type manufacturer required the supply of components and assemblies manufactured by other companies; the acquisition of these items was secured via an extensive network of sub-contractors. In the case of the Avro Lancaster, for example, there were 125 sub-contractors supplying

Rear gun turret of a Halifax bomber. (*Author's collection*)

Avro by the end of 1942, from all parts of the British Isles.[5] A further complication was that the rate of production of new types only allowed a gradual replacement of obsolescent types which led to both old and new aircraft remaining in service concurrently for a considerable period, thus still requiring spares and equipment for both.[6] These challenges remained, albeit for vastly different technologies and for fewer aircraft types, well into the jet age after the Second World War and continued to pose a constant challenge to RAF logisticians well into the twenty first century.

Procurement and Provisioning

The acquisition of military aviation resources is an involved and often lengthy process, usually requiring a disparate range of specialists for both the military customer and the supplying contractor including engineers, public accounts staff, contracts specialists, logisticians, and contractors. Broadly speaking, there are three levels to this process, albeit the associated terminology has changed over time. At the most complete item level is the acquisition of whole assemblies such as aircraft, engines, or vehicles, a process generally referred to as procurement. Complete aircraft—along with their associated navigation, armament, and avionics essential for the fulfilment of their operational role—have come to be known as weapon systems. In parallel with this is the closely aligned activity of initial provisioning, which is the purchase of a range and quantity of spares to 'prime' the supply system, invariably for one to two years following introduction to service; this effectively provides the on-hand stock for the appropriate operating units and for their resupply from the RAF's equipment supply depots. Following the end of the initial provisioning period, a process of spares re-provisioning then takes over for the remainder of the item's life in military service, almost invariably beyond its initial life-cycle.

In the inter-war years and for much of the Second World War, initial and re-provisioning was little more than educated guesswork. The advent of information technology, along with the development of cutting-edge engineering, as well as mathematical and risk-modelling techniques in the 1960s, enabled a more analytical approach to be developed and improved accuracy considerably. Although the twenty-first century has seen the use of computer-based performance simulation and more extensive practical testing has become more commonplace, initial provisioning has always been fraught with several fundamental challenges, which are explored below in the section headed 'Initial Provisioning'.

Broadly speaking, this acquisition process was the main source of supply that 'fuelled' the RAF's inventory.[7] Cost has been and remains a further challenge, with the price of cutting-edge aerospace technology consuming an ever-greater proportion of the RAF's equipment budget. The cost of the Supermarine Spitfire, for example, was in the region of £9,500.[8] By comparison, the modern Eurofighter Typhoon was in the region of £30 million in the 1980s. At component level, the individual cost of some components can be so high that the available budget permits the purchase of a very limited number of spares that have had to be managed as 'high-value' items. Cumulatively, RAF equipment costs can be considerable. In the mid-1960s, the RAF was spending some £70 million on spares; the total stock in Maintenance Command (excluding complete aircraft) was worth some £300 million.[9] In the financial year 1971–1972, DGS (RAF) spent some £354 million in meeting the materiel needs of the RAF, representing half the total support costs of the RAF. At that time, the total asset value in the RAF's ESDs and RAF Supply Squadrons amounted to some £962 million, with an estimated £2,000 million worth of equipment held forward on user-held inventories across the service.[10] It is noteworthy that these figures belong to the Cold War age when the approach to procurement was 'just in case' as opposed to today's approach of 'just in time'.

Procurement

The requirement for a new aircraft type or for the development of those already in service originated in a number of ways.[11] From a war-fighting perspective, the main purpose is to keep ahead of a potential adversary who might need to be deterred or fought. In a broader sense, aircraft and equipment are also required for the wider commitments of the RAF, thereby providing new or a developed capability. The origins of such needs often came from a variety of sources, ranging from fresh intelligence assessments of an enemy's capability and intention to operating experience of RAF squadrons. Additionally, new requirements could arise from technical studies, emerging Air Staff plans, and also unsolicited proposals from industry.[12] The coordinating point within the Air Ministry for these emerging ideas during the inter-war period was within CAS' department, which, by 1934, included an operational requirement (OR) section. The OR staff remained a department within the Air Ministry during the Second World War and continued as such, albeit under different departments in the MOD from 1964.[13] As and when a justifiable new capability arose, a draft OR was raised by the Ministry; this outlined the broad purpose for which the weapon system was required and its required performance level. This was then submitted to the procurement organisation for a technical feasibility analysis prior to the formulation of a formal OR being submitted to a number of manufacturers who might or might not bid for the contract with a suitable product design. Following the selection of a preferred supplier and design, financial approval would then be secured and a contract placed. The invitation to tender from a number of potential suppliers would, in the majority of cases, become a mandatory process in Defence procurement in an effort to introduce competition into pricing. This was not always feasible. Often only one supplier's design would meet the operational requirement in being integrated with the aircraft and its engine, avionics, and weapons systems.

Between 1918 and 1940, both procurement and provisioning for new aircraft, vehicles, and equipment were largely the responsibility of the Air Ministry. Prime Minister Winston Churchill, however, believed that the British rate of aircraft production was slow—a view he had held since before the war. By the first half of 1940, he had come to the conclusion that the answer was to form a separate and independent Ministry of Aircraft Production (MAP) to be responsible for aircraft procurement.[14] Consequently, MAP was formed on 14 May 1940, with Lord Beaverbrook as the minister in charge.[15] Churchill's decision to form MAP at this time, and its influence on producing urgently required fighter aircraft, proved to be a critical success factor in the Battle of Britain. In 1946, MAP was amalgamated with the Ministry of Supply. In further reorganisations, the task was switched to the Ministry of Aviation in 1959, to the Ministry of Technology in 1967, and finally to the Ministry of Aviation Supply in 1970.

In 1971, the Government commissioned Derek Rayner, then the managing director of Marks and Spencer, to investigate ways and means of improving the aerospace industry and procurement for the armed services. One of the fundamental changes recommended in the report that was published in April 1971 was the separation of executive and policy functions. This led to the formation of the MOD Procurement Executive (MOD (PE)) on 2 August 1971, with Derek Rayner as its first chief executive. The new executive became responsible for all defence related procurement, contract supervision, and research and development establishments, but not for support once the weapon system entered service. This was the responsibility of the Engineering and Supply Branches of the Royal Air Force.

At about the same time, responsibility for in-service supply support by the armed services was rationalised. Responsibility for ground weapons and MT for all three services was vested in the Army, responsibility for victualling and maritime craft in the Royal Navy, and responsibility for aircraft spares and for accommodation stores in the RAF. Interestingly, only the RAF had Supply Branch officers involved in provisioning and ordering. The Royal Navy was supported by the DGST (N) organisation manned by civil servants and the Army by civil servants within the ordnance depots. This remained the case until 1990 when further far-reaching changes were to take place.

In 1995, much of MOD (PE) co-located to the newly-built Abbey Wood complex at Bristol and in April 1999, in the wake of SDR 98, became an executive agency of the MOD and renamed the Defence Procurement Agency (DPA). The Defence review also brought further fundamental change with the end of the single-service Logistics organisations, incorporating them into a new tri-service Defence Logistics Organisation (DLO) also formed in April 1999.

The next five years saw both the DLO and the DPA trying to find better ways of working and sharing resources. Further change, though, was precipitated by the Defence Industrial Strategy in 2005, which announced a review of the MOD's arrangements for the acquisition of military capability.[16] In turn, this led to a fresh examination in 2006 of the MOD's ability to undertake what was then termed as 'through life capability management', in the form of the Enabling Acquisition Change review. While this review did acknowledge that time and cost over-runs had improved in the last two years (a problem that had persisted in the post-war period), there were still problems with some of the largest and most complex projects; from the RAF's perspective, the replacement Nimrod programme for example, had experienced a delay of over seven years and a cost over-run of some 35 per cent since project approval.[17] As part of the review's findings, it was recommended that both the DLO and DPA should be merged, becoming DE&S in April 2007; by 2012, most of its staff were co-located at the MOD's Abbey Wood complex near Bristol. This effectively separated logistics (which remained with the three services) from procurement and provisioning.

Much of the work of MOD (PE), from its creation in 1971, was governed by an operating concept known as the 'Downey Cycle', which saw new procurement having to proceed through six key stages, from the original staff target to production by industry. Each of these phases was separated by a period during which the project was reviewed and an assessment made of performance to that point before approval was given for the next stage to commence; this was all intended to ensure that costs were controlled and delays were avoided.[18] Despite the project control mechanisms of the 'Downey Cycle' operating framework, Defence procurement struggled to manage costs and timescales, especially during the 1980s through to the mid-1990s, and the efficiency and effectiveness of the process was the subject of a number of National Audit Office (NAO) reports, many of which identified significant problems with project slippage and cost over-runs. The NAO Major Projects Report in 1997, for example, found that the largest Defence equipment projects at the time were forecast to cost over £3 billion more than originally planned and, on average, would enter operational service over three years late.[19] Of the many views on why Defence procurement had failed to achieve more success during this time is a comment that appeared in the supporting essays of SDR 98, pointing out that during the Cold War, 'there was pressure for projects to be pushed forward into full development and production quickly so as to meet a specific Soviet threat, even though much risk remained'.[20]

There was little surprise that Defence procurement policy became one of the main objectives of the Labour Government's SDR, with a Smart Procurement initiative emerging which aimed to 'establish a new customer–supplier relationship between the MOD and industry'; this, so the review claimed, would introduce a new process which was 'faster, cheaper, and better'. The initiative recognised that procurement was a corporate process that involved many stakeholders, including industry, and a 'through life systems approach' to procurement. Among the many features in the initiative was the requirement for fuller early planning of projects, partnering arrangements with industry, improved estimating and predicting and improved commercial practices.[21] Another feature of the initiative was the replacement of the 'Downey Cycle' with an 'Acquisition Cycle' which had fewer stages and approval

Symbolic of the Cold War: Soviet SA2 missiles on Parade, Moscow, 1978. (*Crown Copyright—Air Historical Branch MoD*)

points.[22] The key difference was that the new cycle enabled more time to be focused on the early concept and assessment phases so that options could be explored and risk reduced by use of testing technology; experience had shown that this element accounted for some 15 per cent of costs.[23]

Initial Provisioning

Initial provisioning, or IP, has always been critical to the support of RAF aircraft, although forecasting what might be required for a brand new aircraft, vehicle or item of equipment, remained a challenge until more sophisticated computerised software started to become available in the 1980s. From 1918, through until the 1960s, IP spares orders were placed by the Air Ministry/MOD's DofE as part of the procurement executive's order with the manufacturer. The order quantity was usually based on an estimate of spares required for a twenty-seven-month period at peacetime maintenance rates, along with four months' supply as additional stock for estimated war rates of operation.[24]

The reliability of a new design can rarely be accurately predicted and it is not until the in-service phase of its life that the required range and scale of spares can become more clearly understood. The suppliers of the aircraft, the engines, and the equipment made recommendations for spares that were then subject to review by the MOD. For many years, the approach to IP was by a range of equipment such as radio or navigation systems, which could have been in service across a number of aircraft types. However, the 1970s started to see provisioning occur on a 'weapon system' basis, starting with the Jaguar aircraft. As described above, the whole IP process, though, was heavily reliant on industry recommending a spares buy for the RAF, although this became increasingly subject to greater scrutiny and validation by the service as more sophisticated modelling and simulation techniques were developed, such as the Systecon 'OPUS' spares optimisation software that the RAF first started using at the RAF's Central Servicing Development Establishment (CSDE) Swanton Morley in about 1986.[25] This software was an important part of the RAF's IP 'tool kit' and enabled provisioning staff to take a much more informed view of the recommendations made by industry; in a number of cases, considerable financial and stock savings were made using this tool. Up until the late 1990s, the CSDE team who ran the OPUS modelling also used software known as 'Scaler', which was a single item model based scaling program written in FORTRAN and maintained in-house. In addition, they also used WARSIM, also a FORTRAN program, for simulating a thirty-day war (then the NATO planning criteria) in order to determine the effectiveness of aircraft fly away packs. In the early days, it was intended that CSDE would use Scaler to determine the budget for a spares solution and then use OPUS to produce the best mix of spares for the same budget but this did not last long and quite quickly Scaler became redundant and OPUS, later OPUS10, became the main tool.[26]

In support of the CSDE modelling team, there were several resource modelling officers who developed and researched new techniques, as well as heading specific modelling tasks. These were further supported by five separate teams (rotary wing, fixed wing, fast jet, Tornado, and Eurofighter), who primarily collected, cleansed, and recorded the maintenance and reliability data primarily taken from the maintenance data system.

By the mid to late 1990s, the RAF's primary modelling 'tool set' was OPUS10 and SIMLOX, a package that simulated operations and maintenance. This was all supported by a range of database systems and computer spreadsheets maintained by the various teams and project managers. The role of the CSDE modelling team, supported by Systecon through its cutting-edge software, was highly significant in the IP process. As an organisation, CSDE progressed from supporting only the RAF in-service fleet and new aircraft entering service to offering wider support to the integrated project teams for other equipment, including some aerospace ground equipment, test equipment, ground radar, ground-based missile systems, and later, Royal Navy and Army projects.[27]

The first stage in the IP process was the production of an IP policy statement. The MOD Supply management branches (SMB) at Harrogate then arranged for contractors to submit IP lists (IPLs), usually for batches of 5,000 items that would comprise a complete breakdown of a particular area or system. The selection of items and quantities was based on servicing policies, engineering assessment, the forward order period (usually thirty-months), the planned peak aircraft establishment, and the contractor's economic order quantity. These IPLs were scrutinised at formal IP meetings, chaired by an IP chairman (usually a Supply Branch squadron leader), and attended by CSDE, SMB range managers, finance staffs, MOD (PE), and contractor-drafting staffs. When agreed and financially approved, the IPL formed the contractual authority for a firm order and the production of spares by the contractor, concurrent with the contractor's production run for the main equipment.[28] Typically, the number of line items bought at IP for a combat aircraft in the 1980s was in the region of 100,000, although some 500,000 items would have been examined in the lead up to that buy. For the Typhoon aircraft, the concept of a phased approach was adopted where support was contracted out during the introductory phase. This enabled the IP for that aircraft to be reduced to 40,000 items, although it was anticipated that this would grow to about 100,000 items over five to seven years as equipment began to mature and the RAF moved to more traditional support policies.[29]

Provisioning of MT vehicles was a more straightforward affair with the RAF responsible for procurement and maintenance requirements for RAF peculiar vehicles (through the deputy director of mechanical transport (RAF) in the MOD); the Army department was responsible as the single service manager for the provisioning and maintenance requirements of common vehicles for the three services. Much of the RAF's provisioning process was based on an annual cycle that took into account three factors: the liability known as the forecast unit establishment (projected over the then ten-year financial planning period), the available assets (taking into account age of vehicles and distribution across the RAF), and the wastage pattern.[30] The Army's role in this process was an early and largely successful move into tri-service rationalisation.

Re-provisioning

Unlike IP, the whole process of re-provisioning (RP) was a more informed exercise and used data accumulated from actual operating experience. It was general practice during the post-Second World War period for RP to start some two years after the in-service date for a new weapon system, by which time a reasonable consumption pattern had been established. Once the calculation process was complete, RP spares requirements would require new contracts to be placed with manufacturers; these, in turn, would provide a standing or 'call-off' contract for replenishment stocks to be ordered by equipment range managers. With the advent of computerised stock control in the 1960s, much of this re-ordering activity became automated, although this still required a sizeable staff of range managers to administer and review specific groups of equipment types. Before the introduction of computer support for this process at MOD Harrogate in the late 1980s, each item they managed required a master provisioning record card to be maintained; it was not unusual to see these cards sitting between bookends, occupying the entire width of each manager's desk. Generally speaking, equipment and supplies were delivered directly, off-contract, to the RAF's equipment depots.

During the inter-war period, RP was a reasonably manageable task within the existing resources of the DofE in the Air Ministry. However, the exponential growth of the size of the RAF's inventory and the corresponding increase in the number of equipment MUs at the beginning of the Second World War led to a pressing need to put in place a provisioning process that could cope with this complexity. By June 1940, the Directorate of Equipment was responsible for a total inventory size of some 500,000 different items.[31] While the dispersal of stock across the depot sites provided a pragmatic and affordable approach to protecting valuable assets, the universal equipment depot concept that was introduced in May 1939, with provisioning calculations being carried out centrally at the Air Ministry in London (and largely from Harrogate when much of the DofE relocated there in September 1939), became untenable.[32] The crux of the problem was that for the provisioning process to work, up-to-date information on the overall inventory (by specific item) was essential. Of particular concern was that fresh stock was not purchased for one depot, when there was already stock elsewhere. With large volumes of equipment being received from industry and large volumes of equipment subsequently being issued to units, it was virtually impossible for one central location to keep track of exactly what the stock balance was for any one item and when reorders of stock needed to be placed. This was further complicated by changes in the overall inventory picture as unserviceable equipment became available again after successful repair. Various approaches to solving this problem were considered by Maintenance Command as early as 1938, with much of the thinking beginning to polarise around a concept that became known as 'master provision'. This work culminated in the formulation of a scheme entitled 'master provisioning for universal equipment depots', which was subsequently approved for implementation in October 1939.[33]

Essentially, the master provisioning concept divided the RAF's inventory into generic groups of equipment such as airframe, engine, and motor transport spares, and allocated provisioning responsibility to a nominated master provision office (MPO). Initially, seven of these were established on the sites of the main equipment MUs at: Nos 7 MU Quedgeley, 14 MU Carlisle, 35 MU Heywood, 16 MU Stafford, 25 MU Hartlebury, and 61 MU Handforth; an additional MPO was also established at Stafford specifically to look after spares sourced from the USA. With the continued expansion of the RAF, the increased number of aircraft types, and individual equipment, along with the progressive increase in demand level and the introduction of new types of equipment depots, a further six MPOs were established in November 1942 at No. 3 MU Milton, No. 68 MU Bolton, No. 216 MU Sutton Coldfield, No. 55 Wing Derby, Wakefield, and Leighton Buzzard.[34] The increase in the number of units in the Middle East led to the formation of an MPO in July 1941 (known as the Middle East Provision Office (MEPO) to avoid confusion with Military Post Office) at No. 107 MU in Egypt.[35] An MPO was also established at RAF Fauld, responsible entirely for munitions and POL. The provisioning task was a sizeable undertaking, not least of which was the sheer number of clerical workers required; by late 1942, this was already in the region of some 3,000 people. Of particular note is that civilians accounted for approximately 60 per cent of the MPO workforce with, typically, some 77 per cent WAAFs (airwomen) at the service manned offices.[36]

Each of the MPOs had, by and large, the same task, which was to calculate when stock replenishment was required. For repairable components, the MPO would issue instructions for the feed-in to repair organisations and would then allocate the repaired item to a specific depot on its return. Where replenishment for non-repairable items was required, and having calculated the quantity required, the MPO would forward details to the Air Ministry's DofE, which would then arrange for orders to be placed through the Ministry's contracts department. In addition to this, the MPOs would transfer equipment between the depots where required, often to ensure that stock was dispersed in line with Maintenance Command's security policy.[37] The theory was one thing, but the practicality was another matter altogether. To carry out its task, each MPO needed to know how much stock was held in each equipment MU, what stock was due to be issued or received from suppliers, and what equipment was in the process of repair. The timely availability of information was therefore crucial to the scheme. The only way this data could be provided at the outbreak of war was by using a paper posting slip, part of a process which required large numbers of clerks to compile and despatch data from the equipment maintenance depots and then for MPO staff to receive and consolidate this data into an overall total; the dispersal of the same stock across a number of depots (with each submitting their own information) required the data for these to be combined into a single figure before stock control calculations could be carried out. To avoid depots notifying the MPOs when they were nearing or actually out of stock, stock transactions were reported as they occurred. The original planning study for the master provision scheme in 1938 had included a recommendation for electro-mechanical equipment to produce data cards (as an alternative to posting slips); the first of these machines were installed at 25 MU Hartlebury in November 1943, but it was not until February 1945 that the last machines required to equip all the depots were received (see Chapter Ten).[38] The master provisioning scheme lasted until the early 1960s when, with the introduction of the RAF's first computerised stock control system, the service developed a largely automated system which used a complex set of algorithms to carry out provisioning and procurement calculations. This enabled much of the RAF's provisioning activity to be conducted from the SMBs at Harrogate.

Taking the Longer View

One of the issues that hindered the effectiveness of acquisition during the post-Second World War period was a lack of coherence between initial procurement and in-service support. Churchill's establishment of the Ministry of Aircraft Production in 1940 (and its successor organisations) had removed the responsibility for procurement from the Air Ministry and placed it in the hands of a separate organisation. This demarcation of responsibility remained a feature well into the twenty-first century, albeit since the mid to late 1990s, a greater awareness of the limitations of this approach began to lead to much better cooperation between the single services and the procurement organisation. Despite the best of intentions, what tended to happen was that the acquisition of a weapon system or equipment was viewed from two distinct perspectives: the procurement organisation was often only interested in the work involved up to the point that the subject equipment was introduced to service, while the RAF Logistics organisation then endeavoured to support it from there on. This led to the widespread (and not unfounded) view that responsibility for weapon system support was effectively 'thrown over a boundary wall' between the two departments, with limited cooperation between either of them.

From the 1980s onwards, more innovative and joined-up thinking in logistics began to develop within the MOD. Of particular influence in this respect was the concept of integrated logistics support (ILS), where acquisition and support processes were viewed as a whole rather than as two discrete elements. This was a concept originally used by the US Army with the key feature that it ensured that the supportability of new equipment was taken into consideration during its design and development. The ILS approach began to be adopted by the UK's MoD for some training aircraft in 1993 and soon formed a mandatory part of most Defence procurement. In theory, this enabled a more holistic approach to logistics to be taken and for the complete life cycle to be considered. At the heart of this concept was logistic support analysis (LSA), whereby a structured approach to understanding system performance enabled the selection of the optimum support policy for a given component. The LSA is a complex process but, in essence, consists of a range of engineering analytical tools which enable the optimum maintenance policy for the subject equipment to be determined. In turn, this enables more informed spares scaling to be undertaken. ILS looked at the whole range of support facilities required and enabled a multi-disciplined master plan to be developed.[39] There is no doubt that ILS offered a more 'through life approach' to support, but it did require more dedicated resources to make it work and was a radically new way of working that was a challenge for an organisation that had developed processes to function in the somewhat polarised 'stove pipes' of MOD (PE) and the RAF.

While ILS was (and remains) a highly effective methodology and did, to some extent, require much closer cooperation between the procurement organisation and the single services, the organisational division in acquisition responsibilities remained until April 2007 when the Defence Procurement Agency became part of DE&S. After some sixty-seven years, this change brought about a much needed and closer organisational relationship in Defence acquisition.

The Development of Collaborative Working

In the post-Second World War period, with numerous Defence reviews endeavouring to find ways of improving efficiency and effectiveness, it was inevitable that the question of more collaborative working between the engineering and logistics disciplines would attract growing attention. Progress towards this aspiration proved to be surprisingly problematical and it took until the autumn of 1989 before a stable and workable structure was approved and implemented. From 1945 through until 1973, the engineering and supply disciplines were headed by their own directors general: for Engineering, this was DG Engineering (DG Eng (RAF), a three-star appointment, and for Equipment the two-star appointment of DGE. The latter became DGS (RAF) in 1970.

The quest to improve RAF operations remained a fact of life for years to come, with perhaps the nature of the relationship between the Equipment and Engineering disciplines attracting greater scrutiny than most topics. In 1970, an Engineer and Equipment Working Party was established to consider if there was a need for closer working between the two disciplines. The party, however, found that the relationship between the two disciplines was generally satisfactory. At MOD Branch level, they noted:

> The complexity of engineering and supply and their interdependence in the joint support of operations is increasing in line with new procedures for procurement of aircraft or equipment from abroad, increased costs and complication of equipment, repair processes involving both branches, parallel involvement in new projects and ADP, MT rationalisation, and joint investigation at the CSDE.[40]

Those factors, it observed, 'point to the need for even closer association in the future and for some changes to make the branches more collectively efficient through combined management with some multiple-annotation posts and co-location of related staffs'.[41] The final report highlighted that working relationships at station and command HQ level were sound but that there was most certainly a need to improve things within the MOD (Air Force Department (AFD)) 'where staffs concerned with policy, planning, new projects, and ADP should be merged and where combined management needs to be applied to control of technical work such as provisioning and arrangements for repair'.[42] The study also recommended that training courses could be improved by providing a more in-depth overview of each Branch to the other and improvements in inter-Branch communication.

As part of the work which resulted in the formation of RAF Support Command in 1973, the Air Force Board approved a recommendation that a joint Engineering and Supply organisation should be formed within the AFD from the staffs of DG Eng (RAF) and DGS (RAF); this was officially formed in November 1973 and headed by a three-star officer known as the controller of Engineering and Supply (CES (RAF)).

There were three branches within the new organisation each headed by a director general (DG): the policy and planning functions became the responsibility of the directorate-general of Engineering and Supply policy and plans (DGESP and P (RAF); the day-to-day management of the engineering and supply functions rested with the directorate-general of Engineering and Supply (DGESM (RAF)); and the deputy directorate of integration studies (DDIS (RAF)) was charged with the practical task of bringing the functions together as well as examining the scope and need for a similar approach at command HQ and at units. The former two-star DGS (RAF) became the new director general of DGESP, with a two-star engineering officer becoming the director general of DGESM (RAF).[43] In practice, it was found that the integration of engineering and supply specialisations had created a series of complicated internal interfaces that proved more complex and time consuming than had been envisaged. Aside from these issues, other changes and evolutionary developments in the RAF did much to relieve the organisational shortcomings. Co-location of staffs within the Old War Office in London and day-to-day working relationships at locations such as Harrogate, Swanton Morley, Hendon, and MOD (PE) continued to strengthen. Consequently, in 1978, the CES (RAF) organisation was effectively disbanded with the professional responsibilities for engineering and supply reverting to the control of a chief engineer (CE (RAF)) and the previous DGS (RAF), both responsible to AMSO.

This working arrangement remained until 1982 when the Government's policy towards the public sector, which was set out in the financial management initiative, placed a much greater emphasis on value for money than before. As part of the wider change that this triggered, the Secretary of State for Defence, Michael Heseltine, implemented a re-organisation in the MOD which, *inter alia*, introduced what was known as the new management strategy (NMS). Notwithstanding the aspirations of the new strategy, problems remained with the various issues that the disbanded CES (RAF) organisation had tried to address. In addition to the separation of acquisition, managed by MOD(PE) from the authorities responsible for in-service support, the latter were further fragmented and operating as 'stove pipes' with most engineering authorities being London-based while the Supply management branches were largely located in Harrogate and Carlisle. Few EAs ventured north, and the expectation was that the SM staff would travel to meetings in London. Many EA decisions were taken and commitments given to Air Staff colleagues without much thought for the procurement process and inevitable lead-times which frequently disappointed the ill-informed Air Staff. There was little constructive dialogue between the SM staff and their accounts colleagues in relation to budgets nor with their contracts management colleagues who had to turn orders into contractual commitments.

A fresh look at the problem took place in 1983 when a study team chaired by Air Marshal Sir Alec Morris examined the issue. In their final report presented in February 1984, the team recommended that a maintenance executive (ME) should be formed.

The 'Morris Report' as it became colloquially known came to the conclusion that decision-making could be improved, and some manpower and financial economies be made, by co-locating staffs working in the EAs and SMBs, with elements of the Post Design Service staff from MOD(PE) and financial representation from part of the MOD's finance organisation. The report recommended that the new executive should be located close to London and HQ STC; Crowthorne, Halton, and Henlow were suggested as possible locations. Although the report was submitted to the Air Force Board Standing Committee it was only afforded limited distribution due to the wider changes then in hand by the Secretary of State for Defence. Consequently, AMSO therefore directed that Air Vice-Marshal (later Air Chief Marshal Sir Michael) Alcock should take a fresh look at the issue and re-asses the recommendations of the Morris Report. While the Alcock Report, as his team's analysis became known, acknowledged the merits of forming a ME, it did much more work on examining the weaknesses of the existing in-service support arrangements to confirm whether or not an executive alone was the answer to the problems identified.

The Alcock Report, though, identified that the quite radical 'big bang' approach in the Morris Report of co-locating the complete range of staffs in one place was highly problematical, not least because of the need to redeploy a large number of MOD civil servants from MOD Harrogate to a new location. Consequently, and to minimise the movement of SMB staff and the involved infrastructure costs, a modified Morris Report option was recommended which confirmed that a ME should be established, but for a weapon system of major operational significance and cost. The main contender for this was the Tornado aircraft which would eventually account for nearly half the front-line strength of the RAF and would consume a significant proportion of the total RAF in-service support budget; in 1985, this amounted to £125 million per year and was rising fast. The Tornado requirement had already been addressed earlier and a Directorate of Tornado Engineering and Supply (DTES) organisation had been formed, albeit with component staffs still split between Harrogate and London. The Alcock Report made a number of recommendations to strengthen this arrangement, along with a transfer of the respective staffs to a new location. The second area which was identified for possible incorporation within a new ME was the management of aero-engines (other than the Tornado's RB199) which was currently split between MOD Harrogate and MOD Carlisle. This too was recommended as a possible 'engine executive' within a new ME. Overall, the Alcock Report recommended that an ideal location for the new ME would be at the redundant MOD site in Harefield which was a former MOD (PE) facility some six-miles north of RAF Uxbridge.[44] The report's recommendations never came to fruition and it would take a further ten years before the very sound principles underpinning the concept could be brought to fruition with the formation of Logistics Command with the author of the Alcock Report as its first Commander-in- Chief in the rank of Air Chief Marshal.

In 1990, AMSO's organisation was restructured as a result of recommendations which emerged from the new management strategy. The new organisation was a significant step forward in the quest for greater collaboration and was structured around the concept of multi-disciplinary groups (MDG) to manage the support of all RAF operational equipment. Due to the complexity of the task, the post of Chief of Logistic Support (RAF) was created; their role was initially to oversee the change process and also to exercise the broader logistics policy functions.[45] The support management task became the responsibility of a DG support management (DGSM), while operational and support infrastructure services became the responsibility of a DG Support Services (DGSS). Both of these posts were held by Supply Branch two-star officers, a net gain of one post at that level for the Branch.[46]

As part of this change, the previous EAs, SMBs, contract branches, and public accounts staff were formed into the new MDGs devoted to specific aircraft types, weapons systems or categories of multi-applicable commodities. To accommodate Supply Branch officers in the airworthiness decision-making chain, which was seen as a key point, a group captain deputy director commanding a MDG always had to have at least one wing commander engineer reporting to him to act as his specialist airworthiness advisor; he could, if required, bypass his immediate superior to a one-star engineer if he felt his professional advice was being disregarded. The finer points of the re-brigading of these staffs was greatly assisted by the work of Touche Ross Consultancy, who were able to gather and interpret data that not only endorsed the approach, but quantified the size of the MDGs and their manning from the various specialisms. Two aircraft MDGs, those to support TriStar and Jaguar, would be commanded by Supply Branch wing commanders and a Supply Branch group captain would become a deputy director within the new organisation and responsible for several MDGs run by Engineer Branch wing commanders. Wing Commander Colin Cummings was selected to lead the Jaguar grouping and was delighted with the opportunity. The preparations for and conduct of the First Gulf War (Operation Granby), the success of the Jaguar force and the speed and effectiveness with which the MDG handled the enhancements to the aircraft, proved the concept. Late in his tour, Colin was told that the Canberra fleet would be added to his portfolio and with it the residual issues of Phantom and Hunter out-of-service work. The addition of this responsibility was a vote of confidence in how the MDGs had matured and the way the Jaguar team was working as a group. Colin resolved the vexed question of airworthiness by the simple expedient of stating that he had 'responsibility' but not 'authority'.[47]

A Defence helicopter support agency was formed in 1991 and structured using the MDG principle. Interestingly, the supply management element was drawn exclusively from MOD Harrogate. It was also envisaged that the MDGs would also have their own contracts staff where required although in the event they kept their independence under the director commercial.

Further rationalisation to the higher organisation of RAF Logistics came in 1994 as a result of the Government's Prospect study with its target of achieving a 20 per cent reduction in the UK armed forces' HQ staffs to match the previous *Options for Change* cuts to the military front-line in 1990. With a backdrop of creating a 'centre of excellence' in RAF Logistics management, a Logistics Command was formed on 1 April 1994 with its combined HQ at RAF Brampton and RAF Wyton in Cambridgeshire. The command was headed by a four-star officer as AOC-in-C, and initially comprised three organisations: the Support Management Group, still under the direction of DGSM (RAF); the Maintenance Group Defence Agency, which was responsible for the depots; and the Communications and Information Systems Group.[48] To further strengthen the collaborative working environment, four purpose-built, open-plan pavilions were constructed at RAF Wyton to house Logistics staff transferred from London, Harrogate, High Wycombe, Stanbridge, and Swanton Morley.[49]

Logistics Command was short-lived and was disbanded at the end of October 1999 as a result of SDR 98 and absorbed into the DLO in April 2000. The relatively short life of the command was by no means a reflection of its effectiveness and in the five and a half years of its existence. It achieved significant rationalisation in logistics real estate and major developments in information system technology. The number of ESDs was reduced with the aim of concentrating storage functions at 16 MU Stafford. From a technology perspective, the command also made major advances in the implementation of the logistics information technology strategy which had the objective of delivering an integrated engineering, supply, and finance IT system to support logistics throughout the RAF (see Chapter Ten). Much work was also done to improve warehouse management systems and the support to the introduction of new equipment while the Command staffs also made a significant contribution to a tri-service project to provide a more comprehensive consignment tracking functionality. A notable feature of the new DLO was that it preserved an 'environmental' grouping for sea, land, and air (each headed by an officer of the respective service), but with integrated project teams (IPT) becoming responsible for a weapon system type(s).[50] For aircraft, this broadly came under the remit of Equipment Support (Air) and headed by an RAF two-star officer based at RAF Wyton. The DLO also made a clear distinction in its organisational grouping, with the environmental IPTs who were seen as interacting with its customers (termed the delivery layer) and the supporting organisations (termed the enabling layer). Higher-level policy and direction rested with a Defence Logistics Board chaired by a new four-star appointment, the Chief of Defence Logistics.

The 'Defence Industrial Strategy' of 2005 announced a review of the MOD's arrangements for the acquisition of military capability.[51] This, in turn, gave rise to the Enabling Acquisition Change study in 2006 which was charged with 'advising whether changes should be made to the MOD's structures, organisation, process or culture and behaviours to facilitate good "through life capability management"'. A key outcome was the merger of the DLO with the Defence Procurement Agency to form DE&S in April 2007. This provided, for the first time, an integrated and unified approach to procurement of equipment and its through-life support. In theory, this change strengthened collaborative working and, with further organisational and functional changes, remains the current Defence organisation responsible for this work.[52]

Understanding the Needs of Aircraft Maintenance

Following the Second World War, the requirement for economy became a much greater driving force in the management of the RAF's resources. The wartime mind-set of 'all-out' effort could no longer be applied as the UK endeavoured to recover economically from the war years. The maintenance of the RAF's aircraft fleet, along with the associated manpower levels, attracted much attention and, in the late 1940s, the RAF introduced what was known as planned flying planned servicing (PFPS). This concept was developed to 'rationalise flying and servicing commitments, and to produce the largest dividends from aircraft and men for any task'.[53] The significant part of this concept was that, when a new operational task arose, a task chart was produced that set out a number of influencing factors such as: the main task, the variable conditions, the administrative requirements, the operational requirements, the flying plan, and the servicing plan, along with the number of aircraft and men required.[54]

In time, aircraft support became defined by the lines of maintenance: first line was defined as activity carried out at RAF operational squadron level; second line, which was minor repair and maintenance and usually carried out at RAF station level in specialist engineering workshops; third line where major repair and maintenance of airframe items was carried out at specialist RAF establishments such as RAF St Athan in South Wales and RAF Sealand; and fourth line for work beyond the capability of the RAF such as upgrade work and carried out by industry. This was not just a framework which governed engineering activity. RAF Logistics invariably had stores located close to the first to third line facilities and also played a key part in the physical feed-in and progression of components for repair or modification at fourth line. This was mirrored at No. 30 MU RAF Sealand where tasking of the repair and maintenance facilities was the responsibility of the Supply Wing, which had both to meet demand from units and ensure spares support of the MU's workshops. This approach to maintenance remained in place until the formation of the DLO when, as part of its change programme launched in 2002, an end-to-end review was carried out by the consulting firm McKinsey and Co. The report from this study, which broadly looked at ways in which the DLO could achieve the treasury-imposed strategic goal by financial year 2005–2006, recommended a rationalised approach to the levels of maintenance. It was thus that in 2003, a more streamlined concept was introduced consisting of 'Forward' where repair is carried out at each operational squadron and 'Depth' which rationalised the number of previous locations to a single 'Depth Hub' such as RAF Marham for the Tornado and RAF Cottesmore for the Harrier.[55]

For good reason, understanding and influencing aircraft reliability became a focus of attention for engineering staffs in the post-war period and by the late 1960s significant progress had been made in quantifying the operational and financial impact of this factor. Indeed, in 1968, one of the RAF's Directors of Mechanical

Engineering commented in *Flight International* that 'cost exercises on a hypothetical frontline force of sixty strike aircraft, costing £800,000 each, showed that a reduction in operational reliability from 95 per cent to 83 per cent would call for twelve more aircraft, at a capital cost of £9.6 million'. From a maintenance perspective, studies on maintenance costs at the time over a fifteen-year period showed that these were running at approximately just over three times the purchase price.[56] It was thus that aircraft reliability and the RAF's approach to maintenance was highly significant to logistics; a clear understanding of this was important in that it enabled a better understanding of current and future equipment and spares requirements.

One of the main factors in achieving effective and economical maintenance from both an engineering and logistics perspective was the provision of data, though it took some time before the logistics organisation's role in this work was recognised by the wider RAF support community. At the heart of the work to provide this information was a dedicated unit, initially formed in January 1947 as the Air Ministry's Servicing Development Unit at RAF Wattisham in Suffolk. By the beginning of 1950, the Unit had become the Central Servicing Development Establishment (CSDE), moving to RAF Swanton Morley in Norfolk in January 1958 where it was to remain until much of the RAF's Logistics and Engineering management organisations relocated to RAF Wyton in 1995.[57] The size of the data collection task which was essential to the analytical task of the various organisations within CSDE was substantial and, by 1968, a separate organisation at Swanton Morley, known as the maintenance data centre, was formed to collate information on engineering faults with aircraft and equipment.[58] By 1978, for example, RAF and RN aircraft were sustaining defects at the rate of 1,400 a day—some half a million a year—which generated a vast quantity of paper defect reports.[59]

One major user of all that data was the Supply Services and Management Studies Wing (SSMW) within CSDE. Under a Supply Branch wing commander, the wing was responsible for calculating likely spares requirements and testing these assumptions with sophisticated mathematical modelling techniques before passing recommendations for purchasing to the RAF's initial provisioning authority in Harrogate. The importance of this supply presence was recognised at the first stage of rationalisation studies in 1993, when OC CSDE declared that as long as CSDE had more than one wing, one would always be commanded by a Supply Branch officer to give a balanced perspective to CSDE's work. Having honed the skills and techniques required for forecasting in Cold War scenarios, SSMW played a crucial role in developing spares packages for enhanced mobility of all units in the mobility and deployed support study of 1993 and, one Friday afternoon in 1991, produced recommendations for the first FAPs for Harrier GR5 operations to deploy four Harriers to Turkey for the first Operation Warden. For all the sophisticated modelling and forecasting techniques available, however, serious account was taken of the judgement of the wing's 120 experienced technicians, whose knowledge was used to refine the outputs from models and simulations. This unique combination of human intelligence, technical judgement and mathematical modelling did much to improve the accuracy of spares forecasting and to validate recommendations from equipment manufacturers. In the case of the E-3 Sentry, some $12 million was saved by reducing the recommendations made by Boeing without detriment to fleet availability. It was also possible, using reliability data from existing types, to build hypothetical aircraft types.

Logistics Research

One of the many recommendations which resulted from SDR 98 was the formation of a tri-service logistics analysis and research organisation (LARO). The RAF element of this largely came from the Logistics Research Wing (LRW) at Hendon, which had been a 'think tank' on inventory control and management techniques. LARO brought LRW and the equivalent from the Army and Royal Navy together and complemented the work being conducted by CSDE. This built on the expertise of the three services and brought together in one organisation their logistics business knowledge, academic expertise and a range of analytical skills. Among the objectives of this new organisation was a research commitment into inventory improvements, optimising costs against system availability and to monitor advances in new technology and commercial logistics models. The establishment of LARO not only focussed the inventory optimisation skills of the three services but provided an independent view and source of advice for the range of weapons system project teams which had begun to form within the DLO at this time.

Managing the Inventory Size

The size of the RAF's inventory was a constant 'headache' for RAF Logistics. By 1988, the inventory had reached its peak post-war size of around 1.6 million line items, but with the number of aircraft type/marks reducing from sixty-six in 1945 to fifty-six in 1982. The increase in the size of the inventory, despite the reduction in aircraft types, reflected aircraft and systems complexity. Efforts continued to reduce the size of the inventory with perhaps the Holland stockholding review of 1989 making the greatest progress in this respect. The size of the inventory fell quite quickly and by the mid to late 1990s had levelled to around 800,000 line items.

The formation of the DLO in 2000 brought a pan-Defence focus to the quest to reduce stock levels, much of which had built up as a result of the reserves of equipment which were required during the Cold War. The SDR of 1998 had set a 20 per cent (£2.2 billion) stock reduction target for non-munitions stocks which was to be achieved by April 2001. The target was actually exceeded with the Air environment achieving savings of some £1 billion, largely through reductions in engine spares for the Tornado,

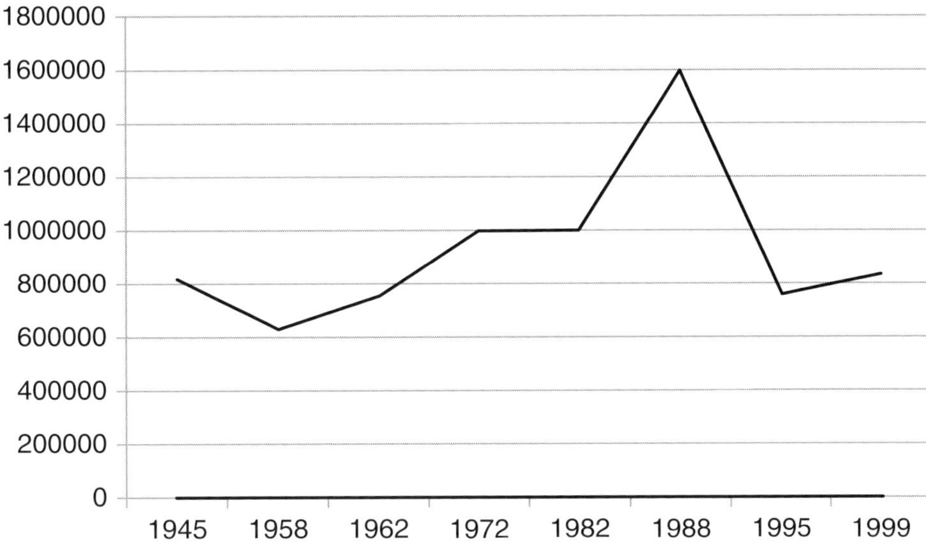

Figure 5: Approximate size of the RAF inventory, 1945–1999.

avionics kits, Nimrod flight control units, and radar installation spares. When the National Audit Office published its report on the MOD's progress in reducing stocks in 2002, the Air environment was holding some £12 billion stock of which £5.4 billion had no forecast demand, including £1 billion of stock which was classed as inactive. More tellingly, of the £6.5 billion where there was a forecast demand, the estimated time taken for this to be issued to users (known as the stock turn) was over sixty years.[60] Work remains ongoing to optimise what is now viewed as a Defence inventory, through a whole range of techniques ranging from the use of more sophisticated analytical software tools improving logistics IT systems and innovative contracting techniques; in the case of the latter, direct supply from industry as and when required, is a concept which reduces the need to hold stock.

Managing the Supply Chain

The end of the Cold War, with the formal dissolution of the USSR in December 1991, saw a marked change in Government spending priorities and in the RAF's operational posture. The *Options for Change* review, announced in July 1990, saw the demise of the Cold War as an opportunity to 'reap the peace dividend' and 'make savings in defence'.[61] It did indeed, and the review outlined, *inter alia*, a reduction in manpower across all three services by about 18 per cent by the mid-1990s, with the RAF to reduce in size from 89,000 to around 75,000. Moreover, two of the four RAF bases in Germany were to close, along with the withdrawal of six RAF squadrons.[62] The RAF Logistics organisation had already recognised that greater effort needed to be made to improve performance and to achieve greater value for money. By 1993, a number of major initiatives were well underway which included the rationalisation of equipment depots and improving the effectiveness of IP through the wider application of ILS to improve equipment reliability, maintainability and availability.

One new approach that also emerged at this time was a concept known as support chain management (SCM), an initiative spearheaded by Wing Commander David Williams. Based on the commercial world's concept of supply chain management, where the various logistics activities between a supplier and customer were managed holistically, the RAF took a slightly wider view to include contracting, maintenance policy, and the management of component repair; this accounted for the subtle change in wording from Supply to Support. Many at the time argued that SCM was not really radical at all and that more collaborative working had already started to achieve the conceptual aims of this initiative. There was some mileage in the view, but developments in logistic IT enabled a much more informed view of the supply (or support) chain to be taken and for the whole logistic function to be considered as a single, integrated process. Much of it affected the policy and planning process and had three core concepts: reducing the size of the inventory to place stock on the shelves as a last resort, awareness of the cost drivers in the total chain and the application of best or better business practice.[63] Within the RAF's Logistics community (the Supply Branch and Trades at the time), the Supply Policy staffs at RAF Brampton, led by Group Captain Glen Morton, managed the implementation through the RAF Supply and Movements Strategy, much of which involved a top to bottom review of the business to adjust it to align with the SCM philosophy.

One particular technique within the new approach was express chain management, a concept that enabled logisticians to 'squeeze more performance out of the support chain than was normally required to support day-to-day task'; much of this involved, for example, the use of dormant contracts with industry and increased output from in-house and commercial manufacturers.[64] The SCM initiative was not an idealistic concept but an attempt to align established military requirements with emerging industrial good practice.

The formation of the DLO was a watershed as far as RAF Logistics was concerned and introduced tri-service management of what gradually became regarded as the Defence inventory, albeit through IPTs that, on the whole, were organised on a weapon system basis. This focus still saw RAF Logistics personnel working in direct support of aircraft types and related equipment(s), in a similar fashion to MDGs prior to the formation of the DLO.

In time, the concept of a defence supply chain developed, which the MOD defines as a 'Defence controlled network of nodes, comprising resources, activities and distribution options that focus on the rapid flow of information, services and materiel between end users and the Strategic Base to generate, sustain and redeploy operational capability'.[65] This new approach to Defence Logistics also saw an end to the majority of the single-service stock control systems with the introduction of a new system known as 'managing the joint deployed inventory and tri-service policy and procedures in a defence logistics support chain manual'; this latter work was evinced by the establishment in 2002 of an RAF Supply Branch group captain as a defence aviation supply policy director, alongside land and sea equivalents under the DG Defence Support Chain based at Andover. It must be said that much of the RAF's Logistics process, governance, and information system expertise was widely acknowledged by the DLO/DE&S as 'best practice' and was incorporated within the Defence approach to managing the inventory in many areas.

The NATO Codification System

The formation of NATO in 1949 brought a much closer working relationship between the member state armed forces. The growth in the number of aircraft being introduced to RAF service at this time also coincided with a much wider sourcing of components from overseas suppliers who were also providing these items to other NATO nations. The RAF's existing domestic reference number (DRN) system, which had been in use since the early 1920s, had proved to be a popular, albeit relatively simple system. It had drawbacks though, in that there was no easy means of checking if new items were already in use and classified with an existing DRN. It was also difficult to match item records with similar items in the other services or Allies.

It became clear that a common, multi-national, stock identification system would be of considerable benefit, and in in the mid-1950s, a NATO codification system was gradually introduced. This system was based on the American federal catalog system and consisted of a series of rules for naming each item of supply with an overall NATO stock number (NSN) consisting of three distinct elements. The first of these was a four number 'family' grouping for items of the same or similar performance or physical characteristics. The second, a number which identified the country which had assigned the NSN and the third a unique seven-digit number for the specific item.[66] Thus, a humble hand hammer codified in the UK would appear as 5120-99-9104650.[67] Notwithstanding the introduction of NATO codification, DRN referenced items remained in use throughout the RAF inventory for many reasons and the application of NATO codification was a very gradual process. It was not cost effective to apply the new system retrospectively and the old RAF system just fell out of use as new items were introduced to service and were NATO codified. The UK's Defence codification authority was based in Glasgow and its director, a senior civil servant, was a member of the NATO main group of codification directors.

Managing Priorities

Among the many commitments of the RAF's Logistics organisation, the support of aircraft has been its main priority and there were many components that could potentially 'ground' individual aircraft if they could not be replaced when unserviceable. With such an enormous volume of equipment flowing through the RAF supply chain, the identification of these spares was critical in order that they could be given due attention in the issue and movement processes to prevent aircraft 'down time'. As already referred to earlier in this book, the AOG system had been in use since before the Second World War and was defined as a 'special system for rapid supply of items essential to render serviceable aircraft, which are in the hands of RAF Squadrons but are grounded for lack of parts'. In such cases, units were authorised to demand such items using the signal message system on their regional or affiliated MU. If stock was available, it was despatched by the fastest possible means. Where stock was not available, it became known as an 'inability' and the requirement was signalled to the appropriate provisioning office, which would check to see if stock was available at another MU and then instruct that depot to make an issue to the demanding unit. Where no stock was held, the provisioning office issued an instruction for diversion of the required item from the supply contractor direct to the demanding unit. This 'Diversion Order' was copied to the Ministry of Aircraft Production, which then managed the requirement, reported progress to the demanding unit or operational command, and also took any necessary steps to obtain supply from salvage or repair.[68] While the supply of spares by Diversion Order met urgent requirements, it did not enable the build-up of stock in the storage depots, a fact which was leading to significant concern within the DofE in the Air Ministry in March 1941. During November and December 1940, a total of 9,532 diversion orders raised, amounting to an average of 156.24 per day (for eight aircraft types including the Spitfire and Hurricane). In a memorandum to the Air Supply Board, DGE commented that 'this practice is highly dangerous in as much as enemy action at a contractors works will immediately make itself felt in the operational efficiency of the Squadrons, and it is to obviate this dangerous position that stocks are necessary in the Depots'.[69] Overall, the AOG and Diversion Order procedures did not solve the spares shortage problems, but enabled the clear identification of requirements (along with an increased level of urgency) which were directly leading to aircraft being grounded.

In the post-war years, the AOG concept remained an important part of priority management and saw some minor refinements, such as the introduction of the 'V' Force on Ground (VOG) category, which was introduced specifically for the management of high priority spares which were grounding any of the Valiant, Victor, or Vulcan aircraft which made up this important Cold War bomber force. Group Captain Andrew Humphries served as a detachment Supply and Movements officer with No. 27 Squadron in Australia in 1972. The squadron was participating in the Sunflower exercises which were to prove that the UK could project conventional airpower around the world. After transiting the USA and the Pacific, the four Vulcans of No. 27 Squadron flew air defence exercises with Singapore and Malaysian air forces over three weeks then redeployed to Darwin to do the same plus conventional bombing range work with the RAAF. Andrew recalled a Vulcan aircraft AOG incident while he was at RAAF Darwin:

> The Vulcan engine door arrived after a week's travelling by civil and RAF air freight. The expense had been enormous and included some considerable organising effort by the staffs of Strike and Air Support Commands. I clambered into the cab alongside my corporal driver of the flatbed truck that carried the enormous packing case. I was determined to be the bearer of the good news when we presented it to the maintenance crew of the grounded aircraft. A Chief Technician and Sergeant emerged from the crew room when our arrival was announced on the flight line. We helped them to remove the plywood box lid—it was a four-man job. The CT leaned right over the complex piece of fuselage snugly supported by struts and wooden brackets in the container and scratched away with a penknife at the paint on the leading edge of a semi-circular air intake to reveal a crack in the metal just like the one in the engine door fitted to the aircraft. My disappointment was palpable 'Oh, not to worry' said the engineer. 'I think they all came cracked from the manufacturer. We mended the original with Araldite and its flying now. I ordered another door just to see if it was in any better state than the one we already had.' In my formative years as a Supply officer, I learned about RAF Engineers from this incident.

The RAF's priority management system was embedded within the day-to-day working of the logistics systems with most units having a priority progression cell, with a similar office at Command level (which worked closely with the aircraft and commodity specific role offices) to provide the all-important liaison with the SMBs at MOD Harrogate. Of the many areas to which RAF unit OC Supply Squadrons needed to pay close attention, priorities—especially AOGs—were probably top of the list and were invariably the subject of quite heated discussion with unit engineering and operations staff. The provision of an all-important delivery forecast was a significant part of managing the effectiveness of RAF operational output.

Managing Stock Losses

So far, this chapter has described the various elements of inventory management in the RAF but one significant topic remains that has often been of considerable political importance—the reconciliation of equipment losses at the conclusion of a conflict. Although regulations stated that war losses should be 'struck off' charge, in the case of Operation Granby in 1991 and in light of the Public Accounts Committee's allegations that 'British equipment found its way into Bosnia', the Department of Internal Audit ruled that only those losses that occurred in direct support of operations could be treated as war losses and the burden of proof would need to be high. HQ STC was therefore tasked with investigating the total RAF equipment discrepancies which amounted to deficiencies of £135,086,199 and surpluses of £69,612,680. This situation had arisen for a variety of reasons, but rapid deployment of squadrons, frequent no-notice moves in-theatre, and a very rapid withdrawal made the control of equipment very difficult. Additionally, inadequate numbers of Supply staff had initially been deployed and the wartime accounting measures used were designed for Cold War operations, not for highly mobile expeditionary warfare. Moreover, in an era of high dependence on Supply information technology, personnel were not trained to use manual accounting. Lastly, there was intermingling of RAF, RN, and Army equipment in-theatre which further added to the accounting confusion.

The reconciliation of the Operation Granby surpluses and deficiencies was the subject of an eighteen-month project led by RAF Logistics Policy and Plans staff. During this time, they examined inventory records at units and depots, cross-checking them with the other services' records of surpluses and deficiencies, studied the results from CSDE's modelling to establish the consumption of aircraft role equipment and finally carried out searches with the Harrogate SMBs on specific items. The final reconciliation revealed total deficiencies at £68,514,988 and surpluses of £44,508,492. The final report found that 'Supply staffs acted with great diligence in husbanding resources While rising to the challenges of the operation and working under adverse conditions'. Moreover, DGSM (RAF) certified that 'the global stock balances were correct and that the deficiencies did not represent physical losses but were in fact accounting errors. On 2 August 1994, the C-in-C RAF Strike Command formally struck-off equipment discrepancies of £68,514,918.10. The findings of the report gave further impetus to the deployable USAS project which is described in Chapter Ten. One example, but one which illustrates the difficulties and costs involved in reconciling stock records at the end of RAF operations, thereby ensuring that the public 'purse' is protected.

Stock Control at the Equipment Depots

The RAF's equipment depots provided the main conduit for the flow of equipment into the service from industry and provided not just buffer stock from which units could replenish, but storage for some of the larger items in the inventory which were beyond unit capacity. With the growth in the number of such depots during the Second World War, the only way which stock could be controlled effectively was through the master provisioning scheme. Generally speaking, some five-months' worth of stock was held at the depots, with a further three-months' worth at RAF bases.[70] All the ESDs had their own stock control and accounting sections, and most had an entire squadron dedicated to stocktaking, an important activity that aimed to check the account on paper with reality on the shelf, both for location and quantity. Some depots had a sizeable packaging squadron that, among many and varied specialist tasks, were able to re-package bulk buys of consumable items into smaller, pre-packed quantities; this often proved to be a more cost-effective means of purchasing and supply. Many of the depots also had a repair and overhaul capability for some equipment types. No. 7 MU at Quedgeley, for example, had an excellent furniture repair line which returned worn and broken furniture to as new condition and was very cost-effective. Group Captain Andrew Humphries recalled how when he was OC Supply and Movements Squadron at RAF Wittering in 1986–1987, they sent lots of old, scruffy wooden furniture to Quedgeley to be refurbished and transformed offices across the station. This was a time when budgetary limitations made modern furniture hard to obtain.

No. 7 MU RAF Quedgeley is worth a specific mention. Subjected to a contracting-out process in the 1980s, it was managed for five or six years by Securicor, who, in the process, 'bought out' the terms and conditions of the largely civil service workforce who had been transferred to them with the contract and had optimised a number of working practices. A Supply Branch Group captain station commander and contract owner was supported directly by a small number of Supply Branch officers and civil servants in a performance monitoring role. On the occasion of contract re-tender, an in-house bid was successful, benefitting from the changes wrought by Securicor. For several years, the unit withstood challenging audits and investigations, consistently demonstrating value for money and cost-effectiveness, being held up as an example of how a public sector organisation could be better value for money than a private sector contractor. Eventually, as a sacrifice to an imposed requirement to reduce numbers within Logistics Command, despite its role going to the private sector and costing more, it was closed in 1996.

With the formation of the DLO, a Defence Storage and Distribution Agency (DSDA) was formed to manage the remaining single service depots as part of the new the defence supply chain; DSDA's agency status was removed in 2010 and it became part of joint support chain services. The closure of the RAF's last equipment supply depot at Stafford in 2006 saw its stocks of equipment relocated to nearby Donnington and Bicester, with stock control becoming a Defence, rather than RAF, responsibility.

Stock Control on RAF Units

As described in Chapter Four, up until the introduction of computerised stock control in the 1960s, stock control on RAF units was a laborious, manual process. In broad terms, the RAF's logistic system relied on its various units, from flying stations and various support units (both at home and overseas), through to the various types of equipment depots, holding and maintaining a set level of stock (establishment). This level was expressed in numerical terms (usually in months) as a lower and an upper limit. The lower or minimum establishment was the point at which a stock replenishment order could be placed and took into account the lead-time from order placement, to receipt of the items; the items remaining in stock served as a 'buffer' stock to meet user demands. Replenishment orders were not permitted to bring the total stock holding above a maximum establishment level, a figure which regulated the total amount of stock holdings in the inventory, thereby limiting excessive cost growth. For most RAF units, the maximum figure was usually three months and the minimum two months. For depots, a similar principle was applied but the calculation was somewhat more complex, taking into account reserve stocks for emergencies and was based on a core stock at the depots amounting to an estimated six months' worth of equipment and fourteen months' worth on order with suppliers.[71] At depot and unit level, equipment due to arrive (known as dues in) or about to be issued (known as dues out) also had to be taken into account.

The Role of Industry: Just a Supplier?

One of the more significant areas of change that the RAF began to experience on its bases at home and overseas was the greater involvement of contractor support. Until the 1970s, the manning on RAF units largely consisted of uniformed personnel along with a significant number of civil servants and locally employed civilians. As far as aircraft maintenance was concerned, this was still largely carried out using the four lines of maintenance concept. The quest to reduce support costs gained greater momentum following the review by John Nott, the Conservative Secretary of State for Defence, in 1981. One of the many issues with which MOD (PE) and the RAF were grappling in this context was the enormous costs involved when carrying out IP for new aircraft entering service. It became clear that a more innovative approach was required and the concept of a contractor providing varying degrees of in-service logistics support began to emerge.

The ideal opportunity for this concept to be introduced in a relatively low risk area came with the decision to develop a replacement for the Jet Provost trainer aircraft in 1984. The decision to procure the replacement turboprop Tucano T1, built under licence by Short Brothers of Belfast, led to an unsolicited proposal by the company to provide most of the logistic support for the aircraft for the first four years of its in-service life. This commitment was highly significant in that it minimised the RAF's investment in spares and other logistic facilities, until enough consumption data became available to make a more informed decision on the optimal support policy for the longer term; the spares buy by Shorts was augmented by production line assets when required. There was an additional benefit in that the package, known as augmented logistics support (ALS), also enabled experience to be gained on contracting logistics services in the support area. To provide a baseline against which Short's performance could be monitored, the company was contracted to ensure that the AOG rate did not exceed 3 per cent of the in-use aircraft fleet or 5 per cent of the in-use aircraft at any one operating RAF station. The concept was a significant change for RAF Logistics and saw, for the first time, a contractor become considerably more involved in the support process. Shorts established an ALS store (essentially a mini depot) at RAF Scampton which was designed to provide supply service to the four RAF units operating the Tucano (Church Fenton, Cranwell, Linton-on-Ouse, and Scampton).

Additionally, forward holding stores were located on the operating units adjacent to the first and second line engineering facilities; these stores were manned by supply personnel from the respective units and were the interface between the contractor and the unit engineering sections. No stocks of Tucano ALS spares were held within the unit Supply Squadrons or the RAF equipment supply depots.[72]

Delivery of the aircraft was delayed and, by the end of the four-year period, not only had steady state operation not been achieved, but the policies for future logistic support were not in place. Consequently, the decision was taken to extend the contract by a further two and a half years to achieve this important balance. The ALS arrangement did take time to bed-in, as might be expected with any form of innovative support arrangement. Lessons were learned by both Shorts and the RAF and, by the end of 1994, an off-the-shelf satisfaction rate of some 95 per cent was being achieved. It was also found that Shorts was able to achieve significantly cheaper purchasing than by in-service agencies. Overall, ALS (or Tucano logistics support as it became following the contract extension) offered significant cost savings to the RAF by transferring the risk and uncertain period of initial provisioning to a contractor. Although the RAF would eventually need to purchase spares to support the Tucano fleet, the consumption data used to calculate the buy was based on actual usage and considerably more accurate than what was often seen as the educated guesswork of traditional methods.[73]

Collaborative Projects[74]

It was not surprising that, given the substantial costs of developing new aircraft, that international collaboration would be considered as a potential means of a more economical approach to acquisition through sharing development costs and, hopefully, reducing acquisition costs by creating larger fleets across participating countries. Subsequent research revealed that while this was so, the additional costs generated by achieving collaboration and inevitable compromises negated some, if not all, of the hoped-for savings, led to delays and even created compromise-inspired operational performance limitations.

Another driver for collaboration was political ambition as, in the 1960s, Britain's political desire to gain membership of the European Union or Common Market led to the military and civil aviation industry becoming a bargaining chip. There are those who argue that Britain gave away its lead in aviation and aerospace technology—an inheritance from the Second World War—through this political horse-trading. Others contend that Britain gave up its technological lead in order to attract funds from the USA. This book is not the place for these debates but will concentrate on the supply chain challenges of international collaboration.

Anglo-French Helicopters

One of the earliest post-Second World War initiatives was taken in February 1967 when the British and French Governments signed a 'Memorandum of Understanding' to collaborate in a joint programme to produce three helicopters: the SA 330 Puma, the SA 341 Gazelle, and the WG.13 Lynx, with Aérospatiale and Westland Helicopters collaborating on airframe production and assembly, Turbomeca and Rolls-Royce on the engines and a number of second tier suppliers in France and in the UK. As part of the wider requirement to provide dedicated RAF personnel to this project in France, the RAF provided MOD (PE) with a Supply Branch squadron leader based at Marignane, some fifteen miles from Marseille, to act as the UK Supply Liaison Officer (UKSLO). This post acted as the link, initially between the respective Defence ministries and the manufacturers, co-located on the premises of Aerospatiale with the state organisation known as SIAR (*Service de Surveillance Industrielle de l'Armement*), responsible for overseeing Aerospatiale's contract for quality and output schedule. Another SIAR team was located at Turbomeca. While this RAF presence was adequate during the phase prior to introduction to service, once the Puma, first, came into service, it was plagued by AOG rates attributable to spares shortages, frequently into double figures and often in excess of 50 per cent of a fleet of less than thirty aircraft. As responsibility for the helicopter fleet moved from Air Support Command to Strike Command in 1972,

Puma helicopter refuelling. (*Crown Copyright—Air Historical Branch MoD*)

pressure on the UKSLO to act as a spares shortage trouble-shooter on behalf of Strike Command became intense; the latter was more accustomed to AOG rates in single figures as part of its NATO generation task and pilot training was being compromised by lack of available aircraft This in turn highlighted the fact that the UKSLO was single-handed and worked for MOD (PE) on production issues, not for Strike Command or the appropriate SMB in the in-service phase. Strike Command's solution was to appoint a bilingual officer specifically as a trouble-shooter, though this at times created tension between the MOD (PE), the SMB in Harrogate, and HQ STC.

Lessons Learned from the Helicopters Project

This experience highlighted three fundamental differences between the UK and, particularly, their French partner which would resurface under the next two collaborative projects: the historical context and impact on the relationship between users and aerospace manufacturers; operational requirements and a key difference between English contract law and that used in European partner countries.

From a historical perspective, and particularly throughout the Second World War, British aviation suppliers had become accustomed to doing whatever it took to support the RAF effort, including where essential, robbing an aircraft or other production lines to meet operational needs. French industry did not have that heritage. During the 1950s and 1960s, as part of the effort to rebuild France's economy after the war, more effort from the French aviation industry went into meeting export orders than its own military orders. Secondly, though part of the NATO political structure, France was outside (though co-operating closely with) the NATO military structure. This meant that France did not have to commit to meeting NATO force generation rates, nor undergo evaluations of the ability to do so. This meant there was a resigned acceptance within the French military that their needs frequently took second place to meeting the needs of export orders. Thirdly, under English contract law there is no concept of a penalty clause. Failure by a supplier to meet contractual commitments leads to remedies that, at their simplest, mean that a disappointed customer might seek to recover in law from the supplier, such funds as are required to put the customer into a position of not having expended funds to achieve the same aim. English courts cannot apply a punitive penalty for failing to meet a requirement. In French contract law (and that of Germany, Italy, and Spain with Tornados and Typhoons in mind), a contract can be drafted so that the supplier will suffer financial penalties for failing to deliver on time. This meant that for the helicopters, it was extremely difficult to divert spares from aircraft production lines to resolve a spares shortage at an RAF airfield, particularly from French production lines which had full order books for Pumas. The RAF had bought only twenty-eight. This situation was to continue with the Jaguar.

Anglo-French Jaguars

The French 'connection' was extended in 1974 when the RAF received the first of its SEPECAT Jaguar GR1s, produced as a joint venture between the French company Breguet Aviation, the British Aircraft Corporation, and Rolls-Royce/SNECMA.[75] Prior to its entry into service, the Jaguar had had a difficult birth. Initially designed to meet a French Naval Aviation specification for a carrier-borne training aircraft, the Jaguar was a partnership between BAC and Breguet Aviation. Breguet was then taken over by Avions Marcel Dassault. For Dassault, the Jaguar was seen as a cuckoo in its inherited nest. Dassault's focus was on building and selling the Mirage, a national product without the complication of international collaboration, and Dassault was less than committed to it. By now, it had metaphorphosed into a ground attack fighter-bomber for the French *Armée de l'Air* and the RAF. The latter set about with help from the BAC, later the BAe, to specify weapons system upgrades and engine power upgrades to make it a more capable weapons system. The French seldom wished to adopt the modifications that were to result in very different aircraft models and capabilities within use in France and in the UK. Interestingly, the British version was to go on to be modified further as an export version and sold well to third party countries, almost despite Dassault.

The supply of French and British-made spares for both the RAF and the French Air Force was provided for under a unique agreement known as FRUGAL (France *Royaume Uni Gestion d'une Association Logistique*), which required both air forces to provide dedicated staffs to the project. This was on a much larger scale than the helicopters with more than 500 aircraft split between the two air forces and was an opportunity to seek opportunities to drive down in-service operating costs.

As a contribution to trying to capture economies of scale and to avoid unnecessary costs for major insurance assemblies which need to be bought to avoid excessive re-jigging costs, once aircraft production lines are closed down, the two Air Forces agreed to categorise all spares as stock or non-stock, each labelled British or French determined by the country of manufacture. Each country had to receive consumption data and needs forecasts from the other; for its stock items, it had to be capable of meeting both air forces' requirements off the shelf. For non-stock insurance buy items, the two air forces agreed on what should be bought and held in the country of manufacture until and when the partner country called for it. This approach had the benefit, perhaps unintended, that each air force went out of its way to meet the needs of its partner and to avoid being found to have failed its partner. It also had the benefit that spares-chasing for AOG situations had the advantage of being a dialogue between the Government representative of the manufacturing country and its native supplier, unlike the helicopters where the dialogue was between a client in one country and the aerospace supplier in the other country. Noticeable throughout the life of the Jaguar, however, was that RAF reliance on determined spares progression was always consistently higher than for their French

Jaguar pictured at RAF Abingdon. (*Crown Copyright—Air Historical Branch MoD*)

Air Force counterparts even when they were using the Jaguar in war zones in Africa While the RAF was training and meeting NATO generation rates.

Reverting to the point about dedicated staffs, the French proceeded to form a team known as ORLOJ (*Organisation Logistique* Jaguar), which within two years was in purpose-built accommodation in Merignac, Bordeaux, together with spares storage and a transportation hub, and encompassing supply management, IT, and accounting staffs. ORLOJ (or more correctly ORLOJ-COGER) was a hybrid organisation headed by an *ingenieur chef de l'armament* (group captain equivalent). The ORLOJ part was manned by French civil servants or *Armée de l'Air* personnel responsible for policy, systems and overseeing the day-to-day operating team. The latter were civilians employed by a company called COGER though most were retired *Armée de l'Air* officers and SNCOs.

Within the UK, No. 16 MU, RAF Stafford was selected as the depot with primary responsibility as the transport hub and for the receipt and subsequent supply of French manufactured spares for the RAF and for the supply of British manufactured spares for the French, using a dedicated road container service which operated between Stafford and Bordeaux. A system of airfreighting was used sparingly for urgently required spares (see Chapter Seven). Both the Carlisle and Quedgeley ESDs, however, retained responsibility for their traditional ranges regardless of source, which caused ORLOJ considerable irritation as it was quite a departure from the principle of dedicated staff to the Jaguar, which they had honoured.

The FRUGAL agreement saw a welcome addition to posting opportunities for RAF Supply Branch officers with the establishment of a liaison officer post (the UK

FRUGAL Liaison Officer (UKFLO)) initially at Velizy, later at Bordeaux, looking after all policy and systems matters between the two Air Forces. The French Air Force had a reciprocal arrangement in the UK at squadron leader or commandant level, the French FRUGAL Liaison Officer (FFLO) located initially at Stafford but later at Harrogate within the SMB responsible for Jaguar spares provisioning and liaison with French partners. When the thorny problem of AOG rates and spares shortages began to surface within the OCU at Lossiemouth, HQ STC established a priority spares progression post for a bilingual flight lieutenant co-located with ORLOJ.

An amusing anecdote relating to this flight lieutenant post was that the requirement was identified by HQ STC in the middle of the C-in-C Strike Command's Economy Project (SCEPO), of which one aspect was that no new posts were to be established within Strike Command. Such was the pressure exerted by the Air Staffs because spares shortages were jeopardising aircrew conversion to the Jaguar, that the HQ STC Supply Officer persuaded DGS (RAF) to reinforce his proposal to the C-in-C to make an exception to his restriction. A young bilingual flight lieutenant was instructed to meet DGS (RAF) in his car at the entrance to HQ STC and had five minutes to convince the director that he was capable of making a difference to spares shortages by being located in France at the ORLOJ organisation in order to facilitate travel to suppliers and to exhort pressure on his French colleagues. He was successful and the requirement was accepted by the C-in-C. This gave birth to a post that went on to ensure that RAF priority spares requirements were afforded priority management which, as explained earlier, was not customary for the French Air Force.

The lack of a dedicated team in the UK to the Jaguar project also manifested itself in the other essential interfaces between ORLOJ and the RAF; IT staffs had to come from Hendon where system changes to the RAF Supply Computer system were complex and painfully slow in the face of rapid changes achieved by the dedicated team at ORLOJ. Engineering input for modifications had to come from London and Swanton Morley, yet all was centralised at ORLOJ. To overcome these drawbacks and to present a coordinated and single point of contact, the RAF appointed a bi-lingual squadron leader at Harrogate who had a team dedicated to supporting the aircraft modifications process and to leading the British delegations for IT, transportation, modifications, systems and policies to bi-national meetings and to supporting the group captain level bi-national senior policy meetings. By this device, the RAF contrived to keep on side with the French organisation and offered a series of judicious postings to Bordeaux and Harrogate for officers with appropriate inter-personal skills. It also kept the French from losing patience with what they saw as a British failure to stick to the original agreement.

One further amusing anecdote concerns the weekly container lorry run from Stafford to Bordeaux and return, carrying UK manufactured and stocked spares to France, returning with French manufactured and stocked spares for the RAF.

Within the agreed split of responsibilities between the two nations, transportation had been allocated to the RAF who chose to contract-out the task rather than use a RAF in-house resource. In those days, before mobile phones and GPS, there was some nervousness surrounding the first run from Stafford to Bordeaux, as well as a desire to record the event for news media as a further manifestation of co-operation between the two air forces. The shine was rather taken off the photo-opportunity when the container vehicle rolled into the ORLOJ hangar at Bordeaux on time- but was coloured a vivid yellow with GEEST bananas in large blue lettering emblazoned on both sides of the container. Having left arranging the container until the last minute, the RAF had contracted for a container lorry and had taken what was available.

Tornado

Just as the Jaguar and its unique supply support arrangement were beginning to settle down and were clearly much more effective than the arrangements for the Anglo-French helicopters, thinking in Whitehall was turning to the same challenges for the next collaborative project—the Tornado. Before considering the supply support arrangements, it is useful to describe the overall project. One of the largest collaborative programmes to emerge in the post-war period was the multirole combat aircraft (MRCA), or the Tornado as it became. The feasibility study for this aircraft was completed in April 1969, with the memorandum of understanding being signed for the development phase in July 1970. At the time, this was the largest European joint industrial venture ever undertaken and involved collaboration between the UK (producing the nose section, rear fuselage, and the tail); the Federal Republic of Germany (producing the centre fuselage, the wings sweep mechanism, and radar); and Italy (producing the wings, flaps, and slats). The design leadership for the RB199 engine rested with Rolls-Royce.[76] Two international consortia were created by the manufacturers to manage cross-border production and manufacture: Panavia for the airframe, avionics and weapons systems and Rolls-Royce for the engines. The RAF eventually ordered 220 of the Interdictor/Strike (IDS) version and 165 of the Air Defence variant.[77] The sheer size of the project required an extensive managerial organisation, not least of which was the coordination of production and assembly. The project was managed through the NATO MRCA development and production organisation (NAMMO), while the day-to-day work in developing and producing the aircraft and spares for in-service support became the responsibility of the NATO MRCA development and production management agency (NAMMA), which was based in Munich.

The RAF's Supply organisation was actively involved in numerous aspects of this project from the outset. Several Supply Branch posts (and Engineer Branch posts) were created within NAMMA, integrated with German and Italian colleagues responsible for receiving orders from the customer nations, placing orders, modifications control, IT systems, and many other supply support tasks. Their primary allegiance was to NAMMA, not to their native countries—something not always appreciated by individuals within their home nations who felt they had 'turned native'.

In the UK, the RAF established an integrated supply and engineering policy staff known as the directorate of Tornado Engineering and Supply (DTES (RAF), headed by an Engineering Branch air commodore, and largely based in MOD London. The supply management and provisioning (initial and re-provisioning) aspects were the responsibility of a group captain at MOD Harrogate with specific branches responsible for an input to the initial provisioning task, amounting to some 300,000 items. In time, and as development and production progressed, existing and some new, dedicated Supply management branches became involved in a wider range of activities such as modifications, technical publications and explosives, bringing more deputy directorates into play, thus compounding the challenges of collaborative working and staying on message.[78]

Collaborative working brought many wider benefits, not least of which was the opportunity to work closely with personnel from other nations. Working with the Germans, for example, brought new perspectives on humour, a factor that often proved to be a key element of any collaborative project. While decisions were generally made on a consensus basis, time and time again, it seemed any permutation of two nations would disagree with the third nation and less than effective compromises were agreed as the only way forward.

The British experience of working with the French on international projects had provided hard-earned lessons that were, at times, well received by German and Italian counterparts, and at other times, were rather resented by them. What was clear was that the NAMMA arrangement for in-service support—another link in the chain between air forces' end-customers and industry—removed that element of customer pressure on industry, which had made the supply arrangements for Jaguar so much more successful than those for the helicopters. The primacy of the production line, as known for the Anglo-French helicopters, was prevalent, particularly when the Tornado was then sold to third party countries. Within the RAF, there was a high level of frustration with spares shortages prejudicing both aircrew conversion and training and, subsequently, aircraft availability to meet NATO generation rates.

Typhoon

The most recent collaborative project that is intended to form the core of the RAF's combat aircraft capability until at least 2030 is the Eurofighter Typhoon. This aircraft was largely intended to replace the Tornado F3 fighter and the Jaguar ground attack aircraft. Originally conceived in 1983 during the Cold War with the future European fighter aircraft programme, the development and production of this aircraft evolved to become a collaboration between the UK, Germany, Italy, and Spain. The story of this project illustrates just how risky and turbulent collaborative programmes can be and the difficulties which they can present for logistics.

While this type of project can undoubtedly make the development of cutting-edge technology more affordable through cost sharing, as described earlier, working with other nations, each of which have their own economic and political agendas, can prove to be problematical. In the case of the Eurofighter, the end of the Cold War reduced European demand for fighter aircraft and debate over the cost and work share, has been particularly difficult, leading to widespread changes to order numbers and aircraft design.[79]

The production of the aircraft is unique in that it is built through four separate assembly lines with each partner company assembling its own national aircraft, but constructing the same parts for all aircraft. The arrangement is, however, a complex mix of manufacturing responsibilities consisting of: the German company Premium AEROTEC building the main fuselage; the Spanish company EADS CASA responsible for the right wing and leading-edge slats; the UK company BAe Systems building the front fuselage, canopy, dorsal spine, tail fin, inboard flaperons, and rear fuselage section; and the Italian company Alenia Aermacchi responsible for the left wing, outboard flaperons, and rear fuselage sections. The four-company Eurojet consortium, consisting of Rolls-Royce (UK), Avio (Italy), ITP (Spain), and MTU Aero Engines (Germany), is responsible for the aircraft's EJ200 engine. The RAF's first batch of aircraft off-contract (tranche one) was for fifty-three F2 variants, with the first squadron at RAF Coningsby taking delivery in 2005 for air defence duties. The requirement to fulfil a potential requirement to deploy on Operation Herrick in Afghanistan saw a UK modification programme on these aircraft to develop an air-to-ground capability, with all aircraft becoming multi-role as the FGR4 in July 2008. A further 107 aircraft are to be delivered to the RAF under tranche two and tranche three, although there are plans for the service to retire its tranche one fleet by 2018.[80]

Similar to the Tornado aircraft programme, an international organisation was established in Munich to manage the project on behalf of the partner nations, known as the NATO European fighter management agency (NEFMA); the RAF Supply Branch at the time provided a wing commander and a squadron leader as part of the agency's Logistics Section. In time, it made sense to provide a more streamlined approach to the international management of both Tornado and the Eurofighter as a number of companies and organisations were involved in both projects. Consequently, both NAMMA and NEFMA were combined in the mid-1990s to form the NATO Eurofighter and Tornado management agency (NETMA) but remained in Munich. The same endemic weaknesses as for NAMMA and the Tornado continued with in-service support always taking a back seat to production with an adverse effect on spares availability.

RAF Typhoon and Russian Bear reconnaissance aircraft. (*Crown Copyright—Air Historical Branch MoD*)

US Sourced Equipment

A further international dimension is where the RAF has bought aircraft from another country, particularly the USA. While equipment had been sourced from the US for many years, it had frequently been for items contracted with a British aircraft or equipment supplier, who in turn ensured the supply of such items from a US sub-contractor. The purchase in the mid-1960s by the MOD of a number of Lockheed C130 Hercules and McDonnell Douglas F4 Phantoms required different supply support arrangements, as did arrangements for the small fleet of Boeing AWACS aircraft.

Phantom F4 and Hercules C130

The RAF initially brought into service 170 F-4 Phantoms, but in the early 1970s, they also received the fifty-two F4K initially used by the Royal Navy's Fleet Air Arm, later purchasing a further fifteen F4J in 1984. The British Phantoms were fitted with a number of British-supplied items including Rolls-Royce Spey engines (apart from the 1984 purchase fitted with Pratt and Whitney engines). For the British-sourced items, normal supply management and provisioning activities took place. The

RAF bought sixty-six C-130 Hercules C1 of which thirty were later 'stretched' to be designated C3 with six converted to airborne re-fueller tankers, designated C1K. At the beginning of 2000, twenty-five C1s were replaced by ten C5 variants and fifteen C5 variants.

For both aircraft types, the source of supply from the USA was an arrangement called the cooperative logistics system (CLS). In essence, the RAF, acting on behalf of its own users and the Fleet Air Arm for its Phantoms, deposited funds with the US Treasury and subsequently placed orders, treated in the same way as both US users of the aircraft and other countries who had bought the aircraft. Issues to the UK were then made once the funds had been drawn down from the RAF's 'deposit', in accordance with agreed timescales. The RAF formed two MOD Supply management branches alongside the ESD at Carlisle to provision items from the USA and positioned a liaison officer in the USA to act progress chasers on behalf of the SMBs.

10

Information Technology

The first use of automated data processing by RAF Logistics occurred during the war when Maintenance Command introduced Hollerith electro-mechanical card-reading machines at the seven main aircraft equipment depots between 1943 and 1945 as part of the master provisioning scheme. Such equipment was already in use at the central ordnance depots at Chilwell, Didcot, and Weedon, as well as by the civilian company Messrs Joseph Lucas Ltd. The ordnance depots, *inter alia*, were using what was known as the 'new NCR' system, a machine produced by the National Cash Register Company, which was used for posting stock cards and producing an overall stock balance. The depot at Didcot was using the 'Hollerith' system produced by the British Tabulating Machine Co. Ltd, which used paper punch-cards. In essence, these machines were used to punch a series of holes on an inserted card for every movement of stock. The specific details of receipts or issues were punched in code and included information such as the section and reference number, quantity, consignee, and terms of issue. The cards were then used to prepare the daily stock journal for the MU concerned and also the posting sheet for onward transmission to the respective MPO. The first machines were installed at No. 25 MU Hartlebury in November 1943, but it was not until February 1945 that the last of the machines required to equip all the depots were received.[1]

Although primitive by modern standards, the introduction of these machines reduced clerical labour, increased accuracy, and provided an easy method of obtaining statistical data for future provisioning. This system, however, was based upon the concept of maintaining depot stocks at a set establishment level and did not take into account equipment that was held forward at RAF stations. Consequently, the service had no 'global' visibility of equipment and this, not surprisingly, led to much duplication and significant waste. Moreover, it was not possible to carry out what in time was to become known as 'asset re-distribution', where spares holdings on one unit could be used to satisfy the demand requirements of another that was in a nil stock situation.

By the early 1950s, the impending introduction of the RAF's V-bomber force was creating a pressing need for something more sophisticated. A new technology was gaining momentum and was able to provide the way forward. The commercial world was beginning to exploit what was then known as electronic data processing (EDP) (see note in the Definitions section at the front of the book). This technology owed much to the advances made during the Second World War with AA range finders, the later bombsights, and the early computer developed by the code-breaking establishment at Bletchley Park, near Milton Keynes. After so many years of manually intensive stock control methods, largely based on 'Dickensian' manuscript ledgers, the Equipment organisation was about to enter the computer age.

The EPAS office at Binbrook had introduced a Remington Rand Foremost accounting machine, which mechanised this entire process (believed to be in May 1956); use of this machine had significantly improved re-provisioning accuracy and reduced the number of stock accounting and re-provisioning clerks from six to four. Its introduction, however, was not an easy one; some 500 man hours were required to change from the manual ledgers to the mechanised process, while machine operators required special training and took eight to nine weeks to become proficient in its use. The machine was also prone to breakdown. Despite this, it made an enormous difference to the stock accounting process.[2] Not surprisingly, the Binbrook study recommended the widespread use of such machines throughout the RAF although limited evidence survives to illustrate just how far this was implemented.

Remington Rand machine at RAF Binbrook. (*Crown Copyright—Air Historical Branch MoD*)

The Woodgate Study

It was against the growing technical developments in the 1950s that the Air Ministry commissioned a study in 1957, to examine how computer technology could improve efficiency in the areas of civilian pay, airmen's pay and records and the RAF Supply system. By this time, the size of the RAF's inventory was rapidly approaching some 630,000 different items and was forecast to be in the region of 750,000 by 1959. As far as the Supply requirement was concerned, Group Captain A. S. Woodgate, who was to later become a commandant of the RAF Supply Control Centre (SCC) at Hendon, headed the study team. Then, as indeed it remains today, the planning to introduce a computer system was a slow and painstaking affair. The work carried out by Woodgate's team was forward-thinking in many respects but perhaps most significant was a concept which would provide the RAF with a fundamental advantage in years to come. At this time, the British Army, Royal Navy, and the United States forces were all working towards introducing EDP for their supply business. All of these had decided to implement computing at their supply depots rather than at their units. However, Woodgate took the completely opposite view and pursued a strategy that provided computer support at unit level first. Of the many problems faced by the study team was that of how the central computer would communicate with remote users. Consideration was given to using telephone lines (the systems of which were entirely manual at this time) during off-peak periods to transfer data collected on punched cards but, for a variety of reasons, this was rejected.

The study also considered using punched paper tape, sent via the telegraph automatic switching system (TASS) or via a private wire alternative. However, the paper tape option was found to be much better in terms of capacity, cost, and availability. The study took three years and by September 1960, the Air Ministry had developed a contract for a computer installation, a completely redesigned RAF Supply system to incorporate the use of such technology, and plans for a new building at RAF Hendon to house the RAF SCC. The contract for the development, manufacture, and installation of the computer complex was placed with Associated Electrical Industries Ltd (AEI) in September 1960.

The First Generation Computer System: AEI 1010

On 1 July 1961, Wing Commander Bill Lydan and Flying Officer Bruce Reed arrived at RAF Hendon and set up what was to become the RAF SCC in old wooden huts. By 1 August, the first Commandant, Air Commodore Victor Roth was appointed and a forecast of March 1962 was given for the completion of the new SCC building.

It was at this time that the unit's badge was also approved with the appropriate motto 'speed with accuracy'. Timescales were tight with AEI's forecast for delivery of the computer system itself only one month later in April 1962. The SCC building

The first RAF SCC at Hendon, 1961. (*Crown Copyright—Air Historical Branch MoD*)

was actually completed and handed over to the RAF in May 1962 for occupation by a relatively small team of fifteen officers and forty-four civilians. However, AEI were experiencing technical difficulties with the system development and were unable to fulfil their original delivery forecast; the key problem was the production of hardware to match a system that was well ahead of its time. There was plenty of work to keep the SCC staff busy, including questions on training, building construction and alteration, fire precautions, personnel requirements, computer programming, and systems analysis among many other issues. Moreover, and perhaps crucially, the hardware delay allowed more time for thorough testing, in manual simulation, step-by-step, of detailed system processes; the SCC programmers were also able to travel to the AEI factory for program testing.[3]

Technical difficulties persisted but in May 1964, AEI were able to deliver the new machine to Hendon, coincidentally also at the same time as the arrival of the third commandant, a certain Air Commodore A. S. Woodgate. However, the installation and testing were a lengthy business and beset by many problems and this on a machine with only twenty-nine kilobytes of memory. It was not until 20 May 1965 that AEI were able to hand over the system to the RAF. Following intensive programme and system training, the AEI 1010 went live on 1 September 1965. On 3 January 1966, the staff of the SCC and the new AEI 1010 computer system assumed initial control of the 4,000 line items required to support the Jet Provost aircraft.

The new-build RAF SCC at Hendon, 1962. (*Crown Copyright—Air Historical Branch MoD*)

By the time of the official opening ceremony by the Minister of Defence for the RAF, the Rt Hon. Lord Shackleton, on 28 June 1966, other ranges had been added, increasing the number of line items controlled to 100,680.

By January 1967, with a year's operation under its belt, the system was acknowledged as one of the largest fully-integrated inventory systems in the world and was supporting 170 RAF stations at home and overseas; its next challenge was take on the 1.4 million different items left in the RAF inventory. It is interesting to note that at the end of its life, a system designed to control 0.75 million items actually had one million on its books. In terms of other benefits, it was estimated that some £80,000 per annum would be saved over the next ten years with a reduction in the RAF manpower requirement of over 1,600 people.[4]

At RAF station level, the equipment accounting process was much more efficient. When a customer required an item of equipment, the requirement (or demand as it is known in the service), was telephoned to the demands clerk in the Equipment Section. The clerk had almost complete visibility of the stock of equipment held (POL and explosives were accounted for separately), with each item being recorded on a stock record card (F1640); these were filed in Section and Reference order in a large steel bin located alongside of his desk, with each card overlapping so that the stock identity numbers could be easily seen. On receipt of the telephone call, he was able to advise the caller whether or not stock was available at the unit by

Formal opening of the RAF SCC, 1966. (*Crown Copyright—Air Historical Branch MoD*)

checking the appropriate card. With the rather obvious need to keep his hands free, the clerk wore a telephone exchange operator's type headset; his number dialler was located on a pull-out shelf situated on the underside of the desk. If stock was available, the clerk would raise a voucher (marked as 'exchange' for Class 'A' or 'B' Stores, 'issue' for Class 'C' Stores or 'initial issue'), clip the voucher to the stock card, and pass it to a corporal for checking who also added what was known as an ABC code to the voucher. If there was no stock available, the clerk raised a separate stock demand. The voucher and card were then passed to what was known as the 'Addlister' clerk (named after the machine they used). The task of this individual was to mathematically add together the ABC code, the reference number, and the quantity required of the item to form a new code number, which was used for checking purposes, later in the process. Following this, the stock card and voucher were passed to a machine operator who would post the transaction to the stock record card using a NCR keyboard accounting machine (KAM) type 31W.

To avoid having to move the punched tape between the unit Equipment Sections and its communication centre, extension spurs were incorporated between the two locations so that the tapes could be transmitted directly. Data accuracy, measured by the lowest number of errors transmitted by units to the SCC, was rewarded by the award of 'data stars', certificates that usually hung on the wall of the machine room and were highly prized. At the Hendon end of the operation was the heart of the

AEI 1010 KAM and operator. (*Crown Copyright—Air Historical Branch MoD*)

system, the AEI 1010 mainframe computer, collectively known as the Supply Central Computer System (SCCS). Initially, there were two mainframe computers (a third was added later) and all records were held on magnetic tape but with punched paper tape for input and output.

For technically-minded readers, it is worth mentioning that since random access devices did not exist at this time, the whole system was batch oriented and therefore offline. The unit inbound paper tapes were read in late each afternoon to magnetic tapes and consolidated and sorted into section and reference order. There then followed a sequence of processes, the principal ones being the UK daily and the overseas daily. Various output tapes were produced and here mention should be made of the low stock (LS) tape. Each day's LS tape, a record of items with little or no stock in the system, superseded that of the previous day, and was used for the next twenty-four hours priority process which was initiated every hour. Another key daily process was the monthly re-provisioning run. Each day, a proportion of the RAF-wide inventory was subject to analysis and printed advices (such as for a routine re-order) were generated for Supply managers. The whole inventory was thus monitored each month.

The hardware details reveal an architecture which now borders on the archaic. What would now be considered as 'memory' was known as the immediate access store (IAS). Into this had to be crammed the operating system, the application program itself, the item record, plus the unit record, maybe also the depot record and a work area. Backing up IAS were two magnetic drums; this concept was imaginatively and rather amusingly described by a former Supply Branch officer, Wing Commander Colin Cummings, as akin to 'a 45-gallon oil drum revolving at high speed with the magnetic tracks about its circumference and a sort of demonic gramophone arm picking up the information when required'.[5] These drums (which would be completely unnecessary today) principally contained lesser-used operating system sub-processes and similar applications sub-processes. Main data storage was provided by a number of magnetic tape decks with control consoles being used to manage over all operations. The control application was planned, designed, programmed, implemented and maintained by a large team of Equipment officers and civil servants; its implementation involved the taking-on of 3.25 million unit and depot records for 750,000 line items on the RAF inventory. Not only did the AEI 1010 provide a major step forward in terms of technology, the business benefit was almost revolutionary representing a major departure from the manually intensive processes that had been in use since the 1920s.

AEI 1010 computer room at Hendon. (*Crown Copyright—Air Historical Branch MoD*)

Depot Computing

With the AEI 1010 system up and running, attention then turned to the question of the ESDs. Although the number of ESDs had greatly reduced, the size of the RAF inventory was beginning to grow quite significantly. Indeed, by 1967, it had increased from 600,000 items to 800,000 with the introduction of the Lockheed Hercules the same year and the McDonnell Douglas Phantom due to enter service later in 1969. The figure was forecast to rise still further. However, similar to RAF units, little had changed in terms of the way these former No. 40 Group units operated since their formation in the late 1930s. The pressure was on to improve the RAF's warehousing operation in order that it could better meet the pressures of an increasingly sophisticated and expanding inventory.

It was not just the scale of the operation that was the challenge, but the way in which the depots went about their business. As part of their original design, stock dispersal was of key concern with the aim of minimising damage from enemy air attack. As described earlier, the majority of the depots operated from a number of geographically dispersed sites, clustered around the main or HQ site. Within this infrastructure, the storage policy had been to group together items by range, such as an aircraft type or version of an aero engine; small, high turnover items were therefore located in the same storage shed as the more bulky, low-turnover items. These specific ranges were invariably stored within a dedicated storage shed on a specific site. The utilisation of storage space was also an issue as space was largely viewed as two dimensional and measured in square rather than cubic feet; consequently, much of the available shed storage space was not being monitored. When it came to issues of equipment, items located on a dispersed site had to be transported to the depot's main site for packing and transportation. The whole concept required high levels of manpower and a sizeable internal transport fleet. With the high turnover items located across the storage sites the issues process in particular was a time-consuming procedure. The concept could be supported in time of war by high levels of manpower but peacetime constraints, with a growing inventory and lower manpower levels, needed a new way of doing business. Given the success of EDP at unit level, it took little imagination to recognise the potential for this technology within the depot environment.

As part of the original AEI 1010 installation, KAMs had been installed at the depots in addition to RAF units for the maintenance of stock records, but proved to be slow and cumbersome in handling the volume of data generated at the depots. Thus, the KAMs were replaced at the depots by the ICL 1903 computer system which first went live at Stafford on 31 October 1968; it was rolled out to the three other depots shortly after. The ICL 1903 had originally been developed by International Computers and Tabulators, a company that had merged, along with the English Electric Computers, to form International Computers Ltd in 1968. The depot computer system (DCS) as it became known allowed transaction vouchers to be produced in stock picking sequence and to automatically and quickly direct paperwork to the appropriate storage point. The savings enabled a number of sub-sites to be closed or to be re-allocated for alternative uses.

In 1978, following a wide-ranging review of the whole Supply ADP System, work started on augmenting the existing ICL 1903 hardware and extending maintenance agreements, prior to replacement at the depots with a new generation of hardware. Between 1979 and 1981, the MS3 staff at HQ RAFSC carried out a series of studies to determine the requirements for what would be known as the ESD ADP replacement system (EARS). Following a highly successful development programme, EARS was officially 'initiated' by the AOC in 'C' RAF Support Command, Air Marshal Sir David Harcourt-Smith on 7 August 1985. The EARS contract was awarded to ICL in September 1983 and by July 1984, the hardware had been installed and accepted. Programming had started in January 1984, and twelve programmers completed the application software, comprising over 184,000 lines of code in just nine months.

The real strength of EARS was its achievement in terms of resilience. The requirement at the two largest of the depots (No. 14 MU Carlisle and No. 16 MU Stafford) was met by the installation of two ICL 2957 processors at each, operating as a dual installation; in the event of the failure of one processor, the other had the capacity to handle the depot's workload with little or no degradation of performance. Additionally, the two depots were linked so that in the event of a total computer failure at one depot, the other would be able to process the workload of the other, albeit at reduced efficiency. Users were connected to the system by visual display units (VDU) that, in turn, were connected in local area networks (LANs) with one master VDU controlling several slave units and their associated printers. Any messages for specific terminals could be diverted to other devices on different LANs in the event of equipment failure. Overall, the 14MU network comprised thirty LANs with a total of fifty-three terminals, distributed throughout the depot in storage locations and supply accounting offices. The 16MU network had twenty-four LANs with a total of fifty-one terminals.[6]

The distributed network also extended to the depots at No. 7 MU Quedgeley and No. 11 MU Chilmark. However, neither of these had their own processor but operated as a series of LANs transacting on their own databases located within a host computer located at No. 16MU. The Quedgeley installation had nine LANs with eleven terminals, while the Chilmark network had five LANs with seven terminals. By 1988, No. 217 MU Cardington was connected to the system at No. 14 MU Carlisle. The external communications to support this overall were complex. The processors at Nos 14 and 16 MUs were connected by high-capacity lines to allow mutual fall-back and also to permit remote programming of the Carlisle computer by the MS3 detachment based at Stafford. Both depots were also independently linked to the RAFSCC at Hendon by private telephone lines, to enable issue orders and advices to be exchanged via punched paper tape or magnetic tape transmission. The installation at Carlisle was also linked to RAF Croughton by private telephone lines to enable demands to be generated and progressed for equipment of American manufacture.

In 1986, the DCS terminal network was expanded to cover MOD SM4 (RAF) at Harrogate and this enabled their staffs to directly input agency demands (demands placed on behalf of out of system users, contractors, and other governments or departments) directly to the DCS rather than pass them to the depots for input. By 1988, many new applications had been developed and introduced to DCS and the expansion had rapidly begun to exceed the original expectations of EARS. With a further £400,000 worth of investment, another hardware upgrade was completed. Computer system storage capacity was increased by the addition of more fixed disk storage and the capacity of each of the four ICL2957 processors was doubled from four to eight megabytes. Two new heavy-duty line printers were added as well as a second-hand ICL2957 processor to enable in-house development to be carried out by the MS3 detachment.

What the technical overview does not tell us, however, is why the RAF Supply System needed such a sophisticated and complex computing environment. By the end of 1988, the RAF inventory consisted of over 1.4 million individual or line items ranging from complete aero engines valued at £1.5 million each to simple nuts and bolts under one pence each. The total value of the inventory at that time was in excess of £4 billion and every month the depots were receiving and issuing some 216,000 consignments of equipment. The business functionality of DCS made an enormous difference to the management of this inventory. The system not only maintained stock accounts (along with transaction histories), but also printed receipt and issue vouchers; in the case of the latter, the computer was able to print in a logical stock picking sequence and to aggregate multiple issues to one issue voucher. DCS also supported a full stocktaking and location checking programme. The development and achievements of DCS were critical to the overall supply operation during the 1970s and 1980s. It was the intention of the RAF to replace the DCS in 1995 with a system known as the warehouse and transport management system (WTMS) as part of the Logistics IT strategy (LITS) but a technical issue prevented this. WTMS (Air), as it became known, worked in conjunction with the old DCS, until August 2005 when DCS ceased operating and WTMS interfaced directly with SCCS. This configuration migrated to a tri-service solution by Boeing Defence UK as part of its major transformation contract, the base inventory and warehouse management services project (BIWMS) in late 2016.

Planning for a Second Generation: The ICL 4/72

Computer technology is a rapidly advancing science and, even in the late 1960s, computer systems were viewed as having only a seven to ten-year life before they needed updating. Consequently, a new development team was formed at the SCC at Hendon headed up by Group Captain J. G. Ireton to consider the AEI 1010's replacement. Affectionately known as 'roaring' Jack, Ireton was one of many Second World War aircrew who had transferred to the Equipment Branch during the post-war rundown of the RAF. During his flying career, he had the claim to fame of being the second pilot in the first Halifax bomber to have been successfully ditched after being shot down during a daylight raid on La Pallice in 1941; he spent the rest of the war as a POW.

What came into being as a result was the ICL 4/72 system, and it was able to take advantage of many further advances in computer system design and technology. In practice, this meant a move from batch processing to real-time processing (in which random events—in this case transactions or enquiries—are actioned as they physically occur). The central system hardware consisted of two central processor units (CPU), which ran the real-time system; a third was added later in 1977. The two CPUs with their associated peripheral equipment were delivered to Hendon in May 1972 and, following tests and trials, were formally taken over by DGS (RAF), on behalf of the RAF on 9 March 1973. The average response time for 90 per cent of messages received (from a worldwide user population) was within ten seconds. User units were provided with VDUs and some 600 were supplied by Cossor Ltd, together with their associated equipment.

ICL 4/72 terminal and civilian operator. (*Crown Copyright—Air Historical Branch MoD*)

The first data input to the ICL4/72 was made from a VDU at RAF Brize Norton on 1 October 1973, using transactions all from Section 26VC—the VC10 airframe. The first transaction was typed in by Group Captain Ireton and within two seconds of him having pressed the 'send' key, a response was received to confirm that stock of the item requested was available. On pressing the 'accept' key, the computer stock balance was updated and a voucher was automatically printed ready for the item to be picked from stock and issued. Although this was a fairly simple transaction, it had taken much hard work to get that far, involving many years of work by RAF systems designers and RAF and civilian programmers. The VC10 data used to initially populate the Hendon processors had been taken from the AEI 1010 and merged into one file; this involved Hendon systems design staff and programmers writing new programs for the operation staff to run. The data then had to be passed through a specially purchased converter (supplied by UCC/Computer Instrumentation) to convert 1010 magnetic tape into an acceptable format. The 4/72 finally went live on 28 April 1975 and was formally inaugurated by CAS, Air Chief Marshal Sir Andrew Humphrey, on 30 June 1975.

The rollout of the ICL 4/72 system was implemented in three distinct phases; the first of these (Phase 1 and 1a) took place between April and November 1975. During this phase, all of the ranges of equipment then under AEI 1010 control were transferred as well as the accounting records of RAF stations not on the AEI 1010 system as well as units of the Army Air Corps. The second phase commenced in January 1976 and over a period of six months brought on to the system ranges of equipment which were hitherto excluded from the AEI 1010—MT spares, accommodation stores, and clothing. A range of management services was also established in this phase as well as the setting up of a data capture scheme for the movement of repairable equipment in and out of second, third, and fourth line repair for eventual use by the SMBs when forecasting forward repair requirements. Another useful function provided in this phase for unit supply squadrons was the capability of generating an annual report on the value of their holdings in stock and in-use on their units. Phase 2 took place during the second half of 1976 with the taking on of articles-in-use (with the exception of married quarter and aircraft inventories). Finally, phase 3 was completed throughout 1977 with the 4/72 taking on responsibility for the ESD Supply ADP System and the introduction of improved methods of cooperative logistics support with the USA, France, Norway, West Germany, and Italy.

The new system represented a significant step forward to users in that it afforded them direct connectivity to the SCCS via VDUs. Essentially, the 4/72 shifted the location of the main stock record from units, where it had originally been held on hand-written ledgers, to the SCC. However, it was not just a simple matter of keeping an accurate stock balance; the system was now much more sophisticated and, in the case of a unit being without stock, the system was now able to carry out a comprehensive stock search throughout the RAF. The whole of the initial

ICL 4/72 computer room at Hendon. (*Crown Copyright—Air Historical Branch MoD*)

process would normally take in the order of five seconds. However, speed was but one consideration as the 4/72 was also able to provide an inventory management facility for units, offer an on-line interrogation facility, manage alternative item and supersession chains and provide a comprehensive management information system (MIS).[7] The availability of this system was also extended to Royal Naval air stations and Army Air Corps units. During its life, the 4/72 underwent four hardware changes and numerous updates within the software.

It is also worth mentioning here that very few organisations at this time really understood real-time stock control and the RAF therefore conducted much of the design, development, programming and research in-house. Although the business world tends to view in-house software development as unfashionable, the RAF has seen many times over since then that it is valuable; the control of process, testing to rigorous standards and business understanding are all key factors in ensuring that the right system is developed. Along with the DCS, the ICL 4/72 installation at the RAFSCC and VDUs at online consumer units in the three services and MOD (procurement executive) formed what became known as the RAF Supply ADP system (RAF SADPS). The overall aim of this was to provide an adequate data processing service to support the most cost-effective supply of materiel for the RAF in both peace and war.

A Third Generation: The Unit Supply ADP System

By 1980, the RAF's inventory had grown significantly and the ICL 4/72 was controlling some 1.5 million items of equipment. By way of comparison, the Army and Royal Navy each had 0.85 million items and British Leyland 0.85 million items. Change, therefore, was in the air again and perhaps even more significantly because of a change in NATO doctrine at the same time from the 'tripwire' strategy to one of 'flexible response', which implied a period of preliminary conventional fighting rather than an immediate nuclear exchange. It was realised that the RAF Logistics organisation would need to be able to operate independently if the link between units and the RAFSCC was disrupted. Operationally, there was a change in the way in which RAF airfields were set up and many, especially those within RAF Germany, were configured for dispersed operations, including the construction of self-contained hardened facilities to improve survivability in war. Thus, many supply squadrons found themselves proud new owners of HESs, which were used to house that part of the station's stock of equipment which was dispersed from the main storage facility. At RAF Laarbruch, for example, HESs were located on each of the four flying squadron sites around the station (see Chapter Four). With the requirement to disperse stocks and the ability to continue Supply operations in the event of disconnection from the RAF SCC, there was a need for a totally new procedural concept, as the existing RAF SADPS was not designed to meet this requirement and the RAF SCCS was perceived as vulnerable. The solution was development of the Unit Supply ADP System (USAS). Programmed by the RAF SCC staffs in the early 1980s, the initial rollout of the system was made to thirty RAF stations, three RN Air Stations, and two Army Air Corps bases from December 1984 to 1986. Housed initially on Honeywell DPS6 hardware, these were replaced in 1992 by DPS600 and then again in 1996 with DPX-20 with a UNIX operating system. Much of the USAS project was driven by the inspired work of Squadron Leader (later Wing Commander) Sam Read and Wing Commander Brian Mitchell who was responsible for designing the interface with the SCC. In 2000, the development and support of USAS was handed over under a phased programme to Steria, based at Hemel Hempstead who undertook a complete rewrite of the application.

This new application was termed USAS2 and was then rolled-out to units from February 2001. Essentially, USAS replicated almost all of the existing RAFS ADPS but enabled units to manage dispersed stocks, calculating establishments for each site (usually a HES) and to move stocks from one part of the unit to another. The system also highlighted if an item required engineering checks before issue (such as aircraft avionic and mechanical components). In terms of design, USAS provided each unit with a stand-alone processor and database. If the SCCS was to cease operations, USAS units could, for as long as their USAS survived, continue to carry out transactions, and control their unit stocks with relatively limited disruption in the short term. Should the RAF SCCS come back online, each USAS processor would update the SCCS with the missing data and bring the system back into alignment. As part of their transition to war process, RAF Germany stations would print off a complete hard copy of their unit records for use in the event of any disruption to the processor, which was usually housed in the main Supply Squadron building; surprisingly, many of these processors were located in 'soft skinned' buildings. The author can recall the sight of the SNCO stock control at RAF Laarbruch during a NATO TACEVAL exercise in 1985, disappearing off to a HES in the back of a van clutching an enormous stack of computer printouts that represented all the unit records; his mission was to take up post as the standby stock controller. As part of the exercise, the TACEVAL staff would often simulate the destruction of the main unit USAS processor and then get the squadron suppliers to locate an item and carry out an issue. With the printout in stock number order, this back-up process was not as lengthy as it might seem. However, one could be forgiven for making comparisons with the stock controller leafing through the printouts in a dingy corner of a HES (they had no windows of course) and the clerk poring over the F1640 equipment accounting ledger back in the 1920s.

At the SCC end, the 4/72 hardware was replaced by two Fujitsu-built ATLAS-10 mainframe computers on 31 January 1985 providing a memory totalling just thirty-two megabytes. The average response times for 95 per cent of messages received was around 0.3 seconds. One CPU provided the real-time processing for RAF units, while the other performed batched processing and provided support services for program development and testing. Two further upgrades took place moving the

USAS Amdahl processors at Stanbridge. (*Crown Copyright—Air Historical Branch MoD*)

SCCS from two Hitachi data system processors onto an Amdahl Omniflex 1015 mainframe in June 2001. These were principally hardware changes; systems and programs were essentially unchanged. The current Amdahl processors provide a system that has one gigabyte of memory, carries out sixty million instructions per second, and can record 648 gigabytes of data onto disk—quite a step forward from that early system put into service at RAF Hendon back in 1966.

A New Home

With the closure of RAF Hendon on 1 April 1987, the RAF SCC relocated to RAF Stanbridge, near Leighton Buzzard in Bedfordshire. Stanbridge had been an RAF unit since 1939 as a communications centre but underwent significant redevelopment for the move of the RAF SCC. The new unit was re-opened on 5 May 1987, and it was quite remarkable that the total system downtime to users was a mere four hours. It will be clear from the preceding chronology of systems upgrades that the 1980s were a period of considerable change, since the advent of USAS meant serious modification to existing transaction processing at the main frame computer itself. The heady mix of hardware replacement, USAS integration, and the relocation of main frame hardware, some events occurring simultaneously, of which hopefully users were completely unaware, taxed the technical staff exceedingly. Following the numerous Defence reviews of the 1990s, the SCC became the RAF Logistics

A new home: RAF SCC Stanbridge. (*Crown Copyright—Air Historical Branch MoD*)

Computer Centre, eventually becoming part of the Logistics applications integrated project team within the Defence communication services agency (DCSA), which was formed in April 1998. With the formation of DE&S in 2007, the DCSA was disestablished as an agency and this responsibility for SCCS transferred to a new organisation, information systems and services.

Deployable USAS

By the time of the first Gulf War in 1991 (Operation Granby), experimental work had been carried out to see if USAS could be installed and operated from remote sites and if communications links would facilitate this. While USAS terminals could be deployed to operational theatres, they were linked to the parent base, rather than directly with the SCC. With the conclusion of Operation Granby, further work was carried out to develop a deployable version of USAS (DUSAS). The inspiration for this came about following an Army exercise in Germany where the Army Air Corps had managed to put their USAS system on the back of a lorry. To provide the communication link, a soldier shinned up a telegraph pole and tapped into the phone line and the unit was able to operate as if they were back at base. Although this caused much consternation back at Hendon in the USAS Wing, the wider possibilities were quickly realised. By March 1995, HQ STC had agreed a DUSAS concept of operations in which it was agreed that a 'proof of concept' trial would be carried out at RAF Leeming and a selected overseas location.[8] It was agreed that an initial purchase of six DUSAS configurations would be made. Of those, it was intended that four would eventually be located at RAFs Leeming, Wittering, Bruggen, and Marham. The remaining two would be used for development and as a HQ STC strategic reserve.

The first deployment of DUSAS was in 1996 to Exercise Purple Star in the USA. The system was eventually rolled-out in 1997 utilising what was known as a 'ruggedised' processor. The components of the system were stored within tough, easily carried cases and were designed to be transported and assembled anywhere in the world and made operational within hours of arrival in theatre. With the introduction of DUSAS2 in October 2001, the components became smaller still and more modularised for even better portability. Connectivity to a communications network would usually be via an in theatre LAN or, if available, by satellite telephones to transmit data to the SCCS. The user interface is identical to that of the static USAS2. By 2005, the RAF had sixteen DUSAS systems, which were routinely operated in the Middle East. Work had also been initiated to see if DUSAS could be used in ships and with deployed Army battalions.

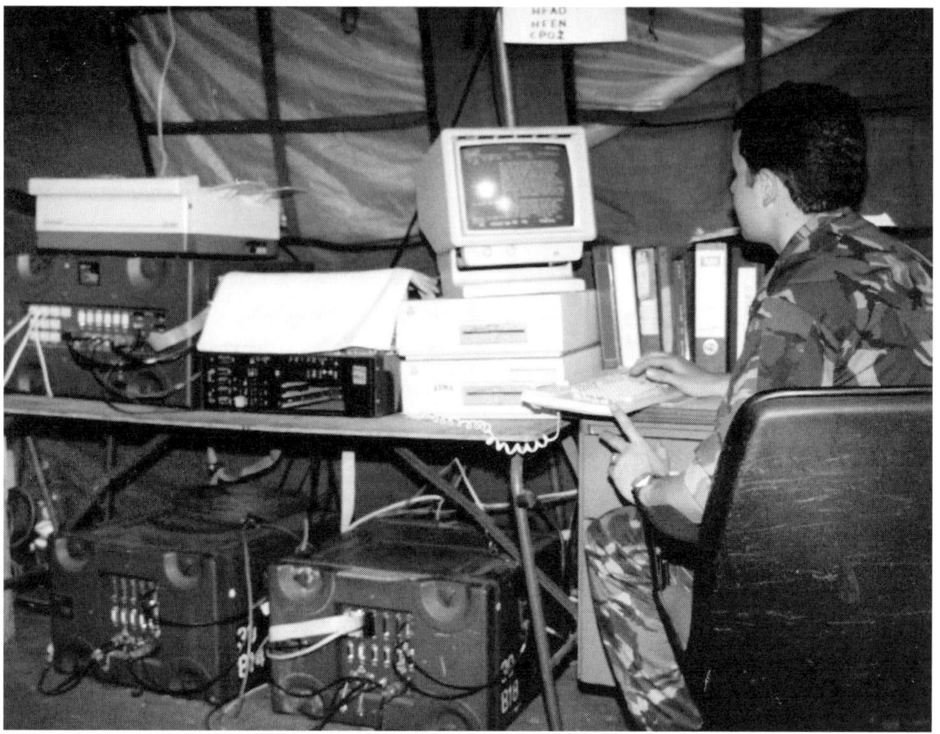

DUSAS in the field. (*Crown Copyright—Air Historical Branch MoD*)

Unit/SCC Interface

In retrospect, one principle element of the general success of the introduction of computer-based systems has been the human face which the SCC presented to its system users. Perhaps only these users are truly qualified to comment, but there is no doubt that the establishment of the SNCO-manned enquiry department Management Advisory Section (MAS) helped gain the confidence and trust of system users and, perhaps more importantly, allowed the SCC itself to understand more clearly the impact of system changes. The MAS team was also responsible for designing the courses, training, and standardising the work of the RAF's base USAS managers (BUSMs). The founder of this incredibly effective and far-sighted function was Flight Sergeant (later WO) Marty King.

Supply Management Terminal Network (SMTN)

A need that was never satisfactorily addressed by the first and second generation computer systems was the availability of sufficient data input devices or online terminals for the SMBs at MOD Harrogate. These branches relied on stock consumption data to carry out the complicated provisioning and procurement of replacement spares. Under the AEI 1010 system, the entire process relied on manual inputs being sent to Hendon for transfer to the central system by keyboard operators. The ICL 4/72 brought an improvement but was initially limited to one online terminal per twenty staff at Harrogate. These were often located away from the immediate work area and were usually heavily utilised. Moreover, the mix of online and offline inputs led to high levels of rejections because of mismatched transactions.

By the late 1980s, it was clear that this arrangement was not going to be satisfactory, and a study team was set up led by Wing Commander Malcolm Oliver. The answer to the problem facing the team lay with British Telecom, who were able to demonstrate that it was possible to use a single remote terminal to connect to many different host computers by tricking the host computers into believing they were communicating with a remote terminal using the correct connectivity protocols. It thus became possible to use the same terminal for connecting to several computers. This concept enabled the SMTN to be developed; this consisted of a desktop terminal that was capable of imitating a number of other terminals. The improvement was significant and more business could be carried out on line; additionally, both error rates and duplication of effort were reduced. The author, based at MOD Harrogate in the early 1990s, recalls the enormous difference SMTN made to the work of SMB staff. For the first time, they had their own desktop terminal and could view, *inter alia*, not only the SCCS, but also DCS and the codification database ISIS through the same screen. SMTN was a revolutionary concept, not only in what it aimed to do—to allow people to access multiple supply chain computer systems on one terminal—but also to overcome huge IT industry leading-edge design and implementation problems. It also provided a link to systems supporting the increasing number of international procurements such as the Tornado support management system, Tornado integrated priority progression system, and the military standard requisitioning process for federal military sales from the USA. The SMTN functionality remains in use although this will be replaced as part of the Boeing Defence UK BIWMS project in 2016–2017.

ADP Support for Aero Engine Management

From the early days of military aviation, the timely availability of aero engines (and their spares) has always been a critical requirement. This was usually a relatively straightforward affair for stock management and engines were identified and accounted for as complete assemblies; their component parts were provisioned as individual items. However, complete aero engines were formally allotted to a unit and, once fitted, were recorded in the aircraft's inventory. From the Second World War, the process was centrally controlled by the Supply Management (SM) 1 organisation at Harrogate. However, by the mid-1960s, a growing number of engines coming into service were of a modular design; this was leading to a significant increase in the number of assets to be controlled. In essence, such engines do not exist as a single entity and are built up of a series of discrete components or modules, each with its own, unique identity. In the case of the SEPECAT Jaguar, which entered RAF front-line service in the early 1970s, its Adour 151 engine consisted of eleven different modules.[9] With this growing complexity and the corresponding need to track the modules, manual accounting was no longer a viable option.

The original intention was that a commercial company would be contracted to provide a total 'turn-key' solution. Unfortunately, the firm originally selected went out of business and it fell to the RAF SCC to provide the answer. In September 1974, a dedicated team was set up within the Supply Research Division at Hendon. The work of this team was another example of an in-house SCC triumph and they were responsible for all of the design, programming and implementation tasks for what became known as the Supply aero-engine record office (SARO) ADP system. Based on an ICL 2903 computer, the solution included a signal reporting system to forward engine defect information to the RAF's maintenance data centre, a file storage system large enough to acquire historical data and with visual display units and printers for the various engine management cells within SARO.

The new ADP System was formally inaugurated at Harrogate by AMSO, Air Marshal Sir Alasdair Steedman on 1 March 1977. It brought significant benefits and dramatically improved the day-to-day management of aero engines. The greatly improved visibility of assets also permitted the identification of engine 'queues' for repair and turn-round times at the various levels of repair to be monitored. It also led to working procedures within SARO being standardised, reducing the clerical task, and eliminating much duplication. The SARO system also enabled the RAF to acquire, maintain, and analyse a vast amount of data derived from statistical information. This, in turn, greatly improved the forecasting of requirements.

In time, the functionality of SARO was subsumed into a number of systems such as the Brandt aero-engine management aid (BAEMMA) and the modular aero-engine management information system (MAEMIS). The Pegasus repairable asset management system (PRAMS) was developed to meet the specific needs of that engine. All of these systems were derived from the principles developed by SARO. In time, the management of RAF aero engines, by and large, was subsumed into the wider engineering asset management component of LITS.

Logistic Information Technology Strategy

By the late 1980s, with growing governmental pressure for the services to be managed in a more business-like manner, it was becoming clear to senior RAF management that its existing engineering and logistic IT systems were out of date and that more modern systems were urgently needed. One of the more specific drivers for change at this time was perhaps the Government's NMS, which, *inter alia*, was triggering much needed organisational change within the MOD. Moreover, by that time, there were well over 100 different systems, with many of them not communicating with one another. It was clear that to deliver the improvements that NMS sought, the RAF needed an integrated system. The RAF's engineers were also experiencing problems with asset management, a capability that had eluded them for some time. They had good reliability data from the CSDE maintenance data centre, but were losing configuration control of complex assets. Most significantly, and in a wider respect, there was next to no inter-communication between supply and engineering systems.

Following an eight-month study published in 1988, the RAF announced its intention to launch a Logistics Information Technology Strategy (LITS) programme. Valued at £430 million, the contract was awarded to IBM (UK) Ltd in July 1994. There were three phases (or 'tranches' as they were known). The first was known as tranche 0; it included early development requirements that were classed as transitional in nature or of more urgent need. Due to the ageing depot computing system, the WTMS application referred to earlier in this chapter was included, as too was a Logistic Support System (LSSys), which was required to support the full integrated logistic support (ILS) process needed for the introduction of new weapon systems, such as the Eurofighter 2000 (Typhoon).[10] The LSSys was a separately approved project, initiated in 1991 and managed by an RAF Supply Officer, Wing Commander Dick Wallis.

Tranche 1 was largely engineering in nature and addressed the requirement to capture data on assets at unit level and providing a much-needed decision support capability for engineering managers. In time, this developed into a highly successful system that enabled electronic asset management, along with a faults database to be maintained and fatigue data to be managed. Tranche 2 was intended to cover supply functionality, concentrating on the replacement of SCCS and USAS. Wider developments in Defence IT management saw the tranche 2 requirement addressed through a tri-service approach; it is described later in this chapter.

ADP Support for POL Management

In many respects, POL had similar problems to explosives when it came to ADP support and early studies recommended that the accounting needs were best met by a separate system from the RAF SADPS. However, before looking at the computing solution itself, the operational need behind the requirement needs some explanation. In the 1970s, the supply management of POL was the responsibility of DD S Pol 10(RAF), a deputy directorate within D of S Pol and Log Plans (RAF). In times of crisis (both in peace and war), the DD was also responsible for the overall management and control of POLOR. It was during 1978, after several activations of

POLOR for various crises, that the DD realised that a major difficulty of the POLOR task was being able to quickly collect, collate and assimilate the POL data required for decision making. This need led to a study which concluded that the POLOR requirement, along with the day-to-day supply management could be met using ADP; by early 1980, a full operational requirement document had been drafted and the proposal became known as the POL Information System (POLIS). Due to Supply Branch ADP expertise being committed to USAS development, however, in-house production of POLIS was not considered feasible. As a result, the OR was released for commercial tender as a 'turnkey' project; the all-inclusive nature of the requirement was rather neatly summed up in an analogy by the deputy project team leader who described the it as 'the concept of a non-driver buying a car—in this instance, not only does the garage customize their choice of vehicle to meet the buyer's requirement, but they also teach him to drive!'[11] The fixed-price contract for POLIS was eventually awarded to Scion Ltd in December 1981.

After a number of development and hardware sourcing difficulties, the solution finally accepted by the MOD consisted of two Digital Equipment Corporation (DEC) 11/750 CPUs (each with two megabytes of memory, two RA60 exchangeable 205-megabyte disc drives, and a TU80 tape drive) and an ORACLE relational database management system. Each of the CPUs was configured to support up to sixteen terminal devices by fibreoptic lines, although the original set-up comprised of eight DEC VT102 visual display terminals and four dot matrix printers. The system was tested using a dummy air force database, prior to being formally loaded with live data. The POLIS installation was inaugurated by DGS (RAF), Air Vice-Marshal A. Beill, on 22 April 1985.

At the time, the POLIS software was seen as one of the most advanced, powerful and flexible packages of its kind and provided a much-needed ADP tool for DD S Pol 10 (RAF). The database contained a wide range of data, including the deployment options of aircraft in peace and war, statistical monitoring of data on POL consumption and even the telephone numbers of POL sections on RAF units.

On a final note, there was an interesting debate surrounding the name of the system. It was discovered early on in the project that the proposed acronym not only sounded like the Scottish pronunciation of the Strathclyde Constabulary, but was also strikingly similar to that of the parliamentary online information system. There was a suggestion to use POLORIS, but it was felt that this might cause international repercussions, particularly at the launching ceremony. Common sense prevailed and the system simply became known as MOD POLIS.

ADP Support for Explosives and Conventional Weapons

When the RAF decided to implement ADP for Supply back in the early 1960s, the Section 12 explosives range was excluded for a number of reasons. Firstly, the range itself was quite small (by comparison to the airframe and engine ranges). Secondly, due to the nature of calculating requirements, explosives were not provisioned in the same way as standard ranges of equipment nor were they accounted for at units in the same way.[12] Thirdly, explosives were not held in the unit Supply Squadron but in explosive storage areas (ESAs); accounting for stock was carried out simultaneously in the Supply Squadron and the ESA. Finally, there were the important questions of dealing with explosives filling data (lot numbers) and security. Visibility of stock holdings would provide an instant 'snapshot' of military capability at both unit and force level. For all these reasons, the explosives range was excluded from both the AEI 1010 and ICL 4/72 and accounting for them remained 'offline'.

During the 1970s, a number of feasibility studies were carried out. It became generally accepted that most of the provisioning calculations were capable of being programmed and placed on a secure automated system. A step nearer came with the Falklands War (Operation Corporate) in 1982 when it was decided that the RAF holdings of explosives should be brought onto ADP control and this was completed in just three weeks using a dummy code system to prevent visibility of actual holdings. However, although this provided stock visibility for units, it did not provide the functionality that the SMBs required to carry out supply management and provisioning. Security proved to be the most significant hurdle and a further enhancement of the ICL 4/72 was ruled out. The answer came in the form of a dedicated microcomputer and this was installed in SM 32(RAF) at Harrogate in October 1984.

The Supply Small Systems Group

The work that had been done to provide dedicated computing support for POL and explosives in the early 1980s had shown that much wider benefit could be realised from the growing availability of microcomputers. These were not the large mainframe systems that were at the heart of the SCCS and DCS, but smaller more self-contained systems with an initial cost under £100,000. Recognising the benefit for logistics, a Supply small systems group was formed at RAF Hendon in January 1986. The group proved to be highly successful and developed many specialist applications that improved efficiency and automated a number of manual processes. It is believed the group moved to Stanbridge when the SCCS relocated there in 1987, and its capability was eventually subsumed within the DCSA in 1998.[13]

Tri-Service IT Management

SDR 98 was also a major turning-point for the single-service approach to logistics IS. The DLO gained a new collective responsibility for managing the extensive and complex panoply of logistics IS that the Royal Navy, Army, and RAF had largely individually funded, developed, and managed since they had adopted such technology in the 1960s. It was hardly surprising that over some forty years, with changing needs and an ever-increasing number of hardware and software developers, that the services had adopted a substantial number of computer applications and systems to manage their individual supply chains. Some of the early attempts to understand the extent of this IS 'landscape' resulted in what became known as the 'spaghetti' diagram—a large sheet of paper that attempted to plot the various IS packages with connecting lines showing any inter-connections. What this early mapping work showed, only too dramatically, was the substantial number of systems and a lack of connectivity between many of them. Moreover, many of the applications were performing virtually the same thing. This backdrop, set against the requirement for the DLO to reduce the cost of its purchasing and logistics budget of £4.6 billion by 20 per cent over its first five years, resulted in work beginning to rationalise logistics IS. The need became more pressing as a result of operating experiences in the First Gulf War (Operation Granby) but perhaps even more significantly in the Second Gulf War (Operation Telic); the MOD's post-campaign report commented:

> It was difficult to monitor the rates at which supplies were consumed, making it hard to determine when resupply would be required. The lack of available information also reduced commanders' confidence in the logistics system, causing units to over-prioritise their requests and re-order equipment already *en route*.[14]

While an element of this shortfall was attributed to the lack of progress in achieving an effective consignment tracking capability, it became clear that a new tri-service stock control system was urgently required. The single-service systems had been developed to support combat operations in Europe where the supply lines of communication from the UK to West Germany were relatively short. Moreover, with the duration of conflicts in the Cold War era seen as likely to be short, stores and supplies were not expected to need much replenishment. The logistics operation to support both conflicts in the Gulf proved to be the exact opposite. The single-service systems were essentially 'stove piped' and had very limited inter-connectivity. As such they did not meet the information system needs of a modern Defence Supply Chain. This lack of coherence was particularly evident in PJHQ as it endeavoured to establish itself as a single command centre for joint operations after its initial formation.

It was thus that in 1998 the Defence Stores Management (DSMS) project was launched with its HQ at Boscombe Down in Wiltshire. While the project utilised the expertise of logisticians from the three services and the software house Indus (using its passport enterprise asset management software), the scope of the task soon proved to be much greater and considerably more complex than initially anticipated and was suspended in January 2002 due to pressure on resources. The successor to this work was the management of the joint deployed inventory (MJDI) project, which aimed to develop a single underpinning logistic information system.

Following a pilot operating capability project that was trialled at RAF Lyneham and RNAS Yeovilton, the system was rolled out to a number of units through the prime contractor Sopra Steria. RAF Logistics personnel had much to offer and were extensively involved in the tri-service system development.

In December 2010, the MOD appointed Boeing Defence UK as its delivery partner for the future logistics information services project, which is an £803 million, eleven-year contract to bring together in one location some 270 legacy logs IS systems, which have been operated by fifty contractors under 120 contracts. Through its BIWMS project, it will provide much needed IS rationalisation and improved technical coherence, reducing the number of data centres from fifteen to two.[15]

Consignment Tracking

Running in parallel with the quest to improve main stock control systems was the issue of consignment tracking—the ability to monitor and identify the location of consignments while they are moving in the supply chain. Under the pre-DLO single service logistic arrangements, the need for precise pin-pointing of consignments in transit was not seen as a pressing requirement. Most of the RAF's equipment was moving over relatively short distances to existing bases using readily monitored transport routes and timescales. Expeditionary operations, however, were very different, involving greater distances through a number of nodal points and to bare base locations. This was further complicated by the multitude of different users that could be using the Defence supply chain at any one time. Experience during both Gulf Wars showed just how important it was to know exactly where stores and supplies were in transit. It became quite commonplace for equipment to be redemanded in frustration, due to the inability of logisticians to advise where urgently required consignments were or how much longer they would take to arrive. The MOD's inability to grip this requirement is perhaps one of the least shining examples of Defence IS management in recent years and has quite rightly been the subject of questions and adverse comment by both the Government's Public Accounts Committee and the National Audit Office in a number of reports since Operation Granby in 1991 and operations in the Balkans in the latter half of the 1990s.

Despite the identification of this serious shortcoming in the three services' management of their supply chains, it was nearly ten years before their logistics organisations were unified following SDR 98. It was not surprising that their efforts to address the problem were not coordinated and this permitted the emergence of two separate systems, separately pioneered by the Royal Navy and the Army. The Navy was slightly ahead of the game and from its work in the late 1980s, went on to introduce the Royal Navy Invoice and Delivery System (RIDELS) in January

1994, closely followed by the Army, which introduced its 'Visibility in Transit Asset Logging' (VITAL) system in December of the same year. Rather than pursue its own project, the RAF subsequently decided to adopt VITAL in 1997 as this was the closest match for its requirements and better suited to tracking consignments into the operational environment. This significantly increased the usage of VITAL and by 2001, it was operating at some 500 per cent of the original planned capacity. Unsurprisingly, this took its toll on system operating efficiency; during the UK's Exercise Saif Sareea II in Oman during September and October 2001, for example, in theatre VITAL users found that it could take as long as fifteen minutes to discover the contents of a single ISO container. This operating experience identified a number of logistics problems, which needed improvement; VITAL was subjected to a refresh programme in April 2002 and successfully overcame the capacity problem.[16]

Planning for the Second Gulf War (Operation Telic) assumed that British operations through Southern Turkey would use an American-operated line of communication. The UK's existing consignment tracking capability at the time, however, was not suitable for this commitment and attempts to try and integrate American and British tracking capabilities would have been prohibitive, both in terms of the time it would have taken and the costs involved. Consequently, the UK MOD adopted elements of the US total asset visibility system (known as TAV(-)) in September 2002, primarily to meet the need of operations in Iraq. The system was retained after the conflict and remains in use with the MOD, although it is mainly used to track major materiel handling assemblies such as ISO containers and aircraft pallets to end users overseas.

The first attempt to unify the tracking capability of the three Services came in 1998 when the MOD launched the DSMS project that, as a complementary project, included the in-transit visibility (ITV) programme, which had the aim of providing a unified Defence solution to consignment tracking. With the DSMS project being cancelled on the grounds of affordability in 2002, the MOD commissioned the management consultancy company McKinsey to examine the consignment tracking requirement as this could not be left to languish; part of their overall recommendations was that a revised capability be pursued to be known as management of materiel in transit (MMiT). This recommendation was taken forward by the MOD and MMiT went live in 2008. This was a much-needed capability that, using a web-based software application, drew data feeds from VITAL, MJDI, and DHL (the MOD's commercial courier). In doing so, it enabled users to view materiel in transit in the Defence supply chain, to and from destinations at home and overseas.

The End of an Era: The Decommissioning of the RAF Supply Central Computer System

The 2010 BIWMS contract with Boeing Defence UK enabled a fresh approach to be taken with the SCCS hardware configuration and in January 2012, work began to replicate the SCCS hardware at a new data centre at Corsham in Wiltshire. Despite a number of technical and practical challenges, including technology obsolescence, hardware scarcity, and a lack of third party expert support, the SCCS was effectively relocated, going live at its new location in 2013; the system was offline for less than sixty hours during the cutover from Stanbridge to Corsham. The new system is largely operated by Boeing's staff some two and a half hours away at Turing House in Milton Keynes. The former location at Stanbridge was officially closed in 2012. The BIWMS project will enable SCCS to be replaced by more modern software and is due to be decommissioned by the end of December 2016. Thus, some forty years of the RAF's SCCS comes to an end, a period that has seen a highly successful cooperation involving combined teams of RAF, civil service, and industry personnel.[17]

The end of an era: SCCS processors at Corsham just before they were decommissioned. (*Boeing Defence UK*)

11

Training and Education

Training and education have always been important to the RAF. Indeed, its 'extreme importance' was clearly articulated by Trenchard in his *Outline Scheme for the Permanent Organisation of the Royal Air Force* in December 1919. It was a requirement, he pointed out, on which 'the whole future of the Royal Air Force depends'.[1] His words did not overstate the case that training and education have been at the heart of the RAF's development of its people through to the present day. This had been particularly significant for the RAF's Logistics discipline where its wide range of sub-skills has demanded an extensive range of training courses. While the service has always encouraged its people to improve their educational qualifications, logistics, particularly after the Second World War, required its specialists to acquire skills which were more commonplace in the commercial sector. This gave rise to what was termed as professionalisation and a number of initiatives and opportunities were made available for RAF's logisticians to gain various academic and professional qualifications in the field. This chapter examines the various types of logistics training and education which have formed an important part of the discipline since 1918.

Officer Training

Following the Armistice in 1918, and as the post-war RAF was reduced in size, the Service progressively vacated many of the privately owned sites and buildings which it had taken-over for the duration of the war. As part of this rationalisation, the Equipment officers' school, which had been housed in various hotels in Reading since August 1917, was relocated to new premises at No. 4 SD at Ruislip, West London.

Due to the new procedures for stores accounting and store keeping, which had been developed throughout 1920, a revised course for officers was developed and the first of these was held to train the new instructors (mostly SNCOs) from December 1920 until February 1921. The inaugural course for Stores officers, following the introduction of this new branch in October 1919, commenced at Ruislip in February 1921. The number of courses grew steadily to the extent that larger accommodation was required and the school therefore moved to No. 1 SD Kidbrooke in October 1922.

By September 1925, the school had become a self-contained unit and was known as the school of Stores accounting and storekeeping; this title reflected the fact that the school was responsible for the training of both officers and airmen.[2] The continual growth of the unit yet again led to space becoming a premium and the school relocated to RAF Cranwell on 1 December 1932, occupying a former annexe of the Sergeants' Mess on West Camp, which had been converted into classrooms and offices.

The move to Cranwell still did not yield all of the additional space required and in December 1936, the officers' course was moved back to Kidbrooke as a detachment from Cranwell and renamed the Equipment training school (officers) in November 1938. The school also became responsible for a detachment at RAF Halton, which had been formed a little earlier in September 1938 and also one at RAF Henlow, which had opened in January 1931 to train officers commissioned from the rank of warrant officer under Air Ministry weekly order 429/30.[3] The courses for officers appointed from civilian life (from January 1933) were twenty-six weeks in duration, whereas the course for former warrant officers was reduced to thirteen weeks.[4] The inter-war period also saw the development of the Branch's first professional qualification with the creation of the explosives specialisation in February 1927. The names of officers so qualified were prefixed by a bold letter 'X' in the Air Force List and were defined as 'qualified to take charge of magazines and explosives'.[5] By January 1939, the expansion programme had generated a number of appointments at various units, which were required to be filled urgently leading to a number of trainee officers being posted prematurely before the end of their course. Consequently, and from May 1939, the course syllabus was revised and shortened from twenty-six to approximately sixteen weeks.[6]

Entrants to the Stores Branch came from quite diverse backgrounds, an interesting example being Arnold Wall, who was to go on and serve throughout the Second World War, eventually retiring as a Group Captain in 1950.[7] Born in New Zealand in 1908, Arnold came to England in 1926 and entered the RAF Cadet College Cranwell in the same year. Qualifying as a pilot with some seventy hours under his belt, Arnold was posted to No. 7 Squadron based at Worthy Down flying Vickers Virginias. Following an armament officers' course in 1929–1930, he was posted to No. 60 Squadron then based in India at Kohat on the North-West Frontier. It was here that his flying career came to an end while flying Wapitis on detachment at Miranshah in Waziristan. During a camera gun training exercise near the aerodrome, he was hit in the eye by a stone thrown at the aircraft by a young goat herder. Having lost his eye, Arnold returned to the UK in December 1931 and the Air Ministry offered him a permanent commission in the Stores Branch, which he accepted. Returning to RAF Cranwell, he joined the School of Stores Accounting and Storekeeping and appears to have enjoyed the six months of training:

> The Cranwell course had nothing to do with the cadet College. It consisted of five ex-civilians aged 23 to 24, one ex-Cranwell cadet who'd been invalided off flying

> and myself, an ex-GD. For three months, we idled and enjoyed ourselves there, then went for three months to the ghastly aircraft depot at Henlow, Herts, where we were joined by five ex-Warrant Officers, a cheerful bunch.

He had a different view of the course itself, however: 'The syllabus was abysmally inadequate, as even I could see; literally nothing beyond stores accounting regulations, word by word, and elementary parade ground foot drill for the ex-civilian chaps'.[8] Of particular interest is that the course at this time was being run for officers from the retired list and one can only assume that this was in anticipation of the significant mobilisation requirement that would come about the following year with the outbreak of the Second World War. Recruiting was also taking place at this time for the Equipment Branch of the RAFVR and was 'open to candidates between the ages of twenty-five to forty, must be physically fit and who have not less than five years' business or industrial experience in the employment of one or more firms of standing'. The initial period of service was set at five years (similar to a present day short service commission) and training was carried out at the RAFVR Centre in Staffordshire House, Store Street, just off Tottenham Court Road in London.

Lack of space continued to be a recurring theme, this time with the space at Kidbrooke being required for Balloon Command. Thus, the school moved yet again in August 1939 to the first of two very short-lived locations in premises vacated by No. 6 Flying Training School at RAF Little Rissington with a detachment at Halton.[9] Six months later in February 1940, the school moved to Loughborough, this time into premises that permitted the detachment at RAF Halton to be closed.[10] Barely four months later, the school relocated to Grange-Over-Sands where it remained until March 1944. Thereafter, it moved to Stannington (April to November 1944), and then Kirkham (December 1944 to July 1945), where it reverted to the title of Equipment officers' course and became part of the RAF School of Administrative Trades on 13 December 1944. Its final wartime move was to RAF Bicester in August 1945.[11]

It was clear that the Equipment Branch had acquitted itself well during the Second World War and its officers had demonstrated their suitability for wider employment within the service. In early 1946, the RAF post-war manning committee recommended to the air member for personnel that the duties of the Equipment Branch should be extended and should include appointments to a number of senior administrative posts. The committee also recommended that potential officers seeking a permanent career should be recruited principally by direct entry from civilian life under a similar procedure to that of the RAF College Cranwell. Secretarial officers were also included in this general concept.

Following a study by an Air Ministry working party convened by the Director General of Training, it was agreed that the standard of training for Equipment and Secretarial cadets should be on the same level as entrants to the GD Branch, with the pattern of training closely aligned with the RAF College. This scheme introduced a dual approach to supply training, consisting of an RAF college and a direct entry scheme. Following approval by the Air Council, the Equipment and Secretarial (E&S) Wing of the RAF College came into being in September 1946; its development was the responsibility of the Commandant of the RAF College within Flying Training Command.[12] The first OC (known as an assistant commandant) was Group Captain R. G. Seymour CBE; as in the pre-war years, accommodation at Cranwell remained a problem and the Wing therefore set up its new home at RAF Digby, just north of Cranwell. Due to insufficient numbers of cadets, the opening of the Wing was deferred until 4 October 1947 when the first entry of cadets for the Equipment and Secretarial Branches was attested in parallel with No. 49 Entry of the GD Branch. In mid-1953, with the accommodation problem at Cranwell resolved, the E&S Wing closed and its cadets were incorporated into their corresponding entries at Cranwell. This far-sighted flight cadet concept continued until 1972, being replaced with the graduate entry scheme, from 1972 to 1974. The importance of this initiative for the future of RAF Logistics (and perhaps to the Administrative/Secretarial Branch) cannot be overestimated. It resulted in future senior officers of the specialisation having started their RAF careers alongside their operational counterparts and in both completing their early training together. This led to much greater mutual trust than would otherwise have been possible. The scheme was later extended to other ground branches of the RAF and has unquestionably contributed greatly to RAF teamwork across all disciplines. Overall, the course consisted of some 528 hours of instruction covering: equipment, movements, explosives, fuels, provisioning, packaging, storage, instructional visits, time for revision, and examinations.

By the late 1960s, Equipment cadets would spend three years at the RAF College, the first two and a half years as flight cadets, followed by six months post-graduate study as pilot officers. The first six months at Cranwell were taken up with general service training, drill, war studies and basic academic subjects. At the same time, non-GD cadets studied the principles of flight, aerodynamics, thermodynamics, and meteorology to give them a broad understanding of aviation-related issues. Long periods closeted in the classroom huts of the E&S Wing absorbing the intricacies of supply control and accounting were punctuated by more appealing activities such as explosives demolition training on Theddlethorpe range and overseas visits courtesy of Transport Command's Hastings, Comet, Britannia, and VC10 aircraft. When not engaged in specialist training, the Equipment cadets trained with and competed on equal terms against their fellow GD, Engineer, Secretarial, and RAF Regiment cadets on the sports field and firing range, on the parade ground and on expeditions as well as in academic and military studies, and more than held their own in terms of trophies and prizes. After three years at Cranwell, the newly commissioned Equipment officers were fully qualified in fuels, explosives and movements as well as basic supply and departed the college to find out how the Air Force and Supply really worked.

Direct entry officers to the Branch trained separately and, similar to the war years, the training school experienced a number of moves. From its last wartime home in Bicester it moved to Hereford in 1948 and then to Digby (1948), Bircham Newton

(1954), Kirton in Lindsey (1959), and Upwood in 1964. This dual approach to Supply officer training finished in 1974 and was then centralised at Cranwell, becoming the Supply Training Group (STG), a component of the Department of Specialist Ground Training (DSGT). The first course to complete training under the new system was number 303 Supply Officers Course (SOC) which commenced training in January 1974. For some unknown reason, the course was always referred to as the initial supply course (ISC) and, through usage rather than any design change, the course name was changed to the ISC in 1979. The syllabus was divided into four modules consisting of: a foundation group, a functional group, a transition-to-war and operations group, and finally, a consolidation and evaluation phase. Students also spent five days on a practical leadership training exercise, usually in Scotland or Wales.

The course underwent many content and structural changes; over the years its duration progressively increased from thirteen weeks in 1974 to eighteen weeks in 1986 and it remained at this level until the middle of 1992. The primary aim of the ISC was to prepare officers for their first tour in the Service and therefore had to cover a wide range of general supply topics. Although management skills were studied, the focus of the course was very much on understanding detailed procedures. During his attendance on the ISC in 1981, the author recalls having to complete and scrutinise supply vouchers (for transactions such as issues, receipts and loans) as part of an office simulator exercise (known as the environmental exercise or ENVEX) and learning how to carry out on-line stock record interrogations using the ICL 4/72 computer terminal. For those requiring more specialist training for their first tour (and also later in their careers) separate courses were run for explosives and fuels at RAF Calshot (later at RAF Hereford), ADP with the Army at Blandford, and air movements at RAF Brize Norton.

Notwithstanding the duration, the basic four-module structure of the ISC remained sound for many years. However, following a study by the Supply Branch sponsor in 1987 entitled 'Supply officer 2000', it was considered that the existing strategy was no longer adequate for the changing needs of the RAF. Consequently, a paper was submitted to the Officers and Aircrew Personnel Committee recommending a new approach to training. In essence, this was to be a three-tier concept, consisting of two Supply officer training (SOT) courses (SOT1 and SOT2) each of twelve weeks duration and a senior Supply course, also of twelve weeks length. The intention was that students would attend SOT1 directly after initial officer training and then enter productive service; they would then return to Cranwell for SOT2 after their first or second tour. The concept was approved and the first SOT1 course commenced training in October 1992. With this change, the old STG became known as just SOT but, with the addition of a number of other specialist courses to its portfolio, it was renamed the Logistics Management Training Squadron (LMTS).

The SOT course was fundamentally different in approach from the ISC and its emphasis was on management of resources rather than understanding detailed procedures. Moreover, the new approach recognised the need for a sound grounding in operational logistics, a lesson subsequently confirmed during the First Gulf War of 1991. Consequently, the fuels, explosives and surface movements aspects in the SOT1 course were greatly enhanced from the previous ISC coverage. The SOT2 course, on the other hand, focused on staff work, with the aim of preparing officers for Command HQ and MOD appointments. The first SOT2 course started training in October 1995, but was only eight weeks long rather than the originally planned twelve weeks. Unfortunately, the SOT2 course did not last long and was replaced by the intermediate Logistics managers course in March 2000, which was intended for junior officers and their civilian equivalents.[13]

The report of the 1999 Defence Training Review, which had a remit to examine all individual training and education for both service and civilian personnel, was published in 2001 and observed that the Defence training estate was too large. A key recommendation of the review, which enabled a much-needed rationalisation, was that a number of Defence colleges or schools were to be formed. It was thus that a new tri-service Defence college of Logistics and Personnel Administration (DCLPA) was formed in April 2004. As part of this rationalisation, a new Supply and Movements Training Wing (SMTW) was formed at RAF Halton, under a Supply Branch wing commander; it became part of the new college. The formation of SMTW brought together LMTS (which remained at Cranwell), the airmen's Supply Training Squadron (STS) at Halton, and the Defence Movements School at RAF Brize Norton under one command. As part of wider work to improve RAF Logistics training, a view developed that greater value could be added if officer and airmen training could be integrated and the SOT element at Cranwell relocated to RAF Halton in April 2005, becoming the SOT Squadron within SMTW. This was the first time that the logistics training of both officers and airmen had taken place on the same unit since 1936. With the renaming of the Supply Branch in 2009, the then SOT course was retitled Logistics officer training (LOT) that, with an ongoing process of continuous improvement to maintain its relevance to an ever-evolving RAF, remains in place to the present day.

The change of Branch name to Logistics in 2009 also included a merger of both the former Supply and Administration (Catering) Branches. This was a challenge for training, as LSTS had to redesign the LOT course to ensure that it would prepare junior Logistics officers who might be required to fill catering appointments and have responsibility for the personnel in the trades of Logistics (chefs) and Logistics (caterer). Initially, this was done by adding a three-week Catering Management module to the existing twenty-one-week long course which included modules for Supply, MT, Fuels, and Mobility. Former junior officers of the Administration (Catering) Branch were given the opportunity of completing the LOT course so that they could fill logistic appointments. At the time of publication, planning work is in hand to relocate SMTW to become part of a new, purpose-built, tri-service logistics training college at Worthy Down near Winchester in Hampshire.

Intermediate Level Training for Officers

For many years, there was no form of intermediate supply training after completion of the basic supply course that was orientated towards unit supply procedures; this basic training did not equip an officer with the skills and knowledge required for staff appointments or for the command of a Supply Squadron. This shortfall was highlighted in 1968 in a report by Air Commodore F. S. R. Johnson entitled 'Review of the Training Requirements of Equipment Officers'. The outcome of the report was the establishment of an advanced supply course, the first of which assembled at the RAF College Cranwell (Supply and Secretarial Wing) in early May 1972. Aimed at senior flight lieutenants and junior squadron leaders, the course was split between professional supply training and management training. The supply element covered topics such as Defence policy, Supply planning, rationalisation, provisioning, and joint service logistics while the management component covered a wide range of topics in both behavioural and management sciences.[14] Curiously, this eight-week course was intended for students between the ages of twenty-nine and thirty-four. Following a syllabus review, the course was lengthened to ten weeks in September 1982 along with a name change to the senior Supply course (SSC); the change of title was to avoid confusion with the abbreviation for the advanced staff course.

With the formation of RAF Logistics Command in 1994, both the Supply and Engineering disciplines were working much more closely with one another, if anything as a result of the physical co-location of the respective staffs at the key sites of RAF Brampton and RAF Wyton. It became clear that there was merit in a conjoined logistics course to help bring both disciplines together and further develop the professionalisation of both. With the approval of the C-in-C, Cranwell was set the task of developing a new course under the leadership of the Director of DSGT, Group Captain Andy Parsons. Very quickly, a twelve-week residential course was designed, eventually entitled the senior Logistics management course (SLMC) and was mostly delivered by visiting lecturers making up the four daily sessions. It was, in effect, a merger of the old SSC and the senior Engineering management course. The content covered a wide range of topics such as operational activities, support, MOD, finance, and contracts, providing a much broader based syllabus. The first course commenced in May 1994 with the intent to run two per year. Two courses of twelve weeks duration per year was fine in the mid-1990s, but became unsustainable as the RAF began reducing in size and the RAF's personnel management agency (PMA) struggled to release senior officers for what was effectively three months. As a result, the opportunity was taken to make up the numbers with overseas students, mainly from the Middle East. This was greatly helped by the Logistics Command C-in-C's encouragement of the Head of the Royal Saudi Air Force (RSAF) to participate in the course and, through BAE Systems sponsorship, send two full colonels on each course.

Although the course was initially a great success, it provided no formal qualification at the end and this fact did not sit comfortably with the RAF's Training

Group Defence Agency, which raised questions about its value, particularly in light of its duration. For a short while, the course was reduced to ten weeks but this proved difficult for BAE and RSAF who had committed (and planned) to provide students for twelve weeks. It was also becoming increasingly difficult for PMA to fill the course with RAF Supply and Engineering Branch officers and it became not uncommon for a course complement to consist of nine overseas students and just three from the RAF; this did not sit well with visiting lecturers. In the event, the course was withdrawn with No. 15 its last in 2006. While this door closed, another opened and a highly successful venture was launched with the University of Lincoln.

The Air and Defence Logistics Staff Course

There was still a need for an intermediate level of training and the University of Lincoln, which specialised in work-based distance learning, expressed an interest in helping to develop a replacement. It was thus that a team from Lincoln (consisting of Dr Malcolm Young, Mr Mike Howitt, and Mr (later Dr) Gary Ramsden) joined forces with Group Captain Richard Fogden and Squadron Leader Jim Nadin (then OC LMTS) to develop a scoping study for a programme of innovative logistics education, but with a qualification at the end. Time was not on their side as they had been given a delivery target of 2007—less than a year to develop a credible military logistics course with a 50 per cent academic content.

Eventually, a proposal was submitted to HQ STC for a new course to be jointly managed with Lincoln; it would challenge the student, but provide them with either a postgraduate diploma or an MSc in logistics management at the end. Each course cohort would comprise of eight specific modules, complemented by a relevant academic topic with a 5,000-word assignment to be written in the intervening period before attending the next module. The cohort would be of a two-year duration, which would allow the student sufficient time to produce and submit their written assignment. The new course, to be known as the air logistics staff course (ALSC), was approved, and the first cohort was launched in 2007 as planned, with six Logistics officers, six Communications officers, and six Aerospace engineer officers embracing the academic structures of strategic management; a highly successful formula of learning was born.

Broadly speaking, the course structure was based on the University of Lincoln's existing Chartered Institute of Logistics and Transport (CILT) accredited MSc logistics management programme and the innovative partnered approach which was developed, combined specialist logistics management delivery from within the MOD, industry, humanitarian agencies, and the academic world. By the time cohort three was launched, LMTS at Cranwell and the University of Lincoln were running three courses at varying levels of student completion. The concept of cohort or module 'hopping' was also introduced, which enabled students to adjust their attendance on the course to take account of short notice postings, overseas detachments or changed personal circumstances. This proved to be particularly popular as it provided much-needed flexibility for students to continue with their studies. It also made life much easier for the RAF's personnel managers and units as students were only absent from their normal place of duty for just a week at a time.

The inaugural visit to LMTS by the new commandant of DCLPA in 2009 witnessed a major change in the direction of logistics education for Defence. Having heard what the ALSC was producing during his briefing by OC LMTS briefing, he turned to his commandant of the Defence Logistics School and said 'the Army needs some of that and now', which effectively gave LMTS and Lincoln six months to develop a revised course that continued to meet the requirements of the RAF, but also those of the Army and Royal Navy. Consequently, the ALSC was developed into a Defence Logistics staff course (DLSC), with students drawn from logistics specialists of all three armed services—MOD, the civil service, and representatives from the Defence industries. Facilitated by LSTS and run mainly at RAF Cranwell, the DLSC has developed into a programme which has met the growing demands for post-graduate logistics education across Defence. Such was its success that by the end of the 2013–2014 academic year, just over 300 students had been enrolled on the programme since its start, with ninety-one having completed MSc degrees.

Much of the success of what is now the DLSC programme is due in no small part to the contribution of Squadron Leader Jim Nadin who had joined the RAF as an airman entrant in 1967. After passing out from RAF Swinderby in Lincolnshire, he went on to complete his Supply accountant training at RAF Hereford. Thus began a forty-seven-year long career in RAF Logistics. He was commissioned in 1984 and served in a variety of Supply appointments until he took redundancy in 1996. He returned to the RAF College Cranwell shortly afterwards with a Reserve Commission and joined the Supply directing staff for the SLMC. In 2002, he took command of the newly formed Logistics Management Training Squadron, continuing in this appointment until his retirement in May 2014. His personal commitment towards steering the professionalisation and development of the Logistics Branch and Trades via a programme of through life academic education, which was available to all, became the foundation of the LMTS vision. The enormous success of the ALSC/DLSC initiative led to LMTS being placed in the final three of the National 2012 CILT professional development award. Jim's services in the pursuit of excellence and for making academic education available to those who wished to accept the challenge at all levels was recognised in 2013 by the University of Lincoln, which awarded him an honorary degree at a ceremony in the magnificent setting of Lincoln Cathedral.

Advanced Pre-Employment Training

In the late 1960s, with much closer working relationships developing with industry and government pressures to achieve better value for money in Defence, the Equipment

Squadron Leader Jim Nadin after receiving his honorary degree at Lincoln Cathedral. (*J. Nadin*)

Branch recognised that there was a growing need for officers with a grounding in modern management techniques. Therefore, financial approval was gained to send a selected number of officers each year to attend the University of Manchester Institute of Science and Technology (UMIST) diploma in management studies course. By the end of the 1970s, there were about twenty-four posts in the Branch that had been annotated with this advanced pre-employment training (APET) requirement.

In time, the UMIST course became a full-blown MSc degree in operations management, although by the mid-1990s, the number of opportunities per year had decreased significantly to just four or five. Similar opportunities for officers specialising in Movements became available at the Universities of Cranfield and Westminster. Due to the length of the courses and the qualification obtained, APET opportunities invariably came with a return of service (amortization) stipulation requiring officers to remain in the service for a specified number of years (usually between two and three) after completion of the course. These opportunities offered unique broadening opportunities for individuals and exposed students, not just to academic thinking on a wide range of topics, but also the chance (often through visits) to see at first-hand how industry conducted its operational business. The author, for example, conducted research with the Sainsbury's supermarket chain, examining how it used barcode technology in its supply chain during his APET MSc course at UMIST in 1996. Qualifications gained through the APET scheme were not intended to develop individuals for higher promotion, as selection for advanced staff training at Staff College was of greater significance in this respect. It did, however, bring much needed expertise into the Branch which proved invaluable as RAF Logistics began to work much more closely with industry partners and suppliers. Having said that, a number of APET qualified did go on to achieve one and two-star rank during their careers.

Airmen and Airwomen Training

During the First World War, the RFC did not have a dedicated school for its storemen and ledger keepers and instruction in these disciplines seems to have taken place amid the general training at Farnborough, along with what must have been a significant amount of on-the-job training. The post-First World War development of more extensive (and complex) store keeping and stores accounting practices and procedures though, soon demanded a more extensive syllabus of training. Consequently, Clerk (Stores) and Storekeepers were trained at the School of Stores Accounting and Store Keeping at No. 4 SD Ruislip, the first courses for them commencing in February 1921.[15] As commented on earlier, the school moved to Kidbrooke in October 1922 and then to RAF Cranwell in December 1932. In December 1936, as a result of the term Equipment being introduced following the renaming of the officers' Stores Branch, the airmen training element of the school was renamed to Equipment Training School (Airmen) (ETS (Airmen)). By then, the airmen's trade had become Equipment assistant.

Although much of the training required airmen to thoroughly understand equipment accounting practices (especially the processing of myriad paper vouchers for receiving and issuing equipment), efforts were made to introduce more imaginative methods of learning. In the period, up to the outbreak of war in 1939, there were four innovations which contributed in this respect. First, and perhaps the most imaginative, was the creation of a 'model' storehouse in early 1923 where airmen could practise what they had learned in a simulated environment. The second innovation, introduced in 1930, was the voucher pack-up, a set of forms and vouchers used for the logistics process, with typewritten user instructions on the reverse of each; this proved to be particularly popular and provided a useful aide memoire for airmen to use when they left the school and joined their first RAF unit. The third initiative, one that was particularly welcomed by both staff and students, was the introduction of a bound volume of printed course notes in 1931; prior to this, notes had been dictated by instructors for students to transcribe into their notebooks—a simple change, but one that freed up time and permitted more time to be allocated to other subjects on the syllabus. The fourth innovation came about following the move of the school to RAF Cranwell in 1933 with it having access to typical RAF unit stores facilities rather than the Stores depot environment that it had experienced at Kidbrooke. Essentially, the course length was increased to four months in duration, enabling students to work for two months of the course in Kidbrooke's main stores complex and each flight of one of the flying squadrons in groups of four to five; they moved between different sections each week. This provided valuable 'work experience' along with the model storehouse.[16]

The degree to which these initiatives were forward thinking is evidenced by the fact that the model storehouse, the voucher pack-up, and pre-printed course notes were still in use in 2014 by SMTW at RAF Halton. The ETS (Airmen) remained at RAF Cranwell following the departure of the ETS (Officers) in April 1936. By 1941, it became clear that accommodation was much in demand at Cranwell, particularly as the radio school was planned to be opened there in the very near future. Consequently, the ETS (Airmen) relocated to RAF Bridlington (a marine craft unit) in May–June 1941, where a new school complex was opened to train both airmen and airwomen; WAAF Equipment assistants had been trained at RAF Melksham up to this date due to accommodation limitations at Cranwell.[17]

As with many wartime requirements, widespread use was made of existing buildings with many facilities requisitioned for the duration of the war. Seaside locations were especially suitable for billeting large numbers of trainees due to the number of hotels and guest houses. This is well-illustrated by the set-up at Bridlington where the school itself was dispersed across the town in various buildings with the HQ in the Alexandra Hotel. The airmen and airwomen were billeted in different houses in the Trinity Road area and took their meals on the sea front in what is now the Cottage Grill restaurant. Most of the equipment training classes were taken in the Grand Pavilion, now the new Leisure World complex, although men and women were segregated.[18] The sizeable volumes of both men and women entering the school by this time led to the creation of two separate training wings respectively within the school in September 1941, primarily for the administration requirements of each. The downside to locating to an east coast position was that it brought the school in much closer proximity to enemy air attacks. Indeed, between December 1941 and May 1942 (during which more detailed figures were kept), some 5,423 training man hours were lost due to air raid alerts along with considerable damage to some of the buildings used by the school in Bridlington, especially following the enemy air raids on the town on 18 June and 16 July 1941.[19] The school remained at Bridlington until August 1942 when accommodation demands necessitated a move to RAF Kirkham as an interim move before relocation to Eastbourne in December 1942. A move to the south east of Britain proved to be even more disruptive and, as it turned out, more tragic than Bridlington in terms of the effects of enemy air raids. Between December 1942 and July 1943, some 9,629 training man hours were lost due to enemy air raids with six trainee Equipment assistants being killed in raids between 15 January and 1 April 1943.[20] The school's final wartime move was to Weston-super-Mare in the south west of the country in July 1943, a considerably safer location where the risk from air raids had virtually disappeared, following the two heavy raids on the town in 1942.

Post-war, the ETS (Airmen) relocated temporarily to RAF St Athan before finding a more permanent location at RAF Hereford in 1946, remaining there for forty-eight years until 1994, when it moved to its current home at RAF Halton. In 1946, the course for Equipment assistants was six months long; on completion of training, the airmen were expected to be capable of working in any area including fuels and explosives, and also as air quartermasters who worked on transport aircraft. By 1948, the course length was reduced to eight weeks and was playing a key role in integrating both national servicemen and regulars. That same year the school also played an important part during the Berlin Airlift, making a major contribution in the training of the many volunteers and pressed men who were required during that emergency.

By 1951, the trade of Equipment assistant had become obsolete and was replaced by the trades of clerk equipment accounting, storeman mechanical, storeman electrical, and instruments and storeman non-technical, all intended for airmen and airwomen up to the rank of SAC. The 'Supplier 1' and 'Supplier 2' courses were also introduced at about the same time. Although this supposedly worked well for a number of years, it became recognised that this number of demarcations restricted flexibility and a more simplified trade structure was adopted with 'supplier accounting' for those employed in supply control and accounting functions and 'supplier materiel' for those employed in storage groups. A 'supplier general' course was introduced later to combine the two elements of the trade.

In 1990, the supply basic training (SBT) 1 and 2 courses were introduced and incorporated what had been, since 1972, the separate trade qualification for Supply controller, which reflected the requirements for the specialist skills of working with the RAF's ADP system. The general concept was that following recruit training, airmen and airwomen would attend SBT 1 followed by a twelve-month period on their first unit, returning to Hereford for SBT2; the concept bears a striking resemblance to that adopted by Supply officer training in 1992. Two trial SBT1 and SBT2 courses were run between 1993 and 1994 before the system was finally implemented. In parallel with this, some 1,800 airmen who had trained under the earlier scheme had to be trained as Supply controllers and gain what was known as the Q-Sup-SC qualification, which was now automatically included in the SBT process.

In the summer of 1994, the school (now known as the Supply Training Squadron (STS)) relocated to RAF Halton and took up residence in the old workshops complex. The explosives and fuels training flights moved in to accommodation in Spreckley Hall. By 1998, STS consisted of four flights: a Supply Training Flight, a Fuels/Explosives Flight, a Course Design Flight, and a Training Coordination Flight. The school was commanded by a squadron leader of the Supply Branch and had a complement of forty-seven, including a number of civilian instructional officers. With the arrival of Supply officer training from Cranwell in 2005, the former STS became part of the new LSTS.

Wider Logistics Training and Education

For many years, the logistics training of officers and airmen after their basic service training was quite simply known as specialist training, including any other courses that they might be required to undertake to gain specific skills or qualifications. As the RAF began to adopt the Defence systems approach to training (DSAT), a standardised approach classified training into phases: phase one included all basic service training courses, phase two included just the former specialist training courses required for individuals to take up their first productive postings, and phase three included a range of even more specialist courses that might be undertaken directly after phase two or later in individual's careers as required by new postings. Within LSTS at RAF Halton, the portfolio in 2008 included courses in explosives, fuels, compressed gasses, cryogenic fluids, and dangerous goods for officers, NCOs, and MOD civilians. The LMTS at Cranwell was offering courses to prepare senior logistic officers for in-command appointments at the RAF's main operating bases and in the Defence logistics environment. By 2009, SMTW was delivering some sixty-five phase two and three courses at its Halton, Cranwell, and Brize Norton sites.

Up to the end of the 1990s, and excluding the APET scheme, the acquisition of additional educational and professional qualifications in logistic and management

Students learning about the finer points of bulk fuel installations. (*Author's collection*)

related subjects was largely a matter of personal pursuit. Certain professional bodies, such as the Institute of Purchasing and Supply and the Institute of Management, did recognise the experience and qualifications of Supply personnel, which enabled many of them to gain various levels of membership.[21] The more rigorous approach to training design offered by DSAT and, perhaps more significantly, the recognition that wider professionalisation was of benefit to the Branch and Trade saw many logistic courses becoming officially accredited by further and higher education establishments as well as professional institutes. The SOT course is perhaps a good example of the additional value added to training courses, which the University of Lincoln accredited from 2003 towards its BSc (Hons) degree programme. The content of both initial officer training and SOT enabled students to achieve part of the first two levels of the degree programme. The balance to achieve the degree could then be completed by work-based distance learning. Similar accreditations were developed with professional institutes.

It was not just officer training which benefitted. In partnership with CILT, SMTW established an award-winning programme to deliver an apprenticeship scheme to offer qualification opportunities from the very early stages of training. New supply trade entrants to the RAF begin their apprenticeship programme by undertaking the CILT level 2 qualification just nine weeks into their careers. The scheme does not cease at level 2; JNCOs can undertake level 3 and SNCOs level 5 qualifications.

Air Movements Training

In the early days of air movements, training for the task was done very much on the job. By early 1944, and the RAF operating ever increasing numbers of Dakota transport aircraft, it had become clear that this needed to be formalized. In September 1944, the deputy senior air staff officer at HQ Transport Command convened a conference at which it was decided that a specialist school needed to be formed. This was subsequently agreed and in November 1944, the Transport Command Traffic Control School was established at RAF St Mawgan in Cornwall.[22] Such was the estimated size of the training task that it was agreed that only officers and SNCOs would initially be trained by the school and that these would provide on the job training for airmen, to the school's standards, at units. Based on the estimate that the RAF would be manning some 200 staging posts worldwide, it was estimated that as many as 600 officers and 1,200 SNCOs would need training in the first year alone. The course was of five weeks duration; three of these were spent at the school, one week at RAF stations, and one week with the BOAC Traffic School at Croydon. The throughput in the early days was considerable, with a planned intake of thirty officers and sixty SNCOs every three weeks, up to a maximum of 1,800 personnel.

In November 1945, the school moved to RAF Bramcote by which time thirteen courses had been completed with 643 officers and 480 SNCOs having successfully completed training. The facilities at Bramcote proved to be far superior to their previous home with mock-up aircraft fuselages housed in a hangar close to the instructional block.[23] The school took on the responsibility for training clerks (movement control) and air movement assistants when these trades were introduced in 1945. As part of rationalisation of training, the school was disbanded in March 1947 with training carried out at the Equipment School at RAF Hereford. This arrangement lasted for seven years when the RAF Movements School was formed at RAF Kidbrooke in January 1954. Her Majesty the Queen granted the school its badge in 1956, which consisted of, at its centre, a swan superimposed on a torch; the swan representing movement by land, sea, and air, with the torch signifying learning. The motto '*ars lenit iter*' roughly translated as 'skill smooths the journey'.

In January 1953, the school moved to RAF Kirton-in-Lindsey but relocated to RAF Abingdon, where it was retitled as the Air Movements Training School. The move to Abingdon enabled a closer relationship with the operational transport squadrons based there, namely the unit Air Movements Squadron and the Air Transport Development Unit. This relationship enabled the school to keep up to date with current operational developments in the air transport world. The school relocated to RAF Brize Norton in March 1972 with its title reverting to the RAF Movements School in August 1974; the change of title reflecting the fact that Movements personnel were involved with both air and surface methods of transportation. In 2002 the professionalism of the RAF Movements School was recognised by becoming affiliated to the Worshipful Company of Carmen, a longstanding Livery Company in the City of London. The company went on to sponsor a prize for the most promising graduate from the Officers' Movements Course each year; the inaugural award was made to Flying Officer Chris Houghton who completed No. 221 Course in December 2001. On 1 April 2004, as part of the continuing implementation of the Defence Training Review, the RAF Movements School became the Defence Movements School, transferring from Strike Command to SMTW within the newly DCLPA.

On completion of recruit training, entrants to the new sub-trade underwent an eight-week course at RAF Brize Norton to train as a Movements Operator which prepared them for their role in handling cargo and passengers and for their documentation. On completion of training, entrants emerged as LACs and each then had to complete one year's service and pass the appropriate examination before promotion to SAC. Once they had completed at least one tour of duty (of up to three years) as Movements operators, they could then be selected for a more advanced training course to qualify as Movements controllers. This was a five-week course which covered the broader aspects of Movements duties including load distribution in aircraft and the theory and practice of compiling documents to determine the correct balance of a loaded aircraft in flight. On successful completion of this course and passing an educational test plus an examination to test their knowledge of RAF administration and organisation, they were then eligible for promotion to corporal.

The transfer of the school to DCLPA brought with it a much wider remit to Defence Movements training to include basic, further, and specialist training to personnel of all three services, overseas students, and civilian staff. By 2008, this included some twenty-five different courses run at RAF Brize Norton and the Princess Royal Barracks at Deepcut in Surrey; the latter reflected the fact that the Army Training Flight of the RLC had become part of the school and was providing soldiers of the RLC their basic and specialist trade training as Movements controllers. Army Movements training was moved to Brize Norton in April 2010. At Brize Norton, the RAF Training Flight was delivering three major courses that included basic Movements training, further Movements training, and officers' Movements training. Under the leadership of Squadron Leader (later Wing Commander) Paul Buxton, much work was done to make training more relevant in the workplace with the disposal of a large proportion of outdated training aids and their replacement by more current items of equipment, not least of which was the complete renovation of the Hercules aircraft cargo hold mock-up to turn it into a more relevant Mk 5 (J-model) version by Pennant International Group PLC. Paul also began a much-needed culture change for the school from what had become a pass or fail approach to a more individualised approach including a psychometric assessment for students on arrival to targeted learning packages to help deliver remedial training. The results of this fresh approach were dramatic and saw the overall pass rate of the basic Movements course alone improve from 75 per cent to around 93 per cent.

Another notable innovation at this time was the introduction of family days for the relatives of students attending the basic Movements training course. From the perspective of the families, it was an opportunity for them to meet the instructors, see the facilities, and try the food. From the school's perspective, it meant that the students could not claim that they wanted to leave training because the accommodation, food, and staff were at fault and allowed the staff to make connections with relatives from the outset. As a result, the school was able to intervene really early on where there were personal issues with students. This initiative had a welcome and positive effect on retention rates within training. The school also took the opportunity to show families the Trade DVD; it was amazing how many of their loved ones had breezily left home to become a mover without ever explaining what that meant. It went down really well with students and relatives, demystified the training, and gave the reputation of military training a real boost.

Training of Civilians in Logistics

While much on the job training took place for civilians on RAF units, the various training schools also ran courses for civilians, as well as offering places on their mainly service oriented courses. Additionally, the Supply Management organisation at Harrogate, and later the DLO site at RAF Wyton, also ran very effective training schools offering a wide range of provisioning and supply management courses to both servicemen and civilians.

PART III
Conclusions

12

The Logistics Journey

While this book has been a work of history, it is the story of a living entity and one that continues to evolve. It has covered a time span of ninety-six years, from the formation of the RAF in April 1918 through to the final withdrawal of British forces from Afghanistan at the end of 2014. The Logistics story in Part One and the specialist perspectives in Part Two have covered a complex range of activities and specialisations, all of which have had their part to play in sustaining air power during this period. While they all stand on their own merits, there are some broad observations which can be made, along with some pointers for the future. Indeed, as suggested by Sir Winston Churchill 'the longer you can look back, the farther you can look forward'. First, though, it is worth examining the past.

Perhaps one of the most noticeable points is identity. Logistics, by whatever name it has been called over the years by the RAF, is not just an activity; it is also a profession. This was clearly acknowledged by Air Commodore Charles Lambe in 1920 when he drove forward the proposal which resulted in the decision to form the RAF's Stores Branch. This, along with the non-commissioned tradesmen and civilians working in the same discipline, established a clear identity for Logistics, one which would endure to the present day. The quest to find the right identity was a long one and led to several changes of name from Stores in the very early days to Equipment in 1936, Supply in 1970, and finally to Logistics in 2009. These changes were not a pursuit of vanity, they were driven by a common factor—the need to reflect accurately what the discipline did and what it was responsible for. In the post-Second World War period, this was important, particularly as the relentless tide of Defence reviews and other governmental initiatives has sought to reduce resources, while still expecting the same level of output. A clear identity helps ensure that planners and operational managers see logistics as a distinct and important component in the wider panoply of support disciplines needed to sustain air power.

The second point is about learning from what has gone before. This was particularly evident just after the First World War when a lot had been learned from the operational logistics of the RFC, much of which was used to shape the emerging RAF Stores organisation. The Second World War was perhaps the best example of where lessons were learned, especially as all three services grappled with the complexities of expeditionary operations such as the invasion of North Africa, Italy, and then France. Where things had not worked well (and there were many), the opportunity was taken to put it right before the next operation. The development of the RAF Beach Squadrons is a clear example of this. By the time of the Normandy landings in 1944, these had evolved into highly capable and self-sufficient force elements and their organisation and operation was progressively honed in light of experience.

The Cold War years were very different; the era of the jet aircraft, inter-continental missiles, and the threat of nuclear war was a whole new world. The relative stability of the years up to the collapse of communism in Europe had largely been influenced by NATO's various nuclear exchange strategies and then just hoping that a nuclear holocaust would never happen; there was little from the past that could help shape this new order. The First Gulf War, though, and the years that followed, found RAF Logistics having to relearn much about supporting expeditionary air operations; this took time to achieve. The development of the ACSSUs and the EAWs, both of which had clear links with similar concepts in the Second World War, are good examples of where the lessons of the past have helped to shape the present and the future.

The third point that emerges from the logistics story is just how much the RAF was at the cutting edge of the discipline. This was particularly evident during the 1960s and 1970s in the field of ADP and later IT, where the service was well ahead not just of its Naval and Army counterparts, but also the commercial sector. While companies such as AEI with the early Supply computer system had done much to enable this, the RAF had also developed a highly credible in-house capability. RAF Logistics in the 1970s and 1980s was also a 'leader in the field' of warehousing, where the high-density storage and distribution facilities at Carlisle and Stafford were well ahead of their time and were viewed with a degree of admiration by many large-scale commercial enterprises.

The fourth point is the need for flexibility and adaptability. A common theme throughout this book has been change, a continual fact of life since 1918. The need to embrace change was clearly demonstrated during the expansion programme of the 1930s as the RAF transitioned from the old world of the biplanes to the new world of the monoplanes and multi-engined bombers. The Second World War was a period of perpetual change, much of which was generated by the uncertainty or 'fog' of war. The theme continued apace after the war, although was largely driven by the various Defence reviews, which tried to grapple with geopolitical influences and diminishing financial resources. The return to expeditionary operations after the Cold War demanded even greater flexibility and adaptability as the RAF reconfigured its logistical resources to meet the challenges of a very different style of warfare.

The fifth point is about vision. Warfare is not a precise art and, despite the earlier point about learning from experience, the past does not always provide the answers for the future. Despite the availability of techniques such as mathematical modeling and consumption pattern analysis for stock control, taking a step back and considering the bigger picture has often had its place. Often, this required judgment and a degree of confidence. The introduction of specialist capabilities such as TSW was not always understood at the time but the perseverance of a number of far-sighted individuals with vision, ensured such capabilities flourished and become an indispensable part of modern RAF Logistics capability. This too can be said of the number of ACSSUs and auxiliary capabilities, which have evolved since 1998.

Many of these points are reflected in the comments made by Air Vice-Marshal Mike Harwood, a former Harrier pilot and one-time station commander at RAF Wittering; having read an extract from the draft manuscript of this book, he commented:

> There are so many lessons therein, about leadership, resilience, the willingness to change/adapt, champions and brick walls, relationships, the value of exercises, and the likelihood of real life 'getting in the way' of that nice, sensible, steady-as-you-go work-up to a declared operational capability.

Thoughts now turn to the future. The departure from Afghanistan has marked yet another watershed for RAF Logistics. The end of 2014 is, in many ways, very similar to the end of 1989 and the end of the Cold War but for slightly different reasons. The Cold War years were relatively stable in terms of logistic commitments but the return to expeditionary warfare from the First Gulf War on has heralded a period of much uncertainty. That was true initially, but logistical activity in Iraq and Afghanistan soon settled down into an enduring, relatively steady-state commitment. From 2014 onwards, a period of true uncertainty returned. The flexibility and adaptability of the new A4 force with its ACSSUs and the EAWs should provide the agility which RAF Logistics will need to meet new challenges—only time will tell. Additionally, the Defence Supply Chain seems to have matured and its joined-up approach should ensure that resources are used effectively. There will, of course, always be the pressure to do more with less.

In 2003, the foreword in the RAF Supply Branch Yearbook commented that its contents were a 'testimony to the variety that characterises our work. It also testifies to versatility, flexibility and professionalism'[1] Of the many virtues of the Logistics Branch and Trades, these are the qualities which have remained constant throughout ninety-six years of service to air power. They will remain the cornerstone of RAF Logistics, sustaining air power well in to the twenty-first century and beyond.

APPENDIX I

Heads of the RAF Logistics Organisation, 1918–2014

Major-General W. S. Brancker: April 1918–November 1918
Major-General E. L. Ellington CB CMG: November 1918–March 1919

RAF Stores Branch

Air Commodore C. L. Lambe CB CMG DSO: June 1919–September 1922
Air Commodore D. Le G Pitcher CMG CBE DSO: January 1923–March 1925
Air Commodore A. M. Longmore CB DSO: April 1925–February 1929
Air Vice-Marshal R. H. Clark-Hall CMG DSO: March 1929–September 1931
Air Commodore A. W. Bigsworth CMG DSO: AFC October 1931–December 1934

RAF Equipment Branch

Air Vice-Marshal J. S. T. Bradley OBE: January 1935–March 1938
Air Vice-Marshal A. G. Garrod OBE MC DFC: April 1938–July 1940
Air Vice-Marshal E. W. Havers CB: July 1940–August 1942
Air Vice-Marshal Sir William. B. Cushion KBE CB: September 1942–November 1946
Air Vice-Marshal T. E. Drowley CB CBE: December 1946–August 1949
Air Vice-Marshal F. N. Trinder CB CBE: September 1949–August 1952
Air Vice-Marshal Sir Leslie Bates KBE CB: September 1952–August 1955
Air Vice-Marshal H. D. Jackman CB CBE: September 1955–February 1958
Air Vice-Marshal Sir Geoffrey Worthington KBE CB: March 1958–February 1961
Air Vice-Marshal Sir Edgar Lowe KBE CB: March 1961–July 1964
Air Vice-Marshal Sir Roderic Salmon KBE CB: August 1964–July 1968
Air Vice-Marshal K. H. Gooding CB OBE: September 1968–March 1971
Air Vice-Marshal F. S. R. Johnson CB OBE: March 1971–December 1973

RAF Supply Branch

Air Vice-Marshal H. C. Southgate CB CBE: December 1973–August 1976
Air Vice-Marshal H. Gill CB OBE: August 1976–April 1979
Air Vice-Marshal D. I. O'Hara CB: April 1979–May 1982
Air Vice-Marshal A. R. Martindale CB: May 1982–October 1984
Air Vice-Marshal A. Beill CB: October 1984–January 1987
Air Vice-Marshal R. C. Allerton CB: January 1987–November 1989
Air Vice-Marshal C. P. Baker CB: November 1989–February 1993
Air Vice-Marshal G. M. Ferguson: February 1993–May 1994

Air Commodore M. P. Crotty CBE: May 1994–April 1995
Air Vice-Marshal P. D. Markey OBE: January 1995–November 1998
Air Commodore N. M. Griffiths: November 1998–Not Known
Air Commodore C. F. Cooper CBE: Not Known–January 2001
Air Commodore P. Whalley CBE ADC: January 2001–April 2003
Air Commodore N. S. Morris: April 2003–December 2004
Air Commodore D. J. Foster: January 2005–December 2007

RAF Logistics Branch

Air Vice-Marshal M. J. G. Wiles CB CBE: December 2007–September 2011
Air Vice-Marshal G. Howard CB: September 2011–July 2015

APPENDIX II

Operational Honours and Awards

Due to the sheer number of honours and awards granted to the RAF's Logistics organisation since 1918, it is not possible to research and list them all within this work. This listing is therefore limited to awards gained for distinguished and gallant service in connection with wartime or operational service for personnel serving in the Stores, Equipment, Supply, or Logistics Branch and connected Trades. They are listed as per the standard order of precedence, as published by the Central Chancery of the Orders of Knighthood. Ranks are as at the date of the award and dates in brackets are those of the official promulgation in *The London Gazette* (LG).

British Awards

George Cross

Hollowday, V., Aircraftsman first class, Equipment Assistant, RAFVR. Awarded for rescuing three aircrew from two separate aircraft crashes (LG: 17 January 1941).

Commander, The Most Excellent Order of the British Empire

Tyzack, J. E., Group Captain, Equipment Branch, RAF. Awarded in recognition of services in planning the landings in Normandy in June 1944 (LG: 19 September 1944).

Distinguished Service Order

George, R. D., Acting Wing Commander, Equipment Branch, RAFVR. Awarded for great gallantry, personal example and coolness whilst under fire during the Salerno landings in September 1943 (LG: 26 May 1944).

Officer, The Most Excellent Order of the British Empire

Armiger, B., Acting Wing Commander, Equipment Branch, Reserve of Air Force Officers (RAFO). Awarded for service as OC No. 2 RAF Beach Squadron, Operation Overlord June 1944 (LG: 29 December 1944).

Faulkner, L. S. N. B., Acting Wing Commander, Equipment Branch, RAFVR. Awarded for service as OC No. 1 RAF Beach Squadron, Operation Overlord, June 1944 (LG: 8 June 1944).

George, R. D., Acting Squadron Leader, Equipment Branch, RAFVR. Awarded for bravery and leadership as CO of the port area of Bone Harbour, North Africa whilst under constant Axis forces attack in the early days of Operation Torch, November 1942 (LG: 2 Jun 1943).

Gore, C. W., Group Captain, Equipment Branch, RAF. Awarded for resolving complicated equipment problems, which arose during the expansion and re-arming of Bomber Command (LG: 14 June 1945).

Maddox, A. J. M., Wing Commander, Supply Branch, RAF. Awarded for distinguished services in Iraq as part of Operation Telic (LG: 31 December 2003).

Maggs, W. J, Acting Wing Commander, Equipment Branch, RAF. Awarded for distinguished services in the Mediterranean Air Command as part of the planning staff for Operation Husky, 1943 (LG: 17 September 1943).

Murphy, J. E. T., Acting Wing Commander, Equipment Branch, RAFO. Awarded for service as OC No. 4 RAF Beach Squadron, Operation Overlord, June 1944 (LG: 29 December 1944).

Primett, M. N., Group Captain, Supply Branch, RAF. Awarded for distinguished services in Iraq as part of Operation Telic, 2004 (LG: 7 September 2004).

Member, The Most Excellent Order of the British Empire

Belmore, D. S., Squadron Leader, Supply Branch, RAF. For services in the First Gulf War (Operation Granby) (LG: 29 June 1991).

Bridges, M. D., Flight Lieutenant, Supply Branch, RAF. For services in the First Gulf War (Operation Granby) (LG: 29 June 1991).

Clinton, E. M., Flight Lieutenant, Supply Branch, WRAF. For services in connection with the Falklands War (Operation Corporate) (LG: 8 October 1982).

Crossman, M., Squadron Leader, Supply Branch, RAF. For services in Northern Ireland (LG: 29 September 2003).

Hewat, C. J. S., Squadron Leader, Supply Branch RAF. For services in the First Gulf War (Operation Granby) (LG: 29 June 1991).

Hills, E. D., Flying Officer, Equipment Branch, RAF. For services as the Equipment Officer with No.1 Squadron, France 1940 (LG: 1 January 1941).

British Empire Medal

Coleman, J., Sergeant, Trade Group 18 (Supply), RAF. For outstanding service with the Tactical Supply Wing during Operation Corporate 1982 (LG: 8 October 1982).

McBey, R. J., Sergeant, Trade Group 18 (Supply), RAF. In recognition of services with the Tactical Supply Wing during Operation Granby 1991 (LG: 29 June 1991.

Harding, J. H., Flight Sergeant, Equipment Assistant, RAF. In recognition of conduct whilst under heavy enemy fire during the Siege of Malta 1942 (LG: 8 June 1942).

Vivian, D. J., Corporal, Trade Group 18 (Supply), RAF. For services in connection with the Falklands War (Operation Corporate) (LG: 8 October 1982).

George Medal

Kings, D. L., Acting Wing Commander, Equipment Branch, RAFVR. Awarded for searching a danger area after an explosion at No. 21 MU RAF Fauld, Staffordshire on 27 November 1944. (LG: 10 April 1945).

Lewin, J. P., Flight Lieutenant, Equipment Branch, RAFO. Awarded for searching a danger area after an explosion at No. 21 MU RAF Fauld, Staffordshire on 27 November 1944 (LG: 10 April 1945).

King's Commendation for Bravery

Lawson, J. A., Flight Lieutenant, Equipment Branch, RAFVR (LG: 1 January 1944).

Queen's Commendation for Bravery

Bennett, A. M., Corporal, believed to be Trade Group 18, RAF (LG: 29 April 2003).
Holsgrove, A. J. S., Senior Aircraftman, Trade Group 18, RAF (LG: 12 October 1993).
Hopkin, C. G., Senior Aircraftman, Trade Group 18, RAF (LG: 6 November 1998).

Mentioned in Despatches

Archbold, E. S. Acting Flight Lieutenant, RAFVR. Awarded for services as Ammunition Officer, 101 Beach Flt, 1 Beach Sqn, Operation Overlord, 1944 (LG: 29 December 1944).
Bailey, E. A., Flying Officer, Equipment Branch RAFVR (LG: 1 January 1945).
Bates, L. J. V., Group Captain, Equipment Branch, RAF (twice mentioned in LG: 1 Jan 1941 and 14 Jan 1944).
Cartmell, B. S., Wing Commander, Equipment Branch, RAF (twice mentioned in LG: 1 January 1941 and 17 September 1943).
Casson, D. R., SAC, Trade Group 18, RAF. Awarded for Northern Ireland (LG: 27 October 1992).
Curtis, W. J. B., Air Commodore, Equipment Branch, RAF (LG: 1 January 1941).
Fry, H. C., Acting Flight Sergeant, Equipment Assistant, RAF. For leadership and gallantry in directing personnel to unload supplies under enemy fire on 6 June 1944 and the days that followed (LG: 29 December 1944).
Gooding, K. H., Wing Commander, Equipment Branch, RAF (twice mentioned LG: 11 June 1942 and 1 January 1945).
George, R. D., Wing Commander. Equipment Branch RAFVR (twice mentioned LG: 14 January 1944 and 8 June 1944).
Gore, C. W., Wing Commander, Equipment Branch, RAF (LG :1 January 1941).
Havers, E. W., Acting Air Vice-Marshal, Equipment Branch, RAF (LG: 1 Jan 1941).
Hills, E. D., Flying Officer, Equipment Branch, RAF (LG: 1 January 1941).
Jackman, H. D., Acting Group Captain, Equipment Branch, RAF (five times mentioned LG: 24 September 1941, 11 June 1942, 1 January 1943, 3 June 1943, and 14 June 1945).
Kearon, N. W., Squadron Leader, Equipment Branch, RAFO (thrice mentioned LG: 24 September 1941, 1 January 1943, and 1 January 1945).
Kings, D. L., Acting Wing Commander, Equipment Branch, RAFVR (LG: 2 June 1943).
Lowe, E. N., Acting Wing Commander, Equipment Branch, RAF (LG: 1 January 1941).
Maggs, W. J., Acting Wing Commander, Equipment Branch, RAF. Awarded for distinguished service at HQ North African Tactical Air Force, whilst preparing the outline logistics plan for the redeployment of Allied squadrons to Algeria in advance of the threatened German breakthrough at Kasserine (LG: 2 June 1943).
Mears, J. H., Flight Lieutenant, Equipment Branch, RAF. Awarded for service with HQ 83 Group during Operation Overlord in 1944 (LG: 28 December 1945).
Priestly, F., Warrant Officer, Equipment Assistant, RAF (LG: 8 June 44).
Rae, H. G. Acting Squadron Leader, Equipment Branch, RAF. Awarded for services as Beach Flight Commander, No. 102 Beach Flight, Operation Overlord, 1944 (LG: 29 December 1944).
Read, F. C., Group Captain, Equipment Branch, RAF (LG: 8 June 1944).
Roth, V. H. B., Wing Commander, Equipment Branch, RAF (LG: 1 Jan 41).
Sandison, R. A., Acting Flight Lieutenant, Equipment Branch, RAF. Awarded for services as Beach Flight Commander, No. 103 Beach Flight, Operation Overlord, 1944 (LG: 29 December 1944).
Thomas, G. P. S., Acting Wing Commander, Equipment Branch, RAF (LG: 1 January1945).
Towers, E., Squadron Leader, Equipment Branch, RAFO. Awarded for services as Beach Flight Commander, No. 104 Beach Flight, Operation Overlord, 1944 (LG: 29 December 1944).

Whitbourn, P. J., Warrant Officer, Trade Group 18, RAF. Awarded for services in Northern Ireland (LG: 27 October 1992).
Woodgate, A. S., Acting Wing Commander, Equipment Branch, RAF (LG: 8 June 1944).
Worthington, G. L., Acting Air Commodore, Equipment Branch, RAF (LG: 1 January 45).

Queen's Commendation for Valuable Service

Bessell, J. C., Air Commodore, Logistics Branch, RAF (LG: January–March 2015).
Jinadu, A. O., Squadron Leader, Supply Branch, RAF (LG: 31 October 2003).
Maddox, A. J. M., Squadron Leader, Supply Branch, RAF (LG: 6 April 2001).
O'Dea, K. L., Air Commodore, Logistics Branch, RAF. (LG: 19 March 2010).

Operational Commendations

Boother, G., Corporal Trade Group 18 (Supply), RAF. Commendation by Commander Task Force 317 (South Atlantic) for services with Tactical Supply Wing during Operation Corporate 1982.
Cromarty, N., Flight Lieutenant, Supply Branch, RAF. Commendation by Commander Task Force 317 (South Atlantic) for services with JHSU during Operation Corporate 1982.
Cruse, C., Wing Commander, Supply Branch, RAF. Commendation by Commander Task Force 317 (South Atlantic) for services with UKMAMS during Operation Corporate 1982.
Harvey, R., Corporal Trade Group 18 (Supply). RAF. Commendation by Commander Task Force 317 (South Atlantic) for services with TSW during Operation Corporate 1982.
McBey, R., Corporal Trade Group 18 (Supply), RAF. Commendation by Commander Task Force 317 (South Atlantic) for services with TSW during Operation Corporate 1982.
Ronan, J., Warrant Officer, Trade Group 18 (Supply), RAF. Commendation by Commander Task Force 317 (South Atlantic) for services with TSW during Operation Corporate 1982.
Sharrock, M. R., Flight Lieutenant, Logistics Branch, RAF. Joint Commander's Commendation. Awarded for work with No.1 Air Mobility Wing in Afghanistan (Operation Herrick) (Operational Awards List No. 37: September 2011).
Stewart, J., Flight Lieutenant, Supply Branch, RAF. Commendation by Commander Task Force 317 (South Atlantic) for services with UKMAMS during Operation Corporate 1982.

Foreign Awards

France: Légion d'Honneur, degree de Chevalier

Marfleet, H., Flying Officer, Equipment Branch RAF. Awarded following his services to the French Government during the Second World War.

France: Croix de Guerre

Bailey, E. A., Flight Lieutenant, Equipment Branch, RAFVR. Awarded for services with No.3 RAF Beach Squadron during Operation Overlord, 1944. Grant of award by the French Government, 17 April 1947.
Fry, H. C., Acting Flight Sergeant, Equipment Trade, RAF. Awarded for services with 101 Beach Flight during Operation Overlord, June 1944. Award was with a gilt star to indicate an award made at corps level.
Woollacott, D., Acting Flight Lieutenant, Equipment Branch, RAFVR. Awarded for services as the ammunition officer with No. 2 Beach Squadron, 104 Flight during Operation Overlord, June 1944. Award was with a gilt star to indicate an award made at corps level.

Greece: Commander of the Order of George I

Jackman, H. D., Air Commodore, Equipment Branch, RAF (LG: 6 September 1946).

Greece: Air Force Cross

Jackman, H. D., Air Commodore, Equipment Branch, RAF (LG: 3 May 1946).

United States of America: Legion of Merit (Degree of Commander)

Sims, F. H., Acting Air Commodore, Equipment Branch, RAF (LG: 26 March 1946)
Worthington, G. L., Acting Air Commodore, Equipment Branch, RAF. Awarded following his work for General Eisenhower at Supreme HQ Allied Expeditionary Force (LG: 5 October 1945).

United States of America: Legion of Merit (Degree of Officer)

Bates, L. J. V., Acting Air Commodore, Equipment Branch, RAF (LG: 9 October 1945).
George, R. D., Wing Commander, Equipment Branch, RAF (LG: 26 September 1944).

United States of America: Legion of Merit (Degree of Legionnaire)

Read, F. C., Group Captain, Equipment Branch, RAF (LG: 15 March 1946).

Endnotes

Preface

1 Sarin, *Military Logistics* (2000), p. 30.
2 Robeson and Copacino, *The Logistics Handbook* (1994), p. 3.
3 NATO, *NATO Logistics Handbook* (2007), p. 4.
4 Van Creveld, *Supplying War* (2004), p. 1.
5 *Ibid.*
6 Peter Dye includes maintenance in his definition of aviation logistics. See Dye, *The Bridge to Airpower* (2015), p. 2.

Chapter One

1 Architect of the RAF: Obituary of Lord Trenchard, *The Aeroplane*, 17 February 1956.
2 Raleigh, *The War in the Air, Vol. 1* (1922), p. 207.
3 Jones, *The War in the Air, Vol. 3* (1931), pp. 258–259.
4 TNA, AIR 2/127, Administration of Royal Naval Air Service and Supply of Material, May 1916.
5 Sykes, *From Many Angles* (1942), p. 216.
6 Raleigh, *The War in the Air, Vol. 1* (1922), pp. 415–416; and Jones, *The War in the Air, Vol. 3* (1931), pp. 257–258.
7 Norris, *The Royal Flying Corps* (1965), p. 49.
8 Edmonds, *Military Operations France and Belgium, 1914* (1922), p. 48. The broad details of which components of the RFC would deploy with an expeditionary force had been determined in late 1913. See also TNA, AIR 1/118/15/40/56, RFC Military Wing: Arrangements for Mobilisation.
9 Jones, *The War in the Air, Vol. 3* (1931), p. 254.
10 Dye, *The Royal Flying Corps Logistic Organisation* (1998), p. 33; and Dye, *France and the Development of British Military Aviation* (2009), pp. 1–12.
11 Jones, *The War in the Air, Vol. 3* (1931), pp. 254–256.
12 Trenchard Museum Archive (TMA), Royal Aircraft Factory, Spare Parts for Aeroplanes: Type R.E.8. (1917). This analysis does not include the aircraft's engine, cockpit components, armaments, undercarriage or the tailplane and rudder assembly.
13 Jones, *The War in the Air, Vol. 3* (1931), p. 252.
14 Figures calculated from Jones, *The War in the Air, Appendices* (1937), Appendix XLI, Table A, pp. 188–189. Seaplanes and Ship Aeroplanes totals have not been included to maintain a like-for-like comparison with the 1914–1918 figures. Engine figures calculated from same source, Appendix XLI, Table B, pp. 190–191.
15 Jones, *The War in the Air, Vol. 3* (1931), p. 253.

16 *Ibid.*, p. 253.
17 War Office, *Statistics* (1922), Part VIII, Section 1, pp. 497–498.
18 Jones, *The War in the Air* (1937), pp. 188–191. The figures quoted include all aircraft types (aeroplanes, seaplanes and ship aeroplanes) for the At Home, Expeditionary, and Eastern theatres.
19 *Ibid.*, p. 154.
20 Edmonds, *Military Operations France and Belgium, 1916* (1922), pp. 102–104.
21 War Office, *Statistics* (1922), pp. 846–847.
22 The Sopwith Camel had a main pressure tank of thirty gallons and a gravity tank of seven gallons. See Pudney, *The Camel Fighter* (1964), p. 21.
23 Edmonds, *Military Operations France and Belgium, 1916* (1922), p. 103 and War Office, *Statistics* (1922), Part XXXII (ii), p. 847.
24 For a much fuller account of RFC logistics see Dye, *The Bridge to Airpower* (2015).
25 Robertson, 'An AID to quality', *Aeroplane Monthly* (1993), p. 64.
26 Dye, *The Bridge to Airpower* (2015), pp. 61–63.
27 *Ibid.*, p. 43.
28 TNA, AIR1/1159/204/5/2459, Distribution of Duties, Equipment Branch, HQ RAF.
29 Raleigh, *The War in the Air, Vol. 1* (1922), p. 213 and TNA, AIR 1/117/15/40/33, Organisation in the R.F.C. for Maintenance in the Field 1914.
30 TNA, AIR 2/5, RFC: System of Store Accounting, Sykes to The Secretary War Office, March 1913.
31 TNA, AIR 1/2398/268/1, Notes on History of R.A.F Stores Branch 1915–1926, p. 2; and AIR 1/506/16/3/43, Parks and Depots at Home 1916.
32 TNA, AIR 1/506/16/3/43, Parks and Depots at Home 1916.
33 Sturtivant *et al.*, *Royal Air Force Flying Training and Support Units* (1997), pp. 46–47; and Anon, 'Aircraft Acceptance Parks', *Aeromilitaria* (1976), pp. 3–6.
34 Dye, *The Royal Flying Corps Logistic Organisation* (1998), p. 33.
35 Jones, *The War in the Air, Vol. 2* (1928), pp. 188-189.
36 Dye, *The Royal Flying Corps Logistic Organisation* (1998), p. 34.
37 *Ibid.*, pp. 33–34.
38 War Office, *Statistics* (1922), Part XVIII, Section 2, Table (iii), p. 613.
39 *Ibid.*
40 War Office, *Statistics* (1922), Part IX, Section 4, Table (i), p. 521.
41 *Ibid.*
42 TNA, AIR 2/5, RFC: System of Store Accounting, Sykes to The Secretary War Office, March 1913.
43 TNA, AIR 10/273, RFC Stores Regulations 1918.
44 TMA, Spare Parts for Aeroplanes: Type R.E.8 (1917).
45 TNA, AIR 10/273, RFC Stores Regulations 1918.
46 *Ibid.*
47 Dye, *Sustaining Air Power* (2006), p. 44.
48 The Royal Flying Corps, *Flight*, 20 July 1912, No. 186 (No. 29, Vol. IV), p. 663. The quartermaster appointment was a traditional Army term for an individual who was responsible for soldier's accommodation, food and clothing.
49 TNA, AIR 2/5, RFC: System of Store Accounting, Sykes to The Secretary War Office, March 1913, pp. 2 and 5–8.
50 Air Ministry, Air Publication (AP) 125, *A Short History* (1936), p. 74.
51 TNA, AIR 1/502/16/3/11, Creation of Equipment Officers, January 1915 and Air Ministry, AP 125, *A Short History* (1936), p. 74.
52 Army List (July 1916).
53 TNA, AIR 1/15/15/1/63, New Syllabus: EOs, School of Instruction.

54 *Ibid.*
55 Robertson, *The Army and Aviation* (1981), p. 68.
56 TNA, AIR 12398/268/1, Kirby to Laing dated 9 November 1926.
57 Jones, *The War in the Air, Vol. 4* (1934), p. 354.
58 Dye, *The Royal Flying Corps and Royal Air Force at St Omer* (2004), p. 81.
59 Jones, *The War in the Air, Vol. 4* (1934), p. 355.
60 Tennant, *In the Clouds Above Baghdad* (1920), pp. 12–13. The spelling of Tanooma is in the source book and is unusual. It is most likely the now At Tannumah, which is on the opposite bank of the river from the current dockyard in the Al Ashar district.
61 Air Ministry, Pam (Air) 328, *Four Lectures on the History of the Royal Air Force*, Second Lecture (1945), p. 9.
62 Grey, *A History of the Air Ministry* (1940), pp. 76–77. For a fuller development of Naval logistics see: Jones, 'Ashore, afloat and airborne' (2007).
63 TNA, AIR 72/1, Air Ministry weekly order (AMWO) 21/1918 dated 3 April 1918.
64 TNA, AIR1/16/15/1/73, Equipment Branch—Memorandum on Organisation dated 18 November 1918.
65 *Ibid.*
66 *Ibid.*
67 TNA, AIR 29/711/17832, ORB for the School of Store Accounting and Storekeeping, 1929, p. 4.
68 *Ibid.*
69 TNA, AIR 10/844, AP 830 dated August 1921.
70 Example taken from TNA, AIR1/2131/207/115/1, Mobilisation Store Table for the Expeditionary Force, A Squadron RFC 18 Aeroplanes, 1916.
71 Eddy and Arnett, *The NATO Codification System* (1998), p. 39.
72 War Office, *Statistics* (1922), Part xxv, Section 3, Table (i), p. 711; and Jones, *The War in the Air, Vol. 6* (1937), p. 74.
73 Air Historical Branch (AHB), *Manning Plans and Policy* (undated), p. 1.
74 RAF Website, Timeline 1918–1929 in raf.mod.uk/history/raftimeline19181929.cfm [accessed 11 October 2015].
75 Bowyer, *RAF Operations* (1988), p. 63.
76 Bailey, *The Arsenal of Democracy* (2013), pp. 28–29.
77 Air Ministry, Pam (Air) 328, *Four Lectures on the History of the Royal Air Force*, Third Lecture (1945), pp. 3–5.
78 Slessor, *The Central Blue* (1956), pp. 51–73.
79 TNA, AIR 5/579, Report on the Royal Air Force in India, August 1922, p. 1. See also Bowyer, *RAF Operations* (1988), p. 62. Bowyer, however, states that the cost of the RAF amounted to £77,000.
80 Smith, *The Royal Air Force, Air Power and British Foreign Policy* (1977), 153–174 (p. 155).
81 'The Great Aircraft Deal', *Flight*, 18 March 1920, No. 586 (No. 12, Vol. XII), p. 308. Initially, these aircraft were held by the Aircraft Disposals Board for the Government but were then bought by the Aircraft Disposals Company Ltd; a key player in this syndicate was the aircraft company Handley Page Ltd, who acted as the selling agent. Once refurbished, large numbers of the aircraft were then sold overseas. By 1925, the company had sold on 2,000 airframes and 3,000 engines, generating a profit of £2,500,000 of which half was returned to the Treasury as per the original agreement: see Barnes, *Handley Page Aircraft* (1976), p. 27. The demobilisation process is also detailed in Saunders, Per Ardua, (1944), p. 281, an account that also relates that 1,000 tons of ball bearings, 350,000 sparking-plugs, and 100,000 magnetos were also disposed of by this means.
82 TNA, AIR 29/959, Milton Aircraft Storage Depot, ORB entry for 1920.
83 Harris, *Bomber Offensive* (1990), p. 19.

84 *Ibid.*, p. 19.
85 *Ibid.*, pp. 19–20. The seriousness of the situation generated a number of articles in the British press at the end of August 1922: Anon, 'RAF Equipment in India: Old Machines and No replacements', *The Times*, 30 August 1922; Anon, 'RAF Equipment in India: The Humour of A Tragedy', *The Times*, 31 August 1922; Anon, 'Indian Air Scandal', *Daily Mail*, 31 August 1922; and Anon, 'Scandal of the Indian Air Force', *Daily Mail*, 31 August 1922.
86 TNA, AIR 5/579, RAF India: Shortage of Equipment, Memorandum to Cabinet and General Action on Sir John Salmond's Report, Part II, Paragraph 64.
87 *Ibid.*, paragraph 64.
88 TNA, AIR 5/579, RAF India: Shortage of Equipment, Memorandum to Cabinet and General Action on Sir John Salmond's Report.
89 Iraq was formerly Mesopotamia until 1922.
90 Rasmusen, *A Visit to Cairo, Baghdad and Basra* (*Part 4*) (1975), p. 11.
91 TNA, AIR 12398/268/1, Notes on History of RAF Stores Branch 1915–1928, p. 4.
92 TNA, AIR 12398/268/1, Notes on History of RAF Stores Branch, p. 4.
93 Air Force List (1920–1929) as at December of each year.
94 TNA, AIR 1/ 2398/268/1, Kirby to Laing.
95 RAF Logistics Heritage Centre (LHCA), BEC 13, Heads of the RAF Equipment and Supply Organisation Since 1918 and TNA, AIR 5/239, Establishment of one 'Stores Branch' in RAF. Air Commodore Lambe became the first head of the RAF's Stores Branch.
96 TNA, AIR 72/1, AMWOs 1919: Order 1158: Stores Officers and TNA, AIR 5/239, Establishment of One 'Stores Branch', CAS to SofS dated 17 October.
97 TNA, AIR 72/2, AMWOs 1920: Order 657: Medical Standards of Fitness for Officers (Stores, Medical, Dental and Chaplains).
98 Overy, *The Morbid Age* (2009), p. xv.
99 TNA, AIR 72/2, AMWOs 1920: Order 537: Stores officers; Emoluments and Conditions of Service and Appendix; Stores Officers Selected for Permanent Commissions.
100 Air Force List, (February 1921), columns 901–911. A large number of these officers had been EOs or AEOs in the RFC.
101 McInnes, 'Sergeant Major Moore, No. 5 RFC and The Balloonatics' *The Journal of Orders and Medals Research Society Vol. 45 No. 2* (2006).
102 TNA, AIR 72/5, AMWOs 1923: Order 621: Conditions of Entry into the Stores Branch for Stores Duties (432081/23) dated 11 October 1923.
103 TNA, AIR 72/5, AMWOs 1927: Order 437: Conditions of Entry into the Stores Branch (763749/27) dated 6 January 1927.
104 TNA, AIR 72/10, AMWOs 1928: Order 426: The Constitution of the General Duties Branch dated 21 June 1928.
105 TNA, AIR 72/13, AMWOs 1930: Order A.428/1930: The Constitution of the Stores Branch dated 8 July 1930.
106 *Ibid.*, p. 28, paragraph 2.
107 *Ibid.*, pp. 28–29, paragraphs 4–7.
108 TNA, AIR 72/13, AMWOs 1930: Order A.429/1930: Appointment of Warrant Officers.
109 AHB, *Manning Plans and Policy* (undated), Appendix 10; and James, *The Paladins*, Table 19, p. 260.
110 TNA, AIR 10/851, Royal Air Force Muster Roll dated 1 April 1918.
111 AHB, *Manning Plans and Policy* (undated), Appendix 10; and James, *The Paladins* (1990), Table 19, p. 260.
112 James, *The Paladins* (1990), Table 19, p. 260; and RAF LHCA, BEC 8, Recruitment Pamphlet 'Are You Satisfied' dated August 1919, p. 6.
113 AHB, *Manning Plans and Policy* (undated), Appendix 10.

114 TNA, AIR 10/844, Instructions for Store Accounting and Store Keeping dated August 1921.
115 *Ibid.*, Appendix III and IV, pp. 195-199 and TNA, AIR 72/4, AMOs 1920: Order 37: Transfer of Stores Accounting Duties to Accountant Officers.
116 TNA, AIR 72/1, AMWOs 1919: Order 908; Warrant Officers, Non-Commissioned Officers and Other Airmen of the Royal Air Force dated 8 August, 1919.
117 TNA, AIR 72/2, AMWOs 1920: Order 885: Storekeepers: New Trade Classification dated 14 October 1920.
118 TNA, AIR 72/21, AMOs 1937: Order A.114: Regrouping and Renaming of the Trade of Storekeeper dated 22 April 1937.
119 TNA, AIR 72/3, AMWOs 1921: Order 570: Airmen Clerks: Abolition of Existing Sub-Classifications dated 14 July 1921.
120 TNA, AIR 72/6, AMWOs 1924: Order 473: Airman Clerks dated 5 June 1924.
121 TNA, AIR 72/19, AMOs 1935: Order A.96: Training of Clerks, Accounting dated 25 April 1935.
122 TNA, AIR 72/5, AMWOs 1923: Order 185: Use of the Term 'Airmen' dated 4 January 1923.
123 The WRAF proper was not formed until 1949. The 1918 version was actually an auxiliary organisation and only lasted two years.
124 TNA, AIR 72/7, AMWOs 1925: Order 499: Stores Administration and Accounting: Introduction of Civilian Station Wardens.
125 Whitley Councils (or Committees) were introduced in 1919 and named after John Henry Whitley who had chaired a committee which had produced a Report on the Relations of Employers and Employees. These councils remained in operation well into the twenty first century.
126 Grey, *A History of the Air Ministry* (1940), pp. 103, 110, 129; and End Charts: The Organisation of the Air Ministry, 1921 and 1930.
127 *Ibid.*, p. 134 and End Charts: The Organisation of the Air Ministry, 1930 and TNA, AIR 2/1704, Directorate of Equipment: Proposed Increases of Staff in 1936, Enclosure 17a dated 19 June 1936.
128 TNA, AVIA 15/113, Proposed Re-Organisation of the Directorate of Equipment 1939, Office Memorandum 76/40.
129 TNA, AIR 2/1704, Directorate of Equipment: Proposed Increases of Staff in 1936, Enclosure 17a.
130 TNA, CAB 23/15/616A, Cabinet Minutes and Papers February 1919–October 1924.
131 Armitage, *The Royal Air Force* (1993), p. 292.
132 Slessor, *The Central Blue* (1956), p. 42. Slessor's particular interest in RAF/Army co-operation can be attributed to the fact that he was appointed as the CO of No. 4 (Army Co-Operation) Squadron in April 1925 just after completing Staff College.
133 TNA, AIR 2/1290, Expeditionary Force–Organisation of Repair Work in the Field, 1932, p. 2
134 *Ibid.*
135 Approximately sixty parks were formed between October 1935 and December 1943.
136 Air Ministry, AP 1301, *Royal Air Force War Manual, Part II* (1928). By 1932, the official definition of an ASP was 'A maintenance unit organised to facilitate rapid distribution to, and holding a reserve of spares and stores for, fighting units'. Air Ministry, AP 1081, RAF Pocket Book 1932 (HMSO: London, 1932), p. 249 refers.
137 TNA, AIR 2/1290, Expeditionary Force: Organisation of Repair Work in the Field, DOSD to DofE dated 15 June 1931.
138 TNA, AIR 10/1473, Royal Air Force Contingent Accompanying an Army Expeditionary Force, Appendix A.

139 *Ibid.*
140 TNA, AIR 2/1290, Expeditionary Force: Organisation of Repair Work in the Field, MT Loading and Allotment Table for No. 1 ASP.
141 Air Ministry, AP 1081, *Royal Air Force Pocket Book 1932* (London: Air Ministry, 1932)

Chapter Two

1 Philpott, *The Royal Air Force, Volume II* (2008), pp. 66–67.
2 TNA, AIR 20/5792, Formation of Mobilisation Committee, notes on the Fifth Meeting held on 22 October 1935, p. 1.
3 TNA, AIR 2/1923, Report on the Equipment Aspect of the Emergency 1935–1936 dated 30 September 1936, Part VII, p. 113.
4 *Ibid.*, p. 13
5 *Ibid.*, Part VII, pp. 113–121.
6 Hawes, 'The Story of the "W" Plan', *Army Quarterly and Defence Journal* 101 (1971), pp. 445–447.
7 Quoted in McKercher, 'Deterrence and the European Balance of Power' *The English Historical Review* Vol. 123, No. 500 (2006), p. 114 and TNA, CAB 23/87, Minutes of a meeting of the Cabinet 27 January 1937.
8 Armitage, *The Royal Air Force* (1993), pp. 67–71.
9 AHB, *The Expansion of the Royal Air Force* (undated), p. 163.
10 *Ibid.*, p. 71.
11 *Ibid.*
12 Slessor, *The Central Blue* (1956), pp. 184–185; and Bailey, *The Arsenal of Democracy* (2013), pp. 30-31.
13 Figures correlated from: Smith, *British Air Strategy Between the Wars* (1984), Appendices, pp. 328–335 and AHB, *The Expansion of the Royal Air Force* (undated), Appendix 1. There was no scheme 'B'. Schemes 'H' and 'J' never actually came into operation and the remaining missing letters represent tentative suggestions, which did not come to fruition. The home based aircraft figures for schemes 'J' and 'M' each contain ten squadrons for the Field Force. All figures exclude the Fleet Air Arm.
14 AHB, *The Expansion of the Royal Air Force* (undated), p. 75.
15 AHB, *Maintenance* (1954), p. 3.
16 Source: Higham, *Armed Forces in Peacetime* (1962), Appendix II, pp. 326–327. Figures include civil aviation which was included in the annual Air Estimates for the period in question.
17 See: Terraine, *The Right of the Line* (1998), pp. 15–45; Coombs, *The Lion has Wings* (1997), pp. 1–91; Armitage, *The Royal Air Force* (1993), pp. 67–74; Dean, *The Royal Air Force and Two World Wars* (1979), pp. 59-81; and Saunders, *Per Ardua* (1944), pp. 315–326.
18 Air Force List (1933–1935) (as of December of each year).
19 Air Force List (1932–1937) (as of December of each year).
20 AHB, *The Expansion of the Royal Air Force* (undated), p. 132; and Richards, *The Fight at Odds* (1953), p. 26. Training Command was further divided into Flying Training Command and Technical Training Command in May 1940.
21 TNA, AIR 72/20, AMOs (Administrative) 1936, Order 713; and *Flight*, Air Ministry Announcements, 'R.A.F. Stores Branch: Change of Title' (19 November 1936), p. 557.
22 Sturtivant *et al.*, *Royal Air Force Flying Training and Support Units* (1997), p. 112.
23 TNA, AIR 1/17/15/1/84, The Formation of the RAF on a Peace Basis, November 1919–July 1920, p. 6.
24 AHB, *Maintenance* (1954), p. 9.

25 *Ibid.*, pp. 9–10
26 Maintenance Command began to assume executive functions on 1 August 1938. TNA, AIR 2/3317, Directorate of Equipment Reorganisation 1938, S.37588/S.9 dated 26 August 1938 refers.
27 No. 42 Group retained this responsibility until it was disbanded in January 1956 with these duties then transferring to No. 40 Group; the latter was absorbed into the general staff structure of Maintenance Command in Jul 1961.
28 TNA, AIR 2/3088, Maintenance Command Establishment dated 8 December 1938.
29 AHB, 'Maintenance Command' (undated), p. 1.
30 TNA, AIR 2/3317, Directorate of Equipment Reorganisation 1938, Air Ministry letter dated 26 August 1938, Attached Memorandum: Organisation of Maintenance Command, pp. 6-7.
31 *Ibid.*, p. 7.
32 TNA, AIR 2/3088, Maintenance Command Establishment dated 8 December 1938.
33 TNA, AIR 72/23, AMOs (Administrative) 1939, Order A.363/39 and RAF Museum web site 'Heraldic Badges: Halloween Edition' at: rafmuseum.org.uk/blog/heraldic-badges-halloween-edition/ (last accessed on 14 January 2016).
34 Thetford, *Aircraft of the Royal Air Force* (1995), pp. 406–407.
35 AHB, *The Expansion of the Royal Air Force* (undated), p. 140.
36 *Ibid.*, p. 140.
37 AHB, *Works* (1956), pp. 288–289.
38 AHB, *The Expansion of the Royal Air Force* (undated), p. 140.
39 Kilcullen, *No. 7 Maintenance Unit* (1996), p. 4.
40 AHB, *Works*, p. 288.
41 Hyde, *British Air Policy* (1976), pp. 319–322.
42 AHB, *Works* (1956), p. 288; and AHB, *14 MU the Original Concept and Design* (undated), p. 3.
43 TNA, AIR 29/960, ORB for No. 4 Stores Depot.
44 AHB, *Maintenance* (1954), p. 37.
45 *Ibid.*
46 Source: AHB, *Maintenance* (1954), p. 21.
47 AHB, *Maintenance* (1954), p. 131.
48 AHB, *Works* (1956), p. 270.
49 Source: Shuttleworth Collection Engineering Hangar, Old Warden, Bedfordshire.
50 AHB, *Maintenance* (1954), p. 131.
51 The octane (or anti-knock) rating of a fuel indicates how much the fuel/air mixture can be compressed before it spontaneously ignites by detonation, producing shock waves which would damage engine components. The higher the rating, the less risk there was of detonation which enabled higher performance engines to be designed, increasing rates of climb, speed and range and enabling more payload to be carried.
52 The Netherlands (or Dutch) West Indies became the Netherlands Antilles in 1954.
53 AHB, *Maintenance* (1954), p. 131.
54 The Oil Board was a consortium of the various oil companies with similar responsibilities to the Royal Navy and the Army.
55 AHB, *Works* (1956), p. 270.
56 *Ibid.*, p. 271.
57 The four main oil companies and their respective share in the construction programme were as follows: Shell Mex and BP Ltd (48 per cent); Anglo-American Oil Co. Ltd (28 per cent); Trinidad Leasehold Ltd (20 per cent); and Carless, Capel and Leonard (4 per cent). Air Ministry, Works (1956), p. 273 refers.
58 AHB, *Works* (1956), p. 273.

59 *Ibid.*, p. 274.
60 *Ibid.*, pp. 274–275.
61 *Ibid.*, p. 271.
62 AHB, *Maintenance* (1954), p. 131.
63 Petroleum Board, *Petroleum at War* (1945), p. 3.
64 Richards, *The Fight at Odds* (1953), p. 19.
65 Hyde, *British Air Policy* (1976), Appendix VI.
66 AHB, *Works* (1956), p. 256.
67 *Ibid.*, p. 256.
68 *Ibid.*, pp. 258–259.
69 Robertson, 'Gas Warfare and the Air', *Air Pictorial* (1989), pp. 64–65.
70 *Ibid.*, p. 65–66.
71 *Ibid.*, p. 66.
72 Terraine, *The Right of the Line* (1998), p. 37.
73 Francis, *British Military Airfield Architecture* (1996), p. 56.
74 AHB, *Works* (1956), pp. 44-45.
75 Francis, *British Military Airfield Architecture* (1996), p. 56.
76 *Ibid.*
77 AHB, *Maintenance* (1954), p. 13.
78 TNA, AIR 2/8788, Report of the Committee on Royal Air Force Administration 1939, p. 1. It was coincidental that this 'Jones' committee shared the same colloquial reference as the 'Jones' report of November 1918.
79 *Ibid.*
80 AHB, *Maintenance* (1954), pp. 13–14.
81 TNA, AIR 2/8788, Report of the Committee on Royal Air Force Administration 1939, pp. 38 and 46.
82 *Ibid.*, pp. 38, 46, and Appendix A.
83 Multi-disciplinary working really came into its own in the late 1980s/1990s within the Maintenance Group Defence Agency and the Support Management Group where Supply, Engineering, Finance and Contracts staff worked alongside each other.
84 TNA, AIR 2/8788, Report of the Committee on Royal Air Force Administration 1939, pp. 39 and 46.
85 *Ibid.*, pp. 53–54.
86 TNA, AIR 2/8788, Report of the Committee on Royal Air Force Administration 1939, pp. 58–59.
87 *Ibid.*, p. 59.
88 *Ibid.*, p. 60.
89 *Ibid.*
90 *Ibid.*
91 *Ibid.*, p. 99.
92 *Ibid.*, p. 99. Tally cards had originally only been used in Stores depots but were brought into use at all units in August 1920.
93 TNA, AIR 72/13, AMWOs 1930: Civilian Order Supplement (No.13/1930) 383; Appointment of Civilian Stores Officers (33336/30) and AIR 72/14, AMOs 1931: Order A.17: Duties of Civilian Stores Officers.
94 James, *The Paladins* (1990), table 21, p. 262.
95 Air Force List (1936). Of a total of seventy-seven Equipment officers on unit establishments, thirty-seven (48 per cent) were retired.
96 TNA, AIR 2/3414, Substitution Officers in Equipment Branch of RAF, undated note from DGE.
97 AIR 2/1923, Report on the Equipment Aspect of the Emergency 1935–1936.

98 AHB, *Manning Plans and Policy* (undated), p. 12.
99 TNA, AIR 2/3414, Substitution Officers in Equipment Branch of RAF, note from CinC Bomber Command (undated).
100 AHB, *Manning Plans and Policy* (undated), p. 12.
101 TNA, AIR 2/3414, Substitution Officers in Equipment Branch of RAF, note by DofE dated October 1938.
102 *Ibid.*, Enclosure 19B: Treasury Chambers letter E.17550/4 dated 28 June 1938.
103 AHB, *Manning Plans and Policy* (undated), p. 15 and Enclosure 2A, p. 3.
104 Air Force List (January 1939). Of a total of 156 Equipment officers on unit establishments, eighty-seven (56 per cent) were retired.
105 TNA, AIR 2/4011, Formation of RAuxAF Equipment Branch, Air Ministry letter dated May 1939.
106 AHB, *Manning Plans and Policy* (undated), Appendix 5.
107 RAF LHCA, Hills papers.
108 *Ibid.*
109 AHB, *Manning Plans and Policy* (undated), Appendix 5.
110 TNA, AIR 2/2220, Civilian Employees at Depots in War: Enclosure 2A, Paragraph 2.
111 *Ibid.*, Enclosure 2A, Paragraph 4.
112 *Ibid.*, Enclosures 2A, Paragraphs 18A and 18B.
113 *Ibid.*, Civilian Employees at Depots in War, memorandum by A. M. S. O.
114 *Ibid.*
115 *Ibid.*
116 TNA, AIR 2/2220, Civilian Employees at Depots in War: Enclosure 18A, Memorandum to AMSO from Air Ministry dated 3 January 1939.
117 Postan, *British War Production* (1952), p. 96.
118 TNA, AIR 2/1973, Storage Units and Stores Depots Conversion from Peace to War Organisation, Air Ministry letter dated 8 February 1939.
119 *Ibid.*
120 *Ibid.*, Enclosures 17a and 21a.
121 *Ibid.*, Part I, p. 5.
122 TNA, AIR 2/3317, Directorate of Equipment Reorganisation 1938, Enclosure 13A.
123 TNA, AIR 2/4236, Proposed Re-organisation of the Directorate of Equipment 1939, enclosure 11A. The majority of staff within DofE 3 remained in London due to their much closer working relationships with other Air Ministry Directorates. The E11 section with its extensive responsibility for movements worked closely with the Directorate of Organisation, the Air Staff, War Office and the Ministry of Shipping; the staff of E14 and E16, responsible for much of the planning function, worked closely with the Directorate of Organisation and E19 worked on a regular basis with the Petroleum Board.

Chapter Three

1 Thetford, *Aircraft of the Royal Air Force* (1995), p. 396.
2 Air Ministry, *Statistics* (1946), Section I, Table I, pp. 1–5.
3 Cited in Logistics Quotations, posted by Naval Supply Systems Command (NAVSUP): au.af.mil/au/awc/awcgate/navy/log_quotes_navsup. pdf [accessed 31 January 2015].
4 TNA, AIR 2/4236, Proposed Re-organisation of the Directorate of Equipment 1939, enclosure 11A, p. 1.
5 TNA, AVIA 15/113, Proposed Re-Organisation of the Directorate of Equipment 1939.
6 TNA, AIR 2/8078, Reorganisation of No.40 Group, C-in-C Maintenance Command to Under Secretary of State dated 8 February 1941 and TNA AIR 2/8185, Reorganisation of Maintenance Command, Memoranda E.40/42 dated 24 June 1942.

7 Each of the UEWs was responsible for a range of locations within a specific geographically defined area: No. 3 UEW covered South East England; No. 7 UEW covered South West England and South Wales; No. 14 UEW covered Northern England and Scotland; No. 16 UEW covered part of the Midlands from Latitude 52° 30' North to Latitude 53° 00' North; No. 25 UEW covered part of the Midlands from the northern boundary of Nos 3 and 7 UEWs north to Latitude 52° 30' North; No. 35 UEW covered North East and North West England from Latitude 53° 30' North to a line just south of Carlisle; and No. 61 UEW covered the Northern part of the Midlands from Latitude 53° 00' North to Latitude 53° 30' North. TNA, AIR 2/8455, Equipment Dispersal at Depots, C-in-C Maintenance Command to AOC in Chief RAF Commands dated 11 April 1942, Appendix B.

8 AHB, *Maintenance* (1954), pp. 136 and 149. Broadly speaking, 55, 56, and 57 Wings covered the geographical areas of the Midlands, Northern England and Scotland and Southern England (including the South East and South West) respectively.

9 The overseas command structure was complex and evolved as the emphasis on the different theatres of war changed. In September 1939, the structure consisted of: RAF Middle East; RAF in Palestine and Transjordan; British Forces in Iraq; British Forces in Aden; RAF Mediterranean; Air Forces in India; and RAF Far East. By January 1945 the structure was based on two main groupings: Mediterranean Air Forces and Air Command South East Asia. Richards, *The Fight at Odds* (1953), Appendix III, and Saunders, *The Fight is Won* (1954), Appendix IV refer.

10 AHB, *Maintenance* (1954), pp. 34–35.

11 RAF LHCA, Hills papers.

12 RAF LHCA, Stamp papers.

13 RAF LHCA, Morss papers.

14 Probert, 'Supply: Two Wartime Examples', *RAF Historical Society Journal* (2005), pp. 35–36.

15 AHB, *Maintenance* (1954), p. 37.

16 *Ibid.*, p. 38. It took several decades more before the RAF started to measure storage buildings in terms of cubic feet and to maximise stacking and racking to enable a better utilisation of capacity.

17 *Ibid.*

18 *Ibid.*, pp. 38–39.

19 *Ibid.*, p. 39.

20 *Ibid.*, p. 154.

21 *Ibid.*

22 TNA, AIR 2/8185, Reorganisation of Maintenance Command, Memoranda E.40/42dated 24 June 1942 and AHB, *Maintenance*, pp. 136–137.

23 AHB, *Maintenance* (1954), p. 137.

24 *Ibid.*, p. 138.

25 TNA, AIR 2/8455, Equipment Dispersal Depots, HQ Maintenance Command letter MC/S.9383 dated 11 April 1942. Although these units were referred to as EPs they were, in fact, allocated an MU identity. Perth and Inverness, for example, became Nos 17 and 79 MUs respectively in June 1941.

26 *Ibid.*, HQ Maintenance Command letter dated 19 June 1942.

27 AHB, *Maintenance* (1954), p. 144; TNA, AIR 2/8455, Equipment Dispersal Depots, HQ Maintenance Command letter dated 19 June 1942; and Air Ministry Memorandum No. 1007 dated 20 May 1941.

28 TNA, AIR 2/8455, Equipment Dispersal Depots, Organisation Memorandum. No. 42.

29 Source: Data extracted from AHB, *Maintenance* (1954), diagram 18, p. 152.

30 TNA AIR 2/8316, Storage Requirements of No. 40 Group 1944–1945, Air Ministry letters S.1371/ADO1 and S101315.

31 RAF LHCA, Birch papers.
32 AHB, *Maintenance* (1954), Appendix 14, Equipment Storage November 1941–December 1944.
33 McCamley, *Secret Underground Cities* (1999), p. 8.
34 AHB, *Maintenance* (1954), pp. 348–351.
35 TNA, AIR 29/973, ORB, HQ No. 14 MU entry dated 26 September 1938.
36 AHB, *Maintenance* (1954), pp. 158–159.
37 McCamley, *Secret Underground Cities* (1999), p. 223; and AHB, *Maintenance*, p. 139.
38 McCamley, *Secret Underground Cities* (1999), pp. 223–224.
39 AHB, *Works* (1956), p. 208.
40 Source data extracted from: TNA files: AIR 29/998, 35 MU Heywood Operational Record Book (ORB); AIR 29/964 and AIR 29/965, 7 MU Quedgeley ORBs; AIR 29/987, 25 MU Hartlebury ORB; AIR 29/973 and AIR 29/974, 14 MU Carlisle ORBs; AIR 29/976, 16 MU Stafford ORB; AIR 29/957, 1 MU Kidbrooke ORB; AIR 29/959, 3 MU Milton ORB; and AIR 29/960, 4 MU Ruislip ORB. Of these units, Nos 3, 7, 14, 16, 25, and 35 MUs were UEDs/AEDs. Nos 1 and 4 MUs, originally formed as EDs, transferred to No. 43 Group in May and June 1940 respectively.
41 Collier, *The Defence of the United Kingdom* (1957), pp. 261–281; and Ray, The *Night Blitz* (1996), pp. 225–232. Contemporary logistics theory considers the manufacturing element as the start of most supply chains.
42 Such intelligence had been gained through the comprehensive listing of RAF units (including their locations) in the Air Force lists up to 1938 and air reconnaissance photographs which had also been taken as early as 1938 by Lufthansa aircraft with concealed cameras. See: Downing, *Spies in the Sky* (2011), p. 337; Royal Commission on the Ancient and Historical Monuments of Scotland (RCAHMS), *Scotland from the Air* (1999), p. 4; Liddell Hart, *History of the Second World War* (1970), p. 121; and Boog, 'German Air Intelligence in the Second World War' in Handel, *Intelligence and Military Operations* (1990), p. 370.
43 Deichmann, *The System of Target Selection* (1955), pp. 11–12.
44 Downing, *Spies in the Sky* (2011), pp. 337–338.
45 Liddell Hart, *History of the Second World War* (1970), p. 121.
46 Boog, *German Air Intelligence*, p. 366.
47 Air Ministry, *Notes for Equipment Assistants* (1944).
48 Air Ministry, *Works* (1956), pp. 277–278.
49 *Ibid.*
50 *Ibid.*, pp. 282–283.
51 TMA, Site Plan of Halton Park Aerodrome (SE 76B) dated 1921.
52 Petroleum Board, *British Oil Distribution in Wartime* (1945), p. 70; Payton-Smith, *Oil* (1971), pp. 332–335 and 408–409; and Edgerton, *Britain's War Machine* (2012), pp. 191 and 199.
53 Source: Petroleum Board, *British Oil Distribution in Wartime* (1945), p. 70.
54 Higham, *Bases of Air Strategy* (1998), p. 138.
55 Thetford, *Aircraft of the RAF* (1995), p. 42.
56 AHB, *Armament, Volume I* (1952), Appendix 18, p. 434.
57 AHB, *Armament, Volume II* (1954), Appendices 6, 7, and 8, pp. 198–203.
58 AHB, *Maintenance* (1954), Appendix 13, p. 441.
59 Chorlton, *Danger Area* (2003), pp. 5–38.
60 *Ibid.*, p. 11.
61 AHB, *Maintenance* (1954), p. 127; and McCamley, Site Record for Llanberis RAF Reserve Depot (Bomb Store) on Subterranea Britannica (2011), subbrit.org.uk/sb-sites/sites/l/llanberis/index.shtml [accessed 1 January 2014].

62 AHB, *Maintenance* (1954), p. 127; Fionn Taylor, The Day the World Blew Up: Fauld Ordnance Explosion 1944 on Mining Website, (2014): healeyhero.co.uk/rescue/individual/fauld_menu.htm [accessed 1 January 2014]; The Fauld Explosion (2007): carolyn.topmum.net/tutbury/fauld.fauldcrater.htm [accessed 7 May 2007]; and Byron Rogers, 'Britain's Biggest Bang', *The Weekend Guardian*, Saturday–Sunday 11–12 March 1989, pp. 1–3.

63 George Medals were awarded to Wing Commander D. L. Kings, Flight Lieutenant J. P. Lewin, and Mr J. C. Salt; the MBE to Flight Lieutenant H. J. Shuttleworth; BEMs to Corporals S. B. Rock and J. S. Peters and Mr H.Coker; and Commendation for Brave Conduct to Mrs M. E. Degg. Third Supplement to *The London Gazette*, Number 37,022 dated 6 April 1945, pages 1,889–1,891 and Fifth Supplement to *The London Gazette*, Number 37,024 dated 6 April 1945, pages 1,897–1,898 refer.

64 TNA, AIR 72/24, AMOs 1940: Order A.703: Clerk, Equipment Accounting, and Clerk, Pay Accounting, Group IV: Re-introduction (592918/36: 26.9.40) dated 26 September 1940; and Stone, 'Royal Air Force Logistics during the Second World War', Appendix 2.

65 The personnel establishment for Equipment Sections varied, depending on the role of the unit in question. A post-war (1956) work study into the Equipment Squadron at RAF Binbrook, a unit which had changed very little in the ten years after the war, shows that the establishment consisted of three officers, forty-two airmen and eight civilians. TNA, AIR 20/10488, Royal Air Force Binbrook Equipment Squadron Study Report, Appendix U to Part I refers.

66 Armitage, *The Royal Air Force* (1993), p. 69.

67 AHB, *Maintenance* (1954), Diagram 18, p. 152.

68 *Ibid.*, Appendix 17, p. 452.

69 Stone, 'Royal Air Force Logistics during the Second World War', Appendix 2.

70 TNA, AIR 72/27, AMOs 1943: Order A.1275.

71 AHB, *The Women's Auxiliary Air Force* (1953), p. 94.

72 TNA, AIR 72/26, AMOs 1942: Order A.1048; and Stone, 'Royal Air Force Logistics during the Second World War, Appendix 2.

73 Stone, 'Royal Air Force Logistics during the Second World War', Appendix 2.

74 Smith, 'The Womanpower Problem in Britain During the Second World War', *The Historical Journal* Vol. 27, No. 4 (1984), pp. 925–945; Smith, 'The Problem of "Equal Pay for Equal Work" in Great Britain during World War II', *The Journal of Modern History*, Vol. 53, No. 4 (1981), pp. 652–672 (p. 654); Escott, *Women in Air Force Blue* (1989), p. 169; and Smith, *Britain in the Second World War: A Social History* (1996), p. 13.

75 AHB, *The Women's Auxiliary Air Force* (1953), pp. 105 and 121.

76 TNA, AIR 2/9247, WAAF Proposal to Have Equipment Officers: paragraph two of the minutes of the seventeenth meeting held on 7 April; Bentley Beauman, *Partners in Blue* (1971), p. 183; and AHB, *The Women's Auxiliary Air Force* (1953), pp. 94–95.

77 *Ibid.*

78 Bentley *Beauman, Partners in Blue* (1971), p. 183; AHB, *The Women's Auxiliary Air Force* (1953), p. 95; and Air Force List (January 1945).

79 AHB, *The Women's Auxiliary Air Force* (1953), p. 113.

80 RAF LHCA, Rothnie papers.

81 TNA, AIR 20/2025, Service Personnel: Strength Returns, September 1939 to June 1946.

82 Nos 4, 5, and 6 ASPs were allocated to the AASF and Nos 1, 2, and 3 ASPs to the Air Component.

83 AHB, *The Campaign in France and the Low Countries* (undated), pp. 114–118.

84 RAF LHCA, Hills papers.

85 RAF LHCA, Hills papers.

86 AHB, *The Campaign in France and the Low Countries* (undated), p. 474.

87 Natkiel, *Atlas of the Second World War* (1985), pp. 48–79.

88 AHB, *Maintenance* (1954), pp. 218–219.
89 Young, *Atlas of the Second World War* (1973), pp. 50–51.
90 AHB, *Maintenance* (1954), p. 209.
91 Young, *Atlas of the Second World War* (1973), pp. 50–51; and AHB, *Maintenance*, p. 210.
92 Young, *Atlas of the Second World War* (1973), pp. 54–63.
93 RAF LHCA, Henry papers.
94 RAF LHCA, Stamp papers.
95 Jefford, *RAF Squadrons* (1988), pp. 222–223.
96 These were 34–38, 40, and 42 ASPs. Sturtivant *et al.*, *Royal Air Force Flying Training and Support Units* (1997), pp. 62–63 refers. Nos 32 and 33 ASPs re-joined the campaign in North Africa after they had returned from Operation Barbarity in Greece during April and May 1941.
97 TNA, AIR 29/784, ORB No. 40 Air Stores Park, entries for November 1941 to June 1942 inclusive.
98 TNA, AIR 29/784, ORB No. 40 Air Stores Park, entries for June 1942 to July 1942 inclusive.
99 TNA, AIR 29/784, ORB No. 40 Air Stores Park, entries for July and August 1942.
100 Young, *Atlas of the Second World War* (1973), pp. 68–69 and 72–73.
101 TNA, AIR 29/784, ORB No. 40 Air Stores Park, entries for 5 and 8 October 1942.
102 The AOG system is described in more detail in Chapter Nine.
103 Young, *Atlas of the Second World War* (1973), pp. 72–73.
104 TNA, AIR 29/784, ORB No. 40 Air Stores Park, entries for 1 November 1942 to 25 February 1943.
105 *Ibid.*, entry for 2 Jan 1943, and Young, *Atlas of the Second World War* (1973), pp. 72–73.
106 TNA, AIR 29/784, ORB No. 40 Air Stores Park, entry for 31 December 1942.
107 *Ibid.*, entry for 31 December 1942 and 2–8 January 1943.
108 Richards and Saunders, *The Fight Avails* (1954), p. 242.
109 Guedalla, *Middle East 1940–1942* (1944), p. 167.
110 Speller, *The Role of Amphibious Warfare* (2001), pp. 19 and 31.
111 War Office, *History of the Combined Operations Organisation* (1956), pp. 140–150.
112 *Ibid.*, p. 142.
113 Fenton, RAF Beach Units: Purpose and Organisation (2015): rafbeachunits.info/Purpose_-_Organisation/purpose_-_organisation.html [accessed 18 January 2016].
114 Speller, *The Role of Amphibious Warfare* (2001), p. 29.
115 *Ibid.*, Combined Operations Pamphlet No. 2: Beach Organisation and Maintenance, dated Autumn 1942.
116 Fenton, RAF Beach Units: Purpose and Organisation (2015): rafbeachunits.info/Purpose_-_Organisation/purpose_-_organisation.html [accessed 18 January 2016].
117 Young, *Atlas of the Second World War* (1973), pp. 70–71 and 78–79.
118 AHB, *The North African Campaign* (undated), Appendix 9; AHB, *Maintenance* (1954), pp. 252–255; and Supplement to *The London Gazette* of 23 March 1949 (Issue 38,569), Despatch Submitted to Commander in Chief Allied Forces on 30 March 1943 by Admiral of the Fleet Sir Andrew Cunningham GCB DSO, Commander in Chief Mediterranean.
119 TNA, AIR 29/438, ORB No. 1 RAF Beach Squadron and AIR 29/18, ORB for Auxiliary Embarkation Units.
120 TNA, AIR 37/99, RAF Beach Units: Administration and Organisation.
121 War Office, *History of the Combined Operations Organisation* (1956), p. 145.
122 Sturtivant *et al.*, *Royal Air Force Flying Training and Support Units* (1997), pp. 63–65.
123 Young-James, *Memoirs of an ASP* (1965), pp. 70–71; and TNA, AIR 29/785, ORB 91 Air Stores Park 1942–1948.
124 RAF LHCA, Harte papers.

125 RAF LHCA, Nancarrow papers.
126 Air Ministry, *Maintenance* (1954), pp. 360–367.
127 *Ibid.*
128 RAF LHCA, Nancarrow papers and TNA, AIR 23/4637, Chief Equipment Officer, Air HQ Far East, Personal War Diary 1941–1942.
129 TNA, Air 2/8920, Greek Awards to RAF.
130 RAFLHCA, George papers.
131 Promulgated in a Supplement to *The London Gazette* dated 26 May 1944.
132 RAF LHCA, Morss papers.
133 Fenton, RAF Beach Units: List of Units:: rafbeachunits.info/List_of_Units/list_of_units.html [accessed 24 March 2015] and TNA, AIR 29/438, ORB No. 1 RAF Beach Squadron.
134 AHB, *Maintenance* (1954), p. 324.
135 Nos. 34, 401, 402, 404, 406 (RCAF), 408 (Polish), 414, and 418 ASPs took part and were allocated to Nos. 2, 83, 84, and 85 Groups. No. 408 (Polish) ASP had originally been formed as 206 MU, a mobile equipment park, in June 1943 to support the Polish Spitfire squadrons based at RAF Northolt and RAF Heston near London. TNA, AIR 2/8185, Reorganisation of Maintenance Command, Maintenance Command Administrative Instruction No. 3/43 dated 18 June 1943 refers.
136 RAF LHCA, Gorddard papers.
137 Ted Inge's account was relayed to the father of Mr Mike Fenton in a letter written in 1990 and is reproduced with permission. A few points of explanation are warranted. The LSI he refers to is a Landing Ship Infantry and the S&W 380 is the widely issued Smith and Wesson revolver. From what can be deduced from the few surviving ORBs, his comment that No. 1 RAF Beach Squadron was probably the first to land is correct. The final point regarding honours and awards is also quite interesting. It was not uncommon in situations where many distinguished themselves, for a quota of certain awards to be allocated to a unit; the fairest way to do this was often by holding a draw. Ted's reference to being lucky in the 'draw for Oak Leaves' is most certainly that he was awarded a Mention in Despatches.
138 War Office, *Notes on Operational Aspects of Mulberry 'B'* (1945), Annex V.
139 TNA, AIR 29/783, ORB for 34 ASP; AIR 29/787, ORBs for 401, 402, 404, 406, 408, and 418 ASPs and AIR 29/1065, ORB for 414 ASP.
140 The definition is from the official history (Payton-Smith, *Oil* (1971), p. 334). Popular history works often incorrectly this as Pipe Line Under the Ocean
141 Searle, *PLUTO* (1995), p. 64; and Bauduin, *Quand l'or noir coulait `a flots* (2004), pp. 9–10.
142 Man, *The Penguin Atlas of D-Day* (1994), pp. 88-105.
143 Neillands, *The Battle for the Rhine* (2005), pp. 70 and 77; and AHB, *Maintenance* (1954), p. 348.
144 AHB, *Maintenance* (1954), p. 353.
145 Neillands, *The Battle for the Rhine* (2005), pp. 70–71
146 *Ibid.*, pp. 157–173.
147 AHB, *Maintenance* (1954), pp. 348–351.
148 TNA, AIR 29/438, ORB No. 5 RAF Beach Unit.
149 TNA, AIR 29/438, ORB No. 6 RAF Beach Unit.

Chapter Four

1 AHB, *Manning Plans and Policy* (Undated), pp. 265–278 and Appendix 4. The Demobilisation Centres were established at Uxbridge, Cardington, Hednesford, Kirkham, and Wythall.

2 Oldaker, *Support in the Sky* (1996), pp. 62–63. These were initially established as purely disposal units, but within only two weeks of formation were re-designated as MUs.
3 Sturtivant *et al*, *Royal Air Force Flying Training and Support Units* (1997), pp. 215–216. All fifteen of these UK units were soon designated as MUs after their formation (Nos 254 to 268 inclusive).
4 TNA, AIR 29/1378, ORB 433 EDD.
5 AHB, *Maintenance* (1954), Appendix 13, p. 441; and Bowles, 'Beauforts Dyke Background' (2006), mod.uk/NR/rdonlyres/52954E9D-A12E (accessed 29 March 2012).
6 RAF LHCA, BEC 6, HQ 42 Group, Group Administrative Instruction No. 138 (1946).
7 RAF LHCA, Drean papers.
8 Bowles, 'Beauforts Dyke Background', (2006), mod.uk/NR/rdonlyres/52954E9D-A12E (accessed 29 March 2012).
9 Thorburn, 'Operation Eclipse', *Air Clues*, Vol. 40, No. 4 (1986), p. 147.
10 HQ BAFO, *An Account of the Part Played by the Royal Air Force in Dissolving the Luftwaffe* (1947), pp. v–viii.
11 Thorburn, 'Operation Eclipse' (1986), *Air Clues*, Vol. 40, No. 4 (1986), p. 147; and Taylor, *Royal Air Force Germany* (2003), pp. 226–227.
12 The number of Air Disarmament Wings within each Group varied. Within 2 Group, there were six; within 83 Group, there were three; and within 84 Group, there were four. See Taylor, *Royal Air Force Germany* (2003), pp. 226–227.
13 HQ BAFO, *An Account of the Part Played by the Royal Air Force in Dissolving the Luftwaffe* (1947), pp. 73 and 79.
14 RAFLHCA, Stamp papers.
15 HQ BAFO, *An Account of the Part Played by the Royal Air Force in Dissolving the Luftwaffe* (1947), p. 113. The quantities of equipment handled by the parks during the duration of Operation Eclipse in tons (deadweight) were: 437 ADDP: 1,202; 438 ADDP: 3,386; and 440 ADDP: 4,036; the latter was the highest as it was handling material from Norway and Denmark.
16 HQ BAFO, *An Account of the Part Played by the Royal Air Force in Dissolving the Luftwaffe* (1947), p. 74.
17 Thorburn, 'Operation Eclipse', *Air Clues*, Vol. 40, No. 4 (1986), p. 150.
18 Natkiel, *Atlas of World War II* (1985), p. 136.
19 Bates, *Japan and the British Commonwealth Occupation Force* (1993), pp. 9 and 63.
20 Young-James, *Memoirs of an ASP* (1965), pp. 70–76.
21 TNA, AIR 20/4373, The Occupation and Disarmament of Japan, Position Report at August 1946.
22 TNA, AIR 2/8788, Report of the Committee on Royal Air Force Administration 1939, pp. 99-102.
23 TNA, AIR 20/9625, AMSO Work Study at RAF Binbrook. and TNA, AIR 20/6617, RAF Tuddenham: Trials of Experimental Station Organisation.
24 TNA, AIR 20/10488, Appendix A to Binbrook Equipment Study Report Part 1. The establishment went from three officers, forty-two RAF, and eight civilians to three officers, thirty-eight RAF and five civilians. This represented a Service manning level of just under 90 per cent.
25 This arrangement lasted until the early 1980s when Supply Squadrons (as the Equipment Sections had then become) were placed under the command of the renamed Technical organisation, the Engineering Wing. By then, more collaborative working and the advent of computerised stock control had removed a lot of the manual intervention in stockholding.
26 TNA, AIR 20/10488, Binbrook Equipment Study Report Part 1, Appendix L and M and TNA, AIR 20/9625, Appendix C to AMSO Work Study at Binbrook.

27 Churchill, *Winston Churchill's Speeches* (2007), p. 420.
28 North Atlantic Military Committee (NATO), Decision on M.C. 14/1, A Report by the Standing Group on Strategic Guidance, Enclosure A (1952) pp. 6–33: nato.int/docu/stratdoc/eng/a521209a.pdf [accessed 19 April 2013].
29 NATO, Final Decision on M.C. 14/2 (Revised), A Report by the Military Committee on the Overall Strategic Concept for the Defense of the North Atlantic Treaty Organisation Area, Enclosure, Section II (1957) pp. 7–10: nato.int/docu/stratdoc/eng/a570523a.pdf [accessed 19 April 2013].
30 Allisstone, 'From Trip Wire to Flexible Response', *Air Clues* (March 1986), p. 83.
31 Maloney, 'Fire Brigade or Tocsin?', *Journal of Strategic Studies*, Vol. 27 (2004), p. 585–613.
32 RAF LHCA, Packman papers.
33 Jackson, *V-Force* (2000), p. 15.
34 Gibson, *Vulcan's Hammer* (2011), pp. 47–53 and 103–108.
35 Allisstone, 'Nuclear Weapons and No. 94 MU' *RAF Historical Society Journal*, No. 35 (2005), pp. 58–60.
36 Brookes, *V Force* (1982), p. 133.
37 Allisstone, 'Post World War II Imperatives for Supply', *RAF Historical Society Journal*, p. 6.
38 Jackson, *V-Force* (2000), p. 102.
39 *Ibid.*, p. 103.
40 Taylor, 'Historical Background', *Royal Air Force in Germany 1945–1993* (1999), pp. 10–13.
41 RAF LHCA, Mobility and Deployed Support Study (1993).
42 Taylor, 'Historical Background', *Royal Air Force in Germany 1945–1993* (1999), pp. 14–15.
43 RAF LHCA, Humphries papers.
44 Sullivan, 'Taceval', *RAF Supply* (1978), pp. 17–18. By the mid-1990s, the evaluations were conducted under three headings: Operations, Support, and Survive-to-Operate.
45 Cocroft *et al.*, *Cold War: Building for Nuclear Confrontation* (2004), p. 63.
46 RAF LHCA, A Study of the RAF Station Supply Organisation, p. 13.
47 Second Line repair was carried out by the unit's Engineering Wing, Third Line repair was conducted at a specialist Service installation such as RAF Sealand, while Fourth Line was conducted back at industry, invariably the equipment manufacturers.
48 Dean, 'Supply Support in a Hardened Environment', *RAF Supply* (1978), p. 29.
49 The identity of critical stock was based on a listing produced by the unit's Engineering Wing.
50 Of the Continental ASPs, Numbers 90, 401, 402, 404, 406(RCAF), 408(Polish), 414, and 418 had all been disbanded by the end of 1946. The personnel and equipment of 34 ASP, however, were absorbed into 431 EP.
51 Sturtivant *et al.*, *Royal Air Force Flying Training and Support Units* (1997), pp. 65–66.
52 RAF LHCA, Noble papers.
53 Taylor, *Royal Air Force Germany* (2003), p. 228; and Sturtivant *et al.*, *Royal Air Force Flying Training and Support Units* (1997), p. 66.
54 Ovendale, *British Defence Policy* (1994). This point also saw NATO's strategic doctrine change from one of 'Massive Retaliation' to 'Flexible Response'.
55 MOD, AP3003 (2004), p. 193.
56 Oldaker, *Support in the Sky* (1996), pp. 37–38.
57 Kilcullen, *No. 7 Maintenance Unit RAF Quedgeley* (1995), pp. 31–32.
58 RAF LHCA, Sefton papers.
59 Beckett and Fentum, 'Support Command Storage and Materials Handling Advisory Team', *RAF Supply* (1975), pp. 16–17.
60 RAF LHCA, Assorted papers on renaming of the Equipment Branch.
61 *Ibid.*

62 Jeffery, 'It's a Fact', *RAF Supply*, Issue 3 (1973), pp. 15–16. The balance of the RAF's manpower at this time was made up of Engineering 50.5 per cent, General Duties 10.6 per cent, Secretarial 6.8 per cent, and all other Branches and Trades 24.6 per cent.
63 The main directorates throughout this period (in addition to DCat and DCA) were: Supply Policy, Supply Systems, SM1, SM2 and Supply Control.
64 RAF LHCA, This is Support Command (1977).
65 RAF LHCA, RAF Mobility in the 1970s (1969), p. 1.
66 RAF LHCA, Air Staff Guidelines for Mobility (1968).
67 RAF LHCA, RAF Mobility in the 1970s (1969), p. 2–5.
68 Air Ministry, AP 3282A, *Trade Structure of the Royal Air Force* (1952)
69 DCI (RAF)) S142/1971 refers.
70 DCI (RAF) S100/1972 refers.
71 RAF LHCA, Report of a Committee on the Future Employment of Civilians in the RAF, Annex D and Appendix B.
72 Dean, *RAF Stafford 50th Anniversary* (2006), pp. 14–15.
73 Smith, 'Maintenance Command Earns a Bonus for the Front Line', *RAF Supply*, pp. 2–4 and 52–55.
74 Allisstone, 'Post World War II Imperatives for Supply', *RAF Historical Society Journal*, No. 35, p. 5.
75 Anon, 'Report from RAF Support Command', *RAF Supply* (1978), pp. 7–10.
76 AHB, *The RAF, Small Wars and Insurgencies* (2011), pp. 1–2.
77 Group Captain A. P. Matthews in a letter to the author dated 19 March 2014.
78 Springett, 'Ascension: Bare Base Revived', *RAF Supply*, Issue 26 (1982), pp. 68–72.
79 Alliston, 'Corporate Miscellany', *RAF Supply* (1982), p. 77.
80 Anon, 'RAF Supply Winning their Biggest Battle', *Air Clues* (1982), pp. 270–271.
81 MBEs were awarded to Flt Lt E. M. Clinton and Mr J. T. Price at Harrogate, the BEM to Cpl D. J. Vivian from RAF Odiham. The commendations were from: AOCinCs Strike Command, and Support Command; AOC Maintenance Units; Commander Task Force 317; C-in-C Task Force; AOC 38 Group and South Atlantic Special Commendations. Anon, 'Supply Honours and Awards' (1982), pp. 3–4 refers.

Chapter Five

1 Taylor, 'A Brief Guide to Previous British Defence Reviews' (2010), p. 9.
2 House of Commons Defence Select Committee, *Frontline First* (1994).
3 Oldaker, *Support in the Sky* (1996), pp. 86–87.
4 Now no longer an agency and part of Joint Support Chain Services.
5 Hayr, 'Logistics in the Gulf War' *The RUSI Journal*, Vol. 136, Issue No. 3 (1991), p. 19. The reference to a 'Joint Tactical Plan' is more likely to have been a 'Joint Theatre Plan'.
6 Crotty, 'Logistics Support in the Gulf War', *Royal Air Force Historical Society Journal*, Vol. 19 (1999) and RAF LHCA, O'Dea papers.
7 Crotty, 'Logistics Support in the Gulf War', *Royal Air Force Historical Society Journal*, Vol. 19 (1999), pp. 86–96. By 1990, two PTPs were held forward, one each at Decimomannu in Sardinia and Goose Bay in Canada to support exercises. Both were recovered to the UK and subsequently deployed to the Gulf.
8 RAF LHCA, O'Dea papers.
9 Crotty, 'Logistics Support in the Gulf War', *Royal Air Force Historical Society Journal*, Vol. 19 (1999), pp. 86–96.
10 National Audit Office (NAO), *Movements of Personnel, Equipment and Stores to and from the Gulf* (1993), p. 16.

11 House of Commons Defence Committee (HCDC), *Lessons of Iraq* (2004), p. 291.
12 Crotty, 'Logistics Support in the Gulf War', *Royal Air Force Historical Society Journal*, Vol. 19 (1999), pp. 86–96.
13 RAF LHCA, O'Dea papers.
14 NAO, Movements of Personnel, Equipment and Stores to and from the Gulf (1993). pp. 1 and 11.
15 Although MDSS claimed to introduce the formal concept of Host Nation Support, a number of former RAF Supply Officers can recall dealing with this idea when working with NATO flank countries as part of the UKMF and ACEMF commitments in the 1980s.
16 MOD, *AP3003, A Brief History* (2004), pp. 296–300.
17 HMSO, *SDR Research Papers 98/91*, p. 15.
18 MOD, *The Strategic Defence Review: Supporting Essays* (1998), p. 11–16.
19 NAO, *Kosovo* (2000), pp. 29–34.
20 BBC News: Flashback to Kosovo's War (2006), news.bbc.co.uk/1/hi/world/europe/5165042.stm [accessed 1 December 2013]; and Crampton, *The Balkans* (2002), pp. 270–277.
21 Tipping, *Key Issues Affecting the Provision of Logistics Support* (2013), p. 1.
22 Lester-Powell, 'Development of No. 85 (Expeditionary Logistics) Wg', RAF Supply Branch Yearbook (2004), p. 32.
23 This was formed by combining its forward support fixed and rotary wing recovery, and transport organisations into a single squadron.
24 No. 42 Wing was formed by transferring-in No. 5001 Squadron from No. 85 (EL) Wing (based at RAF Wittering) and joined by No. 5131 (Bomb Disposal) Squadron (based at RAF Wittering) and No. 93 (Expeditionary Armament) Squadron (based at RAF Marham). No. 71 (Inspection and Repair) Squadron joined the wing in 2014 having moved to Wittering from St Athan. The RAF's deployable medical units (Tactical Medical Wing, No. 612 Squadron and No. 4626 Squadron) joined the A4 grouping but these were transferred out in October 2013 to join a separate command and control arrangement for medical capability.
25 Roberts, 'The A4 Force' (2009), pp. 39–41.
26 Thurston, '85 (Expeditionary Logistics) Wing' (2008), pp. 25–26.
27 Defence Information Note (DIN), 2007DIN05-020, Formation of a Force Headquarters at RAF Wittering, dated 1 April 2007.
28 MOD, *Air and Space Warfare* (2009), p. 2–13.
29 These units were: 121 EAW RAF Coningsby, 122 EAW RAF Cottesmore, 325 EAW RAF Kinloss, 135 EAW RAF Leeming, 125 EAW RAF Leuchars, 140 EAW RAF Lossiemouth, 38 EAW RAF Lyneham, 138 EAW RAF Marham, and 34 EAW at RAF Waddington.
30 MOD, *Air and Space Warfare* (2009), pp. 12–13.
31 Haddican, 'Logistics Capability: EAW', *The Logistician* (2013), 10.
32 NAO, *Support to High Intensity Operations* (2009), p. 19.
33 MOD, *JSP 886, Volume 1, Part 1* (2012), pp. 3–8.
34 Howard, 'Commanding the Joint Force Logistic Component' (2009), pp. 49–52.
35 MOD, *Defence Reform* (2011), p. 9.
36 *Ibid.*, pp. 44–47.
37 Springett, 'Logistics in the Post Cold War Era', *RAF Historical Society Journal*, No. 19 (1999), pp. 97–104.
38 Paulson, 'Logistics Support Centre' (2004), pp. 28–31.
39 MOD, *Delivering Security in a Changing World* (2003).
40 HM Government, *Securing Britain in an Age of Uncertainty* (2010).
41 NAO, *Operation TELIC* (2003), p. 1.

42 MOD, *AP3003, A Brief History* (2004), pp. 290–295; and NAO, *Operation TELIC* (2003), p. 7.
43 *Ibid.*, pp. 39 and 41.
44 MOD, *Operations in Iraq* (2003), p. 42.
45 HCDC, *Operations in Afghanistan* (2011), p. 15.
46 *Ibid.*, p. 18.
47 *Ibid.*, p. 22.
48 *Ibid.*, p. 19.
49 MOD(RAF), Operation Ellamy Overview: raf.mod.uk/news/archive.cfm?storyid=46F56ACD-5056-A318-A814EBC6F3357F66 [accessed 12 November 2016].
50 Group Air Staff Orders mandated that aircrew must keep current in a full range of skills and capabilities, and also mandates the maximum number of flying hours that aircrew are allowed to undertake during any given period.
51 RAF LHCA, Cameron papers.

Chapter Six

1 The author is indebted to Group Captain A. P. Matthews, whose recollections form the core of this description of the development of the TacSF.
2 Gaines and Lowe, 'Harrier Force', *Flight International* (1987), pp. 20–23.
3 Jackson, *Britain's Armed Forces Today: 4, Royal Air Force Germany* (1986), p. 45.
4 Tecklenborg and Rydzynski, *Royal Air Force Gutersloh* (1995), pp. 31–32.
5 Williams, 'Tactical Supply in RAF Germany', *RAF Supply* (1984), p. 27.
6 RAF LHCA. The wider history of TSW has been drawn from the Craven-Griffiths papers (The TSW: Background and initial Start Up dated 22 April 2007) and Packman papers (Tactical Supply Wing History). Additional and more detailed input has been made by Air Commodores A. Spinks and P. Whalley, along with Group Captains N. Cromarty, D. Grant, D. Lester-Powell, C. Markey, and A. Matthews.
7 This became known as AMF (L) for the Helicopter support and AMF (A) in relation to the Harrier support provided by No.1 (Fighter) Squadron.
8 Coleman, *Support to Strike* (undated), p. 22.
9 Anon, 'Have Everything: Will Travel', *Air Clues* (1975), p. 199.
10 *Ibid.*
11 RAFLHCA, Packman papers (Tactical Supply Wing History), Annex A, p. 4.
12 Holsgrove's Commendation was promulgated in Supplement to *The London Gazette*, Number 53,453 dated 12 October 1993, Page 16389 and Bennett's in *The London Gazette*, Number 56,920, Supplement Number 2 dated 28 April 2003, page 5276.
13 Flintham, *High Stakes* (2009), pp. 316–318. A TSW engineering tradesman, Corporal Richard Cassell, was awarded the BEM for his part in the Belize operation in the New Year's Honours List 1976.
14 Corporal G. Boother of TSW was on board the Atlantic Conveyor when it was sunk. He survived and was awarded a Commander Task Force 317 Commendation for shutting down and making safe on-board aircraft refuelling systems before the ship finally went down. Coleman, *Support to Strike*, pp. 44-45 refers.
15 The BEM was awarded to Flight Sergeant J. Coleman and Commendations by Commander Task Force 317 to WO J. Ronan, Corporal G. Boother, Corporal B. McBey, Corporal R. Harvey and Junior Technician I. Harrison.
16 Grant, 'Tactical Refuelling', *Air Clues* (1987), pp. 91–93.
17 *Ibid.*

18 Coleman, *Support to Strike* (undated), p. 25.
19 Anon, 'Flight Safety Awards for TSW Airmen', *RAF Supply* (1986), p. 65.
20 Anon, 'Good Show Award for SAC Donkin', *RAF Supply* (1988), p. 6.
21 Bernard, 'Support to Strike: Tactical Supply Wing Support', *Air Clues* (November 1991), pp. 410–411.
22 *Ibid.*, p. 411.
23 Springett, 'Supply Support for the Support Helicopter Force', *Air Clues* (July 1993), pp. 48–53.
24 Ibid and Allen, *Thunder and Lightning* (1991), p. 47.
25 Springett, 'Supply Support for the Support Helicopter Force', *Air Clues* (July 1993), pp. 48–53.
26 *Ibid.*
27 *Ibid.*, p. 52.
28 TSW only sustained one serious casualty as a result of desert driver training but he subsequently made a full recovery.
29 Springett, 'Supply Support for the Support Helicopter Force', *Air Clues* (July 1993), p. 53.
30 Bernard, 'Support to Strike: Tactical Supply Wing Support', *Air Clues* (November 1991), p. 412.
31 Coleman, *Support to Strike* (undated), pp. 103–107.
32 TSW had the honour of their badge being added to the collection of official RAF badges mounted in the floor of St Clement Danes Church in London in 2012.
33 UK Operations in the Former Yugoslavia came under codenames Oculus, Resolute, Grapple, Lodestar, and Palatine, while the operation in Kosovo in 1999 was codenamed Agricola.
34 Parry, 'TSW Support to UN Ops', *Air Clues* (January 1995), pp. 31–32.
35 Muskett, 'TSW: from UNPROFOR to IFOR', *Beacon View* (Summer 1996), p. 18.
36 The Dayton agreement was so named due to the fact that is was reached at Wright Patterson Air Force base near Dayton, Ohio in the United States.
37 Muskett, 'TSW; from UNPROFOR to IFOR', *Beacon View* (Summer 1996), p. 18–19.
38 Coleman, *Support to Strike* (undated), p. 79.
39 Coleman, *Support to Strike* (undated), pp. 80–81.
40 MOD, *The Strategic Defence Review: Supporting Essays* (1998), p. 7-8.
41 BBC News, Africa: Sierra Leone Profile (2013), news.bbc.co.uk/news/world-africa-14094419 [accessed 1 December 2013]
42 These included the Carriage of Dangerous Goods by Road regulations known as the ADR (from *Accord European Relatif au Transport International des Marchandises Dangereuses par Route*) and the International Maritime Dangerous Goods regulations (IMDG).
43 Anon, 'TSW teams keep the fuel flowing', *RAF News* (2003), p. 3.
44 Maple, 'Tactical Supply Wing', RAF Supply Branch Yearbook (2005), p. 22.
45 *Ibid.*
46 Oshkosh Defense (2013): oshkoshdefense.co.uk/heavy-tactical-vehicles [accessed 30 November 2013].
47 Maple, 'Tactical Supply Wing', RAF Supply Branch Yearbook (2005), p. 23.
48 Smith, 'Tactical Supply Wing: The Op HERRICK Deployment', RAF Supply Branch Yearbook (2006), p. 24.
49 *Ibid.*, p. 25.
50 Atkinson, 'Tactical Supply Wing: Unsung and Unheralded', RAF Logistics Branch Yearbook (2009), pp. 23–24.
51 *Ibid.*, pp. 24–25.
52 The original elements which transferred into TSS included TSW's tactical fuels handling training and the Deployable Supply Group Plans. Additionally, the depot's fork lift training school, its RAF Regiment and Physical Education Flights and the station Training and Learning Centre came under command of TSS.

53 Lester-Powell, 'Development of No. 85 (Expeditionary Logistics) Wg', RAF Supply Branch Yearbook (2004), p. 32.
54 *Ibid.*, pp. 33–34.
55 John, 'A New Perch for the Scabby Crow', RAF Supply Branch Yearbook (2004), pp. 18–20.
56 Lester-Powell, 'Development of No. 85 (Expeditionary Logistics) Wg', RAF Supply Branch Yearbook (2004), p. 34 and information provided by Squadron Leader Roy Brunning and Squadron Leader Beverley Cartwright (RAF Wittering) in January 2017. The Catering Flight became part of the Wittering Support Wing when it left No. 3 MCS.

Chapter Seven

1 Related to the author in a letter by Group Captain David Owens RAF (Retd) as a quote regularly used by a onetime Director of Movements (RAF), Air Cdre Walker.
2 Air Ministry, *AP 1300*, *Royal Air Force War Manual, Part I: Operations* (1940).
3 See: Robertson, *Wheels of the* RAF (1983).
4 TNA, AIR 29/959, ORB No. 3 Stores Depot.
5 Bernard, 'Cost Conscious Attitudes', *RAF Supply* (1982), p. 44.
6 McKernan, 'The Early Bird', (1972), pp. 15–18.
7 Bernard, 'Cost Conscious Attitudes', *RAF Supply* (1982), pp. 43–47.
8 *Ibid.*, p. 44.
9 The STACON service operated on a daily basis for priorities and two containers per week for routine freight. The FRUCON service was weekly, CARCON was based on three containers per week, CYPCON based on first, third and fifth week and the MALCON based on second and fourth week.
10 Cooper, '1+2=4 or Cargo Movement', *RAF Supply*, Issue 14 (1977), pp. 22–23.
11 Delve, *The Source Book of the RAF* (1994), pp. 49–50.
12 Wood and Dempster, *The Narrow Margin* (2010), pp. 105–106.
13 TNA, AIR 2/5379, RAF Motor Transport Companies, Dowding report.
14 *Ibid.*
15 *Ibid.*
16 *Ibid.* By the time the first three companies had formed in mid-July 1940, the vehicle establishment had been increased by the addition of four articulated tenders, six 15 cwt. vans and twelve motor cycles.
17 TNA, AIR 2/5379, RAF Motor Transport Companies, Dowding report.
18 AHB, *The Battle of Britain* (undated), Appendix 8, Table III.
19 TNA, AIR 29/791, ORB No.2 MT Company. The squadron moves were on 6 October 1940: 17 Squadron (Hurricanes) from Debden to Martlesham Heath and 25 Squadron (Blenheims) from Martlesham Heath to North Weald and on 7 October 1940 relocating 25 Squadron from North Weald to Debden.
20 TNA, AIR 2/5379, RAF Motor Transport Companies, Dowding report.
21 *Ibid.*, Enclosure 7A.
22 *Ibid.*, Enclosure 26g.
23 TNA, AIR 29/815, ORB Supply and Transport Columns 8–12, 15, and 16. The flying squadrons operating in Iceland were: 53, 86, 120, 190, 251, 269, 279, and 280. See also Jefford, *RAF Squadrons* (1988) for individual squadron placements.
24 AHB, *Royal Air Force Movements* (undated), p. 6.
25 Blow, *The History of 51 (RAF) MT Company* (1987), p. 6.
26 Young, *Atlas of the Second World War* (1973), pp. 62–63.
27 Blow, *The History of 51 (RAF) MT Company* (1987), pp. 8, 10, and 30.

28 TNA, AIR 29/793, ORB, MT Companies 52–55, 57–59, and 300.
29 TNA, AIR 29/814, ORB, S&TC 2, 4–7; AIR 29/815, ORB, S&TC 8–12, 15–16; AIR 29/816 ORB, S&TC 19–21 and 309, and AIR 29/817, 816, ORB, S&TC 314–317. Those formed in the Middle East and North Africa were Nos 4–7, 10–12, 15–16, and 19–21; those in Sicily and Italy were Nos 8–9 and 310 to 311 and those for North-West Europe were Nos 309, 312 to 314 and 317.
30 Morris, 'No. 2 Mechanical Transport' (1997), p. 393.
31 *Ibid.*, p. 392.
32 Stevenson, '2 MT Leads the Way', *Air Clues* (2003), p. 12; and correspondence with No. 2MT Sqn February 2017.
33 Wolmar, *Engines of War* (2010), p. 183
34 *Ibid.*, p. 229.
35 Robertson, 'Railways and Air Warfare, Part 2' (1987), p. 159.
36 *Ibid.*
37 Corser, *Wings on Rails* (2003), pp. 24, 41, 44, 63, and 69.
38 *Ibid.*, pp. 5, 25, 33 and 40.
39 Saunders, 'The Little Trains of Chilmark', *The Railway Magazine* (1976), p. 117.
40 AHB, *Works* (1956), p. 263 and Corser, *Wings on Rails* (2003), p. 5.
41 Corser, 'Railways and Military Aviation: Part Two', *FlyPast* (1995), p. 26.
42 British Railways, *Facts About British Railways in Wartime* (1943), p. 20.
43 *Ibid.*, p. 10.
44 TNA, AIR 29/987, ORB, 25 MU Hartlebury.
45 Grehan, 'Behind the Offensive', *Britain at War* (2008), p. 20.
46 *Ibid.*, pp. 20–21.
47 RAF LHCA, Pengelly papers.
48 Saunders, 'The Little Trains of Chilmark', *The Railway Magazine* (1976), pp. 116–118.
49 Pitchfork, 'The Evolution of the Air/Sea Rescue Organisation', *Royal Air Force Historical Society Journal* (2007), p. 7–24.
50 RAF LHCA, Hall papers.
51 *Ibid.*
52 Gough and Jones, 'The Mobile Explosives Team', *Air Clues* (1993), p. 307.
53 Briggs, *A Social History of England* (1994), p. 37 and Mathias, *The First Industrial Nation* (1984), pp. 98–102.
54 *Ibid.*, pp. 226–228.
55 Savage, *Inland Transport* (1957), pp. 82–83.
56 AHB, *Maintenance* (1954), p. 163.
57 *Ibid.*, p. 147.
58 Savage, *Inland Transport* (1957), p. 621.
59 *Ibid.*, p. 163.
60 Buckingham, 'The Establishment and Initial Development of a British Airborne Force' (2001), p. 10; Knight, 'British in Iraq' (2003), pp. 9–15; and Cole and Grant, *But Not in Anger* (1979), pp. 7–14.
61 Cole and Grant, *But Not in Anger* (1979), p. 14–15; and Saunders, *Per Ardua*, p. 268.
62 Wynn, *Forged in War* (1996), p. 5.
63 AHB, *Notes on Royal Air Force Early Air Transport Operations* (undated), p. 3.
64 Cole and Grant, *But Not in Anger* (1979), pp. 54–70.
65 Thetford, *Aircraft of the Royal Air Force* (1995), pp. 320 and 324.
66 Bowyer, *RAF Operations* (1988), pp. 144–169 and Jefford, *RAF Squadrons* (1988), Appendix 11, Map 44, pp. 256–257.
67 Cole and Grant, *But Not in Anger* (1979), p. 80; Sturtivant *et al.*, *Royal Air Force Flying Training and Support Units* (1997), p. 191; and Thetford, *Aircraft of the Royal Air Force* (1995), p. 368.

68 Sturtivant *et al*, *Royal Air Force Flying Training and Support Units* (1997), p. 83; and Jefford, *RAF Squadrons* (1988), p. 35.
69 Bond and Taylor, *The Battle for France* (2001), p. 119.
70 Delve, *The Source Book of the RAF* (1994), p. 52; and Jefford, *RAF Squadrons* (1988), pp. 35, 46, and 71.
71 Jefford, *RAF Squadrons* (1988), pp. 46, 57, 65, and 81.
72 Wynn, *Forged in War* (1996), p. 6; and Jefford, *RAF Squadrons* (1988), pp. 57, 65, 71, and 81.These squadrons operated the following aircraft: 117 Squadron: Lockheed Hudson, the Douglas DC2 from February 1943 and Douglas Dakota from June 1943; 173 Squadron: variety of aircraft types; 216 Squadron: Lockheed Hudson and then the Douglas Dakota from April 1943; and 267 Squadron: operating the Lockheed Hudson, Douglas Boston and DC3 from August 1942.
73 Wynn, *Forged in War* (1996), p. 57; Delve, *The Source Book of the R.A.F* (1994), p. 129; and Jefford, *RAF Squadrons* (1988), pp. 35, 71, and 88. The No. 216 Squadron detachment converted to the Douglas Dakota in April 1943, 31 Squadron converted to DC2s in April 1941, the DC3 in April 1942 and Douglas Dakota in April 1943, and 353 Squadron converted to the Douglas Dakota in April 1944.
74 Cole and Grant, *But Not in Anger* (1979), pp. 123–134; and Pitchfork, *Men Behind the Medals* (2003), pp. 139–143. Supply dropping in Burma is also covered in some detail in Annett, *Drop Zone Burma* (2008), pp. 1–201.
75 Wynn, *Forged in War* (1996), p. 6.
76 Havers, 'National Air Communications', *Air-Britain Digest* (1996), pp. 111 and 116.
77 TNA, AIR 2/5054, Formation of an Air Transport Unit.
78 TNA, AIR 35/336, AASF Use of Air Transport and TNA, AIR 27/1573, ORB for No.271 Squadron.
79 TNA, AIR 35/354, Barratt's Despatch on France.
80 TNA, AIR 2/5054, Formation of an Air Transport Unit. The details shown in the Air Ministry file include taskings for the period 1 to 20 September 1940.
81 AHB, *Royal Air Force Movements* (undated), attached memorandum OM 110/41.
82 *Ibid.*, attached memorandum OM 75/42.
83 Delve, *The Source Book of the RAF* (1994), p. 101.
84 *Ibid.*, pp. 107, 118, 121, and 127.
85 Butler, *Air Arsenal North America* (2004), pp. 191–193; and Thetford, *Aircraft of the Royal Air Force* (1995), p. 151.
86 TNA, AIR 37/13, Account of 46 (Transport Support) Group, p. 4. Re-supply missions were also carried out by 38 Group aircraft from 8 June 1944.
87 Fourth Supplement to *The London Gazette*, Air Operations by the Allied Expeditionary Air Force in N.W. Europe from 15 November 1943 to 30 September 1944, Issue 37,838, 2 January 1947, p. 83; and TNA, AIR 37/13, An Account of 46 (Transport Support) Group, pp. 3–5.
88 TNA, AIR 37/13, An Account of 46 (Transport Support) Group, (outbound and inbound tables), p. 62. A UK long ton is equivalent to 2,240 lb.
89 *Ibid.*, p. 64. The British Second Army, for example, had advanced about 250 miles from the River Seine since the end of August 1944. Although the Red Ball Express was predominantly to support American forces, it also ran an operation known as the Red Lion Express which supported British and Canadian forces on Operation Market Garden. Ware, *Red Ball Express* (2007), p. 153.
90 TNA, AIR 14/1025, Air Freight Bomber Command, Eisenhower to AEAF dated 21 September 1944 and minutes of a meeting held at HQ Bomber Command to discuss Using Bomber Command Aircraft for Transportation Supplies to the Continent dated 24 September 1944. Each Halifax aircraft was modified to carry 730 gallons of fuel in 163 jerrycans.

91 Fourth Supplement to *The London Gazette*, Air Operations by the Allied Expeditionary Air Force in N.W. Europe from 15 November 1943 to 30 September 1944, Issue 37,838, 2 January 1947, p. 83.
92 Graham, 'Jungle Supply Pilot', *FlyPast* (undated), p. 26.
93 RAF LHCA, O'Neil papers.
94 AHB, *Britain and the Berlin Airlift* (1998), p. 5.
95 Tusa, *The Berlin Airlift* (1998), p. 168.
96 AHB, *Britain and the Berlin Airlift* (1998), p. 19.
97 Tusa, *The Berlin Airlift* (1998), p. 262.
98 Pearcy, *Berlin Airlift* (1997), p. 67.
99 LHCA, Sullivan papers.
100 AHB, *Britain and the Berlin Airlift* (1998), pp. 16–19.
101 TNA, AIR 10/5067, AP3257, A Report on Operation Plainfare.
102 James, *Defence Policy and the Royal Air Force* (1987), pp. 178, 179, and 181.
103 MOD, *Statement on the Defence Estimates 1964*.
104 MOD, *Statement on the Defence Estimates 1967*.
105 MOD, *Statement on the Defence Estimates 1969*.
106 Ovendale, *British Defence Policy since 1945* (1994), p. 142. Although the Andover C1 became airfield calibration aircraft with No. 115 Squadron, Andover C2 Aircraft continued service with No. 32 Squadron and were used for air transport tasks (along with the BAe 146 Aircraft) until the mid-1990s. The Belfast continued to be used by the MOD as a chartered aircraft (Heavy lift) and was regularly seen at Ascension Island where it was used to bring outsize loads in to be subsequently on-moved by the C130 Falkland Islands Airbridge. It was also used to move outsize equipment for exercises around the world, work now undertaken by C17 and chartered AN124 aircraft
107 MOD, *Statement on the Defence Estimates 1977*.
108 Anon, 'TriStar Tankers: The RAF Goes Widebody', *Air International* (1985), p. 271.
109 Anon, 'The Initial Impact of TriStar Air Transport Operations', *RAF Supply* (1986).
110 Hansard, HC Debate 25 Nov. 55, Vol. 546, columns 1,892–1,902.
111 MOD, *Statement on the Defence Estimates 1967*, Command 3203 (London: HMSO, 1967) and MOD, *Statement on the Defence Estimates 1971*, Command 6735 (London: HMSO, 1971).
112 Movement Control Association Archive (MCAA), MCHS 0259.02: War Office letter 120/Gen/4240(Q(M)2(d)) dated 13 September 1960.
113 The RAF's forerunner was 174 Personnel Transit Centre (formerly Air Trooping and Freight Control Centre) formed in October 1951.
114 MCAA, Smith, R., and Cooke, D., 'MMARS!' (1982).
115 Stewart, 'Joint Service Air Trooping Centre', *RAF Hendon Commemorative Magazine* (1987), pp. 15–16.
116 Cooper, '1+2=4 or Cargo Movement in the RAF', *RAF Supply*, Issue 14 (1977), p. 22.
117 RAF LHCA, The Export from the UK of RAF Cargo under the Open Port and Cargo Allocation Centre Concept (1977).
118 MCAA, Smith, R., and Cooke, D., 'MMARS!' (1982).
119 *Ibid.*
120 Ritchie, 'The Decline of Mobility', *RAF Historical Society Journal*, No. 19 (1999), p. 70.
121 RAF LHCA, Pengelly papers.
122 Lambert, 'UKMAMS at Lyneham', *Air Clues* (September 1974), pp. 452–455.
123 Porter, *UKMAMS: 'Moving in Mysterious Ways'* (1992), p. 12.
124 Lambert, 'UKMAMS at Lyneham', *Air Clues* (September 1974), p. 453.
125 *Ibid.*, p 454.
126 Porter, UKMAMS (1992), pp. 126–127 and 134.
127 Dixon, 'Mobility in Practice', *RAF Supply*, Issue 36 (1988), p. 17.

128 Blore, 'First In, Last Out', *Air Clues* (March 1998), p. 118.
129 Porter, UKMAMS (1992), pp. 66 and 71.
130 *Ibid.*, pp. 124–126.
131 Williams, Briefing Paper on No.4624 Squadron RAuxAF (undated) and correspondence with Wing Commander B. S. Peart in January 2017.
132 TNA, AIR 72/26, AMOs 1942: Order A.482/42.
133 TNA, AIR 72/27, AMOs 1943: Order A.1110.
134 RAF LHCA, BEC 10, Dodimead, E.H., 'It's Not All a Matter of Form' (1945), p. 344.
135 TNA, AIR 72/24, AMOs 1940.
136 TNA, AIR 72/24, AMOs 1945: Order A.869.
137 Air Ministry, AP3282A (1952).
138 Proceedings from an RAF Supply Branch Seminar: Supply and Movements Post-SDR, Towards a Defence Transport and Movements Agency, Presented by Air Cdre PTW Leaning.
139 MOD, DTMA Annual Report and Accounts 2003/2004 (2004), p. 14.
140 MOD, DTMA Annual Report and Accounts 2006 (2006), p. 6.

Chapter Eight

1 RAFLHCA, BEC 5, Provision of POL (1952).
2 Those introduced in the 1950s included the Canberra, Venom, Sabre, Hunter, Swift, Valiant, Jet Provost, Javelin, Vulcan, and Victor. These were followed in the 1960s by the Lightning, Phantom and the Buccaneer. See: Thetford, *Aircraft of the Royal Air Force* (1995), pp. 407–408.
3 Air BP, Avgas vs Jet Fuel bp.com/sectiongenericarticle.do?categoryId=4503818&contentId=57639 [accessed 26 January 2014].
4 RAFLHCA, BEC 5, Current Service POL Developments and Topics (1952), p. 1. Cessation of supplies from refineries in the Iranian city of Abadan came about after Iran nationalised the Anglo-Iranian Oil Company and expelled Western companies from the site.
5 The 91/98 grade AVGAS was decreased to 91/96 in 1951 to bring this in line with the American specification.
6 Air BP, The History of Jet Fuel: bp.com/sectiongenericarticle.do?categoryId=4503664&contentId=57733 [accessed 26 January 2014].
7 FSII was not mixed with the fuel at PSDs as it lost percentage content during transfer by pipeline or bowser to the station, a process known as drag loss.
8 Lloyd, 'Pipeline Supply of Aviation Fuel: Part 2', *RAF Supply*, Issue 21 (1980), pp. 16–17.
9 RAF LHCA, Robertson papers.
10 RAF LHCA, Packman papers.
11 A fuel laboratory was also maintained in the Far East at No. 389 MU, RAF Seletar.
12 RAF LHCA, Jury papers.
13 RAF LHCA, Sefton papers.
14 RAF LHCA, Little papers.
15 Lloyd, 'Pipeline Supply of Aviation Fuel to the RAF: Part 1', *RAF Supply*, Issue 20 (1980), p. 23.
16 RAFLHCA BEC 5, NATO Fuels Lecture (1996).
17 RAF LHCA, Packman papers.
18 The eight other components included: the Norwegian Pipeline System (NOPS), the North European Pipeline System (NEPS), the Central European Pipeline System (CEPS), the Northern Italy Pipeline System (NIPS), the Portuguese Pipeline System (POPS), the Greek Pipeline System (GRPS), the Western Turkey Pipeline System (WTUPS), and the Eastern Turkey Pipeline System (ETUPS).

19 RAF LHCA, NATO Guide to Petroleum Policy in ACE and ACLANT.
20 RAF LHCA, BEC 5, NATO Fuels Lecture (1996).
21 RAF LHCA, BEC 5, CEPS (1996).
22 By 1998, this had become the Central Europe Pipeline Management Agency.
23 RAF LHCA, BEC 5, Fuels notes.
24 Jeffery, 'Supply Versatility', *RAF Supply*, Issue 28 (1983), pp. 24–25.
25 RAFLHCA, BEC 6, Introduction to Compressed Gasses (1952).
26 Cardington had originally manufactured its own hydrogen in the Gas Factory with the unit becoming No. 279 MU in 1948, before being renamed No. 217 MU in 1955.
27 *Ibid.*, pp. 2 and 7.
28 The SD98 was Secret Document 98, maintained by the MOD Air Staff. *Inter alia*, it listed all the types of aircraft used by MOD, their numbers and the fleet's approved annual flying task, and fuel consumption.
29 No. 128 MU for the Middle East, Maintenance Base Seletar for the Far East Air Force, and in the Mediterranean, Malta, and Gibraltar.
30 *Ibid.*, pp. 3–5.
31 MOD, *AP3003* (2004), pp. 220–221.
32 RAF LHCA, Sefton papers,
33 RAF LHCA, Hedges, Spinks and Sutton papers.

Chapter Nine

1 Figures calculated from Jones, *The War in the Air*, Appendices, Appendix XLI: Disposition of Aircraft and Engines on Charge of the Royal Air Force at 31 October 1918, Table A. Aeroplane and Seaplanes (Airframes), pp. 188-189. Seaplanes and Ship Aeroplanes totals have not been included to maintain a like-for-like comparison with the 1914-1918 figures. Engine figures calculated from Jones, *The War in the Air*, Appendices, Appendix XLI, Table B. Engines, pp. 190–191.
2 Thetford, *Aircraft of the Royal Air Force*, pp. 406–408 and RAF Aircraft in Service April. Available at: armedforces.co.uk/raf/listings/l0057.html (accessed 21 January 2017).
3 Trenchard Museum Archive (TMA), Royal Aircraft Factory, Spare Parts for Aeroplanes: Type R.E.8 with RAF 4A Engine (March 1917). This analysis does not include the aircraft's engine, cockpit components, armaments, undercarriage or the tail plane and rudder assembly.
4 TNA, AIR 2/3317, Directorate of Equipment Reorganisation 1938.
5 TNA, AVIA 10/269, AVRO Lancaster sub-contractors.
6 Sperry and Burns, Life Cycle Cost Modelling and Simulation to Determine the Economic Service Life of Aging Aircraft (2001).
7 Other sources include items sourced through the local purchase order procedure and through local manufacture; both of these sources were generally originated at RAF unit level.
8 Mantelli *et al.*, *The Supermarine Spitfire: Aircraft of World War II* (n.4) (2015), p. 14. Although not clear from the source, it is assumed the figures quoted are at 1940s prices.
9 RAF LHCA, CSDE, Improvement of Provisioning (1965), p. 1.
10 Jeffery, 'From the 9th Floor: Where Does Your Money Go?', *RAF Supply*, Issue 4 (1973).
11 This also includes requirements such as engines, weapons, MT vehicles, aircraft ground equipment, airfield equipment and major aircraft systems.
12 RAF LHCA, Air Ministry Training Notes (1956).
13 Sinnott, *The RAF and Aircraft Design 1923–1939* (2001), pp. 24–27. See also: Postan *et al.*, *Design and Development of Weapons* (1963), pp. 46–47.

14 Taylor, *Beaverbrook* (London: Hamish Hamilton, 1972), p. 412.
15 *Ibid*., pp. 414–415.
16 MOD, *The Defence Industrial Strategy* (2005).
17 McKane, *Enabling Acquisition Change* (2006), Section 4 and Figure 4.1.
18 Dunne and Macdonald, *Procurement in the Post Cold War* (2001), pp. 5–6 and Appendix 1. The four other stages between Staff Target and Production were: Feasibility Study, Staff Requirement, Project Definition and Full Development. A seventh stage, Disposal, was added later. See also: MOD, The Strategic Defence Review (1998), Supporting Essay 10: Procurement and Industry, pp. 10.5–10.6.
19 NAO, Ministry of Defence, *Major Projects Report* (1997).
20 MOD, *The Strategic Defence Review* (1998), Supporting Essay 10, paragraph 15.
21 *Ibid*., pp. 10.1–10.2.
22 *Ibid*., pp. 10.5–10.6. The new cycle, more commonly known as the CADMID cycle after its component parts, consisted of: Concept, Assessment, Demonstration, Manufacture, In-Service and Disposal.
23 Dunne and Macdonald, *Procurement in the Post Cold War* (2001), p. 6.
24 TNA, AVIA 46/228, The Spares Problem: Narrative dated 24 July 1951.
25 The software was developed by Systecon in the late 1970s, with the RAF initially ordering OPUS Version 8. The RIU at RAF Henlow and RAF Benson also received copies a few years later.
26 WARISM was re-written as OPSIM in 1997 and then SIMLOX around 2002, part of the Opus suite.
27 Systecon and CSDE information courtesy of Olof Wååk, Phil Sturgess, Phil Bean, and Steve French.
28 Humphrey, 'And in the Beginning', *RAF Supply*, Issue No. 27 (1983).
29 Stubbs, 'To IP or not to IP?', *RAF Supply*, Issue 35, (1987), p. 12.
30 Pocock, 'Provisioning MT Vehicles', *RAF Supply*, Issue 14 (1977).
31 TNA, AIR 20/1832, Ministry of Aircraft Production: Suggested Absorption of DDGE.
32 AHB, *Maintenance* (1954), pp. 152 and 159.
33 *Ibid*., p. 160.
34 TNA, AIR 2/8212, No. 40 Group Organisation: Master Provision.
35 TNA, AIR 29/798, MPO ME Cairo.
36 *Ibid*., Enclosure 1B. The total number of personnel required at that time amounted to 2,657 but the figures excluded the MPO at Stafford (no reason specified). A simple extrapolation to include this, based on typical MPO establishments, would bring the total MPO manpower number to just over the 3,000 mark in November 1942.
37 AHB, *Maintenance* (1954), pp. 39–40 and 159–160 and TNA, AIR 2/3102, Master Provisioning Scheme at Equipment Maintenance Units.
38 TNA, AIR 2/3102, Master Provisioning Scheme at Equipment Maintenance Units.
39 Stubbs, 'To IP or not to IP?', *RAF Supply*, Issue 35, (1987), pp. 12–13.
40 TNA, AIR 20/12459, Engineer and Equipment Working Party Final Report.
41 *Ibid*.
42 *Ibid*.
43 Jeffery, 'It's a Brave New World', *RAF Supply*, Issue 5 (1973).
44 RAF LHCA, A Study of the Proposals for a Maintenance Executive (1985).
45 RAF GAI, Administrative and General, 39/90.
46 DGSM's functional area included: DSM 1, DSM 2, DSM 3, DSM (STC) 4 and 5, DSM (SC) 6, D Catering, and D Defence Codification Authority. DGSS functional area included: D Sigs (Air), D of CC/MIS(RAF), DLIS (RAF), Comdt and D Log Est (RAF).
47 RAF LHCA, Cummings papers.
48 DGSM moved from AMSO's department to AOC in C RAF Logistics Command.

49 HQ Logistics Command, 'Ceremonial to Commemorate the Disbandment of Royal Air Force Logistics Command' (1999). Additional accommodation for senior and mainly policy staffs was provided in the main HQ building at RAF Brampton.
50 The IPTs replaced the former MDGs. From here on, the RAF's Supply Branch relinquished command of any of the new teams.
51 MOD, *The Defence Industrial Strategy* (2005).
52 McKane, *Enabling Acquisition Change* (2006).
53 Harrop, 'Planning for Economy', *Air Clues* (April 1948), pp. 15–20.
54 *Ibid.*
55 NAO, *Transforming logistics support for fast jets* (2007), pp. 4–5.
56 Wharton, 'RAF Aircraft Reliability', *Flight International* (29 February 1968), pp. 299–300.
57 Bowman, *Low Level from Swanton* (1995), pp. 206–225; and Sturtivant *et al*, *Royal Air Force Flying Training and Support Units*, (1997), pp. 58 and 90.
58 Bowman, *Low Level from Swanton* (1995), p. 216.The MDC was replaced by the Maintenance Analysis and Computing Establishment (MACE) in July 1984.
59 Ramsden, 'Managing military aircraft defects', *Flight International* (18 February 1978), p. 425.
60 NAO, *Progress in Reducing Stocks* (2002), pp. 5, 7, and 15.
61 Taylor, *A Brief Guide to Previous Defence Reviews* (2010), p. 8.
62 *Ibid.*, p. 9.
63 RAF LHCA, MOD, Royal Air Force Support Management: Support Excellence (undated), pp. 24–25.
64 Humphries and Rice, 'Support Chain Management in the Royal Air Force', *Supply Chain Management* (2000), pp. 25–28.
65 MOD, JSP, Part 1, p. 4.
66 Eddy and Arnett, 'The NATO Codification System', *The DISAM Journal* (1998), p. 39.
67 The first four figures cover items classed as hand tools, non-edged, non-powered, the second group of two is the nation which codified the item and the last seven figures is the unique identity for the item.
68 TNA, AVIA 10/327, Memorandum on Airframe and Engine Spares.
69 TNA, AVIA 10/181, Air Supply Board March 1941, 76th to 83rd Supply Board Meeting.
70 RAF LHCA, The Organisation of Supply in the Royal Air Force dated November (1988), p. 12; and Buchan, 'Supply: RAF Style', *Air Force Journal of Logistics* (spring 1988), p. 8.
71 TNA, AVIA 46/228, The Spares Problem.
72 Anon, 'Augmented Logistics Support for Tucano', *RAF Supply* (1988), pp. 7–8.
73 RAF LHCA, Tucano Logistics Support: Lessons Learned (1994).
74 The author is indebted to Group Captain D. Forsyth whose recollections form the core of this description of collaborative projects and for earlier inputs in the text of this chapter.
75 SEPECAT: *Société Européenne de Production de l'avion Ecole de Combat et d'Appui Tactique*. The initial order of 165 GR1 aircraft was followed by a further order for thirty-five T2 trainer aircraft.
76 In practice, the production of the aircraft rested with three companies: Panavia which was responsible for the airframe, engine/airframe compatibility and avionics (through the sub-contractor Easams) through: Messerschmitt-Bolkow-Blohm (MBB) in Germany; Aeritalia in Italy and the British Aircraft Corporation in the UK. The RB199-34R engine was the responsibility of Turbo Union which consisted of: Motoren and Turbo Union (MTU) in Germany; Fiat in Italy and Rolls-Royce in the UK. The aircraft gun was the responsibility of Mauser with two sub-contractors who participated in the development of the ammunition and propellant. See Ridley, 'Supply Support for Europe's Largest Aerospace Project', *RAF Supply*, Issue No. 3 (1973), pp. 12–14.
77 De'ath, 'Supply Support for the Tornado', *RAF Supply*, Issue No. 17 (1978), pp. 19.

78 *Ibid.*
79 Royal Air Force Web Site, Equipment, Typhoon FGR4, raf.mod.uk/equipment/typhoon.cfm [accessed 23 June 2016].
80 *Ibid.*

Chapter Ten

1 AHB, *Maintenance* (1954), p. 162 and TNA, AIR 2/3102, Master Provisioning Scheme at Equipment Maintenance Units.
2 TNA, AIR 20/10489, Binbrook Equipment Study Report Part 2, pp. 3, 6, and 9.
3 White, 'The RAF Supply Control Centre', *RAF Hendon Commemorative Magazine* (1987), p. 14.
4 *Ibid.*
5 Cummings, 'The Electronic Era', *RAF Historical Society Journal*, No. 35 (2005), p. 100.
6 Anon, 'Depot Computer System Rejuvenated', *RAF Supply* (1986), p. 57–58.
7 Alternative items are authorised substitutes where the original item in question is not available. Supersession chains are where an item has been brought in to replace the item in question, usually through the modification process. Both of these pieces of information are vital for airworthiness requirements and to ensure the correct item is provided to the customer.
8 RAF LHCA, MDSS: DUSAS Concept of Operations (1995).
9 SEPECAT was an international collaborative venture between the British Aircraft Corporation and Dassault/Breguet.
10 LSSys replaced CSDE's Management Information System (CMIS) which was then used for internal communications, archiving and circulating project reports and supporting the Inception Control and Reporting process (a fore runner of ILS). LSSys was intended to bear the LSA Record which was developed as part of the ILS process.
11 Berry, 'POLIS', *RAF Supply*, Issue 31 (1986), p. 18.
12 The supply management of explosives is quite distinct from non-explosive items and involves lengthy and complex calculations based on factors such as aircraft establishments, war reserve figures, contingency reserves, item life expiry and flying rates.
13 RAF LHCA, Cummings papers.
14 MOD, *Operations in Iraq: Lessons for the Future* (2003), p. 42.
15 NAO, *The Use of Information Technology to Manage the Logistics Supply Chain* (2011), p. 35.
16 NAO, *Exercise SAIF SAREEA II* (2002), p. 23.
17 Boeing, *The Royal Air Force SCCS* (2015).

Chapter Eleven

1 TNA, AIR 1/17/15/1/84, The Formation of the RAF on a Peace Basis, p. 5.
2 TNA, AIR 29/711/17832, Equipment Training School (Airmen) ORB.
3 TNA, AIR 29/712, Equipment Officers' School, Grange over Sands and Stannington (UK) and TNA, AIR 29/711/17832, Equipment Training School (Airmen) ORB.
4 TNA, AIR 72/13, AMWOs 1930: Order 795: Programme of Instructional Courses.
5 TNA, AIR 72/9, AMWOs 1927: Order 2: Qualification of Officers and Air Force List (February 1927), Column 4.
6 TNA, AIR 29/712, Equipment Officers' School, Grange over Sands and Stannington (UK), entry for 27 March 1939 and 3 April 1939.
7 RAF LHCA, Wall papers.

8 *Ibid.*
9 TNA, AIR 29/712, Equipment Officers' School, Grange over Sands and Stannington (UK), entry for August 1939.
10 *Ibid.*, Appendix A.
11 TNA, AIR 29/712, Equipment Officers' School, Grange over Sands and Stannington (UK); AIR 29/1122, RAF School of Administration, Gerrards Cross, Loughborough and Stannington 1937-1945 and AIR 29/1070, No. 246 MU Bicester January–December 1945.
12 Authority was granted in Air Ministry SD 155, serial Number 62/47 for the formation of the Wing from 1st January 1947. Journal of the Royal Air Force College, Winter 1947-8, p. 12 refers.
13 The ILMC was run by LMTS within DSGT at RAF Cranwell. At this time, LMTS was also running an OC Engineering Wing Preparatory Course, a Senior Engineering Officer Induction Course and an OC Supply Squadron Lead-in Course.
14 Todd, "A' Level Supply', *RAF Supply*, Issue No. 1 (1972), pp. 5–6.
15 The training of clerks was initially carried out within the School of Stores Accounting and Store Keeping but, as part of the division of responsibility between the Stores and accountant organisations, the training responsibility transferred to the School of Clerks Accounting at Lympne in October 1931. This school also experienced a series of moves: RAF Cranwell in May 1939, Penarth in June 1941, and Kirkham in June 1944, by which time it had been renamed the School of Administrative Trades. The School also took on the training responsibility for Clerks (Provisioning), Clerks (GD) (Movement Control) and Embarkation Assistants.
16 TNA, AIR 29/711, Equipment Training School (Airmen) ORB.
17 RAF LHCA, BEC 10, RAF Identity within Future Defence Training Schools dated 9 May 2002.
18 RAF LHCA, BEC 10, Correspondence with the Hon. Sec, Bridlington and District Branch Royal Air Forces Association dated 13 January 1989.
19 TNA, AIR 29/711, Equipment Training School (Airmen) ORB.
20 *Ibid.*
21 These later became the Chartered Institute of Procurement and Supply and the Chartered Management Institute respectively.
22 RAF LHCA, BEC 10, RAF Identity within Future Defence Training Schools dated 9 May 2002 and TNA, AIR 29/1130, No. 1 Air Traffic School, St Mawgan.
23 TNA, AIR 29/1130, No. 1 Air Traffic School, St Mawgan.

Chapter Twelve

1 RAF Supply Branch Yearbook (2003), p. 1.

Bibliography

Primary Sources

RAF Logistics Heritage Centre Archive

Private Papers: various documents and correspondence cited by individual's surname
Official Papers: Various documents cited by title
Boxed Ephemera Collection

Movement Control Association Archive

Documents and ephemera collection

The National Archives

Various documents in the following classes: AIR 1, AIR 2, AIR 5, AIR 8, AIR 10, AIR 20, AIR 29, AIR 72, CAB 23, AVIA 10, AVIA 15, and AVIA 46

Shuttleworth Collection

Various items on display at Old Warden, Bedfordshire

Trenchard Museum Archive

Documents and ephemera collection

Official Publications and Books

Air Historical Branch (AHB), *Britain and the Berlin Airlift*, (Innsworth: MOD, 1998)
AHB, *Armament, Volume I, Bombs and Bombing Equipment* (London: Air Ministry, 1952)
AHB, *Armament, Volume II, Guns, Gunsights, Turrets, Ammunition and Pyrotechnics* (London: Air Ministry, 1954)
AHB, *Decoy and Deception* (London: Air Ministry, undated)
AHB, *Maintenance* (London: Air Ministry, 1954)
AHB, *Maintenance Command: 40 Group and 14 MU Carlisle* (London: Air Ministry, undated)
AHB, *Manning Plans and Policy* (London: Air Ministry, undated)
AHB, *Notes on Royal Air Force Early Air Transport Operations* (Unpublished and undated)
AHB, *Royal Air Force Movements during the Second World War* (Unpublished and undated)
AHB, *The Battle of Britain, Volume II* (London: Air Ministry, undated)

AHB, *The Campaign in France and the Low Countries: September 1939–June 1940* (London: Air Ministry, undated)
AHB, *The Expansion of the Royal Air Force 1934–1939* (London: Air Ministry, undated)
AHB, *The North African Campaign November 1942–May 1943* (London: Air Ministry, undated)
AHB, *The RAF, Small Wars and Insurgencies: Later Colonial Operations, 1945–1975* (High Wycombe: HQ Air Command, 2011)
AHB, *The Women's Auxiliary Air Force* (London: Air Ministry, 1953)
AHB, *Works* (London: Air Ministry, 1956)
AHB, *14 MU The Original Concept and Design: May 1938* (London: Air Ministry, undated)
Air Ministry (AM), *Air Publication (AP) 125: A Short History of the Royal Air Force (2nd Edition)* (London: Air Ministry, 1936)
AM, *AP 1081, Royal Air Force Pocket Book 1932* (London: Air Ministry, 1932)
AM, *AP 1300, Royal Air Force War Manual, Part I: Operations* (Provisional) (London: Air Ministry, 1940)
AM, *AP 1301, Royal Air Force War Manual, Part II: Organisation and Administration (Provisional)* (London: Air Ministry, 1928)
AM, *AP 3282A, Trade Structure of the Royal Air Force, Supply* (Vol. 18: Trade Group 18) (London: Air Ministry, 1952)
AM, *Notes for Equipment Assistants and Storekeepers in 40 Group* (London: Air Ministry, 1944)
AM, *Pam (Air) 328: Four Lectures on the History of the Royal Air Force.* (First Edition) (London: Air Ministry, 1945)
HQ BAFO, *An Account of the Part Played by the Royal Air Force in Dissolving the Luftwaffe, Volume 1: February 1944 to December 1946* (London: Air Ministry, 1947)
MOD, *AP3002 (2nd Edition)*, Air and Space Warfare (MOD: London, 2009)
MOD, *AP3003: A Brief History of the Royal Air Force.* (MOD: London, 2004)
MOD, *JSP 886, Volume 1, Part 1* (2012)
NATO, *NATO Logistics Handbook* (Brussels: NATO, 2007)
War Office (WO), *Notes on Operational Aspects of Mulberry 'B'* (London: War Office, 1945)
WO, *Statistics of the Military Effort of the British Empire During the Great War 1914–1920* (London: HMSO, 1922)
WO, Amphibious Warfare HQ, *History of the Combined Operations Organisation 1940–1945* (London: War Office, 1956)

Secondary Sources

Books and Booklets

Allen, C., *Thunder and Lightning: The RAF in the Gulf: Personal Experiences of War* (London: HMSO, 1991)
Annett, R., *Drop Zone Burma: Adventures in Allied Air-Supply 1943–1945* (Barnsley: Pen and Sword, 2008)
Armitage, M., *The Royal Air Force (Second Edition)* (London: Cassell, 1993)
Bailey, G. J., *The Arsenal of Democracy: Aircraft Supply and the Anglo-American Alliance, 1938–1942* (Edinburgh: EUP, 2013)
Barnes, C. H., *Handley Page Aircraft since 1907* (London: Putnam, 1976)
Bates, P., *Japan and the British Commonwealth Occupation Force 1946–52* (London: Brassey's, 1993)
Bauduin, P., *Quand l'or noir coulait `a flots: The Supply Problem of the Allies* (Bayeaux (France): Heimdal, 2004)
Bentley Beauman, K., *Partners in Blue* (London: Hutchinson, 1971)
Blow, B., *The History of 51 (RAF) MT Company (Squadron) 1942–1956* (Leicester: Bryan Blow, 1987)
Boeing Defence UK., *The Royal Air Force Supply Central Computer System (SCCS): Commemorating 40 Years* (Milton Keynes: Boeing Information Services, 2015)

Bond, B. and Taylor, M. D., *The Battle for France and Flanders 1940: Sixty Years On* (Barnsley: Leo Cooper, 2001)

Boog, H., in Handel, M. I. (ed.), *Intelligence and Military Operations* (London: Cass, 1990)

Bowman, M., *Low Level from Swanton* (Walton-on-Thames: Air Research Publications, 1995

Bowyer, C., *RAF Operations 1918–1938*, (London: William Kimber, 1988)

Briggs, A., *A Social History of England* (New Edition) (London: BCA, 1994)

British Railways Press Office, *Facts about Railways in Wartime 1943* (London: British Railways Press Office, 1943)

Brookes, A., *V Force: The History of Britain's Airborne Deterrent* (London: Janes, 1982).

Butler, P., *Air Arsenal North America: Aircraft for the Allies 1938-1945, Purchases and Lend-Lease* (Hinckley: Midland Publishing, 2004)

Chorlton, M., *Danger Area: The Complete History of RAF South Witham 100 Maintenance Unit* (Lincolnshire: Old Forge Publishing, 2003)

Churchill, W. S. (ed)., *Winston Churchill's Speeches: Never Give In!* (London: Pimlico, 2007)

Cocroft, W. D., Thomas, R. J. C., and Barnwell, P. S. (ed)., *Cold War: Building for Nuclear Confrontation 1946: 1989*, (Swindon: English Heritage, 2003)

Cole, C., and Grant, R., *But not in Anger: The RAF in the Transport Role* (London: Ian Allen, 1979)

Coleman, J. M., *Support to Strike: The History of the Royal Air Force Tactical Supply Wing* (Self-published: undated)

Collier, B., *The Defence of the United Kingdom* (London: HMSO, 1957)

Coombs, L. F. E., *The Lion has Wings: The Race to Prepare the RAF for World War II: 1935-1940* (Shrewsbury: Airlife Publishing Ltd, 1997)

Corser, W. J. L., *Wings on Rails: Industrial Railways in the Logistics Support of Britain's Air Defence Forces*, World War Two Railway Study Group Publication No. 2 (Fleet: Arcturus Press, 2003)

Crampton, R. J., *The Balkans since the Second World War* (Harlow: Longman, 2002)

Dean, M., *The Royal Air Force and Two World Wars* (London: Cassell, 1979)

Deichmann, P., *The System of Target Selection Applied by the German Air Force in World War II*, USAF Historical Division Monograph Series (Maxwell AFB (USA): MLRS Books, 1955)

Delve, K., *The Source Book of the RAF* (Shrewsbury: Airlife Publishing Limited, 1994)

Downing, T., *Spies in the Sky: The Secret Battle for Aerial Intelligence During World War II* (London: Little, Brown, 2011)

Dunne. P., and Macdonald, G., *Procurement in the Post Cold War: A Case Study of the UK*, Middlesex University Business School and Coventry University (May 2001)

Dye, P. J., *The Bridge to Airpower: Logistics Support for Royal Flying Corps Operations on the Western Front, 1914–18* (Annapolis (USA): Naval Institute Press, 2015)

Edmonds, J. E., *Military Operations France and Belgium 1914 (August–October 1914)* (London: MacMillan and Co, 1922)

Edmonds, J. E., *Military Operations France and Belgium 1916* (London: MacMillan, 1922)

Escott, B. E., *Women in Air Force Blue* (Somerset: Patrick Stephens Ltd, 1989)

Edgerton, D., *Britain's War Machine: Weapons, Resources and Experts in the Second World War* (London: Penguin Books, 2012)

Flintham, V., *High Stakes: Britain's Air Arms in Action 1945–1990* (Barnsley: Pen and Sword, 2009)

Francis, P., *British Military Airfield Architecture: From Airships to the Jet Age* (Sparkford: The History Press, 1996)

Gibson, C., *Vulcan's Hammer: V-Force Projects and Weapons Since 1945* (Manchester: Hikoki Publications, 2011)

Grey, C. G., *A History of the Air Ministry* (London: Allen and Unwin, 1940)

Guedalla, P., *Middle East 1940–1942: A Study in Air Power* (London: Hodder and Stoughton Ltd, 1944)

Harris, A., *Bomber Offensive* (London: Greenhill Books, 1990)

Higham, R., *Armed Forces in Peacetime Britain, 1918–1940: A Case Study* (London: Foulis and Co. Ltd, 1962)

Higham, R., *Bases of Air Strategy: Building Airfields for the RAF 1914–1945* (Bodmin: Airlife Publishing, 1998)
Humphries, A. and Rice, P., 'Support Chain Management in the Royal Air Force' in Parker, N., *Supply Chain Management* (Management Directions) (Institute of Management, 2000)
Hyde, H. M., *British Air Policy Between the Wars 1918–1939* (London: Heineman, 1976)
Jackson, P., *Britain's Armed Forces Today: 4, Royal Air Force Germany* (Surrey: Ian Allen, 1986)
Jackson, R., *V-Force: Britain's Airborne Nuclear Deterrent* (Shepperton: Ian Allen, 2000)
James, J., *The Paladins: A Social History of the RAF up to the Outbreak of World War II* (Aylesbury: Futura Publications, 1990)
James, T. C. G., *Defence Policy and the Royal Air Force 1956–1963* (London: AHB, 1987)
Jones, H. A., *The War in the Air, Vol. 2* (Oxford: Clarendon Press, 1928)
Jones, H. A., *The War in the Air, Vol. 3* (Oxford: Clarendon Press, 1931)
Jones, H. A., *The War in the Air, Vol. 4* (Oxford: Clarendon Press, 1934)
Jones, H. A., *The War in the Air, Vol. 6* (Oxford: Clarendon Press, 1937)
Jones, H. A., *The War in the Air, Appendices* (Oxford: Clarendon Press, 1937)
Jefford, C. G., *RAF Squadrons*, Shrewsbury: Airlife, 1988)
Kilcullen, B. M., *No. 7 Maintenance Unit RAF Quedgeley: Pre-History and History* (Innsworth: Royal Air Force, 1996)
Liddell Hart, B. H., *History of the Second World War* (London: Pan, 1970)
McCamley, N. J., *Secret Underground Cities* (Barnsley: Leo Cooper, 1999)
Man, J., *The Penguin Atlas of D-Day and the Normandy Campaign* (London: Penguin Books, 1994)
Mantelli-Brown-Kittel-Graf, *The Supermarine Spitfire: Aircraft of World War II* (n.4) (Edizionirei R.E.I, 2015)
Mathias, P., *The First Industrial Nation: An Economic History of Britain 1700–1914* (Second Edition) (London: Methuen, 1984)
Natkiel, R., *Atlas of World War II* (London: Bison Books, 1985)
Neillands, R., *The Battle for the Rhine 1944* (London: Weidenfeld and Nicolson, 2005)
Norris, G., *The Royal Flying Corps: A History* (London: Frederick Muller, 1965)
Oldaker, R., *Support in the Sky: A History of No. 14 Maintenance Unit, Royal Air Force Carlisle* (Carlisle: MOD, 1996)
Overy, R., *The Morbid Age* (London: Penguin Books, 2009)
Ovendale, R., *British Defence Policy Since 1945* (Manchester: MUP, 1994)
Pearcy, A., *Berlin Airlift* (Shrewsbury: Airlife Publishing, 1997)
Petroleum Board, *Petroleum at War: British Oil Distribution in Wartime* (London: William Clowes Ltd, 1945)
Philpott, I. M., *The Royal Air Force: An Encyclopedia of the Inter-War Years Volume II, Re-Armament 1930 to 1939* (Barnsley: Pen and Sword, 2008)
Pitchfork, G., *Men Behind the Medals* (Barnsley: Leo Cooper, 2003)
Porter, J. D., *UKMAMS: 'Moving in Mysterious Ways'* (Northants: Cover2Cover, 1992)
Postan, M. M., *History of the Second World War: British War Production* (London: HMSO, 1952)
Postan, M. M, Hay. D and Scott, J. D., *Design and Development of Weapons: Studies in Government and Industrial Organisation* (London: HMSO, 1963)
Pudney, J., *The Camel Fighter* (London: Hamish Hamilton. 1964)
Raleigh, W., *The War in the Air*. Vol. 1 (Oxford: Clarendon Press, 1922)
Ray, J., *The Night Blitz 1940–1941* (London: Arms and Armour Press, 1996)
Richards, D., *Royal Air Force 1939–1945 Volume I: The Fight at Odds* (London: HMSO, 1953)
Richards, D. and Saunders, H. G., *Royal Air Force 1939–1945 Volume II: The Fight Avails* (London: HMSO, 1954)
Robertson, B., *The Army and Aviation: A Pictorial History* (London: Robert Hale Ltd, 1981)
Robertson, B., *Wheels of the RAF: Vehicles of the Flying Services Through Two World Wars*, (Cambridge: Patrick Stephens, 1983)
Robeson, J. F. and Copacino, W. C. (eds), *The Logistics Handbook* (New York: The Free Press, 1994)

Royal Commission on the Ancient and Historical Monuments of Scotland (RCAHMS), *Scotland from the Air 1939–49 Volume 1: Catalogue of the Luftwaffe Photographs in the National Monuments Record of Scotland* (Edinburgh: RCAHMS, 1999)
Sarin, P. S., *Military Logistics: The Third Dimension* (New Delhi (India): Marias Publications, 2000)
Saunders, H. G., *Per Ardua: The Rise of British Air Power 1911–1939* (London: OUP, 1944)
Saunders, H. G., *Royal Air Force 1939–1945 Volume III: The Fight is Won* (London: HMSO, 1954)
Savage, C. I., *Inland Transport* (London: HMSO, 1957)
Searle, A., *PLUTO: Pipeline Under the Ocean* (Shanklin: Crossprint Design, 1995)
Sinnott, C., *The RAF and Aircraft Design 1923–1939: Air Staff Operational Requirements* (London: Cass, 2001)
Slessor, J., *The Central Blue: Recollections and Reflections* (London: Cassell and Co Ltd, 1956)
Smith, H. L. (ed.), *Britain in the Second World War: A Social History* (Manchester: MUP, 1996)
Smith, M., *British Air Strategy Between the Wars* (Oxford: Clarendon Press, 1984)
Speller, I., *The Role of Amphibious Warfare in British Defence Policy, 1945–56* (Basingstoke: Palgrave, 2001)
Sturtivant, R., Hamlin, J., and Halley, J. J, *Royal Air Force Flying Training and Support Units* (Tunbridge Wells: Air Britain, 1997)
Sykes, F., *From Many Angles: An Autobiography* (London: George Harrap, 1942)
Taylor, A. J. P., *Beaverbrook* (London: Hamish Hamilton, 1972)
Taylor, W., *Royal Air Force Germany since 1945* (Hinckley: Midland Publishing, 2003)
Tecklenborg, M and Rydzynski, W., *Royal Air Force Gütersloh* (Germany: Flöttmann Verlag, 1995)
Tennant, J. E., *In the Clouds above Baghdad*, (London: Cecil Palmer, 1920)
Terraine, J., *The Right of the Line: The Royal Air Force in the European War 1939-1945* (Ware: Wordsworth Editions, 1998)
Thetford, O., *Aircraft of the Royal Air Force Since 1918*, (Ninth Edition) (London: Putnam, 1995)
Tusa, A. and J., *The Berlin Airlift* (Kent: Spellmount Ltd, 1998)
Van Creveld, M., *Supplying War: Logistics from Wallenstein to Patton* (Second Edition) (New York (USA): CUP, 2004)
Ware, P., *Red Ball Express: Supply Line from the D-Day Beaches* (Hersham: Ian Allan Ltd, 2007)
Wolmar, C., *Engines of War: How Wars Were Won and Lost on the Railways* (London: Atlantic Books, 2010)
Wood, D and Dempster, D., *The Narrow Margin: The Battle of Britain and the Rise of Air Power 1930–1940* (Barnsley: Pen and Sword, 2010)
Wynn, H., *Forged in War: A History of Royal Air Force Transport Command 1943–1967* (London: The Stationery Office, 1996)
Young, P (ed.), *Atlas of the Second World War* (London: Military Book Society, 1973)
Young-James, D., *Memoirs of an ASP* (London: Neville Spearman Ltd, 1965)

Journal and Magazine Articles

Alliston, D. R., 'Corporate Miscellany: The Harrogate/Carlisle Connection', *RAF Supply*, Issue No. 26 (1982)
Allisstone, M. J., 'From Trip Wire to Flexible Response: RAF Logistic Sustainability', *Air Clues* (March 1986)
Allisstone, M. J., Nuclear Weapons and No.94 MU, RAF Barnham, *RAF Historical Society Journal*, No. 35 (2005)
Allisstone, M. J., Post World War II Imperatives for Supply, *RAF Historical Society Journal*, No. 35 (2005)
Anon, 'Aircraft Acceptance Parks', *Aeromilitaria*, Issue 1 (1976)
Anon, 'Augmented Logistics Support for Tucano', *RAF Supply*, Issue 38 (1988)
Anon, 'Depot Computer System Rejuvenated', *RAF Supply*, Issue 31 (1986)
Anon, 'Flight Safety Awards for TSW Airmen', *RAF Supply*, Issue 31 (1986)
Anon, 'Good Show Award for SAC Donkin', *RAF Supply*, Issue 36 (1988)

Anon, 'Have Everything: Will Travel, That's the Tactical Supply Wing', *Air Clues* (May 1975)
Anon, 'RAF Supply Winning their Biggest Battle', *Air Clues* (July 1982)
Anon, 'Report from RAF Support Command', *RAF Supply*, Issue 7 (1978)
Anon, 'Supply Honours and Awards', *RAF Supply*, Issue 26 (1982)
Anon, 'The Initial Impact of TriStar Air Transport Operations on the RAF Air Movements Organisation, *RAF Supply*, Issue 32 (1986)
Anon, 'TSW teams keep the fuel flowing 24-hours-a-day', *RAF News* (16 May 2003)
Anon, 'TriStar Tankers: The RAF Goes Widebody', *Air International* (December 1985)
Atkinson, N., 'Tactical Supply Wing: Unsung and Unheralded but a Unique Force Element for Defence', RAF Logistics Branch Yearbook (2009)
Beckett, J. R. and Fentum, S. A., 'Support Command Storage and Materials Handling Advisory Team, *RAF Supply*, Issue 9 (1975)
Bernard, D. C., 'Support to Strike: Tactical Supply Wing Support During Operation Granby', *Air Clues* (November 1991)
Bernard, D. C., 'Cost Conscious Attitudes to Transportation Methods', *RAF Supply*, Issue 26 (1982)
Berry, R. D., 'POLIS: ADP Support for Fuels and Lubricants Management', *RAF Supply*, Issue 31 (1986)
Blore, D. J., 'First In, Last Out: UK Mobile Air Movements Squadron', *Air Clues* (March 1998)
Buchan, A., 'Supply: RAF Style, *Air Force Journal of Logistics* (spring 1988)
Cooper, J. E., '1+2=4 or Cargo Movement in the RAF', *RAF Supply*, Issue 14 (1977)
Corser, W., 'Railways and Military Aviation: Part 2', *FlyPast* (December 1995)
Crotty, P., 'Logistics Support in the Gulf War'. *RAF Historical Society Journal*, No. 19 (1999)
Cummings, C., 'The Electronic Era', *RAF Historical Society Journal*, No. 35 (2005)
Dean, B., 'Supply Support in a Hardened Environment', *RAF Supply*, Issue 17 (1978)
Dean, J. (ed.), RAF Stafford 50th Anniversary (Northants, 2006)
De'ath, J. G., 'Supply Support for the Tornado', *RAF Supply*, Issue No. 17 (1978)
Dixon, R., 'Mobility in Practice: Operation Bushel', *RAF Supply*, Issue 36 (1988)
Dunne, P. and Macdonald G., *Procurement in the Post Cold War: A Case Study of the UK*, Middlesex University Business School and Coventry University (May 2001)
Dye, P. J., 'The Royal Flying Corps Logistic Organisation', *Air Force Journal of Logistics*, Volume XXII, Number 1 (1998)
Dye, P. J., 'The Royal Flying Corps and Royal Air Force at St Omer', *Cross and Cockade International Journal*, Vol. 35, Number 2 (2004)
Dye, P. J., 'Sustaining Air Power: The Influence of Logistics on Royal Air Force Doctrine', *Air Power Review*, Volume 9, Number 2 (2006)
Dye, P. J., 'France and the Development of British Military Aviation', *Air Power Review*, Volume 12, No. 1 (spring 2009)
Eddy, B. and Arnett, S., 'The NATO Codification System: A Bridge to Global Logistics Knowledge, *The DISAM Journal* (1998)
Gaines, M. and Lowe, J., 'Harrier Force', *Flight International* (18 July 1987)
Gough, P. M., and Jones, G. R., 'The Mobile Explosives Team and their Role in the Withdrawal of US Forces from the United Kingdom', *Air Clues*, No. 8 (August 1993)
Graham, R., 'Jungle Supply Pilot', *FlyPast* (undated)
Grant, D., 'Tactical Refuelling: Improvements to the RAF Support Helicopter (SH) Refuelling Concept for the United Kingdom Mobile Force', *Air Clues* (March 1987)
Grehan, J., 'Behind the Offensive', *Britain at War* (October 2008)
Haddican, D., 'Logistics Capability: EAW', *The Logistician*, Issue 3 (May 2013)
Harrop, E. A., 'Planning for Economy', *Air Clues* (April 1948)
Havers, J., 'National Air Communications, September 1939–April 1940', *Air-Britain Digest*, Vol. 48, No. 4 (Winter 1996)
Hawes, L. A., 'The Story of the "W" Plan: The Move of Our Forces to France in 1939', *Army Quarterly*, 101(4) (July 1971)

Hayr, K, 'Logistics in the Gulf War', *RUSI Journal* (1991)
Howard, G., 'Commanding the Joint Force Logistic Component', RAF Logistics Branch Yearbook (2009)
Humphrey, R. J., 'And in the Beginning', *RAF Supply*, Issue 27 (1983)
Jeffery, G. A., 'From the 9th Floor: It's a Fact', *RAF Supply*, Issue 3 (1973)
Jeffery, G. A., 'From the 9th Floor: Where Does Your Money Go?', *RAF Supply*, Issue 4 (1973)
John, D., 'A New Perch for the Scabby Crow', RAF Supply Branch Yearbook (2004)
Jeffery, G. A., 'It's a Brave New World', *RAF Supply*, Issue 5 (1973)
Jeffery, J. L., 'Supply Versatility', *RAF Supply*, Issue 28 (1983)
Knight, I., 'British in Iraq: 1915', *Military Illustrated* (September 2003)
Lambert, J. D., 'UKMAMS at Lyneham', *Air Clues* (September 1974)
Lester-Powell, D., 'Development of No. 85 (Expeditionary Logistics) Wg', RAF Supply Branch Yearbook (2004)
Lloyd, A. G., 'Pipeline Supply of Aviation Fuel to the RAF: Part 1', *RAF Supply*, Issue 20 (1980)
Lloyd, A. G., 'Pipeline Supply of Aviation Fuel to the RAF: Part 2', *RAF Supply*, Issue 21 (1980)
McInnes, I., 'Sergeant Major Moore, No.5 RFC and The Balloonatics', *The Journal of the Orders and Medals Research Society*, Vol. 5, No. 2 (271) (June 2006)
McKercher, B. J. C., 'Deterrence and the European Balance of Power: The Field Force and British Grand Strategy, 1934–1938', *English Historical Review*, Vol. CXXIII, No. 500 (2006)
McKernan, J., 'The Early Bird', *RAF Supply*, Issue 1 (1972)
Maloney, S., 'Fire Brigade or Tocsin? NATO's ACE Mobile Force, Flexible Response and the Cold War', *Journal of Strategic Studies*, 27:4 (2004)
Maple, G., Tactical Supply Wing: Enabling a 'Liquid Lifeline' for Battlefield Helicopters, RAF Supply Branch Yearbook (2005)
Morris, P. L., No. 2 Mechanical Transport: the RAF's Specialist Hauliers, *Air Clues* (Oct 1997)
Muskett, K., 'TSW: from UNPROFOR to IFOR', *Beacon View* (Summer 1996)
Parry, D. W., 'TSW Support to UN Ops in Bosnia-Herzegovina', *Air Clues* (January 1995)
Paulson, J., 'Logistics Support Centre', RAF Supply Branch Yearbook (2004)
Pitchfork, G., 'The Evolution of the Air/Sea Rescue Organisation', *Royal Air Force Historical Society Journal*, Vol. 40 (2007)
Pocock, R. W., 'Provisioning MT Vehicles', *RAF Supply*, Issue 14 (1977)
Probert, H., 'Supply: Two Wartime Examples', *RAF Historical Society Journal*, No.35 (2005)
Ramsden, J. M., 'Managing military aircraft defects', *Flight International* (18 February 1978)
Rasmusen, C. F., *A Visit to Cairo, Baghdad and Basra*, *RAF Supply* Issues 6, 7, 8, and 9 (1974–1975)
Ridley, N. M., 'Supply Support for Europe's Largest Aerospace Project', *RAF Supply*, Issue No. 3 (1973)
Ritchie, S., 'The Decline of Mobility: The RAF and Deployed Operations Since 1945', *RAF Historical Society Journal*, No. 19 (1999)
Roberts, R., 'The A4 Force', RAF Logistics Branch Yearbook (2009)
Robertson, B., 'Railways and Air Warfare: Part 2: Between the Wars', *Air Pictorial* (April 1987)
Robertson, B., 'Gas Warfare and the Air', *Air Pictorial* (February 1989)
Robertson, B., 'An AID to quality', *Aeroplane Monthly* (November 1993)
Saunders, A. F., 'The Little Trains of Chilmark', *The Railway Magazine*, Vol. 122, No.899 (1976)
Smith, H. L., 'The Problem of "Equal Pay for Equal Work" in Great Britain during World War II' *The Journal of Modern History*, Volume 53, Number 4 (December 1981)
Smith, H. L., 'The Womanpower Problem in Britain during the Second World War', *The Historical Journal*, Volume 27, Number 4 (December 1984)
Smith, J., 'Tactical Supply Wing: The Op HERRICK Deployment', RAF Supply Branch Yearbook (2006)
Smith, M., 'The Royal Air Force, Air Power and British Foreign Policy, 1932–37', *Journal of Contemporary History*, Volume 12, Number 1 (January 1977)
Smith, N. F., 'Maintenance Command Earns a Bonus for the Front Line', *RAF Supply*, Issue 3 (1973)

Sperry, K. R. and Burns, K. E., Life *Cycle Cost Modelling and Simulation to Determine the Economic Service Life of Aging Aircraft* (2001), paper presented at the RTO AVT Specialists' Meeting, Manchester, 8–11 October 2001.

Springett, R., 'Ascension: Bare Base Revived', *RAF Supply*, Issue 26 (1982)

Springett, R., 'Supply Support for the Support Helicopter Force in the Gulf War', *Air Clues* (July 1993)

Springett, R., 'Logistics in the Post Cold War Era', *RAF Historical Society Journal*, No. 19 (1999)

Stevenson, T., '2 MT Leads the Way into Iraqi Heartland', *RAF News* (April 18, 2003)

Stewart, I., 'Joint Service Air Trooping Centre', *RAF Hendon Commemorative Magazine* (1987)

Stubbs, K., 'To IP or not to IP? Comment, *RAF Supply*, Issue 35 (1987)

Sullivan, M., 'Taceval', *RAF Supply*, Issue 17 (1978)

Taylor, W. J., 'Historical Background' in *Royal Air Force in Germany 1945–1993* (Brighton: RAF Historical Society, 1999)

Thorburn, G., 'Operation ECLIPSE: The RAF's Part in the Dissolution of the Luftwaffe', *Air Clues*, Vol. 40, No. 4 (April 1986)

Thurston, P., '85 (Expeditionary Logistics) Wing: Change a Plenty in 2007', RAF Supply Branch Yearbook (2008)

Tipping, C., *Key Issues Affecting the Provision of Logistics Support to the UK Armed Forces in Expeditionary Operations*, Occasional Paper Sponsored by IBM (in Conjunction with RUSI) (2013)

Todd, G. P., "A' Level Supply', *RAF Supply*, Issue No. 1 (1972)

Wharton, T., RAF Aircraft Reliability, *Flight International* (29 February 1968)

White, M., *The RAF Supply Control Centre*, *RAF Hendon Commemorative Magazine* (1987)

Williams, R. C., 'Tactical Supply in RAF Germany', *RAF Supply*, Issue 29 (1984)

PhD Theses

Buckingham, W. F., 'The Establishment and Initial Development of a British Airborne Force, June 1940: January 1942', PhD thesis, University of Glasgow (2001)

Jones, B., 'Ashore, afloat and airborne: The Logistics of British Naval Airpower, 1914–1945', PhD thesis, King's College London (2007)

Stone, T., 'Royal Air Force Logistics during the Second World War: Transformation, Sustainment and Flexibility', PhD thesis, University of Exeter (2016)

Official Reports and Papers

House of Commons Defence Committee (HCDC), Third Report of Sessions 2003-4, *Lessons of Iraq: Volume 1* (London, 2004)

HCDC, Fourth Report of Sessions 2010-12, *Operations in Afghanistan* (London 2011)

House of Commons Defence Select Committee, Eighth Report, *Frontline First: The Defence Costs Study*, HC 655, Session 93/94 (London, 1994)

HM Government, *Securing Britain in an Age of Uncertainty: The Strategic Defence and Security Review*, Cm 7948 (London: TSO, 2010)

HMSO, *SDR Research Papers 98/91*

McKane, T., *Enabling Acquisition Change*: An examination of the MOD's ability to undertake Through Life Capability Management (June 2006)

MOD, *Defence Industrial Strategy*, *Defence*, White Paper, Cm 6697 (London: TSO, 2005)

MOD, *Defence Reform: An Independent Report into the Structure and Management of the MOD* (London: TSO, 2011).

MOD, *Delivering Security in a Changing World*, Defence White Paper, Cm 6041-1 (London: TSO, 2003)

MOD, *DTMA Annual Report and Accounts 2003/2004*, HC 695 (London: TSO, 2004)

MOD, *DTMA Annual Report and Accounts 2006*, HC 1552 (London: TSO, 2006)

MOD, Statement on the Defence Estimates 1964, Cmnd 2270 (London: HMSO, 1964)

MOD, Statement on the Defence Estimates 1967, Cmnd 3203 (London: HMSO, 1967)

MOD, Statement on the Defence Estimates 1969, Cmnd 3927 (London: HMSO, 1969)
MOD, Statement on the Defence Estimates 1971, Cmnd 6735 (London: HMSO, 1971)
MOD, Statement on the Defence Estimates 1977, Cmnd 6735 (London: HMSO, 1977)
MOD, *The Strategic Defence Review: Supporting Essays* (London: HMSO, 1998)
MOD, *Operations in Iraq: Lessons for the Future* (London: DGCC, 2003)
National Audit Office (NAO), Report by the Comptroller and Auditor General, MOD, *Movements of Personnel, Equipment and Stores to and from the Gulf* (London: HMSO, 1993)
NAO, Report by the Comptroller and Auditor General, HC 825 Session 2006-2007: 17 July 2007, MOD, *Transforming logistics support for fast jets* (London: TSO, 2007)
NAO, Report by the Comptroller and Auditor General, HC 508 Session 2008-2009: 14 May 2009, MOD, *Support to High Intensity Operations* (London: TSO, 2009)
NAO, Report by the Comptroller and Auditor General, MOD, HC 60 Session 2003-2004: 11 December 2003, MOD, *Operation TELIC: United Kingdom Military Operations in Iraq* (London: TSO, 2003)
NAO, Report by the Comptroller and Auditor General, HC 827, Session 2010-2011: 31 March 2011, MOD, *The Use of Information Technology to Manage the Logistics Supply Chain* (London: TSO, 2011)
NAO, Report by the Comptroller and Auditor General, HC1097, Session 2001-2002: 1 August 2002, MOD, *Exercise SAIF SAREEA II*, (London: TSO, 2002)
NAO, Report by the Comptroller and Auditor General, HC898, Session 2001-2002: 20 June 2002, MOD, *Progress in Reducing Stocks* (London: TSO, 2002)
NAO, Report by the Comptroller and Auditor General, HC530, Session 1999-2000: 5 June 2000, MOD, *Kosovo: The Financial Management of Military Operations* (London: TSO, 2000)
Taylor, C., 'A Brief Guide to Previous British Defence Reviews' (House of Commons Library) SN/IA/5714 dated 19 October 2010

Other Works

Air Force List
Army List
Defence Council Instructions (RAF)
Defence Information Notes
Flight Magazine
Hansard
RAF College Journal
RAF General Administrative Instructions
RAF Internal Briefing Notes
RAF Supply/Logistics Yearbooks
Statements on Defence
The Times

Internet

Air BP: www.airBP.com
British Broadcasting Corporation: www.bbc.co.uk/news
Ministry of Defence: www.mod.uk
NATO: www.nato.int
Naval Systems Command: www.au.af.mil
Oshkosh Defense: oshkoshdefense.co.uk
RAF Beach Units: www.rafbeachunits.info
Royal Air Force: www.raf.mod.uk
Royal Air Force Museum: www.rafmuseum.org.uk

Index

A4 Force 227-229, 241-242, 244, 287, 459
Abbeywood, MOD 368, 375-376
Acquisition 230, 367-399
ACSSU and Minor Unit Basing Study 228, 286
Air Combat Service Support Unit 198, 226-227
Aircraft Equipment Depots 99, 410
Afghanistan 230-233, 237-238, 244, 277-279, 285, 298, 309, 328, 332, 336, 338, 370, 407, 459
Air Ministry 39-40, 44, 46, 51-56, 58-66, 68-70, 74, 77-79, 81, 83-93, 96, 99-101, 103, 105, 111, 113, 116, 121, 133, 148, 166, 190, 195, 290, 293, 299, 307, 312, 316, 358, 361, 372, 374, 377, 380, 389, 394, 412, 439
Air Mobility Wing 228, 332, 336
Airport of Embarkation Wing 328
Air Publication [830] 41, 51, 120, 231
Air Stores Parks 37, 55-58, 95, 116-162, 168, 188, 197, 199, 226, 228, 296, 320
Air Support Command 176, 255, 323, 330, 395, 400
Aircraft on ground 126, 129, 180, 186, 303, 394, 400-404
Airworthiness 147, 386
Alcock Report 385
Altrincham, No. 2 MU 44, 70, 72, 191
Ammunition Depots 72, 85, 108, 137, 178, 199, 299
Architecture, logistics 75
Argosy, Hawker Siddeley 321, 324
Audit 37, 235, 288, 376, 391, 395, 397, 435
Augmented Logistics Support 398
Auxiliary Air Movements 336
Auxiliary Embarkation Unit 136, 141, 147
Avionics 373-374, 391, 405
Barrack and Clothing Depots 90, 98, 166
Barrack Stores 101, 171
Base Inventory and Warehouse Management Services project 420, 429, 435-437
Battle of Britain 6, 94, 102, 294, 312, 375
Beach Bricks/Units/ Squadrons (RAF) 132, 136, 141-147, 148, 151-154, 161, 305
Belfast, Short 260, 322, 324-326, 332, 336
Berlin Airlift 175, 188, 316, 320
Beverley, Blackburn 321
Binbrook Study 169-174
Boeing 218, 257, 326, 336, 390, 408, 420, 429, 435-437
Bomber Command, RAF 82, 94, 117, 172, 177, 179-180, 290, 293, 314, 316
Bosnia Herzegovina 220-222, 242, 269-273, 296, 336-337, 341, 395
Bowser, fuel 105, 184, 203, 257, 262-263, 268, 270, 272, 277, 318, 351-352
Britannia, Bristol 321-323, 441
British Aerospace 213, 402, 407, 444-445
British Pipeline Agency 356
Brize Norton, RAF 204, 216, 219, 227, 229, 237, 260, 275, 324, 327, 331, 335, 343, 351, 364, 422, 442, 451, 453
Bruggen, No. 431 MU 188, 248
Bulk Fuel Installation 183, 253-255, 272, 451, 287, 351, 353-355, 359
Campaigns, France and the Low Countries [1939-1940] 116-122; invasion of North Africa: Operation Torch 130-136; invasion of North West Europe: Operation Overlord 147-158; invasion of Sicily and mainland Italy 140-147; North Africa 122-130
Cardington, No. 217 MU 190, 210, 361, 419

Cargo 38, 75, 165, 184, 204, 213, 227, 255, 281, 283, 293, 301, 305, 308, 313, 318, 324, 326, 330-332, 334-335, 343-344, 366, 453-454
Cargo Allocation Centre 330
Carlisle, No. 14 MU 64, 67, 100, 164, 190, 196, 200, 206, 210, 229, 292, 299, 302, 331, 358, 380, 384, 403, 409, 419, 458
Catering Branch, merger with Logistics Branch 239
Central European Pipeline System 358
Central Servicing Development Establishment 378-379, 383, 389-390, 396, 431
Chemical weapons 73-74, 114, 242
Chilmark, No. 11 MU 72-73, 191, 196, 210, 217, 299, 302-303, 307, 353
Chinook, Boeing 182, 211, 221, 234-235, 238, 249-250, 257, 262, 266-267, 272, 275, 277, 344
Civilian stores officers 58, 81-83
Civilianisation 81, 199, 273
Civilians in logistics 199-201
Classification of stores ('A', 'B' and 'C') 33
Coalition 210, 219, 235, 243, 266-268, 275, 282
Coastal Command, RAF 92, 109, 293-294, 348
Codification 42, 195, 393, 429
Collaborative working 383-387, 392, 406
Computer system, [AEI 1010] 412-417; [ICL 4/72] 420-423; USAS 424-426; Deployable USAS 427; Depot 418-420; Defence Stores Management System 434-435; Management of the Joint Deployed Inventory 435
Computers 34, 171, 363, 379, 416, 425, 429, 433; Supply Small Systems Group 433
Consignment tracking 216, 387, 434-436
Consumables 33, 176, 183, 249
Consumption 29, 41, 68, 87, 96, 113, 149, 165, 172, 262, 267, 357, 363, 379, 396, 398-399, 402, 429, 432, 459
Container services, freight 291-292, 297
Contamination, fuel 207, 352, 366, 354
Contingency Action Group 233
Contractorisation 191, 200
Contractors 121, 191, 200, 244, 277, 287, 307, 359, 372-373, 378, 394, 420, 435
Controller General of Equipment 39-40, 53
Controller of Engineering and Supply 383-384
Cooperative Logistics System 409
Cyprus 174, 189, 201, 216, 238, 240, 242-243, 265-266, 268-269, 292, 316, 327-328, 331, 333, 335, 337, 360, 365
Dakota, Douglas 143, 157, 244, 313, 315, 321, 452
Defects 389
Defence Accommodation Stores 190-191
Defence Clothing and Textiles Agency 209, 230, 338
Defence Codification Authority 195, 393
Defence College of Logistics and Personnel Administration 443, 446, 453
Defence Communications Services Agency 427, 433
Defence Equipment and Support 222, 367, 368, 376, 382, 393, 427
Defence Freight Distribution Group 340
Defence Fuels Group 365-368
Defence Helicopter Support Agency 386
Defence Industrial Strategy 375, 387
Defence Logistics Organisation 222, 230, 235, 238, 292, 340, 342, 365, 367, 375, 387
Defence Procurement Agency 368, 375, 382, 387
Defence Storage and Distribution Agency 225-226, 230, 273, 292, 297, 342
Defence Strategic Fuels Authority 368
Defence Supply Chain 392, 397, 434-436, 459; Operations and Movements 342
Defence Transport and Movements Agency 340-342
Defence Transport and Movements Executive 340
Demand Progression System 186
Denomination of Quantity 171
Density Activity Complex 190
Deployable Supply Group 287
Deputy Director-General of Equipment 90-91, 114, 195, 312
Diesel 73, 252, 257, 299, 350, 355
Dipping, fuel 353
Director General of Supply 163, 195, 209, 362, 374, 383-384, 404, 421, 432
Director General of Support Management 362, 386-387, 396
Director General of Support Services 386
Directorate of Tornado Engineering and Supply 385, 406
Directorate-General of Engineering and Supply 384

Directorate-General of Engineering and Supply Policy and Plans 384
Directorate of Equipment 46, 54, 82, 87, 141, 193-195
Disarmament 58, 163, 166-169, 274
Dispersal, stock/equipment 63, 66, 72, 90, 94, 98, 100, 126, 180, 183, 185-186, 251, 380-381, 418
Disposals 43, 163-165, 167-169, 191
Diversion Order 394
DLO Operations Centre 342
Domestic Reference Number 42, 393
Domestic Supply Flight 173, 192
Electronic Supply/Stores Group or Flight 173, 186
Embarkation Units 132, 136, 151, 153-154, 168, 193, 228, 303-305
End-to-End Review 230
Engineering Authorities 384
Equipment Provisioning and Accounting Section 170, 173, 195
Equipment Assistant 51, 78, 85, 103, 112-115, 120, 125-126, 161, 198, 200, 304, 338
Equipment Branch 50, 62, 78, 81-84, 91, 112, 116, 130, 136, 141, 144, 163-168, 170, 178, 188, 193-195, 197, 239, 251, 256, 320; renaming to 62
Equipment Depot 62, 85, 112, 114, 123, 164, 167, 188-189, 190-191, 216, 301, 379, 380, 392
Equipment Disposal Depots 164-165
Equipment Officers (RFC) 35
Equipment Parks 98-99, 108, 137-138, 166, 188, 199
Equipment Section 30, 49, 78-80, 82, 92-94, 113, 116, 137, 169-170, 172-174, 180, 195, 351, 414-415
Equipment Supply Depot 190, 201, 205, 210, 291-292, 357, 373-374, 387, 396-397, 399, 403, 418
Establishments, stock 41, 172, 363, 424
Expansion Programme 54, 56, 58-62, 64, 68, 70, 75, 78, 81-89, 92, 112, 139, 292-293, 310, 370, 372, 439, 458
Expeditionary Air Wing 229-230, 237, 240-244, 288, 298, 458-459
Expeditionary Logistics Squadron 227-228, 287
Expeditionary Logistics Wing [No. 85] 224-226, 228, 280-288
Expeditionary Operations and Logistics 208, 218, 222, 224-227, 231, 234-235, 244, 247, 308, 326, 370, 435, 458
Explosives Disposal, post-Second World War 165-166
Explosives Storage Area 283, 433
Falkland Islands 202-207, 230, 261, 279, 296, 326, 328, 334, 337, 366
Far East Air Force 189, 251, 351-352, 359
Fauld, No. 21 MU 72-73, 111-112, 299, 363, 380
Fighter Command, RAF 92, 94, 148, 161, 311-312
Fly Away Pack 181, 196-197, 204, 213-214, 248-249, 378, 389
Forward Air Ammunition Park 120
Forward Ammunition Depot 108
Forward Equipment Unit 151
Forward Mounting/ Operating Base 266
Frontline First, Defence Costs Study 209
Fuel, jet engined aircraft 348
Fuel, piston engined aircraft 347-348
Gasses, compressed 190, 193, 360-361, 451
Gateway House 327
General Equipment Park 188
Globemaster C-17, Boeing 218, 223, 234-235, 241, 326, 337, 339, 341, 343
Government Pipeline and Storage System 356-358
Ground Equipment Depot 98-99, 190
Gulf 143, 189, 210-220, 229, 231, 235-237, 244, 265-268, 273, 275-276, 280-284, 296-297, 308, 326, 335-338, 341, 347, 366, 386, 427, 434-436, 443, 458-459
Gutersloh, RAF 182-183, 208, 247-250, 261, 263, 280, 330, 344
Halton, RAF 60, 105, 131, 239-240, 385, 439-440, 443, 449-451
Handforth, No. 61 MU 90, 190, 380
Hardened operating environment 184-186, 424
Harpur Hill, No. 28 MU72-73, 110, 299
Harrogate 88, 90, 191, 201, 206, 222, 378-381, 384-389, 395-396, 401, 404-406, 420, 428-430, 433
Hartlebury, No. 25 MU 64-65, 67, 101, 190, 196, 299-300, 380-381, 410
Hastings, Handley Page 317, 320-321, 441
Heads of the RAF Logistics organisation 460
Hendon, RAF 75, 209, 311, 329-330, 384, 390, 404, 412-413, 415, 419-426, 429-433,
Hercules, Lockheed 205, 211, 213, 234-235, 242-243, 251, 258, 269, 298, 322, 324, 326, 334-335, 339, 350, 360, 408-409, 418, 454

Hereford, RAF 441-442, 446, 450, 453
Heywood, 35 MU 64, 67, 96-97, 101, 190, 299, 380
High Density Storage 190, 458
High Wycombe, RAF 209, 211, 223, 233, 340, 387
Host Nation Support 176-177, 211, 218, 224, 241, 263, 266, 283, 287, 343
Hub and Spoke concept 335
Humanitarian 221, 236, 243, 258, 274, 334, 336, 445
Hydrant, fuel 105, 217, 249, 263
Inability, demand 394
Industry/industrial 56, 59, 78, 85, 96, 102, 166, 193, 200, 216, 230, 292, 349, 362-363, 371, 374-380, 391-401
Initial Provisioning 180, 373, 377-379, 389, 399, 406
Inland Waterways 32, 138, 307-308, 338
Integrated Logistics Support 382, 392, 431
Integrated Project Team 222, 230, 292, 378, 387, 427
Inventory 31, 33, 41, 64, 66, 81, 107, 170, 196, 282, 287, 369, 371, 373, 380, 390-398, 412, 414, 416-418, 420, 424, 429
Iraq 42, 44-45, 60, 71, 107, 210-220, 230, 232, 234-237, 242, 265-268, 275-276, 280-284, 297, 309, 311, 315, 328, 335-338, 341-342, 436, 459
ISIS, codification database 429
Jerrycan 105, 155, 350, 363, 366
Joint Air Delivery Test and Evaluation Unit 343
Joint Air Transport Establishment 343-345
Joint Aircraft Recovery and Transport Squadron 227, 287-288
Joint Force HQ 233
Joint Force Logistics Component 232-233, 280-282, 285
Joint Helicopter Command 223, 225, 228-229, 247, 273, 279, 286, 345
Joint Helicopter Support Unit 344-345
Joint Service 141, 206, 209, 231, 239, 252, 329, 344, 365, 444
Joint Service Air Trooping Centre 209, 329
Joint Service logistics 231-233
Joint Supply Chain 230
Kidbrooke, No. 1 MU 27, 35, 44-47, 67, 84, 92, 101-102, 190, 302, 438, 440, 448, 453
Kosovo 223-224, 272, 274, 297, 336, 341
Ledgers, equipment accounting 34-35, 42, 80, 149, 169-170, 411, 422, 425, 448
Levene, Defence Reform Study 233
Llanberis, No. 31 MU 72, 108, 110
Local Purchase Order 78
Lockheed 234, 311, 322, 324, 408, 418
Locomotives 73, 299-303
Logistic Support Analysis 382
Logistics Support Centre, RAF 233, 240, 283
Logistic Support System 431
Logistics, definition of 7-8
Logistics Branch (RAF) 194, 229, 239, 243, 446, 459; badge and colours 239; renaming to 238
Logistics Command, RAF 210, 223, 230, 239, 358, 385, 387, 397, 444
Logistics Squadron, RAF Gutersloh 248-249
Lubricants 346, 351, 358, 363, 366
Lyneham, RAF 204, 216, 226, 229, 238, 253, 255, 260, 324, 326-328, 331, 334, 336-338, 344
Maintenance Command 62-74, 89-92, 96, 108, 110, 122, 141, 165, 167, 177-178, 195, 199, 252, 285, 294, 374
Maintenance Command Badge 64
Maintenance Group Defence Agency 387
Maintenance Units 62, 64-66, 72, 77-78, 81, 83, 85, 87, 90-91, 94, 100, 102, 113, 123, 126, 129, 133, 136-137, 162, 164, 200
Maintenance, lines of (first, second, third, and fourth) 388
Maintenance Command depots, exposure to enemy air attack 100
Management Advisory Section 428
Marchwood, military port 275
Master Provisioning Office/ Scheme 66, 73, 113, 170, 363, 379-381, 396, 410
Mathematical modelling 378, 389
MAXEVAL 184
Maximum daily off-take 267
Mechanical handling aids 169, 191
Mechanical Supply Group 186
Milton, No. 3 MU 43-44, 64-65, 67, 101, 190
MINEVAL 184
Ministry of Aircraft Production 101, 294, 307, 375, 382, 394
Ministry of Defence 78, 195, 176, 190, 191, 195, 196, 206, 209, 210, 216, 218, 222, 231, 233-236, 244, 252, 266, 270, 287, 328, 335, 339-346, 350, 356, 357-359, 361, 363-366, 374-376, 377-379, 382-383, 385, 387, 391-392, 406, 408, 431-432, 434-436, 443, 444-446

Ministry of Defence (Procurement Executive) 375
Mobile Air Movement Squadron 204, 216, 226, 229, 251, 260, 265, 333-337, 343-344
Mobile Catering Support Unit 226, 228, 286-287
Mobile Explosives Team 306
Mobility 32, 37, 39, 55, 79, 120-121, 128, 130, 161-162, 180, 188, 194, 196, 199, 204, 218, 226, 249, 257, 259, 262, 276, 289, 322, 389, 443
Mobility and Deployed Support Study 218
Mobility in the 1970s, review of 196
Mobility Supply Flight 181, 195-197, 204-205, 226, 260, 273
Modifications 238, 324, 371, 388, 402, 404, 406-407
Morris Report 385
Motor Transport 27, 30, 35, 63, 87, 97, 99, 120-124, 136, 138, 142, 154, 161, 165, 193, 206, 225, 228, 241, 255, 276, 288, 290, 292-299, 304, 312, 328, 346, 375, 379, 383, 443
Movements trade and specialisation 199, 338; air 308-338; IT support 331; rail 299-303; road 290-299; water 303-308
MT Companies 136, 161, 228, 290, 292-299, 304, 312
MT Squadron [No. 2] 206, 225-226, 228, 241-242, 280-286, 294, 296-299
Multi-disciplinary working 78
Munitions 30, 37, 70-74, 88, 91, 94, 107-112, 130, 132, 149, 162-163, 165-169, 176, 182, 191, 208, 210, 213, 217, 227, 235, 248, 295-296, 300-301, 314, 380
Mutual Supply Support 213
NATO 7, 42, 175-177, 182-183, 206, 208-210, 213-214, 218, 221, 224, 236-237, 240-244, 247, 255, 258, 261-263, 271-272, 324, 350, 356, 368, 370, 378, 401, 403, 406, 424-425, 458
NATO codification system 393
NATO pipeline system 263, 358
NATO response strategies 175-176, 424
Navy, Royal 19, 25, 49-50, 92, 131, 166, 177, 203, 205, 223, 239, 257, 266, 270, 273, 289, 291, 304, 306, 335, 348, 363, 372, 375, 378, 390, 408, 412, 434-435, 446
NEFMA and NETMA 407
New Management Strategy 362, 384-385
Nomenclature of stores 42
Northwood, PJHQ 231, 239, 340
Obsolescence 320, 371, 373, 437,
Octane rating, fuel 68, 137, 347-348
Odiham, RAF 206, 229, 251, 255, 261, 267, 344-345,
Oil and Pipelines Agency 356, 358, 366
Operation Granby 210-218, 222, 224, 232, 235-236, 265-268, 272, 296-297, 335-337, 386, 395-396, 427, 434-435
Operation Herrick 237-238, 279, 285, 288, 336, 407
Operation Overlord 147-158
Operation Palatine 222, 337
Operation Resinate (north and south) 220, 297
Operation Telic 220, 232, 234-237, 275-276, 280-284, 297, 336, 341, 434, 436
Options for Change (Defence Review) 188, 208, 210, 222, 232, 296, 386, 391
Packaging 180, 193, 233, 397, 441
Permanent Air Movements Detachments 342-343
Permanent Joint Headquarters 231-232, 233, 240, 284, 339-341, 434
Petrol/petroleum 21, 29, 63, 68, 70, 91, 93, 103, 105, 107, 124, 158, 193, 248, 263, 270, 279, 300, 308, 314, 346-347, 349, 353, 358, 362-363, 366, 368
Petroleum Supply Depot 207, 349, 356-357, 360
Petroleum, Oils and Lubricants 29, 62, 68-70, 88, 103-104, 119, 123, 130, 132, 142, 149, 151, 160, 162, 186, 203, 213, 244, 296, 346-368, 380, 414, 431-432, 433
Pipeline, fuel 69, 104-107, 157, 182, 203, 217, 242, 253, 263, 300, 302, 349-350, 356-360, 364, 366
POL Operations Room and system 203, 364-365, 431-432
Ports 105, 117, 119, 122, 131-132, 136-137, 141, 150-151, 158, 160, 165, 206, 217, 288, 294-295, 300, 303-306, 335, 342
Priority Freight Distribution Service 206, 291-292, 303, 331
Priority progression 186, 395, 429
Procurement 30, 44, 78, 113, 188, 217, 234-235, 292, 361, 365-366, 373-377, 379, 381-384, 387, 429
Professionalisation, logistics 438, 444, 446, 452
Provisioning 51, 54, 64, 66, 73, 77-78, 80, 96, 113, 137, 169-170, 180, 257, 348, 362-363, 373-381, 383, 389, 394, 396, 399, 404, 406, 408, 410-411, 416, 429, 433, 441, 444, 454
Quality control, POL 29, 242, 346, 351, 353-354
Quartermaster 27, 35, 37, 91, 282, 450

Quedgeley, 7 MU 64-65, 96, 101, 190-191, 196, 200, 206, 210, 292, 299, 302, 364, 380, 397, 403, 419
RAF Germany 182, 184, 186, 188, 196, 208-209, 213-214, 217, 247-249, 257, 261, 269, 292, 352-353, 358, 424-425
RAF Supply Central Computer System 416, 420, 422, 424-427, 429, 431, 436
RAF Supply Control Centre 209, 412-416, 419,433
Railways 30, 41, 45, 63, 65, 72, 91, 94, 104, 109-110, 125, 130, 132, 138, 152, 160, 174, 191, 290, 299-303, 307-308, 317, 351
Ranging and scaling 213
Rates of effort 211, 241, 363
Rationalisation 44, 190, 210, 231, 329, 338, 342, 347, 379, 383, 386-387, 389, 392, 435, 438, 443-444, 453
Re-provisioning 373, 379-381, 406, 411, 416
Receipt and Despatch section 75, 173
Refuel/refuellers/refuelling 29, 115, 118, 159, 197, 203, 217, 229, 235, 243, 247, 249, 251, 255-259, 261-279, 287-288, 318, 324, 350, 352-353, 364, 400
Regional Fuels Officer 358
Reliability 377-378, 388-390, 392, 431
Replenishment, stock 41, 44, 172, 359, 363, 379, 381, 397-398, 434
Reprovisioning 373, 379-381, 406, 411, 416
Reserve Ammunition Depots 109
Reservists 85, 216, 336-338
Resupply 5, 37-38, 44, 54-55, 58, 123, 129-130, 133-134, 136, 145, 148, 151, 158, 175-176, 205, 224, 241, 267, 270, 272, 279, 283, 302, 314, 316, 335-336, 350, 373, 434
Royal Logistic Corps 236, 239, 243, 279, 283, 330, 332, 345, 366, 454
Rolls-Royce 400, 402, 405, 407-408
Rotors-turning refuelling 229, 249, 257, 262-264, 272, 274-276, 277, 279
Royal Army Ordnance Corps 120, 203, 253, 353
Royal Auxiliary Air Force 146, 216, 226-228, 275, 288, 326, 336-338
Royal Corps of Transport 344
Royal Engineers 26, 33
Royal Flying Corps 25-27, 29-40, 44-46, 48, 50, 52, 54, 56, 239, 308, 448, 457,
Royal Naval Air Service 25-26, 30, 39, 56, 308
Ruislip, No. 4 MU 44, 64, 66-67, 73, 101, 190, 438, 448
Secondary accounting 170
Section and Reference 42, 410, 414, 416
Senior Air Movements Officer 236, 260, 330-331
Senior Equipment Officer 94, 169-170, 172-173, 181, 353
Serviceability 216, 283, 320
Services Booking Centre 329
Servicing Commandos, RAF 133, 144, 149
Single fuel concept, NATO 252, 350
Smart Procurement initiative 376
South Cerney, Air Mounting Centre 275
Stafford, No. 16 MU 64, 67, 91, 95, 100, 112, 190, 197, 200, 210, 223, 225, 249-250, 252, 273, 291, 296, 304, 331, 380, 387, 403, 419
Stanbridge, RAF SCC 387, 425-426, 433, 437
Standardisation 42, 350, 362
Station Warden 53
Stockholding 34, 44, 66, 96, 98, 149, 170, 173, 206, 390
Stockpiles/stockpiling 149, 164, 176, 213, 218, 301, 318
Stocktaking 37, 51, 396, 420
Storage 31, 45, 53, 63, 65-76, 79, 85, 96-101, 103-111, 116, 125, 128, 139, 164, 167, 173, 178, 181-185, 188, 190, 192, 203, 210, 217, 223, 225, 227, 248, 251, 255, 268, 273, 282, 300, 341, 387, 394, 396, 403, 418-419, 424, 433, 441, 450, 458
Storage and Materials Handling Advisory Team 192
Storekeeping 40-41, 80, 87, 120
Stores Depots 31, 35, 37, 44, 46, 52, 54, 60, 62, 66, 81, 85, 87
Stores Distributing Parks 31, 44
Strategic Defence and Security Review 228, 234, 370
Strategic Defence Review 208, 218, 222, 224, 227, 230, 234, 244, 247, 273, 292, 297, 308, 326, 331, 340, 342, 375, 387, 390, 433, 435
Strike Command, RAF 183-184, 196, 209, 213, 223, 228, 231, 233, 269, 273, 396, 400, 404, 453
Supply and Movements Strategy, RAF 392
Supply and Transport Columns/Sections 117, 119, 123, 136, 149, 151, 228, 296
Supply and Distribution Activity Complex 191
Supply Branch, RAF 140, 163, 192, 194, 208, 219, 233, 238, 251, 307, 340, 358, 375, 379, 386, 389, 392-393, 397, 400, 403, 405, 407, 417, 432, 442-443, 450, 459
Supply Branch, renaming to 193
Supply Chain Management 230, 369, 392
Supply Control and Accounting Flight 173, 195

Supply Management 209, 403, 406, 408, 431, 433
Supply Management Branches 191, 201, 204, 206, 378, 384, 386, 406, 409, 454
Supply Management Terminal Network 428
Supply Squadron 173-174, 180, 183, 185-186, 189, 195, 197, 205, 214, 225, 239, 303, 351, 354, 374, 395, 399, 422, 424, 425, 433, 444
Supply Trade (Group 18) 199, 219, 244, 256, 277, 339, 353, 452
Support Chain Management 7, 392
Support Command, RAF 192, 195, 204, 209, 210, 269, 383, 419
Support, review of in the 1970s 195
Sustainment 7, 162, 233, 242, 298, 341
TACEVAL 183, 185, 261, 425
Tactical Supply Flight 247-250
Tactical Supply Wing 197, 203-206, 211, 217-218, 221, 223, 225-226, 228-229, 236, 238, 250-279
Tally cards 80, 169
Tanker, ocean 69, 158, 203, 207, 242, 252-253, 359
Tanker, road 93, 105, 106, 249, 262, 267-268, 276-277, 281, 283, 297, 349, 351-352, 355, 357
Technical Supply Flight/ Group 173, 195, 351, 360
Training, air movements 452
Training, airmen and airwomen 448
Training, officer 438
Transition-to-War 183, 261, 358
Transport Command, RAF 312-313, 315-316, 318-321, 328, 330
Tri-Service fuels management 365
Tri-Service IT management 433
Tri-Service movement's management 339
TriStar, Lockheed 216, 224, 234-235, 238, 240, 324, 326-327, 336, 339, 386
Turnover, stock/freight/fuel 21, 68, 108, 110, 149, 165, 172, 181, 185, 190
Typhoon, Eurofighter 223, 234, 240, 242, 298, 371, 373, 378-379, 401, 406-407, 431
United Kingdom Mobile Air Movement Squadron 226, 265, 333-336
United States of America 30, 105, 115, 123, 129, 131, 143, 220, 294, 313, 328, 331, 343, 350, 356-358, 367, 380, 395, 399, 408-409, 422, 427, 429
Universal Equipment Wings and Depots 66-67, 90, 95-98, 99, 101, 137, 139
Urgency of need, equipment 66, 394
V-Force 177-181, 183, 197, 291
Vocabulary of stores naming system 42, 87
V-Force on Ground 180, 394
Vouchers, equipment accounting 113, 170, 418, 420, 442, 448
War Manual, RAF 32, 55, 117
War reserves of stock 183, 359
Warehouses 191, 220, 387
Warehousing and Transport Management System 420
Weapons, nuclear 177-178, 182
Women's Auxiliary and Royal Air Force 45, 52, 102, 113-116, 188, 381, 449